HUMAN RESOURCE MANAGEMENT

Fifth Edition

R. WAYNE MONDY, SPHR
McNeese State University

ROBERT M. NOE, SPHR
East Texas State University

In Collaboration With
SHANE R. PREMEAUX, PHR
McNeese State University

ALLYN AND BACON
Boston · London · Toronto · Sydney · Tokyo · Singapore

To My Daughters:
Alyson Lynn and
Marianne Elizabeth
RWM

To:
Joanie
RMN

To My Daughter:
Paige Elizabeth
SRP

A Special Dedication:
To the late Harry N. Mills, Jr., a collaborating author
on previous editions. Harry added a special touch to the
book and will certainly be missed.

Editor-in-Chief, Business and Economics *Rich Wohl*
Senior Editorial Assistant *Sarah Carter*
Editorial-Production Service *Proof Positive/Farrowlyne Associates, Inc.*
Production Administrator *Ann Greenberger*
Composition Buyer *Linda Cox*
Cover Administrator *Linda Dickinson*
Manufacturing Buyer *Louise Richardson*

Library of Congress Cataloging-in-Publication Data

Mondy, R. Wayne.
   Human resource management / R. Wayne Mondy, Robert M. Noe, Shane
R. Premeaux.—5th ed.
      p.   cm.
   Includes bibliographical references and index.
   ISBN 0-205-14218-4
   1. Personnel management—United States. 2. Personnel management.
I. Noe, Robert M. II. Premeaux, Shane R. III. Title.
HF5549.2.U5M66 1992
   658.3—dc20   92-27718
                                                    CIP

Printed in the United States of America

10 9 8 7 6 5 4 3 2 1   95 94 93 92 91

CONTENTS

CHAPTER 7
Selection   206

P·A·R·T T·H·R·E·E

HUMAN RESOURCE DEVELOPMENT   265

CHAPTER 8
**Organization Change and Human Resource
Development   266**

P·A·R·T F·O·U·R

COMPENSATION AND BENEFITS 439

CHAPTER 12
Financial Compensation 440

CHAPTER 13
Benefits and Other Compensation Issues 482

P·A·R·T F·I·V·E

SAFETY AND HEALTH 525

CHAPTER 14
A Safe and Healthy Work Environment 526

PREFACE

The fifth edition of *Human Resource Management* continues to offer a practical and realistic approach to the study of human resource management. While the book is essentially pragmatic, it is balanced throughout by current human resource management concepts. A common theme—the interrelationships among the various human resource functions—runs throughout the book. Each of the functions is described from the standpoint of its relationship to the total needs of human resource management. The book is written primarily for students who are being exposed to human resource management for the first time. It puts the student in touch with the real world through the use of numerous illustrations and company material showing how human resource management is practiced in today's organizations.

Features of the Book

We have included the following features to promote the readability and understanding of important human resource management concepts.

- A model (see Figure 2-1) is developed that provides a vehicle for relating all human resource management topics. We believe that the overview provided will serve as an excellent teaching device.
- A short case study involving human resource management is provided at the beginning of each chapter to set the tone for a discussion of the major topics included within the chapter.
- A brief exercise called "HRM In Action" is included in the body of each chapter. These exercises permit students to make decisions regarding situations that could occur in the business world. A debriefing guide is provided for the instructor in the *Instructor's Resource Manual*.
- A comprehensive exercise called "Developing HRM Skills" is provided at the end of each chapter. These exercises provide for considerable class

participation and group involvement. A comprehensive debriefing guide is provided for the instructor in the *Instructor's Resource Manual.*

- Actual company material is used throughout the book to illustrate how a concept is actually used in organizations.
- Two "Incidents" are provided at the end of each chapter. These short cases highlight material covered in the chapter.
- A comprehensive, continuing case study appears at the end of each of the book's seven parts. This lengthy case study ties all of the human resource functions together.
- Objectives are listed at the beginning of each chapter to highlight the general purpose and key concepts of the chapter.
- Review questions appear at the end of each chapter to test the student's understanding of the material.
- Key terms are listed at the end of each chapter. In addition, a key term is presented in boldface type the first time it is defined or described in the chapter.
- A list of references is provided at the end of each chapter to permit additional in-depth study of selected topics.
- Finally, a glossary of all key terms appears at the end of the book.

Improvements to the Fifth Edition

The previous editions of this book all enjoyed considerable success. Many of our adopters provided us with suggestions for improving the fifth edition. Topics that have been added or have been given additional coverage are provided below.

- Because of the impact of the multinational environment on human resource management, major multinational topics have been added to the following chapters in the book:

    The Globalization of Human Resource Management (Ch. 1)

    Environmental Factors Affecting Multinational Corporations (Ch. 2)

    Implications for Multinational Corporations (Ch. 3)

    The Globalization of Job Design (Ch. 4)

    Global Approaches to HRIS (Ch. 5)

    Strategies for Global Recruitment (Ch. 6)

    The Cost-Benefit Staffing Approach for the Economic Unification of Europe (Ch. 7)

    Global and Joint-Venture Orientation (Ch. 8)

    Global Blending of Cultures and Management Styles (Ch. 9)

    Preparation for the Global Career (Ch. 10)

    Global Performance Appraisal (Ch. 11)

The Impact of Globalization on Financial Compensation (Ch. 12)

Culture Shock—The Ultimate Stressor (Ch. 14)

The Global Sector (Ch. 15)

Global Labor-Management Relations (Ch. 16)

The Role of the Global Human Resource Manager (Ch. 17)

Employee Relations in Times of International Crisis (Ch. 18)

Major Global Human Resource Management Problems (Ch. 19)

- A new section explaining how organizations respond to the external environment has been added to Chapter 2.
- Major new laws, such as the Civil Rights Act of 1991 and the Americans with Disabilities Act, are discussed in Chapter 3.
- The section on employee leasing has been revised, and a new section on automated applicant tracking systems has been added to Chapter 6.
- The segment on drug testing has been updated, and a new section on negligent hiring and retention has been added to Chapter 7.
- In Chapter 8, the sections on coaching and mentoring, behavior modeling, role-playing, and orientation have been substantially rewritten.
- A major section on total quality management (TQM) has been added to Chapter 9.
- The discussion of the Hay Plan has been expanded, and a new section on skill-based pay has been added to Chapter 12.
- A new section entitled "Compensation in Growth Companies" has been added to Chapter 13.
- Chapter 14 has been significantly updated.
- The section entitled "Signs of a Troubled Labor Movement" has been substantially rewritten in Chapter 15.
- A new section entitled "The Glass Ceiling" has been added to Chapter 18.
- In Chapter 19, the sections entitled "The Productivity Challenge" and "Technology Affecting Human Resource Management" have received substantial revision.

All these revisions reflect the latest in HRM practices. They are designed to promote and stimulate student interest. Also, numerous company examples are included to demonstrate how "textbook" concepts are actually being used in leading organizations. We sincerely hope that students of human resource management derive as much pleasure from reading this book as we did from writing it.

Acknowledgements

The assistance and encouragement of many people is normally required in the writing of any book. This was especially true during the writing of *Human Resource Management,* fifth edition. Although it would be virtually impossible to list each person who assisted in this project, we feel that certain people must be credited because of the magnitude of their contribution. We especially appreciate the efforts of the professionals who reviewed this edition. These individuals are Edward Arnold, Auburn University—Montgomery; Walter Bogumil, University of Central Florida; Joseph Culver, University of Texas—Austin; George Davis, Jacksonville State University; and Lynn Scalia, SUNY College—Buffalo.

We express our sincere appreciation to the faculty at McNeese State University and East Texas State University. We would also like to thank Marthanne Lamansky, Debbie VanNetta, and Tina Minter, all very competent and professional individuals, who were always available to ensure that our deadlines were met.

Human resource professionals have offered invaluable assistance to us by providing examples of how their firms practice human resource management. The following individuals have assisted us through each of the four previous editions of this book:

Dr. Paul A. Banas
Manager, Personnel Research
   (Retired)
Ford Motor Company

Robert L. Berra
Senior Vice-President,
   Administration (Retired)
Monsanto Company

Robert E. Edwards, SPHR
Senior Vice-President
Drake Beam Morin, Inc.

Gayla S. Godfrey, SPHR
Division Manager, Pneumotive
   Division
Thomas Industries, Inc.

R. H. Heil
Executive Vice-President,
   Technical Operations
Delta Air Lines, Inc.

Art Hobbs
Vice-President, Corporate
   Relations and Administration
E-Systems, Inc.

Joyce Lawson
Human Resource Management
   Consulting

Susan Marks, SPHR
President
Prostaff Personnel Service

Kathryn D. McKee, SPHR
Senior Vice-President
First Interstate Bank, Ltd.

James G. Parkel, SPHR
IBM Director of Personnel Plans
   and Programs
IBM Corporation

Marsha K. Slaughter
Area Human Resource Manager
Zellerbach, A Mead Company

Barbara A. Sullivan
Executive Vice-President
Encore Temps, Inc.

Dr. Walter W. Tornow, SPHR
Vice-President, Research and
   Publication
The Center for Creative Leadership

Nina E. Woodard, SPHR
Vice-President
First Interstate Bank, Ltd.

Drew M. Young, SPHR
Vice-President (Retired)
ARCO Oil and Gas Company

P·A·R·T O·N·E

INTRODUCTION

Human Resource Research

Human Resource Planning, Recruitment, and Selection

Human Resource Development

Employee and Labor Relations

Human Resource Management

Compensation and Benefits

Safety and Health

CHAPTER 1

HUMAN RESOURCE MANAGEMENT: AN OVERVIEW

CHAPTER OBJECTIVES

1. Distinguish between human resource management and the human resource manager. Describe the functions of human resource management.
2. Describe the changes that have taken place in the human resource field in recent years. Define human resource *executive, generalist,* and *specialist*. Describe the changes that occur in the human resource function as a firm grows larger and more complex.
3. Express the nature of professionalization of human resources and the direction it has taken. Define ethics and relate ethics to human resource management.

As David Curtis, vice-president of human resources for Nelson Enterprises, headquartered in New York City, rose to leave the executive meeting, he realized that his job would be even busier than usual during the next six months. Nelson Enterprises produces high-tech components for both government and private industry, and greater production capacity is needed to meet industry demands. A decision to open a new plant in Mobile, Alabama, had been made at the meeting. David and other members of the council had analyzed numerous sites and had determined that Mobile most closely met their needs. When the plant is completed in a year, 500 new employees must be available and trained. In addition, 75 employees at the New York facility will be transferred to Mobile. It is David's responsibility to ensure that qualified new workers are hired and trained, and that the transferred workers are effectively integrated into the workforce.

Carl Edwards is the supervisor of ten Baby Giant convenience stores in Sacramento, California. As the Baby Giant chain is relatively small (only forty stores), it has no human resource department. Each supervisor is in charge of all employment activities for his or her store. Carl must ensure that only the best people are recruited for positions as store managers and then must properly train these individuals. If one of the managers fails to report for an assigned shift and Carl cannot find a replacement, he is expected to work the shift. It is Friday afternoon and Carl is hurriedly attempting to locate a replacement because one store manager just quit without giving notice.

Judy Lynley is the industrial relations manager for Axton Pneumotives, a small manufacturer of pumps located in Bangor, Maine. The sixty-five machine operators in the firm are unionized. Judy has been negotiating with union leaders for five weeks with little success. The union members have threatened to walk off the job if the contract is not resolved by midnight. However, if Judy's firm agrees to all the union's demands, it will no longer be competitive in the industry because of the higher wage level.

David, Carl, and Judy all have one thing in common; they are deeply involved with some of the challenges and problems related to human resource management. Managers of human resources must constantly deal with the often volatile and unpredictable human element that makes working in this field very challenging. Managing people in organizations is becoming more complex than ever because of rapidly changing and increasingly complicated work environments.

In the first part of this chapter, we distinguish between human resource management and the human resource manager. Next, we review the human resource management functions. We then present topics related to the evolution of human resource management, the globalization of HRM, and the changing world of the chief human resource executive. We make a distinction among human resource executives, generalists, and specialists, and discuss the human resource function in organizations of different size. Finally, we discuss professionalism and ethics in this dynamic discipline.

■ HUMAN RESOURCE MANAGEMENT AND THE HUMAN RESOURCE MANAGER

The field of human resource management changed dramatically during the 1980s and early 1990s, in ways that created a greatly expanded role for the human resource manager. In order to understand this development, we must make a distinction between human resource management and the human resource manager.

Human resource management (HRM) is the utilization of human resources to achieve organizational objectives. Consequently, managers at all levels must concern themselves with human resource management at least to some extent. Basically, managers get things done through the efforts of others, which requires effective human resource management. In a manufacturing firm, for instance, the production manager meshes physical and human resources to produce goods in sufficient numbers and quality; the marketing manager works through sales representatives to sell the firm's products; and the finance manager obtains capital and manages investments to ensure sufficient operating funds. These individuals are called "line" managers because they have formal authority and responsibility for achieving the firm's primary objectives. Although involved in human resource management, they are not human resource managers. They are responsible primarily for specific functional areas of the business. Carl Edwards, the convenience store supervisor in Sacramento, fully understands the challenges that a line manager faces with human resources because he will have to work Friday night if he cannot find a replacement.

A **human resource manager** is an individual who normally acts in an advisory or "staff" capacity, working with other managers to help them deal with human resource matters. In previous editions of this book, the term *personnel manager* denoted the individual who performed staff functions similar to those now performed by the human resource manager. This evolving change in terminology reflects the expanded role of HRM and an increasing awareness that human resources are the key to a successful organization. Although only cosmetic in some instances, this change has been substantive in most cases. Thus, it reflects a new and continually expanding role for the human resource manager.[1] The current functions of many chief human resource managers is illustrated by Kathryn McKee, senior vice-president, human resources for First Interstate Bank, Ltd. As she states, "I am now a strategic partner with line management and participate in business decisions which bring human resources perspectives to the general management of the company."

The human resource manager is primarily responsible for coordinating the management of human resources to help the organization achieve its goals. Jane Kay, formerly vice-president of employee relations for Detroit Edison Company, states, "The human resource manager acts more in an advisory capacity, but should be a catalyst in proposing human relations policies to be implemented by line managers." A senior vice-president for American General Life Insurance Company once said, "The real human resource management game is played by the line manager. The human resource manager's role is to develop policies and programs—the rules of the game—and to function as a catalyst and energizer of the relationship between line management and employees." The distinction between human resource management and the human resource manager is clearly illustrated by the following account:

> Bill Brown, the production supervisor for Ajax Manufacturing, has just learned that one of his machine operators quit. He immediately calls Sandra Williams, the human resource manager, and says, "Sandra, I just had a Class A machine operator quit down here. Can you find some qualified people for me to interview?" "Sure Bill," Sandra replies. "I'll send two or three down to you within the week, and you can select the one that best fits your needs."

In this instance, both Bill and Sandra are concerned with accomplishing organizational goals, but from different perspectives. Sandra, as a human resource manager, identifies applicants who meet the criteria specified by Bill. Yet, Bill will make the final decision as to who is hired because he is responsible for the machine operator's performance. His primary responsibility is production. Hers is human resources. As a human resource manager, Sandra must constantly deal with the many problems related to human resources that Bill and the other managers face. Her job is to help them meet the human resource needs of the entire organization. In some firms her function is also referred to as personnel, employee relations, or industrial relations.

■ HUMAN RESOURCE MANAGEMENT FUNCTIONS

Today's human resource problems are enormous and appear to be ever expanding. The human resource manager faces a multitude of problems, ranging from a constantly changing workforce to coping with the ever-

---

[1] James L. Harvey, "Nine Major Trends in HRM," *Personnel Administrator,* 31 (November 1986), p. 102.

present scores of government regulations.[2] Because of the critical nature of human resource problems, they are receiving increased attention from upper management. Therefore, the human resource executive who is able to deal effectively with those problems often becomes one of the firm's top managers.[3]

Human resource managers develop and work through a human resource management system. As Figure 1-1 shows, six functional areas are associated with effective human resource management: human resource planning, recruitment, and selection; human resource development; compensation and benefits; safety and health; employee and labor relations; and human resource research. A major study conducted for the Society for Human Resource Management confirmed that these areas essentially constitute the field of human resource management.[4] Sound management practices are required for successful performance in each area. We discuss these functions next.

Human Resource Planning, Recruitment, and Selection

An organization must have qualified individuals in specific jobs at specific places and times in order to accomplish its goals. Obtaining such people involves human resource planning, recruitment, and selection.

Human resource planning (HRP) is the process of systematically reviewing human resource requirements to ensure that the required number of employees, with the required skills, are available when needed. Recruitment is the process of attracting such individuals in sufficient numbers and encouraging them to apply for jobs with the organization. Selection is the process through which the organization chooses, from a group of applicants, those individuals best suited both for open positions, and for the company. Successful accomplishment of these three tasks is vital if the organization is to effectively accomplish its mission.

Human Resource Development

Human resource development (HRD) helps individuals, groups, and the entire organization become more effective. Human resource development is needed because people, jobs, and organizations are always changing. The development process should begin when individuals join the firm and continue throughout their careers. Large-scale HRD programs are referred to as organization development (OD). The purpose of OD is to alter the environment within the firm to help employees perform more productively.

---

[2] *Ibid,* p. 28.

[3] James D. Portwood and Robert W. Eichinger, "The Challenge of Human Resource Management: Adding Value," *Human Resource Planning,* 8 (December 1985), p. 209.

[4] Walter W. Tornow, Janis S. Houston, and Walter C. Borman, "An Evaluation of the Body-of-Knowledge," *Personnel Administrator,* 34 (June 1989), p. 140.

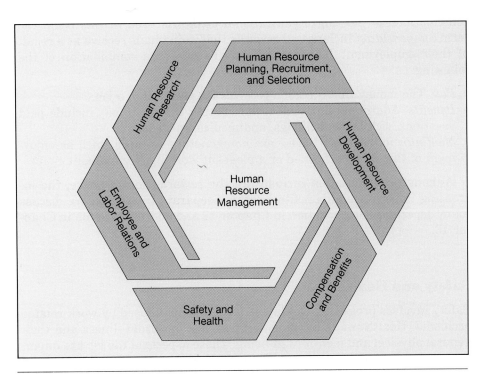

FIGURE 1-1 | The Human Resource Management System

Other aspects of HRD include career planning and performance appraisal. Career planning is a process of setting human resource goals and establishing the means to achieve them. Individual careers and organizational needs are not separate and distinct. Organizations should assist employees in career planning so that the needs of both can be satisfied. Through performance appraisal, employees are evaluated to determine how well they are performing their assigned tasks. Performance appraisal affords employees the opportunity to capitalize on their strengths and overcome identified deficiencies, thereby becoming more satisfied and productive employees.

Throughout this text, but especially in the HRD chapters, we use the term operative employees. **Operative employees** are all workers in an organization except managers and professionals, such as engineers or accountants. Steel workers, secretaries, truck drivers, and waiters are examples of operative employees.

Compensation and Benefits

The question of what constitutes a fair day's pay has plagued management, unions, and workers for a long time. A well-thought-out compensation system provides employees with adequate and equitable rewards for their contributions to meeting organizational goals. As used in this book, the term *compensation* includes all rewards that individuals receive as a result of their employment. The reward may be one or a combination of the following:

- *Pay* The money that a person receives for performing a job.
- *Benefits* Additional financial rewards other than base pay include paid vacations, sick leave, holidays, and medical insurance.
- *Nonfinancial rewards* These are nonmonetary rewards, such as enjoyment of the work performed or a pleasant working environment.

Although compensation includes all the rewards shown above, the increasing importance of benefits warrants separate treatment. We discuss many aspects of compensation in Chapter 12 and address benefits in Chapter 13.

Safety and Health

Safety involves protecting employees from injuries caused by work-related accidents. Health refers to the employees' freedom from illness and their general physical and mental well-being. These aspects of the job are important because employees who work in a safe environment and enjoy good health are more likely to be productive and yield long-term benefits to the organization. For this reason, progressive managers have long advocated and implemented adequate safety and health programs. Today, because of federal and state legislation, which reflect societal concerns, most organizations have become attentive to their employees' safety and health.[5]

Employee and Labor Relations

In 1990, unions represented 16.4 percent of all nonfarm workers and the unionized share of the private workforce had shrunk to only about 12 percent.[6] According to a study presented at a recent National Bureau of Economic Research conference, union membership in the private sector could drop below 5 percent by the year 2000, if present trends continue.[7] Even so, a business firm is required by law to recognize a union and bargain with it in good faith if the firm's employees want the union to represent them. In the past, this relationship was an accepted way of life for many employers. But according to a recent survey of labor-management relations, preventing the spread of unionism and developing effective employee rela-

---

[5] The key law in the area of health and safety is the Occupational Safety and Health Act of 1970. This act is discussed in Chapter 14.

[6] Gene Koretz and Celeste Whittaker, "More Picket Lines, Fewer Rank-And-Filers," *Business Week* (May 7, 1990), p. 24.

[7] *Ibid.*

tions systems are now more important to some managers than achieving sound collective bargaining results.[8]

As Judy Lynley, industrial relations manager for Axton Pneumotives, discovered, dealing with a union often presents difficult problems. During the stressful bargaining process, the union placed Judy in a difficult position. If the workers walk off the job, production stops; but agreeing to all the union's demands may result in pricing the firm's products out of the market. Judy must be a skilled negotiator to solve these problems. When a labor union represents a firm's employees, the human resource activity is often referred to as industrial relations.

Human resource managers in union-free organizations are often quite knowledgeable about union goals and activities. Such organizations typically strive to satisfy all reasonable employee work-related needs. Employees often conclude that a union isn't necessary for them to achieve their personal goals. Remaining union free requires a strong commitment by management and a freely communicative and open environment. In many ways, the commitment necessary to maintain a union-free environment is more demanding on the human resources department than working in a unionized environment is. Organizations that do not make and maintain that commitment are vulnerable to union organizing efforts. The old maxim is still true: "Unions don't organize employees, managers do"—through mistakes, neglect, and, unfortunately, plain greed.[9] The human resource manager, therefore, must create and manage an employee relations system that treats employees positively. The system should allow each individual worker to maintain his or her self-esteem and grow individually within the organization.

Human Resource Research

Human resource research has been increasingly important, and the trend will likely continue. The human resource researcher's laboratory is the entire work environment. Studies may involve every HRM function. For instance, a study related to recruitment may suggest the type of workers most likely to succeed in a particular firm. Or research on job safety may identify the causes of certain work-related accidents.

The reasons for problems such as excessive absenteeism or too many grievances may not be readily apparent. When such problems occur, human resource research can shed light on their causes. In Sweden, the labor force is highly educated and well trained. But the country's high income tax rates reduce the motivational power of pay, even incentive-type pay. Research at Sweden's Volvo factory revealed that the Swedes objected to the grime of the typical automobile factory. The close supervision and machine-paced

---

[8] Alexander B. Trowbridge, "A Management Look at Labor Relations," in *Unions in Transition* (San Francisco: ICS Press, 1988), p. 414.

[9] *Ibid.,* p. 417.

work on the assembly lines were also sore points. So Volvo built more pleasant and colorful factories, where teams of workers were allowed largely to manage themselves. Each team assembles a substantial portion of the car, which is moved from area to area. In the new Volvo plants, morale and productivity are better and absenteeism is lower than in the older factories.[10] Human resource research is clearly an important key to developing the most productive and satisfied workforce possible. As you will see in Chapter 19, numerous quantitative methods are used in human resource research.

Interrelationships of HRM Functions

The functional areas of HRM are not separate and distinct; they are highly interrelated.[11] Management must recognize that decisions in one area will affect other areas—and what those impacts are likely to be. For instance, a firm that emphasizes recruiting and training of a sales force while neglecting to provide adequate compensation is wasting time, effort, and money. In addition, if management is truly concerned about employee welfare, it must ensure a safe and healthy work environment. An added benefit may be keeping the firm union free. The interrelationships among the six HRM functional areas will become more obvious as we address each topic in greater detail.

■ THE EVOLUTION OF HUMAN RESOURCE MANAGEMENT

One of the major changes in business in recent years has been the increased respect and responsibility afforded human resource professionals.[12] In fact, in 1990, the job of human resource manager was identified as one of fifteen fast-track careers.[13] Human resource managers are now expected to provide the direction necessary to meet the many human resource problems and challenges that continue to arise. For example, within the next decade, the content of more than half of all existing jobs is likely to change, and 30 percent of all existing jobs will be eliminated by technological advances.[14] When robots were introduced in the automobile industry, there was a major decrease in the demand for workers who welded or painted, but their introduction created a demand for technicians who could program, install,

---

[10] Jonathan Kapstein and John Hoerr, "Volvo's Radically New Plant: The Death of the Assembly Line?" *Business Week* (August 28, 1989), pp. 92–93.

[11] Robert J. Sahl, "Get It Together! Integrating the HR Department," *Personnel,* 66 (February 1989), p. 39.

[12] Alexander B. Trowbridge, "A Management Look," p. 414.

[13] Michele Morris, "15 Fast-Track Careers," *Money* (June 1990), p. 122.

[14] Eric G. Flamholtz, Yvonne Randle, and Sonja Sackmann, "Personnel Management: The Tenor of Today," *Personnel Journal,* 66 (June 1987), p. 64.

and service the robots.[15] Human resource professionals will have to respond positively to such trends, while keeping an alert eye on their organizations' overall goals.[16]

Not many decades ago, people engaged in human resource work had titles such as "welfare secretary" and "employment clerk." Their duties were rather restrictive and often dealt only with such items as workers' wages, minor medical problems, recreation, and housing.[17] Personnel, as human resources was most commonly called, was generally held in low esteem as a profession, and its organizational position was typically near the bottom of the hierarchy. "In the past," says John L. Quigley, vice-president of human resources for the Dr Pepper Company, "the personnel executive was the 'glad hander' or 'back slapper' who kept morale up in a company by running the company picnic, handling the United Fund drive, and making sure the recreation program went off well." Those days are over in most organizations. The human resource manager's position is no longer a "retirement" position given to managers who cannot perform adequately anywhere else in the organization. Firms have now learned that the human resource department can have a major impact on the organization's overall effectiveness and profitability.

According to the SHRM/Mercer-Meidinger-Hansen survey of some 20,000 human resource professionals in 1,400 organizations of varying size, top human resource executives are generally being paid in line with other upper level managers.[18] As might be expected, salaries of corporate human resource executives depend largely on the size of the organizations employing them. As shown on page 12 in Figure 1-2, the average salary for top executive HRM managers at firms with over 10,000 employees was $196,000, including benefits and incentives. The average salary of human resource managers in firms with between 1,300 and 3,500 employees was $113,000 when benefits and incentives were added to the base salary. For firms with under 250 employees, the salary was $109,000 with benefits and incentives included.

The type of work performed also has a major effect on the pay levels in large companies. Figure 1-3 provides the salaries of top corporate executives in various career options (see page 12). Labor relations and international HR enjoy the highest salaries, while development and employee relations are the lowest.

Education evidently is a major factor in determining the salaries for human resource positions. According to one survey, the median income of all human resource practitioners is 24 percent higher if the employee has earned a bachelor's degree and 10 percent higher still if the employee holds

---

[15] Elizabeth McGregor, "Emerging Careers," *Occupational Outlook Quarterly,* 34 (Fall 1990), p. 22.

[16] Jack F. Gow, "Human Resources Managers Must Remember the Bottom Line," *Personnel Journal,* 64 (April 1985), p. 30.

[17] Henry Eibirt, "The Development of Personnel Management in the United States," *Business History Review,* 33 (August 1969), pp. 348–349.

[18] John D. McMillan and Claire O. Walters, "Dominating the Dollars," *Personnel Administrator,* 33 (August 1988), pp. 26–28.

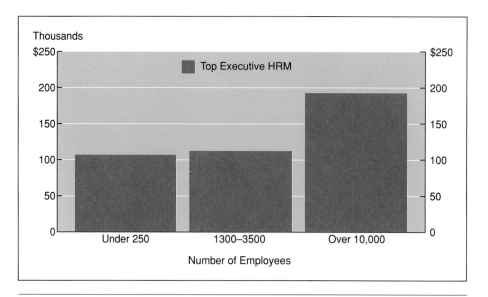

FIGURE 1-2 | Effects of Company Size on HR Salaries

Source: Adapted from "Company Size Affects HR Salaries," *HRMagazine,* 35
(July 1990), p. 46. Reprinted with the permission from *HRMagazine* (formerly *Personnel Administrator*) published by the Society for Human Resource Management, Alexandria, VA.

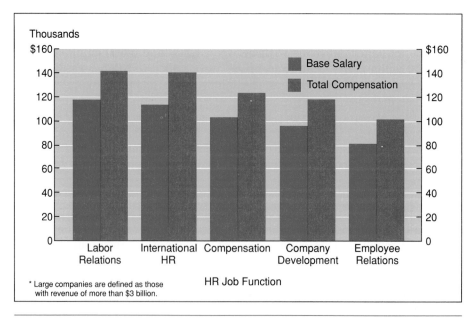

FIGURE 1-3 | HR Job Function Determines Pay Level in Large Companies*

Source: Adapted from "HR Job Function Determines Pay Level in Large Companies," *HRMagazine*, 35 (July 1990), p. 48. Reprinted with the permission
from *HRMagazine* (formerly *Personnel Administrator*) published by the Society for Human Resource Management, Alexandria, VA.

a graduate degree. Length of experience also affects the income of human resource practitioners.[19]

Many human resource professionals now report directly to the CEOs of their companies.[20] Some human resource executives have even become top managers with their firms. These achievements clearly reflect the recently gained respect that chief executive officers and other senior executives have for human resource professionals. The increase in status of the human resource field is not limited to the United States. In his research on Japanese industry, William Ouchi found that in Japan "ordinarily, the most senior and the most respected managing director is in charge of human resources."[21]

■ THE GLOBALIZATION OF HUMAN RESOURCE MANAGEMENT

Twenty years ago, many U.S. multinational corporations had operations in Canada but not in many other countries. Today, most international corporations are becoming truly global. U.S. companies still regularly do business in Canada, but more and more they are doing so in Hong Kong, Singapore, Japan, the United Kingdom, France, and Germany, to name a few. More and more U.S. multinationals are showing interest in doing business in former "Eastern Bloc" countries. This interdependence of national economies has created a global marketplace in which worldwide products and services are bought and sold. The globalization of the marketplace has created special challenges for human resource professionals in the decade of the 1990s.[22]

Among the most serious of the human resource challenges in the global job marketplace is the growing mismatch between emerging jobs that require higher-level skills, and skill levels of the people available to fill them. In the case of American multinationals, human resource management is becoming an even greater challenge because, according to the Commission on Workforce Quality and Labor Market Efficiency, "Unless government and business undertake a vast increase in their investment in human capital, U.S. companies will not be able to hire the types of workers they need to compete in international markets."[23] To compound the problem, managers affiliated with some companies, like General Motors, are learning the techniques that improve the quality of production, but they are not learning to encourage the cooperative attitudes that make operations such as NUMMI and Toyota successful.[24]

---

[19] Steven Langer, "Human Resources: Who Makes What?" *Personnel Journal,* 69 (February 1990), p. 106.

[20] "Anatomy of a Human Resource Executive," *Training,* 22 (May 1985), p. 146.

[21] William G. Ouchi, *Theory Z* (Reading, Mass.: Addison-Wesley, 1981), p. 30.

[22] Mike Fergus, "Employees On the Move," *HRMagazine,* 36 (May 1990), p. 44.

[23] Stephen B. Wildstrom, "A Failing Grade for the American Workforce," *Business Week* (September 11, 1989), p. 22.

[24] Dean Foust, "A Tough Look at General Motors," *Business Week* (September 18, 1989), p. 17.

Coping with human resource problems in the global environment is very complex. American human resource professionals must cope with problems by educating or reeducating much of the American labor force, by carefully reviewing the human resource situation in the host country, by planning to cope with the limitations of the labor situation, and by taking advantage of the strengths of the host country's labor force. Effectively dealing with human resource problems is essential for success in the global marketplace.

■ THE CHANGING WORLD OF THE CHIEF HUMAN RESOURCE EXECUTIVE

The work of the chief human resource executive is affected greatly by top management's human resource priorities and the major changes occurring in management responsibilities and organizational relationships. In one survey, prominent chief human resource officers were asked, "What are the principal human resource areas attracting top management attention?" The results, shown in Figure 1-4, indicate that compensation was the number one concern, with succession planning (planning for the replacement of key employees) a close second.[25] However, each of the areas mentioned by those interviewed are vitally important (and are covered in this book).

The same executives were also asked to identify the major changes occurring in their management responsibilities and organizational relationships.[26] Their responses are summarized as follows:

1. *Greater emphasis and more time spent on human resource strategic planning and management succession planning.* Integrating human resource strategic planning into the corporate strategic planning process is apparently taking on greater importance.
2. *More involvement in all aspects of the business.* Just as the production and finance departments are important to the success of the organization, so too is the human resource department. As a result, it is achieving similar respect. Today's human resource managers must know more than just "personnel." They must have a firm grasp of finance, marketing, operations, and the nature of their firm's business. They must be as profit oriented as any other executive. Merely "liking people" is not enough for the successful human resource manager of the 1990s.
3. *A significant member of the management team.* Top-level managers have begun to realize the vital contributions of effective human resource management.

---

[25] John S. Hellman (ed.), "The Changing World of the CPO" (Spencer Stewart & Associates special report, 1984), pp. 3–4.
[26] *Ibid.,* p. 13.

'TOP FIVE' CONCERNS		PERCENTAGE OF RESPONDENTS
Compensation		84%
Succession Planning		80%
Management Staffing		68%
Human Resource Strategic Planning		40%
Employee Communications		40%
Workforce Management		34%
Benefits		28%
Performance Evaluation		26%
Employee Relations		24%
Personnel Policies		20%
Labor Relations		18%
Training & Development		16%
EEO/Affirmative Action		4%
Other: Reorganization, Corporate Culture and Employee Participation		8%

FIGURE 1-4 | Principal Human Resource Areas Attracting Top Management Attention

Source: John S. Hellman (ed.), "The Changing World of the CPO," a Spencer Stewart & Associates special report, 1984, p. 6. Used with permission.

4. *Key role as consultant to the CEO on organization and succession planning.* Chief human resource officers have become key advisors and counselors to CEOs.
5. *More emphasis on cost-related issues and cost control.* The emphasis here is on workforce management. Chief human resource officers are taking on greater responsibility, facing tougher challenges, and working harder and smarter. But, as one executive stated, the job today is "a lot more fun,"[27] and undoubtedly, a lot more challenging.

---

[27] *Ibid.*

A 1990 SHRM/Mercer survey reports some other anticipated changes:

1. *New specialties in the human resource field are emerging.* Some of these include human resource planning, international human resources, and employee assistance plan (EAP) administration.
2. *Utilization of employee training professionals is increasing.* This emphasis is needed to increase the skills and productivity of the workforce.
3. *Certain compensation and benefits programs are more prevalent.* Many of these new benefits will be discussed in Chapters 12 and 13.
4. *Some human resource programs are being downsized.*[28] The managers of these programs must accomplish more work with less staff.

The only thing that is certain is that the job of the human resource professional is continuously evolving. Yesterday's solutions may not be sufficient for today's challenges.

■ HUMAN RESOURCE EXECUTIVES, GENERALISTS, AND SPECIALISTS

There are various classifications within the human resource profession that you need to recognize and understand. Among them are human resource executives, generalists, and specialists. An **executive** is a top-level manager who reports directly to the corporation's chief executive officer (CEO) or to the head of a major division. A **generalist** (who often is an executive) performs tasks in various human resource-related areas. The generalist is involved in several, or all, of the six human resource management functions. A **specialist** may be a human resource executive, manager, or non-manager who is typically concerned with only one of the six functional areas of human resource management. Figure 1-5 helps clarify these distinctions.

The vice-president of industrial relations shown in Figure 1-5 specializes primarily in union-related matters. This person is both an executive and a specialist. The human resource vice-president is both an executive and a generalist, having responsibility for a wide variety of functions. The manager of compensation and benefits is a specialist, as is the benefits analyst. Whereas an executive is identified by position level in the organization, generalists and specialists are distinguished by their positions' breadth of responsibility.

---

[28] "HR Professionals Sport More Hats Than Ever Before," *Employee Benefits Journal,* 15 (September 1990), p. 9.

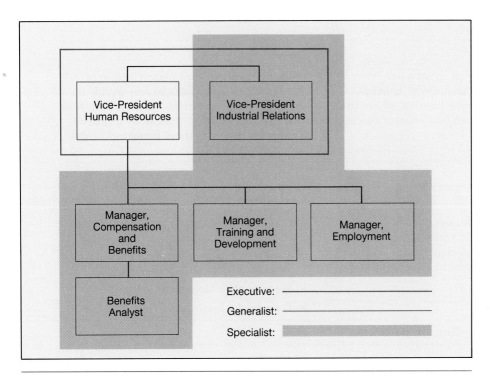

FIGURE 1-5 | Human Resource Executives, Generalists, and Specialists

The distinction between generalists and specialists should be even clearer after studying the Monsanto example in Figure 1-6 on page 18. It lists the type of general work assignments at various levels in the organization for both generalists and specialists. Also interesting are the "two bits of advice" that Monsanto gives generalists and specialists: Career development at the departmental and corporate levels varies considerably, the lines between these assignments for generalists and specialists blur at times, and the career paths for both may not always be "up."

■ THE HUMAN RESOURCE FUNCTION IN ORGANIZATIONS OF VARIOUS SIZES

The human resource function tends to change as firms grow and become more complex—and as the function achieves greater importance. Although the basic purpose of human resource management remains the same, the approach followed in accomplishing its objectives often changes.

Starting Assignment	
Specialist	**Generalist**
Work for a supervisor in an area like labor relations, employment, training, or benefits. This would be at a larger location, where the function is broken down into areas of specialty.	Work for a supervisor or superintendent in several areas. You might be responsible for training, communications, employment, benefits, and safety. This would be at a smaller location with two or three personnel professionals on the staff.
Later Assignments	
Specialist	**Generalist**
Manage one or two areas of responsibility, such as labor relations, training, and development, a combination of employment and benefits. Again, this would be at a larger location.	Manage the total human resource function: ■ For a sub-unit within the location (such as for the maintenance department, or for a geographic area within the location), ■ For a smaller Monsanto location, or ■ For a larger location.
Operating Company/Staff Department	
Specialist	**Generalist**
Manage one or two functions such as human resource planning, compensation, recruiting, or an entire company or staff department.	Manage the total human resource function for a sub-unit within a company (e.g., a division) or for the entire company or staff department.
Corporate	
Specialist	**Generalist**
Work in or manage an entire area of expertise for the corporation, such as labor relations, equal employment opportunity, development, or benefits.	Manage the total corporate human resource function.

Two bits of advice:

■ Don't get hung up on whether you begin your career as a specialist or generalist. The lines between generalist and specialist are not as neat as the chart would indicate. For example, as an employment "specialist," you would become involved daily within questions of labor relations, compensation, human resource planning, equal employment policy, and much more! Or as a small-plant "generalist," you would have to learn the basics of several specialties. Also, the overwhelming odds are that you will get both types of exposure—specialist and generalist—in your career.

■ Career development will not always be "up." It's to the professional's advantage to get as much experience and exposure as possible—and many times, this will mean lateral moves into different areas of specialty.

FIGURE 1-6 | Career Development at Monsanto

Source: Used with the permission of the Monsanto Company.

HRM In Action

Scotty, I know that you are the human resource manager, and I really appreciate your concern for my career, but the position you are offering me as assistant human resource director is, in my opinion, a dead-end job. Recruiters just find employees to fill vacant positions. They don't get involved in other areas of the company, so my achievements could easily go unnoticed and I'd be stuck there forever. Another thing, I have heard that top management really only cares about marketing, production, and finance—not human resources. I appreciate the thought, Scotty, but don't put me in a dead-end job.

How should Scotty respond?

Small businesses seldom have a formal human resource unit and HRM specialists, as Figure 1-7 shows. Rather, other managers handle human resource functions. The focus of their activities is generally on hiring and retaining capable employees.

Some aspects of the human resource function may actually be more significant in small firms than in large organizations. For instance, if the owner of a small business hires her first and only full-time salesperson— and this individual promptly alienates the firm's customers—the business might actually fail. In a larger firm, such an error would be much less devastating.

As a firm grows, a separate staff function may be required to coordinate human resource activities. In a larger firm, the person chosen to do so will be expected to handle most of the human resource activities, as Figure 1-8

FIGURE 1-7 | The Human Resource Function in a Small Business

FIGURE 1-8 | The Human Resource Function in a Medium-sized Firm

implies. For a medium-size firm there is little specialization. A secretary may be available to handle correspondence, but the human resource manager is essentially the entire department.

When the organization's human resource function becomes too much for one person to handle, separate sections often are created and placed under a human resource manager. These sections will typically perform tasks involving human resource development, compensation and benefits, employment, safety and health, and labor relations, as depicted in Figure 1-9.

In still larger firms, the human resource function takes on even more responsibility, permitting even greater specialization. Figure 1-10, an organization chart for the Champion International Corporation, illustrates this condition. The unit responsible for compensation, for example, will most likely include some specialists who concentrate on hourly wages and others who devote their time to salary administration. The employee relations vice-president works closely with top management in formulating corporate policy.

FIGURE 1-9 | The Human Resource Functions in a Medium–Large-sized Firm

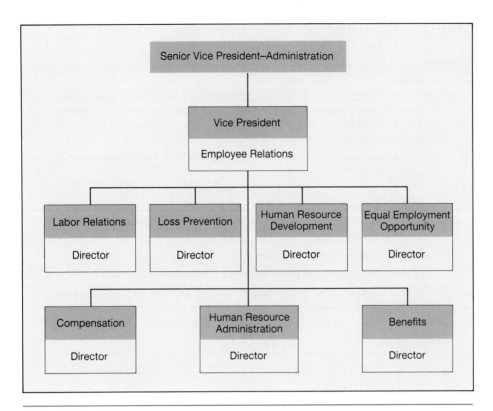

FIGURE 1-10 | The Employee Relations Organization—Champion International Corporation

Source: Used with the permission of Champion International Corporation.

Table 1-1 outlines the duties and responsibilities of Champion's employee relations executive (see page 22). As you can see, the scope of such a position is quite broad, ranging from the coordination, recommendation, and implementation of plans to auditing performance.

■ PROFESSIONALIZATION OF HUMAN RESOURCE MANAGEMENT

A **profession** is characterized by the existence of a common body of knowledge and a procedure for certifying members of the profession. Performance standards are established by members of the profession (self-regulation) rather than by outsiders. Most professions also have effective representative organizations that permit members to exchange ideas of mutual concern. These characteristics apply to the field of human resources, and several well-known organizations serve the profession.[29] Among the more

---

[29] Cheryl Haigley, "Professionalism in Personnel," *Personnel Administrator,* 29 (June 1984), p. 103.

TABLE 1·1 | Champion International Corporation
Corporate Employee Relations

Charter:

To provide operating and staff management with professional centralized services that will assure the competence and continuity of the
company's human resources

Scope:

- To provide expertise and centralized services
- To coordinate plans, recommendations, implementation, and review
  of corporate projects
- To recommend general policies
- To establish functional procedures for designated activities
- To audit performance and compliance with general policies and pro-
  cedures for designated activities

Objectives:

- To provide direction and support to each functional director and his
  or her department
- To require quality and excellence in total performance of function
- To assure that professional positions are occupied by competent
  people who can and do respond to the company's needs and
  requirements

Source: Used with permission of Champion International Corporation.

prominent are the Society for Human Resource Management, the Human
Resource Certification Institute, the American Society for Training and
Development, the American Compensation Association, the National
Human Resources Association, and the International Personnel Manage-
ment Association.

Society for Human Resource Management

The largest national professional organization for individuals involved with
human resource management is the Society for Human Resource Management (SHRM), which was formerly called the American Society for Personnel Administration (ASPA). The name change, which became official in
1990, reflects the increasingly important role that human resource management plays in the overall bottom line of organizations. The basic goals
of the society include defining, maintaining, and improving standards of
excellence in the practice of human resource management. Membership

consists of 42,000 individuals; there are currently more than 435 local chapters and numerous student chapters on university campuses across the country.[30] *HRMagazine* is published monthly by the society as a means of disseminating human resource information.

Human Resource Certification Institute (HRCI)

One of the more significant developments in the field of HRM has been the establishment of the Human Resource Certification Institute, formerly the Personnel Accreditation Institute (PAI), a subsidiary of SHRM.[31] Founded in 1976, HRCI's goal is to recognize human resource professionals through a certification program.[32] This program encourages human resource professionals to continuously update their knowledge and skills. Certification indicates that they have mastered a validated common body of knowledge. The advantages of human resource certification were outlined a number of years ago by a former national president of ASPA, Wiley Beavers.

> First, we would benefit at the college and university level. The development of the body of knowledge required for successful practice in the various areas of personnel would provide invaluable assistance in curricula design. The breakdown of the field into its specialties would also allow students to focus on career directions earlier in their education.
>
> Second, young practitioners would have sound guidelines and information covering areas in which they should be boning up and could avoid the mistakes many of us older types make.
>
> Third, senior practitioners would be encouraged to update their knowledge. (Don't know how many of them will be interested in certification. There will be an appreciable reaction along the lines of: "I don't need to take tests to prove I know what I'm doing. I have already proven it by the job I'm doing." And they will be right in about 50 percent of the cases.)[33]

American Society for Training and Development

Founded in 1944, the American Society for Training and Development (ASTD) has grown to become the largest specialized professional organization in human resources. Its membership exceeds 26,000, and it has over

---

[30] Katherine Gruber (ed.), *Encyclopedia of Associations,* 25th ed., vol. 1: National Organizations of the United States, part 1 (Detroit: Gale Research Company, 1991), p. 291.

[31] Juanita F. Perry, "Accredited Professionals Are Better Prepared," *Personnel Administrator,* 30 (December 1985), p. 48.

[32] Details of the HRCI are shown in the Appendix to this chapter.

[33] Wiley Beavers, "Accreditation: What Do We Need That For?" *Personnel Administrator,* 18 (November 1975), pp. 39–41.

147 local groups.[34] The membership is made up of individuals who are concerned specifically with training and development. The society publishes the *Training and Development Journal* monthly to encourage its members to remain current in the field.

American Compensation Association

The American Compensation Association (ACA) was founded in 1954 and currently has a membership that exceeds 12,000.[35] The ACA is made up of managerial and human resource professionals who are responsible for the establishment, execution, administration, or application of compensation practices and policies in their organizations. The ACA's journal, which contains information related to compensation issues, is the *Compensation Review*.

National Human Resources Association

Founded in 1950, the National Human Resources Association (NHRA), formerly the International Association for Personnel Women (IAPW), was established to expand and improve the professionalism of women in human resource management. Its membership consists of human resource executives in business, industry, education, and government. The NHRA has approximately 1,400 members.[36] NHRA's journal, *Human Resources: Journal of the International Association for Personnel Women,* which disseminates information of interest to its members, is published quarterly.

International Personnel Management Association

The International Personnel Management Association (IPMA) was founded in 1973 and currently has more than 5,600 members. This organization seeks to improve human resource practices by providing testing services, an advisory service, conferences, professional development programs, research, and publications. It sponsors seminars and workshops on various phases of public human resource administration. The organization's journal, *Public Personnel Management,* is published quarterly for those involved in public-agency human resource administration.[37]

---

[34] Katherine Gruber (ed.), *Encyclopedia of Associations,* p. 793.

[35] *Ibid.,* p. 130.

[36] *Ibid.,* p. 291.

[37] *Ibid.,* p. 131.

■ ETHICS AND HUMAN RESOURCE MANAGEMENT

Professionalization of human resource management created the need for a uniform code of ethics. **Ethics** is the discipline dealing with what is good and bad or right and wrong or with moral duty and obligation. According to a recent survey, more companies in the United States are stressing ethical conduct in business. One major reason for this change is that employees are better educated and well versed in the realties of the workplace.[38] Apparently, the attitude has changed from "Should we be doing something in business ethics?" to "What should we be doing in business ethics?"[39] Every day, individuals who work in human resources must make decisions that have ethical implications. Ethical dilemmas, such as whether a manager should recommend against a woman applicant for employment strictly because she will be working exclusively with men, occur frequently and must be correctly addressed. These issues must be dealt with on the basis of what is ethically correct, not just from the standpoint of what will most benefit the organization in the short run.

There are many kinds of ethical codes, and most professions have their own. An example is SHRM's Code of Ethics, shown in Figure 1-11 on page 26. A growing number of firms are establishing ethical codes and communicating these codes to all employees.[40] Few of the numerous codes that exist in our society conflict in principle. They vary primarily in the extent to which they are applied under particular circumstances. It is vitally important that the human resource manager understand those practices that are unacceptable and make every attempt to act ethically in dealing with others.

■ SCOPE OF THIS BOOK

Effective human resource management is crucial to every organization's success. In order to be effective, managers must understand and competently practice human resource management. We designed this human resource management book to give you the following:

■ An insight into the role of human resource management in today's organizations.
■ An understanding of human resource planning, recruitment, and selection.

---

[38] Alan Weiss, "Seven Reasons to Examine Workplace Ethics," *HRMagazine,* 36 (March 1991), p. 71.
[39] Bill Leonard, "Business Ethics Touch HR Issues, Survey Finds," *HR News,* 10 (June 1991), p. 13.
[40] Patricia Buhler, "How Can We Encourage Ethical Behavior?" *Supervision,* 52 (January 1991), p. 3.

As a member of the Society for Human Resource Management, I pledge myself to:

- Maintain the highest standards of professional and personal conduct.
- Strive for personal growth in the field of human resource management.
- Support the Society's goals and objectives for developing the human resource management profession.
- Encourage my employer to make the fair and equitable treatment of all employees a primary concern.
- Strive to make my employer profitable both in monetary terms and through the support and encouragement of effective employment practices.
- Instill in the employees and the public a sense of confidence about the conduct and intentions of my employer.
- Maintain loyalty to my employer and pursue its objectives in ways that are consistent with the public interest.
- Uphold all laws and regulations relating to my employer's activities.
- Refrain from using my official positions, either regular or volunteer, to secure special privilege, gain or benefit for myself.
- Maintain the confidentiality of privileged information.
- Improve public understanding of the role of human resource management.

This Code of Ethics for members of the Society for Human Resource Management has been adopted to promote and maintain the highest standards of personal conduct and professional standards among its members. Adherence to this code is required for membership in the Society and serves to assure public confidence in the integrity and service of human resource management professionals.

FIGURE 1-11 | SHRM Code of Ethics

Source: Reprinted from *Who's Who in HR 1992 Directory,* p. 4. Copyright 1992, The Society for Human Resource Management, Alexandria, Virginia.

- An awareness of the importance of human resource development.
- An appreciation of how compensation and benefits programs are formulated and administered.
- An understanding of safety and health factors as they affect a firm's profitability.
- An opportunity to view employee and labor relations from both unionized and union-free standpoints.
- An understanding of the role of research in human resource management.
- An appreciation of the global dimension of human resource management.

Students often question whether the content of a book corresponds to the realities of the business world. In writing and revising this book, we have drawn heavily on the comments, observations, and experiences of human resource practitioners—and our own extensive research efforts. We cite the human resource practices of leading business organizations to illustrate how theory can be applied in the real world. Our intent is to enable you to experience human resource management in action.

This book is organized under seven parts, as shown in Figure 1-12. Combined, they provide a comprehensive view of human resource management. As you read this book, we hope you will be stimulated to increase your knowledge in this rapidly changing, expanding, and challenging field.

I. Introduction

Chapter 1: Human Resource Management: An Overview
Chapter 2: The Environment of Human Resource Management
Chapter 3: Equal Employment Opportunity and Affirmative Action
Chapter 4: Job Analysis

II. Human Resource Planning, Recruitment, and Selection

Chapter 5: Human Resource Planning
Chapter 6: Recruitment
Chapter 7: Selection

III. Human Resource Development

Chapter 8: Organization Change and Human Resource Development
Chapter 9: Corporate Culture and Organization Development
Chapter 10: Career Planning and Development
Chapter 11: Performance Appraisal

IV. Compensation and Benefits

Chapter 12: Financial Compensation
Chapter 13: Benefits and Other Compensation Issues

V. Safety and Health

Chapter 14: A Safe and Healthy Work Environment

VI. Employee and Labor Relations

Chapter 15: The Labor Union
Chapter 16: Collective Bargaining
Chapter 17: Union-Free Organizations
Chapter 18: Internal Employee Relations

VII. Human Resource Research

Chapter 19: Human Resource Research

FIGURE 1-12 | Organization of This Book

SUMMARY

Human resource management (HRM) is the utilization of the firm's human resources to achieve organizational goals. Human resource managers normally act in an advisory (staff) capacity, working with other managers regarding human resource matters. Human resource managers have the primary responsibility of coordinating the firm's human resource actions through a well-conceived human resource management system. That system embraces six functional areas of effective human resource management: human resource planning, recruitment, and selection; human resource development; compensation and benefits; safety and health; employee and labor relations; and human resource research.

An organization must have qualified individuals available at specific places and times to accomplish its goals. Among the tasks involved in accomplishing this objective are human resource planning, recruitment, and selection.

Human resource development (HRD) is designed to assist individuals, groups, and the entire organization in becoming more effective. Such programs are needed because people, jobs, and organizations are always changing. Development should begin when individuals join the firm and continue throughout their careers. Large-scale HRD programs are referred to as organizational development (OD). Other aspects of HRD are career planning and development and performance appraisal.

The question of what constitutes a fair day's pay has plagued managers for decades. An effective compensation and benefits system rewards employees adequately and equitably for their contributions to the organization. As used in this book, the term *compensation* includes all rewards that individuals receive as a result of their employment.

Safety involves protecting employees from injuries caused by work-related accidents. Health refers to the employees' freedom from illness, and their general physical and mental well-being. A safe and healthy work environment is important not only to employees but also to the organization. Employees who enjoy these conditions are more likely to be productive and provide long-term benefits to the organization.

A business firm is required by law to recognize a union and bargain with it in good faith, if the firm's employees want the union to represent them. However, union-free firms typically strive to satisfy their employees' work-related needs in order to make union representation unnecessary for individuals to achieve their personal goals.

Every human resource management function needs effective research. This need is particularly strong today because of the rapid changes taking place in the HRM field.

In recent years, human resource professionals have been afforded increased respect and responsibility. They are now expected to provide the direction necessary to meet the many HRM problems and challenges of the future.

Within the human resource profession are executives, generalists, and specialists. Executives are top-level managers who report directly to the corporation's CEO or to the head of a major division. A generalist (who often is an executive) performs tasks in many human resource-related areas. A specialist may be an executive, a manager, or a non-manager who is typically concerned with only one of the six functional areas of HRM.

Human resource functions tend to change as firms grow and become more complex—as HRM becomes more important. Although the basic purpose of human resource management remains the same, the approach followed in accomplishing its objectives often changes.

A profession is characterized by the existence of a common body of knowledge and a procedure for certifying members of the profession. Performance standards are established by members of the profession itself (self-regulation). Professional organizations offer their members the chance to exchange ideas and grow. Among the more prominent professional organizations in the field of human resources are the Society for Human Resource Management (formerly the American Society for Personnel Administration), the Human Resource Certification Institute, the American Society for Training and Development, the American Compensation Association, the National Human Resources Association, and the International Personnel Management Association.

Professionalization of human resource management created a need for a uniform code of ethics. Individuals working in human resources must constantly make decisions that have ethical implications. Most professions, organizations, and individuals subscribe to ethical codes of one type or another.

Questions for Review

1. Justify the statement "All managers are involved in human resource management."
2. Distinguish between human resource management and the human resource manager.
3. What human resource management functions must be performed regardless of the organization's size?
4. By definition and example distinguish among human resource executives, generalists, and specialists.
5. How does the human resource function change as a firm grows? Briefly describe each stage of the development.
6. Define *profession*. Do you believe that the field of human resource management is a profession? Explain your answer.
7. Define *ethics*. Why is ethics important to the field of human resource management?

Terms for Review

Human resource management
   (HRM)
Human resource manager
Operative employees
Executive

Generalist
Specialist
Profession
Ethics

INCIDENT 1 ▪ A Day to Remember ▪

The day was one of the happiest in Ed Beaver's life. He had been told that he was being promoted to corporate vice-president for human resources from his present position as human resource manager for his firm's large New York plant. As he leaned back in his office chair, he felt a deep sense of accomplishment. He thought back to the day fifteen years earlier when, fresh out of college, he had joined Duncan Foods as an assistant compensation specialist. He had always wanted to be in human resources, but he got his degree in business management because the university didn't have a human resource curriculum. Ed remembered how tense he was when he arrived at work that first day. College graduates were rarely given the opportunity to start work directly in human resources in those days, and he was the youngest employee in the department.

Ed learned his job well and the older workers quickly accepted him. Three years later he was promoted to the position of compensation manager. Immediately after the promotion he was given the task of designing a new pay system for operative employees. As he remembers, "Designing the system wasn't difficult. Convincing the employees that the new system was better than the old one was the real chore." But he overcame that obstacle.

A few years later Ed moved up again. He was chosen to become the new human resource manager for a small Duncan plant outside Chicago. The move required a major adjustment for his family. At the time Ed's wife remarked, "I sure hated to move in the middle of the school year. And we'd just begun to enjoy our new house." Ed was able to find another house that the family came to like just as well, and the children adjusted quickly. The job was certainly no bed of roses. Six months

after Ed arrived, he led negotiations for a new union contract. He worked night and day for months to develop a contract that would be acceptable to the company and the union. Successful signing of the new agreement was one of his most satisfying experiences.

Four years later, Ed was asked to accept the position of human resource manager for the large New York plant. This plant employed five times as many workers as the Chicago plant and had many different types of problems. After a family discussion, the Beavers were off to new adventures in the Big Apple.

At that moment, Ed's reverie came to an end. He began to realize the challenge that the new job presented to him. As vice-president of human resources for Duncan Foods, he would be responsible for the human resource management activities for fifty plants and warehouses employing 13,000 people. What an overwhelming responsibility he faced! Human resource management had changed greatly during the previous fifteen years, and the rate of change seemed to be accelerating. Ed wondered about these problems and the role he would play in solving them as the new vice-president for human resources.

Questions

1. Trace Ed's progression to vice-president of human resources. Do you believe that this progression qualifies him for the job?
2. What problems do you imagine Ed will face in his new role that he didn't have to deal with as plant human resource manager?
3. What future challenges do you think Ed will confront in the field of human resources?

INCIDENT 2   ▪   Learn What They Really Want   ▪

Marsha Smith was exceptionally happy the day she received word of her appointment as assistant human resource director at Nelson Electronics in Boise, Idaho. Marsha had started working as a recruiter three years earlier. Her degree from the University of Missouri was in human resource administration and she had four years' experience as a human resource specialist with Nelson Electronics.

As she walked to her office, she thought about how much she had learned while working as a recruiter. The first year with Nelson, she went on a recruiting trip to Southern Idaho College, only to find that its placement director was extremely angry with her company. She was visibly upset when the placement director said, "If you expect to recruit any of our students, you people at Nelson had better get your act together." When she questioned the placement director, she learned that a previous recruiter had failed to show up for a full afternoon of scheduled interviews with Southern's students. Marsha's trip ended amicably, though, and she eventually recruited a number of excellent employees from the college.

She learned another important lesson when the production manager asked for some help. "I need you to find an experienced quality control inspector," he said. "I want to make sure that the person has a degree in statistics. Beyond that, you decide on the qualifications." Marsha advertised the position and checked through dozens of résumés in search of the right person. She sent each promising applicant to the production manager. This process went on for six months with the production manager giving various obscure reasons for not hiring any of the applicants. Finally, the production manager called Marsha and said, "I just hired a QC person. He has a degree in history, but he seems eager. Besides, he was willing to work for only fifteen hundred dollars a month."

Marsha learned more with each passing day. She felt that one of her greatest accomplishments was improving the firm's minority recruitment program. She was able to do so, in part, because one of her close friends in school had become a leader in the Black Chamber of Commerce. With his advice, she was able to develop a recruiting program that attracted blacks to Nelson Electronics.

As Marsha began to clean out her desk, she suddenly realized that the learning process was really just beginning. As assistant human resource director, she would be responsible not only for matters related to recruiting, but also for all aspects of human resource management. It was a little scary, but she felt ready.

Questions

1. What lessons can be learned from each of the three situations described?
2. How will the problems that Marsha faces as an assistant human resource director differ from those she handled as a recruiter?

DEVELOPING HRM SKILLS

In every organization, human resource professionals work with many individuals and groups. Cooperation is a must if the tasks involved in human resource management are to be accomplished effectively. The Blue-Green exercise provides those involved in it with an excellent experience of the value of cooperation. This exercise is a good ice breaker and discussion stimulator. The Blue-Green exercise provides students with the opportunity to experience some of the interrelationships that occur in a structured setting, such as an organization or work group.

The Blue-Green exercise is one of the best exercises to use when working with a relatively large group. In fact, it is not recommended for groups of fewer than twelve persons. It has been successfully used with groups as large as forty persons. This exercise works equally well with groups of people who have been working together for some time and with heterogeneous groups whose members barely know one another. Its impact, however, is probably greater when dealing with people who are *supposed* to work together. The language used by the person in charge of conducting the exercise is extremely important, so participants should listen carefully to the rules.

Those who participate in this exercise usually find it quite enlightening; it has been repeated many times over the years. The total group will be divided into four subgroups of as nearly equal size as possible. These subgroups will be called "teams" and designated as Team A-1, Team A-2, Team B-1, and Team B-2. Your instructor will provide the participants with additional information necessary to participate. Enjoy the classic Blue-Green exercise, and experience the first of the experiential exercises provided to expand your educational horizons.

REFERENCES

Axline, Larry L. "Business Ethics: Blackjack or Bust?" *Management Review,* 79 (October 1990), p. 64.

Bavaria, Steve. "Corporate Ethics Should Start in the Boardroom." *Business Horizons,* 34 (January–February 1991), pp. 9–12.

Beilinson, Jerry. "Workforce 2000: Already Here?" *Personnel,* 67 (October 1990), pp. 3–4.

Bhide, Amar, and Howard H. Stevenson. "Why Be Honest If Honesty Doesn't Pay?" *Harvard Business Review,* 66 (September–October 1990), pp. 121–129.

Brown, Rick, and Joseph L. Meresman. "Balancing Stability and Innovation to Stay Competitive." *Personnel,* 67 (September 1990), pp. 49–52.

"Company Size Affects HR Salaries." *HRMagazine,* 35 (July 1990), p. 46.

Dye, Carson F. "10 Rules Define HR's Role." *Personnel Journal,* 69 (June 1990), pp. 83–86.

Herren, Laura M. "The New Game of HR: Playing to Win." *Personnel,* 66 (June 1989), pp. 19–22.

"HR Job Function Determines Pay Level in Large Companies." *HRMagazine,* 35 (July 1990), p. 48.

Hyman, Michael R. "Ethical Codes Are Not Enough." *Business Horizons,* 33 (March–April 1990), pp. 15–22.

Ireland, Karin. "The Ethics Game." *Personnel Journal,* 70 (March 1991), pp. 72–75.

"Issues and Visions." *HRMagazine,* 35 (January 1990), pp. 44–48.

Keaton, Paul N., and Michael J. Semb. "Shaping Up the Bottom Line." *HRMagazine,* 35 (September 1990), pp. 81–86.

Knapp, Jeffrey. "Trends in HR Management Systems." *Personnel,* 67 (April 1990), pp. 56–61.

Kovach, Kenneth A., and John A. Pearce II. "HR Strategic Mandates for the 1990s." *Personnel,* 67 (April 1990), pp. 50–55.

Kromling, Larry K. "Calcomp Reshapes HR for the Future." *Personnel Journal,* 69 (January 1990), pp. 57–63.

Kubiak, Sharon L., Jack L. Simonetti, C. Joseph Sass, and Nick Nykodym. "Making People an Organization's Most Important Resource." *Business,* 40 (October–November–December 1990), pp. 33–35.

Langer, Steven. "Human Resources: Who Makes What." *Personnel Journal,* 69 (February 1990), pp. 102–106.

Lawrence, Stephanie. "HR Trends." *Personnel Journal,* 69 (July 1990), p. 12.

Levitan, Sar A. "We Can Handle It." *HRMagazine,* 35 (April 1990), pp. 39, 42.

Messmer, Max. "Strategic Staffing for the '90s." *Personnel Journal,* 69 (October 1990), pp. 92–97.

Packer, Arnold. "Skills Shortage Looms." *HRMagazine,* 35 (April 1990), pp. 38, 40.

Redwood, Anthony. "Human Resources Management in the 1990s." *Business Horizons,* 33 (January–February 1990), pp. 74–80.

Reilly, Bernard J. "Ethical Business and the Ethical Person." *Business Horizons,* 33 (November–December 1990), pp. 23–27.

Rendero, Thomasine. "HR Panel Takes a Look Ahead." *Personnel,* 67 (August 1990), pp. 14–24.

Robin, Donald P., and Eric Reidenbach. "Balancing Corporate Profits and Ethics." *Business,* 40 (October–November–December 1990), pp. 11–14.

Sheehy, James W. "New Work Ethic Is Frightening." *Personnel Journal,* 69 (June 1990), pp. 28–36.

Shetty, Y. K., and Paul F. Buller. "Regarding Competitiveness Requires HR Solutions." *Personnel,* 67 (July 1990), pp. 8–12.

Shimko, Barbara Whitaker. "All Managers Are HR Managers." *HRMagazine,* 35 (January 1990), pp. 67–70.

Wagel, William H. "On the Horizon: HR in the 1990s." *Personnel,* 67 (January 1990), pp. 11–16.

Wagel, William H., and Hermine Zagat Levine. "HR '90: Challenges and Opportunities." *Personnel,* 67 (June 1990), pp. 18–42.

Weiss, Alan. "Seven Reasons to Examine Work Place Ethics." *HRMagazine,* 36 (March 1991), pp. 69–74.

Woods, Tom H. "Will the Workforce Be the Focus of the 90s?" *Business Forum,* 15 (Spring 1990), p. 3.

APPENDIX

PROFESSIONAL CERTIFICATION

The Human Resource Certification Institute (HRCI) is an affiliate of the Society for Human Resource Management. Since its inception in 1976, the HRCI has granted certification to many human resource professionals. The number of certified individuals will likely increase substantially as the benefits of certification become more apparent.

The Human Resource Certification Institute program provides for two levels of certification: Professional in Human Resources (PHR), and Senior Professional in Human Resources (SPHR). These two levels recognize degrees of expertise and responsibility.

■ ELIGIBILITY

The Human Resource Certification Institute grants certification after an applicant has

1. verified current full-time professional exempt experience in the HR field as either a practitioner, educator, researcher or consultant.
2. passed a comprehensive written examination to demonstrate mastery of knowledge.

To earn the basic generalist designation Professional in Human Resources (PHR), you must have

1. four years of professional HR exempt experience or either two years professional HR exempt experience and a bachelor's degree, or one year professional HR exempt experience and a graduate degree.*
2. passed a comprehensive examination.

To earn the senior generalist designation Senior Professional in Human Resources (SPHR), you must have

1. eight years of professional HR exempt experience or either six years professional HR exempt experience and a bachelor's degree, or five years professional HR exempt experience and a graduate degree.*
2. passed a comprehensive examination.

---

*Degrees must be earned from a higher education institution accredited by a generally recognized college or university accrediting association.

■ BASIC LEVEL CERTIFICATION, PROFESSIONAL IN HUMAN RESOURCES (PHR)

Definitions

The credentialing program established and administered by the Human Resource Certification Institute is intended for those professionals who are currently working in the field. Although that work need not always be exclusively in the HR field, it is expected that work in the field be the main thrust. Therefore, the following general definitions apply:

Practitioner: One whose duties are those normally found in the typical HR/Personnel activity

Educator: One whose principal area of instruction is in the HR/Personnel field in a higher education institution

Researcher: One whose research activities are resticted primarily to the HR/Personnel field

Consultant: One whose consulting activities are predominantly in the HR/Personnel field

The Institute defines professional HR exempt experience as *work that would meet the test for "exempt" as defined by the Fair Labor Standards Act and its amendments.*

■ EXAM COMPOSITION

Functional Areas

1. Employment, placement, and personnel planning
2. Training and development
3. Compensation and benefits
4. Health, safety, and security
5. Employee and labor relations
6. Management practices

The content of HRCI's comprehensive examinations is divided up (by percentage) as follows:

Functional Content Area	PHR Level	SPHR Level
Compensation and Benefits	20%	15%
Employee and Labor Relations	20%	15%
Selection and Placement	20%	15%
Training and Development	20%	15%
Health, Safety, and Security	5%	5%
Management Practices	15%	35%

In addition,

- both exams have a four-hour time limit.
- both exams have 250 multiple-choice questions with each question having four possible answers.
- 70 percent of the questions must be answered correctly to meet the pass requirement.
- questions unanswered are counted as incorrect.

Recertification

Certification is earned by individuals who demonstrate their mastery of the defined body of knowledge. The human resources field, however, is not static. Rapid changes require new and more sophisticated knowledge and behaviors by human resource professionals who wish to grow and develop with their field. Recertification is a method that certified individuals can use to demonstrate their accomplishments in keeping abreast of these changes and to update their knowledge in the field.

Recertification is required within three years of certification. Each subsequent recertification period is also for three years. Senior Professionals in Human Resources who are recertified twice earn this designation for life. There are two ways to become recertified. Testing is one method. The other method involves continuing one's education and professional experience.

Certification examinations are given on the first Saturday of each May and December at designated test sites. Applications must be submitted to the HRCI at least nine weeks in advance of the examination date. For additional certification information, contact the Human Resource Certification Institute, 606 North Washington Street, Alexandria, VA 22314.

CHAPTER 2

THE ENVIRONMENT OF HUMAN RESOURCE MANAGEMENT

CHAPTER OBJECTIVES

1. Identify and describe the external environmental factors that affect human resource management.
2. Identify and describe the internal environmental factors that affect human resource management.
3. Identify and describe external environmental factors that uniquely affect human resource management for multinational corporations.

As Wayne Simmons, vice-president of human resources for Lone Star Manufacturing, returned to his office from the weekly executive staff meeting, he was visibly disturbed. Lone Star, a producer of high-quality telecommunications equipment, is headquartered in Longview, Texas, and has manufacturing plants throughout Texas, Louisiana, and Oklahoma. Wayne had just heard a rumor that an overseas firm had developed a new manufacturing process—one with the potential to cut costs substantially. Should this report prove true, customers might well switch to the cheaper product. The three plants in the Longline Division that produce similar products would then be in serious trouble. The Longline Division had been expanding rapidly, but Wayne knew that demand for Lone Star's product was far from automatic. He also knew that if the new technology was really superior, Lone Star might have to cut back production severely or even close the three plants in the Longline Division. These plants are located in areas that are already experiencing high unemployment because of the depressed price of crude oil. Plant closings would have a devastating effect on the economies of their respective communities. A few workers could be transferred to other locations, but most would have to be laid off. Thus Wayne is now keenly aware of ways in which the external environment can have an impact on Lone Star Manufacturing's operations.

In this chapter, we first identify the environmental factors that affect human resource management. Then, we describe the means by which specific external environmental factors can influence human resource management. Next, we discuss some of the major internal environmental factors that can affect human resource management. Because of the continuing growth of multinational organizations, we devote the final section to describing major external environmental factors that multinational firms confront.

■ ENVIRONMENTAL FACTORS AFFECTING HUMAN RESOURCE MANAGEMENT

Many interrelated factors affect human resource management. Such factors are part of either the firm's external environment or its internal environment (see Figure 2-1). The firm often has little, if any, control over how the external environment affects management of its human resources. These factors impinge on the organization from outside its boundaries. Moreover, important factors within the firm itself also have an impact on how the firm manages its human resources.

Certain interrelationships tend to complicate the management of human resources. For instance, human resource professionals constantly work with people who represent all organizational levels and functional areas. Therefore, they must recognize the different perspectives that these indi-

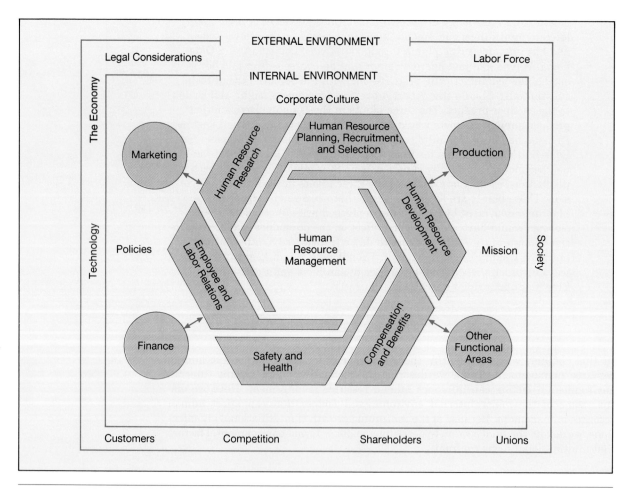

FIGURE 2-1 | The Environment of Human Resource Management

viduals bring to HRM if they are to perform their own human resource tasks properly.

Understanding the many interrelationships implied in Figure 2-1 is essential in order for the human resource professional to help other managers resolve issues and problems. For instance, a production manager may want to give a substantial pay raise to a particular employee. The human resource manager may know that this employee does an exceptional job; he or she should also be aware that granting the raise may affect pay practices in the production department *and* set a precedent for the entire firm. The human resource manager may have to explain to the production manager that such an action isn't an isolated decision. They may have to consider alternative means of rewarding the employee for superior performance, without upsetting the organization's reward system. Perhaps the human resource manager can point to a higher paying position that the employee is qualified to fill.

Whatever the case, the implications of a particular act must be considered in light of its potential impact on a department and the entire organization. Human resource managers must realize the overwhelming importance of the big picture, rather than concentrating on a narrow phase of the company's operation. The basic HRM tasks remain essentially the same regardless of the source of the impact. However, the manner in which those tasks are accomplished may be altered substantially by factors in the external environment.

■ THE EXTERNAL ENVIRONMENT

Those factors that affect a firm's human resources from outside its boundaries comprise the **external environment.** As illustrated in Figure 2-1, external factors include the labor force, legal considerations, society, unions, shareholders, competition, customers, technology, and the economy. Each factor—either separately or in combination with others—can place constraints on the human resource manager's job. Thus the HR manager must always try to identify and consider the impact of such factors.

The Labor Force

The capabilities of its employees determine in a large part how well an organization can perform its mission. The labor force is a pool of individuals external to the firm, from which the organization obtains its workers. As the labor force changes, the composition of the workforce within the organization will also change to some degree. Today's labor force is far different from that of the past. In addition, there has been a slowed growth of the labor supply.[1]

---

[1] Patricia Martin, "Jobs Must Be Marketed," *Personnel Journal,* 70 (April 1991), p. 87.

The projected size of the U.S. labor force in 1995 is some 129 million. This projection represents an increase of about 14 percent from the 1984 level of 114 million. Figure 2-2 shows actual and expected labor force growth rates through 1995. But size alone doesn't tell the entire story. The labor force now includes more working women and older persons. Companies increasingly hire part-time workers, use temporary and "leased employees," and include handicapped people in their workforces. Many new immigrants from developing areas, especially Southeast Asia and Latin America, are also joining the labor force. As Figure 2-3 shows, the breakdown of new entrants in the labor force from 1985 to 2000 is expected to be as follows: U.S.-born white males, 15 percent; U.S.-born white females, 42 percent; U.S.-born nonwhite males, 7 percent; U.S.-born nonwhite females, 13 percent; immigrant males, 13 percent; and immigrant females, 9 percent.[2] It is clear that managing a culturally diverse workforce will be a major challenge for HRM in the 1990s and beyond.

Further complicating the labor force outlook is the estimate that there will not be enough people in the next five to ten years to fill the jobs that the U.S. economy is expected to generate. During the 1990s, the United States will add about 20 million new jobs. For the first five years of this period, the number of workers from 18 to 24 years old who will be available will be about 500,000 less than in 1980.[3] Further complicating this situation is the fact that foreign companies are employing more and more U.S.

[2] William B. Johnston and Arnold E. Packer, *Workforce 2000: Work and Workers for the 21st Century* (Indianapolis: Hudson Institute, Inc., June 1987), p. 95.

[3] Jac Fitz-enz, "Getting—and Keeping—Good Employees," *Personnel,* 67 (August 1990), p. 26.

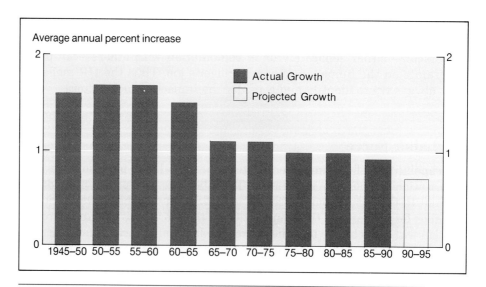

FIGURE 2-2 | Labor Force Growth Rate

Source: U.S. Bureau of the Census.

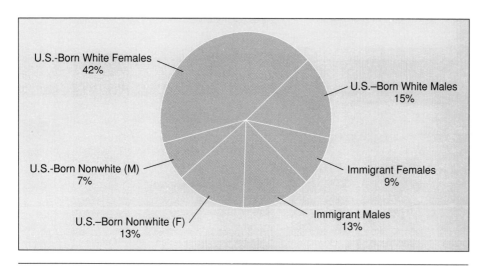

FIGURE 2-3 | New Entrants to the Workforce—Year 2000

Source: Adapted from *Workforce 2000,* published by the Hudson Institute, Inc., p. 95.

employees. In 1991, the number of U.S. workers employed by foreign companies rose to 4.6 million.[4] As may be seen in Figure 2-4 on page 44, the British employ more U.S. workers in their American operations than do the Canadians, Japanese, Germans, Dutch, or the French.

The Nontraditional Household. There is an increasing number of non-traditional households in the United States. These households include those headed by a single parent and those in which both partners work full time. Many women who at one time would have remained at home to care for their children and the household now work outside the home, whether out of the desire for a career or in response to financial necessity. In fact, women are expected to account for over 60 percent of the labor-force growth during the period from 1984 to 1995. Businesses are having to adapt to employees' requirements for flexibility by developing innovative child-care services, benefit plans, and work practices.

Traditionally, child-care needs were viewed as being outside the realm of the business world, a responsibility that workers had to bear and manage alone. This responsibility was particularly difficult for single parents. Even most working-parent couples could not afford a full-time, live-in house-keeper. For many individuals, child care was managed with the help of family or friends.

Today, businesses have begun to see that providing child-care services and workplace flexibility may influence a worker's choice of employers. Many companies have begun providing day-care services for employees.

---

[4] John Hoerr, Leah Nathans Spiro, Larry Armstrong, and James B. Treece, "Culture Shock at Home," *Business Week* (December 17, 1990), pp. 81–84.

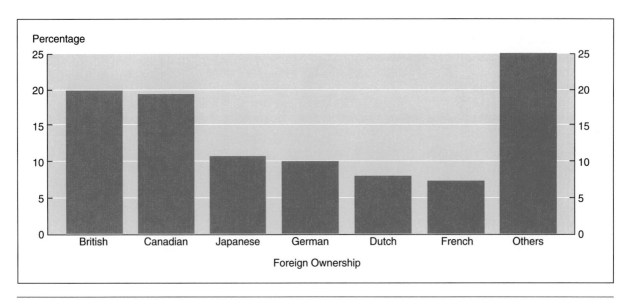

FIGURE 2-4 | Percentage of U.S. Employees at Foreign-owned Companies in the U.S.

Source: U.S. Commerce Department, 1988.

Some companies located in the same building or facility provide joint day-care services. Other companies, such as IBM, provide day-care referral services. More and more companies provide paid maternity leave, and some offer paternity leave. Still other firms give time off for children's visits to a doctor, which can be taken against the parent's sick leave or personal time. Managers need to be sensitive to the needs of this new workforce. At times, they need to be creative in order to accommodate the needs of this extremely valuable workforce segment.

The increasing number of dual-career couples presents organizations with challenges and opportunities. Some firms have revised their policies against nepotism to allow both partners to work for the same company. Other firms have developed policies to assist the spouse of an employee who is transferred. When a firm wishes to transfer an employee to another location, the employee's spouse may be unwilling to give up a good position, or may be unable to find an equivalent position at the new location. Firms have begun to realize that forcing a transfer can lead them to lose valuable employees. Some companies now offer the spouse of a transferred employee assistance in finding a position.[5] Overall, the trend in this society is toward the "nontraditional" household, and firms must develop programs to accommodate the needs of their employees.

---

[5] "Corporate Women," *Business Week* (June 22, 1987), pp. 72–80.

Older Workers. The population of the United States grew older through the 1980s, a trend which is expected to continue through the year 2000. Life expectancies continued to increase; and the baby-boom generation, those born from the end of World War II through 1964, had only half as many children as their parents did.

The trend toward earlier retirement reversed itself in the mid-1980s. This reversal may have been due mainly to the 1986 amendment to the Age Discrimination in Employment Act of 1967. As amended in 1978, the act prohibited age discrimination against individuals between the ages of 40 and 70. The 1986 amendment removed the upper age limitations. As a result of this amendment, firms cannot force employees to retire because of age, no matter how old they are. And many older persons do not want to retire, or even slow down. In addition, as many as one-third of the retirees want to return to full- or part-time work.[6]

The "graying" of the workforce continues to require some adjustments. Some older workers favor a less demanding, although full-time, job; others choose semi-retirement; and still others prefer part-time work. Many of these individuals require retraining as they move through the various stages of their careers. According to Ernie Morris, president of Fred Jones Manufacturing Company in Oklahoma City, "The single most important item in this country for the next ten years will be employee education and retraining."[7]

Part-time Workers. More and more organizations employ part-time workers. In fact, it has been estimated that part-time workers were the fastest growing segment of the workforce after 1970.[8] The use of part-time workers offers a number of advantages. First, it allows access to employees who are available only during certain hours or for a limited number of hours per week. For example, women with small children sometimes work part-time when their children are young. Students may schedule work around their class hours. Second, a company's less than full-time need for a skilled person may be filled, saving on both salary and benefits. Third, part-time workers often are not provided benefits, such as medical insurance and pension programs, thereby saving the company money. However, this advantage has eroded somewhat in recent years. Fourth, part-time workers usually think of their jobs as temporary, so they can be easily hired or laid off as work volume fluctuates. Fifth, if employers restrict employees with demanding family situations to full-time jobs only, the results might include absenteeism, personal business conducted on company time, or the loss of good workers.

Although utilizing part-time workers has many advantages, it often presents unique problems for human resource managers. For example,

---

[6] Joan L. Kelly, "Employers Must Recognize That Older People Want to Work," *Personnel Journal,* 69 (January 1990), p. 44.

[7] Nancy J. Perry, "The New, Improved Vocational School," *Fortune* (June 19, 1989), pp. 127–38.

[8] Harry Bacas, "Desperately Seeking Workers," *Nation's Business* (February 1988), p. 20.

part-time workers require more employee training and orientation, which is both costly and time consuming. Also, they often are not as loyal as full-time employees, sometimes becoming disgruntled as they work alongside full-timers who receive full company benefits. Furthermore, managers must confront the personal problems and complications of a larger work group. Employing part-time workers requires managers to relate to and communicate with different people performing the same job, thus increasing the complexity of the situation. Company policy can lessen some of these problems by giving part-time workers first chance at full-time jobs when they become available. Treating part-time and full-time workers as equally as possible is vitally important in order to tap the part-timers' sense of responsibility and need to feel worthwhile. Overcoming these disadvantages requires that human resource managers exercise extraordinary leadership.

A special case in the use of part-time workers is known as job sharing. **Job sharing** involves filling a job with two or more part-time employees, each working part of a regular work week and sharing the benefits of one full-time worker. Companies such as Walgreens Drugs, New York Life Insurance Company, and Fireman's Fund Insurance Company offer job-sharing arrangements.

Temporary and "Leased" Employees. Skilled professionals who desire to work on a temporary basis are becoming increasingly more available.[9] Also, the corporate takeover fever of the late 1980s caused many firms to cut workforces to bare minimums. They often filled gaps with temporary employees. Some companies use a substantial portion of their compensation budget—as much as 20 percent—on temporary workers in a wide variety of skills.[10]

A special class of temporary workers is known as "leased" employees. **Leased employees** are individuals provided by an outside firm at a fixed hourly rate, similar to a rental fee, often for extended periods. Employee leasing goes beyond the use of short-term "temps" furnished by such agencies as Kelly Services and Manpower.

Managers of temporary or leased workers generally find them to be well qualified and eager to please, though less tied to their employers than traditional employees. Major temporary help and employee-leasing firms have tight reporting systems to ensure that an employee can fit in and do the job intended. Such employees are usually very productive and extremely beneficial to the organization utilizing them.

Persons with Disabilities. According to one estimate, there are approximately 36 million disabled individuals in the United States, not including the mentally handicapped.[11] A handicap, or disability, is a disadvantage

---

[9] Max Messmer, "Strategic Staffing for the '90s," *Personnel Journal,* 69 (October 1990), p. 94.

[10] *Ibid.*

[11] Susan Goff Condon, "Hiring the Handicapped Confronts Cultural Uneasiness," *Personnel Journal,* 66 (April 1987), p. 68.

that limits the amount or kind of work a person can do or makes its achievement unusually difficult.

Laws relating to handicapped workers generally define the terms *handicap* or *disability* quite broadly. More common disabilities include limited hearing or sight, limited mobility, mental or emotional deficiencies, and various nerve disorders. Recent studies indicate that handicapped workers do as well as the unimpaired in terms of productivity, attendance, and average tenure.[12] In fact, in certain high-turnover occupations, handicapped workers had lower turnover rates.

Research suggests that disabled persons can be as productive as the unimpaired in many jobs. A blind person, for example, may be a perfectly competent PBX operator; paraplegics have no disability with regard to most desk jobs. Even when the disabling condition directly affects performance, the handicapped person often compensates for it through extra effort.

Many American firms have long utilized the capabilities of handicapped workers. Passage of the Americans with Disabilities Act requires that virtually all firms not only employ them but also make reasonable accommodations to facilitate their employment.

Immigrants from Developing Areas. Large numbers of immigrants from developing areas, particularly Southeast Asia and Latin America, have settled in many parts of the United States. These immigrants bring with them the attitudes, values, and mores peculiar to their home-country cultures.

Vietnamese settled along the Mississippi, Louisiana, and Texas Gulf Coast in the 1970s and 1980s, after the end of hostilities in Vietnam. At about the same time, thousands of Thais fleeing the upheaval in Thailand came to the Boston area to work and live. New York's Puerto Rican community has long been an economic and political force there. Cubans who fled Castro's regime congregated in southern Florida, especially Miami. A flood of Mexicans and other Hispanics continues across the southern border of the United States. The Irish, the Poles, the Italians, and others who came here in past decades have long since assimilated into—and indeed have become—the culture. Newer immigrants require time to adapt. Meanwhile, they generally take low-paying and menial jobs, live in substandard housing, and form enclaves where they cling to some semblance of the cultures they left.

Wherever they settle, members of these ethnic groups soon begin to become part of the regular workforce, and break out of their isolation in certain occupations. They begin to adopt the English language and American customs. They begin to learn new skills and to adapt old skills to their new country. Human resource managers can place these individuals in jobs appropriate to their skills, with excellent results for the organization.

Young Persons with Limited Education or Skills. Many businesses hire thousands of young, unskilled workers, especially during holiday

---

[12] *Ibid.*

buying seasons. In general, they have limited education—high school or less. Some who have high school diplomas find that their education hardly fits the work they are expected to do. For example, most lack familiarity with computers. Many of these young adults and teenagers have poor work habits. They tend to be tardy or absent more often than experienced or better educated workers. Interviews with supervisors of such workers at J. C. Penney Company and other firms, both large and small, revealed the following recurrent problems with young workers: They do not pay attention to instructions; they will concentrate on the job only for short periods of time; they tend to think that the paycheck is their due for being at the workplace and is unrelated to how much they contribute; they often have transportation problems, such as missing buses or cars that break down frequently; they do not respect their supervisors, often gossiping or speaking openly to other workers; they lack company loyalty; and, to make matters worse, they change jobs frequently.

On the positive side, human resource managers cite these advantages of hiring young, unskilled persons: They work for low wages and few benefits; they are willing to work part-time and during short periods; they can easily be fired if they do not perform; they are exciting, vivacious, and interesting; they generally have high levels of strength, endurance, and energy, which need to be directed to productive purposes; they thrive on competition; they readily respond to praise; they also respond to monetary incentives, especially piece rates; many are physically attractive and make good impressions on customers; and they often have a sincere desire to overcome their shortcomings, especially to get additional education or to gain management experience.

Regardless of whether the positive attributes of such workers outweigh the negative, more workers will be needed in the future, including younger workers with limited skills and education. Because a chronic shortage of qualified workers has been predicted for the future, human resource managers need to view each young worker as a potential long-term employee and carefully avoid stereotyping. Young, unskilled workers can serve as a rich source of permanent employees, even junior managers, and can contribute to productivity.

Managing Diversity. Largely because of this changing workforce, a new concept is weaving its way through many of the leading business organizations: managing diversity. **Managing diversity** means "having an acute awareness of characteristics common to a culture, race, gender, age or sexual preference, while at the same time managing employees with these characteristics as individuals."[13] This philosophy recognizes that individuals of a particular culture may share some general characteristics. In the work environment, these employees should be treated as individuals, while still taking into consideration their cultural differences.

---

[13] Stephenie Overman, "Managing the Diverse Work Force," *HRMagazine,* 36 (April 1991), p. 32.

Legal Considerations

Another significant external force affecting human resource management relates to federal, state, and local legislation and the many court decisions interpreting this legislation. In addition, many presidential executive orders have had a major impact on human resource management. These legal considerations affect virtually the entire spectrum of human resource policies. We highlight in Chapter 3 the most significant of these considerations that affect equal employment opportunity. Laws, court decisions, and executive orders affecting other human resource management activities will be described in the appropriate chapters.

Society

Society may also exert pressure on human resource management. The public is no longer content to accept, without question, the actions of business. Individuals and special interest groups have found that they can effect change through their voices, votes, and other actions. The influence of activists is obvious by the large number of regulatory laws that have been passed since the early 1960s. To remain acceptable to the general public, a firm must accomplish its purpose while complying with societal norms.

A major point that management must consider is that society includes the firm's employees. For instance, if an organization has 10,000 employees, these individuals will influence a larger number of people who are not connected with the firm, including friends and members of an employee's family. Therefore, it behooves a firm to maintain clear and honest communications with its employees so that they understand and appreciate the firm's position.

The general public's attitudes and beliefs can affect the firm's behavior, because those attitudes and beliefs often directly affect profitability. When a corporation behaves as if it has a conscience, it is said to be socially responsible. **Social responsibility** is the implied, enforced, or felt obligation of managers, acting in their official capacities, to serve or protect the interests of groups other than themselves.[14] Many companies develop patterns of concern for moral and social issues. They do so through policy statements, practices, and the leadership of morally strong employees and managers over time. Open-door policies, grievance procedures, and employee benefit programs often stem as much from a desire to do what is right as from a concern for productivity and avoidance of strife.[15]

You may well ask, "Why should a business be concerned with the welfare of society? Its goal is to make a profit and grow." Obviously, a business must make a profit over the long run if it is to survive. But you should also

---

[14] R. Wayne Mondy, Arthur Sharplin, and Shane R. Premeaux, *Management: Concepts, Practices, and Skills,* 5th ed. (Boston: Allyn & Bacon, 1991), p. 76.

[15] Kenneth E. Goodpaster and John B. Matthews, Jr., "Can a Corporation Have a Conscience?" *Harvard Business Review,* 60 (January–February 1982), pp. 132–41.

remember another basic point: If a firm does not satisfy society's needs, then it will ultimately cease to exist. A firm operates by public consent to satisfy society's requirements. Although such issues relate to the organization as a whole, you can easily see how human resource managers might be expected to become involved in them. The organization is a member of the community in which it operates. Just as citizens work to improve the quality of life in their community, the organization should also respect and work with the other members of its community. For instance, a high unemployment rate among a certain minority group may exist within the firm's service area. A philosophy of hiring workers who are capable of being trained as opposed to hiring only qualified applicants may help to reduce unemployment for that group. In the long run, this philosophy will certainly enhance the firm's image, and may actually improve profitability.

Unions

Wage levels, benefits, and working conditions for millions of employees now reflect decisions made jointly by unions and management. A **union** is a group of employees who have joined together for the purpose of dealing with their employer. Unions are treated as an environmental factor because, essentially, they become a third party when dealing with the company. In a unionized organization, the union rather than the individual employee negotiates an agreement with management.

Although unions remain a powerful force, union membership as a percentage of the nonagricultural workforce slipped from 33 percent in 1955 to 16.4 percent in 1990.[16] This trend is expected to continue for a number of reasons, which we discuss in greater detail in Chapter 17. However, as the power and influence of unions continue to decline, the emphasis will likely shift to a human resource system that deals directly with the individual worker and his or her needs.

Shareholders

The owners of a corporation are called **shareholders.** Because shareholders have invested money in the firm, they may at times challenge programs considered by management to be beneficial to the organization. Managers may be forced to justify the merits of a particular program in terms of how it will affect future projects, costs, revenues, and profits. For instance, $50,000 spent on implementing a management development program may require more justification than stating, "Managers should become more open and adaptive to the needs of employees." Shareholders are concerned with how such expenditure decisions will increase revenues or decrease

---

[16] Gene Koretz and Celeste Whittaker, "More Picket Lines, Fewer Rank-And-Filers," *Business Week* (May 7, 1990), p. 24.

costs. Thus management must be prepared to explain the merits of a particular program in terms of its economic costs and benefits.

Another way in which shareholders can influence a company is through shareholder activism. Management has become extremely sensitive to its public image. The last thing most corporations want is criticism of the firm's performance on the front page of a major newspaper or on the evening news. Therefore, corporations have become increasingly sensitive to shareholder pressure.

Competition

Unless an organization is in the unusual position of monopolizing the market it serves, other firms will be producing similar products or services. A firm must maintain a supply of competent employees if it is to succeed, grow, and prosper. But other organizations are also striving for that same objective. A firm's major task is to ensure that it obtains and retains a sufficient number of employees in various career fields to allow the firm to compete effectively. A bidding war often results when competitors attempt to fill certain critical positions in their firms. Because of the strategic nature of their needs, firms are sometimes forced to resort to unusual means to recruit and retain such employees. The poster shown in Figure 2-5 exemplifies the extreme approaches that some organizations have used to recruit qualified workers (see page 52).

Moreover, because of the competitive nature of many businesses, managers may feel considerable pressure to improve their company's compensation system. In order to meet this challenge, many firms not only are improving salaries, but also are emphasizing other forms of rewards. Thus the firm's total financial compensation program has to be considered as part of the overall work environment.

Customers

The people who actually use a firm's goods and services also are part of its external environment. Because sales are crucial to the firm's survival, management has the task of ensuring that its employment practices do not antagonize the customers it serves. For example, consumer boycotts have been triggered by organizations that limited the number of minorities they employed. If a certain minority or ethnic group purchases a large share of the firm's products, the organization should look closely at including a representative proportion of this group in its workforce.

Customers constantly demand high-quality products and after-purchase service. Therefore a firm's workforce should be capable of providing quality goods and services. Sales are often lost or gained because of variances in product quality and follow-up service. These conditions relate directly to the skills, qualifications, and motivations of the organization's employees.

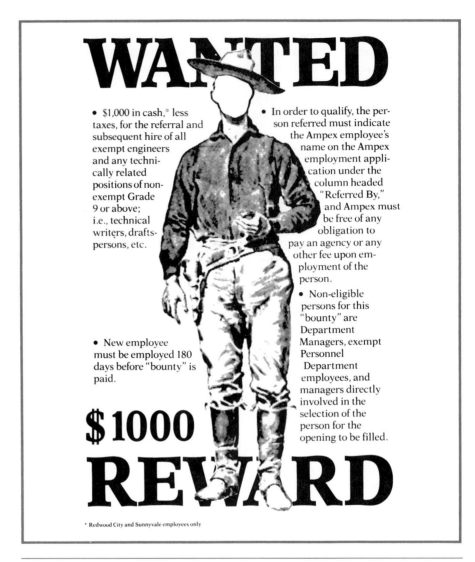

FIGURE 2-5 | A Recruitment Poster

Technology

The rate of technological change is accelerating, and as a result, few firms operate today as they did even a decade ago. Of major concern to those in HRM is the effect that technological changes have had, and will have on businesses. During the next decade, one of the most challenging areas in human resource management will be training employees to keep up with rapidly advancing technology. Products that were not envisioned only a few years ago are now being mass produced, substantially enlarging the tasks of all managers, including human resource managers. New skills are typically not in large supply; recruiting qualified individuals in areas that demand them is often difficult.

As technological changes occur, certain skills also are no longer required. This situation necessitates some retraining of the current workforce. As we mentioned in Chapter 1, within the next decade, more than half of all existing jobs are expected to change and another 30 percent to be eliminated as a result of technological advances.[17] Furthermore, it has been estimated that by the year 2000, 75 percent of all jobs will involve the use of computers.[18] For instance, the traditional role of the secretary has changed substantially since the advent of word processing. Rather than writing or dictating a letter to give to the secretary, some managers are even entering their own letters in word processors and then printing them out.

Partly because of technological change, the industries that will need new employees through 1995 will likely be different from those of today. Figure 2-6 shows that employment in service-producing industries has increased faster than employment in goods-producing industries since 1959—and is expected to continue to do so through 1995. As incomes and living standards have risen, largely because of technological change, consumers' desires for services have grown more rapidly than their desires for goods. By the middle of 1991, 75 percent of all U.S. jobs were service related.[19]

---

[17] Eric G. Flanholtz, Yvonne Randle, and Sonja Sackmann, "Personnel Management: The Tenor of Today," *Personnel Journal,* 66 (June 1987), p. 64.

[18] Marilyn Joyce, "Ergonomics Will Take Center Stage During '90s and into New Century," *Occupational Health and Safety,* 60 (January 1991), p. 31.

[19] Eva Pomice, "Shaping Up Services," *U.S. News & World Report,* 111 (July 22, 1991), p. 42.

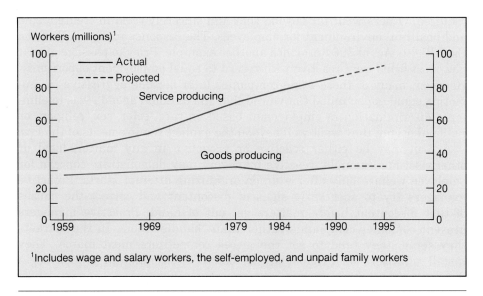

FIGURE 2-6 | Projected Growth of Service-producing versus Goods-producing Industries

Source: U.S. Bureau of Labor Statistics.

The Economy

The economy of the nation—on the whole and in its various segments—is a major environmental factor affecting human resource management. As a generalization, when the economy is booming, it is often more difficult to recruit qualified workers. On the other hand, when a downturn is experienced, more applicants are typically available.

Complicating this situation even further is the fact that one segment of the country may be experiencing a downturn, another a slow recovery, and another a boom. Such was the situation existing in the early 1990s. Some of the northeast states were facing a downturn; Houston, Texas, was gradually recovering; and Salt Lake City was booming.[20]

■ RESPONDING TO THE EXTERNAL ENVIRONMENT: PROACTIVE VERSUS REACTIVE

Managers approach changes in the external environment proactively or reactively. A **proactive response** involves taking action in anticipation of environmental changes. A **reactive response** involves simply reacting to environmental changes after they occur. For example, while the Americans with Disabilities Act of 1990 was weaving its way through Congress, some companies had already implemented its anticipated provisions. Managers of these companies were being proactive. Those who waited until the law went into effect to even plan the required changes were being reactive.

Organizations exhibit varying degrees of proactive and reactive behavior. When OSHA was enacted, some firms did only what the letter of the law required. Others went far beyond that and sincerely tried to create a safe and healthful environment for employees. The response to Title VII of the Civil Rights Act of 1964 provides another example. Prior to passage of that law, most firms were reactive with regard to equal employment opportunity. However, many of these same companies later became aggressive in promoting equal opportunity. Convinced that the national agenda was to eliminate discrimination in employment based on race, color, sex, religion, or national origin, they went well beyond the explicit requirements of the law.

A firm may be either reactive or proactive in any matter, legal or otherwise. For example, reactive managers may demonstrate concern for employee welfare only after a union organizing attempt starts. Proactive managers try to spot early signs of discontent and correct the causes of that discontent before matters get out of hand. Proactive managers prevent customer complaints rather than "handle" them. In the markets they serve, they tend to set the prices competitors must match. They install scrubbers on exhaust stacks before environmental groups begin

---

[20] Patricia Sellers, "The Best Cities for Business," *Fortune,* 122 (October 22, 1990), p. 49.

picketing the plant and before federal regulators file suit. In all matters, proactive managers initiate rather than react. And when an unanticipated environmental change occurs, they go beyond what the change forces them to do.

■ THE INTERNAL ENVIRONMENT

The internal environment also exerts considerable pressure on human resource management. Factors that affect a firm's human resources from inside its boundaries comprise the **internal environment.** As indicated in Figure 2-1 on page 40, the primary internal factors include the firm's mission, policies, corporate culture, management style of upper managers, employees, the informal organization, other units of the organization, and unions. These factors have a major impact in determining the interaction between HRM and other departments within the organization. This interaction has a major effect on overall organizational productivity, so it is vital that the interaction be positive and supportive of the firm's mission.

Mission

Mission is the organization's continuing purpose or reason for being. Each management level should operate with a clear understanding of the firm's mission. In fact, each organizational unit (division, plant, department) should have clear objectives that coincide with that mission.

The specific company mission must be regarded as a major internal factor that affects the tasks of human resource management. Consider two companies, each having a broadly based mission, and envision how certain tasks might differ from one firm to the other. Company A's goal is to be an industry leader in technological advances. Its growth occurs through the pioneering of new products and processes. Company B's goal is one of conservative growth, which involves little risk taking. Only after another company's product or process has proven itself in the marketplace will Company B commit itself.

Company A needs a creative environment to encourage new ideas. Highly skilled workers must be recruited to foster technological advancement. Constant attention to workforce training and development is essential. A compensation program designed to retain and motivate the most productive employees is especially important.

The basic tasks of human resource management are the same for Company B, but the mission dictates that they be altered somewhat. A different kind of workforce will likely be needed. Highly creative individuals may not want to work for Company B. Perhaps because the mission encourages little risk taking, most of the major decisions will be made at higher levels in the organization. Thus management development at lower levels in the organization may receive less emphasis. The compensation program may reflect the different requirements of this particular workforce. As this comparison indicates, a human resource manager must clearly understand the company's mission.

Policies

A **policy** is a predetermined guide established to provide direction in decision making. As guides rather than as hard-and-fast rules, policies are somewhat flexible, requiring interpretation and judgment in their use. They can exert significant influence on how managers accomplish their jobs. For instance, many firms have an "open door" policy that permits an employee to take a problem to the next higher level in the organization if it can't be solved by the immediate supervisor. Knowing that their subordinates can take problems to a higher echelon tends to encourage supervisors to try harder to resolve problems at their levels.

Many larger firms have policies related to every major operational area. Although policies are established for marketing, production, and finance, the largest number of policies often relates to human resource management. Some potential policy statements that affect human resource management are as follows:

- Provide employees with a safe place to work.
- Encourage all employees to achieve as much of their human potential as possible.
- Provide compensation that will encourage a high level of productivity in both quality and quantity.
- Ensure that current employees are considered first for any vacant position for which they may be qualified.

Because policies have a degree of flexibility, the manager is not necessarily required to adhere strictly to the policy statement. Often the tone of a policy guides managers as much as the actual words. Consider, for instance, a policy that ensures that "all members of the labor force have equal opportunity for employment." This policy implies more than merely adhering to certain laws and government regulations. Confronted with this policy, the human resource manager will likely do more than merely conform to the law. Perhaps the manager will initiate a training program to permit hiring of minorities or women who are not totally qualified to perform available jobs. Rather than just seeking qualified applicants, a firm that actively implements this policy goes beyond the minimum required by law.

Corporate Culture

As an internal environmental factor affecting human resource management, corporate culture refers to the firm's social and psychological climate. **Corporate culture** is defined as the system of shared values, beliefs, and habits within an organization that interacts with the formal structure to produce behavioral norms.[21] Managers can, and should, determine the kind of corporate culture they wish to work within and strive to make sure that kind of culture develops. Dennis L. Nowlin, manager of executive development at 3M Corporation, said his company was challenged with "managing a large firm with the value system of a small business." Nowlin added, "We work in a highly technical organization with many technical, research and development, and manufacturing specialists. . . . My personal vision is to get every manager within 3M thinking from a general management perspective."[22]

An infinite variety of cultures could exist, so we probably should view them as a continuum. A closed and threatening culture is at one extreme. In this type of culture, decisions tend to be made at higher levels in the organization; management and subordinates lack trust and confidence in each other; secrecy abounds; and workers aren't encouraged to be creative and solve problems. At the other extreme is an open culture in which decisions tend to be made at lower levels in the organization; a high degree of trust and confidence exists between management and subordinates; communication is open; and workers are encouraged to be creative and to solve problems. In all likelihood, the exact nature of any particular corporate culture falls somewhere between these extremes. Identification of the corporate culture in a firm is important. It affects job performance throughout the organization and consequently affects profitability. We discuss corporate culture in considerable detail in Chapter 9.

Management Style of Upper Managers

Closely related to corporate culture is the way in which the attitudes and preferences of one's superiors affect how a job is done. This situation deserves special emphasis here because of the problems that can result if the managerial style of upper-level managers differs from that of lower-level managers. In general, a lower-level manager must adapt to the style of the boss. It is hard to be open and considerate when the boss believes in just giving orders and having them followed. A lower-level manager's concerns about involving employees in decision making and giving them freedom may be seen as a lack of decisiveness. Even the company president must deal with the management style and attitudes of superiors, in this case, the board of directors.[23] The president may be a risk-taker and want to be aggressive in the marketplace, but the board may prefer a more conservative approach.

---

[21] Mondy et al., *Management,* 5th ed., p. 450.

[22] Stephanie Lawrence, "Voices of HR Experience," *Personnel Journal,* 68, no. 4 (April 1989), pp. 71–72.

[23] Judith H. Dobrzynski, Michael Schroeder, Gregory L. Miles, and Joseph Weber, "Taking Charge," *Business Week* (July 3, 1989), pp. 66–71.

Employees

Employees differ in capabilities, attitudes, personal goals, and personalities, among many other ways. As a result, behavior that a manager finds effective with one worker may not be effective with another. In extreme cases, employees can be so different that it is virtually impossible for them to be managed as a group. In order to be effective, the manager must consider both individual and group differences. A supervisor of experienced workers, for instance, may pay little attention to the technical details of the job and more to encouraging group cooperation, while a supervisor of inexperienced workers may focus mainly on the technical aspects of the task.

Informal Organization

New managers quickly learn that there are two organizations they must deal with in the firm—one formal, the other informal. The formal organization is usually described by an organization chart and job descriptions. Managers know the official reporting relationships. But an informal organization exists alongside the formal one. The **informal organization** is the set of evolving relationships and patterns of human interaction within an organization that are not officially prescribed. Such informal relationships are quite powerful. Assume, for instance, that top management has expressed total commitment to equal employment opportunity. An all-male or all-white work group may still resist the assignment of women or blacks to the group. Unwanted workers may be ostracized or refused the usual friendly assistance in adapting to a new job. In extreme cases, derogatory jokes may be told within earshot of such employees. This kind of behavior places the supervisor in a difficult position, caught between a formal policy and aggressive action arising from the informal organization.

Other Units

Managers must be keenly aware of interrelationships that exist among divisions or departments and should use such relationships to the best advantage. Some of these possible relationships are presented in Figure 2-7. The human resource department helps maintain a competent workforce; the purchasing department buys materials and parts. Because one department precedes another in the flow of work, that department's output becomes the other department's input. Most managers soon discover that cooperation with other departments is necessary if the job is to get done efficiently. Managers who make enemies of other managers may jeopardize the productivity of several departments.

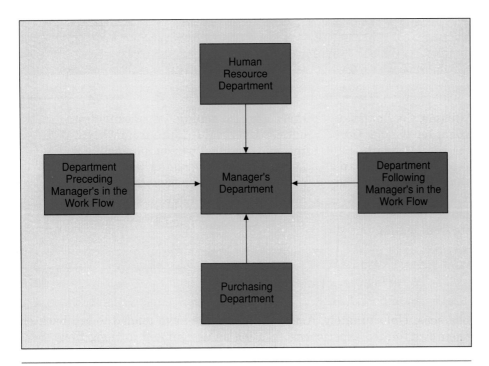

FIGURE 2-7 | Possible Relationships with Other Departments

Unions

Upper management typically negotiates labor-management agreements, but managers throughout the organization must implement the terms of the agreements. In most instances, agreements place restrictions on the manager's actions. For example, a manager may want to shift a maintenance worker to an operator's job temporarily; but if the labor-management agreement specifies the tasks that can and cannot be performed in each job, the supervisor may not be able to make the temporary assignment.

■ ENVIRONMENTAL FACTORS AFFECTING MULTINATIONAL CORPORATIONS

As recently as the early 1980s, management did not fully appreciate the need to adapt business practices to different national environments. However, global competition, air travel, satellite communication technology, and wage differentials have made doing business abroad both necessary and feasible. Companies have responded by establishing more and more operations

HRM In Action

Barbara Williams, the financial vice-president for Bendon Corporation, is speaking with Steve Allen, the vice-president of human resources. "Steve," says Barbara, "The accounting manager has just retired and his replacement must be selected. I would like to promote from within, but there are also qualified applicants from outside the firm. If I hire from within, the best qualified person may not be selected. On the other hand, if I hire from outside the firm, the current employees may not accept the new manager."

How would you respond?

overseas. Unfortunately, American managers have tended to fall back on their own limited experiences, treating an assignment in Hong Kong, Sydney, or Paris much like a stint in Dallas or Atlanta.[24] Some managers thought that international businesses could simply force foreign countries to conform to the companies' usual ways of operating.[25] Today, managers commonly recognize that this way of doing business is unacceptable and that, in fact, the challenge of multinational operations is not easily met. This is especially true with regard to the challenges of human resource management. According to Ellen Brandt, a human resources consultant and journalist, "Human resources executives must acquire a global perspective and global skills."[26]

Earlier in this chapter our discussion focused primarily on environmental factors affecting organizations located and doing business only in the United States. The external environment confronting multinational enterprises is even more diverse and complex than that confronting domestic firms. A **multinational corporation (MNC)** conducts a large part of its business outside the country in which it is headquartered and has a significant percentage of its physical facilities and employees in other countries. Thus, as illustrated in Figure 2-8, multinational operations add another environmental layer to human resource management. Although the basic HRM tasks remain essentially the same, the manner in which they are accomplished may be altered substantially by the multinational's external environment.

---

[24] Phillip R. Harris, "Employees Abroad: Maintain the Corporate Connection," *Personnel Journal,* 65 (August 1986), p. 108.

[25] Geert Hofstede, "The Cultural Relativity of Organizational Practices and Theories," *Journal of International Business Studies,* 24 (Fall 1983), p. 75.

[26] Ellen Brandt, "Global HR," *Personnel Journal,* 70 (March 1991), pp. 38–39.

Legal Considerations

Not only must the multinational corporation adhere to the federal, state, and local legislation of its parent country, it must also obey the laws of the host country. However, there is no comprehensive system of international law or courts requiring that the MNC understand in detail the laws of each host country. The United States, United Kingdom, Canada, Australia, and New Zealand have developed their legal systems from English common law. Under it, judges are extremely important, for they are guided by principles

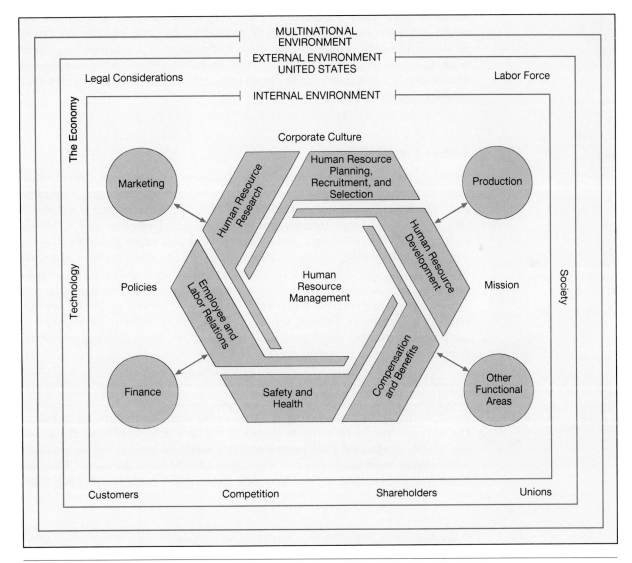

FIGURE 2-8 | Human Resource Management in the Multinational Environment

declared in previous cases. In most of Europe, Asia, and Africa, the legal systems are based on civil law, and judges play a lesser role because the legal requirements are codified. The civil servant has greater power under civil law than under the common law. Although the United States is a highly legalistic country and American MNCs tend to carry U.S. law with them, those involved in human resource management must realize that international law recognizes the rights of nations to regulate conduct within their own borders.[27]

Human resource professionals must also be acutely aware that the legal systems of other countries can differ considerably. For example, the Japanese dislike laws, lawyers, and litigation. In France, lawyers are prohibited from serving on boards of directors by codes of the legal profession. The vastness and sheer complexity of varying legal systems throughout the world demonstrate clearly the intricate and demanding legal environment in which the MNCs operate. In order to function in a manner consistent with the host country, those involved in human resource management should become familiar with the legal requirements of the host country that relate to human resources.

Labor Force

In filling key managerial, technical, or professional positions abroad, multinational corporations can choose from among three basic types of employees: (1) parent country nationals (PCNs), (2) host country nationals (HCNs), and (3) third country nationals (TCNs). Until the 1950s, MNCs routinely filled key foreign posts with trusted and experienced employees from PCNs. Recently, stronger nationalistic feelings and the ever rising cost of reassigning PCNs have led companies to alter their policies and employ more HCNs.[28] Additionally, some firms have used TCNs. For example, one U.S.-based firm received a contract to build highways in Saudi Arabia, using workers from Turkey and Italy. Still, many companies attempt to keep parent country employees in at least half the identified key positions, particularly in the financial area.

Using workers from the parent nation of the MNC ensures a greater degree of consistency and control in the firm's operations around the world. However, this approach is not without its costs because PCNs may have great difficulty understanding cultural differences and adapting to life in the host country. In an attitude survey of workers in forty-nine multinationals, HCNs contended that parent country workers tended not to question orders from headquarters even when they should have done so.[29] Unquestioning attitudes and actions enabled these individuals to advance their

---

[27] Joan Biskupic, "Lawmakers Seek Bias Shield for Workers Overseas," *Congressional Quarterly Weekly Report,* 49 (March 30, 1991), p. 801.

[28] Neil B. Krupp, "Overseas Staffing for the New Europe," *Personnel,* 67 (July 1990), pp. 20–23.

[29] Yoram Zeira, "Overlooked Personnel Problems of Multinational Corporations," *Columbia Journal of World Business,* 10 (Summer 1975), pp. 96–103.

own long-term interests in the firm by getting better evaluations from headquarters and easing repatriation at the end of their tours of duty. In addition, the common practice of rotating key employees frequently intensified the problem of understanding and adapting to local cultures. However, using PCNs facilitates communications with headquarters because both parties are of the same culture.

Utilizing workers from the host country in key positions usually improves the MNC's relations with the government of the host country. It also fosters quicker and more accurate adaptation to the requirements of the host country. Disadvantages include a lessened degree of centralized control and increased communication problems with headquarters. In addition, if the HCNs perceive that the opportunity for higher-level positions is blocked for ethnic reasons, they will use the MNC to gain experience and then move to a higher position with a national firm in the host country. Properly balancing the type of key employees stationed in the host country is often a complex and difficult human resource task, but it is one that is crucial to the success of an MNC. If predictions of a world labor shortage are correct, the difficulty and complexity of this task may be substantially increased.[30] However, regardless of the obstacles, human resource professionals must locate the best people and then help assure that those people are properly motivated to accomplish the goals of the multinational corporation.[31]

Society

The significant societal norms—customs, beliefs, values, attitudes, and habits—of one nation differ at least to some extent from those of other countries. If the multinational corporation is to operate in many nations, it will necessarily have to adapt some of its managerial practices to the specific and unique expectations and situations of each of those nations. Attitudes concerning work, risk taking, change introduction, line authority, and material gain will differ. Professionals working in human resource management should never assume that the attitudes within the parent country will be similar to those in various host countries.

Lack of cultural sensitivity has limited the transfer of successful U.S. management practices to foreign countries. The same is true for some foreign MNCs doing business in the United States. When Renault built plants in the United States, it had to adapt to the U.S. work ethic. Primarily, U.S. workers tend to prefer less direct supervision than do the French, so Renault adapted its management style to better accommodate U.S. employees.

To help assure managerial success, human resource professionals must provide special knowledge and sensitivity training to employees who are

---

[30] Louis S. Richman, "The Coming World Labor Shortage," *Fortune* (April 9, 1990), p. 70.

[31] Reuben Mark, "Partnerships Will Be the Thrust of the 1990s," *Fortune* (March 26, 1990), p. 23.

preparing for global assignments. Unfortunately, only 34 percent of the companies recently studied had host country orientation programs, and only 17 percent provided cross-cultural training.[32]

In certain societies, authority is viewed as a natural right and is not questioned by subordinates. In other cultures, authority must be earned and is granted to those who have demonstrated the ability to lead. In some cultures, work is good and moral; in others, it is to be avoided. Accumulating wealth in some nations is proper behavior; in others, riches are to be avoided. David McClelland discovered that basic attitudes toward achievement correspond somewhat to rates of economic development. If a nation's citizens are willing to commit themselves to the accomplishment of tasks deemed worthwhile and difficult, a country tends to benefit economically. McClelland contends that how persons perceive their ability to influence the future has a definite impact on the behavior of a country's workforce.[33] If the basic belief is fatalistic—what will be, will be—the importance of planning and organizing for the future is undervalued.

Interclass mobility and sources of status also vary. If people have little hope of moving up socially and economically in a society, fatalism and an absence of a drive for achievement are likely results. In many instances, the MNC will have to adapt and conform to the societal norms of the host country in order to operate successfully. Obviously, human resource management is directly affected by societal concerns and, therefore, such concerns must be carefully considered by the MNC managers.

Unions

The future of unionism abroad seems much brighter than that of domestic unionism. According to economist Richard Freeman, interest in unionism fell in some countries in the 1980s, but no country's unions suffered the consistent and swift drop experienced by those in the U.S.[34] Factors such as the decline in union membership in the U.S. since the 1950s, the lack of government support for employee organizations in countries that do not have free-market economies, and the troubled labor movements in other industrialized free nations, dim the prospects for worldwide unionism.[35] During the past decade, many Western democracies have become more politically conservative, one result being a decline in unionism. Conservative legislation and administration of this legislation may also limit the growth of union organizing efforts.[36]

---

[32] Mike Fergus, "Employees on the Move," *HRMagazine,* 36 (May 1990), p. 44.

[33] Peter Wright, David Townsend, Jerry Kinard, and Joe Iverstine, "The Developing World to 1990: Trends and Implications for Multinational Business," *Long Range Planning,* 15 (May 1982), p. 122.

[34] Gene Koretz, "Why Unions Thrive Abroad—But Wither in the U.S." *Business Week* (September 10, 1990), p. 26.

[35] Joseph Krislov, "Unions in the Next Century: An Exploratory Essay," *Journal of Labor Research,* 7 (Spring 1986), pp. 165–166.

[36] *Ibid.,* p. 169.

Unions in industrialized nations with free-market economies seem to be yielding to management demands for enhanced productivity, often doing so without the benefit of increased compensation. In some countries, union demands for higher wages are gradually taking a backseat to concerns for retraining, improved working conditions, and job security. Many foreign unions are becoming less adversarial in their approaches toward management, instead keying on worker councils and participative decision making.[37] Germany is a perfect example of an industrialized nation in which many employees are quitting unions because of the unions' lack of flexibility in dealing with management.[38]

The pressures of a global economy are creating the need for greater productivity at reduced or capped wage levels, which greatly limits a union's attractiveness to employees. The state of unionism worldwide can have a dramatic impact on the competitiveness of MNCs. Therefore, MNC managers must consider the impact of unionism throughout the world when making many human resource decisions.

Shareholders

At first glance, MNC goals may not appear much different from those of domestic businesses. The typical goals of survival, profit, and growth are indeed similar. Shareholders must be satisfied with their return on investment, or they will seek other investment opportunities. An MNC seeks to produce and distribute products throughout the world in return for a satisfactory return on its invested capital. It survives, grows, and remains attractive to shareholders by maintaining its technological advantages and minimizing risk.

However, the MNC differs from the domestic firm because of the potential clash of its goals with those of the economic and political systems of the various countries within which it operates. Some may coincide; some may not. Because most countries want improved standards of living for their people, goals such as a trained labor force, full employment, reasonable price stability, a favorable balance of payments, and steady economic growth are fairly common.

In achieving some of these goals, the interests of the MNC and those of the host country overlap. For example, a new MNC in a country will usually create new jobs, thereby contributing to a higher level of employment, increased income, and economic growth. Thus an MNC may provide an out for political leaders accused of having contributed to unemployment in their countries.[39] Although the MNC usually contributes to the accomplishment of such goals, it may not do so at the rate expected by the host country,

---

[37] Gene Koretz, "Why Unions Thrive," p. 26.

[38] Gail Schares, "Are Labor Leaders Asking for the Moon?" *Business Week* (September 19, 1988), p. 50.

[39] J. O. Enitame, "Do Multinationals Create Wealth?" *International Management,* 37 (January 1983), p. 48.

which can create problems. In the final analysis, the interests of shareholders must be protected, regardless of whether the firm is a domestic or multinational corporation.

Competition

Competition to the United States in a multinational environment comes from many directions, such as Japan and the recently unified Europe. The worldwide economy is continually opening up markets abroad and increasing the nature of worldwide competition. Predictions are that Mexico is about to dramatically alter the nature of competition in North America. American producers are moving into Mexico, and it may become the most popular location for U.S. manufacturers who are faced with global competition and pricing pressures.[40] In the past, U.S. firms had the luxury of viewing competition as primarily American. This is no longer true, however. These same firms now find themselves competing with corporations in many countries. Furthermore, MNCs may find themselves competing with other multinationals and host country firms for the same personnel. This situation further compounds the HRM tasks and emphasizes the importance of HRM in multinational corporations.

Customers

In this new global environment, potential customers may exist in any country in the world. Cultivating them often requires new, and sometimes innovative, HRM approaches. For example, fundamental selling skills transcend cultural barriers. However, the perception of the salesperson differs from country to country, and the manner in which the sale is culminated often differs.[41] Consequently, the way in which the sales force is prepared could mean the difference between success and failure. Therefore, HRM professionals must make every attempt to ensure that key personnel who directly influence customers are properly prepared to represent the MNC. Human resource professionals should provide appropriate cross-cultural adaptation training to those individuals who will interface with foreign customers.[42]

Technology

Although the host country has power as a result of national sovereignty, MNCs are not helpless. Their power lies primarily in the ability to grant or withhold needed economic resources and technological knowledge. Other

---

[40] Ellen Brandt, "Global HR," pp. 38–39.

[41] Brian H. Flynn, "The Challenge of Multinational Sales Training," *Training and Development Journal,* 41 (November 1987), p. 54.

[42] Mark E. Mendenhall and Gary Oddon, "The Overseas Assignment: A Practical Look," *Business Horizons,* 31 (September–October 1988), pp. 78–79.

MNCs will observe the treatment accorded by the host country, which will affect their decisions to invest in that country. Should the host country have enterprises with investments in the parent country, retaliation can be threatened. If the parent country provides foreign economic aid, it can also be used as leverage in promoting equitable treatment for the MNC.

Transfer of technological expertise is the primary advantage of multinational enterprises. Many MNCs operate in high-technology industries, such as petroleum, pharmaceuticals, tires, electronics, and motor vehicles. There are fewer MNCs in such fields as cotton, textiles, and cement. The technological gap that exists in some nations provides a unique opportunity for the MNC to transfer high technology from the parent country. The reverse can also be true. The existing situation in a country will dictate the nature of the technology required to accomplish its goals. Obviously, the vast range of environments, goals, and technologies precludes any significant generalizations for multinationals. However, we can say that the strength of most MNCs lies in their ability to operate highly complex technologies.

Of course, transferring technologies profitably requires specially designed strategies. Among the factors that must be considered are the laws of the host country, the stability of the region, and financial incentives.[43] Obviously, the technological nature of the operation will have a direct bearing on certain aspects of human resource management. Basically, human resource managers must maintain the personnel needed to support the level of technology employed by the MNC, and provide assistance to those who must adapt to a high-tech work environment.

The Economy

The economy of the world and of various countries in the world is a major environmental factor affecting human resource management in the multinational environment. As a broad generalization, when the economy is booming, it is often more difficult to recruit qualified workers. On the other hand, when a downturn is experienced, more applicants are typically available. One country could be experiencing an upturn and another a downturn.

---

[43] Peter Wright et al., "The Developing World," p. 119.

SUMMARY

Many interrelated factors affect human resource management. Effective HRM requires careful consideration of all environmental variables. The external environment affects a firm's human resources from outside the organization. The internal environment affects the firm's human resources from inside. In addition, certain interrelationships complicate the management of human resources.

Factors in the external environment include the labor force, legal consid-erations, society, unions, shareholders, competition, customers, technology, and the economy. Each, separately or in combination with others, can impose constraints on the human resource manager's job.

The capabilities of a firm's employees determine largely how well an organization can perform its mission. The organization obtains its workers from a labor pool that is external to the firm. To some degree, as the labor force changes so will the composition of the organization's workforce. The labor force with which today's human resource managers have to deal is far different from that of the past.

The size of the labor force alone does not tell the entire employment story. The labor force now includes more working women, single parents, and older persons. Many companies hire part-time workers, often for shared jobs. The use of temporary and "leased" employees is also increas-ing. Handicapped employees are being included in the workforce in increas-ing numbers, and this trend may accelerate due to the passing of the Americans with Disabilities Act. Many new immigrants from developing areas, especially Southeast Asia and Latin America, continue to swell the U.S. labor force.

Another significant external force affecting human resource manage-ment relates to federal, state, and local legislation and court decisions interpreting this legislation. In addition, many presidential executive or-ders have had a major impact on human resource management. These legal considerations affect virtually the entire spectrum of human resource poli-cies and practices.

Society may also exert pressure on human resource management. The public is no longer content to accept, without question, the actions of business. Increasingly, firms must accomplish their purposes while meeting societal norms. Social responsibility is the implied, enforced, or felt obliga-tion of managers, acting in their official capacities, to serve or protect the interests of groups other than themselves.

Wage levels, benefits, and working conditions for millions of employees now reflect decisions made jointly by unions and management. A union is a group of employees who have joined together for the purpose of dealing with their employer. Unions are external factors because, essentially, they become a third party when dealing with the company. In a unionized organization, the union rather than the individual employee negotiates an agreement with the firm.

The owners of a corporation are called shareholders. Because sharehold-ers have invested in the firm, they may challenge programs considered by management to be beneficial to the organization. Managers may be forced to justify the merits of a particular program in terms of how it will affect future projects, costs, revenues, and profits.

Unless an organization is in the unusual position of monopolizing the market it serves, other firms will be producing similar goods or services. For a firm to succeed, grow, and prosper, it must be able to maintain a supply of competent employees.

Customers are those who actually use a firm's products and also are part of the external environment. Because sales are crucial to the firm's survival, management must ensure that its employment practices and employees do not antagonize its customers.

Change is occurring at an ever-increasing rate, and few firms operate today as they did even a decade ago. Of major concern to those in HRM is the effect that technological changes have had and will have on businesses.

The internal environment also exerts considerable pressure on human resource management. Internal factors include the firm's mission, policies, and corporate culture. Mission is the organization's continuing purpose or reason for being. A policy is a predetermined guide established to provide direction in decision making. Corporate culture is defined as the system of shared values, beliefs, and habits within an organization that interacts with the formal structure to produce behavioral norms.

A multinational corporation (MNC) conducts a large part of its business outside the country in which it is headquartered and has a significant percentage of its physical facilities and employees in other countries. Another layer is added to the environment that affects human resource management in a multinational climate. Although the basic HRM tasks remain essentially the same, the manner in which the tasks are accomplished may be altered substantially by the multinational's external environment.

Questions for Review

1. What is meant by the statement "The human resource manager's job is not accomplished in a vacuum"?
2. What factors make up the external environment of human resource management? Briefly describe each of these factors.
3. How is the composition of the U.S. labor force expected to change during the next decade?
4. What internal environment considerations exert pressure on the human resource manager?
5. How could changes in an organizational policy affect the human resource professional's work? Give an example.
6. Define *corporate culture*. What effect could it have on human resource management?
7. Describe how the external environmental factors for a multinational corporation affect human resource management.

Terms for Review

External environment
Job sharing
Leased employees
Managing diversity
Social responsibility
Union
Shareholders
Proactive response

Reactive response
Internal environment
Mission
Policy
Corporate culture
Informal organization
Multinational corporation (MNC)

INCIDENT 1   ■   A Japanese View of the Trade Imbalance   ■

Throughout the mid-1980s, the U.S. trade deficit with Japan grew worse. The Japanese share of American markets steadily increased, especially in automobiles and electronics. But very few products or services flowed the other way. The steadily growing stock of U.S. dollars in Japanese hands was used to buy up an increasing number of shares of U.S. companies. Labor unions and politicians complained about the loss of American jobs. Citizens expressed fear that the Japanese would come to own too much of American industry. Corporations complained that they were shut out of a potentially profitable foreign market.

The United States accused the Japanese of "dumping" products (that is, selling items in the United States for less than the cost of production). Another complaint frequently heard was that the Japanese government erected every conceivable trade barrier to keep American products out of Japan, while American markets were essentially open to Japanese products.

But George Tanaka, senior vice-president of Toyonoka Electronics, said that the problems were Americans' own fault. Tanaka described what he saw as the "real" source of U.S. trade balance problems.

"In a nutshell, in Japan we treat customers as God and you only say, 'The customer is king.' Let me explain. Toyonoka sells microwave ovens in the United States. I have been trying for over a year to find an American company to make some of the parts we need. We want to have the parts shipped to Japan for installation in United States-bound ovens. That would improve your trade balance. It would also allow us to take advantage of present favorable exchange rates.

"But I cannot find anyone who will produce the quality we need to stay competitive. American managers tell me, 'This is as good as we can do. You will have to change your operation to make the parts work.' In Japan, of course, suppliers value contracts like this and do all they can to meet our specifications. I am under a great deal of pressure to buy American. But American firms just do not seem to care about our needs.

"The same kind of attitude surfaces when I ask about shipping schedules. In our factories, we practice 'just-in-time' inventory control. Japanese suppliers deliver the parts we need just when we need them—and in small quantities. I know United States companies have to ship long distances. So we are willing to accept larger shipments and be somewhat flexible about delivery dates. But no American firm I have talked to will guarantee even the week of delivery. They say there are too many variables involved—strikes, raw materials shortages, shipping problems. In Japan, a supplier would not ask me to worry about those things. I am the customer.

"The language also presents a problem. United States firms will not bother to use Japanese. They refuse to even print installation instructions and invoices in any language but English. This is especially grating since we take the time to learn even the American dialect of English. Can any American imagine buying a Toyonoka stereo or a Mazda automobile with the owner's manual written in Japanese? We take care of those problems because Americans are our valued customers."

Mr. Tanaka went on to reemphasize that American companies could sell as much in Japan as Japan sells in the United States if they gave Japanese customers proper regard.

Questions

1. Does Mr. Tanaka's "ugly American" argument have some validity?
2. What are the external environmental factors that both Japanese and U.S. companies encounter?

INCIDENT 2 ▪ Getting By? ▪

As the human resource director for KBH Stores in St. Louis, Missouri, Virginia Stutes knew that she had her work cut out for her. Company management was moving forward on a goal of opening ten new stores in twelve months. KBH already employed 480 people in thirty-five stores, in addition to the headquarters staff of thirty-one. Virginia knew that staffing the ten new stores would require hiring and training about 150 people. She felt that her own small office was inadequately funded and staffed to handle this task. She sat at her desk, mulling over how to present a recommendation for her own staffing needs.

One of her concerns was broaching the subject with her boss because she had not officially been told of the expansion plans. Virginia had learned about them through the office grapevine. While she did not like being kept in the dark, she was not surprised that she hadn't been told. Glenn Sullivan, the president of KBH, was noted for his autocratic leadership style. Virginia had been warned early on that Glenn told subordinates only what he wanted them to know and that he expected everyone who worked for him to follow orders without question. He was not an unkind person, though, and Virginia had always gotten along with him well enough. She had never confronted Mr. Sullivan about anything, so it was with some concern that she approached him in his office later that day.

"Mr. Sullivan," she began, "I hear that we are going to be opening ten new stores next year."

"That's right, Virginia," said Mr. Sullivan. "We've already arranged the credit lines and picked out several of the sites."

"What about staffing?" asked Virginia.

"Well, I assume you will take care of that, Virginia, when we get to that point."

"What about my own staff?" asked Virginia. "I think I am going to need at least three or four more people. And we are already crowded for space. So I hope you plan to expand the human resource office."

"Not really," said Mr. Sullivan. "The new demands on the human resource staff will be temporary. It wouldn't be cost effective to hire and train additions to your staff that will only be cut the next year. I am counting on you to plan the expansion staffing within our current proposed budget allowances for the human resource office. It may require some reallocation, but I am sure you can handle that."

Questions

1. What should Virginia do? Explain.
2. Describe the elements of the internal environment that the case highlights. How does each affect Virginia?

Developing HRM Skills

This is an exercise involving Jesse Heard, the human resource manager at Parma Cycle Company; Gene Wilson, the corporate planner; and Edmont Fitzgerald, the controller. Parma Cycle Company is one of only three companies in the United States that actually manufactures complete bicycles. Most of Parma's competitors import parts from other countries and simply assemble bicycles here. Parma Cycle currently employs about 800 workers at wages well above the average wage levels in the area. Most of these workers are machine operators and assemblers. Parma Cycle Company is experiencing severe difficulties competing with less expensive bicycles, and the time had come for Parma to lower its costs.

Jesse Heard, the human resource manager, is faced with a dilemma. He feels obligated to find the best quality labor at the best available price, but he is also concerned about the workers, some of whom have been with Parma Cycle for many years. Even though the highly favorable labor market allows replacement of many of them with other workers at lower pay, he hesitates to do so. Yesterday, Jesse received an angry call from the president, Mr. Burgess, who told him to meet with the corporate planner and the controller to come up with a unified recommendation for taking advantage of the improved labor market.

Gene Wilson never really had much power at Parma Cycle, although his title, corporate planner, sounds impressive enough. Primarily, he maintains a chart room and keeps track of various trends. He basically agrees that Parma Cycle Company is headed downhill because of depressed markets and an inability on the part of company managers to decrease unit costs. In his opinion, the most important asset that Parma Cycle has is a trained and loyal workforce. While many of the workers could be replaced with lower paid workers, he is afraid that this would destroy the team spirit that now exists at Parma Cycle. He believes that workers are more likely than ever to respond to financial incentives, such as some kind of piece-rate program or bonus system.

Edmont Fitzgerald, an Ohio State University graduate in finance, believes that, above all, the corporation is an economic entity. He believes that market forces will take care of those workers who really wish to contribute to the economy. He believes in purchasing all resources, including labor, at the lowest possible price. He views the current situation as an opportunity to decrease costs radically. The union is weak, jobs are scarce, and there is a surplus of skilled workers in the area.

Three students will serve as the Parma Cycle management: one as Jesse Heard, the human resource manager; one as Edmont Fitzgerald, the controller; and one as Gene Wilson, the corporate planner. All students not playing roles in the exercise should carefully observe the behavior of its participants. Your instructor will provide the participants with the necessary additional information that they will need.

REFERENCES

Becker, Gary S. "The Long-Term Unemployed Need Long Term Help." *Business Week* (May 20, 1991), p. 22.

Beilinson, Jerry. "Workforce 2000: Already Here?" *Personnel,* 67 (October 1990), pp. 3–4.

Bernstein, Aaron. "The Case of the Climbing Welfare Rolls." *Business Week* (May 13, 1991), p. 40.

Brant, Ellen. "Global HR." *Personnel Journal,* 70 (March 1991), pp. 38–44.

Caudron, Shari. "Monsanto Responds to Diversity." *Personnel Journal,* 69 (November 1990), pp. 72–80.

Cooper, James C., and Kathleen Madigan. "Downbeat Job Numbers Will Keep the Economy Playing the Blues." *Business Week* (March 25, 1991), pp. 19–20.

Elliot, Ronald D. "The Challenge of Managing Change." *Personnel Journal,* 69 (March 1990), pp. 40–49.

Fergus, Mike. "Employees on the Move." *HRMagazine,* 36 (May 1990), pp. 44–46.

Foegen, J. H. "The Ability Gap." *Business Horizons* (July–August 1990), pp. 45–46.

Foxman, Loretta D., and Walter L. Polsky. "HR Approaches for the Age of Globalization." *Personnel Journal,* 70 (April 1991), pp. 38–41.

Garrison, Stephen A. "Wanted: Eight Million Educated Workers." *Fortune,* 121 (March 26, 1990), p. 56.

Hoerr, John. "Business Shares the Blame for Workers' Low Skills." *Business Week* (June 25, 1990), p. 71.

Howard, Patricia Digh. "Worldshrink." *HRMagazine,* 36 (January 1991), pp. 42–43.

Ireland, Karin. "The $100 Billion High." *Personnel Journal,* 70 (February 1991), p. 85.

Koretz, Gene. ". . . And Jobs May Get Even Scarcer for Ghetto Youths." *Business Week* (December 10, 1990), p. 18.

Koretz, Gene. "Professional Workers: Can America Keep Its Edge?" *Business Week* (April 2, 1990), p. 23.

Koretz, Gene. "Women Still Earn Less, But They've Come a Long Way." *Business Week* (December 24, 1990), p. 14.

Kovach, Kenneth A., and John A. Pearce II. "HR Strategic Mandates for the 1990s." *Personnel,* 67 (April 1990), pp. 50–55.

Kubiak, Sharon L., Jack L. Simonetti, C. Joseph Sass, and Nick Nykodym. "Making People an Organization's Most Important Resource." *Business,* 40 (October–November–December 1990), pp. 33–35.

Lawrence, Stephanie. "HR Trends." *Personnel Journal,* 69 (July 1990), p. 12.

Lesher, Richard. "Business-Government Relations in the 1990s." *Business Horizons,* 33 (January–February 1990), pp. 20–25.

Messmer, Max. "Strategic Staffing for the '90s." *Personnel Journal,* 69 (October 1990), pp. 92–97.

Packer, Arnold. "Skills Shortage Looms." *HRMagazine,* 35 (April 1990), pp. 38, 40.

Powell, Gary N. "Upgrading Management Opportunities for Women." *HRMagazine,* 35 (November 1990), pp. 67–70.

Recio, Irene. "Beyond Day Care: The Company School." *Business Week* (May 20, 1991), p. 142.

Redwood, Anthony. "Human Resources Management in the 1990s." *Business Horizons,* 33 (January–February 1990), pp. 74–80.

Reynolds, Calvin, and Rita Bennett. "The Career Couple Challenge." *Personnel Journal,* 70 (March 1991), pp. 46–48.

Reynolds, Calvin. "HR Must Influence Global Staff Strategy." *HRNews* (March 1991), pp. C1–C2.

Richman, Louis S. "The Coming World Labor Shortage." *Fortune,* 121 (April 9, 1990), pp. 70–77.

Sachs, Robert. "A Productive Workforce: The Final Frontier of Competitive Advantage?" *Business Forum,* 15 (Spring 1990), pp. 5–7.

Wagel, William H. "On the Horizon: HR in the 1990s." *Personnel,* 67 (January 1990), pp. 11–16.

Woodford, Karen. "Child Care Sours at America West." *Personnel Journal,* 69 (December 1990), pp. 46–47.

Woods, Tom H. "Will the Workforce Be the Focus of the 90s?" *Business Forum,* 15 (Spring 1990), p. 3.

"Work Force 2000." *HRMagazine,* 36 (April 1991), pp. 40–41.

CHAPTER 3

EQUAL EMPLOYMENT OPPORTUNITY AND AFFIRMATIVE ACTION

Chapter Objectives

1. Explain the major laws affecting equal employment opportunity.
2. Explain Presidential Executive Orders 11246 and 11375.
3. Identify and briefly describe some of the major Supreme Court decisions that have had an impact on equal employment opportunity.
4. Explain the purpose of the Equal Employment Opportunity Commission.
5. Describe the *Uniform Guidelines on Employee Selection Procedures* and the additional guidelines that have been adopted.
6. Explain adverse impact.
7. Describe affirmative action programs.

"I agree with you Phyllis," said Art Kurth, supervisor of the maintenance division of Allied Chemical. "Mary Martin is by far the best qualified to fill that vacant position in my department. She has done similar work at Olin for seven years and comes highly recommended. I really want to hire her, but do you think a woman could survive with that crew? They might not work with her, and you know how important cooperation is in that job. Remember what happened when we hired that woman a couple of years ago. She lasted a week before she walked out crying and didn't return."

Phyllis Jordon, human resource manager of Allied, was visibly upset when she heard Art's comments. Ten years ago when she joined Allied, she might have expected something like that, but not now. Allied has an aggressive nondiscrimination policy. "Listen, Art," she said, "I still recommend that you hire her. I know that you can find a way to see that she fits in. From all I can gather, she is a top-notch worker, and Allied is lucky to have an applicant of that quality. I'll help you make this work."

In this chapter, we provide an overview of the major equal employment opportunity legislation that has had an impact on human resource management. We first discuss the significant equal employment opportunity laws affecting human resource management. Then we describe the importance of Presidential Executive Orders 11246 and 11375. Next, we review significant Supreme Court decisions and describe the Equal Employment Opportunity Commission. Then we discuss the *Uniform Guidelines on Employee Selection Procedures* and address the issue of adverse impact. We devote the remainder of the chapter to affirmative action programs and the legal aspects of human resource management in the multinational environment.

■ EQUAL EMPLOYMENT OPPORTUNITY: AN OVERVIEW

The concept of equal employment opportunity has undergone much modification and fine-tuning since the passage of the Civil Rights Act of 1964. Congress has passed numerous amendments to that act and has passed other acts, as oversights in the initial act surfaced. Major Supreme Court decisions interpreting the provisions of the act have also been handed down. Executive orders were signed into law which further strengthened equal employment opportunity. Now nearly three decades have passed, and equal employment opportunity has become a part of the workplace.

Although continuing efforts are required, equal employment opportunity has come a long way since the early 1960s. Today, the majority of businesses do attempt to make employment decisions based on who is the best qualified, as opposed to whether an individual is of a certain gender, race, religion, color, national origin, or age. By and large, the laws, the Supreme Court decisions, and the executive orders have provided organizations—both public and private—the opportunity to tap the abilities of a workforce that was largely underutilized before the mid-1960s.

■ LAWS AFFECTING EQUAL EMPLOYMENT OPPORTUNITY

Numerous national laws have been passed that have had an impact on equal employment opportunity. The passage of these laws reflects society's attitude toward the changes that should be made to give everyone an equal opportunity for employment. We briefly describe the most significant of these laws in the following sections.

Civil Rights Acts of 1866 and 1871

The Civil Rights Act of 1866 is based on the Thirteenth Amendment to the Constitution and prohibits racial discrimination in the making and enforcement of contracts, which could include hiring and promotion decisions. Private employers, unions, and employment agencies are all covered under this act. The 1871 act is based on the Fourteenth Amendment and prohibits deprivation of equal employment rights under state laws. State and local governments are included. There is virtually no effective statute of limitation on filing charges under these acts.[1]

---

[1] Howard C. Lockwook, "Equal Employment Opportunities," in Dale Yoder and Herbert G. Heneman (eds.), *Staffing Policies and Strategies* (Washington, D.C.: Bureau of National Affairs, Inc., 1979), pp. 4–252.

Title VII of the Civil Rights Act of 1964— Amended 1972

One law that has greatly influenced human resource management is Title VII of the 1964 Civil Rights Act, as amended by the Equal Employment Opportunity Act of 1972. This legislation prohibits discrimination based on race, color, sex, religion, or national origin. Title VII covers employers with fifteen or more employees for at least twenty calendar weeks in the year in which a charge is filed, or the year preceding the filing of a charge, who are engaged in an industry affecting interstate commerce. Included in the definition of employers are state and local governments, schools, colleges, unions, and employment agencies. The act created the Equal Employment Opportunity Commission (EEOC), which is responsible for its enforcement.

Age Discrimination in Employment Act of 1967— Amended in 1978 and 1986

As originally enacted, the Age Discrimination in Employment Act (ADEA) prohibited employers from discriminating against individuals who were from 40 to 65 years of age. The 1978 amendment provided protection for individuals who were at least 40, but less than 70 years old. A 1986 amendment made employer discrimination against anyone over 40 years of age illegal. The latest amendment not only gives older employees the option to continue working past age 70, but the health care provision of the amendment also provides them with an additional incentive to continue to do so.[2] The act pertains to employers with twenty or more employees for twenty or more calendar weeks (either in the current or preceding calendar year); unions of twenty-five or more members; employment agencies; and federal, state, and local government subunits. Administration of the act was transferred from the U.S. Department of Labor to the EEOC in 1979.

Enforcement begins when a charge is filed, but the EEOC can review compliance even if no charge is filed. The Age Discrimination in Employment Act differs from Title VII of the Civil Rights Act in that it provides for a trial by jury and carries a possible criminal penalty. The trial-by-jury provision is important because juries may have great sympathy for older people who may have been discriminated against. The criminal penalty provision means that a person may receive more than lost wages if discrimination is proved. The 1978 amendment also makes class action suits possible.

The Older Workers Benefit Protection Act (OWBPA), an amendment to the Age Discrimination in Employment Act, was signed into law on October 16, 1990.[3] The amendment overturned the Supreme Court's decision in

---

[2] Michael R. Carrell and Frank E. Kuzmits, "Amended ADEA's Effects on HR Strategies Remain Dubious," *Personnel Journal,* 66 (May 1987), p. 112.

[3] Rory Judd Albert and Neal S. Schelberg, "Highlighting the OWBPA," *Pension World,* 27 (January 1991), p. 40.

Public Employees Retirement System of Ohio v. Betts and adopted an equal benefit or equal cost philosophy. This act prohibits discrimination in the administration of benefits on the basis of age, but also permits early retirement incentive plans as long as they are voluntary.[4]

Rehabilitation Act of 1973

The Rehabilitation Act covers certain government contractors and subcontractors and organizations that receive federal grants in excess of $2,500. Individuals are considered handicapped if they have a physical or mental impairment that substantially limits one or more major life activities or if they have a record of such impairment. If a contract or subcontract exceeds $50,000, or if the contractor has fifty or more employees, an affirmative action program must be prepared. In it, the contractor must specify reasonable steps that are being taken to hire and promote handicapped persons. The Office of Federal Contract Compliance Programs (OFCCP) administers the act.

This act is expected to have even more impact in the future because the definition of *handicapped* has not been thoroughly tested by the courts. As more and more cases go to court, additional ailments will probably be labeled as handicapping conditions. For example, in *Vickers v. Veterans Administration* it was determined that a person who is hypersensitive to tobacco smoke is handicapped.[5] It is also possible that AIDS victims will be included under the act in the future.

Pregnancy Discrimination Act of 1978

Passed as an amendment to Title VII of the Civil Rights Act, the Pregnancy Discrimination Act prohibits discrimination in employment based on pregnancy, childbirth, or related medical conditions. The basic principle of the act is that women affected by pregnancy, and related conditions, must be treated the same as other applicants and employees on the basis of their ability or inability to work. A woman is therefore protected against such practices as being fired or refused a job or promotion merely because she is pregnant or has had an abortion. She usually cannot be forced to take a leave of absence as long as she can work. If other employees on disability leave are entitled to return to their jobs when they are able to work again, so too are women who have been unable to work because of pregnancy.

The same principle applies in the benefits area, including disability benefits, sick leave, and health insurance. A woman unable to work for pregnancy-related reasons is entitled to disability benefits or sick leave on

---

[4] Robert J. Noble, Esq., "To Waiver or Not to Waiver Is the Question of OWPWA," *Personnel,* 68 (June 1991), p. 11.

[5] George E. Stevens, "Exploding the Myths About Hiring the Handicapped," *Personnel,* 63 (December 1986), p. 57.

the same basis as employees unable to work for medical reasons. Also, any health insurance provided must cover expenses for pregnancy-related conditions on the same basis as expenses for other medical conditions. However, health insurance for expenses arising from an abortion is not required except where the life of the mother would be endangered if the fetus were carried to term or where medical complications have arisen from an abortion.

In a class action suit originally filed in 1978 but settled in July 1991, American Telephone & Telegraph Company agreed to settle a pregnancy discrimination suit with the EEOC for $66 million. This suit was the largest cash recovery in the agency's history and involved more than 13,000 present and former female AT&T workers. The 1978 suit charged that Western Electric required pregnant workers to leave their jobs at the end of their sixth month of pregnancy, denied them seniority credit, and refused to guarantee them a job when they returned.[6]

Immigration Reform and Control Act of 1986

The Immigration Reform and Control Act (IRCA) established criminal and civil sanctions against employers who knowingly hire an unauthorized alien. The act further makes hiring anyone without verifying employment authorization and identity unlawful. Employers who unlawfully hire an illegal alien will be subject to fines of $250–$2,000 per worker for the first offense; $2,000–$5,000 for the second offense; and $3,000–$10,000 for the third offense. In addition, employers who fail to comply with the record-keeping provisions of the law are subject to a penalty of $100–$1,000 for each individual they fail to document, even if the individual is legally entitled to be employed. Moreover, when dealing with the national origin provision of the Civil Rights Act, IRCA reduces the threshold coverage from fifteen to four employees. The effect of this extension of the 1964 law will be to curtail hiring actions of some businesses. They may choose to hire only U.S. citizens and thereby avoid any potential violation of IRCA. However, many foreign nationals are in this country legally (many who are legal immigrants awaiting citizenship); refusing to hire them would violate their civil rights.[7]

The Americans with Disabilities Act (ADA)

The Americans with Disabilities Act (ADA), passed in 1990, prohibits discrimination against "qualified individuals with disabilities." Persons discriminated against because they have a known association or relationship with a disabled individual also are protected. The ADA defines an

---

[6] John J. Keller, "AT&T Will Settle EEOC Lawsuit for $66 Million," *The Wall Street Journal,* 88, no. 13 (July 18, 1991), p. B8.

[7] Art L. Bethke, "The IRCA: What's an Employer to Do?" *Wisconsin Small Business Forum,* 6 (Fall 1987), p. 26.

"individual with a disability" as a person who has, or is regarded as having, a physical or mental impairment that substantially limits one or more major life activities, and has a record of such an impairment, or is regarded as having such an impairment. The ADA prohibits discrimination in all employment practices, including job application procedures, hiring, firing, advancement, compensation, training, and other terms, conditions, and privileges of employment. It applies to recruitment, advertising, tenure, layoff, leave, fringe benefits, and all other employment-related activities.

The employment provisions apply to private employers, state and local governments, employment agencies, and labor unions. Employers with twenty-five or more employees are covered beginning in July 1992. Employers with fifteen or more employees will be covered beginning July 26, 1994.[8] The full impact of this new law is yet to be fully determined. For example, some believe that obesity may emerge as a life-style that is protected under the act.[9]

Civil Rights Act (CRA) of 1991

The CRA of 1991 amended the Civil Rights Act of 1964 and had the following purposes:

1. To provide appropriate remedies for intentional discrimination and unlawful harassment in the workplace.
2. To codify the concepts of *business necessity* and *job related* pronounced by the Supreme Court in *Griggs v. Duke Power Co.*, and in the other Supreme Court decisions prior to *Wards Cove Packing Co., Inc. v. Atonio.*
3. To confirm statutory authority and provide statutory guidelines for the adjudication of disparate impacts under Title VII of the Civil Rights Act of 1964.
4. To respond to recent decisions of the Supreme Court by expanding the scope of relevant civil rights statutes in order to provide adequate protection to victims of discrimination.

Under this act, a complaining party may recover punitive damages if the complaining party demonstrates that the company engaged in a discriminatory practice with malice or with reckless indifference to the law. However, the following limits, based on the number of people employed by the company, were placed on the amount of the award:

- Between 15 and 100 employees—$50,000
- Between 101 and 200 employees—$100,000
- Between 201 and 500 employees—$200,000
- More than 500 employees—$300,000

---

[8] "The Americans with Disabilities Act: Questions and Answers," (Washington, D.C.: U.S. Government Printing Office, 1991), p. 1.

[9] Christine D. Keen, "Lifestyle Disabilities Could Become a Civil Rights Frontier," *HRNews*, 9 (October 1990), p. 7.

In each case, employees must be with the firm for twenty or more calendar weeks in the current or preceding calendar year.

With regard to burden of proof in disparate impact cases, an unlawful employment practice passed on disparate impact is established under this title *only* if a complaining party demonstrates that a respondent uses a particular employment practice that causes a disparate impact on the basis of race, color, religion, sex, or national origin; and the company fails to demonstrate that the challenged practice is job related for the position in question and consistent with business necessity. The act also extends the coverage of the Civil Rights Act of 1964 to extraterritorial employment. However, the act does not apply to United States companies operating in another country *if it would violate* the law of the foreign country. Furthermore, the act reverses the following Supreme Court decisions: *Patterson v. McLean Credit Union, Martin v. Wilks,* and *Wards Cove Packing Co., Inc. v. Atonio.*

The act mandates the establishment of the Equal Employment Opportunity Commission's Technical Assistance Training Institute (TATI) and enhances Title VII's provisions regarding education and outreach. The TATI provides technical assistance and training regarding the laws and regulations enforced by the commission. The commission is charged with carrying out educational and outreach activities (including dissemination of information in languages other than English) targeted to individuals who historically have been victims of employment and have not been equitably served by the commission. The act also extends the nondiscrimination principles to Congress and other government agencies, such as the General Accounting Office and the Government Printing Office.

Also included in the CRA of 1991 is the Glass Ceiling Act of 1991. The purpose of this act is to establish a Glass Ceiling commission to study the manner in which businesses fill management and decision-making positions, the developmental and skill-enhancing practices used to foster the necessary qualifications for advancement to such positions, and the compensation programs and reward structures currently utilized in the workplace. It also established an annual award for excellence in promoting a more diverse skilled workforce at the management and decision-making levels in business.

State and Local Laws

Numerous state and local laws also affect equal employment opportunity. A number of states and some cities have passed fair employment practice laws prohibiting discrimination on the basis of race, color, religion, gender, or national origin. Even prior to federal legislation, several states had anti-discrimination legislation relating to age and gender. For instance, New York protected individuals between the ages of 18 and 65 prior to the 1978 and 1986 ADEA amendments, and California had no upper limit on protected age. However, when EEOC regulations conflict with state or local civil rights regulations, the legislation more favorable to women and minorities applies.

■ EXECUTIVE ORDER 11246, AS AMENDED BY EO 11375

An **executive order (EO)** is a directive issued by the president and has the force and effect of laws enacted by Congress. In 1965 President Lyndon B. Johnson signed EO 11246. This EO makes it the policy of the government of the United States to provide equal opportunity in federal employment for all qualified persons. It prohibits discrimination in employment because of race, creed, color, or national origin. The EO also requires promoting the full realization of equal employment opportunity through a positive, continuing program in each executive department and agency. The policy of equal opportunity applies to every aspect of federal employment policy and practice.

A major provision of EO 11246 requires adherence to a policy of nondiscrimination in employment as a condition for the approval of a grant, contract, loan, insurance, or guarantee. Every executive department and agency that administers a program involving federal financial assistance must include such language in its contracts. Contractors must agree not to discriminate in employment because of race, creed, color, or national origin during performance of a contract.

Affirmative action, stipulated by EO 11246, requires employers to take positive steps to ensure employment of applicants and treatment of employees during employment without regard to race, creed, color, or national origin. Human resource practices covered relate to employment, upgrading, demotion, transfer, recruitment or recruitment advertising, layoffs or termination, rates of pay or other forms of compensation, and selection for training, including apprenticeships. Employers are required to post notices to this effect in conspicuous places in the workplace. In the event of contractor noncompliance, contracts can be canceled, terminated, or suspended in whole or in part, and the contractor may be declared ineligible for future government contracts. In 1968, EO 11246 was amended by EO 11375, which changed the word *creed* to *religion* and added sex discrimination to the other prohibited items. These EOs are enforced by the Department of Labor through the Office of Federal Contract Compliance Programs (OFCCP).

■ SIGNIFICANT U.S. SUPREME COURT DECISIONS

Knowledge of the law is obviously important for human resource managers. However, they must be aware of and understand much more than the words in the law itself. The manner in which the courts interpret the law is also vitally important. And interpretation continuously changes, even though the law may not have been amended. Discussions of some of the more significant U.S. Supreme Court decisions affecting equal employment opportunity follow.

Griggs v. Duke Power Company

A major decision affecting the field of human resource management was rendered on March 8, 1971. A group of black employees at Duke Power Company had charged job discrimination under Title VII of the Civil Rights Act of 1964. Prior to Title VII, the Duke Power Company had two work-forces, separated by race. After passage of the act, the company required applicants to have a high school diploma and pass a paper-and-pencil test to qualify for certain jobs. The plaintiff was able to demonstrate that, in the relevant labor market, 34 percent of the white males but only 12 percent of the black males had a high school education. The plaintiff was also able to show that people already in those jobs were performing successfully even though they did not have high school diplomas. No business necessity could be shown for this educational requirement.

In an 8–0 vote, the Supreme Court ruled against Duke Power Company and stated, "If an employment practice which operates to exclude Negroes cannot be shown to be related to job performance, the practice is prohibited." A major implication of the decision is that when human resource management practices eliminate substantial numbers of minority or women applicants, the burden of proof is on the employer to show that the practice is job related. This court decision significantly affected the human resource practices of many firms.

Albermarle Paper Company v. Moody

In August 1966, a class action suit was brought against Albermarle Paper Company and the plant employees' labor union. A permanent injunction was requested against any policy, practice, custom, or usage at the plant that violated Title VII. In 1975, the Supreme Court, in *Albermarle Paper Co. v. Moody,* reaffirmed the idea that any test used in the selection process, or in promotion decisions, must be validated if it is found that its use has had an adverse impact on women and minorities. The employer has the burden of proof for showing that the test is valid. Subsequently, the employer must show that any selection or promotion device actually measures what it is supposed to measure.

Phillips v. Martin Marietta Corporation

In this 1971 case, the Court ruled that the company had discriminated against a woman because she had young children. The company had a rule prohibiting the hiring of women with school-age children. The company argued that it did not preclude all women from job consideration—only those women with school-age children. Martin Marietta contended that this was a business requirement. The argument was obviously based on stereotypes and was rejected. A major implication of this decision is that a firm

HRM In Action

Jack Johnson, human resource manager for Zoomer Electronics, was speaking to the production manager, Philip Lewis, regarding the person to hire to fill a newly created position. Jack started the conversation by saying, "Of all the applicants, Betty Jones scored highest on the tests. Her previous work experience is right in line with our needs, and her references check out great. What do you think, Philip?"

Philip replied, "I don't know. We've never had a woman in that position, and I don't know if she could handle the job. Besides, she is only 25 years old and recently married. I'll bet she wants to have kids."

How should Jack respond?

cannot impose standards for employment only on women. For example, a firm cannot reject divorced women if it does not also reject divorced men. Neither application forms nor interviews should contain questions for women that do not also apply to men.

Weber v. Kaiser Aluminum and Chemical Corporation

In 1974, the United Steelworkers of America and Kaiser Aluminum and Chemical Corporation entered into a master collective bargaining agreement covering terms and conditions of employment at fifteen Kaiser plants. The agreement contained an affirmative action plan designed to eliminate conspicuous racial imbalances in Kaiser's then almost exclusively white craft workforce. Black craft hiring goals equal to the percentage of blacks in the respective local labor forces were set for each Kaiser plant. To enable plants to meet these goals, on-the-job training programs were established to teach unskilled production workers—black and white—the skills necessary to become craft workers. The plan reserved 50 percent of the openings in these newly created in-plant training programs for black employees.

In 1974, only 1.83 percent (5 out of 273) of the skilled craft workers at the Gramercy, Louisiana, plant were black, even though the labor force in the Gramercy area was approximately 39 percent black. Thirteen craft trainees, of whom seven were black and six were white, were selected from Gramercy's production workforce. The most junior black selected for the program had less seniority than several white production workers whose bids for admission were rejected. Brian Weber subsequently instituted a class action suit alleging that the action by Kaiser and USWA discriminated against him and other similarly situated white employees in violation of Title VII. Although the lower courts ruled that Kaiser's actions were illegal because they fostered reverse discrimination, the Supreme Court reversed the decision, stating that Title VII does not prohibit race-conscious affirmative action plans. Since the affirmative action plan was voluntarily agreed to by the company and the union, it did not violate Title VII.

Dothard v. Rawlingson

At the time Rawlingson applied for a position as correctional counselor trainee, she was a 22-year-old college graduate whose major course of study had been correctional psychology. She was refused employment because she failed to meet the minimum height and weight requirements. In this 1977 case, the Supreme Court upheld the U.S. District Court's decision that Alabama's statutory minimum height requirement of five feet two inches and minimum weight requirement of 120 pounds for the position of correctional counselor had a discriminatory impact on women applicants. The contention was that minimum height and weight requirements for the position of correctional counselor were job related. However, the Court stated that this argument does not rebut *prima facie* evidence showing that these requirements have a discriminatory impact on women, whereas no evidence was produced correlating these requirements with a requisite amount of strength thought essential to good performance. The impact of the decision is that height and weight requirements must be job related.

University of California Regents v. Bakke

This Supreme Court decision involved the first major test involving reverse discrimination. The University of California had reserved sixteen places in each beginning medical school class for minority persons. Allen Bakke, a white man, was denied admission even though he scored higher on the admission criteria than some minority applicants who were admitted. The Supreme Court ruled 5–4 in Bakke's favor. As a result, Bakke was admitted to the university and later received his degree. But, at the same time, the Court reaffirmed that race may be taken into account in admission decisions.

American Tobacco Company v. Patterson

This 1982 Supreme Court decision allows seniority and promotion systems established since Title VII to stand, although they unintentionally hurt minority workers. Under *Griggs v. Duke Power Co.*, a *prima facie* violation of Title VII may be established by policies or practices that are neutral on their face and in intent, but that nonetheless discriminate against a particular group. A seniority system would fall under the *Griggs* rationale if it were not for Section 703 (h) of the Civil Rights Act. That section provides:

Notwithstanding any other provision of this subchapter, it shall not be an unlawful employment practice for an employer to apply different standards of compensation, or different terms, conditions, or privileges of employment pursuant to a bona fide seniority or merit system, . . . provided that such differences are not the result of an intention to discriminate because of race, color, religion, sex, or national origin, nor shall it be an unlawful employment practice for an employer to give and to act upon the results of any professionally developed ability test provided that such test, its administration or action upon the results is not designed, intended or used to discriminate because of race, color, religion, sex, or national origin. . . ."

Thus the court ruled that a seniority system adopted after Title VII may stand, even though it has an unintended discriminatory impact.

Firefighters Local Union #1984 v. Carl W. Stotts

The U.S. Supreme Court ruled on June 12, 1984, on the relationship between affirmative action and last-hired, first-fired seniority. Essentially, when seniority systems are involved, only individuals who can prove that they are victims of discrimination by an employer may benefit from affirmative action. In May 1981, the City of Memphis, Tennessee, had a budget deficit and had to lay off some employees. The city decided that the fairest policy was to use the last-hired, first-fired seniority system. Stotts appealed to the U.S. District Court for an order forbidding a layoff of any black employee. Both the District Court and the Appeals Court ruled in favor of Stotts, but the Supreme Court overturned the ruling.

Meritor Savings Bank v. Vinson

The first sexual harassment case to reach the U.S. Supreme Court was the June 1986 case, *Meritor Savings Bank v. Vinson*. In ruling for the plaintiff, one of the outcomes from the case was that Title VII is not limited to discrimination having only economic or tangible effects. In this case, the plaintiff had obtained two promotions based on merit, even though sexual harassment was involved. The Court also ruled on whether an employee's voluntary participation in sexual acts with a manager constitutes a valid defense for an employer to a Title VII complaint. Here they said that the appropriate test is whether the sexual activity was "unwelcomed," not whether the employee voluntarily engaged in sexual activity with her manager.[10]

---

[10] Frederick L. Sullivan, "Sexual Harassment: The Supreme Court's Ruling," *Personnel,* 63 (December 1986), pp. 37–38.

City of Richmond v. J. A. Croson Co.

The City of Richmond adopted a Minority Business Utilization Plan requiring prime contractors awarded city construction contracts to subcontract at least 30 percent of the dollar amount of each contract to one or more "Minority Business Enterprises" (MBEs), which the plan defined to include a business from anywhere in the country at least 51 percent of which is owned and controlled by black, Spanish-speaking, Oriental, Native-American, Eskimo, or Aleut citizens. After J. A. Croson Co. was denied a waiver and lost its contract, it brought suit alleging that the plan was unconstitutional under the Fourteenth Amendment's Equal Protection Clause. On January 23, 1989, the Supreme Court affirmed a Court of Appeals ruling that the city's plan was not justified by a compelling governmental interest because the record revealed no prior discrimination by the city itself in awarding contracts, and the 30 percent set-aside was not narrowly tailored to accomplish a remedial purpose. The decision forced thirty-six states and many cities and counties to review their programs.

Wards Cove Packing Co., Inc. v. Atonio

Jobs at the petitioners' Alaskan salmon canneries are of two general types: unskilled "cannery jobs" on the cannery lines, which are filled predominantly by nonwhites; and "noncannery jobs," most of which are classified as skilled positions and filled predominantly with white workers. Virtually all of the latter positions pay more than cannery positions. The nonwhite cannery workers filed suit under Title VII of the Civil Rights of 1964, contending that the company's hiring and promotion practices were responsible for the workforce's racial stratification, and that they had been denied employment as noncannery workers on the basis of race. The District Court rejected these claims, finding, among other things, that nonwhite workers were overrepresented in cannery jobs because many of those jobs were filled under a hiring hall agreement with a predominantly nonwhite union. The Court of Appeals ultimately reversed the decision, holding that respondents had made out a *prima facie* case of disparate impact in hiring for both skilled and unskilled noncannery jobs, relying solely on respondents' statistics that showed a high percentage of nonwhite workers in cannery jobs and a low percentage of such workers in noncannery positions. In 1989 the Supreme Court ruled that the Court of Appeals erred in its ruling that a comparison of the percentage of cannery workers who are nonwhite and the percentage of noncannery workers who are nonwhite makes out a *prima facie* disparate-impact case. This ruling made it more difficult for minorities and women to win cases based on statistics. The ruling essentially reversed *Griggs* by shifting to workers the burden of providing that there is no business necessity for a challenged employment practice.[11] However, this Supreme Court decision was reversed by the Civil Rights Act of 1991.

---

[11] Joan Biskupic, "Behind the Fight Over Quotas Lie Divisive Racial Issues," *Congressional Quarterly Weekly Report,* 49 (June 1, 1991), p. 1444.

Martin v. Wilks

On June 12, 1989, the Supreme Court ruled that a voluntary settlement in the form of a consent decree between one group of employees and its employer cannot possibly "settle," voluntarily or otherwise, the conflicting claims of another group of employees who do not join the agreement. This 5–4 decision said that court-approved affirmative action settlements can be reopened when white male employees allege reverse discrimination. Black individuals and a branch of the NAACP brought actions in U.S. District Court against the City of Birmingham, Alabama, and the Jefferson County Personnel Board, alleging that the defendants had engaged in racially discriminatory hiring and promotion practices in violation of Title VII of the Civil Rights Act of 1964 and other federal laws. Consent decrees were eventually entered that included goals for hiring blacks as firefighters and for promoting them. Respondent white firefighters subsequently brought suit in the District Court against the city and the board, alleging that because of their race, they were being denied promotions in favor of less qualified blacks in violation of federal law. This Supreme Court decision was also reversed by the Civil Rights Act of 1991.

Patterson v. McLean Credit Union

Patterson, a black woman, was employed by McLean Credit Union as a teller and file coordinator for ten years until she was laid off. Thereafter, she brought suit under the Civil Rights Act of 1866 alleging that McLean had harassed her, failed to promote her to accounting clerk, and then discharged her, all because of her race. The Court ruled that since the 1866 act is restrictive in its scope to forbidding racial discrimination in the "make[ing] and enforce[ment]" of contracts, it cannot be construed as a general prescription of discrimination in all aspects of contract relations. Thus, Patterson's racial harassment claim is not actionable with the possible exception of her claim that McLean's refusal to promote her was discriminatory. The 1866 act was not overturned but was made more restrictive. This Supreme Court decision was reversed by the Civil Rights Act of 1991.

■ EQUAL EMPLOYMENT OPPORTUNITY COMMISSION

As we mentioned previously, Title VII of the Civil Rights Act, as amended, created the Equal Employment Opportunity Commission. Under Title VII, filing a discrimination charge initiates EEOC action. Charges may be filed by one of the presidentially appointed EEOC commissioners, by any aggrieved person, or by anyone acting on behalf of an aggrieved person. Charges must be filed within 180 days of the alleged act. However, the time is extended to 300 days if a state or local agency is involved in the case.

As you can see in Figure 3-1, when a charge is filed, the EEOC typically proceeds in the following manner. First, an attempt at no-fault settlement is made. Essentially, the organization charged with the violation is invited to settle the case with no admission of guilt. Most charges are settled at this stage.

Failing settlement, the EEOC investigates the charges. Once the employer is notified that an investigation will take place, no records relating to the charge may be destroyed. During the investigative process, the employer is permitted to present a position statement. After the investigation has been completed, the district director of the EEOC will issue a "probable cause" or "no probable cause" statement.

The next step involves attempted conciliation. In the event this effort fails, the case will be reviewed for litigation potential. Some of the factors

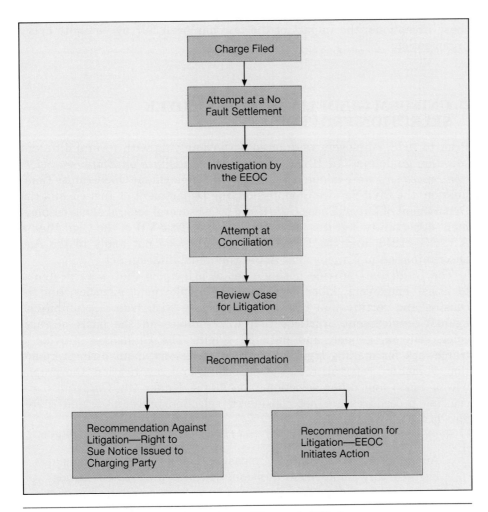

FIGURE 3-1 | EEOC Procedure Once a Charge Is Filed

that determine whether the EEOC will pursue litigation are (1) the number of people affected by the alleged practice, (2) the amount of money involved in the charge, (3) other charges against the employer, and (4) the type of charge. Recommendations for litigation are then passed on to the general counsel of the EEOC. If the recommendation is against litigation, a right to sue notice will be issued to the charging party.

It is important to note that the Civil Rights Act of 1964 prohibits retaliation against employees who have opposed an illegal employment practice. The act also protects those who have testified, assisted, or participated in an investigation of discrimination.

There are certain exceptions to the coverage of Title VII. These exceptions include (1) religious institutions, with respect to the employment of persons of a specific religion in any of the institution's activities; (2) aliens; and (3) members of the Communist Party. Noncitizens are not protected from discrimination because of their lack of citizenship. However, they are protected from discrimination because of their national origin. Even with these exceptions, the impact of the law has been felt by virtually every organization.

■ UNIFORM GUIDELINES ON EMPLOYEE SELECTION PROCEDURES

Prior to 1978, employers were faced with complying with several different selection guidelines. In 1978, the *Uniform Guidelines on Employee Selection Procedures* were adopted by the Equal Employment Opportunity Commission, the Civil Service Commission, the Department of Justice, and the Department of Labor. These *Guidelines* cover several federal equal employment opportunity statutes and EOs including Title VII of the Civil Rights Act, EO 11246, and the Equal Pay Act. They do not apply to the Age Discrimination in Employment Act or the Rehabilitation Act.

The *Guidelines* provide a single set of principles that were designed to assist employers, labor organizations, employment agencies, and licensing and certification boards in complying with federal prohibitions against employment practices that discriminate on the basis of race, color, religion, gender, and national origin. The *Guidelines* provide a framework for making legal employment decisions about hiring, promotion, demotion, referral, retention, licensing and certification, the proper use of tests, and other selection procedures. Under the *Guidelines*, recruiting procedures are not considered selection procedures, and therefore are not covered.

Regarding selection procedures, the *Guidelines* state that a test is:

> Any measure, combination of measures, or procedures used as a basis for any employment decision. Selection procedures include the full range of assessment techniques from traditional paper and pencil tests, performance tests, testing programs or probationary periods and physical, education, and work experience

requirements through informal or casual interviews and unscored application forms.

Using this definition, virtually any instrument or procedure used in the
selection decision is considered a test.

The Concept of Adverse Impact

Prior to the issuance of the *Uniform Guidelines on Employee Selection
Procedures* in 1978, the only way to prove job relatedness was to validate
each test. The *Guidelines* do not require validation in all cases. Essentially,
it is required only in instances where the test or other selection device
produces an adverse impact on a minority group. Under the *Guidelines*,
adverse impact has been defined in terms of selection rates, the selection
rate being the number of applicants hired or promoted, divided by the total
number of applicants.[12] **Adverse impact,** a concept established by the
Uniform Guidelines, occurs if women and minorities are not hired at the
rate of at least 80 percent of the best-achieving group. This has also been
called the four-fifths rule, which is actually a guideline subject to interpretation by the EEOC. The groups identified for analysis under the guidelines are (1) blacks, (2) Native Americans (including Alaskan natives),
(3) Asians, (4) Hispanics, (5) women, and (6) men.

The following formula is used to compute adverse impact for hiring:

$$\frac{\text{Success rate for women and minority applicants}}{\text{Success rate for best–achieving group applicants}} = \text{Determination of adverse impact}$$

The success rate for women and minority applicants is determined by
dividing the number of members of a specific group *employed* in a period by
the number of women and minority *applicants* in a period. The success rate
for best-achieving group applicants is determined by dividing the number
of people in the best-achieving group *employed* by the number of the best-
achieving group *applicants* in a period.

Using the formula, let's determine whether there has been an adverse
impact in the following case. During 1992, 400 people were hired for a
particular job. Of the total, 300 were white and 100 were black. There were
1,500 applicants for these jobs, of whom 1,000 were white and 500 were
black. Using the adverse impact formula, we have:

$$\frac{100/500 \;=\; 0.2}{300/1,000 \;=\; 0.3} = 66.67\%$$

We conclude that adverse impact exists.

Evidence of adverse impact involves more than the total number of
minority workers *employed*. Also considered are the total number of quali-

---

[12] David E. Robertson, "New Directions in EEO Guidelines," *Personnel Journal,* 57 (July 1978),
p. 361.

fied *applicants*. For instance, assume that 300 blacks and 300 whites were hired. But there were 1,500 black applicants and 1,000 white applicants. Putting these figures into the adverse impact formula, we conclude that adverse impact still exists.

$$\frac{300/1,500 = 0.2}{300/1,000 = 0.3} = 66.67\%$$

Thus it is clear that firms must monitor their recruitment efforts very carefully. Obviously, firms should attempt to recruit qualified individuals because once in the applicant pool, they will be used in computing adverse impact.

Assuming that adverse impact is shown, employers have two avenues available to them if they still desire to use a particular standard. First, the employer may validate a selection device by showing that it is indeed a predictor of success. If the device has proved to be a predictor of job performance, business necessity has been established. If the firm's selection device has not been validated, business necessity may be demonstrated in another manner: The employer can show a strong relationship between the selection device and job performance, and that if it did not use this procedure, the firm's training costs would become prohibitive.

The second avenue available to employers should adverse impact be shown is the bona fide occupational qualification (BFOQ) defense. The BFOQ defense means that only one group is capable of performing the job successfully. As you might expect, the BFOQ defense has been narrowly interpreted by the courts because it almost always relates to sex discrimination. For instance, courts have rejected the concept that because most women cannot lift fifty pounds, all women would be eliminated from consideration for a job requiring heavy lifting.

Creators of the *Guidelines* adopted the bottom-line approach in assessing whether a firm's employment practices are discriminatory. For example, if a number of separate procedures is used in making a selection decision, the enforcement agencies will focus on the end result of these procedures to determine whether adverse impact has occurred. Essentially, the EEOC is concerned more with what is occurring than how it occurred. They admit that discriminatory employment practices that cannot be validated may exist. However, the net effect, or the *bottom line*, of the selection procedures is the focus of their attention.

■ ADDITIONAL GUIDELINES

Since the *Uniform Guidelines* were published in 1978, they have been modified several times. Some of these changes reflect Supreme Court decisions; others clarify implementation procedures. Three major changes—*Interpretative Guidelines on Sexual Harassment, Guidelines on Discrimination Because of National Origin,* and *Guidelines on Discrimination Because of Religion*—merit additional discussion.

Interpretative Guidelines on Sexual Harassment

In a recent survey, 42 percent of the women and 15 percent of the men reported that they had been sexually harassed on the job.[13] Today, one of the most fervently pursued civil rights issues relates to sexual harassment.[14] As previously mentioned, Title VII of the Civil Rights Act generally prohibits discrimination in employment on the basis of gender. The EEOC has also issued interpretative guidelines that state that employers have an affirmative duty to maintain a workplace free from sexual harassment. The OFCCP has also issued similar guidelines. Managers in both for-profit and not-for-profit organizations should be particularly alert to the issue of sexual harassment. The EEOC issued the guidelines because of the belief that sexual harassment continues to be a widespread problem. Table 3-1 on page 94 contains the EEOC's definition of sexual harassment.

According to these guidelines, employers are totally liable for the acts of their supervisors, regardless of whether the employer is aware of the sexual harassment act. Where coworkers are concerned, the employer is responsible for such acts if the employer knew, or should have known, about them. The employer is not responsible when it can show that it took immediate and appropriate corrective action on learning of the problem.

Another important aspect of these guidelines is that employers may be liable for acts committed by nonemployees in the workplace if the employer knew, or should have known, of the conduct and failed to take appropriate action. Firms are responsible for developing programs to prevent sexual harassment in the workplace. They must also investigate all formal and informal complaints alleging sexual harassment. After investigating, a firm must take immediate and appropriate action to correct the situation.[15] Failure to do so constitutes a violation of Title VII, as interpreted by the EEOC.[16]

There have been numerous sexual harassment court cases. In *Miller v. Bank of America*, a U.S. Circuit Court of Appeals held an employer liable for the sexually harassing acts of its supervisors, even though the company had a policy prohibiting such conduct, and even though the victim did not formally notify the employer of the problem. Another U.S. Circuit Court of Appeals ruled that sexual harassment, in and of itself, is a violation of Title VII. The court ruled that the law does not require the victim to prove that she or he resisted harassment and was penalized for that resistance. As previously mentioned, the first sexual harassment case to reach the U.S. Supreme Court was the June 1986 case of *Meritor Savings Bank v. Vinson*. In the *Vinson* decision, the Supreme Court recognized for the first time that Title VII could be used for offensive environment claims.[17]

---

[13] Kelly Flynn, "Preventive Medicine for Sexual Harassment," *Personnel,* 68 (March 1991), p. 17.

[14] Michele Galen, "Ending Sexual Harassment: Business Is Getting the Message," *Business Week* (March 18, 1991), p. 98.

[15] Robert K. McCalla, "Stopping Sexual Harassment Before It Begins," *Management Review,* 80 (April 1991), p. 44.

[16] *Ibid.*

[17] Stacey J. Garvin, "Employer Liability for Sexual Harassment," *HRMagazine,* 36 (June 1991), p. 107.

TABLE 3-1 | EEOC Definition of Sexual Harassment

Unwelcome sexual advances, requests for sexual favors, and other verbal or physical conduct of a sexual nature that occur under any of the following situations:

1. When submission to such contact is made either explicitly or implicitly a term or condition of an individual's employment.

2. When submission to or rejection of such conduct by an individual is used as the basis for employment decisions affecting such individual.

3. When such conduct has the purpose or effect of unreasonably interfering with an individual's work performance or creating an intimidating, hostile, or offensive working environment.

Guidelines on Discrimination Because of National Origin

The EEOC broadly defined discrimination on the basis of national origin as the denial of equal employment opportunity because of an individual's ancestors or place of birth; or because an individual has the physical, cultural, or linguistic characteristics of a national origin group. Because height or weight requirements tend to exclude individuals on the basis of national origin, firms are expected to evaluate their selection procedures for adverse impact, regardless of whether the total selection process has an adverse impact based on national origin. Height and weight requirements are, therefore, exceptions to the bottom-line concept. As Table 3-2 shows, the EEOC has identified certain selection procedures that may be discriminatory.

TABLE 3-2 | Selection Procedures That May Be Discriminatory with Regard to National Origin

1. Fluency-in-English requirements: One questionable practice involves denying employment opportunities because of an individual's foreign accent or inability to communicate well in English. When this practice is continually followed, the Commission will presume that such a rule violates Title VII and will closely study it. However, a firm may require that employees speak only in English at certain times if business necessity can be shown.

2. Training or education requirements: Denying employment opportunities to an individual because of his or her foreign training or education; or practices that require an individual to be foreign trained or educated may be discriminatory.

Harassment on the basis of national origin is a violation of Title VII. Employers have an affirmative duty to maintain a working environment free from such harassment. Ethnic slurs and other verbal or physical conduct relating to an individual's national origin constitute harassment when this conduct (1) has the purpose or effect of creating an intimidating, hostile, or offensive working environment; (2) has the purpose or effect of unreasonably interfering with an individual's work performance; or (3) otherwise adversely affects an individual's employment opportunity.

Guidelines on Discrimination Because of Religion

Employers have an obligation to accommodate religious practices unless they can demonstrate a resulting undue hardship. Consideration is given to identifiable costs in relation to the size and operating costs of the employer and the number of individuals who actually need the accommodation. These guidelines recognize that regular payment of premium wages constitutes undue hardship, whereas these payments on an infrequent or temporary basis do not. Undue hardship would also exist if an accommodation required a firm to vary from its bona fide seniority system.

These guidelines identify several means of accommodating religious practices that prohibit working on certain days. Some of the methods suggested include voluntary substitutes, flexible scheduling, lateral transfer, and change of job assignments. Some collective bargaining agreements include a provision that each employee must join the union or pay the union a sum equivalent to dues. When an employee's religious beliefs prevent compliance, the union should accommodate the employee by permitting that person to make an equivalent donation to a charitable organization.

■ AFFIRMATIVE ACTION PROGRAMS

An **affirmative action program (AAP)** is an approach that certain organizations with government contracts develop to demonstrate that workers are employed in proportion to their representation in the firm's relevant labor market. The need for affirmative action programs was created by EO 11246, as amended by EO 11375, and placed enforcement with the OFCCP. An affirmative action program may be voluntarily implemented by an organization. In such an event, goals are established and action is taken to hire and move minorities and women upward in the organization. In other situations, an AAP may be mandated by the OFCCP. The degree of control the OFCCP will impose depends on the size of the contract. Contracts of $10,000 or less are not covered. The first level of control involves contracts that exceed $10,000 but are less than $50,000. These contractors are governed by the equal opportunity clause, as shown in Table 3-3 on page 96.

The second level of control occurs if the contractor (1) has fifty or more employees; (2) has a contract of $50,000 or more; (3) has contracts which, in any twelve-month period total $50,000 or more, or reasonably may be expected to total $50,000 or more; or (4) is a financial institution that

TABLE 3-3 | Equal Opportunity Clause—Government Contracts

1. The contractor will not discriminate against any employee or applicant for employment because of race, color, religion, sex, or national origin. The contractors will take affirmative action to ensure that applicants are employed, and that employees are treated during employment, without regard to their race, color, religion, sex, or national origin. Such action shall include, but not be limited to the following: Employment, upgrading, demotions, or transfer; recruitment or recruitment advertising, layoff or termination; rates of pay or other forms of compensation; and selection for training, including apprenticeship. The contractor agrees to post in conspicuous places, available to employees and applicants for employment, notices to be provided by the contracting officer setting forth the provisions for this nondiscrimination clause.

2. The contractor will in all solicitations or advertisements for employees placed by or on behalf of the contractor, state that all qualified applicants will receive consideration for employment without regard to race, color, religion, sex, or national origin.

3. The contractor will send to each labor union or representative of workers with which he has a collective bargaining agreement or other contract or understanding, a notice to be provided by the agency contracting officer, advising the labor union or workers' representative of the contractor's commitments under section 202 of Executive Order 11246 of September 24, 1965, and shall post copies of the notice in conspicuous places available to employees and applicants for employment.

4. The contractor will comply with all provisions of Executive Order 11246 of September 24, 1965, and of the rules, regulations, and relevant orders of the Secretary of Labor.

5. The contractor will furnish all information and reports required by Executive Order 11246 of September 24, 1965, and by the rules, regulations, and orders of the Secretary of Labor, or pursuant thereto, and will permit access to his books, records, and accounts by the contracting agency and the Secretary of Labor for purposes of investigation to ascertain compliance with such rules, regulations, and orders.

6. In the event of the contractor's noncompliance with the nondiscrimination clauses of this contract or with any of such rules, regulations, or orders, this contract may be canceled, terminated or suspended in whole or in part and the contractor may be declared ineligible for further Government contracts in accordance with procedures authorized in Executive Order 11246 of September 24, 1965, or by rule, regulation, or order of the Secretary of State, or as otherwise provided by law.

7. The contractor will include the provisions of paragraphs (1) through (7) in every subcontract or purchase order unless exempted by rules, regulations, or orders of the Secretary of Labor issued pursuant to section 204 of Executive Order 11246 of September 24, 1965, so that such provisions will be binding upon each subcontractor or vendor. The contractor will take such action with respect to any subcontract or purchase order as may be directed by the Secretary of Labor as a means of enforcing such provisions including sanctions for noncompliance: *Provided, however,* that in the event the contractor becomes involved in, or is threatened with litigation with a subcontractor or vendor as a result of such direction, the contractor may request the United States to enter into such litigation to protect the interests of the United States.

Source: Federal Register, 45, no. 251 (Tuesday, December 30, 1980), p. 86230.

serves as a depository for government funds in any amount, acts as an issuing or redeeming agent for U.S. savings bonds and savings notes in any amount, or subscribes to federal deposit or share insurance. Contractors meeting these criteria must develop a written affirmative action program for each of its establishments and file an annual EEO-1 report (see Figure 3-2 on page 98). The affirmative action program is the major focus of EO 11246. It requires specific steps to guarantee equal employment opportunity. Prerequisite to development of a satisfactory AAP is identification and analysis of problem areas inherent in employment of minorities and women, and an evaluation of opportunities for utilizing these employees.

The third level of control on contractors is in effect when contracts exceed $1 million. All previously stated requirements must be met and, in addition, the OFCCP is authorized to conduct preaward compliance reviews. The purpose of a compliance review is to determine whether the contractor is maintaining nondiscriminatory hiring and employment practices. The review also ensures that the contractor is utilizing affirmative action to guarantee that applicants are employed, placed, trained, upgraded, promoted, terminated, and otherwise treated fairly without regard to race, color, religion, gender, national origin, veteran status, or handicap during employment. In determining whether to conduct a preaward review, the OFCCP may consider the items presented in Table 3-4 on page 100.

If an investigation indicates a violation, the OFCCP first tries to secure compliance through persuasion. If persuasion fails to resolve the issue, the OFCCP serves a notice to show cause or a notice of violation. A show cause notice contains a list of the violations, a statement of how the OFCCP proposes that corrections be made, a request for a written response to the findings, and a suggested date for a conciliation conference. The firm usually has thirty days to respond. Successful conciliation results in a written contract between the OFCCP and the contractor. In a conciliation agreement, the contractor agrees to take specific steps to remedy noncompliance with the EO. Firms that do not correct violations can be passed over in the awarding of future contracts.

The procedures for developing affirmative action plans were published in the *Federal Register* of December 4, 1974. These regulations are referred to as Revised Order No. 4. The OFCCP guide for compliance officers, outlining what to cover in a compliance review, is known as Order No. 14.

The OFCCP is very specific about what should be included in an affirmative action program. A policy statement has to be developed that reflects the CEO's attitude regarding equal employment opportunity, assigns overall responsibility for preparing and implementing the affirmative action program, and provides for reporting and monitoring procedures. The policy should state that the firm intends to recruit, hire, train, and promote persons in all job titles without regard to race, color, religion, gender, or national origin, except where gender is a bona fide organizational qualification (BFOQ). The policy should guarantee that all human resource actions involving such areas as compensation, benefits, transfers, layoffs, returns from layoff, company-sponsored training, education, tuition assistance, and social and recreational programs will be administered without regard to race, color, religion, gender, or national origin.

Joint Reporting Committee

- Equal Employment Opportunity Commission
- Office of Federal Contract Compliance Programs (Labor)

EQUAL EMPLOYMENT OPPORTUNITY
EMPLOYER INFORMATION REPORT EEO–1

Standard Form 100
(Rev. 5–84)
O.M.B. No. 3046–0007
EXPIRES 3/31/85
100–211

Section A—TYPE OF REPORT
Refer to instructions for number and types of reports to be filed.

1. Indicate by marking in the appropriate box the type of reporting unit for which this copy of the form is submitted (MARK ONLY ONE BOX).

(1) ☐ Single-establishment Employer Report

Multi-establishment Employer:

(2) ☐ Consolidated Report (Required)

(3) ☐ Headquarters Unit Report (Required)

(4) ☐ Individual Establishment Report (submit one for each establishment with 50 or more employees)

(5) ☐ Special Report

2. Total number of reports being filed by this Company (Answer on Consolidated Report only) _____

Section B—COMPANY IDENTIFICATION (To be answered by all employers)

OFFICE USE ONLY

1. Parent Company

   a. Name of parent company (owns or controls establishment in item 2) omit if same as label

   a.

Name of receiving office		Address (Number and street)	
			b.

City or town	County	State	ZIP code	b. Employer Identification No.								

2. Establishment for which this report is filed. (Omit if same as label)

   OFFICE USE ONLY

   a. Name of establishment

   c.

Address (Number and street)	City or Town	County	State	ZIP code	d.

b. Employer Identification No.							(Omit if same as label)	e.

Section C—EMPLOYERS WHO ARE REQUIRED TO FILE (To be answered by all employers)

☐ Yes ☐ No   1. Does the entire company have at least 100 employees in the payroll period for which you are reporting?

☐ Yes ☐ No   2. Is your company affiliated through common ownership and/or centralized management with other entities in an enterprise with a total employment of 100 or more?

☐ Yes ☐ No   3. Does the company or any of its establishments (a) have 50 or more employees AND (b) is not exempt as provided by 41 CFR 60–1.5, AND either (1) is a prime government contractor or first-tier subcontractor, and has a contract, subcontract, or purchase order amounting to $50,000 or more, or (2) serves as a depository of Government funds in any amount or is a financial institution which is an issuing and paying agent for U.S. Savings Bonds and Savings Notes?

➤ If the response to question C–3 is yes, please enter your Dun and Bradstreet identification number (if you have one): ☐☐☐☐☐☐☐☐☐

☐ Yes ☐ No   4. Does the company receive financial assistance from the Small Business Administration (SBA)?

NOTE: If the answer is yes to questions 1, 2, or 3, complete the entire form, otherwise skip to Section G.

NSN 7540–00–180–6384

FIGURE 3-2 | Equal Employment Opportunity Employer Information Report (EEO-1)

SF 100 Page 2

Section D—EMPLOYMENT DATA

Employment at this establishment—Report all permanent full-time or part-time employees including apprentices and on-the-job trainees unless specifically excluded as set forth in the instructions. Enter the appropriate figures on all lines and in all columns. Blank spaces will be considered as zeros.

JOB CATEGORIES		OVERALL TOTALS (SUM OF COL. B THRU K)	MALE						FEMALE				
			WHITE (NOT OF HISPANIC ORIGIN)	BLACK (NOT OF HISPANIC ORIGIN)	HISPANIC	ASIAN OR PACIFIC ISLANDER	AMERICAN INDIAN OR ALASKAN NATIVE		WHITE (NOT OF HISPANIC ORIGIN)	BLACK (NOT OF HISPANIC ORIGIN)	HISPANIC	ASIAN OR PACIFIC ISLANDER	AMERICAN INDIAN OR ALASKAN NATIVE
		A	B	C	D	E	F		G	H	I	J	K
Officials and Managers	1												
Professionals	2												
Technicians	3												
Sales Workers	4												
Office and Clerical	5												
Craft Workers (Skilled)	6												
Operatives (Semi-Skilled)	7												
Laborers (Unskilled)	8												
Service Workers	9												
TOTAL	10												
Total employment reported in previous EEO–1 report	11												

(The trainees below should also be included in the figures for the appropriate occupational categories above)

Formal On-the-job trainees	White collar	12											
	Production	13											

NOTE: Omit questions 1 and 2 on the Consolidated Report.
1. Date(s) of payroll period used: 2. Does this establishment employ apprentices?
                                                   1 ☐ Yes   2 ☐ No

Section E—ESTABLISHMENT INFORMATION (Omit on the Consolidated Report)

1. Is the location of the establishment the same as that reported last year? 1 ☐ Yes 2 ☐ No 3 ☐ No report last year	2. Is the major business activity at this establishment the same as that reported last year? 1 ☐ Yes 2 ☐ No 3 ☐ No report last year	OFFICE USE ONLY

3. What is the major activity of this establishment? (Be specific, i.e., manufacturing steel castings, retail grocer, wholesale plumbing supplies, title insurance, etc. Include the specific type of product or type of service provided, as well as the principal business or industrial activity.)

Section F—REMARKS

Use this item to give any identification data appearing on last report which differs from that given above, explain major changes in composition or reporting units and other pertinent information.

Section G—CERTIFICATION (See Instructions G)

Check one   1 ☐ All reports are accurate and were prepared in accordance with the instructions (check on consolidated only)
             2 ☐ This report is accurate and was prepared in accordance with the instructions.

Name of Certifying Official	Title	Signature	Date
Name of person to contact regarding this report (Type or print)	Address (Number and street)		

Title	City and State	ZIP code	Telephone Area Code	Number	Extension

All reports and information obtained from individual reports will be kept confidential as required by Section 709(e) of Title VII
WILLFULLY FALSE STATEMENTS ON THIS REPORT ARE PUNISHABLE BY LAW, U.S. CODE, TITLE 18, SECTION 1001.

FIGURE 3-2 | *Continued*

TABLE 3-4 | Factors That the OFCCP May Consider in Conducting a Preaward Review

1. The past EEO performance of the contractor, including its current EEO profile and indications of underutilization.
2. The volume and nature of complaints filed by employees or applicants against the contractor.
3. Whether the contractor is in a growth industry.
4. The level of employment or promotional opportunities resulting from the expansion of, or turnover in, the contractor's workforce.
5. The employment opportunities likely to result from the contract in issue.
6. Whether resources are available to conduct the review.

Revised Order No. 4 is quite specific with regard to dissemination of a firm's EEO policy, both internally and externally. An executive should be appointed to manage the firm's equal employment opportunity program. This person should be given the necessary support by top management to accomplish the assignment. Revised Order No. 4 specifies the minimum level of responsibility associated with the task of EEO manager.

An acceptable AAP must include an analysis of deficiencies in the utilization of minority groups and women. The first step in conducting a utilization analysis is to make a workforce analysis.

The second step involves an analysis of all major job groups. An explanation of the situation is required if minorities or women are currently being underutilized. A job group is defined as one or more jobs having similar content, wage rates, and opportunities. Underutilization is defined as having fewer minorities or women in a particular job group than would reasonably be expected by their availability. The utilization analysis is important because the calculations determine whether underutilization exists. For example, if the utilization analysis shows that the availability of blacks for a certain job group is 30 percent, the organization should have at least 30 percent black employment in that group. If actual employment is less than 30 percent, underutilization exists, and the firm should set a goal of 30 percent black employment for that job group.

The primary focus of any affirmative action program is on goals and timetables: The issue is how many, by when. Goals and timetables developed by the firm should cover its entire affirmative action program, including correction of deficiencies. These goals and timetables should be attainable; that is, they should be based on results that the firm, making good-faith efforts, could reasonably expect to achieve.

Both human resource managers and line managers should be involved in the goal-setting process. Goals should be significant and measurable, as well as attainable. Two types of goals must be established regarding underutilization: annual and ultimate. The annual goal is to move toward elimination of underutilization, whereas the ultimate goal is to correct all underutilization. Goals should be specific in terms of planned results, with timetables for completion. However, goals should not establish inflexible quotas that must be met. Rather, they should be targets that are reasonably attainable.

Employers should also conduct a detailed analysis of job descriptions to ensure that they accurately reflect job content. In addition, job specifications should be validated, with special attention given to academic, experience, and skills requirements. If a job specification screens out a disproportionate number of minorities or women, the requirements must be professionally validated in relation to job performance. Thus a comprehensive job analysis program is required.

When an opening occurs, everyone involved in human resource recruiting, screening, selection, and promotion should be aware of the opening. In addition, the firm should evaluate the entire selection process to ensure freedom from bias. And individuals involved in the process should be carefully selected and trained in order to minimize bias in all human resource actions.

Firms should observe the requirements of the *Uniform Guidelines*. Selection techniques other than tests can also be used improperly and thus discriminate against minorities and women. Such techniques include unscored interviews, unscored or casual application forms, use of arrest records and credit checks, and consideration of marital status, dependency, and minor children. Where data suggest that discrimination or unfair exclusion of minorities and women exists, the firm should analyze its unscored procedures and eliminate them if they are not objective and valid. Some techniques that can be used to improve recruitment and increase the flow of minority and women applicants are shown in Table 3-5 on page 102.

■ IMPLICATIONS FOR MULTINATIONAL CORPORATIONS

Domestic firms obviously are greatly affected by statutes, executive orders, and court decisions—and must abide by them or face legal consequences. However, multinational corporations headquartered in the United States must obey the laws of the host country. When operating in the multinational environment, U.S.-based firms often find their human resource policies to be in conflict with the laws and accepted norms of the host country. For instance, the influence of Title VII of the Civil Rights Act of 1964, as amended, has been felt by virtually all firms operating in the United States. But most countries in the world do not have such laws prohibiting discrimination. In fact, some countries practice overt discrimination against certain groups whose members would be protected if they were employed in the United States.

In 1991 the Supreme Court ruled that when Congress passed the Civil Rights Act of 1964, it did not want the statute to apply outside of the United States. Chief Justice William H. Rehnquist did acknowledge that it was

TABLE 3-5 | Techniques to Improve Recruitment of Minorities and Women

- Identify referral organizations for minorities and women.
- Hold formal briefing sessions with representatives of referral organizations.
- Encourage minority and women employees to refer applicants to the firm.
- Include minorities and women on the Personnel Relations staff.
- Permit minorities and women to participate in Career Days, Youth Motivation Programs, and related activities in their community.
- Actively participate in job fairs and give company representatives the authority to make on-the-spot commitments.
- Actively recruit at schools having predominant minority or female enrollments.
- Recruiting efforts at all schools should use special efforts to reach minorities and women.
- Special employment programs should be undertaken whenever possible for women and minorities. These might include technical and nontechnical co-op programs, "after school" and/or work-study jobs, summer jobs for underprivileged, summer work—study programs, and motivation, training, and employment programs for the hardcore unemployed.
- Pictorially present minorities and women in recruiting brochures.
- Help wanted advertising should be expanded to include the minority news media and women's interest media.

Source: Federal Register, 45, no. 251, (Tuesday, December 30, 1980), p. 86243.

"plausible" that Congress wanted antibias laws to apply internationally, but he also wrote that there was no "persuasive" evidence of such an intent.[18] This ruling is in line with international law, which recognizes the rights of nations to regulate conduct within their own borders.[19] However, the Civil Rights Act of 1991 extended the coverage to extraterritorial employment unless it violates the law of the foreign country in which such workplace is located. The full impact of this law will be determined by the courts.

---

[18] Joan Biskupic, "Lawmakers Seek Bias Shield for Workers Overseas," *Congressional Quarterly Weekly Report,* 49 (March 30, 1991), p. 801.

[19] Susan B. Garland, "Were Civil Rights Laws Meant to Travel?" *Business Week* (January 21, 1991), p. 36.

SUMMARY

The concept of equal employment opportunity has evolved considerably since passage of the Civil Rights Act of 1964. Numerous amendments, and even other acts, have been passed when voids were found in the initial act. Major Supreme Court decisions have interpreted the provisions of these statutes. Presidential executive orders further strengthened the quest for equal employment opportunity.

The 1866 and 1871 Civil Rights Acts, based on the Thirteenth and Fourteenth Amendments to the Constitution, represented early efforts to outlaw discrimination in the workplace. Title VII of the 1964 Civil Rights Act, as amended by the Equal Employment Opportunity Act of 1972, has had a major impact on HRM. These laws prohibit discrimination based on race, color, sex, religion, or national origin. The Age Discrimination in Employment Act (ADEA), as amended, prohibits employers from discriminating against individuals because of age. The Rehabilitation Act covers certain government contractors and subcontractors and organizations that receive federal grants in excess of $2,500. Passed as an amendment to Title VII of the Civil Rights Act, the Pregnancy Discrimination Act prohibits discrimination in employment based on pregnancy, childbirth, or related medical conditions. The Immigration Reform and Control Act of 1986 established criminal and civil sanctions against employers who knowingly hire an illegal immigrant, and made it unlawful to hire anyone without verifying employment authorization and identity.

Presidential executive orders (EOs) apply to governmental agencies and have the force and effect of laws enacted by Congress. In 1965, EO 11246 made it federal policy to provide equal opportunity in federal employment for all qualified persons. It not only prohibits discrimination in employment, but it also requires promoting the full realization of equal employment opportunity through a positive, continuing program in each executive department and agency.

The manner in which the courts interpret the law is vitally important. Important Supreme Court decisions related to equal employment opportunity and affirmative action include: *Albermarle Paper Co. v. Moody, Griggs v. Duke Power Co., Phillips v. Martin Marietta Corporation, Weber v. Kaiser Aluminum and Chemical Corporation, Dothard v. Rawlingson, University of California Regents v. Bakke, American Tobacco Co. v. Patterson, Firefighters Local Union #1984 v. Carl W. Stotts, Meritor Savings Bank v. Vinson, City of Richmond v. J. A. Croson Co., Wards Cove Packing Co., Inc., v. Atonio, Martin v. Wilks,* and *Patterson v. McLean Credit Union.*

Title VII of the Civil Rights Act, as amended, created the Equal Employment Opportunity Commission. Under Title VII, filing a discrimination charge initiates EEOC action. Charges may be filed by one of the appointed EEOC commissioners, by any aggrieved person, or by anyone acting on behalf of an aggrieved person.

In 1978, the *Uniform Guidelines on Employee Selection Procedures* were adopted by the EEOC, the Civil Service Commission, the Department of Justice, and the Department of Labor. The guidelines provide a single set of principles designed to assist employers, labor organizations, employment agencies, and licensing and certification boards in complying with federal prohibitions against discriminatory employment practices. The fundamental principle underlying the guidelines is that employer policies or practices that have an adverse impact on the employment opportunities of any protected race, gender, or ethnic group are illegal under Title VII and/or EO 11246 unless justified by business necessity. Adverse impact occurs when members of protected groups receive unequal consideration for employment. Specifically, adverse impact occurs if women and minorities are not hired at the rate of at least 80 percent of the best-achieving group. Three major changes in the *Uniform Guidelines* were the Interpretative Guidelines on Sexual Harassment, Guidelines on Discrimination Because of National Origin, and Guidelines on Discrimination Because of Religion.

An affirmative action program (AAP) is developed by an organization to demonstrate that women and minorities are employed in proportion to their representation in the firm's labor market. The need for affirmative action programs was created by the signing of Executive Order 11246, as amended by 11375, and placed enforcement with the OFCCP.

Firms in the United States are greatly affected by statutes, executive orders, and court decisions. But, when an organization headquartered in the United States goes multinational, the laws of the host country must be obeyed. Firms operating in the multinational environment often find their human resource policies to be in conflict with the laws and accepted norms of the host country and must adapt to them.

Questions for Review

1. Briefly describe the following laws: (a) Title VII of the Civil Rights Act of 1964, as amended in 1972 and 1991; (b) Age Discrimination in Employment Act of 1967, as amended in 1978 and 1986; (c) Rehabilitation Act of 1973; (d) Pregnancy Discrimination Act of 1978; (e) Immigration Reform and Control Act of 1986; and (f) Civil Rights Act of 1991.
2. What is a Presidential executive order? Describe the major provisions of EO 11246, as amended by EO 11375.
3. What is the purpose of the Office of Federal Contract Compliance Programs?
4. Discuss the significant U.S. Supreme Court decisions that have had an impact on equal employment opportunity.
5. What is the purpose of the *Uniform Guidelines on Employee Selection Procedures*?
6. Distinguish between adverse impact and affirmative action programs.
7. How does the EEOC define sexual harassment?

Terms for Review

Executive order (EO)
Affirmative action

Adverse impact
Affirmative action program (AAP)

INCIDENT 1   ■   So, What's Affirmative Action?   ■

Supreme Construction Company began as a small commercial builder located in Baytown, Texas. Until the 1980s, Alex Boyd, Supreme's founder, concentrated his efforts on small, free-standing shops and offices. Up to that time Alex never employed more than fifteen people.

In 1985 Alex's son, Michael, graduated from college with a degree in construction and immediately joined the company full time. Mike had worked on a variety of Supreme jobs while in school, and Alex felt his son was really cut out for the construction business. Mike was given increasing responsibility and the company continued its success, although with a few more projects—and a few more employees—than before. In 1988 Mike approached his father with a proposition: "Let's get into some of the bigger projects now. We have the capital to expand and I really believe we can do it." Alex approved and Supreme began doing small shopping centers and multistory office buildings in addition to its traditional specialization. Soon, employment had grown to seventy-five employees.

In 1991, NASA released construction specifications for two aircraft hangars to be built southeast of Houston. Although Supreme had never done any construction work for the government, Mike and Alex considered the job within the company's capabilities. Michael worked up the $582,000 bid and submitted it to the NASA procurement office.

Several weeks later the bids were opened. Supreme had the low bid. However, the acceptance letter was contingent on submission of a satisfactory affirmative action program.

Questions

1. Explain why Supreme must submit an affirmative action program.
2. Generally, what should the program be designed to accomplish?

INCIDENT 2   ■   Retire?   ■

Les Partain, human resource development manager for Gazelle Corporation, was 64 years old in 1991 and had been with the firm for over thirty years. He had been in his current job twelve years. During those years he had received excellent performance reports.

Six months before Les's sixty-fifth birthday, he and Bennie Helton, the human resource director, were enjoying a cup of coffee together. "Les," said Bennie, "I'll bet you and the missus are looking forward to retirement. You can certainly look back on a fine career at Gazelle."

"Gee, Bennie, I really appreciate that, but I've never felt better in my life. I figure that I have at least five more good years. There are many other things I would like to do for the department before I retire. We can do a lot in the next five years."

Bennie was surprised, to say the least. He had assumed that Les would retire, since his longevity would give him maximum retirement benefits. Later that day he discussed the matter with Jim Altic, the company president and a longtime friend. He told Jim, "My gosh, I had no idea that Les intended to hang on. We really need a younger, more aggressive person in that job. The human resource development department is more important than ever and Les's old ideas just won't cut it anymore."

Questions

1. What should Bennie do about this situation? Discuss.
2. What actions should Bennie have taken in the past to avoid his current predicament?

DEVELOPING HRM SKILLS

Many laws have been passed and court decisions rendered that affect the everyday actions of human resource managers. Past decisions may no longer apply. Human resource managers have a responsibility to ensure that actions affecting human resource management adhere to both the letter and intent of the law. Unfortunately, not everyone may share this view, which is when problems occur. In this situation, the human resource manager and a dock foreman for New York-based Hoffa Loading and Storage Company are having a disagreement on the necessity of hiring women dock workers.

The human resource manager must talk to the dock foreman concerning future hiring practices. The dock foreman is aware that the firm follows the policy of affirmative action; however, he rejects virtually every woman that is sent over to the docks. On the rare occasion that he does hire a woman, she does not last very long. The human resource manager realizes that this hiring practice puts the dock foreman in a somewhat precarious position, but this is the way things have to be.

The dock foreman is quite disgruntled about the company's directive to hire women on the dock. He thinks that the human resource manager and the bosses upstairs do not understand that on the dock, men are needed—red-blooded American men. The foreman believes that his men are the best dock workers on the pier and wants to keep the situation as it is. They have always exceeded the tonnage moved by any other group and they work very well together. Every worker pulls his own weight. He also believes that women are just going to mess things up and that the wives of his dock workers do not want their husbands working with women.

Certainly, a potential for conflict exists in this situation. Two individuals will participate in this exercise: one to serve as the human resource manager and the other to play the role of dock foreman. All students not playing a role should carefully observe the behavior of both participants. Your instructor will provide the participants with necessary additional information that they will need.

REFERENCES

Albert, Rory Judd, and Neal S. Schelberg. "Highlighting the OWBPA." *Pension World,* 27 (January 1991), pp. 40–43.

Becker, Gary S. "What Keeps Older Workers Off the Job Rolls?" *Business Week* (March 19, 1990), p. 18.

Biskupic, Joan. "Behind the Fight Over Quotas Lie Divisive Racial Issues." *Congressional Quarterly Weekly Report,* 49 (June 1, 1991), pp. 1442–45.

Biskupic, Joan. "Democrats Scramble for Cover Under GOP 'Quota' Attacks." *Congressional Quarterly Weekly Report,* 49 (May 25, 1991), pp. 1378–80.

Biskupic, Joan. "Lawmakers Seek Bias Shield For Workers Overseas." *Congressional Quarterly Weekly Report,* 49 (March 30, 1991), p. 801.

Biskupic, Joan. "Supporters of Anti-Job-Bias Bill Need a Winning Strategy." *Congressional Quarterly Weekly Report,* 49 (March 16, 1991), pp. 683–85.

Dwyer, Paula and Tim Smart. "The Price of Discrimination May Well Go Up." *Business Week* (August 13, 1990), p. 34.

"EEOC Issues Undocumented Alien and Title VII Policy Statement." *Personnel Journal,* 68 (July 1989), p. 14.

Flynn, Kelly. "Preventive Medicine for Sexual Harassment." *Personnel,* 68 (March 1991), p. 17.

Galen, Michele and others. "Ending Sexual Harassment: Business Is Getting The Message." *Business Week* (March 18, 1991), pp. 98–100.

Garland, Susan B. "Disabling a Bill for the Disabled." *Business Week* (February 19, 1990), p. 45.

Garland, Susan B., and Lisa Driscoll. "Can the Feds Bust Through the 'Glass Ceiling'?" *Business Week* (April 29, 1991), p. 33.

Israel, David, and Greg McConnell. "New Law Protects Older Workers." *HRMagazine,* 36 (March 1991), pp. 77–78.

Kelly, Joan L. "What Went Wrong?" *Personnel Journal,* 69 (January 1990), pp. 44–47.

Lesher, Richard. "Business-Government Relations in the 1990s." *Business Horizons,* 33 (January–February 1990), pp. 20–25.

"Line Up: Why Women Have Not Moved Faster." *Stores,* 72 (September 1990), p. 37.

Matusewitch, Eric. "Pitfalls of Informal Affirmative Action." *Personnel Journal,* 69 (January 1990), pp. 84–90.

McCalla, Robert K. "Stopping Sexual Harassment Before It Begins." *Management Review,* 80 (April 1991), pp. 44–46.

McDenzie, Richard B. "Government Policies in the 1990s." *Business Horizons,* 33 (January–February 1990), pp. 26–32.

Murphy, Betty Southard, Wayne E. Barlow, and D. Diane Hatch. "Employee Benefit Plans Under ADEA." *Personnel Journal,* 68 (September 1989), pp. 22–23.

Murphy, Betty Southard, Wayne E. Barlow, and D. Diane Hatch. " 'Reasonable Woman' is New Standard For Sexual Harassment." *Personnel Journal,* 70 (May 1991), pp. 34–36.

Nelson-Horchler, Joani. "The Best Man for a Job Is a Man!" *Industry Week,* 240 (January 7, 1991), pp. 50–52.

Nobile, Robert J., Esq. "To Waiver or Not to Waiver Is the Question of OWPWA." *Personnel,* 68 (June 1991), p. 11.

Pati, Gopal C., and Gay Stubblefield. "The Disabled Are Able to Work." *Personnel Journal,* 69 (December 1990), pp. 30–34.

Powell, Gary N. "Upgrading Management Opportunities for Women." *HRMagazine,* 35 (November 1990), pp. 67–70.

Raisner, Jack. "When Workplace Relationships Cause Discrimination." *HRMagazine,* 36 (January 1991), pp. 75–76.

Reminger, Richard T. "At Risk EEO Complaints Are on the Rise, but Most Companies Are Doing Little to Fight Back." *Personnel Journal,* 70 (March 1991), pp. 51–54.

Schiller, Zachary, and Mark Landler. "Ending Sexual Harassment: Business Is Getting the Message." *Business Week* (March 18, 1991), pp. 98–100.

Segal, Jonathan A. "New Rules for Waivers by Older Workers." *HRMagazine,* 36 (April 1991), pp. 84–88.

Smart, Tim. "After the Election, Civil Rights May Get a Fighting Chance." *Business Week* (November 5, 1990), p. 52.

Smart, Tim, and Susan B. Garland. "Why Business Is Suddenly Gunning for the 1990 Civil Rights Act." *Business Week* (May 14, 1990), p. 49.

Wendt, Ann C., and William M. Slonaker. "Confronting and Preventing Employment Discrimination." *Supervision,* 52 (March 1991), pp. 3–5.

"Where Are Women Making It?" *Stores,* 72 (September 1990), p. 38.

CHAPTER 4

JOB ANALYSIS

Chapter Objectives

1. Define *job analysis* and explain the reasons for conducting job analysis.
2. State the types of information required for job analysis, describe the various job analysis methods, and explain the components of a well-designed job description and job specification.
3. Describe the newer methods available for conducting job analysis and describe how job analysis helps to satisfy various legal requirements.
4. Explain job design, job enrichment, and job enlargement.

"Mary, I'm having trouble figuring out what kind of machine operators you need," said John Anderson, the human resource director at Gulf Machineries. "I've sent four people for you to interview who seemed to meet the requirements outlined in the job description. You rejected all of them."

"To heck with the job description," replied Mary. "What I'm concerned with is finding someone who can do the job. And, the people you sent me couldn't do the job. Besides, I've never even seen the job description."

John took a copy of the job description to Mary and went over it point by point. They discovered that either the job description never fit the job, or the job had changed a great deal since it was written. For example, the job description specified experience on an older model drill press while the one in use is a new digital machine. Workers had to be more mathematically oriented to effectively use the new machine.

After hearing Mary describe the qualifications needed for the machine operators' job, and explaining the duties they perform, John said, "I think that we can now write an accurate description of the job, and using it as a guide, find the right kind of people. Let's work more closely so this kind of situation won't happen again."

The situation just described reflects a very common problem in human resource management: The job description did not adequately define the duties and skills needed to perform the job. Therefore, it became virtually impossible for John Anderson, the human resource director, to locate people with the required skills. Job analysis was critically needed to resolve the problem. As we stress throughout the remainder of this book, job analysis is the most basic function of human resource management.

We begin the chapter by defining job analysis and describing its importance to all human resource functions. Next, we discuss job analysis methods and the types of data gathered in the process. We then explain the use of job analysis data in preparing job descriptions and job specifications. We next describe newer methods for conducting job analysis and conclude the chapter by reviewing the legal implications of job analysis and the globalization of job design.

■ JOB ANALYSIS: A BASIC HUMAN RESOURCE TOOL

A **job** consists of a group of tasks that must be performed for an organization to achieve its goals. A job may require the services of one person, such as that of president, or the services of seventy-five, as might be the case with data entry operators in a large firm.

In a work group consisting of a supervisor, two senior clerks, and four word processing operators, there are three jobs and seven positions. A **position** is the collection of tasks and responsibilities performed by one person; there is a position for every individual in an organization. For instance, a small company might have 25 jobs for its 75 employees, whereas in a large company 2,000 jobs may exist for 50,000 employees. In some firms, as few as 10 jobs constitute 90 percent of a workforce.[1]

Job analysis is the systematic process of determining the skills, duties, and knowledge required for performing jobs in an organization.[2] It is an essential and pervasive human resource technique. The purpose of job analysis is to obtain answers to six important questions:

1. What physical and mental tasks does the worker accomplish?
2. When is the job to be completed?
3. Where is the job to be accomplished?
4. How does the worker do the job?
5. Why is the job done?
6. What qualifications are needed to perform the job?

Job analysis provides a summary of a job's duties and responsibilities, its relationship to other jobs, the knowledge and skills required, and working conditions under which it is performed. Job facts are gathered, analyzed, and recorded as the job exists, not as the job should exist.[3] The latter function is most often assigned to industrial engineers, methods analysts, or others. Job analysis is conducted after the job has been designed, the worker has been trained, and the job is being performed.

Job analysis is performed on three occasions. First, it is done when the organization is founded and a job analysis program is initiated for the first time. Second, it is performed when new jobs are created. Third, it is used when jobs are changed significantly as a result of new technology, methods,

---

[1] Donald W. Myers, "The Impact of a Selected Provision in the Federal Guidelines on Job Analysis and Training," *Personnel Administrator,* 26 (July 1981), p. 45.

[2] R. Wayne Mondy, Robert M. Noe, and Robert E. Edwards, "What the Staffing Function Entails," *Personnel,* 63 (April 1986), p. 55.

[3] John C. Crystal and Richard S. Deems, "Redesigning Jobs," *Training and Development Journal,* 37 (February 1983), p. 45.

procedures, or systems. The majority of job analyses are performed because of changes in the nature of jobs. Job analysis information is used to prepare both job descriptions and job specifications.

The **job description** is a document that provides information regarding the tasks, duties, and responsibilities of the job. The minimum acceptable qualifications that a person should possess in order to perform a particular job are contained in the **job specification.** We discuss both types of documents in greater detail later in the chapter.

■ REASONS FOR CONDUCTING JOB ANALYSIS

As Figure 4-1 on page 112 shows, data derived from job analysis have an impact on virtually every aspect of human resource management. A major use of job analysis data is in the area of human resource planning. Merely knowing that the firm will need 1,000 new employees to produce goods or services to satisfy sales demand is insufficient. Each job requires different knowledge, skills, and ability levels. Obviously, effective human resource planning must take these job requirements into consideration.

Employee recruitment and selection would be haphazard if the recruiter didn't know the qualifications needed to perform the job. Lacking up-to-date job descriptions and specifications, employees would have to be recruited and selected for a job without clear guidelines, and this practice could have disastrous consequences. Such a practice is virtually unheard of when firms procure raw materials, supplies, or equipment. For example, even when ordering a copying machine, the purchasing department normally develops precise specifications. Surely, the same logic should apply when searching for a firm's most valuable asset!

Also, job specification information often proves beneficial in identifying human resource development needs. If the specification suggests that the job requires a particular knowledge, skill, or ability—and the person filling the position does not possess all the qualifications required—training and/or development is probably in order. It should be directed at assisting workers in performing duties specified in their present job descriptions or preparing them for promotion to higher level jobs. With regard to performance appraisal, employees should be evaluated in terms of how well they accomplish the duties specified in their job descriptions. A manager who evaluates an employee on factors not included in the job description is left wide open to allegations of discrimination.

In the area of compensation, the relative value of a particular job to the company must be known before a dollar value can be placed on it. The more significant its duties and responsibilities, the more the job is worth relatively. Jobs that require greater knowledge, skills, and abilities should be worth more to the firm. For example, the relative value of a job that calls for a master's degree normally would be higher than that of a job that requires only a high school diploma.

Information derived from job analysis is also valuable in identifying safety and health considerations. For example, employers are required to state whether a job is hazardous. The job description/specification should

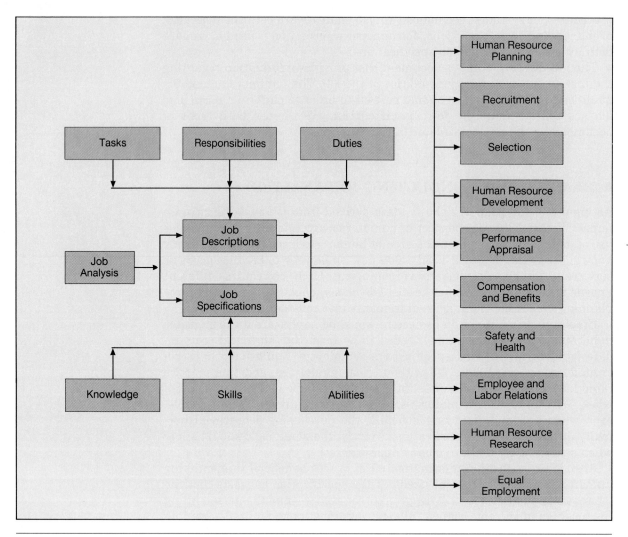

FIGURE 4-1 | Job Analysis: The Most Basic Human Resource Management Tool

respond to this requirement. In addition, in certain hazardous jobs, workers may need specific information about the hazards in order to perform the jobs safely.

Job analysis information is also important to employee and labor relations. When employees are considered for promotion, transfer, or demotion, the job description provides a standard for comparison of talent. Regardless of whether the firm is unionized, information obtained through job analysis can often lead to more objective human resource decisions.

When human resource research is undertaken, job analysis information provides the researcher with a starting point. For example, if the human resource manager is trying to identify factors that distinguish successful employees from mediocre employees, the researcher needs to study only those employees who have similar job descriptions/specifications.

Finally, having properly accomplished job analysis is particularly important for supporting the legality of employment practices. Job analysis data are needed to defend, for example, decisions involving promotion, transfers, and demotions.

Thus far, we have described job analysis as it pertains to specific HRM functions. However, in practice these functions are interrelated. In fact, job analysis provides the basis for tying the functional areas together and the foundation for developing a sound human resource program.

■ TYPES OF JOB ANALYSIS INFORMATION

Considerable information is needed for successful accomplishment of job analysis. The job analyst identifies the job's actual duties and responsibilities and gathers the other types of data shown in Table 4-1 on page 114. Note that work activities, worker-oriented activities, and the types of machines, tools, equipment, and work aids used in the job are important. This information is used later to help determine the job skills needed. In addition, the job analyst looks at job-related tangibles and intangibles, such as the knowledge needed, the materials processed, and the goods made or services performed.

Some job analysis systems identify job standards. Work measurement studies may be needed to determine, for example, how long it takes to perform a task. With regard to job content, the analyst studies the work schedule, financial and nonfinancial incentives, and physical working conditions. Since jobs are often performed in conjunction with others, organizational and social contexts are noted. Specific education, training, and work experience pertinent to the job are also identified.

■ JOB ANALYSIS METHODS

Job analysis has traditionally been conducted in a number of different ways because organizational needs and resources for conducting job analysis differ.[4] Selection of a specific method should be based on the ways in which the information is to be used (job evaluation, pay increases, development, and so on) and the approach that is most feasible for a particular organization. We describe the most common methods of job analysis in the following sections.

Questionnaires

Questionnaires are typically quick and economical to use. The job analyst may administer a structured questionnaire to employees, who identify the tasks they perform. However, in some cases employees may lack verbal

---

[4] Ronald A. Ash and Edward L. Levine, "A Framework for Evaluating Job Analysis Methods," *Personnel*, 57 (November–December 1980), pp. 53–54.

TABLE 4-1 | Types of Data Normally Gathered in Job Analysis

Summary of Types of Data Collected Through Job Analysis*

1. Work activities
  a. Work activities and processes.
  b. Activity records (in film form, for example).
  c. Procedures used.
  d. Personal responsibility.

2. Worker-oriented activities
  a. Human behaviors, such as physical actions and communicating on the job.
  b. Elemental motions for methods analysis.
  c. Personal job demands, such as energy expenditure.

3. Machines, tools, equipment, and work aids used

4. Job-related tangibles and intangibles
  a. Knowledge dealt with or applied (as in accounting).
  b. Materials processed.
  c. Products made or services performed.

5. Work performance†
  a. Error analysis.
  b. Work standards.
  c. Work measurements, such as time taken for a task.

6. Job context
  a. Work schedule.
  b. Financial and nonfinancial incentives.
  c. Physical working conditions.
  d. Organizational and social contexts.

7. Personal requirements for the job.
  a. Personal attributes such as personality and interests.
  b. Education and training required.
  c. Work experience.

*This information can be in the form of qualitative, verbal, narrative descriptions or quantitative measurements of each item, such as error rates per unit of time or noise level.

†All job analysis systems do not develop the work performance aspects.

Source: Reprinted by permission of Marvin D. Dunnette.

skills, which makes this method less useful. Also, some employees may tend to exaggerate the significance of their tasks.

A portion of a job analysis questionnaire used by First Interstate Bancorp is presented in Figure 4-2 on page 116. Although the entire questionnaire consists of six sections, only Section III, Position Skills and Knowledge, is shown.

Observation

When using the observation method, the job analyst usually watches the worker perform job tasks and records his or her observations. This method is used primarily to gather information on jobs emphasizing manual skills, such as those of a machine operator. It can also help the analyst identify interrelationships between physical and mental tasks. However, observation alone is usually an insufficient means of conducting job analysis, particularly when mental skills are dominant in a job. For instance, observing a financial analyst at work would not reveal much about the requirements of the job.

Interviews

An understanding of the job may also be gained through interviewing both the employee and the supervisor. Usually the analyst interviews the employee first, helping the worker describe the duties performed. Then the analyst normally contacts the supervisor for additional information, to check the accuracy of the information obtained from the worker, and to clarify certain points.

Employee Recording

In some instances, job analysis information is gathered by having the employees describe their daily work activities in a diary or log. Again, the problem of employees exaggerating job importance may have to be overcome. However, valuable understanding of highly specialized jobs, such as a recreation therapist, may be obtained in this way.

Combination of Methods

Usually, an analyst does not use one job analysis method exclusively. A combination of methods is often more appropriate. For instance, in analyzing clerical and administrative jobs, the analyst might use questionnaires supported by interviews and limited observation. In studying production jobs, interviews supplemented by extensive work observation may provide the needed data. Basically, the analyst should employ the combination of techniques needed to conduct an effective job analysis.

■ CONDUCTING JOB ANALYSIS

The person who conducts job analysis is interested in gathering data on what is involved in performing a particular job. The people who participate in job analysis should include, at a minimum, the employee and the employee's immediate supervisor. Large organizations may have one or more job analysts, but in small organizations line supervisors may be

Job Analysis Questionnaire

First Interstate Bancorp

Name _____

Position Title _____

Affiliate _____

Division/Group/Unit _____

City and State _____

Immediate Manager _____

General Instructions

This questionnaire is designed to provide information about your current position. It is *not* intended to measure your performance or productivity. It is a tool for analyzing and describing your job.

The questionnaire consists of six sections.
- **Section I** deals with the tasks and activities that comprise your job.
- **Section II** asks you to compare various job dimensions, which are groupings of similar tasks.
- **Section III** covers the skills and knowledge required to perform the tasks and activities of your position.
- **Section IV** identifies specific scope measures of your position.
- **Section V** focuses on individual factors that you bring to your job.
- **Section VI** includes additional factors which may have an impact on your position.

Because this questionnaire covers a broad range of affiliates and jobs, a number of the questions may not apply to your position. However, *if you perform tasks that are not covered by the questionnaire, space has been provided for you to write them in.* Whether you perform a large number of tasks or only a few is not important. What is essential is that you respond to *all* of the questions (for example, you may perform certain financial management tasks, although you are in a marketing function), and in a manner which best describes your position as it is typically performed by you.

In responding to the questions, please use the following definitions:
- **affiliate** refers to an individual bank (e.g., First Interstate Bank of Arizona) or a nonbank subsidiary (e.g. First Interstate Services Company).
- **customer** means any individual or group, inside or outside the company, with which you deal on a client or customer basis. For example, an affiliate bank can be a customer for the data processing unit, a small business can be a customer for the venture capital group, and an individual or a corporation can be a customer for a bank.
- **unit** is the organizational group in which you report or for which you have responsibility. This could be a functional group, a department, or a division of a company. For example, for a Cashier position, the unit might be the Cashier's Department; for a VP Operations, the unit might be the Operations Department; for a VP Administration, the unit might be the Administration Division; or for a Chief Executive Officer, the unit would be the entire bank.

The questionnaires will be returned directly to Towers, Perrin, Forster & Crosby (TPF&C), so all responses on this form will remain confidential. However, to ensure that the information about your position is accurate and consistent, you and your immediate manager will review the results of TPF&C's analysis of the questionnaire.

Please follow the specific instructions at the beginning of each section. Read each section in full before attempting to complete it so that you can respond as accurately as possible.

Thank you for your efforts in participating in this study.

FIGURE 4-2 | A Job Analysis Questionnaire

Source: Used with the permission of First Interstate Bancorp.

Section III: Position Skills and Knowledge

This section focuses on the type and depth of skills and knowledge that are 1) required to perform your job, and 2) that you may possess.

For each of the skills listed, you are asked to rate two items: the **level required** and the **level you possess.** In the appropriate boxes, write the number that best describes the skill or knowledge level, according to the following scale:

0 = Job neither requires nor do I possess skill/knowledge.
1 = Familiarity with skill/knowledge.
2 = General working skill/knowledge.
3 = Advanced skill/knowledge.
4 = Unique expertise in skill/knowledge.

In the first column of boxes, identify the **level of skill/knowledge required** to successfully perform your present job.

In the second column of boxes, identify the **level of skill/knowledge** that **you possess,** regardless of whether the job requires it.

The third column identifies sources of skills and knowledge. To indicate where you acquired each skill or knowledge that is required for the performance of your current position, identify up to, but no more than, two sources. Mark 1 in the column that represents the primary source. Mark 2 in the column that represents the secondary source.

- Level required for position
- Level you possess
- On-the-job training
- College/university
- Formal banking program
- Internal training program
- External training program

A. Planning, Policies, Procedures

1 Organization design
2 Short-term planning (setting budgets, goals, etc.)
3 Strategic planning
4 Pricing fee structuring

B. Business Development / Marketing

5 Market research (identifying markets, competitive analyses and evaluation)
6 Market analysis (client needs, trends, strategies, etc.)
7 Marketing tools (advertising, promotional campaigns, etc.)
8 Products services (bank unit services, systems, etc.)
9 Marketing sales

C. Customer Relations

10 Customer industry (objectives, economics, trends, etc.)
11 Customer counsel/problem solving
12 Account management
13 Profit analysis

For every statement:
• If a task is not part of your job, mark X in the first box
• If a task is a part of your job, rate:

Relative Time Spent   Relative Importance
1 : Very small amount   A   Unimportant
2 : Small amount   B   Minor importance
3 : Moderate amount   C   Important
4 : Large amount   D   Very important
5 : Very large amount   E   Crucial

- Not part of the job
- Relative time spent
- Relative importance

A. Planning

1   Develops business planning activities
2   Directs business planning activities
3   Develops annual unit goals and objectives
4   Approves annual unit goals and objectives
5   Develops longer-range strategic goals
6   Approves longer-range strategic goals
7   Develops specific strategy and action plans for unit
8   Approves specific strategy and action plans for unit
9   Reviews approves and monitors business plans
10 Prepares profit plans and updates
11 Approves profit plans and updates
12 Prepares operating budgets
13 Approves operating budgets
14 Approves requests for nonbudgeted items
15 Develops plans to improve administrative efficiency
16 Approves plans to improve administrative efficiency
17 Integrates the plans of other organizational units
18 Coordinates with other units to meet predetermined schedules
19 Proposes new or customized programs, services, products and research
20 Approves new or customized programs, services, products and research
21 Identifies impact of external conditions on unit
22 Coordinates units in the development of plans and programs
23 Monitors progress of specific projects
24 Recommends revisions to the unit organizational structure
25 Approves revisions to the unit organizational structure
26 Evaluates and recommends approval of affiliate facility projects
27 Recommends potential mergers, acquisitions or relocations
28 Approves potential mergers, acquisitions or relocations
29 Other: please list task(s) and check boxes

a _____
b _____
c _____

From the above list of Planning tasks, please mark the numbers of the three most important tasks in rank order:

1 _____
2 _____

B. Policies and Procedures

30 Formulates and recommends policies or procedures for others to follow
31 Approves policies or procedures for others to follow
32 Reviews agreements or documentation for compliance with appropriate policies and standards
33 Directs the establishment of review or control procedures
34 Evaluates operating policies or procedures against desired objectives
35 Develops or maintains standards for service
36 Develops quality control programs and procedures
37 Approves quality control programs and procedures
38 Formulates or recommends pricing policies
39 Approves pricing policies
40 Develops methods and procedures to evaluate business strategies
41 Establishes planning guidelines and procedures
42 Directs creation, handling and disposition of official records
43 Directs safeguarding of records and documents
44 Approves procedures for automating existing manual systems
45 Other: please list task(s) and check boxes

a _____
b _____
c _____

From the above list of Policies and Procedures tasks, please mark the numbers of the three most important tasks in rank order:

1 _____
2 _____
3 _____

FIGURE 4-2   *Continued*

responsible for job analysis. Organizations that lack the technical expertise often use outside consultants to perform job analysis.

Before conducting job analysis, the analyst learns as much as possible about the job by reviewing organizational charts and talking with individuals acquainted with the jobs to be studied. Before beginning, the supervisor should introduce the analyst to the employees and explain the purpose of the job analysis. Although employee attitudes about the job are beyond the job analyst's control, the analyst must attempt to develop mutual trust and confidence with those whose jobs are being analyzed. Failure in this area will detract from an otherwise technically sound job analysis. Upon completion of job analysis, two basic human resource documents—job descriptions and job specifications—can be prepared.

■ JOB DESCRIPTION

Information obtained through job analysis is crucial to the development of job descriptions. Recall that we previously defined the job description as a document that states the tasks, duties, and responsibilities of the job. Job descriptions should be both relevant and accurate.[5] They should provide concise statements of what employees are expected to do on the job and indicate exactly what employees do, how they do it, and the conditions under which the duties are performed.[6]

Among the items frequently included in a job description are:

- Major duties performed.
- Percentage of time devoted to each duty.
- Performance standards to be achieved.
- Working conditions and possible hazards.
- Number of employees performing the job and whom they report to.
- The machines and equipment used on the job.

The contents of the job description vary somewhat with the purpose for which it will be used. Let's consider the sections most commonly included in a job description.

Job Identification

The job identification section includes the job title, department, reporting relationship, and a job number or code. A good title will closely approximate the nature of the work content and will distinguish that job from

---

[5] Donald C. Busi, "The Job Description: More Than Bureaucratic Control," *Supervisory Management,* 35 (October 1990), p. 5.

[6] Hubert S. Field and Robert D. Gatewood, "Matching Talent with the Task: To Find the Right People, First Define the Jobs You Want Them to Do," *Personnel Administrator,* 32 (April 1987), p. 113.

others. Unfortunately, job titles are often misleading.[7] An "executive secretary" in one organization may be little more than a highly paid clerk, whereas a person with the same title in another firm may practically run the company. For instance, one former student's first job after graduation was with a major tire and rubber company as an "assistant district service manager." Because the primary duties of the job were to unload tires from trucks, check the tread wear, and stack the tires in boxcars, a more appropriate title would probably have been "tire checker and stacker."

One information source that assists in standardizing job titles is the *Dictionary of Occupational Titles* (DOT).[8] The DOT includes standardized and comprehensive descriptions of job duties and related information for over 200,000 occupations. Such standardization permits employers in different industries and parts of the country to match more accurately job requirements with worker skills.

An example of a DOT definition—for a "branch manager," occupational code 183.137-010—is provided in Figure 4-3 on page 120. The first digit of the code identifies one of the following major occupations:

- 0/1 Professional, technical, and managerial
- 2 Clerical and sales
- 3 Service
- 4 Farming, fishing, forestry, and related
- 5 Processing
- 6 Machine trade
- 7 Bench work
- 8 Structural work
- 9 Miscellaneous

For the branch manager, the major classification would be "managerial" occupations. Thus, this example has a code "1."

The next two digits represent breakdowns of the general occupation category.

Digits four through six describe the job's relationship to data, people, and things. For the branch manager, a code "1" for data would be "coordinating," a code "3" for people would be "supervising," and a code "7" for things would be "handling."

The final three digits indicate the alphabetical order of titles within the six-digit code group. These codes assist in distinguishing a specific occupation from other similar ones. The alphabetical order for "branch manager" is indicated by the digits 010.

---

[7] James N. Baron and William T. Bilby, "The Proliferation of Job Titles in Organizations," *Administrative Science Quarterly,* 31 (December 1986), p. 561.

[8] U.S. Department of Labor, *Dictionary of Occupational Titles,* 4th ed. (Washington, D.C.: U.S. Government Printing Office, 1977).

FIGURE 4-3 | The Parts of the *Dictionary of Occupational Titles* Definition

Source: U.S. Department of Labor, *Dictionary of Occupational Titles.*

Date of the Job Analysis

The job analysis date is placed on the job description to aid in identifying job changes that would make the description obsolete. Some firms have found it useful to place an expiration date on the document. This practice ensures periodic review of job content and minimizes the number of obsolete job descriptions.

Job Summary

The job summary provides a concise overview of the job. It is generally a short paragraph that states job content.

Duties Performed

The body of the job description delineates the major duties to be performed. Usually one sentence beginning with an action verb such as *receives, performs, establishes,* or *assembles* adequately explains each duty.

■ JOB SPECIFICATION

Recall that we defined *job specification* as a document containing the minimum acceptable qualifications that a person should possess in order to perform a particular job. Items typically included in the job specification are educational requirements, experience, personality traits, and physical abilities. In practice, job specifications are often included as a major section of job descriptions. Figure 4-4 is an actual job description provided by General Mills, Inc. As you can see, the qualifications needed for the job of

POSITION TITLE			POSITION NUMBER 217
SECRETARY II			APPROVAL RHS
DIVISION OR STAFF DEPARTMENT All	LOCATION All	REPORTS TO	EFFECTIVE DATE May 1992
DEPARTMENT OR ACTIVITY	SECTION	POINTS 165	GRADE 6	REVISES

JOB SUMMARY
Performs clerical and administrative duties for a manager and often one or more staff members of a major function.

NATURE OF WORK
Performs a wide variety of office duties including most of the following:
a. Data entry of correspondence, reports, manuscripts, graphs, charts, etc., from notes, dictating machine, and/or hand written drafts proficiently and with minimum direction and instructions.
b. Receiving telephone calls and visitors skillfully and handling incoming mail efficiently.
c. Originating routine correspondence and handling inquiries, and routing non-routine inquiries and correspondence to proper persons.
d. Establishing and maintaining department files and records.
e. Assuming responsibility for arranging appointments and meetings, screening calls, and handling personal and confidential matters for superior.
f. Assembling, organizing, processing, and evaluating data and reports; operating office machines needed for accomplishing this.
g. Performing administrative duties and special projects as directed, such as collecting and compiling general reference materials and information pertaining to company, division, or department practices and procedures.

Works independently, receiving a minimum of supervision and guidance on established office procedures. Relieves supervisor of minor administrative details. May have some light work direction over others in department. Structure is light and most work is not checked.

QUALIFICATIONS
High school education or its equivalent plus three years of clerical experience, including one year with the Company, and a word processing skill of at least 60 WPM. Demonstrated proficiency in English grammar, punctuation, spelling, and proper word usage. Must be able to anticipate problems and use sound judgment and tact in handling confidential matters, screening telephone calls and visitors, and scheduling superior's time. Must have the ability to acquire a thorough knowledge of the organization's policies, procedures, and personnel in order to relieve superior of specified administrative duties. A basic figure aptitude and/or a working knowledge of certain word processing packages may be necessary depending on the specific job.

FIGURE 4-4 | A Job Description

Source: Used with the permission of General Mills, Inc.

HRM In Action

I can't determine what kind of computer programmer you need, Alex," said Bob Sanders, the human resource director. "Every applicant I sent down was proficient in FORTRAN, just like the job description stated."

"Get real, Bob," replied Alex. "We haven't required FORTRAN in ten years. The person I need has to be up-to-date on the latest software. None of those people you sent me were qualified."

How would you respond?

"Secretary II" include entering data at the rate of at least sixty words per minute and demonstrated proficiency in English grammar, punctuation, spelling, and proper word usage. This type of information is extremely valuable in the recruiting and selection process.

After jobs have been analyzed and the descriptions written, the results should be reviewed with the supervisor and the worker to ensure that they are accurate, clear, and understandable. The courtesy of reviewing results with employees also helps to gain their acceptance. Because the job description and job specification are often combined into one form, we use the term *job description* in this book to include both documents.

■ OTHER JOB ANALYSIS METHODS

Many attempts have been made to provide more systematic methods of conducting job analysis. We describe several of these next.

Department of Labor Job Analysis Schedule

The U.S. Department of Labor established a method of systematically studying jobs and occupations called the **job analysis schedule (JAS).** Its basic content is shown in Figure 4-5. When the JAS method is used, information is gathered by a trained analyst.

A major component of the JAS is the Work Performed Ratings section. Here, what workers do in performing a job with regard to data (D), people (P), and things (T) is evaluated. Subdivisions of these three categories are shown in Table 4-2 on page 126. Each is viewed as a hierarchy of functions, with those higher in the category being more difficult. The codes in the Worker Functions section represent the highest level of involvement in each of the three categories.

JOB ANALYSIS SCHEDULE

1. Estab. Job Title   DOUGH MIXER

2. Ind. Assign.   (bake. prod.)

3. SIC Code(s) and Title(s)   2051 Bread and other bakery products

Code   520.782   Oper. Control p. 435   WTA Group   DOT Title   Ind. Desig.

4. JOB SUMMARY:

Operates mixing machine to mix ingredients for straight and sponge (yeast) doughs according to established formulas, directs other workers in fermentation of dough, and cuts dough into pieces with hand cutter.

5. WORK PERFORMED RATINGS:

	D	P	(T)
Worker Functions	Data	People	Things
	5	6	2

Work Field   148 - Cooking, Food Preparing

M.P.S.M.S.   384 - Bakery Products

6. WORKER TRAITS RATINGS:

GED   1 (2) 3   4   5   6
SVP   1   2   3 (4) 5   6   7   8   9
Aptitudes   G 3 V 3 N 3 S 3 P 3 Q 4 K 3 F 3 M 3 E 4 C 4

Temperaments   D F I J (M) P R S (T) V
Interests   (1a) 1b 2a 2b 3a 3b 4a (4b) 5a (5b)
Phys. Demands   S L M (H) V 2 (3) (4) 5 (6)
Environ. Cond.   (I) O B 2 3 4 (5) 6 7

7. General Education

   a. Elementary   6   High School _____ Courses _____

   b. College   None   Courses _____

8. Vocational Preparation

   a. College   None   Courses _____

   b. Vocational Education   None   Courses _____

   c. Apprenticeship   None

FIGURE 4-5 | A Department of Labor Job Analysis Schedule

Source: U.S. Department of Labor, Manpower Administration, *Handbook for Analyzing Jobs.* Washington, D.C.: U.S. Government Printing Office, 1972, pp. 42–45.

d. Inplant Training   None _____

e. On-the-Job Training   Six Months _____

f. Performance on Other Jobs   DOUGH-MIXER HELPER - One Year

9. Experience   One Year as DOUGH-MIXER HELPER

10. Orientation   Four Hours

11. Licenses, etc.   Food Handlers Certificate Issued by the Health Department

12. Relation to Other Jobs and Workers

Promotion: From   DOUGH-MIXER HELPER   To   BAKER

Transfers: From   None   To   None

Supervision Received   By BAKER

Supervision Given   DOUGH-MIXER HELPER

13. Machines, Tools, Equipment, and Work Aids - Dough-mixing machine; balance scales; hand scoops; measuring vessels; portable dough troughs.

14. Materials and Products

Bread dough

15. Description of Tasks:

1. Dumps ingredients into mixing machine: Examines production schedule to determine type of bread to be produced, such as rye, whole wheat, or white. Refers to formula card for quantities and types of ingredients required, such as flour, water, milk, vitamin solutions, and shortening. Weighs out, measures, and dumps ingredients into mixing machine. (20%)

FIGURE 4-5 | *Continued*

The JAS component Worker Traits Ratings relates primarily to job requirement data. The topics general education (GED), specific vocational preparation (SVP), Aptitudes, Temperaments, Interests, Physical Demands, and Environmental Conditions are included. The Description of Tasks section (item 15) provides a specific description of the work performed. Both routine tasks and occasionally performed tasks are included.

Functional Job Analysis

Functional job analysis (FJA) is a comprehensive job analysis approach that concentrates on the interactions among the work, the worker, and the organization. This approach is a modification of the job analysis schedule.

2. Operates mixing machine: Turns valves and other hand controls to set mixing time according to type of dough being mixed. Presses button to start agitator blades in machine. Observes gauges and dials on equipment continuously to verify temperature of dough and mixing time. Feels dough for desired consistency. Adds water or flour to mix measuring vessels and adjusts mixing time and controls to obtain desired elasticity in mix. (55%)

3. Directs other workers in fermentation of dough: Prepares fermentation schedule according to type of dough being raised. Sprays portable dough *Trough* with lubricant to prevent adherence of mixed dough to trough. Directs DOUGH-MIXER HELPER in positioning trough beneath door of mixer to catch dough when mixing cycle is complete. Pushes or directs other workers to push troughs of dough into fermentation room. (10%)

4. Cuts dough: Dumps fermentated dough onto worktable. Manually kneads dough to eliminate gases formed by yeast. Cuts dough into pieces with hand cutter. Places cut dough on proofing rack and covers with cloth. (10%)

5. Performs miscellaneous duties: Records on work sheet number of batches mixed during work shift. Informs BAKE SHOP FOREMAN when repairs or major adjustments are required for machines and equipment. (5%)

---

16. Definition of Terms
Trough - A long, narrow, opened vessel used for kneading or washing ingredients.

17. General Comments
None

---

18. Analyst   Jane Smith   Date   3/21/92   Editor   John Rilley   Date   3/30/92

Reviewed By   Alexandra Purcey   Title, Org.   Foreman, Bake Shop

FIGURE 4-5 | *Continued*

It is a worker-oriented method of describing jobs that identifies what a person actually does rather than his or her responsibilities.[9] The fundamental elements of FJA follow:

1. A major distinction is made between what gets done and what workers do to get things done. It is more important in job analysis to know the latter. For instance, a word processing operator doesn't just enter data; a number of other tasks must be performed in accomplishing the job.
2. Each job is concerned with data, people, and things.
3. Workers function in unique ways as they relate to data, people, and things.

---

[9] Felix M. Lopez, Gerald A. Kesselman, and Felix E. Lopez, "An Empirical Test of a Trait-Oriented Job Analysis Technique," *Personnel Psychology,* 35 (August 1981), p. 480.

TABLE 4-2 | Worker Function Scale for Job Analysis Schedule

Data (4th digit)	People (5th digit)	Things (6th digit)
0 Synthesizing	0 Monitoring	0 Setting-up
1 Coordinating	1 Negotiating	1 Precision working
2 Analyzing	2 Instructing	2 Operating— controlling
3 Compiling	3 Supervising	3 Driving—operating
4 Computing	4 Diverting	4 Manipulating
5 Copying	5 Persuading	5 Tending
6 Comparing	6 Speaking— signaling	6 Feeding— offbearing
7 No significant relationship	7 Serving	7 Handling
8	8 No significant relationship	8 No significant relationship

Source: U.S. Department of Labor, *Dictionary of Occupational Titles.*

4. Each job requires the worker to relate to data, people, and things in some way.
5. Only a few definite and identifiable functions are involved with data, people, and things (refer again to Table 4-2).
6. These functions proceed from the simple to the complex. The least complex function of data would be comparing, and the most complex would be synthesizing. In addition, the assumption is that if an upper level function is required, all the lower level functions are also required.
7. The three hierarchies for data, people, and things provide two measures for a job. First, there is a measure of relative complexity in relation to data, people, and things—in essence, the amount of interrelationship among the three functions. Second, there is a measure of proportional involvement for each function. For instance, 50 percent of a person's time may be spent in analyzing, 30 percent in supervising, and 20 percent in operating.[10]

One study determined that FJA was a useful technique for defining the work of heavy-equipment operators. Therefore, the knowledge, skills, and abilities required for the job could be easily communicated to the courts and the public.[11]

---

[10] Ernest J. McCormick, "Job Information: Its Development and Application," in Dale Yoder and Herbert S. Heneman (eds.), *Staffing Policies and Strategies* (Washington, D.C.: The Bureau of National Affairs, 1979), pp. 54–58.

[11] Howard C. Olson, Sidney A. Fine, David C. Myers, and Margarette C. Jennings, "The Use of Functional Job Analysis in Establishing Performance Standards for Heavy Equipment Operators," *Personnel Psychology,* 34 (Summer 1981), p. 351.

Position Analysis Questionnaire

The **position analysis questionnaire (PAQ)** is a structured job analysis questionnaire that uses a checklist approach to identify job elements. Some 194 job descriptors relate to job-oriented or worker-oriented elements. Advocates of the PAQ believe that its ability to identify job elements, behaviors required of job incumbents, and other job characteristics makes this procedure applicable to analysis of virtually any type of job. Each job descriptor is evaluated on a specified scale such as extent of use, amount of time, importance of job, possibility of occurrence, and applicability.

With the aid of a computer program, each job being studied is scored relative to the thirty-two job dimensions. The score derived represents a profile of the job, which can be compared with standard profiles to group the job into known job families; that is, jobs of a similar nature. In essence, the PAQ identifies significant job behaviors and classifies jobs. Using the PAQ, job descriptions can be based on the relative importance and emphasis placed on various job elements.

The PAQ is completed by an employee or employees familiar with the job being studied—typically an experienced job incumbent or the immediate supervisor. The profiles and job descriptions are then prepared by a job analyst.[12]

Management Position Description Questionnaire

The **management position description questionnaire (MPDQ)** is a method of job analysis designed for management positions and uses a checklist to analyze jobs. It contains 208 items that are related to the concerns and responsibilities of managers.[13] These 208 items have been reduced to thirteen primary job factors:

1. Product, market, and financial planning
2. Coordination of other organizational units and workers
3. Internal business control
4. Products and service responsibility
5. Public and customer relations
6. Advanced consulting
7. Autonomy of action
8. Approval of financial commitment
9. Staff service
10. Supervision
11. Complexity and stress
12. Advanced financial responsibility
13. Broad human resource responsibility

---

[12] Donald L. Caruth, Robert M. Noe III, and R. Wayne Mondy, *Staffing the Contemporary Organization.* (New York: Praeger Publishers, 1990), p. 100.

[13] W. W. Tornow and P. R. Pinto, "The Development of Management Job Taxonomy: A System for Describing, Classifying and Evaluating Executive Positions," *Journal of Applied Psychology,* 11 (1976), pp. 410–418.

The MPDQ has been used to determine the training needs of individuals who are slated to move into managerial positions. It has also been used to evaluate and set compensation rates for managerial jobs and to assign these jobs to job families.

Guidelines Oriented Job Analysis

The **guidelines oriented job analysis (GOJA)** responds to the growing amount of legislation affecting staffing and involves a step-by-step procedure for describing the work of a particular job classification.[14] It is also used for developing selection tools, such as application forms, and for documenting compliance with various legal requirements.

There are three versions of GOJA. The original method, *full* GOJA, is very detailed and requires approximately twenty hours to analyze a job completely. Its use is most appropriate when there is a high probability of discrimination suits. Next, *brief* GOJA was developed after the *Uniform Guidelines* were published in order to reduce the amount of time required to complete a job analysis. To reduce the amount of time required still further, a third version, *simplified* GOJA, was developed. Only about two to four hours are required to complete this job analysis form. The GOJA obtains the following types of information: (1) machines, tools and equipment; (2) supervision; (3) contacts; (4) duties; (5) knowledge, skills, and abilities; (6) physical and other requirements; and (7) differentiating requirements.

Occupational Measurement System[15]

Because of the many technological advances that are presently taking place, new and innovative job analysis methods are being developed.[16] The occupational measurement system is one such technique. The **occupational measurement system (OMS)** enables organizations to collect, store, and analyze information pertinent to human resources by means of a computer database. The computer provides fast turnaround and more accurate job analysis, job descriptions, and evaluations. The computer also makes feasible the use of multiple regression statistical techniques that increase objectivity and hence responsiveness to potential discrimination claims.

The OMS is designed to work with task-based information. Task-based job evaluation uses structured job analysis questionnaires covering work performed within the organization as the basic input document. The ques-

---

[14] Stephen E. Bemis, Ann Holt Belenky, and Dee Ann Soder, *Job Analysis: An Effective Management Tool* (Washington, D.C.: The Bureau of National Affairs, 1983), p. 42.

[15] Information for this section was furnished by First Interstate Bancorp.

[16] Kaye L. Aho, "Understanding the New Job-Analysis Technology," *Personnel,* 66 (January 1989), p. 38.

tionnaires are developed from a number of different sources, including a database of industry job tasks, the organization's job descriptions, and job experts within the firm's workforce. The system includes a booklet with instructions and general information. The questionnaire contains items specifically tailored to the category of positions covered. Responses are given in data entry or optical scanning format. Sample items from a questionnaire are shown in Figure 4-6 on page 130.

The OMS is used to analyze the information obtained in the job analysis questionnaire. The OMS is an integrated computer software system specifically designed to process, analyze, and display task-based information. The following are a few of the reports generated by OMS:

1. A functional and a detailed task-level job description. The job descriptions contain the functions performed by each employee, job, or job classification, the specific tasks covered by those functions, and the amount of time spent on the functions and tasks.
2. Skill and knowledge levels required to perform a function or job, those possessed by the incumbents, and the differences between the two, if any, along with identified training needs.
3. Costs of production, both in terms of performance and supervision.

■ JOB ANALYSIS AND THE LAW

Effective job analysis is essential to sound human resource management as an organization recruits, selects, and promotes employees. In particular, HRM has focused on job analysis because selection methods need to be clearly job related.[17] Legislation requiring thorough job analysis includes the following acts.

Fair Labor Standards Act: Employees are categorized as exempt or nonexempt, and job analysis is basic to this determination. Nonexempt workers must be paid time and a half when they work more than forty hours per week. Overtime pay is not required for exempt employees.

Equal Pay Act: In the past (and to some extent today) men were often paid higher salaries than women, even though they performed essentially the same job. If jobs are not substantially different, similar pay must be provided. When pay differences exist, job descriptions can be used to show whether jobs are substantially equal in terms of skill, effort, responsibility, or working conditions.

Civil Rights Act: As with the Equal Pay Act, job descriptions may provide the basis for adequate defenses against unfair discrimination charges in initial selection, promotion, and all other areas of human resource administration. When job analysis is not performed, defending certain

---

[17] Donald W. Myers, "The Impact of a Selected Provision in the Federal Guidelines on Job Analysis and Training," *Personnel Administrator,* 26 (July 1981), pp. 41–45.

For Every Statement:

■ If a task is part of your job, mark X in the first box.

■ If you PERFORM and/or SUPERVISE a task, rate it using the adjacent RELATIVE TIME SPENT scale:

1 = An extremely small amount of time.
2 = Between levels 1 and 3.
3 = A small amount of time.
4 = Between levels 3 and 5.
5 = A moderate amount of time.
6 = Between levels 5 and 7.
7 = A large amount of time.
8 = Between levels 7 and 9.
9 = An extremely large amount of time.

Relative time spent SUPERVISING ———

Relative time spent PERFORMING ———

Part of job ———

Relative time spent SUPERVISING ———

Relative time spent PERFORMING ———

Part of job ———

CREDIT ADMINISTRATION

1. Works with officers on national accounts to solve credit problems.

2. Responds to inquiries from branches regarding consumer regulations.

3. Establishes goals for delinquency ratios, charge-offs and recoveries.

4. Maintains annual forecasts for nonaccrual loans and other nonperforming assets.

5. Develops loan policy and procedures.

6. Recommends loan policy and procedures.

7. Maintains annual forecasts of commercial, consumer and real estate loan losses.

8. Prepares reports on branch compliance with consumer regulations.

9. Recommends interest rates for loans.

10. Reviews periodicals for changes to consumer protection laws.

11. Reviews analysis reports and financial statement spreads.

12. Performs commercial credit investigations.

13. Prepares credit memos.

14. Prepares loan write-ups.

15. Assembles and interprets debtor credit information.

16. Surveys collateral status for credit extension on potential and current customers.

17. Contacts credit agencies to secure credit reports and special services.

FIGURE 4-6 | A Job Analysis Questionnaire

Source: Used with the permission of First Interstate Bancorp.

qualifications established for the job is usually difficult. For instance, stating that a high school diploma is required without having determined its necessity through job analysis leaves the firm open to possible discrimination charges.

Occupational Safety and Health Act: Job descriptions are required to specify "elements of the job that endanger health, or are considered unsatisfactory or distasteful by the majority of the population." Showing the job description to the employee in advance is a good defense.

■ JOB DESIGN

When a problem occurs, the usual response is to blame the worker, but often the real culprit is job design. Many believe that the manner in which the job is accomplished is fixed. This is often not the case, but the boss looks to the worker first as the cause of the problem. Many times jobs can be redesigned with a substantial improvement in productivity.[18] The challenge is to increase worker productivity by finding ways to "unlock the potential that exists in the overwhelming majority of our workforce."[19]

J. Richard Hackman and Greg R. Oldham contend that the quality of work life can be improved, while at the same time increasing or maximizing worker productivity.[20] They challenge several long-held assumptions, such as the following statements:

- The basic nature of work is fixed and cannot be changed.
- Technology and work processes determine job design.
- All that management can do is properly select and train workers.

Accordingly, they believe, job design should focus on enhancing employee productivity and not be constrained by long-held assumptions.

Job design is the process of determining the specific tasks to be performed, the methods used in performing these tasks, and how the job relates to other work in the organization. In their book, *Work Redesign,* Hackman and Oldham assert that if managers want to achieve a high level of motivation, they must give reliable feedback on performance to employees. Workers must also sense that they are accountable for specific results and feel that the job has meaning beyond pay.[21] Many workers get more satisfaction from completing an entire task or an identifiable part of a process than from producing indistinguishable and seemingly unrelated pieces of work. In spite of its bright promise, however, job design alternatives face some realistic constraints.

---

[18] Michael A. Campion, "How Do You Design a Job?" *Personnel Journal,* 68 (January 1989), p. 43.

[19] Robert H. Guest, "Review of Work Redesign," *Harvard Business Review,* 24 (January–February 1981), pp. 46–47, 52.

[20] *Ibid.,* p. 46.

[21] J. Richard Hackman and Greg R. Oldham, *Work Redesign.* (Reading, Mass.: Addison-Wesley, 1980).

Technology has an impact on job design. The type of equipment and tools, as well as particular work layout and methods, used in producing goods or services tends to act as a constraint. Technology may make job redesign difficult and expensive, but not impossible.

Economic factors also affect job design. If management believes that redesigning jobs can improve output and the level of worker satisfaction, it must also consider the adequacy of the firm's other resources. Although job redesign may be desirable, its cost may be prohibitive. A manager must continually balance the benefits of job design with its costs.

Job design is also affected by laws and government regulations. Management may want to design a job in a way that could increase worker performance, but in doing so would violate labor laws or environmental or safety standards.

If a company has a union, job design can be affected by the philosophy, policies, and strategies of the union. Typically, the contract between the company and the union specifies and defines the types of jobs and the duties and responsibilities of workers. Unions generally have opposed work redesign experiments. They have perceived them to be attempts by management to squeeze more work out of the worker without increasing wages. Also, unions may view job redesign as a threat to their power and position with the workers. However, in recent years unions have become more flexible in order to maintain job security for their members.

Other important considerations for job design include the abilities, attitudes, and motivation of the firm's employees. Obviously, the design of particular jobs depends on the abilities or training potential of employees. Designing a job that would be far more complex than the ability level of employees available to do it wouldn't make sense unless they are willing to be trained, or new employees with the necessary capabilities can be hired.

Finally, management philosophy and organizational goals and strategies may determine the degree to which job redesign is possible. Top management must be committed to the concept of job redesign. Job redesign may give employees greater authority in determining how their jobs are performed and how they are managed. Job enrichment and job enlargement are two ways of enhancing jobs through job design and can result in greater employee productivity.

Job Enrichment

Strongly advocated by Frederick Herzberg, **job enrichment** refers to basic changes in a job's content and level of responsibility, providing a greater challenge to the worker. In this approach to job design, the employee is given a chance to experience greater achievement, recognition, responsibility, and personal growth.

Many job enrichment programs have improved job performance and employee satisfaction. AT&T, Polaroid, Texas Instruments, Monsanto, Weyerhaeuser, Corning Glass, and many other firms have achieved excellent results with job enrichment programs. In most of these cases, productivity and job satisfaction increased, and employee turnover and absentee-ism decreased.[22]

According to Herzberg, job enrichment efforts should be based on the following principles.

1. *Increasing job demands:* Changing the job to increase the levels of difficulty and responsibility.
2. *Increasing a worker's accountability:* Allowing more worker control and authority over the work, while retaining the manager's ultimate ac-countability.
3. *Providing work scheduling freedom:* Within limits, allowing workers to schedule their own work.
4. *Providing feedback:* Making timely periodic reports on performance directly to the worker.
5. *Providing new learning experiences:* Creating opportunities for new personal experiences and growth.[23]

Job Enlargement

There is a basic distinction between job enrichment and job enlargement. **Job enlargement** changes the scope of a job to provide a greater variety of tasks for the worker to perform; it expands duties horizontally. For example, instead of knowing how to operate only one machine, a worker is taught to operate two or even three with the same level of responsibility. Job enrichment, on the other hand, involves increased responsibility; this is a vertical extension of duties.

Employee-Centered Work Redesign

An innovative concept designed to link the mission of the company with the job satisfaction needs of employees is **employee-centered work redesign.** Here, employees become involved in redesigning their work to benefit both the organization and themselves. Workers can propose innovative changes in their job design to make the job more satisfying. They also must show how these changes improve the accomplishment of the goals of the unit as a whole—improved quality, productivity, and so on. With this approach, the contribution of each employee is recognized, and simultaneously the focus remains on effective accomplishment of the organizational mission.[24]

---

[22] See "Case Studies in the Humanization of Work," in *Work in America: Report of Special Task Force to the Secretary of Health, Education, and Welfare* (Cambridge, Mass.: MIT Press, 1973), Appendix, pp. 188–200.

[23] Frederick Herzberg, "One More Time: How Do You Motivate Employees?" *Harvard Business Review,* 22 (Winter 1979), p. 59.

[24] Stephen L. Perlman, "Employees Redesign Their Jobs," *Personnel Journal,* 69 (November 1990), pp. 37–40.

■ THE GLOBALIZATION OF JOB DESIGN

Redesigning the way jobs are done is a strategy to increase global quality and productivity. One example of the positive impact of job redesign is the General Motors–Toyota NUMMI joint venture in Fremont, California. Before the NUMMI joint venture, General Motors' Fremont plant had one of the worst records in the company for poor labor relations and defective production. The plant was a typical assembly-line operation in which workers and supervisors tried to push as many parts as possible down the line and let quality control inspectors discover the defects at the end of the line.[25]

Four years after the joint venture started, its productivity and quality levels rivaled Japan's best and exceeded anything in the U.S. automobile industry. The question arises as to what caused these changes. It can't be the workers, since they are still members of the United Auto Workers (UAW), and they are paid union-scale wages and benefits. Nor did the change spring from the introduction of advanced robotics. It occurred because of a revolutionary team-production system run by the workers themselves. Each worker is responsible for quality control and for ensuring that no car moves on to the next station unless every job already done on it is perfect. The system was worked out between the plant's Japanese and U.S. managers and the UAW members on the assembly line.[26]

Conflict is common in international alliances, especially when they involve high-technology companies and human egos. NUMMI's lessons for these alliances are simple ones:

- Involve all parties in the effort to redesign jobs.
- Be willing to listen, and be receptive to new ideas.
- Learn from each other's strengths and weaknesses.[27]

SUMMARY

A job consists of a group of tasks that must be performed for an organization to achieve its goals. The systematic process of determining the duties and skills required for performing the organization's jobs is referred to as job analysis. Job analysis is the most basic human resource management tool. Without a properly conducted job analysis, satisfactorily performing the other human resource functions would be difficult, if not impossible.

Job analysis information is used to prepare both job descriptions and job specifications. A job description specifies the tasks, duties, and responsibil-

---

[25] Wayne F. Cascio and Manuel G. Serapio, Jr., "Human Resources Systems in an International Alliance: The Undoing of a Done Deal?" *Organizational Dynamics,* 19 (Winter 1991), pp. 68–69.

[26] *Ibid.*

[27] *Ibid.*

ities associated with a job. A job specification states the knowledge, skills, and abilities a person must possess in order to perform the job.

Job analysis may be conducted in several different ways. When using questionnaires, the job analyst has employees identify the tasks they perform in accomplishing the job. The job analyst actually watches the employee work and records observations when using the observation method. The job analyst may also gain an understanding of the job by interviewing both the employee and the supervisor. In some instances, job analysis information is gathered by having employees describe their daily work activities in a diary or log. Finally, the analyst may use a combination of any of these methods. Basically, the person who conducts job analysis is interested in gathering data about what is involved in performing a particular job.

The sections most commonly used in a job description are (1) job identification, (2) date of the job analysis, (3) job summary, and (4) duties performed. Some of the items often included in the job specification section are requirements for education, experience, personality traits, and physical abilities.

In recent years, attempts have been made to provide more systematic methods for conducting job analysis. These newer approaches include (1) U.S. Department of Labor job analysis schedule (JAS), (2) functional job analysis (FJA), (3) position analysis questionnaire (PAQ), (4) management position description questionnaire (MPDQ), (5) guidelines oriented job analysis (GOJA), and (6) occupational measurement system (OMS). Job analysis has become a focus of HRM because selection methods need to be job related.

Job design is the process of determining the specific tasks to be performed, the methods used in performing these tasks, and how the job relates to other work in the organization. Job enrichment refers to basic changes in the content and level of responsibility of a job to provide a greater challenge to the worker. Job enlargement involves changes in the scope of a job to provide greater variety to the worker.

Questions for Review

1. What is the distinction between a job and a position? Define job analysis.
2. Discuss what is meant by the statement "Job analysis is the most basic human resource management tool."
3. Describe the traditional methods used to conduct job analysis.
4. List and briefly describe the types of data that are typically gathered when conducting job analysis.
5. What are the basic components of a job description? Briefly describe each.
6. What are the items typically included in a job specification?
7. Briefly describe each of the following: (a) U.S. Department of Labor job analysis schedule (JAS); (b) functional job analysis (FJA); (c) position analysis questionnaire (PAQ); and (d) management position description questionnaire (MPDQ).
8. Describe how effective job analysis can be used to satisfy each of the following statutes: (a) Fair Labor Standards Act; (b) Equal Pay Act; (c) Civil Rights Act; and (d) Occupational Safety and Health Act.
9. Distinguish among job design, job enrichment, and job enlargement.

Terms for Review

Job	Management position description
Position	questionnaire (MPDQ)
Job analysis	Guidelines oriented job analysis
Job description	(GOJA)
Job specification	Occupational measurement
Job analysis schedule (JAS)	system (OMS)
Functional job analysis	Job design
(FJA)	Job enrichment
Position analysis questionnaire	Job enlargement
(PAQ)	Employee-centered work redesign

INCIDENT 1 ■ Who Needs Job Descriptions? ■

John Case, accounting supervisor, was clearly annoyed as he approached his boss, Gerald Jones. He began, "Gerald, this note you sent me says I have to update descriptions for all ten of the jobs in my department within the next two weeks."

"Well, what's the problem with that?" asked Gerald.

John explained, "This is a waste of time, especially since I have other deadlines. It will take at least thirty hours. We still have two weeks of work left on the internal audit reviews. You want me to push that back and work on *job descriptions?* No way.

"We have not looked at these job descriptions in years. They will need a great deal of revision. And as soon as they get into the hands of the employees, I will get all kinds of flack."

"Why would you get flack for getting the job descriptions in order?" asked Gerald. John answered, "This whole thing is a can of worms. Just calling attention to the existence of job descriptions will give some people the idea that they don't have to do things that aren't in the description. And if we write what the people in my division really do, some jobs will have to be upgraded and others downgraded, I'll bet. I just can't afford the morale problem and the confusion right now."

Gerald replied, "What do you suggest, John? I have been told just to get it done, and within two weeks." "I don't want to do it at all," said John, "but certainly not during the audit period. Can't you just go back up the line and get it put off until next month?"

Questions

1. What have John and Gerald forgotten to do prior to the creation of job descriptions? Why is that step important?
2. Evaluate John's statement, "Just calling attention to the existence of job descriptions will give some people the idea that they don't have to do things that aren't in the description."

INCIDENT 2   ■   A Job Well Done   ■

As Professor Sharpland toured the Plymouth Tube Company plant in Pontiac, New Jersey, he became more and more impressed with his young guide, Jim Murdoch. Jim was the assistant human resource director at Plymouth Tube and was primarily responsible for job analysis. An industrial engineer was assigned full-time to the human resource department to assist Jim in job design. Professor Sharpland had been retained by the human resource director to study Plymouth Tube's job analysis system and to make recommendations for improvements. He had gone through the files of job descriptions in the human resource office with Jim and found them, in general, to be complete and directly related to the jobs performed.

One of the first stops on the tour was the office of the weld mill supervisor, a 10-foot by 10-foot room out on the factory floor with glass windows on all sides. As Jim approached, the supervisor, Roger Dishongh, was outside his office. "Hi, Jim," he said. "Hello, Roger," said Jim. "This is Professor Sharpland. Could we look at your job descriptions and chat with you for a moment?" "Sure, Jim," said Roger, opening the door. "Come on in and have a seat and I'll get them out." From their vantage point, the men in the office could see the workers in the weld mill area. As they reviewed each job description it was possible to observe every worker actually performing the work described. Roger Dishongh was familiar with each of the jobs. He was very knowledgeable about the job descriptions themselves, having contributed in preparing or revising each of them. "How are the job descriptions related to the performance evaluations here?" asked Professor Sharpland. "Well," answered Roger, "I only evaluate the workers on the items specified in the job descriptions, which were determined through careful job analysis. Limiting performance evaluations to those items encourages me to correct the job descriptions when something changes and they no longer accurately describe the job. Jim has conducted training sessions for all the supervisors so that we understand the relationships among job analysis, job descriptions, and performance evaluations. I think it's a pretty good system."

Jim and Professor Sharpland went on to several other areas of the plant and found similar situations. Jim seemed to have a good relationship with each of the supervisors as well as with the plant manager and the three mid-level managers they visited. As they headed back to the front office, Professor Sharpland was considering the comments that he would soon make to the plant manager.

Questions

1. What desirable attributes of job analysis are evident at Plymouth Tube Company?
2. What kind of report do you think Professor Sharpland should present to the plant manager?
3. Describe the relationship that might exist between the industrial engineer and the assistant human resource director regarding job analysis.

DEVELOPING HRM SKILLS

Developing and updating job descriptions is an integral part of the job of any human resource professional. Without properly designed job descriptions, performing necessary human resource management activities is extremely difficult. This exercise will permit you to gain a better appreciation of what is involved in preparing job descriptions. Job descriptions may vary even when the job analysis information is similar.

As a senior human resource specialist at Pedal Cycle Company, you have been involved in job analysis planning for the new plant in Springfield, Missouri. Most of the job analysis data has been gathered, and now it is time to prepare specific job descriptions. You have been given a stack of job analysis information sheets and assigned the task of writing job descriptions based on this information. When the assistant human resource director, Ed Deal, handed you the data sheet, he said, "I'd like for you to do the first one, and then bring it to me and we'll go over it together."

The initial job description will be for the position of **Spot Welder. Work Activities** primarily involve welding parts together. All parts consist of thin steel pieces weighing less than two pounds. The preformed pieces to be welded together are taken from numbered bins surrounding the spot welder, placed in position on the machine, and welded. **Relationship With Other Workers** is fairly standard for a factory floor worker. Other machine operators running similar machines are within view, twenty to thirty feet away. The crane operator moves the parts bins to this work station and away as required, placing them wherever specified by the operator. There is little time for social interaction on the job. **Degree of Supervision** involved in fairly standard in this industry. The spot welder supervisor supervises twelve operators, all doing essentially the same job. Operators are expected to do their jobs with very little supervision, consulting the supervisor infrequently. **Records and Reports** are not generated as part of this job. **Skill and Dexterity Requirements** are marginal. In order to meet the standard times, the worker must be able to take two parts from separate bins, place them together in the correct position and complete the part within 3.2 seconds. **Working Conditions** are not ideal; the work station is relatively crowded, the operator is required to wear safety goggles, and ambient temperature varies from 60° F to 80° F in summer. The noise level is about 60 decibels, safe but distracting, and the lighting is excellent.

Each participant will use the **Pedal Cycle Company's Job Description Form** and develop an appropriate job description. Several class members can participate in this exercise. Your instructor will provide the participants with additional information necessary to complete the exercise.

REFERENCES

Aho, Kaye L. "Understanding the New Job-Analysis Technology." *Personnel,* 66 (January 1989), pp. 38–40.

Baron, James N., and William T. Biolby. "The Proliferation of Job Titles in Organizations." *Administrative Science Quarterly,* 31 (December 1986), pp. 561–586.

Buckham, Robert H. "Applying Role Analysis in the Workplace." *Personnel,* 54 (February 1987), pp. 53–56.

Busi, Donald C. "The Job Description: More Than Bureaucratic Control." *Supervisory Management,* 35 (October 1990), p. 5.

Campion, Michael A. and Paul W. Thayer. "How Do You Design a Job?" *Personnel Journal,* 68 (January 1989), pp. 43–46.

Davidson, Jeffrey P. "What's My Job Again?" *Management World,* 15 (July–August 1986), pp. 24–26.

Field, Hubert S., and Robert D. Gatewood. "Matching Talent with the Task: To Find the Right People, First Define the Jobs You Want Them to Do." *Personnel Administrator,* 32 (April 1987), pp. 113–123.

Friedman, Lee, and Robert J. Harvey. "Can Raters with Reduced Job Descriptive Information Provide Accurate Position Analysis Questionnaire (PAQ) Ratings?" *Personnel Psychology,* 39 (Winter 1986), pp. 779–790.

Green, Samuel B., and Thomas Stutzman. "An Evaluation of Methods to Select Respondents to Structured Job-Analysis Questionnaires." *Personnel Psychology,* 39 (August 1985), pp. 543–565.

Kennedy, William R. "Train Managers to Write Winning Job Descriptions." *Training and Development Journal,* 41 (April 1987), pp. 52–55.

Koretz, Gene. "Professional Workers: Can America Keep Its Edge?" *Business Week* (April 2, 1990), p. 23.

Lawler, Edward E. III. "Let the Workers Make White-Knuckle Decisions." *Fortune,* 121 (March 26, 1990), pp. 49–52.

Markovitz, Jarroid. "Managing the Job Analysis Process." *Training and Development Journal,* 41 (August 1987), pp. 64–67.

Mondy, R. Wayne, Robert M. Noe, and Robert E. Edwards. "What the Staffing Function Entails." *Personnel,* 63 (April 1986), pp. 55–58.

Perlman, Stephen L. "Employees Redesign Their Jobs." *Personnel Journal,* 69 (November 1990), pp. 37–40.

Rea, Peter, Julie Rea, and Charles Moomaw. "Use Assessment Centers in Skill Development." *Personnel Journal,* 69 (April 1990), pp. 126–131.

Sahl, Robert J. "Get It Together! Integrating the HR Department." *Personnel,* 66 (February 1989), pp. 39–45.

P·A·R·T O·N·E

CASE I

Parma Cycle Company: An Overview

According to the National Sporting Goods Association, over 23 million Americans participate in bicycling. This makes it third among sports activities, behind swimming and exercise walking. Sales of bicycles in the United States recently exceeded 12 million a year, up over 50 percent in just a decade. But imports accounted for all of the gain. Domestic sales of U.S.-made bicycles fell throughout the 1980s.

Parma Cycle Company of Parma, Ohio, a Cleveland suburb, is one of only three companies that actually manufacture complete bicycles in the United States. Most of Parma's competitors import parts from other countries and simply assemble bicycles here. Even Parma finally began to import many parts, mainly from Italy, Japan, and, more recently, Korea. Parma Cycle employed about 800 workers in the late 1980s, most of them machine operators and assemblers. Cuyahoga County, where Parma is located, suffered from auto industry layoffs in the early 1980s. But conditions steadily improved during the late 1980s, with unemployment falling below the national average of about 5.5 percent. The county population in 1989 exceeded 1.4 million, with Cleveland accounting for about half. Per capita income in Cleveland was near the national average at $8,000 in 1985, but the figure was about 30 percent higher for the county as a whole.

Bicycles are typically classified into eight types, including one-speed, low-priced multispeed, sport, touring, and all-terrain bicycles. Parma Cycle made only one-speed and low-priced multispeed bicycles, leaving the premium types to Schwinn, Panasonic, Peugeot, and a host of other competitors. Parma dis-

tributed bicycles under its own name through distributors to small retailers. However, most of the bicycles Parma manufactured were purchased by large national retailers and marketed under those retailers' house names. A few bicycles were exported to Europe and South America, but Parma found it difficult to compete in the international market with Japanese and Italian manufacturers.

Parma Cycle Company, Inc., is a publicly held corporation, although 30 percent of its shares are controlled by a major recreational conglomerate corporation. There have been rumors of a takeover from time to time but none ever materialized. Because of depressed earnings in the late 1980s, Parma's stock declined from $27 per share to $13 per share. Interest rates increased significantly during the same period. The company found it costly, therefore, to raise funds to purchase the new machines that have been developed for bicycle manufacturing. A high-performance racing cycle was planned for introduction in the early 1990s. But a research and development program aimed at cutting the cost of producing that bicycle was canceled because of the high cost of financing.

Jesse Heard is the human resource director. He went to work at Parma Cycle in 1966. His first job was as a painter, when painting was done with a hand-held spray gun. He was later promoted to supervisor and worked in several departments at the plant. Parma encourages its supervisors to advance their education. Because the company paid for college tuition, fees, as well as books, Jesse had gone on to college. In 1976, he received his bachelor's degree in personnel administration from Case Western University in Cleveland. Jesse was immediately promoted to a job in the human resource department and three years later became the human resource director.

In May 1987, the Equal Employment Opportunity Commission received a complaint about employment practices at Parma. It was alleged that while the proportion of blacks in the Cleveland area approached 25 percent, only 8 percent of the Parma Cycle workforce was black. There were only two black managers above the level of supervisor. Jesse Heard was advised of the complaint. He felt that the company was doing everything it should with regard to equal opportunity.

The company had an affirmative action program and encouraged managers to employ blacks, other minority group members, and women. In fact, Jesse's efforts to encourage the employment of women and minorities had

provoked some managers to complain to the company president, his immediate superior.

In general, the working environment at Parma Cycle was a good one. The company had a relatively flat organizational structure with few managerial levels, as shown in Figure I-1.

Most of Parma's workers are of European stock and are acclimated to working in a factory environment. Beginning in 1978, the company conducted periodic management training seminars in which managers were taught to be sensitive to workers and cooperative with one another. The management philosophy was always one of decentralized authority. Managers, like Jesse Heard, were essentially responsible for their own operations.

As a result of an aggressive safety program, there was only one fatal accident at Parma during the 1980s, and work-related injuries remained well below the industry average. In

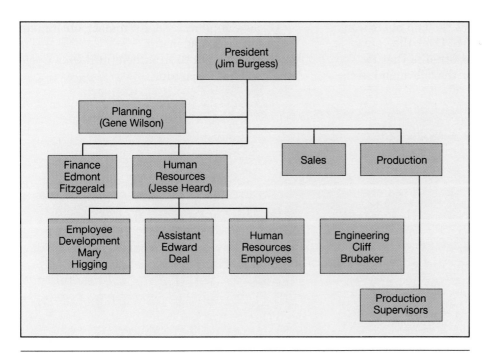

FIGURE I-1 | Parma Cycle Company: Organization Chart

1980 the ventilation system in the factory was modernized. The lighting is good, by Cleveland area standards, and the health and safety officer once remarked that the air was cleaner inside the factory than outside. Gene Wilson, the corporate planner, said that he believed the company spent too much money on employee safety and working conditions and that this was a reason for Parma's declining profits. The company's mission had not changed since 1960, when it was stated as: "To enhance the wealth of the common shareholder through efficient production and aggressive marketing of bicycles while contributing to the well-being of our workers and the stability of the Cleveland economy."

Parma's workforce was unionized, with the local union being a member of the National Association of Machinists. Employee recruitment was done primarily through referrals from current workers. Selection was based on personal interviews, evaluation of job-related application forms, and, for certain jobs, a basic skills test conducted by the supervisor. The supervisor made the final hiring decision. Workers must join the union before the end of a three-month probationary period. Over the years, the union won wages and benefits that remained about average for the Cleveland area.

The Cleveland factory was laid out, coincidentally, like a bicycle wheel, with component manufacturing departments representing the tire and spoke areas, and assembly being done in the center of the factory, representing the hub. The factory work was neither especially difficult nor complicated. Technology for the bicycles Parma made changed very little over the years, and most of the jobs became standardized. However, growing foreign competition caused an increasing emphasis on productivity and a heightened concern for quality. Consequently, workers were encouraged to put forth additional effort, and production standards were raised to the point where many employees complained of the faster work pace. The productivity improvement program was carried forward with the union's assistance. The union justified its participation on the basis of saving jobs. The last strike at Parma occurred in 1976.

Questions

1. Discuss the external environment of Parma Cycle Company and its impact on human resource management.
2. Is the internal environment at Parma Cycle a good one? Explain.

HUMAN RESOURCE PLANNING, RECRUITMENT, AND SELECTION

Human Resource Research

Human Resource Planning, Recruitment, and Selection

Human Resource Development

Human Resource Management

Employee and Labor Relations

Compensation and Benefits

Safety and Health

CHAPTER 5

HUMAN RESOURCE PLANNING

Chapter Objectives

1. Explain the human resource planning process and define the basic terms used in forecasting.
2. Describe some human resource forecasting techniques and explain how human resource requirements are forecasted.
3. State what a firm can do when a surplus of workers exists and explain how human resource availability is forecasted.
4. Describe the importance of a human resource information system.

Mark Swann, the marketing director for Sharpco Manufacturing, commented at the weekly executive directors' meeting, "I have good news. We can get the large contract with Medord Corporation. All we have to do is complete the project in one year instead of two. I told them we could do it."

Linda Cane, vice-president of human resources, brought everyone back to reality by asserting, "As I understand it, our present workers do not have the expertise required to produce the quality that Medord's particular specifications require. Under the two-year project timetable, we planned to retrain our present workers gradually. With this new time schedule, we will have to go into the job market and recruit workers who are already experienced in this process. We may need to analyze this proposal further to see if that is really what we want to do. Human resource costs will rise considerably if we attempt to complete the project in one year instead of two. Sure, Mark, we can do it, but with these constraints, will the project be cost effective?"

In the above instance, Mark failed to take into account the importance of human resource planning in his projections. In today's fast-paced, competitive environment, failure to recognize the importance of human resource planning will often destroy an otherwise well thought-out plan.

This chapter will explain the role and nature of human resource planning in organizations today. First, we define human resource planning and describe the human resource planning process. We then review terminology of forecasting and examine some human resource forecasting techniques. Next, we discuss forecasting human resource requirements and availability. We then examine action to be taken when a firm has a surplus of workers, and we follow up with an example of effective human resource planning. The final sections of the chapter are a discussion of the human resource information system and global approaches to HRIS.

■ THE HUMAN RESOURCE PLANNING PROCESS

Human resource planning (HRP) is the process of systematically reviewing human resource requirements to ensure that the required number of employees, with the required skills, are available when they are needed.[1] It is the process of matching the internal and external supply of people with job openings anticipated in the organization over a specified period of time. However, there is a growing mismatch between emerging jobs and the people available to fill them. The labor pool is changing as U.S. companies try to cope with rapid technological change and increasing globalization of the economy.[2] As previously mentioned, human resource planning is increasingly being recognized as an important activity.

The human resource planning process is illustrated in Figure 5-1. Note that strategic planning—which requires consideration of both the external and internal environment—precedes human resource planning. **Strategic planning** is the determination of overall organizational purposes and objectives and how they are to be achieved.[3] There is a growing realization among professional managers of the importance of including human resource management in the strategic planning process. Essentially, human resource planning should be linked to organizational strategy.[4] In fact, in this decade, human resource planning will become an even more important aspect of strategic planning.[5]

According to a recent survey of top-level executives, the best methods of improving quality and overall productivity are directly related to human resource issues. As may be seen on page 148 in Figure 5-2, motivation, culture, and education were rated as the best methods for increasing productivity. Employees must be adequately motivated, prepared to deal with the existing corporate culture, and appropriately educated to cope with the challenges of their jobs. These and other human resource issues are the keys for improving quality and productivity.[6] This fact reveals the absolute necessity for integrating HRP into a firm's strategic plans.

After organizational strategic plans have been formulated, human resource planning can be undertaken. Strategic plans are reduced to specific quantitative and qualitative human resource plans. For example, note in Figure 5-1 that human resource planning has two components: requirements and availability. Forecasting human resource requirements involves determining the number and type of employees needed, by skill level and location. These projections will reflect various factors, such as production

---

[1] R. Wayne Mondy, Robert M. Noe, and Robert E. Edwards, "What the Staffing Function Entails," *Personnel,* 63 (April 1986), pp. 55–56.

[2] Walter Kiechel III. "Love, Don't Lose, the Newly Hired." *Fortune* (June 6, 1988), pp. 271–274.

[3] R. Wayne Mondy, Arthur Sharplin, and Shane R. Premeaux, *Management: Concepts, Practices, and Skills,* 5th ed. (Boston: Allyn & Bacon, 1991), p. 165.

[4] Lincoln Akin Norton, "Link HR to Corporate Strategy," *Personnel Journal,* 70 (April 1991), p. 75.

[5] Jeffrey O. Nyweide, "Simply Sophisticated," *Management World,* 16 (April–May 1987), p. 34.

[6] Y. K. Shetty and Paul F. Buller, "Regaining Competitiveness Requires HR Solutions." *Personnel,* 67 (July 1990), pp. 8–12.

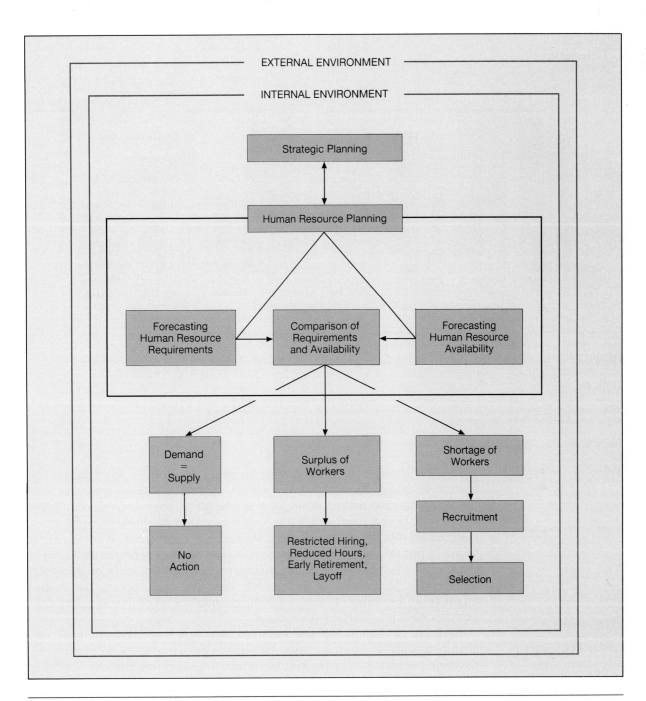

FIGURE 5-1 | The Human Resource Planning Process

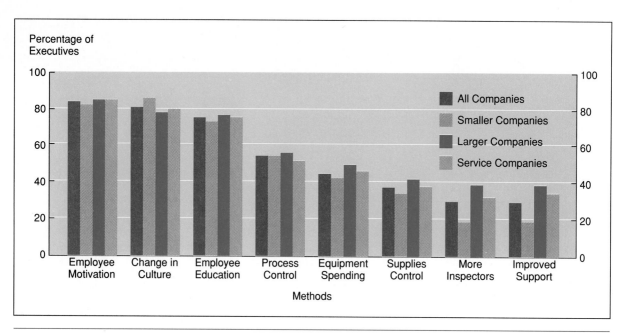

FIGURE 5-2 | Most Effective Method for Improving Quality and Productivity

plans and changes in productivity. In order to forecast availability, the human resource manager looks to both internal sources (presently employed employees) and external sources (the labor market). When employee requirements and availability have been analyzed, the firm can determine whether it will have a surplus or shortage of employees. Ways must be found to reduce the number of employees if a surplus is projected. Some of these methods include restricted hiring, reduced hours, early retirements, and layoffs. If a shortage is forecast, the firm must obtain the proper quantity and quality of workers from outside the organization. External recruitment and selection is required.

Because conditions in the external and internal environments can change quickly, the human resource planning process must be continuous. Changing conditions could affect the entire organization, thereby requiring extensive modification of forecasts. Planning in general enables managers to anticipate and prepare for changing conditions, and HRP in particular allows flexibility in the area of human resource management. During the past ten years, various factors have caused some organizations to downsize (reduce the size of their workforces).[7] Human resource planning allows workforce reductions with a minimum of disruption.

---

[7] Colin P. Silverthorne, "Planning for a Smaller Organization: A Guide for HR Managers," *Personnel,* 64 (March 1987), p. 60.

HRM In Action

C ynthia, what do you mean by saying that I'm going to have to justify my need for the typesetter's position? One of my ten employees in this job just quit, and I want a replacement now. We've had ten typesetters in my department for the thirteen years that I've been here, and probably a long time before that. If we've needed them in the past, certainly we will need them in the future." This is the beginning of a conversation between Richard Wiley, a first-line supervisor with Allen Industries, and Cynthia Larger, its human resource manager.

How should Cynthia respond?

■ TERMINOLOGY OF FORECASTING

Four basic terms are used in forecasting. First, the **long-term trend** is a projection of demand for a firm's products, typically five years or more into the future. As Figure 5-3 shows, the hypothetical long-term trend is for increased sales: Sales are expected to double during the period shown. Early recognition of such a trend is crucial. A firm may not be able to fill

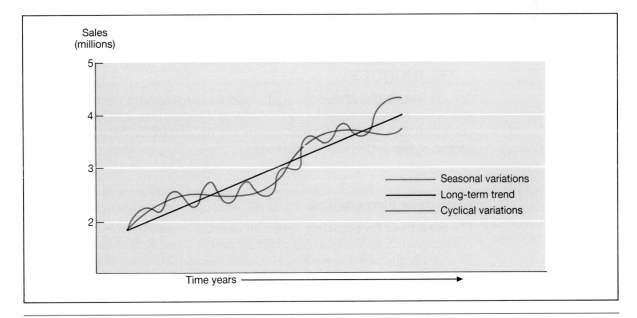

FIGURE 5-3 | Forecasting Terminology Example

the positions necessary to support such sales levels quickly if considerable training and development are required. Some employees may need extensive training and development before they are capable of taking on new or added responsibilities. Proper estimation of long-term trends, therefore, is essential for organizational success.

Second, **cyclical variations** are reasonably predictable movements about the trend line that occur over a period of more than a year. Cyclical variations may be caused by war, elections, changes in economic conditions and consumer demand, and societal pressures. These variations typically last between one and five years. Anticipating cyclical demand is important because of the potential for severe peaks and valleys. Extra people may be required to meet high cyclical demand, even though a stable long-term demand has been forecast. Conversely, although the long-term forecast may be upward, conditions such as a short-term recession may require a temporary workforce reduction.

Third, **seasonal variations** are reasonably predictable changes that occur over a period of a year. Seasonal variations follow cyclical variations, but may fluctuate drastically (see Figure 5-3 on page 149). These variations occur within a twelve-month period and are of most immediate concern to many firms. Electric shavers are sold primarily during the holiday season, whereas motorboats are sold primarily in the spring. Seasonal demand can have a major impact on a firm as it attempts to stabilize its workforce and still meet production and inventory requirements.

Finally, **random variations** are changes without pattern. Even the most sophisticated forecasting techniques cannot anticipate such changes. Management must therefore anticipate and plan for long-term trends, cyclical variations, and seasonal variations—and be ready to deal with random variations.

■ HUMAN RESOURCE FORECASTING TECHNIQUES

Several techniques of forecasting human resource requirements and availability are currently used by those in the profession. Some of the techniques are qualitative in nature, and others are quantitative. We describe next several of the better known methods.

Zero-Base Forecasting

The **zero-base forecasting** approach uses the organization's current level of employment as the starting point for determining future staffing needs. Essentially the same procedure is used for human resource planning as for zero-base budgeting, whereby each budget must be rejustified each year.[8]

---

[8] Ernie A. Kurbis, "The Case for Zero-Base Budgeting," *CA Magazine,* 119 (April 1986), p. 104.

If an employee retires, is fired, or leaves the firm for any other reason, the position is not automatically filled. Instead, an analysis is made to determine whether the firm can justify filling it. Equal concern is shown for creating new positions when they appear to be needed. The key to zero-base forecasting is a thorough analysis of human resource needs.

Bottom-Up Approach

Some firms use what might be called the bottom-up approach to employment forecasting. It is based on the reasoning that the manager in each unit is the most knowledgeable about employment requirements. In the **bottom-up approach,** each successive level in the organization—starting with the lowest—forecasts its requirements, ultimately providing an aggregate forecast of employees needed. Human resource forecasting is often most effective when managers periodically project their human resource needs, comparing their current and anticipated levels, and giving the human resource department adequate lead time to explore internal and external sources.[9]

Use of Predictor Variables

Another means of forecasting human resource requirements is to use past employment levels to predict future requirements. **Predictor variables** are factors known to have had an impact on employment levels. One of the most useful predictors of employment levels is sales volume. The relationship between demand and number of employees needed is a positive one. As you can see on page 152 in Figure 5-4, a firm's sales volume is depicted on the horizontal axis and the number of employees actually required is shown on the vertical axis. In this illustration, as sales increase, so does the number of employees. Using this method, managers can approximate the number of employees required at different demand levels.

With the increased use of computers and statistical software packages, human resource managers have at their disposal an important forecasting tool: regression analysis. **Regression analysis** is used to predict one item (known as the dependent variable) through knowledge of other items (known as the independent variables). When there is one dependent variable and one independent variable, the process is called simple linear regression. When there is more than one independent variable, the technique is called multiple regression.

Regression is often used because of the direct relationship between demand for a firm's goods and/or services and employment levels. However, in most instances, the employment level is determined by several

---

[9] John F. DeSanto, "Work Force Planning and Corporate Strategy," *Personnel Administrator,* 28 (October 1983), p. 34.

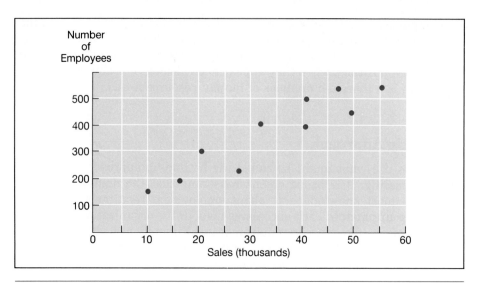

FIGURE 5-4 | The Relationship of Sales Volume to Number of Employees

independent variables, and multiple regression is required. Instead of predicting employment levels solely on the basis of sales, an analyst might also use other variables, such as productivity of the workforce. Multiple regression often produces results superior to those obtained from simple linear regression because it recognizes that a variety of factors may influence future employment levels.

Simulation

Simulation is a technique for experimenting with a real-world situation through a mathematical model representing that situation. A model is an abstraction of the real world. Thus a simulation model is an attempt to represent a real-world situation through mathematical logic in order to predict what will occur. Simulation assists the human resource manager by permitting the asking of many "what if . . ." questions without having to make a decision with real-world consequences.

In human resource management, a simulation model might be developed to represent the interrelationships among employment level and many other variables. The manager could then ask "what if . . ." questions such as:

- What would happen if we put 10 percent of the present workforce on overtime?
- What would happen if the plant utilized two shifts? Three shifts?

The purpose of the model is to permit the human resource manager to gain considerable insight into a particular problem before making an actual decision.

■ FORECASTING HUMAN RESOURCE REQUIREMENTS

A **requirements forecast** is an estimate of the numbers and kinds of employees the organization will need at future dates in order for it to realize its stated goals. Before human resource requirements can be projected, demand for the firm's goods or services must first be forecast. This forecast is then converted into people requirements for the activities that will be required to meet this demand. For a firm that manufactures personal computers, activities might be stated in terms of the number of units to be produced, number of sales calls to be made, number of vouchers to be processed, or a variety of other activities. For example, manufacturing 1,000 personal computers each week might require 10,000 hours of work by assemblers during a 40-hour week. Dividing the 10,000 hours by the 40 hours in the work week gives 250 assembly workers needed. Similar calculations are performed for the other jobs needed to produce and market the personal computers.

■ FORECASTING HUMAN RESOURCE AVAILABILITY

Forecasting requirements provides managers with the means of estimating how many and what types of employees will be required. But there is another side to the coin.

> A large manufacturing firm on the West Coast was preparing to begin operations in a new plant. Analysts had already determined that there was a large long-term demand for the new product. Financing was available and equipment was in place. But production did not begin for two years! Management had made a critical mistake: It had studied the demand side of human resources but not the supply side. There weren't enough qualified workers in the local labor market to operate the new plant. New workers had to receive extensive training before they could move into the newly created jobs.

Determining whether the firm will be able to secure employees with the necessary skills and from what sources is called an **availability forecast.** It helps the human resource manager to determine whether the needed employees may be obtained from within the company, from outside the organization, or from a combination of the two sources.

Internal Sources of Supply

Many of the workers that will be needed for future positions may already work for the firm. If the firm is small, management probably knows all the workers well enough to easily match their skills and aspirations with the company's needs. If, for instance, the firm is creating a new sales position, it may be common knowledge that Mary Garcia, a five-year employee with the company, has both the skills and desire to take over the new job. This unplanned process of matching people and positions may be sufficient for smaller firms. As organizations grow, however, the matching process becomes increasingly difficult. Both management and skills inventories increasingly are being used by human resource professionals and organizations that take human resources seriously.[10]

Management Inventories. Managerial talent is an essential resource in every organization. Thus firms maintain better data on managers than they do on nonmanagers' skills. A **management inventory** contains detailed information about each manager and is used to identify individuals who have the potential to move into higher level positions. Essentially, this type of inventory provides information for replacement and promotion decisions. It would likely include data such as:

- Work history and experience
- Educational background
- Assessment of strengths and weaknesses
- Developmental needs
- Promotion potential at present and with further development
- Current job performance
- Field of specialization
- Job preferences
- Geographic preferences
- Career goals and aspirations
- Anticipated retirement date
- Personal history, including psychological assessments

Succession Planning. Because of the tremendous changes that will confront management in the 1990s, succession planning takes on more importance than perhaps ever before. In view of these expected changes, organizations need to develop a profile of the type of individuals who can effectively lead the organization both now and in the future.[11] Many companies are doing this; in a 1990 survey of over 400 boards of large U.S. companies, nearly three-quarters of the firms questioned had a succession plan.[12]

One of the outcomes of a management inventory is a succession plan, which can be most useful in human resource planning. Detroit Edison calls its chart a Career Planning Inventory Organization Review Chart. As you can see in Figure 5-5, the chart shows a manager in the top box with immediate subordinates in the lower boxes. Information shown on the chart includes the following.

Position Box: The position title and incumbent's name appear in each box. The symbol ☆ preceding the name identifies incumbents who will

---

[10] John Lawrie, "Skill Inventories: Pack for the Future," *Personnel Journal,* 66 (March 1987), p. 127.

[11] James E. McElwain, "Succession Plans Designed to Manage Change," *HRMagazine,* 36 (February 1991), p. 67.

[12] "Heirs and Races," *The Economist,* 318 (March 9, 1991), p. 69.

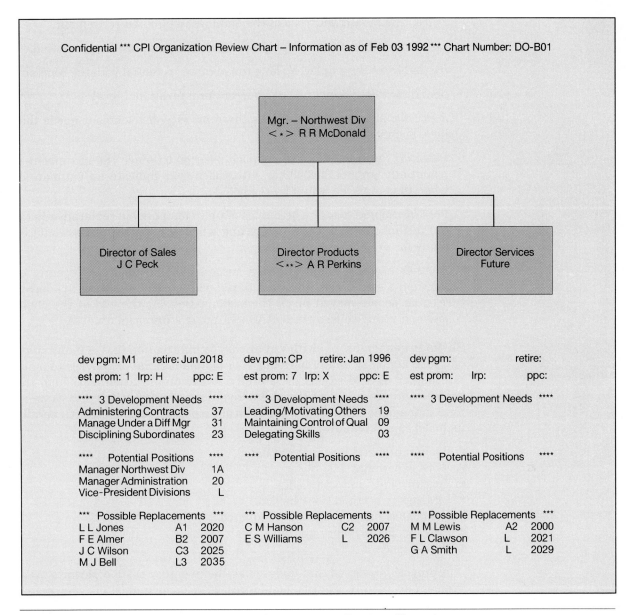

Confidential *** CPI Organization Review Chart – Information as of Feb 03 1992 *** Chart Number: DO-B01

Mgr. – Northwest Div
< * > R R McDonald

Director of Sales
J C Peck

Director Products
< ** > A R Perkins

Director Services
Future

dev pgm: M1 retire: Jun 2018	dev pgm: CP retire: Jan 1996	dev pgm: retire:	
est prom: 1 lrp: H ppc: E	est prom: 7 lrp: X ppc: E	est prom: lrp: ppc:	

**** 3 Development Needs ****
Administering Contracts   37
Manage Under a Diff Mgr   31
Disciplining Subordinates   23

**** 3 Development Needs ****
Leading/Motivating Others   19
Maintaining Control of Qual   09
Delegating Skills   03

**** 3 Development Needs ****

****   Potential Positions   ****
Manager Northwest Div   1A
Manager Administration   20
Vice-President Divisions   L

****   Potential Positions   ****

****   Potential Positions   ****

*** Possible Replacements ***
L L Jones   A1   2020
F E Almer   B2   2007
J C Wilson   C3   2025
M J Bell   L3   2035

*** Possible Replacements ***
C M Hanson   C2   2007
E S Williams   L   2026

*** Possible Replacements ***
M M Lewis   A2   2000
F L Clawson   L   2021
G A Smith   L   2029

FIGURE 5-5 | Career Planning Inventory Organization Review Chart

retire between 1991 and 1995, indicating that short-range planning is required. The symbol ☆☆ preceding the name identifies incumbents who will retire between 1996 and 2002, indicating that long-range planning is required. If the word *Open* appears in the box, the position is unfilled; if *Future* appears, the position is anticipated but does not yet exist.

dev pgm: Identifies the particular development program in which the employee participates.

retire: The month and year of the employee's planned retirement.

est prom: Indicates the employee's estimated potential for promotion.

lrp: Indicates the employee's long-range career potential with the company.

ppc: Indicates the incumbent's current organizational level.

3 Development Needs: Describes three priority development needs that have been identified.

Potential Positions: The title of each position to which the incumbent is potentially promotable, along with codes that indicate an estimate of when the employee would be ready.

Possible Replacements: The names of up to ten possible replacements for the incumbent, with codes indicating when the replacements would be ready for promotion to this position.

Another example of an effective succession plan occurred recently at NCR when a senior vice-president of finance retired. Following his departure, nine people moved up in the organization. At the end of the chain reaction, a young college student was hired as a financial analyst.[13]

Skills Inventories. A **skills inventory** is information that is maintained on the availability and preparedness of nonmanagerial employees to move into higher level positions or laterally in the organization. Although the process and the intent of the skills inventory are essentially the same as for a management inventory, the information differs somewhat. Generally included in a skills inventory are:

- Background and biographical data
- Work experience
- Specific skills and knowledge
- Licenses or certifications held
- In-house training programs completed
- Previous performance appraisal evaluations
- Career goals

A properly designed and updated skills inventory system permits management to readily identify employees with particular skills and match them insofar as possible to the changing needs of the company.

External Supply

Unless a firm is experiencing declining demand, it will have to recruit some employees from outside the organization. However, finding and hiring new employees capable of performing immediately is usually quite difficult. The best source of supply varies by industry, firm, and geographic location. Some organizations find that their best sources of potential employees are

---

[13] *Ibid.*

colleges and universities. Others get excellent results from vocational schools, competitors, or even unsolicited applications.

If the company has information revealing where its present employees were recruited, it can develop statistics and project the best sources. For instance, a firm may discover that graduates from a particular college or university adapt well to the firm's environment and culture. One large farm-equipment manufacturer has achieved excellent success in recruiting from regional schools located in rural areas. Managers in this firm believe that since many students come from a farming environment, they can adapt more quickly to the firm's method of operation.

Other firms may discover from past records that the majority of their more successful employees lived no more than twenty miles from their place of work. This information may suggest concentrated recruiting efforts in that particular geographic area.

Forecasting can assist not only in identifying where potential employees may be found but also in predicting the type of individuals that will likely succeed in the organization. A regional medical center—located far from any large metropolitan area—reviewed its employment files of registered nurses. It discovered that RNs born and raised in smaller towns adapted better to the medical center's small-town environment than those who grew up in large metropolitan areas. After studying these statistics, management modified its recruiting efforts.[14]

However, forecasting has many pitfalls, and examples of improper forecasting are numerous. Managers of one large convenience store chain were disturbed by their unusually high employee turnover rate. When they analyzed their recruiting efforts, they discovered that the large majority of short-term employees had merely seen a sign in the store window announcing that a position was available. These individuals, often unemployed at the time, were highly transient. The source of supply virtually guaranteed a high turnover rate. When they discovered this fact, the managers found new sources of supply, which significantly reduced turnover.

■ SURPLUS OF EMPLOYEES

When a comparison of requirements and availability indicates a worker surplus, restricted hiring, reduced hours, early retirements, or layoffs may be required to correct the situation.

Restricted Hiring

When a firm implements a restricted hiring policy, it reduces the workforce by not replacing employees who leave. New workers are hired only when overall performance of the organization may be affected. For instance, if a

---

[14] Wayne Mondy and Harry N. Mills, "Choice Not Chance in Nurse Selection," *Supervisor Nurse,* 9 (November 1978), pp. 35–39.

quality control department that consisted of four inspectors lost one to a competitor, this individual probably would not be replaced. However, if the firm lost all its inspectors, it would probably replace at least some of them to ensure continued operation.

Reduced Hours

Reaction to declining demand can also be made by reducing the total number of hours worked. Instead of continuing a forty-hour week, management may decide to cut each employee's time to thirty hours. This cutback normally applies only to hourly employees because management and other professionals typically are salaried, not paid on an hourly basis.

Early Retirement

Early retirement of some present employees is another way to reduce the number of workers. Some employees will be delighted to retire, but others will be somewhat reluctant. The latter may be willing to accept early retirement if the total retirement package is made attractive enough. A key point to remember is that because of the Age Discrimination in Employment Act, as amended, retirement can no longer be mandated by age.

Layoffs

At times, a firm has no choice but to lay off part of its workforce. A layoff is not the same as being fired, but it has the same short-term effect—the worker is no longer employed. When the firm is unionized, layoff procedures are usually stated clearly in the labor-management agreement. Typically, workers with the least seniority are laid off first. If the organization is union-free, it may base layoff on a combination of factors, such as seniority and productivity level. When managers and other professionals are laid off, the decision is likely to be based on ability, although internal politics may be a factor.

■ HUMAN RESOURCE PLANNING: AN EXAMPLE

The human resource planning model presented in Figure 5-1 on page 147 is a generalized one. Each firm must tailor human resource planning to fit its specific needs. Figure 5-6 shows the human resource planning process for Honeywell, Inc. We discuss each element of the plan in the following sections.

Organizational Goals

To be relevant, a human resource planning process should be clearly tied to the organization's strategic goals. It must rest on a solid foundation of information about sales forecasts, market trends, technological advances,

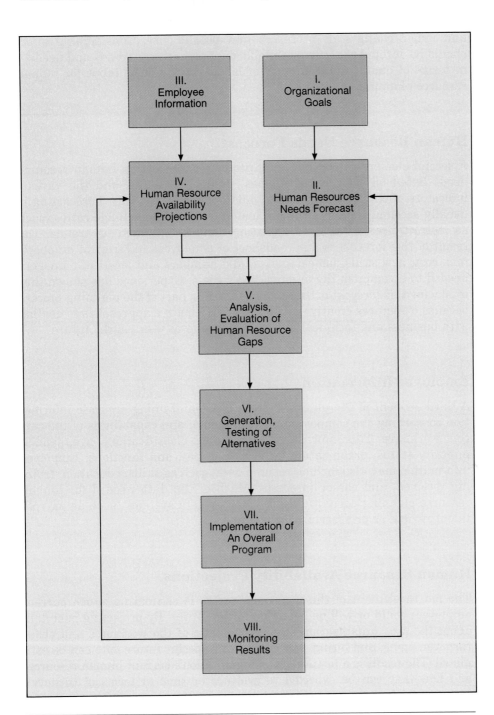

FIGURE 5-6 | Elements of a Human Resource Plan

Source: Used with the permission of Honeywell, Inc.

and major changes in processes and productivity. Considerable effort should be devoted to securing reliable data on business trends and needs—in terms of quantity and quality of labor—as the basic input for human resource planning.

Human Resource Needs Forecast

A second element in the planning process is forecasting human resource needs based on business strategies, production plans, and the various indicators of change in technology and operating methods. Forecasting is usually accomplished by utilizing historical data and reliable ratios (such as indirect/direct labor) and adjusting them for productivity trends. The result of this forecast is a spreadsheet of employees in terms of numbers, mix, cost, new skills, job categories, and numbers and levels of managers needed to accomplish the organization's goals. Experience has shown that producing this forecast is the most challenging part of the planning process because it requires creative and highly participative approaches to dealing with business and technical uncertainties several years in the future.

Employee Information

A third element of the planning process is maintaining accurate information concerning the composition, assignments, and capabilities of the current workforce. This information includes job classifications, age, gender, minority status, organization level, rate of pay, and functions. Employee information may also include résumé data, such as skills, education, training received, and career interests. Much of the data needed for human resource planning currently exists in other data systems (such as payroll, talent review, or professional development).

Human Resource Availability Projections

The fourth element of the planning process is estimating which current employees could or will be available in the future. By projecting past data about the size, organization, and composition of the workforce and about turnover, aging, and hiring, availability at a specific future date can be estimated. The result is a picture of the organization's current human resources and how they can be expected to evolve over time in terms of turnover, retirement, obsolescence, promotability, and other relevant characteristics.

Analyzing and Evaluating Human Resource Gaps

The fifth element of the planning process is comparing what is needed with what is available in terms of numbers, mix, skills, and technologies. This comparison permits the human resource manager to determine gaps and evaluate where the most serious mismatches are likely to be. This type of analysis should help management address issues such as the following:

- Are imbalances developing between projected human resource require-ments and availability?
- What is the effect of current productivity trends and pay rates on work-force levels and costs?
- Do turnover problems exist in certain jobs or age levels?
- Are there problems of career blockage and obsolescence?
- Are there sufficient high-potential managers to fulfill future needs?
- Is there a shortage of any critical skills?

Such an analysis permits development of long-range plans for recruiting, hiring, training, transferring, and retraining appropriate numbers and types of employees.

Generating and Testing Alternatives

The analysis of human resources should reveal much about a wide range of policies and practices, such as staffing plans, promotion practices and policies, EEO plans, organization design, training and development pro-grams, salary planning, and career management. This phase of the process explores the implications of the analysis and generates alternatives to current practices and policies. Some of the more comprehensive human resource planning systems utilize modeling to simulate the types and organization of employees that would result from specific changes in em-ployment strategies or policies. Testing of complex alternatives and antici-pated consequences is usually performed on a computer model. However, manual systems should be utilized if computers aren't available.

Implementing an Overall Human Resource Program

After the optimal alternative for addressing the organization's human re-source issues has been chosen, it is translated into operational programs with specific plans, target dates, schedules, and resource commitments. The analytical steps described—from considering organizational goals to generating and testing alternatives—should shape an organization's staff-ing plan, EEO plan, human resource development activities, mobility plans, productivity programs, bargaining strategies, and compensation programs.

Monitoring Results

The final element in any human resource planning process is to provide a means for management to monitor results of the overall program. This step should address questions such as the following:

- How well is the plan working?
- Is it cost effective?
- What is the actual versus planned impact on the workforce?
- Where are the plan's weaknesses?
- What changes will be needed during the next planning cycle?

■ HUMAN RESOURCE INFORMATION SYSTEMS

A **human resource information system (HRIS)** is any organized approach for obtaining relevant and timely information on which to base human resource decisions. An effective HRIS is crucial to sound human resource decision making; it typically employs computers and other sophisticated technologies to process data that reflect the day-to-day operations of a company, organized in the form of information to facilitate the decision-making process.

An HRIS should be designed to provide information that is:

- *Timely*—A manager must have access to up-to-date information.
- *Accurate*—A manager must be able to rely on the accuracy of the information provided.
- *Concise*—A manager can absorb only so much information at any one time.
- *Relevant*—A manager should receive only the information needed in a particular situation.
- *Complete*—A manager should receive complete, not partial, information.

The absence of even one of these characteristics reduces the effectiveness of an HRIS and complicates the decision-making process. Conversely, a system possessing all these characteristics enhances the ease and accuracy of the decision-making process. An effective HRIS also produces several important reports and forecasts related to business operations.

Routine Reports. Business data summarized on a scheduled basis are referred to as routine reports. Weekly and monthly employment status reports may be sent to the general manager, whereas quarterly reports may be forwarded to top management.

Exception Reports. Exception reports highlight variations in operations that are serious enough to require management's attention. One type of exception report is the quality-exception report, which is completed when the number of product defects exceeds a predetermined maximum. The human resource manager may be interested in this type of information in order to identify additional training needs.

On-Demand Reports. An on-demand report provides information in response to a specific request. The number of engineers with five years' work experience who speak fluent Spanish is an example of an on-demand report that the human resource manager could request from the database.[15]

---

[15] Janet Bensu, "Use Your Data Base in New Ways," *HRMagazine,* 35 (March 1990), pp. 33–34.

Forecasts. A forecast applies predictive models to specific situations. Managers need forecasts of the number and types of employees required to satisfy projected demand for the firm's product.

Creating the HRIS

Let's consider four steps in designing an HRIS that will provide the types of output just discussed and also conform to the HRIS criteria presented. These steps are not separate and distinct—in fact, they overlap considerably. Development of an HRIS is not merely a matter of properly designing the system. Without a major commitment from top management, creating a smoothly functioning and operational HRIS is virtually impossible. However, following the four steps can result in a HRIS design that could become quite an effective system if supported strongly by top management.

Study the Present System. In defining requirements or assessing the existing information system, three questions need to be answered: (1) What is the present flow of information? (2) How is the information used? (3) How valuable is this information to decision making?[16] A prime example of a flawed system was encountered by Art Simmons. Art was employed as a consultant to develop a human resource information system for a national forest products firm. In studying the firm's existing system, Art was amazed to discover a large amount of duplication and wasted effort. Some weekly reports were essentially useless for decision making. In addition, two employees had to work a total of eight hours weekly to prepare one particular report. If the report was late, the vice-president's secretary would send a strongly worded reprimand to the delinquent division chief. However, when the information arrived at headquarters, it was neatly filed and never used. Numerous questions regarding this practice finally revealed that about five years ago this type of information was requested—as a one-time report. Preparation of the report had continued through the administrations of three vice-presidents because no one thought to stop it.

Develop a Priority of Information That Managers Need. Once the current system is thoroughly understood, it is used to develop information priorities. A manager must have certain information in order to make proper decisions. Other information is nice to have but isn't essential to the manager's decision making. The HRIS design must ensure provision of high-priority information. Data having a lower priority should be generated only if the benefits exceed the costs of producing it.

One approach is to have individual managers develop their own priority lists and then integrate them into a list for the entire organization. Certain departments may discover that the information they identify as top priority will be far down the list for the organization as a whole. In such cases the needs of the entire organization may well be the controlling factor.

---

[16] Timothy R. Adams, "Buying Software Without the Glitches," *HRMagazine,* 35 (January 1990), pp. 40–42.

Develop the New Information System. The organization-wide priority list should govern the design of the HRIS. Information judged not worth the cost should not be included. A system of required reports should be developed and diagrammed. The entire organization is treated as a unit to eliminate duplication of information.

Choose a Computer. Today, it is reasonable to assume that the HRIS of most organizations will be computerized. Because of the increasing reliance on computers, the human resource manager should be computer literate. The presence of computers is far too pervasive and their usefulness far too great for human resource managers to ignore their capabilities. Human resource software for personal computers is almost always the responsibility of the human resource department.[17]

An Illustrative HRIS

Historically, the accounting information system was the first to be established in a firm, and the human resource information system was often the last. Firms now realize that a properly developed HRIS can provide tremendous benefits to the organization.

Figure 5-7 presents an overview of the human resource information system designed for one organization. Utilizing numerous types of input data, the HRIS makes available many types of output data that have far-reaching human resource planning and operational value. The HRIS ties all human resource information together into a system. Data from various input sources are integrated to provide the needed outputs. Information needed in the firm's human resource decision-making process is readily available when the system is properly designed. For instance, many firms are now studying historical trends to determine the best means of securing qualified applicants. In addition, complying with statutes and government regulations would be extremely difficult were it not for the modern HRIS. As the human component of the firm gains greater importance, the use of the HRIS is likely to expand.

One firm that has pioneered the development of human resource information systems is Information Science Incorporated (InSci). Founded in 1965, InSci was the first company to engage in the commercial development of computer-based human resource information systems. InSci's comprehensive concept of human resource management consists of human resource, payroll, pension, health claim, flexible compensation, and decision support systems. Today more than 1,000 organizations, including half of *Fortune*'s top 100 and 45 of the nation's largest banks, rely on InSci systems to help them manage their human resources effectively. One major advantage of the InSci system is its ability to provide management with information in the form required for planning.

---

[17] Timothy V. Welo, "HR Computer Study: Who Buys? What? How? and Why?," *Personnel,* 67 (February 1990), pp. 36–94.

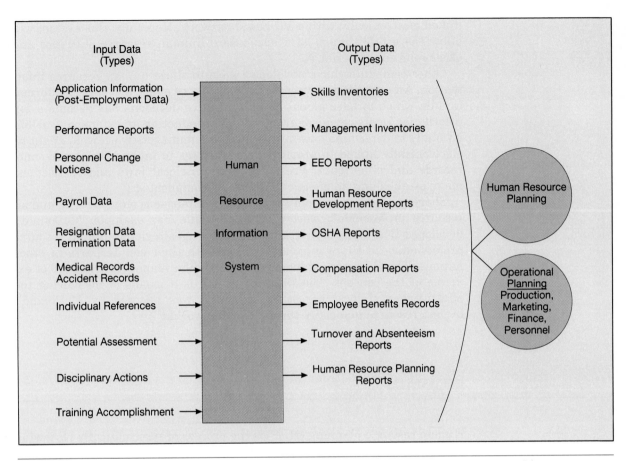

FIGURE 5-7 | A Human Resource Information System

Global Approaches to HRIS

Developing an effective global HRIS is virtually essential because of the complexity involved in managing a global labor force. The degree to which a human resource professional can globalize his or her function is dependent on many factors, and one of the most important factors is an effective HRIS. Information concerning the many factors affecting human resources must be shared. This information must be relevant and timely to assure that the best human resource decisions are made.

According to Ralph W. Stevens, vice-president of personnel and employee relations for the Denver-based Hamilton Oil Corporation, human resource professionals in each location must be experts on local laws, customs, salary structures, and so on. It is also essential that they have quality information. Through an effective HRIS, his company's human resource management approach is becoming much more integrated. Presently, Stevens shares information with his international counterparts by telephone, fax, and telex. Beginning in 1992, all human resource managers were linked electronically with a PC-based network. Hopefully, this system will allow the establishment of a database of human resource statistics and other relevant material.[18]

Other companies have developed ways to share human resource information. An organized approach for obtaining relevant and timely information on which to base global human resource decisions has become a top priority for Dow's chemical group. Dow is conducting an extensive feasibility study to determine how human resource managers worldwide might be electronically linked to provide greater access to international personnel records and other data. Presently, however, local laws and restrictions make establishing an effective HRIS very complicated.[19]

Sharing information from a centralized database is only one way human resource professionals worldwide share data. For example, McDonald's developed Best Bets, a program that encourages regional human resource professionals to share innovative plans with their counterparts in other nations. The P-Factor established by Canadian managers is a perfect example of the concept. The P-Factor, which is a means of measuring the effectiveness of local personnel practices, was adopted by McDonald's human resource managers throughout the world.[20]

SUMMARY

Human resource planning (HRP) is the process of systematically reviewing human resource requirements to ensure that the required number of employees, with the required skills, are available when they are needed. Strategic planning is the determination of overall organizational purposes and goals and how they are to be achieved. Strategic plans affect every major department and activity, including human resources.

After strategic plans have been formulated, human resource planning can be undertaken. Strategic plans are reduced to specific quantitative and qualitative human resource plans. Human resource planning has two components: requirements and availability. Forecasting human resource requirements involves determining the number and type of employees needed, by skill level and location. These projections are based on various factors, such as production plans and changes in productivity. In forecasting the availability of human resources, the organization looks to both internal sources (the present employees) and external sources (the labor market). After requirements and availability have been analyzed, management can determine whether there will likely be a surplus or shortage of employees in the future. Ways must be found to reduce the number of

---

[18] Ellen Brandt, "Global HR," *Personnel Journal,* 70 (March 1991), pp. 38–39.

[19] *Ibid.,* p. 42.

[20] *Ibid.,* p. 43.

employees if a surplus of workers is projected. These methods include restricted hiring, reduced hours, early retirements, and layoffs. If a shortage is forecast, the firm must look outside the organization to recruit and select the proper quantity and quality of workers.

Four basic terms are used in forecasting. First, the long-term trend represents the expected demand for a firm's goods or services, typically five years or more into the future. Second, cyclical variation is a reasonably predictable movement about the trend line that occurs over a period of more than a year. Third, seasonal variations are reasonably predictable changes that occur over a period of a year. Finally, random variations are changes for which there are no patterns.

Several techniques of forecasting human resource requirements and availability are currently in use by human resource professionals. The zero-base forecasting approach uses the organization's current level of employment as the starting point for determining future staffing needs. The bottom-up approach is a forecasting method that progresses upward from lower organizational units to ultimately provide an aggregate forecast of employment needs for the organization. Another method is to use past employment levels as a predictor of future requirements. Regression analysis is used to predict one item (the dependent variable) through knowledge of other items (the independent variables). Simulation is a technique for testing alternatives on a mathematical model representing a real-world situation.

A management inventory contains information about each manager for use in identifying individuals having the potential to move into higher level positions. A skills inventory is information maintained on the availability and readiness of nonmanagerial employees to move into higher level or lateral positions.

A human resource information system (HRIS) is any organized approach for obtaining relevant and timely information on which to base human resource decisions. An effective HRIS typically employs computers and other sophisticated technologies to maintain and process information reflecting the day-to-day human resource operations. An HRIS organizes data and outputs to facilitate the decision-making process.

Questions for Review

1. Describe the human resource planning process.
2. Identify and define the basic terms used in demand forecasting.
3. Identify and briefly describe the methods used to forecast human resource needs.
4. Distinguish between forecasting human resource requirements and availability. Use definitions and examples.
5. What actions could a firm take if it had a worker surplus?
6. Distinguish between a management inventory and a skills inventory. What are the essential components of each?
7. What is the purpose of a human resource information system? What are the basic steps that should be considered in developing an HRIS?

Terms for Review

Human resource planning (HRP)	Regression analysis
Strategic planning	Simulation
Long-term trend	Requirements forecast
Cyclical variations	Availability forecast
Seasonal variations	Management inventory
Random variations	Skills inventory
Zero-base forecasting	Human resource information
Bottom-up approach	system (HRIS)
Predictor variables	

INCIDENT 1   ▪   A Degree for Meter Readers?   ▪

Judy Anderson was the personnel recruiter for South Illinois Electric Company (SIE), a small supplier of natural gas and electricity for Cairo, Illinois, and the surrounding area. The company had grown rapidly during the last half of the 1980s, and this growth was continuing in the 1990s. Recently, SIE purchased the utilities system serving neighboring Mitchell County. The expansion concerned Judy. The company workforce had increased by 30 percent the previous year and Judy had found it a struggle to recruit enough qualified job applicants. She knew that the new expansion would intensify the problem.

Meter readers were of particular concern. The tasks required in meter reading are relatively simple. A person drives to homes served by the company, finds the gas or electric meter, and records its current reading. If the meter has been tampered with, it is reported. Otherwise no decision making of any consequence is associated with the job. The reader performs no calculations. The pay was $8.00 per hour, high for unskilled work in the area. Even so, Judy had been having considerable difficulty keeping the thirty-seven meter reader positions filled.

Judy was thinking about how to attract more job applicants when she received a call from the human resource director, Sam

McCord. "Judy," Sam said, "I'm unhappy with the job specification calling for only a high school education for meter readers. In planning for the future we need better educated people in the company. I've decided to change the education requirement for the meter reader job from a high school diploma to a college degree." "But, Mr. McCord," protested Judy, "the company is growing rapidly. If we are to have enough people to fill those jobs we just can't insist on finding college applicants to perform such basic tasks. I don't see how we can meet our future needs for this job with such an unrealistic job qualification." Sam terminated the conversation abruptly by saying, "No, I don't agree. We need to upgrade all the people in our organization. This is just part of a general effort to do that. Anyway, I cleared this with the president before I decided to do it."

Questions

1. Should there be a minimum education requirement for the meter reader job? Discuss.
2. What is your opinion of Sam's effort to upgrade the people in the organization?
3. What legal ramifications, if any, should Sam have considered?

INCIDENT 2   ■   A Busy Day   ■

Dave Johnson, human resource manager for Eagle Aircraft, had just returned from a brief vacation in Cozumel, Mexico. Eagle is a Wichita, Kansas, maker of small commercial aircraft. Eagle's workforce in 1992 totaled 236. Dave's friend Carl Edwards, vice-president of marketing, stopped by to ask Dave to lunch, as he often did. In the course of their conversation Carl asked Dave's opinion on the president's announcement concerning expansion. "What announcement?" was Dave's response.

Carl explained that there had been a special meeting of the executive council to announce a major expansion, involving a new plant to be built near St. Louis, Missouri. He continued, "Everyone at the meeting seemed to be completely behind the president. Joe Davis, the controller, stressed our independent financial position; the production manager had written a complete report on the equipment we are going to need, including availability and cost information. And I have been pushing for this expansion for some time. So I was ready. I think it will be good for you too, Dave. The president said he expects employment to double in the next year."

As Carl left, Rex Schearer, a production supervisor, arrived. "Dave," said Rex, "the production manager jumped on me Friday because maintenance doesn't have anybody qualified to work on the new digital lathe they are installing." "He's right," Dave replied. "Maintenance sent me a requisition last week. We'd better get moving and see if we can find someone." Dave knew that it was going to be another busy Monday.

Questions

1. What should Dave do, if anything, about being kept in the dark about the expansion? Explain.
2. Discuss any additional problems highlighted by the case and tell what should be done to solve them.

DEVELOPING HRM SKILLS

This exercise is designed to give participants experience in dealing with some aspects of planning that a typical human resource manager faces. Students will also be exposed to some of the activities that human resource managers confront on a daily basis. The old axiom, "plan your work and work your plan," will probably have new meaning after this exercise.

You are the human resource manager at a large canning plant. Your plant produces several lines of canned food products that are shipped to wholesale distributors nationwide. You are responsible for the human resource activities at the plant.

It is Monday morning, August 30. You have just returned from a week-long corporate executives' meeting at the home office. The meeting was attended by all human resource managers from every one of the company's plants. You returned with notes from the meeting and other materials you were given concerning the company's goals and plans for the next six months. When you arrive at your office (an hour early), you find your "in basket" full of notes, messages, and other correspondence.

The material provided to participants represents your notes and information from the meeting, plus what was in your "in basket." You must go through these and be prepared for the meeting the plant manager has scheduled for 8:00 A.M. It is now 7:30 A.M. Remember, you need to deal with some items immediately, some later today, and some tomorrow or later in the week. You will need to sort, prioritize, and set up your plan of activities. Participants will sort the material and information according to some priority in order to sequence handling issues properly. After sorting, participants can address each item concerning the action they plan to take. The participants will do the following on each item:

1. Note when it is to be handled.
2. Note who is to handle it, if not themselves.
3. Note what is to be done or who is to be informed.
4. If a meeting is to be called, set up an agenda.
5. If a memo or notice is to be sent out, write it.

Your instructor will provide the participants with additional information necessary to participate.

REFERENCES

Anthony, Peg, and Lincoln Akin Norton. "Link HR to Corporate Strategy." *Personnel Journal,* 70 (April 1991), pp. 75–86.

Aronoff, Craig E., and John L. Ward. "Succession: A New Image." *Nation's Business,* 78 (July 1990), pp. 45–46.

Blair, Edward. "Bootstrapping Your HRIS Capabilities." *Personnel Administrator,* 33 (February 1988), pp. 68–72.

Brant, Ellen. "Global HR." *Personnel Journal,* 70 (March 1991), pp. 38–44.

Brown, Rick, and Joseph L. Meresman. "Balancing Stability and Innovation to Stay Competitive." *Personnel,* 67 (September 1990), pp. 49–52.

Cashman, Margaret E., and James C. McElroy. "Evaluating the HR Function." *HRMagazine,* 36 (January 1991), pp. 70–73.

Clifton, Robert G. "A Critical Issue: Who Will Succeed You?" *Industrial Distribution* (August 1990), p. 58.

Fischer, Robert L. "HRIS Quality Depends on Teamwork." *Personnel Journal,* 70 (April 1991), pp. 47–51.

Foxman, Loretta D., and Walter L. Polsky. "HR Approaches for the Age of Globalization." Personnel Journal, 70 (April 1991), pp. 38–41.

Francis, Barton C. "Succession Planning for Closely Held Businesses." *Journal of Accountancy,* 171 (April 1991), pp. 83–85.

Goodman, Joan E. "Does Your HRS Speak English?" *Personnel Journal,* 69 (March 1990), pp. 76–83.

Goodrich, Jonathan N. "Telecommuting in America." *Business Horizons,* 33 (July–August 1990), pp. 31–37.

Hoerr, John. "Sharpening Minds for a Competitive Edge." *Business Week* (December 17, 1990), pp. 72–78.

Keaton, Paul N., and Michael J. Semb. "Shaping Up the Bottom Line." *HRMagazine,* 35 (September 1990), pp. 81–86.

Knapp, Jeffrey. "Trends in HR Management Systems." *Personnel,* 67 (April 1990), pp. 56–61.

Kossek, Ellen Ernst. "Why Many HR Programs Fail." *Personnel,* 67 (May 1990), pp. 50–53.

Kovach, Kenneth A., and John A. Pearce II. "HR Strategic Mandates for the 1990s." *Personnel,* 67 (April 1990), pp. 50–55.

Kromling, Larry K. "Calcomp Reshapes HR for the Future." *Personnel Journal,* 69 (January 1990), pp. 57–63.

Kubiak, Sharon L., Jack L. Simonetti, C. Joseph Sass, and Nick Nykodym. "Making People an Organization's Most Important Resource." *Business,* 40 (October–November–December 1990), pp. 33–35.

Kustoff, Marc. "The Role of Human Resources Information Systems in Personnel." *Personnel,* 63 (November 1986), pp. 68–70.

Lawrie, John. "Skill Inventories: Pack for the Future." *Personnel Journal,* 66 (March 1987), pp. 127–130.

MacAdam, Maureen. "HRIS: Document What You're Doing." *Personnel Journal,* 69 (February 1990), pp. 56–63.

McElwain, James E. "Succession Plans Designed to Manage Change." *HRMagazine,* 36 (February 1991), pp. 67–71.

Messmer, Max. "Strategic Staffing for the '90s." *Personnel Journal,* 69 (October 1990), pp. 92–97.

Miller, Marc S. "Up & Running." *Personnel,* 67 (November 1990), p. 23.

Moellring, Genevieve. "Integrate HRIS and Payroll." *Personnel Journal,* 70 (February 1991), pp. 79–82.

Mondy, R. Wayne, Robert M. Noe, and Robert E. Edwards. "What the Staffing Function Entails." *Personnel,* 63 (April 1986), pp. 55–58.

Nardoni, Ren. "Planning Promotes HRIS Success." *Personnel Journal,* 70 (January 1991), pp. 61–65.

Nkomo, Stella M. "The Theory and Practice of HR Planning: The Gap Still Remains." *Personnel Administrator,* 31 (August 1986), pp. 71–81.

Overman, Stephanie. "Different World Brings Challenge." *HRMagazine,* 35 (June 1990), pp. 58–60.

Perry, Stephen G. "The PC-Based HRIS." *Personnel Administrator,* 33 (February 1988), pp. 60–63.

Pollard, John R. "HRIS: Time Is of the Essence." *Personnel Journal,* 69 (November 1990), pp. 42–44.

Sahl, Robert J. "Get It Together! Integrating the HR Department." *Personnel,* 66 (February 1989), pp. 39–45.

Shetty, Y. K., and Paul F. Buller. "Regaining Competitiveness Requires HR Solutions." *Personnel,* 67 (July 1990), pp. 8–12.

Silverthorne, Colin P. "Planning for a Smaller Organization: A Guide for HR Managers." *Personnel,* 64 (March 1987), pp. 60–66.

Tinsley, Dillard B. "Future Flash: Computer Facilitates HR Function." *Personnel,* 67 (February 1990), pp. 32–35.

CHAPTER 6   RECRUITMENT

CHAPTER OBJECTIVES

1. Describe the recruitment process, explain why it is so closely related to human resource planning, and identify actions that a firm might consider before resorting to outside recruitment.
2. Describe the external and internal factors that can influence the recruitment process, and explain internal recruitment methods.
3. Identify the various sources and methods available to an organization for external recruiting.
4. State what should be done to ensure that recruitment efforts meet legal requirements.

Dorothy Bryant, recruiting supervisor for International Manufacturing Company, had been promoted to her position after several years as a group leader in the production department. One of Dorothy's first assignments was to recruit two software design engineers for International. After considering various recruitment alternatives, Dorothy placed the following ad in a local newspaper with a circulation in excess of 1,000,000:

> EMPLOYMENT OPPORTUNITY
> FOR SOFTWARE DESIGN ENGINEERS
> Progressive firm in growth industry has
> 2 positions available for software design engineers.
> 3 years of computer-related experience desired.
> Apply Today! Send your résumé, in
> confidence, to: D. A. Bryant, International
> Manufacturing Co., P.O. Box 1515, Alexandria, VA 22314

More than 300 applications were received in the first week, and Dorothy was elated. However, when she reviewed the applicants, it appeared that few people possessed the desired qualifications for the job.

Dorothy has learned the importance of proper recruiting practices. She obviously failed to include important job requirements in her newspaper advertisement. As a result, an excessive number of unqualified persons applied. Determining the proper means to encourage potential employees to apply for employment is extremely important. Tapping appropriate sources of applicants and utilizing appropriate recruitment methods are essential to maximize recruiting effectiveness.

We begin this chapter by describing the recruitment process, strategies for global recruitment, and alternatives to recruitment. Next, we describe the external and internal environments of recruitment. Then, we present methods used in external and internal recruitment, and how methods should be tailored to sources. We devote the final portion of the chapter to recruiting efforts under the law.

■ THE RECRUITMENT PROCESS

Recruitment is the process of attracting individuals on a timely basis, in sufficient numbers and with appropriate qualifications, and encouraging them to apply for jobs with an organization.[1] Applicants with qualifications most closely related to job specifications may then be selected. However, in practice, recruitment is often very demanding and seldom so straightforward. Recruitment today is like marketing consumer products—tough and competitive. Unless a sufficient number of qualified prospects apply, a firm cannot have a truly selective employment system.

In most medium-sized and large organizations, the human resource department is responsible for the recruitment process. In small firms, recruitment is likely the responsibility of individual managers. Regardless of who is responsible for the recruitment process, it is an essential function of every firm. Benefit cost control, compensation, and training have been cited as the current primary HRM issues. However, many experts believe that recruitment and retention will be top challenges of the 1990s.[2]

As you can see in Figure 6-1, when human resource planning indicates a need for employees, the firm may evaluate alternative ways to meet this demand through the recruitment process. When other alternatives are not appropriate, the recruitment process starts. Frequently, recruitment begins when a manager initiates an employee requisition. The **employee requisition** is a document that specifies job title, department, the date the employee is needed for work, and other details (see Figure 6-2 on page 176). With this information, the human resource manager can refer to the appropriate job description to determine the qualifications the person to be recruited needs. At times, firms continue to recruit even when they have no vacancies. This practice permits them to maintain recruitment contacts and to identify exceptional candidates for future employment.

The next step in the recruitment process is to determine whether qualified employees are available within the firm (the internal source) or must be recruited from external sources, such as colleges, universities, and other organizations. Because of the high cost of recruiting, organizations need to utilize the most productive recruitment sources and methods available. **Recruitment sources** are where qualified individuals can be found. **Recruitment methods** are the specific means by which potential employees can be attracted to the firm. When the sources of potential employees

---

[1] R. Wayne Mondy, Robert M. Noe, and Robert E. Edwards, "What the Staffing Function Entails," *Personnel,* 63 (April 1986), pp. 54–58.

[2] Jac Fitz-enz, "Getting—and Keeping—Good Employees," *Personnel,* 67 (August 1990), p. 25–28.

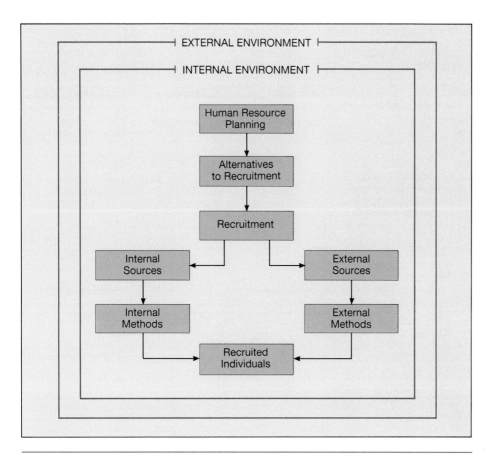

FIGURE 6-1 | The Recruitment Process

have been identified, appropriate methods for either internal or external recruitment are used to accomplish recruitment objectives.

Companies may discover that one recruitment method is superior to another for locating potential executive talent. For instance, one large equipment manufacturer determined that medium-sized, state-supported colleges and universities located in rural areas were good sources of potential managers. Other firms may arrive at a different conclusion. Thus in order to maximize recruiting effectiveness, utilizing recruitment sources and methods tailored to each organization's needs is vitally important.

■ STRATEGIES FOR GLOBAL RECRUITMENT

As the globalization of the world economy intensifies, U.S. corporations have found it more difficult to assure the uninhibited flow of adequate human capital to the multinational organization. Recruiting individuals with appropriate qualifications and encouraging them to apply is essential

JOB NUMBER	JOB TITLE	DATE OF JOB VACANCY	DATE REPLACEMENT NEEDED

PLEASE CHECK	☐ Permanent	☐ Temporary	☐ Part-Time
	☐ Exempt	☐ Nonexempt	If Nonexempt, Enter Job Class

REASON FOR REQUEST: What management or employee action(s) caused the opening?	
BRIEF DESCRIPTION OF MINIMUM QUALIFICATIONS FOR THE JOB CANDIDATES:	
BRIEF DESCRIPTION OF JOB DUTIES:	

LOCATION NAME	
DATE	MANAGER'S SIGNATURE

FIGURE 6-2 | An Employee Requisition

for global success.[3] The essence of global business success is finding and employing the best people. Once the global business strategy is outlined, human resource professionals must develop a corresponding recruiting strategy. The sooner human resource professionals are consulted in reference to recruitment and selection, the better. In fact, establishing the global business strategy and the recruiting and staffing strategies concurrently will often result in a more effective overall strategy.

If an international joint venture is anticipated, it is very helpful to specify the recruitment and staffing policies in the joint contract.[4] Such contractual

---

[3] John P. Senko, "Dollar-Wise, Pound-Foolish Controlling Expatriate Execs' Costs," *Management Review,* 80 (March 1991), p. 38.

[4] Wayne F. Cascio and Manuel G. Serapio, Jr., "Human Resources Systems in an International Alliance: The Undoing of a Done Deal?" *Organizational Dynamics,* 19 (Winter 1991), p. 69.

requirements help limit friction between partners. In lieu of contractual agreements, the partners should formulate written "house rules" on recruitment and staffing. House rules should provide guidelines for recruitment and staffing and a basis for settling disputes. Effective recruitment and staffing is essential for global success, and therefore, the adoption of guidelines to assure effectiveness should be given serious consideration.[5]

■ ALTERNATIVES TO RECRUITMENT

Even when human resource planning indicates a need for additional or replacement employees, a firm may decide against jumping immediately into recruitment efforts. Recruitment and selection costs are high. For example, one organization estimates the median cost-per-hire for a new employee to be $15,017, with a high-end cost of $27,030.[6] Often included in the calculation are costs of the search process, interviewing, agency fee payment, and relocation and processing of the new employee. Although selection decisions are not irreversible, once employees are placed on the payroll, they may be difficult to remove, even if their performance is marginal. Therefore, a firm should consider its alternatives carefully before engaging in recruitment. Alternatives to recruitment commonly include overtime, subcontracting, temporary employees, and employee leasing.

Overtime

Perhaps the most commonly used method of meeting short-term fluctuations in work volume is through the use of overtime. Overtime may help both employer and employee. The employer may benefit by avoiding recruitment, selection, and training costs. The employee may benefit from a higher rate of pay.

Along with the obvious advantages of using overtime are potential problems. Many managers believe that when they work employees for unusually long periods of time, the company pays more and receives less in return. Employees may become fatigued and lack the energy to perform at a normal rate, especially when excessive overtime is required.

Two additional potential problems are related to the use of prolonged overtime. Employees may, consciously or not, pace themselves so that overtime will be assured. They may also become accustomed to the added income resulting from overtime pay. Employees may even elevate their standard of living to the level permitted by this additional income. Then, when overtime is no longer required, and the paycheck shrinks, employees may become disgruntled.

---

[5] *Ibid.*, p. 69.

[6] Margaret Magnus, "Is Your Recruitment All It Can Be?" *Personnel Journal,* 66 (February 1987), pp. 54–63.

Subcontracting

Even though a long-term increase in demand for its goods or services is anticipated, an organization may still decide against further hiring. Rather, the firm may choose to subcontract the work to someone else. This approach has a special appeal when the subcontractor actually has greater expertise in producing certain goods or services. This arrangement often has considerable benefits for both parties.

Temporary Employees

The total cost of a permanent employee is generally estimated at 30 to 40 percent above gross pay. This does not include, among other things, the costs of recruitment. To avoid some of these costs and to maintain flexibility as workloads vary, many organizations utilize temporary employees. During certain periods in the past, as many as nine of ten companies in this country used temporary-help services. Temporary-help companies assist their clients by handling excess or special workloads. They assign their own employees to their customers and fulfill all the obligations normally associated with an employer.[7] The expenses of recruitment, absenteeism and turnover, and employee benefits are avoided. Suppose that the supervisor of the word processing department has an immediate, but short-term, need for six secretaries. Rather than recruit and hire additional employees, the supervisor calls a local organization that supplies temporary workers. This firm immediately sends the employees needed. These secretaries remain on the payroll of the temporary-help organization, which bills the using firm for their services. To illustrate the rapidly increasing popularity of firms specializing in providing "temps," one executive of a temporary-help firm stated, "In the last two years, our business has gone from $15 million to $45 million."[8]

Employee Leasing[9]

As discussed in Chapter 2, an alternative to recruitment that is growing in popularity is employee leasing. Using this approach, a firm formally terminates some or most of its employees. A leasing company then hires them, usually at the same salary, and leases them back to the former employer, who becomes the client. The employees continue to work as before, with the client supervising their activities. The leasing company, however, assumes all responsibilities associated with being employer, including human resource administration.

---

[7] Charles W. L. Deale, "How to Choose a Temporary Help Service: A Guide to Quality Supplemental Staffing," *Personnel Administrator,* 25 (December 1980), p. 56.

[8] Margaret Magnus, "Is Your Recruitment All It Can Be?" p. 63.

[9] Paul N. Keaton and Janine Anderson, "Leasing Offers Benefits to Both Sides," *HRMagazine,* 35 (July 1990), p. 53.

A primary advantage of employee leasing to the client is being free from human resource administration, including maintaining a benefit program. Another advantage of employee leasing is that it provides a way of avoiding union-organizing activities or the requirement to recognize and bargain with an existing union. If the leasing company does not qualify as an "employer" under the National Labor Relations Act, employee leasing permits a firm to escape any requirement to recognize a representative of leased workers.

Advantages of leasing also accrue to the employees. Since leasing companies provide workers for many companies, they often enjoy economies of scale that permit them to offer excellent, low-cost benefit programs. In addition, there are often greater opportunities for job mobility. Since leasing firms operate throughout the nation, if a spouse is relocated, the leasing company may offer the employee a job in the new location. Also, if a client organization suffers a downturn in business, the leasing company can transfer employees to another client, avoiding both layoff and loss of seniority.

A potential disadvantage to the client is that Congress may further reduce the tax-shelter benefits of employee leasing initially provided by the Tax Equity and Fiscal Responsibility Act of 1982. Another possible difficulty is that employee loyalty may be eroded since workers receive pay and benefits from the leasing company. Regardless of the disadvantages, use of employee leasing is growing. Currently, about 75,000 employees are being leased. It is estimated that 20 percent of the 4.4 million businesses in the U.S. with fewer than 35 employees will be attracted to employee leasing, resulting in 10 million leased employees by the year 2000. Larger companies have also begun using employee leasing to a greater extent. It provides them with a body of well-trained, long-term employees that can expand or contract as business conditions dictate.[10]

■ EXTERNAL ENVIRONMENT OF RECRUITMENT

As with the other human resource functions, the recruitment process doesn't take place in a vacuum. Factors external to the organization can significantly affect the firm's recruitment efforts. Of particular importance is the demand for and supply of specific skills in the labor market. If demand for a particular skill is high relative to supply, an extraordinary recruiting effort may be required. For instance, demand for technical salespeople is likely to be greater than the supply, relative to the demand-supply relationship for nontechnical sales representatives.

When the unemployment rate in an organization's labor market is high, the firm's recruitment process may be simplified. The number of unsolicited applicants is usually greater, and the increased size of the labor pool provides a better opportunity for attracting qualified applicants.

---

[10] John Ross, "Effective Ways to Hire Contingent Personnel," *HRMagazine,* 36 (February 1991), p. 53.

Conversely, as the unemployment rate drops, recruitment efforts must be increased and new sources explored.

Local labor market conditions are of primary importance in recruitment for most nonmanagerial, many supervisory, and even some middle-management positions. However, recruitment for executive and professional positions often extends to the national market. Although the recruiter's day-to-day activities provide a feel for the labor market, accurate employment data—found in professional journals and U.S. Department of Labor reports—is essential.

Legal considerations also play a significant role in recruitment practices in the United States. The individual and the employer first make contact during the recruitment process. Therefore, nondiscriminatory practices at this stage are absolutely essential. We discuss this topic later in this chapter.

The firm's corporate image is another important factor that affects recruitment. If employees believe that their employer deals with them fairly, the positive word-of-mouth support they provide is of great value to the firm. It assists in establishing credibility with prospective employees. Good reputations earned in this manner can result in more and better qualified applicants seeking employment with the firm. Prospective employees are more inclined to respond positively to the organization's recruitment efforts if the firm is praised by employees. The firm with an untarnished public image is one believed to be a "good place to work," and the recruitment efforts of such a firm are greatly enhanced.

■ INTERNAL ENVIRONMENT OF RECRUITMENT

Although the labor market and the government exert powerful external influences, the organization's own practices and policies also affect recruitment. A major internal factor that can greatly aid recruitment is human resource planning. In most cases, a firm cannot attract prospective employees in sufficient numbers and with the required skills overnight. Examining alternative sources of recruits and determining the most productive methods for obtaining them takes time. After identifying the best alternatives, the human resource manager can make appropriate recruitment plans.

An organization's promotion policy can also have a significant impact on recruitment. Basically, an organization can stress a policy of promotion from within its own ranks or a policy of filling positions from outside the organization. Depending on the circumstances, either approach may have merit.

Promotion from within is the policy of filling vacancies above entry-level positions with current employees. When an organization emphasizes promotion from within, its workers have an incentive to strive for advancement. When employees see coworkers being promoted, they become more aware of their own opportunities. Motivation provided by this practice often improves employee morale.

Another advantage of internal recruitment is that the organization is usually well aware of its employees' capabilities. An employee's job performance may not, by itself, be a reliable criterion for promotion. Nevertheless, many of the employee's personal and job-related qualities will be known. The employee has a track record, as opposed to being an "unknown quantity." Also, the company's investment in the individual may yield a higher return. Still another positive factor is the employee's knowledge of the firm, its policies, and its people.

Yet it is unlikely that a firm can (or would even desire to) adhere rigidly to a practice of promotion from within. The vice-president of human resources for a major automobile manufacturer offers this advice: "A strictly applied 'PFW' policy eventually leads to inbreeding, a lack of cross-fertilization, and a lack of creativity. A good goal, in my opinion, is to fill 80 percent of openings above entry-level positions from within." Frequently, new blood is needed to provide new ideas and innovation that must take place for firms to remain competitive. In such cases, even organizations with promotion from within policies may opt to look outside the organization for new talent. In any event, a promotion policy that first considers insiders is great for employee morale and motivation and is often beneficial to the organization.

Policies related to the employment of relatives may also affect a firm's recruitment efforts. The content of such policies varies greatly, but it is not uncommon for companies to have policies that discourage the employment of close relatives. This is especially true when their assignments would place them in the same department, under the same supervisor, or in supervisor-subordinate roles.

■ METHODS USED IN INTERNAL RECRUITMENT

Management should be able to identify current employees who are capable of filling positions as they become available. Helpful tools used for internal recruitment include management and skills inventories and job posting and bidding procedures. As we mentioned in Chapter 5, management and skills inventories permit organizations to determine whether current employees possess the qualifications for filling open positions. As a recruitment device, these inventories have proved to be extremely valuable to organizations when they are kept up-to-date. Inventories can be of tremendous value in locating talent internally and supporting the concept of promotion from within.

Job posting is a procedure for informing employees that job openings exist. **Job bidding** is a technique that permits employees who believe that they possess the required qualifications to apply for a posted job. Table 6-1 on page 182 shows the procedure that a medium-sized firm might use. Larger firms often provide employees with a weekly list of job openings. Any qualified employee is encouraged to apply. Figure 6-3 shows an example of this approach (see page 183).

The procedure followed by Texas Instruments minimizes the complaint commonly heard in many companies that insiders never hear of a job opening until it has been filled. Implementation of a job posting and bidding system avoids this problem. It reflects an openness that most employees

TABLE 6-1 | Job Posting and Bidding Procedure

Responsibility	Action Required
Human resource assistant	1. Upon receiving a *Human Resource Requisition,* write a memo to each appropriate supervisor stating that a job vacancy exists. The memo should include a job title, job number, pay grade, salary range, a summary of the basic duties performed, and the qualifications required for the job (data to be taken from job description/specification).
	2. Ensure that a copy of this memo is posted on all company bulletin boards.
Supervisors	3. Make certain that every employee who might qualify for the position is made aware of the job opening.
Interested employees	4. Contact the human resource department.

generally value highly. In addition, this system can assist in college recruitment efforts. A firm that offers freedom of choice and encourages career growth has a distinct advantage over those organizations that don't.

However, a job posting and bidding system does have some negative features. An effective system requires the expenditure of considerable time and money. When bidders are unsuccessful, someone must explain to them why they weren't chosen. If care has not been taken to ensure that the most qualified applicant is chosen, the system will lack credibility. Even successful implementation of such a system can't completely eliminate complaints.

■ EXTERNAL SOURCES OF RECRUITMENT

At times, a firm must look beyond itself to find employees, particularly when expanding its workforce. The following circumstances require external recruitment: (1) to fill entry-level jobs; (2) to acquire skills not possessed by current employees; and (3) to obtain employees with different backgrounds to provide new ideas. As Figure 6-4 on page 184 shows, even when promotions are made internally, entry-level jobs must be filled from the outside. Thus after the president retires, a series of internal promotions is made. Ultimately, however, the firm has to recruit externally to fill the entry-level position of salary analyst. If the president's position had been filled from the outside, the chain-reaction of promotions from within would not have occurred. Depending on the qualifications desired, employees may be attracted from a number of outside sources.

1. If you are interested in any of the opportunities listed below, please complete a "Job Opportunity Request" form and submit it to your Job Opportunity Office. Forms may be obtained from your personnel department.
2. Each opportunity will be held open for consideration of TIers for one week. To be considered, your Job Opportunity Request must be received in your site Job Opportunity Office by no later than seven days from the date of this Bulletin.
3. To qualify for a job, you must satisfy all requirements of the job and you must list these qualifications on your Job Opportunity Request form. A résumé or additional information may be attached if desired but the required qualifications as described in the job posting must be listed on the Job Opportunity Request form.
4. Each opportunity is coded to indicate payment of transfer expenses in accordance with Personnel Procedure PM 2-3-4 (Transfer Expenses of TI Personnel) as follows:
    CR—Candidates urgently needed. Transfer expenses including Home Guarantee Program paid.
    ER— Internal and external candidates are being sought locally and nationally. Transfer expenses paid as listed in PM 2-3-4.
    LR— Adequate local supply of qualified people. TIers in other locations may bid with understanding that no transfer expenses will be paid by TI.
    For details of transfer expenses paid for by each of the above classifications, see your administrator.
5. JOB GRADES—On jobs in locations other than your own, see your personnel administrator for comparison with your grading system.
6. If you do not receive an answer to your Job Opportunity Request by four weeks from the date of this Bulletin, call Job Opportunity at Dallas Expressway 5336. Remember the Job Number in requesting information about your Job Opportunity Request.

NON-EXEMPT
ADMINISTRATIVE

EQUIPMENT

CLK, GEN   (JPN)01DN2040
                           (JRC)0922723053
DUTIES: Prfm gen cler tasks; oper IBM PC; oper calcul; some typg; maint logs, files, etc. MIN SKILL REQD: Prfm cler tasks. JG53: 1–3 yrs rel expr. JG55: 3–5 yrs rel expr. SECURITY CLEARANCE REQD Grd 53/55 LR–CC922
CLK, GEN   (JPN)01DN2011
                           (JRC)0988723053
DUTIES: Oper various types of reprod/copy equip. Asst in oper of classified document contrl syst to include registration, transfer, filg % destruction of classified matl. Typg ability reqd. Wrk hrs 10:30 a.m.–7:00 p.m. MIN SKILL REQD: JG53: type 40–50 WPM, 1–5 yrs rel expr. JG55: type 50–60 WPM, 3–5 yrs rel expr. SECURITY CLEARANCE REQD. Grd 53/55 LR–CC988 s/lor Rotg

SECRETARY   (JPN)01DN2016
                           (JRC)0431731053
DUTIES: Sec duties Contract Admin includg hvy data entry, typg, filg, handlg classified documents, hvy phone liaison (cust/TI). JG53: over 1 yr dir rel expr. JG55: over 3 yrs dir rel expr MIN SKILL REQD: Typg 50–60 WPM. IBM PC expr helpful. Abil to wrk under pressure & get along well w/others. Dependable, mature. Contracts or purchasing expr helpful. MIN EDUC REQD: Some bus schl &/or coll prefd. SECURITY CLEARANCE REQD. Grd 53/55 LR–CC431
WORD PROCESS   (JPN)01DN2032
OPER   (JRC)0713723053
DUTIES: Data entry of draft copy, reprod copy & finished copy to meet contract data reqmts. Train on Word Procg Typg syst. Reqs attention to detail & sustained concentration f/long periods of time; abil to follow written, oral & mach-coded instructions. Prfm other rel duties as reqd. MIN SKILL REQD: JG53: 1–3 yrs rel expr & 40–50 WPM data entry. JG55: 3–5 yrs rel expr & 60 WPM typg. SECURITY CLEARANCE REQD. Grd 53/55 LR–CC713

FIGURE 6-3 | An Example of Texas Instruments' Job Posting System

Source: Texas Instruments, Inc.

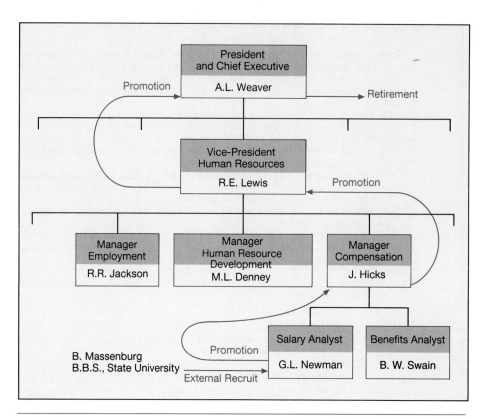

FIGURE 6-4 | Internal Promotion and External Recruitment

High Schools and Vocational Schools

Organizations concerned with recruiting clerical and other entry-level operative employees often depend heavily on high schools and vocational schools. Many schools have outstanding training programs for specific occupational skills, such as home-appliance repair and small-engine mechanics. Some companies work with schools to ensure a constant supply of trained individuals with specific job skills. In some areas, companies even loan employees to schools to assist in the training programs.

Community Colleges

Many community colleges are sensitive to the specific employment needs in their local labor markets and graduate highly sought-after students with marketable skills. Typically, community colleges have two-year programs designed for both a terminal education and preparation for a four-year university degree program. Many community colleges also have excellent mid-management programs combined with training for specific trades. In addition, career centers often provide a place for employers to contact students, thereby facilitating the recruitment process.

Colleges and Universities

Colleges and universities represent a major recruitment source for many organizations. Potential professional, technical, and management employees are typically found in these institutions. Firms commonly send recruiters to campuses to interview prospective employees.

Placement directors, faculty, and administrators can be extremely helpful to organizations in their search for recruits. Many firms cultivate these resources. For instance, the large retailer Bloomingdale's has improved greatly its image on campuses by making personal contact with business professors and providing grants for studies and internships. In fact, many firms are becoming more college relationship oriented as opposed to college recruitment oriented. To make this shift, companies must be willing to provide financial resources (for scholarships, materials, equipment, and research), as well as professional expertise and classroom speakers. Such efforts give the firm exposure in more than just a recruitment context.[11]

Because on-campus recruitment is mutually beneficial, both employers and universities should take steps to develop and maintain close relationships. When a company establishes recruitment programs with educational institutions, it should continue those programs year after year to maintain an effective relationship with each school. It is important that the firm know the school and that the school know the firm.

Competitors and Other Firms

Competitors and other firms in the industry or geographic area may be the most important source of recruits for positions in which recent experience is highly desired. The fact that approximately 5 percent of the working population, at any one time, is either actively seeking or receptive to change of position emphasizes the importance of these sources. Furthermore, one of every three people—especially managers and professionals—changes jobs every five years.[12]

Even organizations that have strong policies of promotion from within must occasionally look elsewhere (which includes competitors) to fill important positions. When Cessna Aircraft entered the business-jet market, it needed a top sales executive with experience in this field. Cessna was able to lure a successful executive from Pan American World Airways to run its marketing operations.[13] Other organizations are valuable sources of high-quality talent, and raiding often occurs.

Smaller firms, in particular, look for employees who have been trained by larger organizations that have the necessary developmental resources. For instance, an optical firm believes that its own operation is not large

---

[11] Margaret Magnus, "Is Your Recruitment All It Can Be?" p. 58.

[12] Dan Lionel, "Dow Jones Tests Recruitment Weekly," *Editor and Publisher* (May 24, 1980), p. 29.

[13] Richard R. Conarroe, *Executive Search: A Guide For Recruiting Outstanding Executives* (New York: Van Nostrand Reinhold, 1976), p. 8.

enough to provide extensive training and development programs. Thus, a person recruited by this firm for a significant management role is likely to have held at least two positions previously with a competitor.

The Unemployed

The unemployed often provide a valuable source of recruits. Qualified applicants join the unemployment rolls every day for various reasons. Companies may go out of business, cut back, or be merged with other firms, leaving qualified workers without jobs. Employees are also fired sometimes merely because of personality differences with their bosses. Not infrequently, employees become frustrated with their jobs and simply quit.

Self-Employed Workers

Finally, the self-employed worker may also be a good potential recruit. Such individuals may constitute a source of applicants for any number of jobs requiring technical, professional, administrative, or entrepreneurial expertise within a firm.

■ EXTERNAL METHODS OF RECRUITMENT

By examining recruitment sources, a firm determines where potential job applicants are. It then seeks to attract them by specific recruitment methods. Recruitment methods such as advertising, employment agencies, and employee referrals may be effective in attracting individuals with virtually every type of skill. Recruiters, special events, and internships are used primarily to attract students, especially those attending colleges and universities. Also, executive search firms and professional organizations are particularly helpful in the recruitment of managerial and professional employees.

Advertising

Advertising communicates the firm's employment needs to the public through media such as radio, newspaper, television, and industry publications. In determining the content of an advertising message, a firm must decide on the corporate image it wants to project. Obviously, the firm should give prospective employees a clear and honest picture of the job and the organization. At the same time, the firm should attempt to appeal to the self-interest of prospective employees, emphasizing the unique qualities of the job. The advertisement must tell them why they should be interested in that particular job and organization. The message should also indicate how an applicant is to respond: apply in person, by telephone, or submit a résumé.

The firm's previous experience with various media should suggest the approach to be taken for specific types of jobs. The least expensive form of advertising that provides the broadest coverage is probably the newspaper advertisement. Many firms use help-wanted advertising, and studies indicate that approximately 40 percent of all jobs are filled through recruitment advertising.[14] The greatest problem with its use is the large number of unqualified individuals who respond to such ads. This situation increases the likelihood of poor selection decisions.

Although no one bases a decision to change jobs on an advertisement, an ad creates awareness, generates interest, and encourages a prospect to seek more information about the firm and the job opportunities that it provides.[15] Examination of the Sunday edition of any major newspaper reveals the extensive use of advertising in recruiting practically every type of employee.

Certain media attract audiences that are more homogeneous in terms of employment skills, education, and orientation. Advertisements placed in publications such as *The Wall Street Journal* relate primarily to managerial, professional, and technical positions. The readers generally are individuals who are qualified for many of the positions advertised. Focusing on a specific labor market minimizes the likelihood of receiving marginally qualified or even totally unqualified applicants.

Virtually every professional group publishes a journal that is widely read by its members. Advertising for a human resource executive position in *HRMagazine,* for example, would be an excellent choice because it is read almost exclusively by human resource professionals.

Trade journals are widely utilized, but their use presents some problems. For example, regional editions are not offered, so the journals may be useless to the employer who wants to avoid paying relocation expenses. Also, they lack scheduling flexibility. Their deadlines are usually thirty days prior to the issue date, and may be even further in advance for four-color material. Since staffing needs cannot always be anticipated far in advance, the use of trade journals for recruitment obviously is not too helpful at times.

Recruitment advertisers assume that qualified prospects who read job ads in newspapers and professional and trade journals are dissatisfied with their present jobs to the extent that they will pursue opportunities advertised. This is not always the case, especially for those qualified individuals who are not actively considering a job change. Therefore, in high-demand situations, the firm needs to consider all available media resources.[16]

Other media that can also be used include radio, billboards, and television. These methods are likely to be more expensive than newspapers or journals, but they have been used with success in specific situations. For

---

[14] James W. Schreier, "Deciphering Messages in Recruitment Ads," *Personnel Administrator,* 28 (March 1983), p. 35.

[15] Rick Stoops, "Recruitment," *Personnel Journal,* 63 (December 1984), p. 60.

[16] Dan Lionel, "Dow Jones Tests," p. 29.

instance, a regional medical center used billboards successfully to attract registered nurses. One large manufacturing firm achieved considerable success in advertising for production trainees by means of spot advertisements on the radio. A large electronics firm used television to attract experienced engineers when it opened a new facility and needed more engineers immediately. Thus in situations where hiring needs are urgent, television and radio may provide good results; although by themselves, they may not be sufficient. Broadcast messages can alert people to the fact that an organization is seeking recruits, but they are limited in their ability to provide much more information than the general type of job available and company address and phone number. For this reason, broadcasting and print media are often used together to attract qualified applicants.

Some human resource executives believe that recruitment advertising does not receive a fair share of the firm's advertising budget. For many companies, there is an astounding difference between the amount of money spent and marketing research done for product advertising versus employee recruitment advertising. A great deal of effort goes into motivating somebody to buy a tube of toothpaste that only costs a dollar. Yet, a human resource department must motivate somebody to leave the security of a current job, and in some cases, move to a distant city. This requires at least as much effort, thought, and talent.[17]

Employment Agencies—Private and Public

An **employment agency** is an organization that helps firms recruit employees and, at the same time, aids individuals in their attempts to locate jobs. These agencies perform many recruitment and selection functions for the employer. The tasks that employment agencies perform have proven quite beneficial to many organizations.

Private employment agencies are utilized by firms for virtually every type of position. However, they are best known for recruiting white-collar employees. Although some parts of the industry have a bad reputation, a number of highly reputable employment agencies have operated successfully for decades. Difficulties that occasionally occur stem from a lack of industry standards. The quality of a particular agency depends on the professionalism of its management. Even though problems may exist, private employment agencies offer an important service in bringing qualified applicants and open positions together. They should not be overlooked by either the organization or the job applicant. Individuals are often turned off by the one-time fees that agencies charge. However, the fee is frequently paid by the employer. An example of a typical employment agency fee schedule is shown in Table 6-2. Fee percentages are based on gross salary.

---

[17] Tracy E. Benson, "Ready, Aim, Hire," *Industry Week,* 24 (February 4, 1991), p. 16.

TABLE 6-2 | Typical Employment Agency Fee Schedule

Annual Gross Salary	Fee*	Annual Gross Salary	Fee*
$ 0–$9,999	10%	20,000–20,999	21
10,000–10,999	11	21,000–21,999	22
11,000–11,999	12	22,000–22,999	23
12,000–12,999	13	23,000–23,999	24
13,000–13,999	14	24,000–24,999	25
14,000–14,999	15	25,000–25,999	26
15,000–15,999	16	26,000–26,999	27
16,000–16,999	17	27,000–27,999	28
17,000–17,999	18	28,000–28,999	29
18,000–18,999	19	29,000+	30
19,000–19,999	20		

*The employment agency's fee is normally a percentage of the
employee's salary for the first year.

The public employment agencies operated by each state receive overall policy direction from the U.S. Employment Service. Public employment agencies are best known for recruiting and placing individuals in operative jobs. But recently they have become increasingly involved in matching people with technical, professional, and managerial positions. Some public agencies utilize computerized job matching systems to aid in the recruitment process. Public employment agencies provide their services without charge to either the employer or prospective employee.

Recruiters

The most common use of recruiters is with technical and vocational schools, community colleges, colleges, and universities. The key contact for recruiters on college and university campuses is often the director of student placement. This administrator is in an excellent position to arrange interviews with students possessing the qualifications desired by the firm. Placement services help organizations utilize their recruiters efficiently. Qualified candidates are identified, interviews are scheduled, and suitable rooms are provided for interviews.

The company recruiter plays a vital role in attracting applicants. The interviewee often perceives the recruiter's actions as a reflection of the character of the firm. If the recruiter is dull, the interviewee may think the company dull; if the recruiter is apathetic, discourteous, or vulgar, the interviewee may well attribute all these negative characteristics to the firm. Recruiters must always be aware of the image they present at the screening interview because it makes a lasting impression.

Recruiters determine which individuals possess the best qualifications and therefore should be encouraged in their interest in the firm. In making this determination, the recruiter becomes involved with the interviewee in two-way communication about the company, its products, its general organizational structure, its policies, its compensation and benefits program, and the position to be filled. The recruiter will also ask the prospect numerous questions, which may range from "What position do you want to occupy five years from now?" to "How will your employment benefit our firm?" Although such questions may be difficult to answer, the recruiter expects the prospect to respond in some logical manner. Other questions may be more predictable, such as those relating to grades, extracurricular activities, employment while attending school, and hobbies.

Considering the importance of the occasion, the interview is often short—about thirty minutes on average. Recruiters may spend over half this time discussing the student's high school and college education. Information sought and topics that may reveal this information are as follows:[18]

Information Sought	**Topics**
Intelligence and aptitudes	Grades
	Amount of effort to achieve grades
	College board scores
Motivation	Effort spent on academic work
Judgment and maturity	Decisions involving choice of college and major field
Analytical power	Reasons for subject preferences
Leadership and ability to get along with people	Participation in extracurricular activities

An applicant should prepare for the recruitment interview. In order to make a good impression, the prospect must do some homework on the company. The school's placement service often has literature that generally describes the organization and its operations. In addition, library research may yield information about the company's sales volume, number of employees, products, and so on. Prospects armed with facts such as these can confidently engage the recruiter in conversation and ask relevant questions. Other things being equal, an informed prospect has a competitive advantage.

Numerous college placement offices have installed the visual equivalent of a jukebox to handle recruiting messages from companies. The proliferation of videodisk equipment allows organizations to utilize playback machines and disks at campus locations. In the near future, the high cost of travel for screening interviews may be reduced through the use of cable and satellite communications.[19]

---

[18] Richard A. Fear, *The Evaluation Interview,* 3rd ed. (New York: McGraw-Hill, 1984), pp. 74–75.

[19] Roy G. Foltz, "Recruiting Communications," *Personnel Administrator,* 26 (February 1981), p. 14.

Special Events

Holding **special events** is a recruiting method that involves an effort on the part of a single employer, or group of employers, to attract a large number of applicants for interviews. Job fairs, for example, are designed to bring together applicants and representatives of various companies. One convention held exclusively for women attracted 90 firms and about 4,000 prospects from 16 states. The president of the sponsoring organization stated, "Employers want good women but often don't know how to get them. Women want good jobs and don't know how to go about it."[20] From an employer's viewpoint, a primary advantage of job fairs is the opportunity to meet a large number of candidates in a short time—usually one or two days. More than a dozen commercial firms operate job fairs, but government agencies, charitable organizations, and business alliances also frequently sponsor them. Job fairs provide a recruitment method that offers the potential for a much lower cost per hire than traditional approaches.[21]

Internships

An **internship** is a special form of recruiting that involves placing a student in a temporary job with no obligation by the company to permanently hire the student or by the student to accept a permanent position with the firm following graduation. An internship typically involves a temporary job for the summer months or a part-time job during the school year. In many instances, students alternate their schedules by working full-time one semester and becoming full-time students the next. During the internship, the student gets to view business practices firsthand. At the same time, the intern contributes to the firm by performing needed tasks. Through this relationship, a student can determine whether a company would be a desirable employer. Similarly, the firm can make a sound judgment regarding the candidate's qualifications. Internships provide opportunities for students to bridge the gap from business theory to practice.

Internships have also proved useful in moving minorities into the workforce. Bob Edwards, senior vice-president for Drake Beam Morin, Inc., describes a program he helped implement for a former employer:

> The successful integration of our office workforce after the Civil Rights legislation in 1964 required innovative approaches to selection as well as placement of minorities. The business leaders in the city were not yet confident that an acceptable solution could be found to answer the critics of integration or those advocates who did not want to weaken their companies' performance by active compliance. We elected to deal with this important issue

---

[20] "Career Conventions Open Doors to Jobs," *Nation's Business* (December 1981), p. 86.

[21] Gloria Glickstein and Donald C. Z. Ramer, "The Alternative Employment Marketplace," *Personnel Administrator,* 33 (February 1988), p. 101.

by strengthening our high school internship program. Business-minded students in this program were provided full-time summer jobs in our home office prior to their senior year and were moved to part-time jobs through their final school term.

Our approach provided:

1. Summer employment to a predominantly minority population.
2. Part-time employment, without giving any employment test, to high school students that more accurately reflected the demands of an adult work environment.
3. Maximum discretion for the student, as the company required no commitment beyond the school term.
4. Maximum discretion for the company, as full-time employment could be offered to those students who performed well on the internship jobs.
5. Up-to-date information for high school teachers and administrators on industry needs and hard data to motivate student development.

In summary, we integrated our workforce with performers and minimized management reluctance to enter an unknown and, in some situations, a feared adventure with a population whose background was different from their own. Our success with this approach was evidenced by the size of our employee minority population and their presence at all levels of responsibility.

Local communities also view favorably firms that offer internships. Internships serve as an effective public relations tool that provides visibility for the company name. As one recruiting manager stated, "There should be more internships to give students hands-on exposure. Internships provide an opportunity to give a little and get back a lot, especially in terms of productivity."[22]

Executive Search Firms

Executive search firms may be used by organizations in their recruitment efforts to locate experienced professionals and top-level executives when other sources prove inadequate. **Executive search firms** are organizations that seek the most qualified executive available for a specific position and are generally retained by the companies needing specific types of individuals.

In the past ten years, the executive search industry has evolved from a basic recruitment service to a highly sophisticated profession serving a greatly expanded role. Search firms now assist organizations in determining their human resource needs, establishing compensation packages, and revising organizational structures.

---

[22] Austin Weber, "Internships Offer Something to Root For," *Data Management,* 24 (May 1986), p. 8.

Most executive search firms differ from employment agencies and job advisory consultants in that they do not work for individuals. Retainer search firms work for corporations and governmental agencies, which pay the fees. These firms normally search in strict confidence for executives to fill upper management positions.[23] For example, Korn/Ferry International, a prominent firm of this type, has thirty-one offices around the world, of which thirteen are in the United States. They concentrate on executives earning in excess of $60,000.[24] Contingency search firms, which grew out of the employment agency industry, focus on lower management positions for which confidentiality is not so important or situations in which multiple openings for a position exist. Unlike retainer search firms, these organizations are paid only when an individual is placed.[25]

An executive search firm's representatives often visit the client's offices and interview the company's management. This enables them to gain a clear understanding of the company's goals and the job qualifications required. After obtaining this information, they contact and interview potential candidates, check references, and refer the best qualified person to the client for the selection decision. The search firm's fee is generally a percentage of the individual's compensation for the first year. Expenses, as well as the fee, are paid by the client.

The key problem in executive searches is poor communication between the client and the search firm. Face-to-face meetings are highly desirable in enabling the parties to agree on the specifications for the executive position. Competent executive search firms will be successful in their searches 70 to 80 percent of the time.[26]

The relationship between a client company and a search firm should be based on mutual trust and understanding. In order to be successful, the search firm must understand in detail the nature of the client's operations, the responsibilities of the position being filled, and the client's corporate culture. Similarly, the client must understand the search process, work with the consultant, and provide continuous, honest feedback.[27]

Professional Associations

Finance, marketing, accounting, and human resource professional associations provide recruitment and placement services for their members. The Society for Human Resource Management, for example, operates a job referral service for members seeking new positions and employers with positions to fill.

---

[23] Norman E. Van Maldegiam, "Executive Pursuit," *Personnel Administrator,* 33 (September 1988), p. 95.

[24] Interview with J. Alvin Wakefield, senior vice-president and partner, Korn/Ferry International, August 9, 1982.

[25] Norman E. Van Maldegiam, "Executive Pursuit," p. 95.

[26] Thomas A. Byrnes, "Why an Executive Search Fails," *Personnel Journal,* 60 (December 1981), pp. 922–923.

[27] Robert LoPresto, "Ethical Recruiting," *Personnel Administrator,* 31 (November 1986), pp. 90–91.

Employee Referrals

Many organizations have found that their employees can assist in the recruitment process. Employees often actively solicit applications from their friends and associates. In some organizations, especially where certain skills are scarce, this approach has proven quite effective. For example, one survey found that 27.8 percent of professional hires and 57.2 percent of management hires were from employee referrals.[28]

Unsolicited Applicants

If an organization has the reputation of being a good place to work, it may be able to attract qualified prospects even without extensive recruitment efforts. Acting on their own initiative, well-qualified workers may seek out a specific company to apply for a job. Unsolicited applicants who apply because they are favorably impressed with the firm's reputation often prove to be valuable employees.

Automated Applicant Tracking Systems

The use of computers in HRM has greatly facilitated many functions. Among these is a means for automating applicant tracking systems. In an automated system, information can be drawn from a firm's database to produce fast and accurate requisitions. Next, applicant information can be accessed from the database. In seconds, the few individuals who meet specific selection criteria can be identified out of a group of many applicants. The selection procedure, discussed in the next chapter, can also be facilitated. With a few simple keystrokes, managers can get a detailed picture of each candidate's background.

An automated tracking system streamlines the recruitment process and permits managers to spend more time finding high-quality candidates. A firm gains a sophisticated means of handling all steps of the process, from generating routine correspondence to tracking requisitions and scheduling interviews. Such a system provides detailed documentation of hiring practices and is a tremendous help in meeting EEO guidelines.[29]

Résumé Databases

Résumé database services, which are operated by several independent networks, obtain detailed information on job seekers' professional and educational backgrounds. These data are then fed into a central database, which is accessed by corporate clients using their own terminals. When an

---

[28] Margaret Magnus, "Is Your Recruitment All It Can Be?" p. 55.

[29] Peg Anthony, "Track Applicants, Track Costs," *Personnel Journal,* 69 (April 1990), pp. 75–81.

individual's background matches an open position, the client may obtain a copy of the potential employee's résumé to review. The use of computer technology greatly facilitates the process of matching candidates with positions and dramatically reduces paperwork costs.[30]

■ TAILORING RECRUITMENT METHODS TO SOURCES

Because each organization is unique in many ways, the types and qualifications of workers needed to fill positions vary greatly. Thus successful recruitment must be tailored to the needs of each firm. In addition, recruitment sources and methods often vary according to the type of position being filled.

Figure 6-5 shows a matrix that depicts methods and sources of recruitment for a data processing manager (see page 196). A human resource professional must first identify the source (where prospective employees are) before choosing the methods (how to get them). Suppose, for example, that a large firm has an immediate need for an accounting manager with a minimum of five years' experience. Most likely, such an individual is employed by another firm, very possibly a competitor, or is self-employed. The recruiter must then choose the method (or methods) of recruitment that offers the best opportunity for attracting qualified candidates. Perhaps the job can be advertised in the classified section of *The Wall Street Journal, National Employment Weekly,* or *The CPA Journal.* Or an executive search firm may be used to locate a qualified person. In addition, the recruiter may attend meetings of professional accounting associations. In all likelihood, other methods would be of little or no value in this case.

Suppose now, for example, that a firm needs twenty entry-level machine operators, whom the firm is willing to train. High schools and vocational schools would probably be good recruitment sources. Methods of recruitment might include newspaper advertisements, public employment agencies, sending recruiters to vocational schools, and employee referrals.

The specific recruitment methods used will depend on external environmental factors, including market supply and job requirements. Each organization should maintain employment records and conduct its own research in order to determine which recruitment sources and methods are most appropriate under various circumstances.

■ RECRUITMENT UNDER THE LAW

In spite of equal opportunity laws, some human resource practices that have an unequal impact on women and minorities are deeply embedded in some organizations. Some traditional employment systems, such as

---

[30] Gloria Glickstein and Donald C. Z. Ramer, "The Alternative Employment Marketplace," p. 102.

SOURCES	METHODS OF RECRUITING										
	Advertising	Private employment agencies	Public employment agencies	Recruiters	Special events	Internships	Executive search firms	Unsolicited applications	Professional associations	Employee referrals	Unsolicited applicants
High schools											
Vocational schools											
Community colleges											
Colleges and universities											
Competitors and other firms	X	X					X		X		
Unemployed											
Self-employed											

FIGURE 6-5 | Methods and Sources of Recruitment for a Data Processing Manager

employee referrals, perpetuate the effects of past discrimination even after the original practices have been discontinued. The result, though not necessarily conscious, is a continuation of what has been labeled systemic discrimination.[31] Courts have found that some employment practices, regardless of intent, have resulted in discrimination against women and minorities. In addition, gender stereotypes may contribute to beliefs that members of one sex either do not prefer, or perform less well in, certain jobs compared to members of the other sex. To offset the effects of past discrimination in employment, firms may need to use new recruitment approaches.

As we discussed in Chapter 3, equal employment opportunity, as provided by federal legislation, prohibits considering such characteristics as race, gender, and disabilities in employment decisions. In other words,

---

[31] Gary N. Powell, "The Effects of Sex and Gender on Recruitment," *Academy of Management Review,* 12 (October 1987), p. 732.

HRM In Action

Mark Smith and Debra Coffee, two executives from competing firms, met at their annual product conference. They were discussing the effect of civil rights legislation on their firms. Mark said, "I don't think we will have any difficulty at our company. I'm told that our workforce is composed of 35 percent minorities."

"Sounds good," Debra replied, "How many of your minorities fill middle-management positions?" After thinking a moment, Mark said, "I believe we have one over in maintenance."

As a human resource professional, how would you respond?

these attributes are not to be a factor when decisions such as firing, promoting, and discharging employees are made. On the other hand, affirmative action may be mandated by executive order or court order. In this case, special provisions must be made to recruit, train, retain, and promote members of protected groups, such as women and blacks. Affirmative action does require that such factors as race and gender be considered in employment decisions.[32]

Some groups are opposed to the concept of affirmative action and may even charge that it results in so-called reverse discrimination. There is another side to the story, however. Because of past unequal opportunity, women and minorities may not respond to traditional recruitment methods. These groups may be omitted altogether from the typical recruitment process unless specific action is taken to attract them. If this action is not taken, there is a question as to whether women and minorities will ever be adequately represented in the workforce. Therefore, any organization that adopts affirmative action (either voluntarily or by mandate) must implement recruitment and other employment programs that give special treatment to women and minorities. These programs must be carefully monitored to assure their effectiveness.

Analysis of Recruitment Procedures

To ensure that its recruitment program is nondiscriminatory, a firm must analyze its recruitment procedures. For example, it might be wise to stop using employee referral or unsolicited applicants as primary recruitment

---

[32] Gerard P. Panaro, *Employment Law Manual* (Boston: Warren, Gorham & Lamont, 1990), p. 5-2–5-5.

methods. These actions may perpetuate the composition of the organization's workforce. In cases where minorities and women are not well represented at all levels, the courts have ruled that reliance on these particular practices is discriminatory.

In identifying sources of continuing discrimination, it is helpful to develop a record of applicant flow. In fact, this record may be mandatory if the firm has been found guilty of discrimination or operates under an affirmative action program. An applicant flow record includes personal and job-related data concerning each applicant. It indicates whether a job offer was extended and, if no such offer was made, an explanation of the decision. Such records enable the organization to analyze its recruitment and selection practices and take corrective action when necessary.

Utilization of Minorities, Women, and Handicapped Individuals

Recruiters should be trained in the use of objective, job-related standards because they occupy a unique position in terms of encouraging or discouraging minorities, women, and the handicapped to apply for jobs. Qualified members of these groups may be utilized effectively in key recruitment activities, such as visiting schools and colleges and participating in career days. They also are in an excellent position to provide valuable input for recruitment planning and can effectively serve as referral sources. Pictures of minority, female, and handicapped employees in help-wanted advertisements and company brochures give credibility to the message, "We are an equal opportunity employer."

Advertising

With few exceptions, jobs must be open to all individuals. Therefore, gender-segregated advertisements, for example, should not be used unless gender is a bona fide occupational qualification. The BFOQ exception provided in Title VII of the Civil Rights Act requires that qualifications be job related. This definition is narrowly interpreted by EEOC and the courts. The burden of proof is on the employer to establish that the requirements are essential for successful performance of the job. Other advertising practices designed to provide equal opportunity include:

1. Ensuring that the content of advertisements does not indicate preference for any race, gender, or age or that these factors are a qualification for the job.
2. Utilizing media that are directed toward minorities, such as appropriate radio stations.
3. Emphasizing the intent to recruit without regard to race, gender, or handicapped status by including the phrase "Equal Opportunity Employer, M/F/H" in job ads (see Figure 6-6).

CORPORATE CONTROLLER

Sureway Development Company offers an outstanding opportunity for an individual with a degree in accounting and a minimum of 4 years experience. Background should include financial analysis and budgeting. Real estate development experience preferred and/or CPA. Please contact Mary Smith 555/255-1656.

Equal Opportunity Employer M/F/H

FIGURE 6-6 | A Newspaper Ad Stressing Equal Employment Opportunity for Men, Women, and Handicapped Individuals

Employment Agencies

An organization should emphasize its nondiscriminatory recruitment practices when utilizing employment agencies. Even when private agencies, which are also covered under Title VII, are retained, jobs at all levels should be listed with the state employment service. These agencies can provide valuable assistance to organizations seeking to fulfill affirmative action goals. In addition, agencies and consultant firms that specialize in minority and women applicants should be contacted.

Other Suggested Affirmative Recruitment Approaches

Personal contact should be made with counselors and administrators at high schools, vocational schools, and colleges with large minority and/or female enrollments. Counselors and administrators should be made aware that the organization is actively seeking minorities and women for jobs that they have not traditionally held. Also, they should be familiar with the types of jobs available and the training and education needed to perform these jobs. The possibilities for developing internships and summer employment for minorities and women should be carefully investigated. Firms should develop contact with minority, women's, and other community organizations. These organizations include National Association for the Advancement of Colored People, League of United Latin American Citizens, National Urban League, American Association of University Women, Federation of Business and Professional Women's Talent Bank, National Council of Negro Women, and the Veterans Administration. The EEOC's regional offices will assist employers in locating appropriate local agencies.

SUMMARY

Recruitment is the process of attracting individuals on a timely basis, in sufficient numbers and with appropriate qualifications, and encouraging them to apply for jobs with an organization. When human resource planning indicates a need for employees, a firm should first evaluate alternatives to hiring additional workers. Common alternatives to recruitment include overtime, subcontracting, temporary employees, and employee leasing.

When these other alternatives won't meet the demand, the recruitment process starts. Frequently, recruitment begins when a manager initiates an employee requisition. It specifies job title, department, the date the employee is needed for work, and other details. With this information, the human resource manager can refer to the appropriate job description to determine the qualifications needed by the person to be recruited.

The next step is to determine whether qualified employees are available within the firm (the internal source) or must be recruited externally from sources such as colleges, universities, and other organizations. Because of the high cost of recruiting, organizations must be assured that they are utilizing the most productive recruitment sources and methods. Recruitment sources are places where qualified individuals can be found. Recruitment methods are the specific means by which potential employees are attracted to the firm. After identifying the sources of potential employees, the human resource manager chooses the appropriate methods for internal and/or external recruitment.

External factors can significantly affect a firm's recruitment efforts. Of particular importance is the demand for, and supply of, specific skills in the labor market. If demand for a particular skill is high relative to supply, an extraordinary recruitment effort may be required. When the unemployment rate in the firm's labor market is high, its recruitment process may be simplified. Legal considerations and the firm's corporate image also play significant roles in recruitment practices in the United States.

An organization's promotion policy can also have a significant impact on recruitment. Basically, an organization can utilize two promotion approaches: a policy of promotion from within or a policy of filling positions from outside the organization. Depending on the circumstances, each approach may have merit.

Tools used for internal recruitment include management and skills inventories and job posting and bidding procedures. Management and skills inventories indicate whether current employees possess the qualifications needed for promotion. Job posting informs employees of job openings. Job bidding permits employees who believe that they possess the required qualifications to apply for a posted job.

Candidates for jobs may be attracted from various outside sources. Firms often depend heavily on high schools and vocational schools when recruiting clerical and other entry-level operative employees. Many community colleges are sensitive to specific employment needs in local labor markets and graduate highly sought-after students. Colleges and universities represent a major source of recruitment for many organizations. Competitors and other firms in the same industry or geographic area may be the most important source of recruits for positions in which recent experience is highly desired. The unemployed and the self-employed may also be good sources of recruits.

Recruitment methods such as advertising, employment agencies, and employee referrals may be effective in attracting individuals with virtually every type of skill. Recruiters, special events, and internships are used primarily to attract college and university students. Also, executive search firms and professional organizations are particularly useful in the recruitment of managerial and professional employees.

In spite of equal opportunity laws, some human resource practices that have an unequal impact on women and minorities are deeply embedded in some organizations. Some traditional recruitment methods, such as employee referrals, perpetuate the effects of past discrimination even after the original practices have been discontinued. The result is a continuation of what has been labeled systemic discrimination.

To ensure that its recruitment program is nondiscriminatory, a firm must analyze its recruitment procedures. Continuing to use employee referral or unsolicited applicants as primary recruitment methods may perpetuate the present composition of the firm's workforce. For situations in which minorities and women are not well represented at all levels, the courts have ruled that reliance on these particular practices is discriminatory.

Questions for Review

1. Describe the basic components of the recruitment process.
2. What are some actions that can be taken prior to engaging in recruitment?
3. List and discuss the various external and internal factors that may affect recruitment.
4. What is meant by the term *internal recruitment?* Describe the advantages and disadvantages of internal recruitment.
5. Describe the methods commonly used in internal recruitment. Briefly define each.
6. Discuss the reasons for an external recruitment program.
7. Distinguish between sources and methods of external recruitment. Identify various sources and methods of external recruitment.
8. Explain the difference between an executive search firm and an employment agency.
9. How can a firm improve its recruiting efforts under the law?

Terms for Review

Recruitment	Job bidding
Employee requisition	Advertising
Recruitment sources	Employment agency
Recruitment methods	Special events
Promotion from within	Internship
Job posting	Executive search firms

INCIDENT 1 ▪ Right Idea, Wrong Song ▪

Robert Key was human resource manager at Epler Manufacturing Company in Greenfield, Wisconsin. He was considering the need to recruit qualified blacks for Epler when Betty Alexander walked into his office. "Got a minute?" asked Betty. "I need to talk to you about the recruiting trip to Michigan State next week." "Sure," Robert replied, "but first I need your advice about something. How can we get more blacks to apply for work here? We're running ads on WBEZ-TV along with the classified ads in the *Tribune*. I think you and John have made recruiting trips to every community college within 200 miles. We've encouraged employee referral, too, and I still think that's our most reliable source of new workers. But we just aren't getting any black applicants."

From the president on down, the management at Epler claimed commitment to equal employment opportunity. According to Robert, the commitment went much deeper than posting the usual placards and filing an "affirmative action program" with the federal government. Still, the percentage of black employees at Epler remained at only 5 percent, while the surrounding community was 11 percent black. Epler paid competitive wages and had a good training program.

One need was for machine operator trainees. The machines were not difficult to operate, and there was no educational requirement for the job. There were also several clerical and management trainee positions open.

Questions

1. Evaluate the current recruitment effort. How could Robert better the firm's goal of equal employment?

INCIDENT 2   ▪   Time to Do Something?   ▪

Five years ago when Bobby Bret joined Crystal Productions as a junior accountant, he felt that he was on his way up. He had just graduated with a B+ average from college, where he was well liked by his peers and the faculty and had been an officer in several student organizations. Bobby had shown a natural ability to get along with people as well as to get things done. He remembered what Roger Friedman, the controller at Crystal, had told him when he was hired, "I think you will do well here, Bobby. You've come highly recommended. You are the kind of guy that can expect to move right on up the ladder."

Bobby felt that he had done a good job at Crystal, and everybody seemed to like him. In addition, his performance appraisals had been excellent. However, after five years he was still a junior accountant. He had applied for two senior accountant positions that had come open, but they were both filled by people hired from outside the firm. When the accounting supervisor's job came open two years ago, Bobby had not applied. He was surprised when his new boss turned out to be a hotshot graduate of State University, whose only experience was three years with a "Big Eight"

accounting firm. Bobby had hoped that Ron Greene, a senior accountant he particularly respected, would get the job.

On the fifth anniversary of his employment at Crystal, Bobby decided it was time to do something. He made an appointment with the controller. At that meeting Bobby explained to Mr. Friedman that he had worked hard to obtain a promotion and shared his frustration about having been in the same job for so long. "Well," said Mr. Friedman, "you don't think that you were all that much better qualified than the people that we have hired, do you?" "No," said Bobby, "but, I think I could have handled the senior accountant job. Of course, the people you have hired are doing a great job too." The controller responded, "We just look at the qualifications of all the applicants for each job and, considering everything, try to make a reasonable decision."

Questions

1. Explain the impact of a promotion-from-within policy on outside recruitment.
2. Do you believe that Bobby has a legitimate complaint? Explain.

DEVELOPING HRM SKILLS

Human resource managers have the responsibility for preparing job descriptions. From these job descriptions, profiles of the types of individuals needed to fill various positions in the firm can be developed and recruitment efforts can be designed. The human resource manager must determine where the best applicants are located (recruitment sources) and how to entice them to join the organization (recruitment methods). This exercise is designed to provide an understanding of the relationship between recruitment sources and methods.

Each participant will identify both recruitment sources and methods for the job description. The job description is for a **Human Resource Assistant,** who reports to the Manager of Employee Relations and Recruitment, in the human resource department. **Accountability Objective** for the position is fairly standard. This position is accountable for performing employment activities for the off-site claims division in order to staff the organization with proficient, suitable personnel, and provide effective administration of human resource policies and procedures. The successful applicant will have a four-year college degree, preferably in business administration, but needs little or no experience because the candidate selected for the position will be placed in a six-month training program before assuming these duties and functions. Span of control is limited to two

people, one clerk and one secretary. Primary duties of the incumbent include recruitment and interviewing of applicants for employment, and performing the basic employment function, which includes screening, recruiting, and interviewing candidates (clerical, technical, and professional), devising recruiting ads, performing reference checks, and administering standard skills tests where applicable.

The incumbent will function independently as a counseling source, and is expected to create an atmosphere of impartiality and equity, and will probably choose the appropriate method of communicating information to location personnel. The incumbent may also assess training needs for on-site personnel. In order to make personnel recommendations, the incumbent must be capable of maintaining an updated knowledge of all areas of human resources, a knowledge base of the external environment, and an awareness of the internal climate. Knowledge of the employment marketplace, as well as hiring practices and legal considerations, is required. Excellent interpersonal skills and the ability to establish rapport are also required.

Participants will attempt to determine the most appropriate recruitment sources and methods for the job description that will be given to them. Your instructor will provide the participants with additional information necessary to complete the exercise.

REFERENCES

Anthony, Peg. "Track Applicants, Track Costs." *Personnel Journal,* 69 (April 1990), pp. 75–81.

Avery, Susan. "Shorthanded? Hire a Temp." *Purchasing,* 108 (March 22, 1990), pp. 70–71, 75–76.

Benson, Tracy E. "Ready, Aim, Hire." *Industry Week,* 24 (February 4, 1991), p. 16.

Drucker, Peter F. "Getting Things Done." *Harvard Business Review,* 4 (July–August 1985), pp. 22–26.

Feuer, Dale. "Adverse Impact: Can Your Hiring System Pass the Test?" *Training,* 22 (March 1985), pp. 111–112.

Fitz-enz, Jac. "Getting—and Keeping—Good Employees." *Personnel,* 67 (August 1990), pp. 25–28.

Greenlaw, Paul S. "Affirmative Action or Reverse Discrimination." *Personnel Journal,* 61 (September 1985), p. 81.

Halcrow, Allan. "Scaling the Recruitment Wall." *Personnel Journal,* 70 (April 1991), pp. 69–72.

Hallett, Jeffrey J. "Why Does Recruitment Cost So Much?" *Personnel Administrator,* 31 (December 1986), pp. 22–24.

Herren, Laura M. "The New Game of HR: Playing to Win." *Personnel,* 66 (June 1989), pp. 19–22.

Keaton, Paul N., and Janine Anderson. "Leasing Offers Benefits to Both Sides." *HRMagazine,* 35 (July 1990), pp. 53, 55, 56, 58.

Koch, Jennifer. "Apple Ads Target Intellect." *Personnel Journal,* 69 (March 1990), pp. 107–114.

Koch, Jennifer. "Recruitment Ads with Flair." *Personnel Journal,* 68 (October 1989), pp. 46–55.

Layne, Stevan P. "A Closer Look at Hiring and Firing." *Security Management,* 33 (June 1989), pp. 49–52.

Leibowitz, Zandy B., Nancy K. Schlossberg, and Jane E. Shore. "Stopping the Revolving Door." *Training and Development Journal,* 45 (February 1991), pp. 43–50.

LoPresto, Robert. "Ethical Recruiting." *Personnel Administrator,* 31 (November 1986), p. 90–92.

Magnus, Margaret. "Is Your Recruitment All It Can Be?" *Personnel Journal,* 66 (February 1987), pp. 54–63.

Magnus, Margaret. "Recruitment Advantages." *Personnel Journal,* 65 (August 1986), pp. 58–79.

May, Bess Ritter. "Help Concerning Temporary Help." *Supervision,* 50 (September 1989), pp. 6–8.

Mondy, R. Wayne, Robert M. Noe, and Robert E. Edwards. "What the Staffing Function Entails." *Personnel,* 63 (April 1986), pp. 55–58.

Phillips, Douglas J. "The Price Tag on Turnover." *Personnel Journal,* 69 (December 1990), pp. 58–61.

Powell, Gary N. "The Effects of Sex and Gender on Recruitment." *Academy of Management Review,* 12 (October 1987), pp. 731–743.

Ross, John. "Effective Ways to Hire Contingent Personnel." *HRMagazine,* 36 (February 1991), pp. 52–54.

Schenkel-Savitt, Susan, and Steven P. Seltzer. "Recruitment as a Successful Means of Affirmative Action." *Employee Relations Law Journal,* 13 (Winter 1987), pp. 165–179.

Springer, Felix J., and Albert Zakarian. "Managing with Legal Employment Background Checks." *Pension World,* 26 (June 1990), p. 15.

Webb, Susan L. "Sexual Harassment: Court Costs Rise for Persistent Problem." *Management Review* (December 1984), pp. 25–28.

CHAPTER **7**   SELECTION

CHAPTER OBJECTIVES

1. Explain how environmental factors affect the selection process.
2. Describe the importance of the preliminary interview and the application for employment in the selection process.
3. State the role of tests and the importance of interviewing in the selection process.
4. State why reference checks and background investigations are conducted, describe the reasons for preemployment physical examinations, and explain the considerations related to acceptance or rejection of job applicants.
5. Explain selection and utility analysis, and describe human resource planning, recruitment, and selection in the multinational environment.

Bill Jenkins is the printing shop owner/manager of Quality Printing Company. Because of an increase in business, shop employees have been working overtime for almost a month. Last week, Bill put an ad in the newspaper to hire a printer. Three people applied for the job. Bill considered only one of them, Mark Ketchell, to be qualified. Bill called Mark's previous employer in Detroit, who responded, "Mark is a diligent, hardworking person. He is as honest as the day is long. He knows his trade, too." Bill also found that Mark had left Detroit after he was divorced a few months ago and that his work had deteriorated slightly prior to the divorce. The next day, Bill asked Mark to operate one of the printing presses. Mark did so competently, and Bill immediately decided to hire him.

Mary Howard is the shipping supervisor for McCarty-Holman Warehouse, a major food distributor. One of Mary's truck drivers just quit. She spoke to the human resource manager, Tom Sullivan, who said that he would begin the search right away. The next day an advertisement appeared in the local paper for the position. Tom considered three of the fifteen applicants to be qualified and called them in for an initial interview. The next morning Tom called Mary and said, "I have three drivers who look like they can do the job. When do you want me to set up an interview for you with them? I guess you'll want to give them a driving test at that time." Mary interviewed the three drivers and gave them each a driving test and then called Tom to tell him her choice. The next day the new driver reported to Mary for work.

These incidents provide only a brief look at the all-important selection process. In the first instance, Bill Jenkins, as owner/manager of a small printing shop, handled the entire selection process himself. In the second instance, Tom, the human resource manager, was heavily involved in the selection process, but Mary, the shipping supervisor, made the actual decision. However, knowledge of the selection process was important in both situations.

We begin the chapter with a discussion of the selection process and the environmental factors that affect it. Then, we describe the preliminary interview and review of the application for employment. Next, we cover administration of selection tests, validity studies, cutoff scores, and psychological testing. In the ensuing sections, we present the employment interview, methods of interviewing, the interviewer, interview planning, and the interview process. We follow those topics with a discussion of reference checks, background investigation, and polygraph tests. We then describe factors related to the selection decision, physical examination, and acceptance or rejection of job applicants. We devote the remainder of the chapter to selection and utility analysis and human resource planning, recruitment, and selection in the multinational environment.

■ THE SELECTION PROCESS

Whereas recruitment encourages individuals to seek employment with a firm, the purpose of the selection process is to identify and employ the best qualified individuals for specific positions. **Selection** is the process of choosing from a group of applicants the individual best suited for a particular position. As you might expect, a firm's recruitment efforts have a significant impact on the efficiency of the selection process. The organization may be forced to employ marginally acceptable workers if recruitment attracts only a few qualified applicants.

Employee selection is perhaps the most significant task that managers perform. As Peter Drucker has stated, "No other decisions are so long lasting in their consequences or so difficult to unmake. And yet, by and large, executives make poor promotion and staffing decisions. By all accounts, their batting average is no better than .333: At most, one-third of such decisions turn out right; one-third are minimally effective, and one-third are outright failures."[1] However, if mediocre or poor performers are hired, a firm cannot be successful long even if it has perfect plans, a sound organizational structure, and finely tuned control systems. These organizational factors are not self-actuating. Competent people must be available to ensure that organizational goals are attained.

One indicator of the importance of selection decisions is that the entire process has been valued as high as $500,000 per hire. While this figure may appear to be excessive, it is important to consider the productivity difference between high and low performers. This differential has been estimated

---

[1] Peter F. Drucker, "Getting Things Done: How to Make People Decisions," *Harvard Business Review,* 63, no. 4, (July–August 1985), p. 22.

to be as high as 3 to 1.[2] A firm that selects qualified employees can reap substantial benefits, which may be repeated every year the employee is on the payroll.

The importance of obtaining qualified people for key positions has caused corporate America to adopt a hiring, or sign-on, bonus—a practice previously limited to sports and movie stars. One study indicated that 42 percent of 1,422 human resource professionals surveyed granted sign-on bonuses to candidates to assure that they accepted the job offer. This approach is not currently common. However, it is becoming increasingly popular in fields in which there is a critical shortage of qualified people.[3]

The selection process affects, and is also affected by, the other human resource functions. For instance, if the selection process only provides the firm with marginally qualified workers, the organization may have to develop an extensive training program. If the compensation package is inferior to those provided by the firm's competition, attracting the best qualified applicants may be difficult or impossible.

The goal of the selection process is to properly match people with jobs. If individuals are overqualified, underqualified, or for any reason do not "fit" either the job or organization, they will probably leave the firm. While some turnover may be positive for an organization, it can become extremely expensive. A high turnover rate makes it almost impossible to achieve superior performance. For example, product research and development is delayed, manufacturing loses efficiency, and marketing penetration is slowed. It is these hidden consequences of turnover, not the visible costs of recruitment, relocation, and training, that constitute the major costs. Two studies conducted almost a decade apart indicate that such expenses, although they are rarely measured, account for 80 percent or more of turnover costs.[4]

As we emphasized in Chapter 4, job analysis provides data for preparing job descriptions and specifications, which in turn are essential for making good selection decisions. However, a real problem exists when selection criteria are different from what is actually required by the job.[5] Therefore, human resource managers must continually update job descriptions and specifications to ensure that only properly qualified employees are recruited.

Figure 7-1 on page 210 shows the selection process in general. It typically begins with the preliminary interview, after which obviously unqualified candidates are rejected. Next, applicants complete the firm's application for employment, and then they progress through a series of selection tests, the employment interview, and reference and background checks.

---

[2] Vandra L. Huber, Gregory B. Northcraft, and Margaret A. Neale, "Effects of Decision Strategy and Number of Openings on Employment Selection Decisions," *Organizational Behavior and Human Decisions Processes,* 45 (April 1990), p. 276.

[3] Milton N. Dossin and Nancie L. Merritt, "Sign-On Bonuses Score for Recruiters," *HR-Magazine,* 35 (March 1990), p. 42.

[4] J. Douglas Phillips, "The Price Tag on Turnover," *Personnel Journal,* 69 (December 1990), pp. 58–61.

[5] Joseph D. Levesque, "Selecting and Managing Competent Managers," *Personnel Administrator,* 30 (March 1985), p. 64.

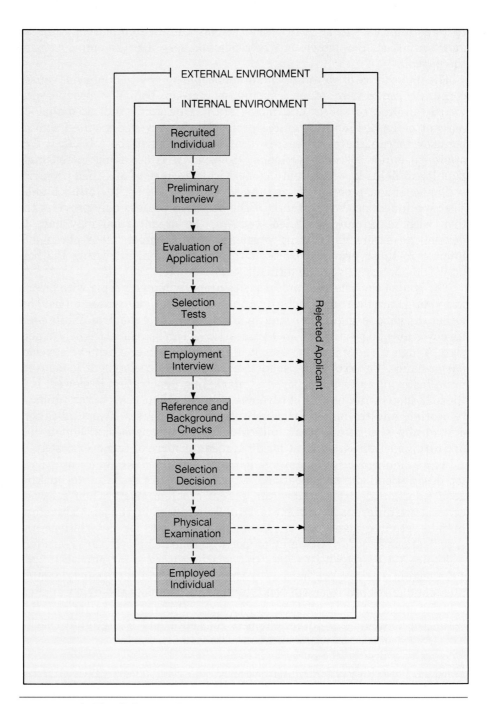

FIGURE 7-1 | The Selection Process

The successful applicant receives a company physical examination. The individual is employed if the physical examination is satisfactory. Several external and internal factors have an impact on the selection process, and the manager must take them into account in making selection decisions.

■ ENVIRONMENTAL FACTORS AFFECTING THE SELECTION PROCESS

A permanent, standardized screening process could greatly simplify the selection process. However, development of such a process—even if it were possible and desirable—would not eliminate deviations to meet the unique needs of particular situations. As one human resource manager expressed it, "The only thing certain is that exceptions will be made." And exceptions are often made in accordance with the following environmental factors.

Legal Considerations

As we described in Chapter 3, legislation, executive orders, and court decisions have had a major impact on human resource management. However, merely having knowledge of the legal aspects of selection is often insufficient. All human resource managers should also be aware of which selection criteria to avoid, based on the law and court decisions. Table 7-1 identifies selection criteria that obviously should not be used because of their discriminatory potential (see pages 212–215).

Speed of Decision Making

The time available to make the selection decision can have a major effect on the selection process. Suppose, for instance, that the production manager for a manufacturing firm comes to the human resource manager's office and says, "My only quality control inspectors just had a fight and both resigned. I can't operate until those positions are filled." Speed is crucial in this instance, and two interviews, a few phone calls, and a prayer may constitute the entire selection process. On the other hand, selecting a university dean may take an entire year, with considerable attention being devoted to careful study of résumés, intensive reference checking, and hours of interviews. Regardless of whether the process is casual and hurried or more careful and deliberate, errors will be made.

Organizational Hierarchy

Different approaches to selection are generally used for filling positions at different levels in the organization. For instance, consider the variations in hiring a top-level executive and in hiring a person to fill a clerical position. Extensive background checks and interviewing would be conducted to

TABLE 7-1 | Hiring Criteria and Standards to Avoid

Gender

Hiring persons based on whether they are men or women is unlawful. The only exception is a case in which gender is a bona fide occupational qualification (BFOQ). However, the use of BFOQs has been narrowly interpreted by EEOC and the courts. The specification of a man versus a woman must be made in view of whether gender is absolutely job related. For example, if the job in question is for an attendant for a women's restroom, gender can legitimately be specified.

Presuming that a particular job is physically too demanding for a woman to perform is also ill-advised. Instead, women applicants should be given the opportunity to prove that they can perform the job. For example, if a job requires frequent lifting of a fifty-pound object, an employer may require applicants to demonstrate that they—both men and women—can regularly lift the required weight.

National Origin

Information regarding an applicant's national origin should not be sought. In addition, other data that might be used to determine national origin should not be requested. Questions regarding an applicant's place of birth and the place of birth of parents, grandparents, or spouse fall into this category.

Marital Status

This is a difficult selection standard to defend and should be avoided. Although asking marital status is not by itself illegal under federal law, the standard has often been applied differently to women than to men.

Disabilities

The passage of the Americans with Disabilities Act (ADA) will cause large and small firms to reevaluate their hiring practices as well as their physical workplaces. Virtually all employers must provide equal employment opportunities to disabled persons who are qualified. This may include making reasonable accommodations for them.

Religion

Discrimination based on religious beliefs is generally unlawful. The only exception is when the employer is a religious corporation, association, educational institution, or society. Questions regarding the applicant's religious denomination, religious affiliation, church, parish, or religious holidays observed are generally ill-advised. Another form of discrimination occurs when individuals' religious beliefs cause them to be away from work before sundown, on Saturdays, or at other times. When this occurs, these practices should be reasonably accommodated unless undue hardships are imposed on the employer.

Race

Race is very rarely a legal employment requirement. Therefore selection decisions should be made without regard to this factor.

Age

Questions asked about an applicant's age or date of birth may be ill-advised in light of the Age Discrimination in Employment Act as amended. However, a firm may ask for age information to comply with the child labor law. For example, the question could be asked, "Are you under the age of 18?" With this exception, an applicant should not be asked his or her age or date of birth. Also, questions about the ages of children, if any, could be potentially discriminatory because a close approximation of the applicant's age often is obtained through knowledge of the ages of the children.

Pregnancy

Discrimination in employment based on pregnancy, childbirth, or complications arising from either is illegal. Questions regarding a woman's family and childbearing plans should not be asked. Similarly, questions relating to family plans, birth control techniques, and the like may be viewed as discriminatory because they are not also asked of men.

Physical Requirements

Specifications that set a minimum height or weight should be used only when these characteristics are necessary for performing a particular job. Hispanics, Asians, and Pacific Islanders are generally shorter and smaller than others, and women are generally smaller than men. Therefore nonjob-related physical requirements would tend to reject a disproportionate number of individuals in certain groups.

Standards relating to the ability to lift a certain amount of weight also should not be used unless they are clearly job related. At times, it may be feasible for the employer to redesign the job to overcome a weight-lifting requirement.

Credit Record

An individual's poor credit rating has been found to be an improper standard for rejecting applicants for cases in which this has a disproportionate negative effect on women and minorities. Members of certain groups are more likely to have credit problems than others. Therefore the standard should not be used unless the employer has a business necessity for obtaining the information. Inquiries about charge accounts, credit references, and home or car ownership should not be made unless they are job related.

Background of Spouse

Basing employment decisions on the background of a spouse is very difficult, if not impossible, to support. Some employers believe that they need to know what the spouse does for a living in making selection decisions. Merely asking this type of question may be interpreted as sex discrimination. In certain instances, women have been turned down for employment because the employer believed that a woman with a working husband would be denying an unemployed man the opportunity for a job.

TABLE 7-1 | *Continued*

Care of Children
Employers have, at times, denied employment to women who have nonschool-age children. If this standard is imposed on women and not on men, it amounts to sex discrimination. While it may be true that some women find it difficult to work and take care of children at the same time, the same can be said for men. A person should be evaluated on his or her ability to perform a particular job. The U.S. Supreme Court has clearly decided this issue.
Arrest Record
In our system of justice, an arrest is not an indication of guilt. Standards related to arrest records have been found to constitute race or national origin discrimination because the arrest rate for minority group members tends to be higher than that for nonminorities. Therefore this selection criterion can rarely be used as a justification for rejecting applicants from certain minority groups.
Conviction Record
Unlike an arrest record, a conviction record is an indication of guilt. Even though some minorities have a greater conviction rate than nonminorities, this standard may be used if it is job related. It would be quite acceptable to reject a job applicant who had been convicted of robbery if the job required handling of large sums of money. On the other hand, it would be difficult to justify rejecting an applicant for a laborer job if that individual had only been convicted for failure to pay alimony.
Work Experience Requirements
Experience requirements should be reviewed to ensure that they are actually job related. Many women and minorities have not been in the labor force long enough to gain extensive work experience. Requiring that a person have, for example, ten years' work experience may tend to eliminate a large portion of women and minorities and would be discriminatory if this experience is not actually needed to perform the job.

verify the character and capabilities of the applicant for a high-level position. However, an applicant for a clerical position would most likely take only a word processing test and perhaps have a short employment interview.

Applicant Pool

The number of applicants for a particular job can also affect the selection process. The process can be truly selective only if there are several qualified applicants for a particular position. However, only a few applicants with

Garnishment Record

As with arrest and conviction records, members of certain minority groups have had their wages garnished more than nonminorities. Therefore, if knowledge of this information cannot be shown to be job related, it should not be used as an employment standard.

Dress and Appearance

Employers have the right to establish standards relating to dress and appearance. This is especially true in situations in which the applicant is dealing directly with the public. Requiring hair to be a certain length has been found by the courts to be nondiscriminatory except when standards have varied by gender. Care should be taken when rejecting applicants strictly on their appearance. A person's appearance may be related to a special dress and style typical of a certain group.

Education Requirements

Nonjob-related educational standards should not be used because of their potential for discrimination. For example, the ability to speak English should be required only if it is job related. A disproportionate number of certain minorities have not graduated from high school or college. Stating that a job requires a college degree when it could be accomplished effectively by a high school graduate can potentially be discriminatory.

Any educational standard may be difficult to defend. Therefore it may be advisable to focus on the knowledge, skills, and abilities needed to perform the job.

Relatives Working for the Company (Anti-nepotism Rule)

Standards established about an applicant's relatives working for the company may be discriminatory if they result in reducing employment opportunities for women and members of minorities. Some firms have rules that prohibit hiring the spouse of a current employee. On the surface, this rule appears to affect men and women similarly. In reality, because men have normally been in the labor force longer, the rule reduces employment opportunities much more for women. Therefore anti-nepotism rules should be avoided unless they can be shown to be a business necessity.

highly demanded skills may be available. The selection process then becomes a matter of choosing whoever is available. Expansion and contraction of the labor market also exert considerable influence on availability and thus the selection process.

The number of people hired for a particular job compared to the individuals in the applicant pool is often expressed as a **selection ratio,** or

$$\text{Selection ratio} = \frac{\text{Number of persons hired to fill a particular job}}{\text{Number of available applicants}}$$

A selection ratio of 1.00 indicates that there is one applicant for each position. Having an effective selection process is difficult if this situation exists. People who might otherwise be rejected are often hired. The lower the ratio falls below 1.00, the more alternatives the manager has in making a selection decision. For example, a selection ratio of 0.10 indicates that there are ten applicants for each position.

Type of Organization

The sector of the economy in which individuals are to be employed—private, governmental, or not-for-profit—can also affect the selection process. A business in the private sector is heavily profit oriented. Prospective employees are screened with regard to how they can help achieve profit goals. Consideration of the total individual, including personality factors, is involved in the selection of future employees for this sector.[6]

Government civil service systems typically identify qualified applicants through competitive examinations. Often, a manager is allowed to select only from among the top three applicants for a position. A manager in this sector frequently does not have the prerogative to interview other applicants.

Individuals being considered for positions in not-for-profit organizations (such as the Scouts, YMCA, or YWCA) confront a different situation. The salary level may not be competitive with private and governmental organizations. Therefore a person who fills one of these positions must not only be qualified but also dedicated to this type of work.

Probationary Period

Many firms use a probationary period, which provides for the evaluation of an employee's ability based on performance. This may be either a substitute for, or a supplement to, the use of tests. The rationale is that if an individual can successfully perform the job during the probationary period, tests may not be needed. However, newly hired employees should be monitored to determine whether the hiring decision was a good one. Employees who voluntarily leave should have an exit interview. The results of this interview should be shared with all managers who are involved in the selection process.[7]

Even though a firm may be unionized, a new employee typically is not protected by the union-management agreement until after a certain probationary period. This period is typically from sixty to ninety days. During that time, an employee may be terminated with little or no justification. When the probationary period is over, terminating a marginal employee may prove to be quite difficult. When a firm is unionized, it becomes

---

[6] Sampo V. Paunonen, Douglas N. Jackson, and Steven M. Oberman, "Personnel Selection Decisions: Effects of Applicant Personality and the Letter of Reference," *Organizational Behavior and Human Decision Processes,* 40 (August 1987), p. 97.

[7] Alan Weiss, "Select, Don't Settle," *Training,* 24 (September 1987), p. 90.

especially important for the selection process to identify the most productive workers. Once they come under the union-management agreement, its terms must be followed in changing the status of a worker.

■ PRELIMINARY INTERVIEW

The selection process often begins with an initial screening of applicants to eliminate those who obviously do not meet the position's requirements. At this stage, the interviewer asks a few straightforward questions. For instance, a position may require a degree in petroleum engineering and considerable work experience. If an applicant has no experience and a degree in an unrelated field, any further discussion regarding this particular position will prove useless for both the firm and the applicant.

In addition to eliminating obviously unqualified job applicants quickly, a preliminary interview may produce other positive benefits for the firm. It is likely that the position for which the applicant applied is not the only one available. A skilled interviewer will know about other vacancies in the firm and may be able to steer the prospective employee to another position. A person who does not qualify for one position may be capable of performing well in another. For instance, an applicant may obviously be unqualified to fill the advertised position of senior programming analyst but be well qualified to work as a computer operator. This type of interviewing not only builds goodwill for the firm but also can maximize recruitment and selection effectiveness.

■ REVIEW OF APPLICATION FOR EMPLOYMENT

The next step in the selection process may involve having the prospective employee complete an application for employment. The employer then evaluates it to see whether there is an apparent match between the individual and the position. A well-designed and properly used application form can be a real time-saver. It can be used much more effectively than résumés to reduce dozens of applicants to a few bona fide candidates. The application, creatively constructed to reveal a candidate's true qualifications, is making a comeback as a selection tool.[8]

The specific type of information requested on an application for employment may vary from firm to firm, and even by job type within an organization. An application form typically contains sections for name, address, telephone number, military service, education, and work history.

An employment application form must reflect not only the firm's informational needs but also EEO requirements. An excellent example of a properly designed application form is provided in Figure 7-2 on pages 218–219. Potentially discriminatory questions, such as gender, race, age, and number of children living at home, have been eliminated from the form.

---

[8] Bradford D. Smart, "Progressive Approaches for Hiring the Best People," *Training and Development Journal,* 41 (September 1987), p. 49.

FIGURE 7-2 | An Application for Employment

Source: General Electric Company

Employment History

Please read carefully before starting. List all employment starting with present or most recent employer. Account for all periods, including unemployment and service with the Armed Forces. Also include relevant voluntary and/or part-time work experience. Use additional sheet if necessary.

Employer	Dates		Hourly Rate/Salary	
	From	Month	Year	Starting	$	per
Address	To	Month	Year	Final	$	per
Job Title	Describe Major Duties			
Department				
Supervisor	Reason For Leaving			

Employer	Dates		Hourly Rate/Salary	
	From	Month	Year	Starting	$	per
Address	To	Month	Year	Final	$	per
Job Title	Describe Major Duties			
Department				
Supervisor	Reason For Leaving			

Employer	Dates		Hourly Rate/Salary	
	From	Month	Year	Starting	$	per
Address	To	Month	Year	Final	$	per
Job Title	Describe Major Duties			
Department				
Supervisor	Reason For Leaving			

Employer	Dates		Hourly Rate/Salary	
	From	Month	Year	Starting	$	per
Address	To	Month	Year	Final	$	per
Job Title	Describe Major Duties			
Department				
Supervisor	Reason For Leaving			

Interviewer's Comments:

Interviewed By: _____ Date: _____

Page 2   Continue on Next Page

Affirmative Action

Special Employment Notice To Disabled Veterans, Vietnam Era Veterans And Individuals With Physical Or Mental Handicaps:

Government contractors are subject to Section 402 of the Vietnam Era Veterans Readjustment Act of 1974 which requires that they take affirmative action to employ and advance in employment qualified disabled veterans and veterans of the Vietnam Era (i.e., served more than 180 days between August 5, 1964 and May 7, 1975), and Section 503 of the Rehabilitation Act of 1973, as amended, which requires government contractors to take affirmative action to employ and advance in employment qualified handicapped individuals.

Please Check Below If You Are A:

☐ Vietnam Era Veteran
☐ Disabled Veteran
☐ Handicapped Individual

And wish to be considered under our Affirmative Action Program(s). **Submission of this information is voluntary.**

Please read this carefully before signing:

Employee Release and Privacy Statement

I understand that the General Electric Company requires certain information about me to evaluate my qualifications for employment and to conduct its business if I become an employee. Therefore, I authorize the Company to investigate my past employment, educational credentials and other employment-related activities. I agree to cooperate in such investigations, and release those parties supplying such information to the Company from all liability or responsibility with respect to information supplied.

I agree that the Company may use the information it obtains concerning me in the conduct of its business. I understand that such use may include disclosure outside the Company in those cases where its agents and contractors need such information to perform their functions, where the Company's legal interests and/or obligations are involved, or where there is a medical emergency involving me. I understand, however, that the Company intends to protect the confidentiality of personal information it obtains concerning me. Consequently, personal information in Company record-keeping systems, other than the fact and location of past or present Company employment, the dates of employment, or the job name or description of general duties, will not otherwise be disclosed outside the Company with a personal identifier without my consent. Further, the Company will require its agents and contractors to safeguard personal information disclosed to them by the Company.

I understand that any employment with the Company would not be for any fixed period of time and that, if employed, I may resign at any time for any reason or the Company may terminate my employment at any time for any reason in the absence of a specific written agreement to the contrary.

I understand that any false answers or statements made by me on this application or any supplement thereto or in connection with the above-mentioned investigations will be sufficient grounds for immediate discharge, if I am employed.

_____
Applicant's Signature: Date:

FIGURE 7-2 | *Continued*

The information contained in a completed application for employment is compared to the job description to determine whether a potential match exists between the firm's requirements and the applicant's qualifications. As you might expect, this comparison is often difficult. Applicants frequently attempt to present themselves in a positive, somewhat unrealistic light. Comparing past duties and responsibilities with those needed for the job the applicant is seeking isn't always easy. A person with the title of "manager" in one firm may actually have performed few managerial tasks, whereas a person with the same title in another firm may have had a great deal of managerial responsibility.

Some companies now have terminals in their lobbies on which applicants can complete a job application form. A few human resource departments are setting up optical scanning programs that can handle the first-level screening of applications. These programs could also scan applications for other jobs that the applicants may not know they are qualified to fill. This approach would not only be more objective but also less expensive.[9]

Over the years, much effort has been devoted to using employment application data to assist in spotting individuals who will succeed and those who won't. Research results over the past fifty years suggest that the application can be a valuable predictor for certain types of positions. One technique for identifying factors that differentiate successful from less successful employees is the **weighted application blank (WAB).** The WAB is an approach used to analyze variables such as long- and short-term employees, productive and less productive employees, and satisfied and less satisfied employees. One variable, years on the last job, is shown in Figure 7-3. First, the percentage difference between short- and long-term workers is computed. Then a weight is assigned, based on the percentage difference. After the weights for all variables on the application have been calculated, applicants can be screened on the basis of their point totals. Using the WAB, applicants with the highest point totals are considered to have the greatest potential for success.

At times, the WAB has proved to be quite accurate. In spite of the WAB's ability to determine which factors are important for predicting tenure and job success, the overwhelming majority of U.S. firms continue to use traditional application forms.[10] And, in some instances, the WAB's benefits have been only marginal. Because this approach has produced some unsatisfactory results, many human resource researchers have turned to other quantitative techniques for evaluating employment application data, such as regression analysis and discriminant analysis (discussed in Chapter 19).

---

[9] Jac Fitz-enz, "Getting—and Keeping—Good Employees," *Personnel,* 67 (August 1990), p. 27.

[10] Daniel G. Lawrence, Barbara L. Salsburg, John G. Dawson, and Zachary D. Fashman, "Design and Use of Weighted Application Blanks," *Personnel Administrator,* 27 (March 1982), p. 47.

	Percentage Responding			
Item	Short-term	Long-term	Difference	Weight
Years on the Last Job				
No response	4	12	+ 8	0
Less than 1	50	0	−50	−5
1–1 1/2	7	35	+28	+2
1 1/2–2 1/2	37	12	−25	−2
2 1/2–3	0	6	+ 6	0
More than 3	2	35	+33	+3

FIGURE 7-3 | An Example of a Weighted Application Blank
Question

■ ADMINISTRATION OF SELECTION TESTS

Selection tests are often used to assist in assessing an applicant's qualifications and potential for success. The popularity of selection tests declined sharply following enactment of the Civil Rights Act and subsequent court decisions. For instance, in *Griggs v. Duke Power Company,* the U.S. Supreme Court ruled that preemployment requirements, including tests, must be related to job performance. In *Albermarle Paper v. Moody,* the Supreme Court ruled that any test used in the selection process or in promotion decisions must be validated if its use has had an adverse impact on women or minorities. For a selection test to be considered nondiscriminatory, it must conform to the *Uniform Guidelines.* The general standard is that if the use of test results has an adverse impact on women or minorities the employer will be required to show that it is job related; that is, the employer must validate the test.

By curtailing test usage, some employers apparently felt that they would be immune from legal requirements for valid instruments. Clearly, however, all the tools used in making selection and other employment decisions are subject to the same validity requirements. Although many individuals distrust tests, they may well be the most valid instrument available. Recognition of this—and increased awareness of the interview's vulnerability—has recently led to a resurgence of test usage in the selection process.[11]

Evidence suggests that the use of tests is more widespread in the public sector than in the private sector and in medium-sized and large companies than in small companies—and that large organizations are likely to have trained specialists to run their testing programs.[12] A survey of companies

---

[11] "Employee Selection Tests: Upping the Odds for Success," *Personnel,* 57 (November–December 1980), p. 48.

[12] "Ability Tests: They Can Provide Useful Information About the Probability of an Applicant's Performing Successfully on the Job," *Across the Board,* 19 (July–August 1982), p. 27.

that use selection tests revealed that more than 80 percent use them for office positions, 20 percent for production positions, and only 10 percent for sales and service positions.[13]

Advantages of Selection Tests

Selection tests help managers make better hiring decisions. One example of the contribution of effective selection tests to productivity is provided by the Philadelphia Police Department. Labor savings in this 5,000-member organization from the use of cognitive ability tests to select officers has been estimated to be $18 million for each year's hires.[14]

In an earlier study, using a computer programming test as an example, it was suggested that if all 18,498 programmers employed by the federal government had been selected by the use of a specific test, the productivity gain would have been $1.2 billion. If use of this procedure were to include all programmers employed in the public and private sectors, the productivity gain would have been $10.78 billion.[15]

Disadvantages of Selection Tests

Job performance is related primarily to an individual's ability and motivation to do the job. Selection tests may accurately predict an applicant's ability to perform the job, but they are less successful in indicating the extent to which the individual will want to perform it. For one reason or another, many employees with high potential never seem to reach it. The factors related to success on the job are so numerous and complex that selection may always be more of an art than a science.

Another potential problem, related primarily to personality tests and interest inventories, has to do with applicants' honesty. An applicant may be strongly motivated to respond to questions untruthfully or provide answers that he or she believes the firm expects. To prevent this occurrence, some tests have built-in lie detection scales.

A common problem is test anxiety. Applicants often become quite anxious when confronting yet another hurdle that might eliminate them from consideration. The test administrator's reassuring manner and a well-organized testing operation should serve to reduce this threat. Actually, although a great deal of anxiety is detrimental to test performance, a slight amount is helpful.[16]

---

[13] *Ibid.*

[14] John E. Hunter and Frank L. Schmidt, "Ability Tests: Economic Benefits versus the Issue of Fairness," *Industrial Relations,* 21 (Fall 1982), p. 293.

[15] Frank L. Schmidt, John E. Hunter, Robert C. McKenzie, and Tressie W. Muldrow, "Impact of Valid Selection Procedures on Work-Force Productivity," *Journal of Applied Psychology,* 64 (1979), p. 624.

[16] Anne Anastasi, *Psychological Testing,* 5th ed. (New York: Macmillan, 1982), pp. 36–37.

The dual problems of hiring unqualified or less qualified candidates and rejecting qualified candidates will continue regardless of the procedures followed. Organizations can minimize such errors through the use of well-developed tests administered by competent professionals. Nevertheless, selection tests rarely, if ever, are perfect predictors. Using even the best test, errors will be made in predicting success. For this reason, tests alone should not be used in the selection process but rather in conjunction with other tools.

Characteristics of Properly Designed Selection Tests

Properly designed selection tests are standardized, objective, based on sound norms, reliable, and—of utmost importance—valid. We discuss the application of these concepts next.

Standardization. **Standardization** refers to the uniformity of the procedures and conditions related to administering tests. In order to compare the performance of several applicants on the same test, it is necessary for all to take the test under conditions that are as close to identical as possible. For example, the content of instructions provided and the time allowed must be the same, and the physical environment must be similar. If one person takes a test in a noisy room and another takes it in a quiet environment, differences in test results are likely. Differences in conditions may affect an applicant's performance. Even though test administration procedures may be specified by a test's developers, test administrators are responsible for ensuring standardized conditions.

Objectivity. **Objectivity** in testing is achieved when everyone scoring a test obtains the same results. Multiple-choice and true-false tests are said to be objective. The person taking the test either chooses the correct answer or does not. Scoring these tests is a highly mechanical process, which lends itself to machine grading.

Norms. A **norm** provides a frame of reference for comparing an applicant's performance with that of others. Specifically, a norm reflects the distribution of many scores obtained by people similar to the applicant being tested. The scores will tend to be distributed according to the normal probability curve presented in Figure 7-4 on page 224. Standard deviations measure the amount of dispersion of the data. A normalized test will have approximately 68.3 percent of the scores within ±1 standard deviation from the mean. Individuals scoring in this range would be considered average. Individuals achieving scores outside the range of ±2 standard deviations would probably be highly unsuccessful or highly successful, based on the particular criteria used.

When a sufficient number of employees are performing the same or similar work, employers can standardize their own tests. Typically this is not the case, and a national norm for a particular test must be used. A

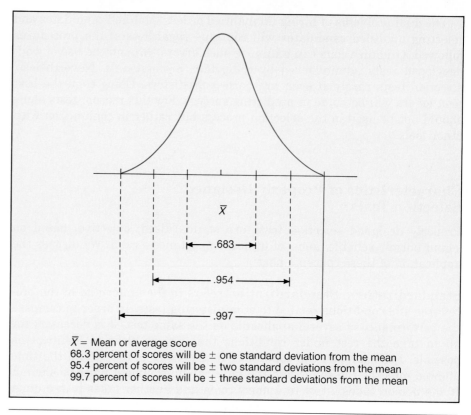

$\overline{X}$ = Mean or average score
68.3 percent of scores will be ± one standard deviation from the mean
95.4 percent of scores will be ± two standard deviations from the mean
99.7 percent of scores will be ± three standard deviations from the mean

FIGURE 7-4 | A Normal Probability Curve

prospective employee takes the test, the score obtained is compared to the norm, and the significance of the test score is determined.

Reliability. Reliability is the extent to which a selection test provides consistent results. Reliability data reveal the degree of confidence that can be placed in a test. If a test has low reliability, its validity as a predictor will also be low. But the existence of reliability does not in itself guarantee validity.

To ensure its usefulness, the test's reliability must be verified. The **test-retest method** is a method of determining selection test reliability by giving the test twice to the same group of individuals and correlating the two sets of scores. A perfect positive correlation is +1.00. The closer the reliability coefficient is to perfection, the more consistent the results, and therefore the more reliable the test. Problems with this method for determining reliability include the cost of administering the test twice, employees recalling test questions, and the learning that may take place between tests.

Similar to the test-retest method, the **equivalent forms method** tests reliability by correlating the results of tests that are similar but not identical. This approach overcomes some of the difficulties encountered with the test-retest method, but developing two forms of a test can be expensive. To overcome this weakness somewhat, the split-halves method may be used. The **split-halves method** tests reliability by dividing the results of a test into two parts and then correlating the results of the two parts. The one-time administration of the test has the obvious advantage of minimizing costs. Also, there is no opportunity for learning or recall, which would distort the second score.

Validity. The basic requirement for a selection test is that it be valid. **Validity** is the extent to which a test measures what it purports to measure. If a test cannot indicate ability to perform the job, it has no value as a predictor. For this reason, validity has always been a proper concern of organizations that use tests. Because our society is committed to equal employment opportunity, greater emphasis has been given in recent years to the validation process.

Validity is commonly reported as a correlation coefficient, which summarizes the relationship between two variables. For example, these variables may be the score on a selection test and some measure of employee performance. A coefficient of 0 shows no relationship, while coefficients of either +1.0 or −1.0 indicate a perfect relationship, one positive and the other negative. Naturally, no test will be 100 percent accurate, yet organizations strive for the highest feasible coefficient. If a test is designed to predict job performance and validity studies of the test indicate a high correlation coefficient, most prospective employees who score high on the test will probably later prove to be high performers. As we previously stated, the ability to select better qualified individuals will help increase the firm's productivity.

Employers are not required to automatically validate their selection tests. Generally speaking, validation is required only when the selection process as a whole results in an adverse impact on women or minorities. Validation of selection tests is expensive. However, an organization cannot know whether the test is actually measuring the qualities and abilities being sought without validation.

■ TYPES OF VALIDATION STUDIES

The *Uniform Guidelines* established three approaches that may be followed to validate selection tests: criterion-related validity, content validity, and construct validity.[17]

---

[17] Dwight R. Norris and James A. Buford, Jr., "A Content Valid Writing Test: A Case Study," *Personnel Administrator,* 25 (January 1980), p. 40.

Criterion-Related Validity

Criterion-related validity is determined by comparing the scores on selection tests to some aspect of job performance as determined, for example, by performance appraisal. Performance measures might include quantity and quality of work, turnover, and absenteeism. A close relationship between the score on the test and job performance suggests that the test is valid.

There are two basic forms of criterion-related validity: concurrent and predictive validity. With **concurrent validity,** the test scores and the criterion data are obtained at essentially the same time. For instance, all currently employed telemarketers may be given a test. Company records contain current information about each employee's job performance. If the test is able to identify productive and less productive workers, one could say that it is valid. A potential problem in using this validation procedure results from changes that may have occurred within the work group. For example, the less productive workers may have been fired, and the more productive employees may have been promoted out of the group.

Predictive validity involves administering a test and later obtaining the criterion information. For instance, a test might be administered to all applicants but test results not used in the selection decision; employees would be hired on the basis of other selection criteria. After employee performance has been observed over a period of time, the test results are analyzed to determine whether they differentiate the successful and less successful employees. Predictive validity is considered to be a technically sound procedure. However, because of the time and cost involved, its use is often not feasible.

Content Validity

Although statistical concepts are not involved, many human resource practitioners believe that content validity provides a sensible approach to validating a selection test. **Content validity** is a test validation method whereby a person performs certain tasks that are actually required by the job or completes a paper-and-pencil test that measures relevant job knowledge. Thorough job analysis and carefully prepared job descriptions are needed when this form of validation is used.

The classic example of the use of content validity is giving a typing test to an applicant whose primary job would be to type. In *Washington v. Davis,* the Supreme Court supported content validity, and its use will likely grow in the future.

Construct Validity

Construct validity is a test validation method that determines whether a test measures certain traits or qualities that are important in performing the job. For instance, if the job requires a large amount of persistence, such as in some forms of life insurance sales, a test would be used to measure persistence. However, traits or qualities needed on the job must first be carefully identified through job analysis.

■ CUTOFF SCORES

After a test has been shown to be valid, an appropriate cutoff score must be established. A **cutoff score** is the score below which an applicant will not be selected. Cutoff scores will vary over time because they are directly related to the selection ratio. The more individuals applying for a job, the more selective the firm can be and therefore the higher the cutoff scores can be. Cutoff scores should normally be set to reflect a reasonable expectation of acceptable proficiency.

An example of what would likely occur if a validated test were administered to prospective employees is shown in Figure 7-5 on page 228. The firm's experience indicates that individuals who score 40 and above on the test will be successful. Those who score below 40 will be less successful. Note that test results do not precisely predict performance. A small number of individuals who scored below the cutoff score of 40 proved to be good workers. Also, some applicants scoring above 40 proved to be less successful. However, the test appears to be a reasonably good predictor of success. It is because of this gray area that test results should serve as only one of several criteria in the selection decision. The setting of a cutoff score to determine who will be screened out may have adverse impact. If so, the *Uniform Guidelines* require an employer to justify the initial cutoff score used.

■ TYPES OF EMPLOYMENT TESTS

Individuals differ in characteristics related to job performance. These differences, which are measurable, relate to cognitive abilities, psychomotor abilities, job knowledge, work samples, vocational interests, personality, drugs, and AIDS. We discuss tests to measure these differences next.

Cognitive Aptitude Tests

Cognitive aptitude tests measure an individual's ability to learn, as well as to perform a job. This type of test is particularly appropriate for making a selection from a group of inexperienced candidates. Job-related abilities may be classified as verbal, numerical, perceptual speed, spatial, and reasoning.

Psychomotor Abilities Tests

Psychomotor abilities tests measure strength, coordination, and dexterity. The development of tests to determine these abilities has been accelerated by miniaturization in assembly operations. Much of this work is so

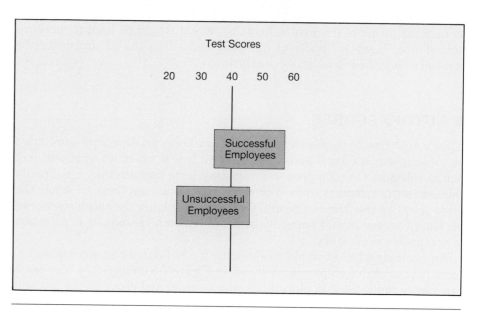

FIGURE 7-5 | An Example of Results from a Validated Test

delicate that magnifying lenses must be used, and the psychomotor abilities required to perform the tasks are critical. While standardized tests are not available to cover all these abilities, it is feasible to measure those that are involved in many routine production jobs and some office jobs. **Finger dexterity** is the ability to make precise, coordinated finger movements, such as those performed by an electronics assembler or a watchmaker. **Manual dexterity** involves the coordinated movements of both hands and arms, such as those required by large assembly jobs. **Wrist-finger speed** is the ability to make rapid wrist and finger movements, such as those required in inspector-packer and assembly operation jobs. **Aiming** is the ability to move the hands quickly and accurately from one spot to another, which is important in jobs such as electronic parts assembly.

Job Knowledge Tests

Job knowledge tests are designed to measure a candidate's knowledge of the duties of the position for which he or she is applying. Such tests are commercially available but may also be designed specifically for any job, based on the data derived from job analysis. While such tests frequently involve written responses, they may be administered orally. Regardless of the form, they contain key questions that serve to distinguish experienced, skilled workers from those with less experience or skill.

Job knowledge tests, based on job analysis information, must be designed specifically for unique jobs. When in-house specialists are not available, consultants are often utilized to design the tests.

Job knowledge tests are by definition job related, but they do present some problems. For example, heavy equipment may not easily be moved to a testing site, untrained applicants may injure themselves or damage expensive equipment, and the economy of group testing isn't always feasible.

Work-Sample Tests

Work-sample tests require an applicant to perform a task or set of tasks representative of the job.[18] The evidence to date concerning these tests is that they produce high predictive validities, reduce adverse impact, and are more acceptable to applicants.[19]

Vocational Interest Tests

Vocational interest tests indicate the occupation in which a person is most interested and is most likely to receive satisfaction from. These tests compare the individual's interests with those of successful employees in a specific job.

Interests appear to be stable over a long period of time and have been related to success in some fields. However, interests must not be confused with aptitudes or abilities. Tests for these characteristics should accompany the administration of an interest test. Moreover, answers to interest test questions can easily be faked. Although interest tests may possibly have some application in employee selection, their primary use has been in counseling and vocational guidance.

Personality Tests

As selection tools, personality tests have not been as useful as other types of tests. They are often characterized by low reliability and low validity. Because some personality tests emphasize subjective interpretation, the services of a qualified psychologist are required to administer them. Additional research is needed before personality tests can be used with confidence as a selection tool.

---

[18] I. T. Robertson and R. M. Mindel, "A Study of Trainability Testing," *Journal of Occupational Psychology*, 53 (June 1980), p. 131.

[19] I. T. Robertson and R. S. Kandola, "Work Sample Tests: Validity, Adverse Impact, and Applicant Reaction," *Journal of Occupational Psychology*, 55 (1982), p. 180.

Drug Testing

A major 1990 survey found that 23 percent of the responding companies require some type of substance abuse testing as a condition of employment. In addition, 11 percent are considering requiring testing. Table 7-2 shows the extent of testing in various types of companies that either currently require substance abuse tests or are considering their use. As the table indicates, drug testing appears to be most common in utility/transportation/communication firms, with 73 percent of these organizations requiring or considering tests.[20]

In two cases decided in 1989, the U.S. Supreme Court upheld drug testing required by federal agencies. These cases stemmed from Fourth Amendment challenges.[21] Although these cases did not apply directly to private sector employers, the decisions are nevertheless important. First, one can anticipate that drug testing conducted by private sector employers under similar circumstances will be upheld. If drug testing can pass rigorous Fourth Amendment scrutiny, it should also be defensible under normal invasion of privacy claims. In addition, federal rules, regulations, and programs tend to become models for private sector behavior.[22]

Testing for Acquired Immune Deficiency Syndrome (AIDS)

One survey found that only 1.5 percent of the responding firms reported AIDS antibody testing of job applicants. The same study indicated that a slightly higher percentage of smaller companies (50–99 employees) than of larger firms conduct these tests. A possible explanation is the prohibitive cost for large firms. Less than 1 percent of health service companies test for AIDS, whereas over 12 percent of utilities/transportation/communication firms and over 19 percent of public administration organizations do so. We discuss AIDS further in Chapter 14.

■ THE EMPLOYMENT INTERVIEW

The **employment interview** is a goal-oriented conversation in which the interviewer and applicant exchange information. The employment interview, along with letters of recommendation, continues to be the primary method used to evaluate applicants.[23] It is utilized by virtually every com-

---

[20] Joseph E. McKendrick, Jr., "Latest AMS Foundation Survey Finds: One-Third of Nation's Employers Have or Are Considering Drug Testing," *Management World,* 19 (March/April 1990), p. 3.

[21] The Fourth Amendment prohibits the government from conducting unreasonable searches or seizures.

[22] Gerard P. Panaro, *Employment Law Manual* (Boston: Warren, Gorham & Lamont, 1990), pp. 4–28.

[23] Sampo V. Paunonen, Douglas N. Jackson, and Steven M. Oberman, "Personnel Selection Decisions," p. 96.

TABLE 7-2 | Companies with or Considering Drug Testing

Type	Percentage
Utilities/transportation/communication	73
Manufacturing/construction	61
Retail	41
Insurance	19
Banking/finance	18
Nonprofit/government	15
Services	15
Other	18
Total—all industries	34

Source: Joseph E. McKendrick, Jr., "Latest AMS Foundation Survey Finds: One-Third of Nation's Employers Have or Are Considering Drug Testing," *Management World,* 19 (March/April 1990), p. 3. Reprinted with permission from the Administrative Management Society, Washington, DC, copyright 1990.

pany in the United States.[24] The employment interview is especially significant because the applicants who reach this stage are the most promising candidates.[25] They have survived the preliminary interview, scored satisfactorily on selection tests, and fared well in reference and background checks. At this point, the candidates appear to be qualified, at least on paper. Every seasoned manager knows, however, that appearances can be quite misleading. Additional information is needed to indicate whether the individual is willing to work and can adapt to that particular organization.[26]

Legal Implications of Interviewing

For a number of years following the enactment of the Civil Rights Act, many employers stopped using tests and relied even more heavily on the employment interview as a selection tool. This change in practice was based on the false assumption that legal validity requirements applied only to tests.[27] But the definition of a test in the *Uniform Guidelines* included "physical, education and work experience requirements from informal or casual interviews." Since the interview is clearly a test, it is subject to the same validity requirements as any other step in the selection process,

---

[24] Gary P. Latham, Lise M. Saari, Elliott D. Pursell, and Michael A. Campion, "The Situational Interview," *Journal of Applied Psychology,* 65 (August 1980), p. 422.

[25] Richard A. Fear and James F. Ross, *Jobs, Dollars—and EEO: How to Hire More Productive Entry-Level Workers* (New York: McGraw-Hill, 1983), p. 113.

[26] *Ibid.*

[27] James G. Goodale, *The Fine Art of Interviewing* (Englewood Cliffs, N.J.: Prentice-Hall, 1982), p. 41.

should adverse impact be shown. For the interview, this constraint presents special difficulties. To begin with, few firms are willing to pay the cost of validating interviews. They can be validated only by a long-term follow up—a method that requires collecting much data over a long period of time.[28] However, significant evidence indicates that if two managers in a firm interview the same applicant at different times, the outcomes will differ.[29]

The interview is perhaps more vulnerable to charges of discrimination than any other tool used in the selection process. In most cases, there is little or no documentation of the questions asked or the answers received. The interviewer may tend to ask irrelevant questions that would never appear on an application form. Some interviewers are inclined to ask questions that are not job related and that reflect their personal biases. They probably reason that this practice will go uncriticized because there is no written or verbal record of the interview. Nevertheless, interviewing in this manner is risky and can lead to charges of discrimination. Since an interview is a test, all questions should be job related. In the Appendix to this chapter, we further discuss potential interviewing problems.

Objectives of the Interview

Employment interviews have several basic objectives. It is important that at least the following objectives be successfully achieved.

Obtain Additional Information from the Applicant. The interview is an essential method of obtaining additional information about the applicant to complement the data provided by other selection tools. The interview permits clarification of certain points, the uncovering of additional information, and the elaboration of data needed to make a sound selection decision.

Provide Information Regarding the Firm. General information about the job, company policies, its products, and its services should be communicated to the applicant during the interview. If the interviewee is adequately prepared, this information will not come as a surprise.

Sell the Company. The employment interview provides an excellent opportunity for selling the company to the applicant. The interviewer should do so in a realistic manner, not through rose-colored glasses. Describing the company as a virtual utopia may well result in a disappointed employee or even an ex-employee.

---

[28] Robert L. Decker, "The Employment Interview: Are We Seeing the Demise of Another Management Prerogative?" *Personnel Administrator,* 27 (November 1981), p. 71.

[29] James G. Goodale, "The Neglected Art of Interviewing," *Supervisory Management,* 26 (July 1981), p. 2.

Make New Friends. The applicant should leave the interview with a positive attitude about the company. If treated properly, the interviewee will not change this attitude even if no job offer is made. The interview should never serve to make the applicant feel inadequate.

Content of the Interview

The specific content of employment interviews varies greatly by organization and the level of the job. However, the following general topics appear fairly consistently in employment interviews: technical competence (often revealed through academic achievement and occupational experience), personal qualities (such as interpersonal competence), and potential, which includes the candidate's career orientation.[30]

Academic Achievement. The interviewer should try to discover any underlying factors related to academic performance. For example, a student who earned only a 2.28/4.0 GPA may turn out to be a very bright individual who, because of financial difficulties, might have worked virtually full time while still participating in a variety of activities. On the other hand, a student who received a 3.8/4.0 GPA may not be a well-rounded individual and may be a weak candidate for the position.

Personal Qualities. Personal qualities normally observed during the interview include physical appearance, speaking ability, vocabulary, poise, adaptability, and assertiveness. Even though he or she may have personal preferences, the interviewer should make every effort to keep nonjob-related personal biases out of the selection process.

Because of the legal ramifications, permitting the applicant's personal characteristics to influence the selection decision would obviously be unwise, unless they were BFOQs. Physical appearance might very well be an occupational qualification if the job being filled were that of an actress who is to portray the early career of Glenn Close. Speaking ability, vocabulary, and poise may be job-related qualifications if the job is that of a sportscaster. Assertiveness may be required for the successful performance of a credit collector's job.

Occupational Experience. Exploring an individual's occupational experience requires finding out about the applicant's skills, abilities, and willingness to handle responsibility. Job titles in one organization do not necessarily represent the same job content in another. Successful performance in one job does not guarantee success in another. At the same time, past performance does provide some indication of the employee's ability and willingness to work.

---

[30] Gary T. Hunt and William F. Eadie, *Interviewing: A Communication Approach* (New York: Holt, Rinehart and Winston, 1987), p. 170.

Interpersonal Competence. To a degree, an interviewer may observe an applicant's interpersonal competence. However, the interviewer may be witnessing an Academy Award performance by a candidate displaying an "I like people" nature. For this reason, the interviewer may need to ask questions regarding the applicant's interpersonal relationships with family and friends and how he or she behaves in other social and civic situations. The primary cause of failure in performing jobs is not the lack of technical ability but rather shortcomings in interpersonal competence. Even though an individual may be a highly skilled worker, if he or she cannot work well with other employees, chances for success are slim.

Career Orientation. Questions about a candidate's career objectives may help the interviewer determine whether the applicant's aspirations are realistic. The odds are rather great that a recent college graduate who expects to become a senior vice-president within six months will become quickly dissatisfied.

In addition to determining an applicant's career goals, the interviewer should present an honest and accurate description of career prospects in the organization. Deception may well prove counterproductive if the applicant is hired and later becomes dissatisfied as the truth unfolds. The firm may lose a substantial investment in the form of recruitment, selection, and training.

Types of Interviews

Interviews may be classified as highly structured at one extreme and as having virtually no structure at the other. In practice, interviews usually fall between these extremes. Regardless of structure, interviews should solicit the following types of information from applicants: (1) ability to perform the job, (2) motivation to stay on the job, and (3) adaptability to the job situation.[31]

The Unstructured (Nondirective) Interview. In the **unstructured interview,** the interviewer asks probing, open-ended questions. This type of interview is comprehensive, and the interviewer encourages the applicant to do much of the talking. The nondirective interview is often more time-consuming than more structured interviews, yet some interviewers believe that it has greater effectiveness in obtaining significant information. The nature of the nondirective interview requires a highly trained and skillful interviewer who asks open-ended questions such as:

What do you believe are your primary strengths? Your main weaknesses?

How will our company benefit by having you as an employee?

---

[31] Barbara Felton and Sue Ries Lamb, "A Model for Systematic Selection Interviewing," *Personnel,* 59 (January–February 1982), p. 43.

Where do you want to be in this firm five years from now?

What was your most significant contribution in your last job?

The specific answers may not be as important to the interviewer as how the applicant answers the questions and the thought process leading to the response. The nondirective interview consists of a highly subjective appraisal of the candidate. Research conducted on traditional selection interviews indicates very low reliability and little or no validity.[32] Various types of errors have contributed to this poor performance (see the Appendix to this chapter), and therefore the use of such an approach may not be extremely effective in many interview situations.

The Structured (Directive or Patterned) Interview. The **structured interview** consists of a series of job-related questions that are consistently asked of each applicant for a particular job.[33] Use of structured interviews increases reliability and accuracy by reducing the subjectivity and inconsistency of unstructured (nondirective) interviews.

Interviewers should follow a structured, systematic interview procedure in order to obtain the information necessary to evaluate the candidate fairly and objectively.[34] The advantages of structure are diminished, however, if the interviewer asks each of the questions perfunctorily. This approach could easily result in an overly formal setting and severely impair the candidate's ability or desire to respond.

A structured job interview typically contains four types of questions. **Situational questions** pose a hypothetical job situation to determine what the applicant would do in that situation. **Job knowledge questions** probe the applicant's job-related knowledge. These questions may relate to basic educational skills or complex scientific or managerial skills. **Job-sample simulation questions** involve situations in which an applicant may be required to actually perform a sample task from the job. When this isn't feasible, a simulation of critical job aspects may be utilized. Also, answering these types of questions may require physical activity.

The last type of question used in structured interviews deals with worker requirements. **Worker requirements questions** seek to determine the applicant's willingness to conform to the requirements of the job. For example, the interviewer may ask whether the applicant is willing to perform repetitive work or move to another city. The nature of these questions serves as a realistic job preview and may aid in self-selection.

A properly designed patterned interview will contain only job-related questions. An illustration of a patterned interview guide for discussing work experience is provided in Table 7-3 on page 236. Each question should be asked for a specific purpose.

---

[32] Elliott D. Pursell, Michael A. Campion, and Sara R. Gaylord, "Structuring Interviewing: Avoiding Selection Problems," *Personnel Journal,* 59 (November 1980), p. 908.

[33] *Ibid.*

[34] Alan Weiss, "Select, Don't Settle," p. 90.

TABLE 7-3 | Portion of a Patterned Interview Guide

Work Experience	
Cover:	**Look for:**
Earliest jobs: part-time, temporary	Relevance of work
Military assignments	Sufficiency of work
Full-time positions	Skill and competence
	Adaptability
Ask:	Productivity
Things done best? Done less well?	Motivation
Things liked best? Liked less well?	Interpersonal relations
Major accomplishments? How achieved?	Leadership
Most difficult problems faced? How handled?	Growth and development
Ways most effective with people?	
Ways less effective?	
Level of earnings?	
Reasons for changing jobs?	
What learned from work experience?	
What looking for in job? In career?	

Source: Reproduced from *The Interviewer's Manual* by special permission. Copyright © 1980, by Drake Beam Morin, Inc. All rights reserved.

■ METHODS OF INTERVIEWING

Interviews may be conducted in several ways. In a typical employment interview, the applicant meets one-on-one with an interviewer. As the interview may be a highly emotional occasion for the applicant, meeting alone with the interviewer is often less threatening.

Unlike a one-on-one interview, in a **group interview** several applicants interact in the presence of one or more company representatives. This approach, while not mutually exclusive of other interview types, may provide useful insights into the candidates' interpersonal competence as they engage in group discussion. This technique is often used because it saves time for busy professionals and executives.

In a **board interview,** one candidate is interviewed by several representatives of the firm. Although a thorough examination of the applicant is likely, the interviewee's anxiety level is often quite high. A vice-president of industrial relations for an aircraft firm stated, "We use a three-person board to screen each applicant, asking a series of questions designed to ferret out the individual's attitudes toward former employers, jobs, etc. Then, a week later, we bring successful applicants and their spouses in for a family-night meeting with top management and their spouses, where we further screen them while discussing the company and employee benefits." Naturally, the amount of time devoted to a board interview will differ depending on the type and level of job.

Most interview sessions are designed to minimize stress on the part of the candidate. However, the **stress interview** intentionally creates anxiety to determine how an applicant will react in certain types of situations. The stress interview should be used only by highly trained and skilled interviewers. Interviewers for some types of sales jobs subject applicants to stress situations in order to determine how they will react under pressure. For instance, on the first interview, everything might progress smoothly. The applicant is led to believe that all he or she has to do is come back for the second interview and the job offer will be made. However, during the second interview, events progress a bit differently. The individual might have to wait in the outer office for a considerable period of time before the interview begins. This tactic allows the candidate's anxiety to build. Then the interviewer might begin with a statement such as, "Mr. Noles, I appreciate your interest, but we just don't believe there is any need to continue this interview. Your qualifications just don't appear to match our needs." The purpose of this approach is to see how the applicant will react when confronted with an unexpected situation. Individuals who are able to turn this situation around may demonstrate that they can become successful sales representatives, for example.

Another point of view relative to stress interviews relies on evidence indicating that the stress interview is not only inconsiderate but is also ineffective. Proponents of this view feel that information exchange in a stressful environment is often distorted and misinterpreted. These critics maintain that the data obtained are not the type of information upon which to base a selection decision.[35] In any event, it seems clear that the stress interview is not appropriate for the majority of situations.

The Interviewer, Interview Planning, and the Interview Process

The interviewer should possess a pleasant personality, empathy, and the ability to listen and communicate effectively. He or she should respect those who have different personal attributes and backgrounds. Interviewers must be aware of stereotyped views of the capabilities of women and minorities. Everyone has biases, and some are not bad. However, those based on a false value system about people tend to be destructive.[36] Consequently, these biases have no place in the interview process. Interviewers should also have a solid knowledge of actual job requirements so that they can properly assess the applicant's qualifications.

---

[35] Susan Gribben, "A Guide to the Hiring Process," *CA Magazine,* 115 (September 1982), p. 85.
[36] Joseph D. Levesque, "Selecting and Managing Competent Managers," p. 67.

In addition, interview planning is essential to effective employment interviews. The physical location of the interview should be both pleasant and private, providing for a minimum of interruptions. The interviewer should become familiar with the applicant's record by reviewing the data collected from other selection tools. In preparing for the interview, a job profile should be developed based on the job description. After job requirements have been listed, it is helpful to have an interview checklist that includes these hints:

- Compare applicant's résumé with job requirements.
- Develop questions related to qualities sought.
- Prepare a step-by-step scenario of how to present the position, company, division, and department.
- Determine how to ask for examples of past applicant behavior, not what future behavior might be.[37]

The interview process should begin with a warm and sincere welcome for the candidate, and rapport should be quickly developed. Because people can often talk most easily about themselves, it is a good practice for the interview to begin in this manner. After this initial icebreaker, the interviewer can proceed to ask relevant, job-related questions. The interviewer should never ask leading questions, such as, "You didn't do too well in statistics, did you?" Rather, questions should be asked in a manner that permits the applicant some flexibility in answering.

When the interviewer has obtained the necessary information and answered the applicant's questions, the interview should be concluded. At this point, the interviewer should tell the applicant that he or she will receive notification of the selection decision shortly. Unfortunately, this promise is often broken, and this may destroy a positive relationship between the applicant and the organization.

Realistic Job Previews[38]

Many applicants have unrealistic expectations about the prospective job and employer. This inaccurate perception, which may have negative consequences, is often encouraged by firms that present themselves in overly attractive terms. To correct this situation, a realistic job preview should be given to applicants early in the selection process and definitely before a job offer is made.

A **realistic job preview (RJP)** conveys job information to the applicant in an unbiased manner, including both positive and negative factors. This approach helps applicants develop a more accurate perception of the job

---

[37] James M. Jenks and Brian L. P. Zevnik, "ABCs of Job Interviewing," *Harvard Business Review,* 67 (July–August 1989), p. 38–39.

[38] John P. Wanous, "Tell It Like It Is at Realistic Job Previews," in Kendrith M. Rowland, Manual London, Gerald R. Ferris, and Jay L. Sherman (eds.), *Current Issues in Personnel Management* (Boston: Allyn & Bacon, 1980), pp. 41–50.

and the firm. Research results suggest that newly hired employees who received RJPs have a greater rate of job survival and higher job satisfaction. At the same time, use of this technique should not reduce the flow of qualified applicants. A comparison of the results of traditional preview procedures and realistic preview procedures is shown in Figure 7-6. Note that traditional procedures result in low job survival and dissatisfaction, whereas RJPs help to overcome these difficulties.

■ REFERENCE CHECKS

Information contained in the completed application for employment is at times incorrect or colored to present the applicant in a more favorable light. **Reference checks** provide additional insight into the information furnished by the applicant and allow verification of its accuracy. Most individuals who apply for jobs have to submit several references. References are normally checked by letter, by telephone, or both. When reference letters are used, the writer usually describes the nature of the job for which the applicant is being considered. Information requested from the reference is typically limited to dates of employment, job title, absentee record, promotions and demotions, compensation, and reason for termination.[39] As you might expect, written reference checks raise numerous problems. In

---

[39] G. Bruce Knecht, "Screening Out Thieves Before They're Hired," *Dun's Business Month,* 120 (October 1982), p. 70.

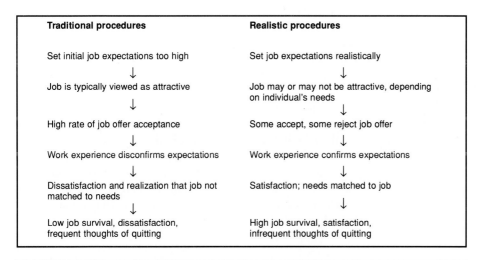

FIGURE 7-6 | Typical Consequences of Job Procedures

fact, many companies dispense with reference checks because they are concerned that the practice might be discriminatory or be perceived as an invasion of privacy. A study conducted by the National Consumers League in 1990 found that about 80 percent of the job seekers stated that the firms they wanted to join intruded into their private lives by asking inappropriate questions.[40]

The Privacy Act of 1974 has had a major impact on obtaining references. The act was passed to provide an individual certain safeguards against an invasion of personal privacy but is limited to the federal government and its contractors. It applies to all executive departments, the military, independent regulatory agencies, government corporations, and government-controlled corporations. Any private business that has a contract with any of these agencies is also covered for the duration of the contract. The purpose of the act is to limit the amount and type of information that federal agencies maintain in records about individuals and to control dissemination of that information to other agencies. Individuals must be permitted access to any personal records concerning them, and those covered by this act have the legal right to review reference checks that have been made regarding their employment unless the individual waives this right. There have been instances in which applicants have sued and won court cases when it was proven that the reference was biased.

Today many organizations refuse to release any information except dates of employment and salary. Even this information is often withheld without the former employee's written authorization. Furthermore, previous employers may "whitewash" a record by emphasizing positive factors and not mentioning negative factors, even if the applicant had been fired.[41] Comments regarding the reason for termination and job performance are often not included in a written response.

Another difficulty is that the applicant provides the names of the references. Applicants will carefully select their references in order to present a positive image. An applicant is not likely to use a person who would give an unfavorable response. Therefore the majority of references are biased in a positive manner.

Perhaps because of the bias associated with written references, many reference checkers use the telephone. They reason that a more objective appraisal will result if there is no documentation of the conversation. Still, they must be careful of the type of questions they ask. However, if the respondent desires to elaborate on a particular topic, the reference checker should certainly encourage further discussion. Basically, the reference checker should always remember that comments from a reference can be biased.

---

[40] Arthur Bragg, "Checking References," *Sales and Marketing Management,* 142 (November 1990), p. 68.

[41] Bradford D. Smart, "Progressive Approaches for Hiring the Best People," p. 51.

■ BACKGROUND INVESTIGATION

Although a reference check often verifies certain statements on the application blank, it frequently does not. Performing a background investigation of the applicant's past employment history may be necessary. This background investigation may be helpful in determining whether past work experience is related to the qualifications needed for the new position. As we previously noted, job titles may not accurately reflect the nature of past work experience.

Another reason for background investigations is that credential fraud has increased in recent years. Some 7–10 percent of job applicants are not what they present themselves to be.[42] Some applicants are not even who they say they are. They may also exaggerate their skills, education, and experience when given the chance. One firm recently gave applicants a list of equipment and asked them to identify the items they were qualified to operate. A high percentage of the candidates indicated they could operate equipment that doesn't exist.[43]

It has become increasingly important to conduct a reasonable background investigation in order to avoid charges of negligent hiring. Although it is expensive, the investigation may provide information critical to the selection decision since almost every qualification an applicant lists can be verified.[44]

■ NEGLIGENT HIRING AND RETENTION

Negligent hiring is one of the hottest issues in current HRM law. An employer can be held responsible for an employee's unlawful acts if it does not reasonably investigate applicants' backgrounds and then assigns potentially dangerous persons to positions where they can inflict harm. A firm should not go overboard with the investigation, however, because invasion of privacy is a possibility. Negligent retention involves keeping persons on the payroll whose records indicate strong potential for wrongdoing.

In the last ten years, employers have begun to be held responsible for actions outside the scope of their employees' duties. For example, if an employer hired a manager of an apartment complex without investigating the person's background and the individual later assaulted a tenant, the employer could be held responsible for the action. Employers are required by law to provide employees a safe place to work. This duty has been extended to providing safe employees because the courts have reasoned that a dangerous worker is comparable to a defective machine.

Negligent hiring cases often involve awards in the hundreds of thousands of dollars. In addition, they are likely to be upheld on appeal. The

---

[42] Scott T. Rickard, "Effective Staff Selection," *Personnel Journal,* 60 (June 1981), p. 477.

[43] Stevan P. Payne, "A Closer Look at Hiring and Firing," *Security Management,* 33 (June 1989), p. 50.

[44] Kurt W. Decker, "The Rights and Wrongs of Screening," *Security Management,* 34 (January 1990), p. 46.

primary consideration in negligent hiring is whether the risk of harm from a dangerous employee was reasonably foreseeable. The nature of the job also has a critical bearing on the employer's obligation. If the job gives employees access to homes or property (as in the case of meter readers, security guards, and exterminators), the hiring firm may be found to have an obligation to make a reasonable investigation into the person's background. Professions that involve an even higher degree of care include landlords, common carriers, workers in hospitals and other patient care facilities, and taxi drivers.[45]

A case in point is a Fort Worth cab company. One of its drivers picked up a young mother and her daughters at a bus station and took them to a deserted area, where he raped and robbed the mother. The young woman sued the cab company and won a judgment of $4,500,000 for "negligent hiring."[46] The Texas Supreme Court determined a reasonable background investigation would have made it quite clear that the cab driver should not have been hired. He had been previously convicted of robbery and forgery and, before that, had been arrested and charged for using a hammer to assault a woman. To avoid cases of this sort, employers should consider the type of interaction employees have with customers. Employers should also make reasonable background investigations and keep written records of the investigations.[47]

■ POLYGRAPH TESTS

For many years, another means used to verify background information has been the polygraph, or lie detector, test. One purpose of the polygraph was to confirm or refute the information contained in the application blank. However, on July 27, 1988, the Employee Polygraph Protection Act was passed, and it went into effect December 27, 1988. This act severely limited the use of polygraph tests. It made it unlawful for any employer engaged in or affecting commerce, or in the production of goods for commerce, to use a polygraph test. However, the act does not apply to governmental employers, and there are limited exceptions for ongoing investigations and for drug security, drug theft, or drug diversion investigations.

■ THE SELECTION DECISION

After obtaining and evaluating information about the finalists, the manager must take the most critical step of all: making the actual hiring decision. The other stages in the selection process have been used to narrow

---

[45] James W. Fenton, Jr., "Negligent Hiring/Retention Adds to Human Resources Woes," *Personnel Journal,* 69 (April 1990), p. 62; and Stephanie Overman, "A Delicate Balance Protects Everyone's Rights," *HRMagazine,* 35 (November 1990), pp. 36–39.

[46] Caleb S. Atwood and James M. Neel, "New Lawsuits Expand Employer Liability," *HRMagazine,* 35 (October 1990), p. 74.

[47] Joseph W. Ambash, "Knowing Your Limits: How Far Can You Go When Checking an Applicant's Background?" *Management World,* 19 (March/April 1990), pp. 8–10.

the number of candidates. The final choice will be made from among those still in the running after reference checks, selection tests, background investigations, and interview information have been evaluated. The individual with the best overall qualifications may not be hired. Rather, the person whose qualifications most closely conform to the requirements of the open position should be selected.[48] If an organization is going to invest thousands of dollars to recruit, select, and train an employee, it is important for the manager to hire the most qualified available candidate for the position.[49]

Human resource professionals are heavily involved in all phases leading up to the final employment decision. However, the person who normally makes the final selection is the manager who will be responsible for the performance of the new employee. In making this decision, the operating manager may or may not ask the advice of the human resource manager. The role of HRM in this process is to provide service and counsel to help the operating manager make the selection decision. The rationale for permitting the supervisor to make the final selection is simple: Managers should be allowed to select the individuals for whom they will be responsible.

In certain instances, however, the human resource manager serves in a strong advisory capacity. For example, if the organization is under pressure from the federal government to employ more women and minorities, a recommendation by the human resource manager may carry additional weight.

■ PHYSICAL EXAMINATION

After the decision has been made to extend a job offer, the next phase of the selection process involves a physical examination for the successful applicant. Typically, a job offer is contingent on the applicant's passing of this examination. The purposes of the physical examination are several. Obviously, one reason is to screen out individuals who have a contagious disease. The exam also assists in determining whether an applicant is physically capable of performing the work. For instance, if the work is physically demanding and a heart problem is detected, the individual will likely be rejected. Finally, physical examination information may be used to determine whether certain physical capabilities differentiate successful from less successful employees. A physical examination can also be used to establish a record of preexisting physical conditions for insurance and workers' compensation purposes.

Human resource managers should be aware of the legal liabilities related to physical examinations. The *Uniform Guidelines* state that these

---

[48] Hall A. Acuff, "Quality Control in Employee Selection," *Personnel Journal,* 60 (July 1981), p. 563.

[49] Robert Goddard, Jeremy Fox, and W. E. Patton, "The Job-Hire Sale," *Personnel Administrator,* (June 1989), p. 120.

examinations should be used to reject applicants only when the results show that job performance would be adversely affected.

The Rehabilitation Act of 1973 and the Americans with Disabilities Act of 1990 do not prohibit employers from requiring physical examinations. However, they have encouraged employers considering hiring covered employees to examine carefully each job's physical requirements. The acts require employers to take affirmative action to hire qualified handicapped persons who, with reasonable accommodation, can perform the essential components of a job.

■ ACCEPTANCE OF JOB APPLICANTS

Assuming that the physical examination fails to uncover any disqualifying medical problems, the applicant can be employed. The starting date normally is based on the wishes of both the firm and the individual. If currently employed by another firm, the individual customarily gives between two and four weeks' notice. Even after this notice, the individual may need some personal time to prepare for the new job. This transition time is particularly important if the new job requires a move to another city. Thus the amount of time before the individual can join the firm is often considerable—but necessary.

The firm may also want the individual to delay the date of employment. If, for example, the new employee's first assignment upon joining the firm is to attend a training school, the organization may request that the individual delay joining the firm until the school begins. This practice, which would only benefit the company, should not be abused, especially if an undue hardship would be placed on the individual.

■ REJECTION OF JOB APPLICANTS

Applicants may be rejected during any phase of the selection process. In this section, we focus on the applicants who for various reasons were not offered employment. When someone applies for a position, that person is essentially saying, "I think I am qualified for the job. Why don't you hire me?" Tension builds as the applicant progresses through the selection process. If the preliminary interview shows that the applicant clearly is not qualified, the ego damage is likely to be slight. The company may even be able to steer the individual to other jobs in the firm that better match his or her qualifications.

For most people, the employment interview is not one of the most enjoyable experiences. Taking a test that could affect an individual's career often causes hands to become moist and perspiration to break out on the forehead. Suffering through all this only to be told, "There does not appear to be a proper match between your qualifications and our needs" can be a painful experience. Most firms recognize this fact and attempt to let the individual down as easily as possible. But it is often difficult to tell people that they will not be hired.

HRM In Action

ulie Thompson, the production manager for Ampex Manufacturing, called her friend, Bill Alexander, in human resources, to ask a favor. "Bill, I have a friend I'd like you to consider for the new sales manager's position. I really like the fellow and would appreciate anything you could do."

"Tell me about the person," said Bill.

"He just graduated from State University with a degree in history, I believe. He has no real work experience, but I am sure he could learn quickly. His parents are real good friends of mine, and I sure would like to help him out."

How would you respond?

When considerable time has been spent on the individual in the selection process, a company representative often sits down with the applicant and explains why another person was offered the job. But if there were many applicants, time constraints may force the firm to notify individuals by letter that they were not chosen. However, a rejection letter can still be personalized. A personal touch will often reduce the stigma of rejection and the chance that the applicant will feel negatively about the company. An impersonal letter is likely to cause the opposite reaction. If the selection was made objectively, most individuals can, with time, understand why they were not chosen.

■ SELECTION AND UTILITY ANALYSIS

Determining the ratio of benefits to costs for any selection technique is referred to as **utility analysis.** Each step in the selection process involves a cost. If tests are to be used, they need to be validated. Professionals are required to administer the tests, interpret the results, and explain the results to management. In addition, employment applications that are job related for particular job classes need to be developed. Properly conducted reference checks and background investigations require trained checkers. Even the preliminary interview requires that an individual be trained and time provided to perform the task properly. All these tasks require time, effort, and money.

Even though substantial costs are involved in developing, implementing, and using a job-related selection process, the benefits are likely to outweigh the costs. If individuals are placed in positions for which they are not suited, dissatisfaction is inevitable. Numerous hidden costs are involved. For example, before discovering that the individual was not suited for the job, considerable supervisory effort may have been expended. The quality and quantity of work in the department may suffer. And the new employee may have a negative impact on other workers. If the worker then leaves the firm, the recruitment and selection process must start all over to find a replacement. If training has been provided, it is wasted and must be provided again when a replacement is hired. Turnover costs associated with a poor selection process can be substantial.

Formal utility analysis attempts to assign dollar values to the various selection activities.[50] Managers are first asked to estimate the dollar value of hypothetical performance levels. They are then asked to estimate the performance level they expect to be achieved by the firm's selection activities. Managers seldom do a formal utility analysis but often perform informal utility analysis as they estimate the benefits and costs of employing a particular applicant.[51]

■ STAFFING IN THE MULTINATIONAL ENVIRONMENT

One of the most difficult human resource management problems for the multinational organization is that of selecting suitable people to be sent on foreign assignments. Inappropriate selections are often made, which negatively affect the multinational operation. A National Industrial Conference Board survey has called staffing overseas executive positions the second-most serious problem facing multinational corporations.[52] Although specific failure rates vary by country and company, an estimated 25 percent of Americans selected for overseas assignments are obvious failures and return home prematurely. Approximately the same number are hidden failures or marginal performers.[53] Some firms have experienced a 60 to 90 percent failure rate in certain countries.[54]

After being carefully selected for the assignment and briefed on the new job and locale, employees based in the United States do business in familiar surroundings. However, the multinational environment is often unfamiliar, and doing business as it has always been done may be ineffective. The tasks of everyday living may also be very different and unnerving.[55] Poor selection, coupled with the stress of living and working overseas, are documented contributors to mental breakdown, alcoholism, and divorce.

---

[50] Frank L. Schmidt, John E. Hunter, and Kenneth Pearlman, "Assessing the Economic Impact of Personnel Programs on Workforce Productivity," *Personnel Psychology,* 35 (1982), pp. 333–347.

[51] Kendrith M. Rowland and Gerald R. Ferris, *Personnel Management* (Boston: Allyn & Bacon, 1982), p. 134.

[52] Philip R. Harris, "Employees Abroad: Maintain the Corporate Connection," *Personnel Journal,* 65 (August 1986), pp. 107–108.

[53] Allen L. Hixon, "Why Corporations Make Haphazard Overseas Staffing Decisions," *Personnel Administrator,* 31 (March 1986), p. 91.

[54] Prabhu Guptara, "Searching the Organization for the Cross-Cultural Operators," *International Management,* (August 1986), pp. 39–40.

[55] Philip R. Harris, "Employees Abroad," pp. 107–108.

There are three primary reasons why U.S. workers sent overseas fail: (1) their families are misjudged, or are not even considered at the time of selection; (2) they are selected because of their domestic track records; or (3) they lack adequate cross-cultural training.[56] To overcome these obstacles human resource managers should plan carefully to ensure that selectees possess certain basic characteristics. Obviously, they must be technically qualified to do the job.[57] Unfortunately, however, U.S. firms seem to focus their selection efforts on the single criterion "technical competence" at the expense of other criteria. For example, few firms administer tests to determine the relational/cross-cultural/interpersonal skills of their selectees. Other contributing factors are also needed:

- A real desire to work in a foreign country.
- Spouses and families who have actively encouraged the person to work overseas.
- Cultural sensitivity and flexibility.
- A sense for politics.

Several surveys of overseas managers have revealed that the spouse's opinion and attitude should be considered the most important screening factor. Cultural sensitivity is also essential to avoid antagonizing host country nationals unnecessarily.

The selection process should measure and evaluate the candidate's expertise broadly. Psychological tests, stress tests, evaluations by the candidate's superiors, subordinates, peers, and acquaintances, and professional evaluations from licensed psychologists can all aid in ascertaining the candidate's current level of interpersonal and cross-cultural skills. The candidate's spouse and children should undergo modified versions of the selection process, since the family members confront slightly different challenges overseas than do employees.[58]

In selecting individuals for overseas assignments, management must recognize that no one style of leadership will be equally effective in all countries. People in various countries have widely divergent backgrounds, education, cultures, and religions—and live within a variety of social conditions and economic and political systems. Human resource managers must consider all these factors because they can have a rather dramatic effect on the working environment of the person selected.

An appropriate management approach for the multinational corporation must be based on common sense and informed conjecture. It seems

[56] Allen L. Hixon, "Why Corporations Make Haphazard Overseas Staffing Decisions," p. 91.

[57] Gurudutt M. Baliga and James C. Baker, "Multinational Corporate Policies for Expatriate Managers: Selection, Training, Evaluation," *SAM Advanced Management Journal,* 50 (Autumn 1985), p. 32.

[58] Mark E. Mendenhall, Edward Dunbar, and Gary R. Oddou, "Expatriate Selection, Training and Career-Pathing: A Review and Critique," *Human Resource Management,* 26 (Fall 1987), pp. 331–345.

reasonable that a successful international manager should possess the following qualities, among others:

- A basic knowledge of history, particularly in countries of old and homogeneous cultures.
- An understanding of the basic economic and sociological concepts of various countries.
- An interest in the host country and a willingness to learn and use its language.
- A respect for differing philosophical and ethical approaches to living.

Basically, individuals transferred overseas should have a desire to function, as well as possible, in the host country's environment.

■ THE COST-BENEFIT STAFFING APPROACH FOR THE ECONOMIC UNIFICATION OF EUROPE

Global staffing strategies for operating in the environment of the 1992 economically unified Europe (EC 92) must focus on hiring the most appropriate people. In addition to employing the most suitable workforce, human resource professionals must also assemble a cost-effective workforce. As is indicated from the information in Figure 7-7, the most expensive employee except for those from Belgium is ordinarily a U.S. citizen, although the cost gap between U.S. citizens and U.S. foreign employees is narrowing.[59]

Human resource professionals who staff for EC 92 must continually work to control cost. To fully utilize a cost-benefit strategy, human resource professionals should employ local nationals whenever possible, concentrate on foreign service employees in low-allowance and low–tax cost locations (such as the United Kingdom), and minimize relocation cost by reshuffling overseas employees whenever possible. Some companies try to cut costs overseas by employing such strategies as hiring single employees rather than those with spouses or children. Although discriminating on the basis of marital status does not violate Title VII of the Civil Rights Act of 1964, it does violate some U.S. state laws. Human resource professionals should carefully consider such approaches prior to their utilization.[60]

The methods for selecting a cost-effective international staff will continue to evolve. Human resource professionals in the "New Europe" must constantly search for innovative methods for employing a qualified but cost-effective workforce. However, they must never focus on cost to the detriment of selecting appropriate candidates. Such an approach may result in the selection of individuals who fail to perform satisfactorily. Failures are even more costly than any initial selection expense. One human resource professional estimates that the cost of a failed expatriate employee is three times the individual's salary, not including the price of lost productivity.[61]

---

[59] Neil B. Krupp, "Overseas Staffing for the New Europe," *Personnel,* 67 (July 1990), p. 23.

[60] *Ibid.*

[61] Mike Fergus, "Employees on the Move," *HRMagazine,* 36 (May 1990), p. 45.

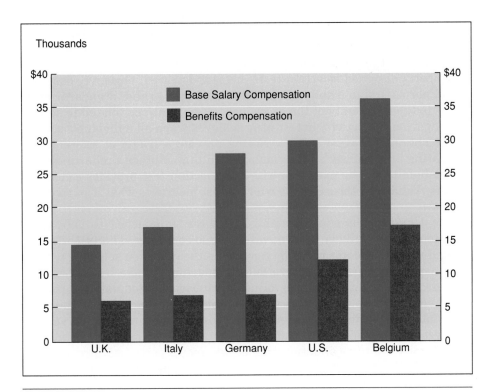

FIGURE 7-7 | Costs of Employing Local Nationals

Source: Adapted from Neil B. Krupp, "Overseas Staffing for the New Europe,"
Personnel, 67 (July 1990), p. 23. Reprinted, by permission of publisher, from
Personnel, July/1990 © 1990. American Management Association, New York.
All rights reserved.

SUMMARY

Selection is the process of choosing from a group of applicants those individuals best suited for a particular position. The selection process often begins with an initial screening of applicants to eliminate those who obviously do not meet the position's requirements. The next step may involve having the prospective employee complete an application for employment. The employer evaluates it to see whether the individual's qualifications match the position's requirements. A well-designed and properly used application form is much more effective than résumés in reducing dozens of applicants to a few bona fide candidates.

Selection tests are often used to help assess an applicant's qualifications and potential for success. Although selection tests may accurately predict an applicant's ability to perform a job, they cannot indicate the extent to which the individual will want to perform it. Another potential problem related primarily to personality tests and interest inventories has to do with the applicant's honesty. There may be a strong motivation for the applicant to respond to questions untruthfully or provide answers that he or she believes the firm expects.

Properly designed selection tests are standardized, objective, based on sound norms, reliable and—of utmost importance—valid. Standardization refers to the uniformity of the procedures and conditions related to administering tests. Objectivity in testing is achieved when all individuals scoring a test obtain the same results. Norms provide a frame of reference for comparing an applicant's performance with that of other similar individuals. Reliability is the extent to which a selection test provides consistent results. Validity is the extent to which a test measures what it purports to measure.

The *Uniform Guidelines* established three approaches to validation: criterion-related validity, content validity, and construct validity. Criterion-related validity is determined by comparing the scores on selection tests to some aspect of job performance as determined, for example, by performance appraisal. There are two basic forms of criterion-related validity: concurrent and predictive. With concurrent validity, the test scores and the criterion data are obtained at essentially the same time. Predictive validity involves administering a test and later obtaining the criterion data. Content validity is a test validation method whereby a person performs certain tasks actually required by the job or completes a paper-and-pencil test that measures relevant job knowledge. Construct validity is a test validation method to determine whether a test measures certain traits or qualities that have been identified as important in performing the job. After a test has been validated, an appropriate cutoff score must be established. An applicant scoring less than the cutoff score will be disqualified. Characteristics related to job performance, which are measurable, include cognitive aptitudes, psychomotor abilities, job knowledge, work samples, vocational interests, and personality. Some firms also test applicants for AIDS and for drug use.

The employment interview is a goal-oriented conversation in which the interviewer and applicant exchange information. The specific content of employment interviews varies greatly, but the following general topics appear fairly consistently in employment interviews: technical competence, personal qualities, and career potential.

Interviews may be conducted in several ways. In a group interview, several applicants interact with one or more company representatives. In a board interview, one candidate is interviewed by several company representatives. The stress interview intentionally creates anxiety to determine how an applicant will react in certain types of situations. A realistic job preview (RJP) conveys unbiased job information to the applicant.

Reference checks provide additional insight into the applicant and are used to verify the accuracy of the information provided. Often a background investigation of the applicant's past employment history is necessary.

Based on all the information obtained, the manager must take the critical step of making the actual hiring decision. The other stages in the selection process have been used to narrow the number of candidates, and the final decision will be a choice from among those still in the running.

After the decision has been made to extend a job offer, the successful candidate takes a physical examination. Typically, a job offer is contingent on the candidate's successful passing of the physical examination. Assuming that no disqualifying medical problems are discovered during the physical examination, the applicant can now be employed.

Negligent hiring and retention of individuals with questionable character are currently hot HRM topics. Employers are advised to make a reasonable background investigation of persons who will occupy jobs in which they could possibly inflict harm on others. During the past decade, employers have begun to be held responsible for employee actions that are outside the scope of the employee's duties. Employers are especially vulnerable to lawsuits if a reasonable background investigation has not been conducted.

One of the most difficult human resource management problems for the multinational organization is that of selecting the appropriate people for foreign assignments. Inappropriate selections are often made, which have negative impacts on multinational operations. In selecting individuals for overseas assignments, management must recognize that no one style of leadership will be equally effective in all countries. People selected must respect and be comfortable with the backgrounds, education, cultures, religions, social conditions, and economic and political systems of the country in which they will work.

Questions for Review

1. What basic steps are normally followed in the selection process?
2. Identify and describe the various factors outside the control of the human resource manager that could affect the selection process.
3. What would be the selection ratio if there were 15 applicants to choose from and only 1 position to fill? Interpret the meaning of this selection ratio.
4. If a firm wants to use selection tests, how should the tests be used to avoid discriminatory practices?
5. What is the general purpose of the preliminary interview?
6. What types of questions should be asked on an application form?

7. What basic conditions should be met if selection tests are to be used in the screening process? Briefly describe each.
8. Briefly describe the objectives of the employment interview.
9. Define each of the following terms:
   a. nondirective interview
   b. structured interview
   c. group interview
   d. board interview
   e. stress interview
10. What is the purpose of reference checks and background investigations?
11. What are the reasons for administering a physical examination?
12. Describe the most important factors in selecting someone for an overseas assignment.

Terms for Review

Selection
Selection ratio
Weighted application blank (WAB)
Standardization
Objectivity
Norm
Reliability
Test-retest method
Equivalent forms method
Split-halves method
Validity
Criterion-related validity
Concurrent validity
Predictive validity
Content validity
Construct validity
Cutoff score
Cognitive aptitude tests
Psychomotor abilities tests
Finger dexterity

Manual dexterity
Wrist-finger speed
Aiming
Job knowledge tests
Work-sample tests
Vocational interest tests
Employment interview
Unstructured interview
Structured interview
Situational questions
Job knowledge questions
Job-sample simulation questions
Worker requirements questions
Group interview
Board interview
Stress interview
Realistic job preview (RJP)
Reference checks
Utility analysis

INCIDENT 1   ■   Business First!   ■

As production manager for Thompson Manufacturing, Jack Stephens has the final authority to approve the hiring of any new supervisors who work for him. The human resource manager performs the initial screening of all prospective supervisors and then sends the most likely candidates to Jack for interviews.

One day recently, Jack received a call from Pete Peterson, the human resource manager: "Jack, I've just spoken to a young man who may be just who you're looking for to fill that final line supervisor position. He has some good work experience and it appears as if his head is screwed on straight. He's here right now and available if you could possibly see him." Jack hesitated a moment before answering. "Gee, Pete," he said, "I'm certainly busy today but I'll try to squeeze him in. Send him on down."

A moment later Allen Guthrie, the new applicant, arrived at Jack's office and introduced himself. "Come on in, Allen," said Jack. "I'll be right with you after I make a few phone calls."

Fifteen minutes later Jack finished the calls and began talking with Allen. Jack was quite impressed. After a few minutes Jack's door opened and a supervisor yelled, "We have a small problem on line number 1 and need your help." Jack stood up and said, "Excuse me a minute, Allen." Ten minutes later Jack returned, and the conversation continued for ten more minutes before a series of phone calls again interrupted them.

The same pattern of interruptions continued for the next hour. Finally Allen looked at his watch and said, "I'm sorry, Mr. Stephens, but I have to pick up my wife." "Sure thing, Allen," Jack said as the phone rang again. "Call me later today."

Questions

1. What specific policies should a company follow to avoid interviews like this one?
2. Explain why Jack, not Pete, should make the selection decision.

INCIDENT 2 ▪ Should We Test? ▪

"Mrs. Peacock, I've decided that we should quit using selection tests altogether," said John Barnes, the human resource manager. "I'm not sure there are any that could be defended if we ever got a discrimination complaint." John had just read a report of a court decision finding a large company nearby guilty of discriminatory employment practices. Essentially, the company had been using tests designed to measure general intelligence as a screening device for all categories of employees. The court held that the tests caused certain groups to be eliminated from employment consideration.

The tests that John's firm, Miller Chemical Company, used were aptitude tests, carefully designed for specific jobs. For example, the test for a certain mechanical mixer operator job included questions about the relative weights of various liquids and solids, the ways in which emulsions were formed, and the dangers involved in working with rotating machinery. No study had been done, however, to determine the relationship between performance on the test and success on the job. Most of the managers felt that the interviews and references were more valuable than the tests. Besides, John thought that validation

of the tests would be too expensive and time consuming.

As John was thinking about all of this, Nancy Peacock called back. "Mr. Barnes," she said, "I've been thinking about your decision to eliminate our tests. Do we still have enough to go on in making an employment decision?" "Not really," said John, "but I don't know what else we can do to be safe. A discrimination suit could tie us up for months. The tests may not be any more discriminatory than interviews, but I don't think that interviews can get us into trouble. The same thing is true of applications and reference checks. It would just be harder for the EEOC to attack us on those points." "Then I suppose the decision is final?" asked Nancy. "I've thought about it a lot, Mrs. Peacock," said John, "and I suppose it is."

Questions

1. Do you agree with the rationale for John's decision? Explain.
2. Under what circumstances might Miller Chemical have been required to validate the tests?

Developing HRM Skills

Selecting the best person to fill a vacant position is one of the most important tasks of human resource management. As all managers recognize, many factors must be considered in order to ensure proper selection. The selection decision you will be dealing with in this exercise is necessary because George Hendricks has just been promoted, and before he starts his new job, he must determine his replacement. George's firm is an affirmative action employer, and presently there are few women in management. George has some excellent employees to choose from, but there are many factors to consider before a decision can be made. The people upstairs made it perfectly clear that they expect George to select an individual who can perform as well as he did over the last six years. The people he worked with on the line made it clear that they want Sam. The women on the line have indicated, to everyone who will listen, that it is time for a female supervisor, in at least one division. But it is George's decision, and he must select the best person, regardless of any criticism he may receive.

Sam Philips, an employee of the company for the past eleven years, is one possible candidate. He wants this promotion, needs the higher pay, wants the respect and influence to be gained, and admires the nice office that George has now. Sam is recognized as one of the most technically capable individuals in the division. He is from the old school of thought: We get things done through discipline, and we don't put up with people allowing their personal problems to interfere with work.

Frieda Lott, an employee for seven years, is another candidate for the promotion. She wants the promotion primarily because she can do a good job and represent the women on the line. She was an excellent student in college and believes she can deal effectively with the personal problems of others. She is recognized as technically capable and has an undergraduate degree in management.

Fred Rubble, an employee of the company for six years, is the final candidate. He believes he should get the promotion primarily because he can do the best job. Fred is very capable but not quite as familiar with all the technical aspects of the job as Frieda or Sam. He has an associate degree in liberal arts, but he is taking business classes at night. Fred is also actively involved in the community and has held various civic offices.

Four individuals will have roles in this exercise: one to serve as George Hendricks, the current supervisor, and three to be the candidates for the promotion. Your instructor will provide the participants with additional information necessary to complete the exercise.

REFERENCES

Ambash, Joseph W. "Knowing Your Limits: How Far Can You Go When Checking an Applicant's Background?" *Management World,* 19 (March–April 1990), pp. 8–10.

Atwood, Caleb S., and James M. Neel. "New Lawsuits Expand Employer Liability." *HRMagazine,* 35 (October 1990), pp. 74–75.

Berger, Raymond M., and Donna H. Tucker. "How to Evaluate a Selection Test." *Personnel Journal,* 66 (February 1987), pp. 88–90.

Bottorf, Dana. "The Velvet Boot." *New England Business,* 9 (October 19, 1987), pp. 21–25.

Bragg, Arthur. "Checking References." *Sales and Marketing Management,* 142 (November 1990), pp. 68–70.

Briscoe, Dennis R., and Susan Harwood. "Improving the Interview Process." *Personnel,* 61 (September 1987), pp. 18–20.

Byrne, John A. "Why Headhunters Are Hunting Each Other." *Business Week* (January 14, 1991), p. 43.

Decker, Kurt H. "The Rights and Wrongs of Screening." *Security Management,* 34 (January 1990), pp. 44–49.

Dossin, Milton S., and Nancie L. Merritt. "Sign-On Bonuses Score for Recruiters." *HRMagazine,* 35 (March 1990), pp. 42–43.

Fagiano, David. "Interviewing for Style." *Management Review,* 79 (November 1990), p. 4.

Fenton, James W., Jr. "Negligent Hiring/Retention Adds to Human Resources Woes." *Personnel Journal,* 69 (April 1990), pp. 62–73.

Fitz-enz, Jac. "Getting—and Keeping—Good Employees." *Personnel,* 67 (August 1990), pp. 25–28.

Goddard, Robert, Jeremy Fox, and W. E. Patton. "The Job-Hire Sale." *Personnel Administrator,* 34 (June 1989), pp. 120–124.

Jenks, James M. "Protecting Privacy Rights." *Personnel Journal,* 66 (September 1987), p. 123.

Jenks, James M., and Brian L. P. Zevnik. "ABCs of Job Interviewing." *Harvard Business Review,* 67 (July–August 1989), pp. 38–39, 42.

Kowal, Dennis M. "Emphasize Integrity Assessment in Interviews." *Personnel Journal,* 69 (June 1990), pp. 66–71.

Krupp, Neil B. "Overseas Staffing for the New Europe." *Personnel,* 67 (July 1990), pp. 20–25.

McKee, Thomas E., and Paul E. Bayes. "Why Audit Background Investigations?" *Internal Auditor,* 11 (October 1987), p. 53.

McKendrick, Joseph E., Jr. "Latest AMS Foundation Survey Finds: One-Third of Nation's Employers Have or Are Considering Drug Testing." *Management World,* 19 (March–April 1990), pp. 2–4.

Martinez, Michelle Nelly. "Creative Ways to Employ People with Disabilities." *HRMagazine,* 35 (November 1990), pp. 40–44, 101.

Martinez, Michelle Nelly. "Making Room for Work/Family Positions." *HRMagazine,* 35 (August 1990), pp. 45–47.

Mercer, Michael W., and John J. Seres. "Using Scorable Interview Tests in Hiring." *Personnel,* 61 (June 1987), p. 57.

Messmer, Max. "Strategic Staffing for the '90s." *Personnel Journal,* 69 (October 1990), pp. 92–97.

Miceli, Marcia P. "Effects of Realistic Job Previews on Newcomer Affect and Behavior." *Journal of Organizational Behavior Management,* 8 (Spring–Summer 1986), pp. 73–88.

"Negligent Hiring Costs Companies." *Supervisory Management,* 35 (March 1990), p. 2.

Overman, Stephanie. "A Delicate Balance Protects Everyone's Rights." *HRMagazine,* 35 (November 1990), pp. 36–39.

Paunonen, Sampo V., Douglas N. Jackson, and Steven M. Oberman. "Personnel Selection Decisions: Effects of Applicant Personality and the Letter of Reference." *Organizational Behavior and Human Decision Processes,* 40 (August 1987), p. 97.

Segal, Jonathan A. "Follow the Yellow Brick Road." *HRMagazine,* (February 1990), pp. 83–86.

Smart, Bradford D. "Progressive Approaches for Hiring the Best People." *Training and Development Journal,* 41 (September 1987), pp. 46–53.

Waerdt, Lois Vander. "Taking Nothing for Granted—Check Applicants' Background and References—Thoroughly." *Management World,* 9 (March–April 1990), pp. 5–7.

APPENDIX   POTENTIAL INTERVIEWING PROBLEMS

One source alone lists almost a dozen serious problems associated with unstructured interviews.[1] Although each of the following potential interviewing problems can be satisfactorily dealt with, they nevertheless threaten the success of employment interviews.

■ LACK OF GOALS

A management axiom is that clearly stated goals are essential if meaningful activity is to take place. This requirement is no less essential for the interviewing process. Goals for the selection interview are tied to both the job to be filled and the qualifications of the applicant. Unfortunately, individuals are often selected on the basis of whim, with less consideration for the skills, knowledge, and abilities required to perform the job.

In order to effectively conduct an interview, the interviewer must know the job's content and the human requirements for satisfactorily performing the job. As we previously discussed, this information is obtained from job analysis. Without it, the interviewer cannot set goals, ask pertinent questions, or make rational judgments about candidates.

■ PREMATURE JUDGMENTS (FIRST IMPRESSION BIAS)

Some researchers have established that the first few minutes of personal meetings typically provide the most lasting impressions of ourselves to others. This being the case, an interviewer should consciously resist the temptation to make quick decisions about applicants. When the interviewer does make a premature judgment, he or she will likely spend the remaining interview time searching for information to support the decision already made. This practice represents not only wasted time but a foolhardy approach to selection. A more appropriate technique is to objectively gather all needed data, analyze it, and then make an evaluation.

---

[1] Terry W. Mullins and Ronald H. Davis, "A Strategy for Managing the Selection Interview Process," *Personnel Administrator,* 26 (March 1981), pp. 66–67.

■ INTERVIEWER DOMINATION

When interviewers dominate the conversation, collecting job-related information about the candidate is hindered. In successful interviews, relevant information must flow both ways: Thus interviewers must develop listening skills. Listening is essential for effective communication, but studies have shown that most of us listen with about 25 percent efficiency.[2] One of the most common errors made by an interviewer is talking too much. The applicant should be permitted to talk about 75 percent of the time during a job interview.[3] People listen in different ways, but all listening methods do not provide satisfactory results. Individuals can engage in marginal listening, giving the speaker only part of their attention. When people do this, they may understand only a part of what is said. But what about the remainder? Often the most essential part of what was said is not heard, in which case it obviously will not be understood.

A second type of listening is referred to as evaluative. In this case, while the speaker is talking, the listener starts formulating his or her response or rebuttal to what is being said. Once again, parts of the speaker's message are not even received, and portions that were received are often misunderstood.

A third type of listening is called empathic. Here, the listener makes an effort to enter the mind of the speaker. The listener attempts to put aside personal biases and his or her own frame of reference. While all transmissions must ultimately be evaluated, the evaluation is not made prematurely. It is delayed until the entire message has been received and a sincere effort has been made to understand what the speaker means. Empathic listening is difficult. Yet, it is this approach that permits understanding, and therefore communication, to take place.

From the firm's viewpoint, the objective of the employment interview is to acquire sufficient information for making an informed choice. If the interviewer dominates the conversation, dispenses facts, or merely outlines the parameters of the position, he or she will not succeed. A primary interviewing goal is to gather information. To do so, interviewers must question and listen.

■ INCONSISTENT QUESTIONS

Various applicants may be asked different questions by the same or different interviewers. When this happens, all the applicants are not judged on the same basis, and charges of discrimination may result. If interviewers ask applicants essentially the same questions and in the same sequence, a better foundation is provided for comparing the qualifications of the applicants, and higher reliability should occur.[4]

---

[2] Joel P. Bowman and Bernadine P. Branchaw, *Business Communication* (Chicago: The Dryden Press, 1987), p. 587.

[3] Charles Denova, "The Job Interviewer and the Supervisor," *Supervision,* 45 (September 1983), p. 26.

[4] Paul S. Greenlaw and John P. Kohl, "Selection Interviewing and the New Uniform Federal Guidelines," *Personnel Administrator,* 25 (August 1980), p. 78.

■ CENTRAL TENDENCY

The central tendency error occurs when an interviewer rates virtually all candidates as average. In this instance, the interviewer fails to differentiate between strong and weak candidates.

■ HALO ERROR

The type of bias known as halo error occurs when an interviewer is overly impressed with one or more personal characteristics and permits this bias to unduly affect his or her opinion of the applicant. For example, an interviewer who places a high value on neatness or communication skill may automatically favor candidates who rate high on these attributes, without due regard for other abilities that may relate more directly to job requirements.

■ CONTRAST EFFECTS

An error in judgment may occur when, for example, an interviewer meets with several poorly qualified applicants and then confronts a mediocre candidate. By comparison, the last applicant may appear to be better qualified than he or she actually is and, as a result, receive a higher rating than deserved.

■ INTERVIEWER BIAS

All individuals, through their experiences, have acquired certain biases. These biases can totally disrupt the interviewing process, which should be as objective as possible. Thus interviewers must know themselves, acknowledge and understand their own prejudices, and learn to deal with those prejudices. If he or she is unable to do this, the interviewer's attitude—perhaps at the unconscious level—can lead to unfair treatment of candidates. For example, research has indicated that interviewers terminate interviews with physically handicapped applicants sooner than they do with nonhandicapped candidates.[5] With the implementation of the Americans with Disabilities Act, this practice is clearly discriminatory.

Another example of such bias is stereotyping; the interviewer sometimes has a preconception of the ideal candidate. Some interviewers may not believe that women or blacks, for example, are qualified to handle executive positions because they do not match the interviewers' stereotypes. They may view such individuals as best suited for secretarial, clerical, or more

---

[5] Robert L. Dipboye, "Self-Fulfilling Prophecies in the Selection-Recruitment Interview," *The Academy of Management Review,* 7 (October 1982), p. 52.

menial jobs. Although actions based on these stereotyped views are illogical and clearly illegal, they do occur and, as a result, qualified candidates may be eliminated from the selection process.

■ LACK OF INTERVIEWER TRAINING

Employment interviews are often conducted by line managers who interview infrequently. Typically, they are not well trained in interviewing techniques. This deficiency is compounded by the other pressures of their jobs. As a result, interview goals may not be clearly formulated, and these interviewers may not be prepared to answer questions asked by the candidate.

■ BEHAVIOR SAMPLE

It has been suggested that even if an interviewer spent a week with an applicant, the sample of behavior would be too small to properly assess the candidate's qualifications. Furthermore, not only is the sample of behavior inadequate, the candidate's behavior during an interview is also seldom typical or natural.[6]

■ NONVERBAL COMMUNICATION

Words are the most important symbols used in communication. As a result, employment interviews tend to focus on them. However, facial expressions and body movements can often convey meaning very effectively. The interviewer should remember that nonverbal communication accounts for about 80 percent of the information-gathering process.[7] An interviewer should be aware of his or her nonverbal behavior, which might transmit unintended signals. For example, the interviewer may glance at the clock to determine how much time is left for the interview. The applicant may interpret this action as meaning "the interview is over." Other actions that often occur during the interview and common interpretations of them by applicants are shown in Table A-1.

Often interviewers are not fully aware of their nonverbal behavior. They should make a conscious effort to view themselves as applicants do in order to avoid sending inappropriate or unintended signals.

---

[6] Robert L. Decker, "The Employment Interview: Are We Seeing the Demise of Another Management Prerogative?" *Personnel Administrator,* 27 (November 1981), p. 72.

[7] Dennis M. Kowal, "Communication: Emphasize Integrity Assessment in Interviews," *Personnel Journal,* 69 (June 1990), p. 66.

TABLE A-1 | Nonverbal Communication

Behavior	Possible Interpretation
Sitting stiffly behind desk	*This is a very formal meeting. I'd better not reveal too much of myself.*
Reading the application form	*This interviewer doesn't even know who I am.*
Nodding head	*You understand what I'm saying.*
Frequent glancing out the window	*This person would rather be someplace else.*
Receiving telephone calls	*This manager is too busy to see me.*
Frowning	*My answer to that question didn't go over very well.*

■ INTERPRETATION OF BEHAVIOR

An additional problem in assessing an applicant is that of interpreting his or her behavior. Suppose, for example, that during a stress interview in which the interviewer makes insulting remarks, the candidate simply gets up and walks out or decides to sue. Should this be interpreted as (1) an indication that the candidate is well informed, that is, knows his or her rights; (2) an indication of immaturity and insecurity; or (3) an indication of stupidity, in that the candidate has lost a chance of a job? No one, including the "experts," has satisfactorily solved this problem.[8]

■ INAPPROPRIATE QUESTIONS

A basic requirement in employee selection is that the questions asked be job related. During an interview, it is very easy for an interviewer to innocently ask questions that have answers which reveal irrelevant information about women or minorities. Employers must be extremely cautious in asking questions that are generally considered risky from a legal viewpoint.

At this point, litigation has revolved around two basic themes. First, do questions give the impression of a discriminatory attitude? For example, are women asked about marital status, child care, and so on? Another example would be a male interviewer referring to female employees as "girls." Second, does the question have the effect of creating an adverse impact on women or minorities?[9]

---

[8] Robert L. Decker, "The Employment Interview," p. 72.

[9] Richard D. Arvey and James E. Campion, "The Employment Interview: A Summary and Review of Recent Research," *Personnel Psychology,* 35 (1982), p. 289.

P·A·R·T T·W·O

CASE II

Parma Cycle Company:
Workers for the New Plant

Gene Wilson, the corporate planner at Parma Cycle Company, was ecstatic as he talked with the human resource director, Jesse Heard, on that Tuesday morning in early 1992. He had just received word that the board of directors had approved the plan for Parma's new southern plant, to be located in Clarksdale, Mississippi. "I really appreciate your help on this, Jesse," Gene said. "Without the research you did on the human resource needs for the new plant, I don't think that it would have been approved." "We still have a long way to go," said Jesse. He continued, "There's no doubt that we can construct the building and install the machinery, but getting skilled workers in Clarksdale, Mississippi, may not be so easy." "Well," said Gene, "the results of the labor survey that you did in Clarksdale last year indicate that we'll be able to get by. Anyway, some of the people here at Parma will surely agree to transfer."

Clarksdale, population 25,000, is the county seat of Coahoma County, in the Mississippi River delta below Memphis, Tennessee. Per capita income in the county hovered above $7,000 a year, far below the national average and less than half the level in the Parma, Ohio, area.

"When is the new plant scheduled to open?" asked Jesse. Gene replied, "The building will be finished in June, the machinery will be in by July, and the goal is to be in production by September." "Gosh," said Jesse, "I'd better get to work."

A few minutes later, back in his office, Jesse considered what the future held at Parma Cycle. The company had been located in Parma, Ohio, a Cleveland suburb, since its

founding. It had grown over the years to become the nation's third largest bicycle manufacturer. The decision to open the Clarksdale plant had been made in hopes of cutting production costs, through lower wages, and improving quality. Although no one ever came right out and said it, it was assumed that the new plant would be nonunion. The elimination of union work rules was expected to be a benefit.

The state of Mississippi had offered a ten-year exemption from all property taxes. This was a significant advantage because tax rates for Cleveland area industries were extremely high. Jesse was pleased that he had been involved in the discussions from the time that the new plant had been first suggested. Even with all the advanced preparation he had done, he knew that the coming months would be extremely difficult for him and his staff.

As Jesse was thinking about all this, his assistant, Ed Deal, walked in with a bundle of papers. "Hi, Ed," said Jesse, "I'm glad you're here. The Clarksdale plant is definitely on the way and you and I need to get our act together." "That's great," said Ed. "It's quite a coincidence, too, because I was just going over this stack of job descriptions, identifying which ones might be eliminated as we scale back at this plant." Jesse said, "Remember, Ed, we are not going to cut back very much here. Some jobs will be deleted and others added. But out of the 800 positions here, I'll bet that not more than 40 will actually be cut." "So, what you are saying is that we basically have to staff the plant with people we hire from the Clarksdale area?" Ed asked. Jesse replied, "No, Ed, we will have some people here who are willing to transfer even though their jobs are not being eliminated. We will then replace them with others we hire in the Cleveland area. Most of the workers at Clarksdale, though, will be recruited from that area."

"What about the management team?" asked Ed. "Well," said Jesse, "I think the boss already knows who the main people will be down there. They are managers we currently have on board plus a fellow we located at a defunct three-wheeler plant in Mound Bayou, Mississippi."

"Who will be the human resource director down there?" asked Ed. "Well," replied Jesse, "I don't think I'm talking out of school by telling you that I plan to recommend you for the job." After letting that soak in for a minute, Ed said, "It's no secret I was hoping for that. When will we know for sure?"

"There's really not much doubt," said Jesse. "I'm so sure that I've decided to put you in charge of human resources for the whole project. During the next two weeks I'd like you to put together a comprehensive plan. I want a detailed report of the people we will need, including their qualifications. Secondly, we need more information about the labor supply in Clarksdale. Finally, I'd like for you to come up with a general idea of who might be willing to transfer from this plant. They are really going to be the backbone of our workforce at Clarksdale."

"Okay, Jesse, but I'll need a lot of help," said Ed as he gathered his papers and left. As Jesse watched Ed leave he thought he noticed a certain snappiness about Ed's movements that had not been there before.

Questions

1. What procedures should be followed in determining the human resource needs at the new plant?
2. How might Jesse and Ed go about recruiting workers in Clarksdale? What about managers?

HUMAN RESOURCE DEVELOPMENT

Human Resource Research

Human Resource Planning, Recruitment, and Selection

Human Resource Development

Employee and Labor Relations

Human Resource Management

Safety and Health

Compensation and Benefits

CHAPTER 8

ORGANIZATION CHANGE AND HUMAN RESOURCE DEVELOPMENT

CHAPTER OBJECTIVES

1. Describe the organization change sequence, accompanying difficulties, and ways to reduce resistance to change.
2. Define human resource development (HRD), list the general purposes of HRD, describe factors influencing HRD, and explain the human resource development process.
3. Explain how HRD needs are determined and HRD objectives are established, describe the various management development methods, and explain the HRD methods specifically available for operative employees.
4. Describe problems associated with implementation of HRD programs, explain the importance of HRD evaluation, and describe the significance of employee orientation.

Marian Lillie, an experienced accountant, competently handled the administrative tasks for an automobile dealership for over ten years. She was familiar with all aspects of the business. Two months ago, the dealership was sold to a young man who had graduated from a prominent university in the Northeast. Soon after he assumed control of the firm, he automated every conceivable administrative function. Marian was not consulted at any point in the process. She was, however, presented with a procedures manual when the project was completed. Later she was overheard telling a coworker, "I know this new system is not going to work."

Imagining Marian Lillie's opposition to changes that she doesn't understand isn't difficult. Based on her last statement, she isn't likely to support the changes, which were made without her consultation.

We devote the first portion of this chapter to a discussion of organization change and to defining human resource development (HRD). Then we describe factors that influence HRD. Next, we address elements of the HRD process, which include determining HRD needs, establishing objectives, selecting methods and media, and implementing and evaluating the HRD program. We devote the final portion of the chapter to employee orientation.

■ ORGANIZATION CHANGE

Change involves moving from one condition to another, and it may affect individuals, groups, or even an entire organization. All organizations will experience change at one time or another. The most prominent changes occurring today in business include the following:

- Changes in organizational structure caused by mergers, acquisitions, rapid growth, and downsizing.
- Changes in technology and the way people work, resulting largely from computerization.
- Changes in employees—a diverse workforce consisting of these groups:
  - Older workers
  - More women
  - More minorities
  - Highly educated employees
  - Illiterate people
  - Many different ethnic groups[1]

Everyone is ultimately affected by change. Those who want to learn about human resource development must first understand the change sequence, the accompanying difficulties, and ways to reduce resistance to change.

The Change Sequence

Change for the sake of change is seldom justified. Some degree of stability is needed to allow employees to accomplish assigned tasks. Even too many rational changes over a short period of time may leave workers bewildered and confused.[2] Change can also be a source of mental and physical problems, regardless of whether the change has favorable or unfavorable consequences. It is a contributing factor for most mental and physical health problems, as it destroys homeostasis.[3]

Because of the impact of change on the organization and its employees, change should be undertaken only when a real need for it exists. Of course, circumstances in the internal or external environments may make change desirable or even necessary (see Figure 8-1). Basically, the impetus for change comes from a belief that the organization and its human resources can be more productive and successful after change occurs. But if change is to be successfully implemented, it must be approached systematically. Many managers tend to feel that "we have always done it this way, so why

---

[1] Marcia Kleiman, "Ease the Stress of Change," *Personnel Journal,* 68 (September 1989), p. 107.

[2] H. Kent Baker and Stephen R. Holmberg, "Stepping Up to Supervision: Coping with Change," *Supervisory Management,* 27 (March 1982), p. 23.

[3] George S. Everly, Jr., "Managing Change Demands Three Simple, Personal Steps," *Data Management,* 22 (September 1984), p. 21.

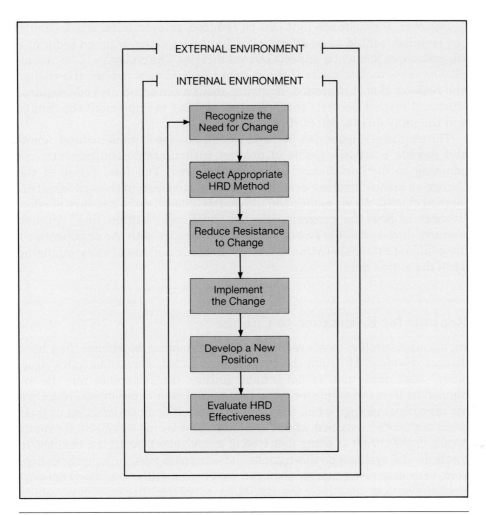

EXTERNAL ENVIRONMENT

INTERNAL ENVIRONMENT

Recognize the
Need for Change

Select Appropriate
HRD Method

Reduce Resistance
to Change

Implement
the Change

Develop a New
Position

Evaluate HRD
Effectiveness

FIGURE 8-1 | The Organization Change Sequence

argue with success?" However, a firm's past success does not guarantee future prosperity. Once the need for change has been recognized, an HRD method tailored to the particular situation can be selected.

Reducing resistance to change is crucial to success. At times, this may be extremely difficult because it usually requires shifts in attitudes. Although Marian Lillie may not overtly resist a change and risk losing her job, the new owner could have prepared her better to accept the change and work to make it successful. Many times resistance to change is substantial. Consider, for instance, a machine operator who has been using one piece of equipment over a long period of time and has just been told that she will have to learn another skill. In this situation, the machine operator may become quite anxious and vigorously oppose any proposed changes in her work routine.

However, if resistance to it can be reduced, or even eliminated, change can be implemented more effectively. Change may stem from an order or a suggestion, or it may be undertaken voluntarily. The change will be accomplished more satisfactorily if the person involved in it desires the change and believes that it is needed. Bringing about a change in attitude requires trust and respect between the person attempting to implement the change and the individual(s) affected by the change.

The change sequence does not end when a change is implemented. A new and flexible position capable of dealing with present requirements and adapting to further change must be developed. The final phase of the change sequence involves evaluating the effectiveness of the specific HRD method chosen. As we mentioned previously, one primary measure of effectiveness is how the program affected the firm's "bottom line." Human resource development is an ongoing process because both the organization's internal and external environments are dynamic and are always impinging upon the status quo.

Reasons for Resistance to Change

In business circles, employees' "natural" resistance to change has been discussed widely. Although change is often resisted, sometimes quite vigorously,[4] such opposition is not innate. Rather, the resistance may be explained in terms of employee expectations and past experiences. Individuals may resist change when they feel that it will deny satisfaction of their basic needs. For instance, one of the most frightening prospects for many people is the threat of being deprived of employment. At times, changes in methods and systems do downgrade and eliminate jobs. In a more positive vein, they may also generate the need for greater skills. Yet, many employees believe that they lack the flexibility to adjust. Because most adults derive their primary income from their work, they would be economically unable to obtain the basic necessities of life if they were unemployed. Therefore, it is easy to understand the threatening nature of change.

Many changes in organizations are perceived as disrupting established social groups. In fact, there may be an inordinate fear that change will disturb established friendships. Because numerous social needs are satisfied on the job, any threat to these relationships may be resisted.

The potential threat to a person's status in the organization may also be a powerful reason for resisting change. Many workers literally invest their lives in their jobs. They are likely to resist any change that they perceive as upsetting their standing in the organization or their sense of importance. For instance, the master machinist, when faced with new automation in his firm, may fear that his high-level skill will no longer be needed and that his prestige will be lowered. Regardless of the reasons individuals resist change, management must take action to minimize the loss of productivity

---

[4] Rensis Likert and Jane Gibson Likert, *New Ways of Managing Conflict* (New York: McGraw-Hill, 1976), p. 245.

associated with change. Productivity and accuracy generally do decline during periods of change. Instead of thinking about their work, employees are worrying about their survival or loss of status. They are also absent more, either because of illness or because they are looking for another job.[5]

In summary, the prospect of change can conceivably threaten every level of human need. This feeling of being threatened often causes employees to resist change. The resistance is not "natural" but is based on reasons that are perceived as being quite logical.

Reducing Resistance to Change

In order for a firm to gain general acceptance of a needed change, management must be aware of ways to lessen resistance. Although negative attitudes cannot be overcome overnight, the following approaches can serve to increase employees' acceptance of change.

Building Trust and Confidence. The degree of employee trust and confidence in management relates directly to past experiences. If employees have suffered in the past as a result of change, they may reasonably attempt to avoid future changes. When management has misrepresented the effects of change, resistance tends to be even greater. For example, when faced with the prospect of having to reduce the workforce, management may assure employees that layoffs will be based on individual performance. However, if previous layoffs appeared to be determined by seniority or favoritism, employees may not believe that current actions will be any different.

Conversely, management builds trust by dealing with employees in an open and straightforward manner. Workers who are told that they need additional training will accept the idea much more readily if they have confidence in management. The desired level of trust cannot be achieved quickly. Rather, it results from a long period of fair dealing by the firm's management.

Developing Open Communication. An estimated 90 percent of "confidential" information in most organizations is not truly confidential. It is withheld from employees because of management's unwillingness to share information.[6] Such managers create a climate that breeds mistrust and fear. Any rumor of planned changes may then become extremely distorted, with the firm's employees programed to fear the worst.

By sharing information with employees, management can take a giant step toward developing open communications. In speaking to this point, Louis Lunborg, former chairman of the board of Bank of America, once stated the following:

---

[5] Marcia Kleiman, "Ease the Stress of Change," p. 107.

[6] Justin G. Longnecker, *Principles of Management and Organizational Behavior,* 3rd ed. (Columbus, Ohio: Charles E. Merrill, 1973), p. 479.

People want to know several things. They want to know what their own job is all about, why they are doing what we ask them to do, what good it does anybody, and above all, how well they are doing it. And then they want to know what's going on. If they see strange things happening or hear rumors that something new is about to happen, they want to know about it.

If you don't tell them, you're saying, "It's none of your business," and that in turn means, "I just don't think you are important enough." It is the deadliest thing you can do to people.[7]

Managers must recognize that subordinates are human beings and deal with them accordingly. Their informational needs should be recognized and reasonably met, whenever possible.

Employee Participation. People such as Marian Lillie are more inclined to accept changes if they are given the opportunity to participate in the planning. For instance, suppose that management determines that a department's operating budget must be cut by 25 percent. The department's manager may more readily accept this change if permitted to help determine the extent of the cuts and where they should be made. Participation is also more effective when permitted in the early planning stages. For example, an employee might not feel too involved if brought in on a change the day before it is to be implemented. Another caution regarding participation relates to the effect of the change on the individuals involved. If the change will have a negative impact—for example, if their jobs are in jeopardy—then management should not have them participate in their own demise.[8]

Generally speaking, participation can be helpful in minimizing resistance to change. In some cases resistance can be eliminated. In fact, developing a participative climate within which employees aggressively seek change is often possible. In order to achieve such an atmosphere, it is necessary to remove, or at least minimize, the employees' fears of being unable to satisfy their personal needs. Managers must be convinced that their own actions—not the employees' inherent nature—are most often responsible for attitudes toward change. Only then can human resource development programs be effective.

■ HUMAN RESOURCE DEVELOPMENT: DEFINITION AND SCOPE

Human resource development (HRD) is planned, continuous effort by management to improve employee competency levels and organizational performance through training, education, and development programs. The broad scope of the HRD function is reflected in its three components:

---

[7] Louis B. Lunborg, "Managing for Tomorrow," *Information and Records Management* (April 1971), p. 72. Reprinted by permission.

[8] Leonard Ackerman, "Whose Ox Is Being Gored?" *HRMagazine,* 36 (February 1991), p. 96.

training, education, and development.[9] **Training** includes those activities that serve to improve an individual's performance on a currently held job or one related to it.[10] Showing a worker how to operate a lathe or a supervisor how to schedule daily production are examples of training. U.S. business firms spend more than $200 billion a year on formal and informal job-related training. They educate more people each year than all educational institutions combined. The recent explosion in the need for training stems from the need to adapt to rapid changes in technology, improve the quality of products and services, and increase productivity to remain competitive.[11] **Education** consists of learning new skills, knowledge, and attitudes that will enable the employee to assume a new job involving different tasks at some future time.[12] Seminars designed to develop communication or leadership skills fall into this category. Training and education both focus on either currently held jobs or predetermined different jobs within the organization. **Development** involves learning oriented to both personal and organizational growth but is not restricted to a specific present or future job.[13] It prepares employees to keep pace with the organization as it changes and grows. Developing human resources has become crucial with the rapid advances in technology. "High tech" has made the need for development quite apparent.[14] As jobs grow increasingly complex and impersonal, the need for improved human relations within a firm also becomes increasingly significant. Largely because of this, training and development should be conducted on a continuous basis.

The connection between economic survival and productivity has become obvious in the last decade, with the result that increased productivity has become a strategic goal for many firms.[15] In fact, the primary purpose of HRD is to improve worker productivity and the firm's profitability. Most organizations invest in HRD because they believe that higher profits will result—which often happens. Training frequently improves workers' skills and boosts their motivation. This, in turn, leads to higher productivity and increased profitability.[16] According to a book on corporate trends, "The recognition that people are a company's critical resource—and its greatest storehouse of knowledge—is creating a boom in corporate training and education."[17]

---

[9] Leonard Nadler and Garland D. Wiggs, *Managing Human Resources Development* (San Francisco: Jossey-Bass Publishers, 1989), p. 3.

[10] *Ibid.,* p. 5.

[11] Philip J. Harkins and David Giber, "Linking Business and Education Through Training," *Training and Development Journal,* 43 (October 1989), p. 69.

[12] Leonard Nadler and Garland D. Wiggs, *Managing Human Resources Development,* p. 6.

[13] *Ibid.,* p. 7.

[14] Benjamin B. Tregoe and John W. Zimmerman, "Needed: A Strategy for Human Resource Development," *Training and Development Journal,* 38 (May 1984), p. 78.

[15] George J. McManus, "Team Concept Stressed in Productivity Confab," *Iron Age* (December 7, 1981), p. 47.

[16] Michael Godkewitsch, "The Dollars and Sense of Corporate Training," *Training: The Magazine of Human Resources Development,* 24 (May 1987), pp. 79–81.

[17] John Naisbitt and Patricia Aburdene, *Re-inventing the Corporation* (New York: Warner Books, 1985), p. 165.

Another major goal of HRD is to prevent obsolescence of skills at all levels in the company. Not only can effective HRD programs play a vital role in achieving this goal, they can also upgrade employees' skills to qualify them for promotion. The organization is responsible for helping employees upgrade their skills based on employee aptitudes and interests, in addition to meeting the needs of the company. Human resource development costs should be accepted for what they are—an investment in human resources.

■ THE HUMAN RESOURCE DEVELOPMENT PROCESS

Major adjustments in the external and internal environments necessitate corporate change. The general human resource development process that helps facilitate change is shown in Figure 8-2. Once the need for change is recognized, the process of determining training, education, and development needs begins. Essentially two questions must be asked. The first is, "What are our training needs?" The second is, "What do we want to accomplish through our HRD efforts?" The objectives might be quite narrow if limited to the supervisory ability of a manager. Or they might be so broad as to include improving the management skills of all first-line supervisors.

After stating the process objectives, management can determine the appropriate methods and media for accomplishing them. Various methods and media are available; the selection depends on the nature of HRD goals. Naturally, HRD must be continuously evaluated in order to properly facilitate change and accomplish organizational objectives.

Probably the most common function of an HRD process revolves around training. Increasingly, training departments are being considered as profit centers rather than overhead. The training manager at Hewlett-Packard's Business Computer Sales Center has commented, "We present our contribution to division management, along with the other groups. We are measured on the results we show—more training provided, more skills learned, more quickly." A training department that is evaluated on results achieved *must* think like a profit center.[18] Training, as with all HRD functions, requires continuous reevaluation.

■ FACTORS INFLUENCING HUMAN RESOURCE DEVELOPMENT

Several of the most important factors that influence training and development are shown in Figure 8-3 on page 276. How these factors are addressed often determines whether a firm achieves its HRD objectives.

---

[18] Chris Lee, "Training Profiles: The View from Ground Level," *Training: The Magazine of Human Resources Development,* 23 (October 1986), p. 76.

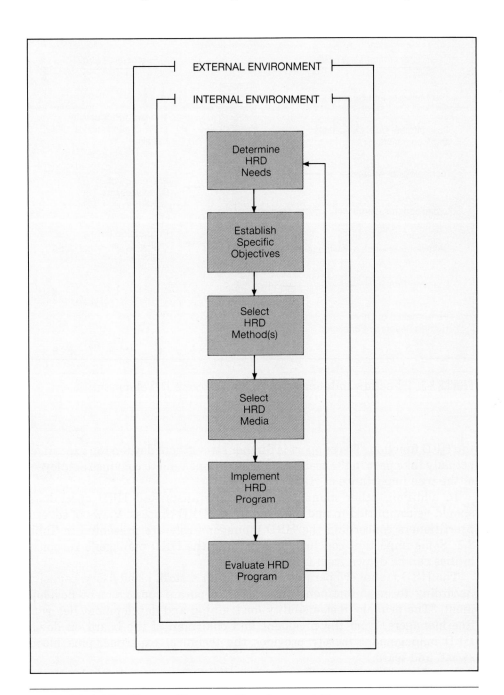

FIGURE 8-2 | The Human Resource Development Process

First and foremost, training and development programs must have top management's full support. This support must be real—not merely lip service—and it should be communicated to the entire organization. True support becomes evident when executives provide the resources needed for

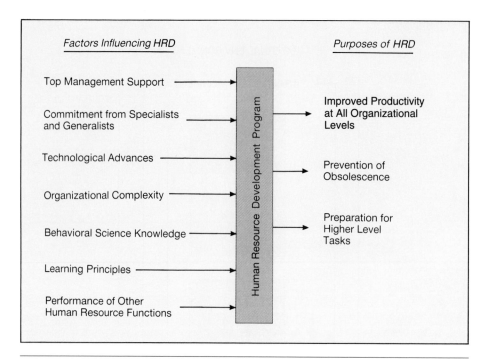

FIGURE 8-3 | Factors Influencing Human Resource Development

the HRD function. The support is further strengthened when top executives actually take part in the training. These actions tend to convince employees of the true importance of HRD programs.

In addition, other managers, both generalists and HRD specialists, should be committed to and involved in the HRD process. Views of several practitioners concerning the HRD manager's role are presented in Table 8-1. Some important conclusions regarding the HRD manager's responsibilities can be drawn from these comments.

The HRD manager operates essentially in a staff, or advisory, capacity. According to one prominent director of corporate management development, "The primary responsibility for training and development lies with line managers, from the president and chairman of the board on down. HRD management merely provides the technical expertise, plus blood, sweat, and tears."

In order to ensure effective programs, HRD managers must show management that there will be a tangible payoff if resources are committed to this effort. One firm, Florida Power Corporation, has a battle cry, "No more training for training's sake." The company designed a new system, which focuses on specific job objectives and ensures that training is provided—but only when needed.[19]

---

[19] *Ibid.*

TABLE 8-1 | Today's Role of the Human Resource Development Manager

Executive	Comments
Senior Advisor, Personnel Development, Chevron Corporation	Principal role is to be a consultant to managers to help identify: (1) operating problems or potential problems; (2) scenarios or alternative courses of action to solve these problems or prevent them from occurring; and (3) feedback processes to see that on-job results are consistent with stated management goals.
Director of Personnel, Fotomat Corporation	The role varies greatly, depending on the industry and the individual in the job. My perception is that the role is becoming more important and is expanding into nontraditional training and development functions.
District Manager, Training, Ohio Bell Telephone Company	The role of the training/development manager is a staff function that must prove to the line organization and users that the services provided are job relevant, and will improve productivity, lower costs, and increase profits.
Manager, Employee Development and Planning, The Upjohn Company	Plan, develop, and administer programs that meet the needs of line managers in assisting their people to obtain the knowledge and skills they need to perform their present jobs satisfactorily; prepare employees for future jobs in the company; and assist them in achieving their personal goals.

Some form of cost-benefit analysis should be made prior to implementing any HRD program. The program should be job related, improve productivity, lower costs, and increase profits. The following statement stresses the importance of accomplishing this task:

This is the era of "pursuit of excellence," "high performance," and "the right stuff." When quality is returning to popularity, it is important to review, rethink, and perhaps reshape the building blocks of our corporate reputation for training effectiveness. It is helpful to examine anew the trail between training effectiveness and our reputation for being/for doing (what we are and what we achieve).[20]

A major role of the HRD manager is to assist people in obtaining the knowledge and skills they need for present and future jobs and to assist them in attaining personal goals. Learning is a self-determined activity, and all development is self-development. The HRD manager explains the type of training available, shows how it can be accomplished, and provides encouragement to ensure its successful accomplishment.

In recent years, the increasingly rapid changes in products, systems, and methods have had a significant impact on job requirements. Thus employees face the need to constantly upgrade their skills and to develop an attitude that permits them not only to adapt to change, but also to accept and even seek it.

Many organizations have grown to gigantic size in terms of the number of employees, sales volume, and diversity of products. This growth has resulted in extremely complex organizational structures and a high degree of specialization. These conditions necessitate greater operating interdependence. More than ever, people must interact with groups of peers, subordinates, and superiors to perform their jobs successfully.

During the past several decades, a vast amount of new knowledge has emerged from the behavioral sciences. Much of it relates directly to human resource management. Today's managers must be aware of this knowledge and be capable of utilizing it. The HRD function faces a substantial task in keeping pace with behavioral science developments and informing others in the organization about them.

Human resource development specialists must know more than the topic to be presented in a training program. They must also have some understanding of basic learning principles. The purpose of training is to change employee behavior, and information must be learned if change is to occur. Although much remains to be discovered about the learning process, several generalizations may be helpful in understanding this phenomenon. Some general concepts—fundamentals related to learning—are shown in Table 8-2.

Most of these concepts relate to the management and development of human resources. For example, behavior that is rewarded (reinforced) is more likely to recur. In applying this thought to managing people, management should strive to ensure that the firm's pay system rewards productivity. In addition, HRD specialists need to praise trainees for their accomplishments. Failure to provide the desired feedback on their performance—according to this concept—would not encourage learning.

From the human resource manager's viewpoint, successful accomplishment of other human resource functions can have a significant impact on

[20] Chip R. Bell, "Building a Reputation for Training Effectiveness," *Training and Development Journal*, 38 (May 1984), p. 50.

TABLE 8-2 | General Learning Concepts

- Behavior that is rewarded (reinforced) is more likely to recur.
- This reinforcement, to be most effective, must immediately follow the desired behavior and be clearly connected with that behavior.
- Mere repetition, without reinforcement, is an ineffective approach to learning.
- Threats and punishment have variable and uncertain effects on learning. Punishment may disturb the learning process.
- The sense of satisfaction that stems from achievement is the type of reward that has the greatest transfer value to other situations.
- The value of an external reward depends on who dispenses the reward. If the reward giver is highly respected, the extrinsic reward may be of great value; if not, it may be without value.
- Learners progress in an area of learning only as far as they need to in order to achieve their purposes.
- Individuals are more likely to be enthusiastic about a learning situation if they themselves have participated in the planning of the project.
- Autocratic leadership has been found to make members more dependent on the leader and to generate resentment in the group.
- Overstrict discipline tends to be associated with greater conformity, anxiety, shyness, and acquiescence; greater permissiveness is associated with more initiative and creativity.
- Many people experience so much criticism, failure, and discouragement that their self-confidence, level of aspiration, and sense of worth are damaged.
- When people experience too much frustration, their behavior ceases to be integrated, purposeful, and rational.
- People who have met with little success and continual failure are not apt to be in the mood to learn.
- Individuals tend to think best whenever they encounter an obstacle or intellectual challenge which is of interest to them.
- The best way to help people form a general concept is to present an idea in numerous and varied situations.
- Learning from reading is aided more by time spent recalling what has been read than by rereading.
- Individuals remember new information that confirms their previous attitudes better than they remember new information that does not confirm their previous attitudes.
- What is learned is more likely to be available for use if it is learned in a situation much like that in which it is to be used, and immediately preceding the time when it is needed.
- The best time to learn is when the learning can be useful. Motivation is then at its strongest peak.

HRD. For instance, if recruitment and selection efforts attract only un-skilled workers, an extensive HRD program may be needed to train entry-level workers. Training and development efforts may also be influenced by the firm's compensation package. A firm with a competitive program may find it easier to attract qualified workers, which substantially influences the type of training required. Also, a competitive compensation plan may help lower the turnover rate, thereby minimizing the need to train new workers.

A firm's employee relations efforts can also influence the HRD program. Workers want to feel that the company is interested in them. One way to express this interest is through management's support of HRD. The HRD process can also train managers to deal more effectively with employees and their problems. Managers can be taught to treat employees as individuals and not merely as numbers.

The emphasis a firm places on its employees' health and safety can also affect the HRD process. Heavy emphasis in this area can pave the way for extensive training programs throughout the organization. Providing a healthy and safe work environment can benefit all other human resource functions as the firm gains a reputation as a rewarding place to work.

■ DETERMINING HUMAN RESOURCE DEVELOPMENT NEEDS

The first step in the HRD process is to determine training, education, and development needs. In today's highly competitive business environment, undertaking programs simply because "other firms are doing it" is asking for trouble. Rather, a systematic approach to addressing bona fide needs must be undertaken.

Three types of analysis are required in order to determine an organization's HRD needs: organization analysis, task analysis, and person analysis.[21] In this context, organization analysis examines the entire firm to determine where training, education, and development should be conducted. The firm's strategic goals and plans should be studied along with the results of human resource planning.

In conducting task analysis, two primary factors should be determined—importance and proficiency. Importance relates to the relevance of specific tasks and behaviors in a particular job and the frequency with which they are performed. Proficiency is the employees' competence in performing these tasks. Job descriptions, performance appraisals, and interviews or surveys of supervisors and job incumbents should provide the data needed.[22]

Person analysis, which focuses on the individual employee, deals with two questions: "Who needs to be trained?" and "What kind of training is

---

[21] Kenneth N. Wexley and Gary P. Latham, *Developing and Training Human Resources in Organizations,* 2nd edition (New York: HarperCollins Publishers, Inc., 1991), p. 36.

[22] Kenneth M. Nowack, "A True Training Needs Analysis," *Training and Development Journal,* 45 (April 1991), p. 69.

needed?" The first step in a person analysis is to compare employee performance with established standards. If the person's work is acceptable, training may not be needed. If the employee's performance is below standard, further investigation will be needed to identify the specific knowledge and skills required for satisfactory job performance.[23]

In addition, tests, role playing, and assessment centers may be helpful in conducting person analyses. The results of career planning programs may also prove to be quite revealing.

■ ESTABLISHING HUMAN RESOURCE DEVELOPMENT OBJECTIVES

Clear and concise objectives must be formulated for HRD. Without them, designing meaningful HRD programs wouldn't be possible. Worthwhile evaluation of a program's effectiveness would also be difficult at best. The following statement of purposes and objectives is from a segment of a training program designed by the Chevron Corporation.

Employment Compliance

Purpose. To provide supervisor with:

1. Knowledge and value of consistent human resource practices.
2. The intent of EEO legal requirements.
3. The skills to apply them.

Objectives. Be able to:

1. Cite the supervisory areas affected by EEO laws on discrimination.
2. Identify acceptable and nonacceptable actions, according to EEO laws.
3. State how to get help on EEO and Affirmative Action matters.
4. Describe why we have discipline and grievance procedures.
5. Describe our discipline and grievance procedures, including who is covered.

As you can see, the purpose is clearly established first. Managers would have little difficulty in determining whether this is the type of training a subordinate needs. The specific learning objectives leave little doubt of what should be learned from the training. Action words such as *cite, identify, state,* and *describe* are used to disclose the specific content of the program. With these types of objectives, the HRD specialist may determine whether a person has obtained the necessary knowledge. For instance, a trainee either can or cannot state how to get help on EEO and Affirmative Action matters.

---

[23] *Ibid.*

■ SELECTING HUMAN RESOURCE DEVELOPMENT METHODS

When a person is working on a car, some tools are more helpful in doing certain tasks than others. The same logic applies when considering various HRD methods. Note the diverse methods shown in Table 8-3. Some apply strictly to managers and entry-level professionals, others to operative employees, and several can be used in the training and development of both managers and operative employees. We include methods that apply to both management and operative employees under management development.

Again referring to Table 8-3, note that HRD methods are used both on and off the job. Often it is not feasible to learn while doing. Thus, although a large portion of training and development takes place on the job, many HRD programs occur away from the work setting.

■ MANAGEMENT DEVELOPMENT

A firm's future lies primarily in the hands of its management. This group performs certain functions that are essential to the organization's survival and prosperity. Managers must make the right choice in most of the numerous decisions they make. Otherwise, the firm will not grow and may even fail. One unnerving statistic is that between six or seven of every ten American managers have significant shortcomings in their managerial abilities.[24] For these reasons, it is imperative that managers keep up with the latest developments in their respective fields and—at the same time—manage an ever-changing workforce operating in a dynamic environment. Thus many organizations emphasize training and development programs for managers. **Management development** consists of all learning experiences provided by an organization to impart and upgrade skills and knowledge required in current and future managerial positions. First-line supervisors, middle managers, and executives may all be expected to participate in management development programs. These programs are offered in-house, by professional organizations, and by colleges and universities. In-house programs are planned and presented by a firm's HRD specialists from the human resource department. Line managers are also frequently utilized to conduct segments of a program.

Professional organizations and universities are additional sources of management development programs. Organizations such as the Society for Human Resource Management and the American Management Association conduct conferences and seminars in a number of specialties. Numerous universities also provide management training and development programs. At times, colleges and universities possess expertise not available within business organizations. In some cases, academicians and management practitioners can advantageously present HRD programs jointly. A recent

---

[24] Paul G. Wilhelm, "Employment at Will Harms Productivity," *HRMagazine,* 35 (September 1990), p. 88.

TABLE 8-3 | Human Resource Development Methods

Method	Utilized for			Conducted	
	Managers and entry-level professionals	Operative employees	Both	On the job	Off the job
Coaching/mentoring			X	X	
Business games	X				X
Case study	X				X
Conference method	X				X
Behavior modeling	X				X
In-basket training	X				X
Internships	X			X	
Role playing	X				X
Job rotation			X	X	
Programmed instruction			X		X
Computer-based training			X		X
Classroom lecture			X		X
On-the-job training		X		X	
Apprenticeship training		X		X	
Simulators		X			X
Vestibule training		X			X

survey revealed the most frequently mentioned reasons to conduct management training outside the company:

- An outside perspective
- New viewpoints
- Possibility of taking executives out of the work environment
- Exposure to faculty experts and research
- Broader vision

The most frequently mentioned reasons for keeping management training inside the company are listed below:

- Training that is more specific to needs
- Lower costs
- Less time
- Consistent, relevant material
- More control of content and faculty
- Helps develop organizational culture and teamwork[25]

---

[25] Philip J. Harkins and David Giber, "Linking Business and Education Through Training," *Training and Development Journal,* 43 (October 1989), p. 69.

Basically, companies have various management development options. A recent survey of organizations with 100 or more employees revealed numerous types of training currently being used. These data are shown in Table 8-4. As you can see, management skills/development was the most popular type of training, followed by technical skills/knowledge, supervisory skills, communication skills, and basic computer skills. Management skills/development training was provided by 86.2 percent of the responding firms. Almost 14 percent provided this type of training solely in-house, and over 16 percent used outside sources such as universities and consultants. Over 56 percent of the firms used both in-house and outside trainers for their management skills/development.[26]

Regardless of whether programs are presented in-house or by an outside source, a number of methods are utilized in imparting knowledge to managers. We discuss these methods next.

Coaching and Mentoring

Coaching is an on-the-job approach to management development in which the manager is given an opportunity to teach on a one-to-one basis. Some firms create "assistant to" positions for this purpose. An individual placed in this type of staff position becomes an understudy to his or her boss. In addition to having the opportunity to observe, the subordinate will also be assigned significant tasks requiring decision-making skills. To be productive, coach-counselor managers must have a thorough knowledge of the job and how it relates to the firm's goals. They should also have a strong desire to share information with the understudy and be willing to take the time—which can be considerable—for this endeavor. The relationship between the supervisor and subordinate must be based on mutual trust and confidence for this approach to be effective.

Mentoring is an on-the-job approach to management development in which the trainee is given the opportunity to learn on a one-to-one basis from more experienced organizational members. The mentor is usually an older, experienced executive located anywhere in the organization who serves as a host, friend, confidant, and advisor to a new firm member. The relationship may be formally planned or it may develop informally. The concept of mentoring has some prestigious advocates such as Ortho Pharmaceutical Corporation, Bell Labs, AT&T, and the Internal Revenue Service. Mentoring has received considerable attention, most of which has emphasized its advantages. There have even been suggestions that mentoring is necessary to "make it to the top."

Mentoring has sometimes been compared to a blind date because the individuals involved won't necessarily like each other. An inherent problem exists because of the pyramidal hierarchy in organizations: There will always be fewer mentors than individuals needing mentoring.[27]

---

[26] Jack Gordon, "Where the Training Goes," *Training,* 27 (October 1990), p. 52.

[27] Peter Kizilos, "Take My Mentor, Please!" *Training,* 27 (April 1990), p. 50.

TABLE 8-4 | General Types of Training

Types of Training	Providing (%)	In-House Only (%)	Outside Only (%)	Both (%)
Management Skills/Development	86.2	13.6	16.2	56.4
Technical Skills/Knowledge	83.0	28.3	4.7	49.9
Supervisory Skills	82.4	17.8	11.8	52.8
Communication Skills	78.2	21.6	13.1	43.5
Basic Computer Skills	74.5	23.5	12.1	38.9
New Methods/Procedures	72.6	37.9	4.4	30.4
Customer Relations/Services	70.8	22.2	12.3	36.3
Executive Development	69.1	7.4	25.1	36.7
Clerical/Secretarial Skills	68.2	17.9	16.5	33.7
Personal Growth	65.6	12.9	14.1	38.6
Employee/Labor Relations	56.4	17.7	13.0	25.7
Wellness	52.8	18.6	11.4	22.8
Sales Skills	47.5	15.0	7.4	25.1
Customer Education	45.2	21.2	4.0	19.9
Remedial Basic Education	35.1	9.3	11.6	14.1

Source: Jack Gordon, "Where the Training Goes," *Training,* 27 (October 1990), p. 52. Reprinted with permission from the Oct. 1990 issue of *Training* Magazine. Copyright 1990, Lakewood Publications Inc., Minneapolis, MN, (612) 333-0471. All rights reserved.

For mentoring to work, the parties' interests must be compatible, and they must understand each other's psyches. Getting teachers and students together can obviously have advantages. In a mentoring relationship this combination has the potential for positive results.[28]

Business Games

Simulations that represent actual business situations are referred to as **business games.** These simulations attempt to duplicate selected factors in a particular situation, which are then manipulated by the participants. Business games involve two or more hypothetical organizations competing in a given product market. The participants are assigned such roles as president, controller, and marketing vice-president. They make decisions affecting price levels, production volumes, and inventory levels. Their

---

[28] Don Barnes, "What Is This Thing Called Mentoring?" *National Underwriter,* 94 (May 28, 1990), p. 9.

decisions are manipulated by a computer program, with the results simulating those of an actual business situation. Participants are able to see how their decisions affect other groups and vice versa. The best part about this type of learning is that if a decision is made that costs the company $1 million, no one gets fired, and still the business lesson is learned.

Case Study

The **case study** is a training method that utilizes simulated business problems for trainees to solve. The individual is expected to study the information given in the case and make decisions based on the situation. If the student is provided a case involving an actual company, he or she would be expected to research the firm to gain a better appreciation of its financial condition and environment. Typically, the case study method is used in the classroom with an instructor who serves as a facilitator.

Conference Method

The **conference method,** or discussion method, is a widely used instructional approach that brings together individuals with common interests to discuss and attempt to solve problems. Often the leader of the group is the supervisor. The group leader's role is to keep the discussion on course and avoid the tendency of some individuals to get off the subject. As problems are discussed, the leader listens and permits group members to solve their own problems. Individuals engaged in the conference method, although in training, work to solve actual problems that they face in their everyday activities.

Behavior Modeling

Behavior modeling has long been a successful training method that utilizes live demonstrations or videotapes to illustrate effective interpersonal skills and how managers function in various situations. The trainees observe the model's actions. Behavior modeling has been used successfully to train supervisors in such tasks as conducting performance appraisal reviews, correcting unacceptable performance, delegating work, improving safety habits, handling discrimination complaints, overcoming resistance to change, orienting new employees, and mediating between conflicting individuals or groups.[29]

As an example, a supervisor may act out his or her role in disciplining an employee who has been consistently late in reporting to work. Since the

---

[29] William M. Fox, "Getting the Most from Behavior Modeling Training," *National Productivity Review,* 7 (Summer 1988), p. 238.

situations presented are typical of the firm's problems, the participants are able to relate the behavior to their own jobs. The concept of behavior modeling has been around for a long time. For example, most linguists agree that learning language is imitative. Consider for a moment how most of us learn to drive a car, hit a golf ball, or mow the lawn. We probably learned by observing others doing these activities. To get the most from behavior modeling, however, it is helpful to learn various rules that guide our behavior other than by simply mimicking the behavior of others. For example, Table 8-5 provides various learning points that have been established for guiding the behavior of one who is demonstrating (via videotape) how to handle a complaining employee. The trainee observes the behavior and makes notes in the appropriate column indicating the places in the videotape where learning points are demonstrated.

To be most effective, the individual who models the particular skill to be taught should possess certain characteristics. He or she should

TABLE 8-5 | Handling a Complaining Employee

Learning Points	Indicate Below Places in Videotape Where Learning Points Are Modeled
Encourage full description of the complaint by listening non-judgmentally without hostility or defensiveness. (Check your understanding of the full complaint by "mirroring" or restating what employee has said.)	
Communicate that you understand employee's viewpoint and feelings.	
If you cannot accommodate the employee, explain why, non-defensively, and explain how you will handle the matter (or you may explain that you need to check with others or obtain additional information).	
If applicable, plan a specific follow-up meeting date.	

Source: William M. Fox, "Getting the Most from Behavior Modeling Training," *National Productivity Review,* 7, no. 3 (Summer 1988), p. 238. Reprinted with permission from *National Productivity Review.* Copyright 1988 by Executive Enterprises, Inc., 22 West 21st Street, New York, NY 10010-6904. All rights reserved.

have status in the firm, be of the same gender and race, and have a friendly and helpful attitude. The trainee should physically practice the skill to test his or her understanding of each component. Finally, follow-up meetings to reinforce the learning helps to assure that it does not diminish with disuse.[30]

In-Basket Training

In-basket training is a simulation in which the participant is given a number of business papers such as memoranda, reports, and telephone messages that would typically cross a manager's desk. The papers, presented in no particular order, call for actions ranging from urgent to routine handling. The participant is required to act on the information contained in these papers. In this training method, assigning a priority to each particular situation precedes making decisions called for in each situation.

Internships

As we mentioned in Chapter 6, an internship program is a recruitment method whereby university students divide their time between attending classes and working for an organization. Internships can also serve as an effective training method.

From the employer's viewpoint, an internship provides an excellent means of viewing a potential permanent employee at work. Internships also provide advantages for students. The experience they obtain through working enables them to integrate theory learned in the classroom with the practice of management. At the same time, the interns' experience will help them determine whether that type of firm and job appeals to them.

Role Playing

In **role playing**, participants are required to actually respond to specific problems they may encounter in their jobs. Rather than hearing about how a problem might be handled, or even discussing it, they learn by doing. Role playing is often used in management development. It may be effectively utilized to teach such skills as interviewing, grievance handling, performance appraisal, conference leadership, team problem solving, effective communication, and analyzing leadership styles. Role playing incorporates several theoretical learning approaches, including the following:

1. Active participation
2. Modeling

---

[30] *Ibid.*

3. Knowledge of results (feedback from other participants)
4. Practice[31]

In one type of role playing, the leader assigns roles and tells the "actors" how they feel, and each attempts to behave according to these feelings.[32] Or participants may choose specific roles in a situation and then act them out. For example, a trainee might play the role of a supervisor who is required to discipline an employee for substandard performance. Another participant would play the role of the employee. The individual in the supervisory role would then proceed to take whatever action is deemed appropriate. This action then provides the basis for discussion and comments by the group. Role reversal—an exchange of roles by the participants—is an effective version of role playing, which provides trainees with a different perspective of the problem. It helps them develop empathy, a quality vitally needed by managers. The Experiencing Human Resource Management section at the end of each chapter is a role playing exercise that demonstrates the benefits of this training approach.

Job Rotation

Job rotation involves moving employees from one job to another to broaden their experience. This breadth of knowledge is often needed for performing higher level tasks. Consider this example:

> Roy Jackson's firm is grooming him to fill the position of plant controller at the company's new branch plant. Roy is expected to assume his new responsibilities within the next six months. In preparing Roy for his new job, the vice-president for finance and the human resource director have decided that he needs additional experience in credit operations and accounts receivable. They have arranged for him to spend three months in each of these departments prior to his move to the new plant.

As you might expect, Roy's temporary assignments will not make him an expert in either area. He will, however, gain an overview of these functions, which will assist him in his new position.

Rotational training programs help new employees understand the variety of jobs within their fields. However, there are some potential problems. The new hires may have such short assignments that they feel like "tourists" in the department, and not really a part of the workforce.[33] Since they often do not develop a high level of proficiency, they can lower the overall

---

[31] Kenneth N. Wexley and Gary P. Latham, *Developing and Training Human Resources in Organizations* (New York: HarperCollins Publishers, Inc., 1991), pp. 271–272.

[32] John S. Randall, "Methods of Teaching." In Lloyd Baird, Craig Eric Schneir, and Dugan Laird (eds.), *The Training and Development Sourcebook* (Amherst, Mass.: Human Resource Development Press, 1983), p. 128.

[33] Milan Moravec and Kevin Wheeler, "Speed New Hires into Success," *Personnel Journal,* 68 (March 1989), p. 74–75.

productivity of the work group. In addition, employees who observe or have to work with an individual rotating through their department may resent a "fast-track" employee who may in time become their boss.

Programmed Instruction

A teaching method that provides instruction without the intervention of an instructor is called **programmed instruction (PI).** In PI, information is broken down into small portions (frames). The learner reads each frame in sequence and responds to questions, receiving immediate feedback on response accuracy. If correct, the learner proceeds to the next frame. If not, the learner repeats the frame. Primary features of this approach are immediate reinforcement and the ability of learners to proceed at their own pace. Programmed instruction material may be presented in a book or by more sophisticated means, such as computers.

Computer-Based Training

Computer-based training takes advantage of the speed, memory, and data manipulation capabilities of the computer for greater flexibility. For example, a student's response may determine the difficulty level of the next frame in a PI session. This information can be selected and displayed almost instantaneously.

The increased speed of presentation and less dependence on an instructor are advantages of this training approach. However, some students object to the absence of a human facilitator. Another primary disadvantage is the cost of software. However, with enough trainees, the cost may quickly reach an acceptable level. Computer-based training appears to be much more than a fad. A recent study indicated that almost half of all firms with fifty or more employees use computers in connection with their training efforts.[34] Although used primarily to teach technical skills, a growing number of firms are using computer-based training for subjects such as management and sales skills.[35]

Classroom Lecture

The classroom lecture is effective for certain types of employee training. The lecturer may convey a great deal of information in a relatively short time. The effectiveness of lectures can be improved when groups are small enough to permit discussion, the lecturer is able to capture the imagination of the class, and audiovisual equipment is used in a timely and appropriate manner.

---

[34] Jack Gordon, "Where the Training Goes," p. 53.

[35] Carlene Reinhart, "How Do You Determine the Use of New Training Technologies?" *Training and Development Journal,* 41 (August 1987), p. 22.

■ MANAGEMENT DEVELOPMENT PROGRAMS AT IBM

At IBM, formal management development programs are conducted for three groups of individuals: new managers, middle managers, and executives. These groups are described as follows:

New managers—those appointed to their first level of management responsibility.

Middle managers—those who are responsible for managing managers.

Executives—those who have reached top-management positions and those who are considered to have potential for such responsibility.

An overview of the programs provided for these management groups is provided in Figure 8-4 on page 292. In addition to providing training early in the manager's career, IBM emphasizes regular and continuous development. For example, annual training programs have been initiated to ensure that IBM's managers have an opportunity to receive at least one week of formal training each year.[36] More and more organizations are expected to implement management development programs for their employees in the future.

■ SUPERVISORY MANAGEMENT TRAINING PROGRAMS: AN ILLUSTRATION

Many firms conduct supervisory training programs. They consider such training to be necessary for their first-line managers to perform to their maximum potential. An overview of a supervisory training program developed by Chevron Corporation for its first-line managers is shown in Figure 8-5 on page 293. This program is designed to provide new supervisors with the skills and knowledge they need to manage people effectively. The training program is also available to supervisors with long-term service to update their knowledge. The program has three phases: presession activities; a five-day, live-in session; and postsession activities.

Several weeks prior to the live-in session participants are asked to engage in the following activities, which will prepare them for involvement in the program:

1. Identify productive and nonproductive activities.
2. Discuss the basic elements of their jobs with their bosses.
3. Select a major opportunity or problem that both the participant and the boss are committed to deal with (this becomes an action plan).
4. Send a sample of an employee evaluation to the training program coordinator.

---

[36] Ken Macher, "The Politics of Organizations," *Personnel Journal,* 65 (February 1986), p. 83.

New Manager School

All individuals appointed to the initial level of management responsibility, after receiving basic orientation to their job by their immediate managers, are enrolled, usually within one month, in a one-week basic training program.

The objectives of this training are:

Developing a deeper awareness of the basic policies and practices by which the company is managed.

Learning the practical application of these policies and practices.

Acquiring the basic management concepts, skills and techniques.

Included in the program are such subjects as A Business and Its Beliefs, Performance Planning, Counseling and Evaluation, and Managing Individuals.

Middle Management Training

Individuals newly appointed to the responsibility of managing managers attend, usually within ninety days, a week-long program.

The objectives of such training are:

Defining the role of the manager of managers.

Learning the organization, delegation, and control skills required of this level of management.

Understanding the interrelationship of the various business functions within the company.

Acquiring a knowledge of, and appreciation for, the issues and challenges of the business environment.

Included in the program are such subjects as Transition to Middle Management, Business Management Issues, People Management, and Leadership Styles.

Executive Development

Managers who have been appointed to executive-level positions, and those identified as having potential to be promoted to such positions, receive formal training at internally conducted programs as well as out-company programs.

The earliest of this series of company-conducted internal programs is scheduled within a year of the individual being included in the executive resource category. These classes, usually of three to four weeks duration, have objectives related to these areas:

The IBM Company: its organization, missions, management system; its policies, practices, and strategies; and its current issues and challenges.

Management Practices: leadership and decision making, general management concepts, functional integration, and management of change.

External Environment: international economic, political, and social changes; the current relationship of business, government, and other institutions.

Included in the programs are such courses as Finance, Marketing, Human Resources, Environmental Analysis and Strategic Thinking, Goals and Means of Our Economy, and Business Ethics.

In addition, individuals attend external training programs conducted by colleges, universities, and other institutions. Such programs include concentration on general management, leadership, government relations, and the humanities. Attendance at such internal and external executive development programs is scheduled at intervals to complement on-the-job experiences.

FIGURE 8-4 | IBM's Management Development Programs

Source: Used with the permission of International Business Machines Corporation.

Presession Activities	Five-Day, Live-In Session Activities			Postsession Activities
	Support subjects	Key course subjects	Program evaluation	
Time Analysis	Why We Are Here	Performance Planning and Review	Formulate an Action Plan Project	Approval and Implementation of an Action Plan Project
Work Analysis	Analyzing Performance Problems	Documentation Skills		
Performance Planning Discussion	Training	Employee Ranking	Rank Session's Topics	Possible Performance Planning and Review Discussions
Selecting an Action Plan Project	Special Health Services	Salary Administration	Evaluate Program	Follow-up Questionnaire to Participant and Boss
Writing a Performance Evaluation	Time Management	Employee Development		
Interview with Coordinator	Employment Compliance			
Time:	*Time:*	*Time:*	*Time:*	*Time:*
Completed Prior to Start of Program	1 1/2 days →	2 1/2 days →	1 day →	2–4 months after program →

FIGURE 8-5 | An Overview of Chevron Corporation's Supervisory Training Program

Source: Used with the permission of the Chevron Corporation.

The five-day, live-in session comprises the heart of the program. It begins on a Sunday night with a social get-together, dinner, and business meeting. Participants are asked to tell briefly about their jobs and discuss their action plans. A top-management representative meets with the group during this initial meeting to discuss the role of the supervisor, the purpose of the program, and expected on-the-job results.

During this main session, a number of support subjects and key course subjects are presented. At the same time, information is provided concerning laws and company policies and practices. Brief descriptions of the purposes of support subjects and key course subjects are presented in Table 8-6. Action plan projects are worked with during the program evaluation phase, and the results are used to measure the program's value.

The postsession phase of the program consists of implementing the action plans. Further attempts are also made to relate the program's impact to the supervisor's job performance. At this point, training needs that are not being met are emphasized. Appropriate changes are made to ensure that the training program continues to have practical value to both the employee and the company.

■ TRAINING METHODS FOR ENTRY-LEVEL PROFESSIONAL EMPLOYEES

Firms have a special interest in college-trained employees hired for entry-level professional positions, including management trainees. For example, General Electric conducts programs for new employees in numerous fields. One such program is the information systems manufacturing program (ISMP). This is a two-year program combining rotational work assignments with graduate-level seminars. It prepares employees to design, program, and implement integrated computerized and manual information systems.

General Electric's ISMP emphasizes challenging work assignments in such areas as programming, systems analysis and design, computer center operation, project management, and functional work. The length of these assignments varies, and individual progress is determined by employee performance and demonstrated potential.

A candidate for ISMP must have taken at least two computer science courses in college and have a bachelor's degree in one of the following majors or related fields: computer science, industrial engineering, accounting, mathematics, business administration, industrial management, or management information systems. Selection for the ISMP is based on a careful review of the employee's course curriculum, academic records, leadership in extracurricular activities, and work experience.

Other training programs for college graduates may have more or less structure than GE's ISMP. However, most of them also emphasize training provided on the job. "Hands-on" experience, alone or in combination with other methods, appears to be an essential component of these programs.

TABLE 8-6 | Chevron Corporation's Supervisory Training Program's Purposes for a Five-Day, Live-In Session

Support Subjects	Key Course Subjects
Why we are here	**Performance planning and review**
To orient participants with top management views of the role of a supervisor, the purpose of this program, and what on-job results are expected to occur.	To increase supervisory productivity and efficiency by creating better: • Communications • Understanding of the job • Planning and allocation of time • Data for evaluating employees' work performance
Analyzing performance problems	Documentation skills
To provide supervisors with the skills necessary to analyze a performance discrepancy so that they can determine the best solution.	To improve writing skills of supervisors in order that they may better manage their human resources.
Training	Employee ranking
To provide supervisors with the skill and knowledge to effectively train others.	To provide supervisors with the skill and knowledge needed to objectively evaluate employee performance on the job.
Special health services	Salary administration
To provide supervisors with an expanded awareness of their responsibilities in the area of Special Health Services and with information and skills to deal with the troubled employee.	To review the basics of salary administration so that supervisors can provide meaningful inputs to higher management and provide feedback to employees about salary decisions.
Time management	Employee development
To provide skills in how to better manage and use time.	To assist supervisors in their role of developing employees both within their current jobs and for future jobs as appropriate.
Employment compliance	
To teach supervisors the value of consistent personnel practices and the skills to apply them, as well as the intent of EEO legal requirements.	

Source: Used with the permission of the Chevron Corporation.

HRM In Action

Lon Williams, the training and development manager, was studying the weekly training schedule when he heard a tap at his door. "Got a minute, Lon?" asked Scotty Needham, production manager.

"Sure, come on in," said Lon. "What've you got?"

"You may know that I recently hired Brit Salvo, a retired Marine officer who wanted to begin his second career with us. Brit's military record was excellent, and I was shocked when I heard through the grapevine about his high-handed methods. Apparently he still thinks he's in the Marines the way he bosses people around. When I spoke to Brit, he said, 'I've been successful for twenty years managing people and using these exact methods.' Lon, something has to be done. Do you have any ideas?"

How would you respond?

■ TRAINING METHODS FOR OPERATIVE EMPLOYEES

Unlike managers, operative employees do not make their contributions to the firm through the efforts of other people. They are, always, the "other people." Their contributions are direct and, collectively, essential to the production of goods and services. Organizations rely heavily on their executive secretaries, senior clerks, systems analysts, and other operative employees. Every position in an organization is necessary or it would not (or should not) exist. Therefore, training and development for operative employees must also be given high priority.

In this section, we discuss HRD methods that apply to the training of operative employees. However, these are not the only available methods; they are just an overview of methods commonly utilized. Recall the methods listed in Table 8-3 that are applicable to both management and operative employees (see page 283).

On-the-Job Training

On-the-job training (OJT) is an informal approach to training that permits an employee to learn job tasks by actually performing them. Although some may not consider OJT to be a bona fide training method, it is the most commonly used approach to HRD. With OJT, there is no problem in later transferring what has been learned to the task. Individuals may also be more highly motivated to learn because they are acquiring the knowledge needed to perform their jobs. At times, however, the emphasis on production may tend to detract from the training process. The trainee may feel so much pressure to perform that learning is negatively affected.

Both the manager and the trainee must recognize that OJT is a joint effort. In addition, the manager must create a climate of trust and open communication to make OJT effective.

Apprenticeship Training

Another approach, **apprenticeship training,** combines classroom instruction with on-the-job training. Such training is traditionally used in craft jobs, such as those of plumber, barber, carpenter, machinist, and printer. While in training, the employee earns less than the master craftsperson who is the instructor. The training period varies according to the craft, as shown in Table 8-7 on page 298. For instance, the apprenticeship training period for barbers is two years; for machinists, four years; and for pattern makers, five years.

Simulators

Simulators are training devices of varying degrees of complexity that model the real world. They range from simple paper mock-ups of mechanical devices to computerized simulations of total environments. Human resource development specialists often use simulated sales counters, automobiles, and airplanes.[37] Although simulator training may be less valuable than on-the-job training for some purposes, it has certain advantages. A prime example is the training of airline pilots: Simulated training crashes do not cost lives or deplete the firm's fleet of jets.

Vestibule Training

Vestibule training takes place away from the production area on equipment that closely resembles equipment actually used on the job. For example, a group of lathes may be located in a training center where the trainees will be instructed in their use. A primary advantage of vestibule training is that it removes the employee from the pressure of having to produce while learning. The emphasis is on learning the skills required by the job.

---

[37] Dugan Laird, *Approaches to Training and Development,* 2nd edition (Reading, Mass.: Addison-Wesley, 1985), p. 217.

TABLE 8-7 | Selected Apprenticeable Occupations Classified by Length of Apprenticeship

Two years	Barber Cosmetician	Four years	Boilermaker Carpenter
Two to three years	Brewer Butcher Roofer		Machinist Printing press operator Tailor
Two to four years	Bindery workers	Four to five years	Electrical worker
Three years	Baker Bricklayer Photographer		Lithographer
		Four to eight years	Die sinker
Three to four years	Airplane mechanic Leatherworker	Five years	Lead burner Pattern maker
	Operating engineer Sheet-metal worker	Five to six years	Electrotyper Photoengraver
Three to five years	Draftsperson/ designer		Stereotyper

Source: U.S. Department of Labor, *The National Apprenticeship Program* (Washington, D.C.: U.S. Government Printing Office), pp. 9–27.

■ JOB TRAINING PARTNERSHIP ACT

Administered by the Employment and Training Administration of the Department of Labor, the **Job Training Partnership Act (JTPA)** provides job training and employment services for economically disadvantaged adults and youth, dislocated workers, and other persons who face exceptional employment hurdles. The act became operational in 1983 with the goal of moving the unemployed into permanent, unsubsidized, self-sustaining jobs. An overview of selected programs included within the JTPA is shown in Table 8-8.

■ USE OF VARIOUS HUMAN RESOURCE DEVELOPMENT METHODS

A study of organizations with 100 or more employees revealed the percentage of firms using various training methods (see Figure 8-6 on page 300). As may be seen, the top two methods are videotapes and lectures. Even though firms are slightly more likely to use videotapes than lectures, the figures do not imply that employees as a whole spend more time watching videos than listening to lectures. The question on the survey was "Do you use it?" not "How much do you use it?" Figure 8-6 also shows that other

TABLE 8-8 | Selected Programs Included within the Job Training Partnership Act

Job corps	A federally administered employment and training program for seriously disadvantaged youth between the ages of 16 and 21. The program's goal is to prepare youth for productive employment and entrance into vocational and technical schools, junior colleges, or other institutions for further education and training.
Adult and youth programs	Provides participants (primarily economically disadvantaged youth and adults) with various job-related services including classroom and on-the-job training. This program is administered through a block grant to the states.
Summer youth employment and training programs	Provides disadvantaged youth with jobs, training, and education services during the summer months.
Assistance for dislocated workers	Provides aid to experienced workers who have become unemployed due to economic and technological change. A number of services are provided to the participants including training and job search assistance.
Migrant and seasonal farmworker programs	Job training and supportive services are provided to farmworkers and their families in an attempt to combat chronic unemployment, underemployment, and substandard living conditions.
Native American programs	A variety of employment related services are provided to Native Americans who are without jobs.
Pilot and demonstration projects	These projects provide job training, employment opportunities, and other services to people with specific disadvantages.

Source: "Job Training," *Congressional Digest,* 67 (February 1988), p. 37.

methods used by more than 50 percent of responding organizations include one-on-one instruction, slides, role plays, and audiotapes.[38]

■ SELECTING HUMAN RESOURCE DEVELOPMENT MEDIA

Organizations have utilized various media to enhance their training programs. As used in this context, **media** are special methods of communicating ideas and concepts in training and development. These media include videotapes, films, closed-circuit television, slide projectors, overhead and opaque projectors, flip charts, and chalkboards.

Some critics have referred to audiovisual aids as "gadgetry for its own sake." Yet, these devices play an essential role in training and

---

[38] Jack Gordon, "Where the Training Goes," pp. 54–55.

Videotapes	88.7%
Lectures	84.1%
One-on-One Instruction	72.2%
Role Plays	55.6%
Slides	54.4%
Audiotapes	53.0%
Films	47.8%
Games/Simulations	46.4%
Case Studies	46.4%
Self-Assessment/Self-Testing Instruments	39.8%
Noncomputerized Self-Study Programs	25.9%
Video Conferencing	11.6%
Teleconferencing (Audio Only)	8.5%
Computer Conferencing	4.3%

FIGURE 8-6 | Frequency of Use of Human Resource Development Methods

Source: Jack Gordon, "Where the Training Goes," *Training,* 27 (October 1990) p. 54. Reprinted with permission from the Oct. 1990 issue of *Training* Magazine. Copyright 1990, Lakewood Publications Inc., Minneapolis, MN, (612) 333-0471. All rights reserved.

development.[39] In fact, 75 percent of what we learn is learned by sight, whereas about 75 percent of what we hear is forgotten within two days.[40]

Various forms and uses of audiovisual media are described briefly in Table 8-9. Audiovisual aids are valuable supplements to training methods.

[39] Max H. Forster, "Training and Development Programs, Methods, and Facilities." In Dale Yoder and Herbert G. Heneman, Jr. (eds.) *ASPA Handbook of Personnel and Industrial Relations: Training and Development* (Washington, D.C.: The Bureau of National Affairs, 1977), pp. 5–53.

[40] Martin M. Broadwell, *The Supervisor as an Instructor,* 3rd edition (Reading, Mass.: Addison-Wesley, 1978), p. 85.

TABLE 8-9 | Audiovisual Media

Films
Films are useful due to their versatility. They combine many elements such as color, motion, action, plot, and musical scoring. Films provide a wide range of topics available for rental at a relatively low cost but are very expensive for an organization to produce.
Slide Projectors
Slide projectors are commonly used, with slide–tape presentations becoming more popular. In these programs, the projector may be advanced automatically by an inaudible signal from one stereo channel.
Overhead Projectors
An overhead projector, providing an image on a screen by passing light through a transparency, can be used to provide colorful visual presentations. The trainer can maintain eye contact in an undarkened room and the trainee may take notes.
Audiotapes
There are several types of audiotape systems on the market, and the running time varies from sixty minutes (thirty minutes per side) to two hours.
Video
The instant-replay capability of video makes it a particularly valuable medium for use in training programs. Most of the advantages of film are inherent in video.
Flip Charts, Chalkboards, and Slap Boards
These relatively inexpensive pieces of equipment can assist the trainer in emphasizing major points. One type of chalkboard permits the use of a colored ink pen, and the ink may be easily erased.

Source: Adapted from Devin O'Sullivan, "Audiovisuals and the Training Process." In Robert L. Craig (ed.), *Training and Development Handbook, A Guide to Human Resource Development,* 2nd ed. (New York: McGraw-Hill, 1976). Reprinted by permission.

For example, a lecture might be greatly enhanced by use of an overhead projector or a short film. These media can assist in gaining and maintaining trainee interest and attention. Various applications of audiovisual media are not mutually exclusive. The use of more than one type of audiovisual aid (multimedia) may be appropriate for many training sessions. An example would be a slide–tape presentation.

■ IMPLEMENTING HUMAN RESOURCE DEVELOPMENT PROGRAMS

A perfectly conceived training program can fail if management can't convince the participants of its merits. Participants must believe that the program has value and will help them achieve their personal and professional goals. The credibility of HRD specialists may depend on a series of successful programs.

Implementing HRD programs is often difficult. One of the reasons is that many managers are action oriented and frequently feel that they are too busy for HRD. According to one management development executive, "Most busy executives are too involved chopping down the proverbial tree to stop for the purpose of sharpening their axes. . . . " Another difficulty in program implementation is that qualified trainers must be available. In addition to possessing communication skills, the trainers must know the company's philosophy, its objectives, its formal and informal organization, and the training program's goals. Human resource development requires more creativity than perhaps any other human resource specialty.

A new program must be monitored carefully, especially during its initial phases. Training implies change, which employees may resist vigorously. Others may sit back waiting, perhaps even hoping, that the program will fail. Participant feedback is vital at this stage because there will be "bugs" in any new program. The sooner these problems are resolved, the better the chances for success.

The HRD manager often has unique problems in implementing training programs. For example, it may be difficult to schedule the training around present work requirements. Unless the employee is new to the firm, he or she undoubtedly has specific full-time duties to perform. Although it is the line manager's job to have positions covered while an employee is in training, the HRD manager must assist with this problem.

Another difficulty in implementing HRD programs is record keeping. Records should be maintained on all training the employee receives and how well he or she performs during training and on the job. This information is important in terms of measuring program effectiveness and charting the employee's progress in the company.

Training conducted outside the organization requires considerable coordination. Consider the coordination required to get managers from all parts of the country to participate in an HRD program in Storrs, Connecticut. The logistics and costs involved in this type of undertaking can be significant.

In order to deal with these factors, a relatively new approach has been developed. **Teletraining** utilizes teleconferencing (with or without video) to train people in their own locations rather than bringing them together at one place. This approach can complement existing professional development training programs and, in many instances, make it possible to economically reach individuals who would not otherwise have access to training.[41]

---

[41] Mary E. Boone and Susan Schulman, "Teletraining: A High-Tech Alternative," *Personnel*, 62 (May 1985), p. 4.

■ EVALUATING HUMAN RESOURCE DEVELOPMENT

Corporate America spends more than $40 billion a year on employee training. Yet, there is no clear consensus within the training community on how to determine its value.[42] Obviously, the credibility of HRD can be greatly enhanced by showing that the organization benefits tangibly from such programs. Thus the HRD department must document its efforts and clearly show that it provides a valuable service. The documentation should be in the form of memoranda to management, written reports of activities, and any other evidence that indicates a quality product.[43]

Organizations have taken several approaches to determining the worth of specific programs. These involve evaluations of (1) the participants' opinions of the program, (2) the extent to which participants have learned the material, (3) the participants' ability to apply the new knowledge, and (4) whether the stated training goals have been achieved.

Participants' Opinions

Evaluating an HRD program by asking the participants' opinions of it is an inexpensive approach that provides an immediate response and suggestions for improvements. The basic problem with this type of evaluation is that it is based on opinion rather than fact. In reality, the trainee may have learned nothing, but perceive that a learning experience occurred.[44] For example, Tom Dickson has just completed a three-day executive seminar in Honolulu. At the conclusion of the program, Tom was given a brief questionnaire that, in essence, asked him whether the seminar was beneficial. It is difficult to imagine Tom or any of his fellow participants downgrading this training program. Even if it had been conducted in a less exotic location, a brief break from the hectic part of an executive's job can be a welcome relief. Participants' perceptions of the value of such programs may prove useful, but they must be interpreted cautiously.

Extent of Learning

Some organizations administer tests to determine what the participants in an HRD program have learned. The most widely accepted evaluation procedure is referred to as the pretest-posttest, control group design.[45] In this procedure, the same test is used before and after training. It also calls for

---

[42] James R. Cook and Carol M. Panza, "ROI: What Should Training Take Credit For?" *Training: The Magazine of Human Resources Development,* 24 (January 1987), p. 64.

[43] Jack Asgar, "Give Me Relevance or Give Me Nothing," *Training,* 27 (July 1990), p. 49.

[44] John Dopyera and Louise Pitone, "Decision Points in Planning the Evolution of Training," *Training and Development Journal,* 37 (May 1983), p. 67.

[45] John H. Zenger and Kenneth Hargis, "Assessing Training Results: It's Time to Take the Plunge!" *Training and Development Journal,* 36 (January 1982), pp. 13–14.

both a control group (which does not receive the training) and an experimental group (which does). Trainees are randomly assigned to each group. Differences in pretest and posttest results between the groups are then attributed to the training provided.

Behavioral Change

Tests may indicate fairly accurately what has been learned, but they give little insight into desired behavioral changes. For example, it is one thing for a manager to learn about motivational techniques but quite another matter for this person to apply the new knowledge. Consider the situation involving Pat Sittel:

> Pat Sittel sat in the front row at the supervisory training seminar her company sponsored. The primary topic of the program was delegation of authority. As the lecturer made each point regarding effective delegation techniques, Pat would nod her head in agreement. She thoroughly understood what was being said over the three-day period of the seminar. At the end of the program, Pat returned to her department and continued the management style she had followed for ten years—little delegation of authority. Although she had understood the material presented in the seminar, Pat's failure to apply what she had learned did not benefit the organization.

Accomplishment of HRD Objectives

Still another approach to evaluating HRD programs involves determining the extent to which stated objectives have been achieved. For instance, if the objective of an accident prevention program is to reduce the number and severity of accidents by 15 percent, comparing accident rates before and after training provides a useful measurement of success. However, many programs dealing with broader topics are more difficult to evaluate. A group of executives may, for example, be sent to a state university for a one-week course in management and leadership development. "Before" and "after" performance appraisals of the participants may be available. Following the course, the managers may actually perform at a higher level, but other variables may distort the picture. For instance, a mild recession may force the layoff of several key employees; a competing firm may be successful in luring away one of the department's top engineers; or the company president could pressure the employment director to hire an incompetent relative. These and many other factors could cause the performance level of the group to decline, even though the managers had benefited from the HRD program.

In evaluating HRD programs, managers should strive for proof that the program is effective. While such proof may be difficult to establish, the effect on performance should at least be estimated to show whether the training achieved its desired purpose.[46] In spite of problems associated with evaluation, the human resource manager must continue to strive for solid evidence of HRD's contributions in achieving organizational goals.

■ ORIENTATION

The initial HRD effort designed for employees is orientation. **Orientation** is the guided adjustment of new employees to the company, the job, and the work group. It is the most prevalent type of formal training in U.S. organizations.[47] Comprehensive orientation makes many of the other tasks associated with human resource management easier.

In an orientation program, requirements for promotion will likely be explained. Rules, the infraction of which may lead to potential disciplinary action, will be stated. The mechanics of promotion, demotion, transfer, resignation, discharge, layoff, and retirement should be spelled out in policy handbooks and given to each new employee. Also, a summary of employee benefits is often provided.

To perform effectively, new employees need information that permits them to do their jobs and information that will help them understand their coworkers' behavioral patterns. In this regard, peers have been found to serve as excellent information agents. There are several reasons for their success in performing this function. For one thing they are accessible to the newcomers and often more approachable than the boss. Peers also tend to have a high degree of empathy for new people. In addition, they have the organizational experience and technical expertise to which new employees need access.[48]

Several themes seem to apply to successful orientation programs. The first is that significant and measurable goals are set for them. The goals might relate to such factors as the time required to master the new job, anxiety reduction, units produced per hour, absenteeism, tardiness, and turnover. Goals such as these have been successfully achieved by such organizations as Texas Instruments, Corning Glass Works, Disneyland, and Walt Disney World.

Another point is that orientation should be the joint responsibility of the training staff and the line supervisor. The new hire is primarily concerned about the job and his or her supervisor. Until anxiety about these factors is reduced, the corporate message cannot be communicated.

---

[46] James R. Cook and Carol M. Panza, "ROI: What Should Training Take Credit For?" p. 64.

[47] Jack Gordon, "*Training* Magazine's Industry Report 1986," *Training: The Magazine of Human Resources Development,* 23 (October 1986), p. 28.

[48] Debra R. Comer, "Peers as Providers," *Personnel Administrator,* 34 (May 1989), pp. 84–86.

Successful orientation programs also tend to have a high degree of senior management involvement both in developing the program and implementing it. Actually, for any type of program to be successful, top management support is essential.[49]

Purposes of Orientation

A new employee's first few days on the job may be spent in orientation. Orientation programs are designed basically for new employees. An estimated 60–80 percent of an organization's current workforce is new not only to the job, but also to the job market. These new workers include a large number of late entries or reentries of women, men and women who were self-employed, recent graduates, and people who have made radical career changes.[50] Many of these individuals are inexperienced and have anxieties about entering the organization. An effective orientation program can do much to reduce these anxieties. Orientation has three primary purposes, which we discuss next.

Easing the New Employee's Adjustment to the Organization. Orientation helps the new employee adjust to the organization, both formally and informally. Formally, the organization wants the employee to become productive as rapidly as possible. In order to facilitate this process, the employee needs to know specifically what doing the job involves. Explanations concerning the job by the supervisor can do much to speed this process.

Many of the benefits of orientation relate to the informal organization. New employees are not automatically greeted with open arms. There may be a certain amount of hazing and kidding. Older workers may want to make sure that the new employee knows his or her place. A mistake or slowness in accomplishing tasks may encourage joking comments such as, "The last person who messed up like that was fired the next day" or "If you can't produce any more than that, there's no need to stay here." Taking such remarks seriously may make the new employee wonder whether he or she made the proper decision in accepting the job.

In order to reduce the anxiety that new employees experience, attempts should be made to integrate the person into the informal organization. Perhaps a senior employee—not the supervisor—can be assigned the task of showing the new person the "ropes." High turnover is often associated with the failure of workers to informally accept new employees. It is a lonely feeling to be on a job when you feel unwanted by peers.

New employees characteristically have enthusiasm, creativity, and commitment. Much of this can be lost through an inept orientation program

---

[49] Ron Zemke, "Employee Orientation: A Process, Not a Program," *Training,* 26 (August 1989), pp. 33–38.

[50] Mark S. Tauber, "New Employee Orientation: A Comprehensive Systems Approach," *Personnel Administrator,* 26 (January 1981), p. 65.

that fails to integrate new hires into the work group. On the other hand, an effective program enhances the employment relationship and provides the foundation for employee motivation, commitment, and productivity.[51]

Members of certain groups may also experience rejection from the informal work group. Women, blacks, and other minorities often have to actively seek acceptance into the work group. Initial job turnover may be higher among these individuals than for those in the more traditional work group.

Providing Information Concerning Tasks and Performance Expectations. Another purpose of orientation is to provide specific information about tasks and performance expectations. Employees want and need to know precisely what is expected of them. Thus new employees should be informed of the standards that they must meet in order to qualify for pay raises, and the criteria for promotion. Rules of the company and of the particular department to which the individual is assigned should also be explained.

Creating a Favorable Impression. A final purpose of orientation is to create a favorable impression on new employees of the organization and its work. Doubts may arise after employees begin their new jobs. The new employee may begin to wonder, "Did I make the right decision?" The orientation process can do much to allay such fears.

Stages in Effective Orientation

There are essentially three different stages in an effective orientation program.[52] During the first stage, general information about the organization is provided. Matters that relate to all employees, such as a company overview, review of company policies and procedures, and salary, are presented. A checklist for new employees is often used to ensure that certain information is provided to the new hire. One such checklist is shown in Figure 8-7 on page 308. It is also helpful for the new employee to know how his or her department fits into the overall scheme of the company's operations. Orientation programs should also provide information about how the products or the services of the company benefit society as a whole. Another purpose of this stage is anxiety reduction. New employees are informed of some of the possible hazing games that longer term employees may play. The human resource department may be heavily involved in this stage.

The employee's immediate supervisor usually is responsible for the second stage of orientation. Topics and events covered include an overview of the department, job requirements, safety, a tour of the department, a

---

[51] Pamela A. Kaul, "First Impressions Last," *Association Management,* 41 (May 1989), p. 18.

[52] Diana Reed-Mendenhall and C. W. Millard, "Orientation: A Training and Development Tool," *Personnel Administrator,* 25 (August 1980), pp. 42–44.

NEW EMPLOYEE CHECKLIST

NAME _____ EMPLOYMENT DATE _____

POSITION TITLE _____ DEPARTMENT _____

PAY GRADE _____ APPOINTMENT TYPE: PT _____ FT _____ SUPERVISOR _____

PROBATIONARY PERIOD ENDS _____

FIVE MONTH PERFORMANCE APPRAISAL DUE _____

INFORMATION PROVIDED:

_____ Orientation packet   By: _____ Date _____

_____ I.D. card   By: _____ Date _____

_____ Staff handbook   By: _____ Date _____

_____ Grievance guide   By: _____ Date _____

_____ Retirement information   By: _____ Date _____

_____ Life insurance   By: _____ Date _____

_____ Disability insurance   By: _____ Date _____

_____ Health insurance   By: _____ Date _____

I understand that an exit interview with a Human Resource Department representative is required of all terminating employees receiving benefits.

I have received the information checked above, understand my employment status, and have been fully informed about my insurance options and benefits.

I have chosen not to enroll in HEALTH, LIFE, DISABILITY insurance. (Circle those you are not enrolling in.)

_____
Employee Signature   Date

_____
Human Resource Representative   Date

Effective Date _____

FIGURE 8-7 | Checklist for a New Employee

---

question and answer session, and introductions to other employees. It is crucial that the supervisor clearly explain performance expectations and specific work rules at this point. It is also important for the supervisor to ease the new hire into social acceptance by the work group as quickly as possible.

The third stage involves evaluation and follow-up, which are conducted by the human resource department in conjunction with the immediate supervisor. The new employee does not go through the orientation program simply to be forgotten. During the first week or so, the supervisor works with the new employee to clarify information and make sure of integration into the work group. Human resource professionals assist supervisors to ensure that this vital third step is accomplished.

Training the Supervisor

One of the most vital aspects of an orientation program is training supervisors to conduct orientation properly.[53] Human resource professionals can provide the new hire with organizational information, but it is the supervisor who must successfully integrate the employee into the work setting.

The supervisor should first express confidence that new employees are going to do well on the job. New hires often begin work not fully convinced that they are capable of doing the job. Supervisors need to reassure these individuals that the company would not have hired them if it didn't believe that they could do the job.

Second, supervisors need to explain both the good and bad points of the job. During the orientation period, managers often spend most of their time emphasizing the positive aspects of the job, leaving the new employees to learn of the negative features on their own. Studies have verified that good employee understanding of the job lowers turnover rates. Ideally, new employees will have received a realistic job preview, and will not face any unpleasant surprises at this time.

Third, the supervisor should inform the new hire of what he or she likes and dislikes in job performance. Every supervisor has particular preferences—usually small things that they react to favorably or unfavorably. Knowing these preferences, employees can more easily adapt to a particular work situation. For example, a supervisor who is a stickler for neatness should communicate this fact to new hires.

Fourth, the supervisor should describe both the standards set by the company and any unique customs of the employee's particular work group. All company rules, especially those pertaining to the new hire's section, should also be explained.

Finally, the supervisor should introduce the new employee to members of the work group. Any informal group leader should be identified. Here again, an attempt should be made to minimize the number of surprises that the employee will encounter. Starting off on the wrong foot with leaders of the informal organization can hurt the new employee's chances for quick acceptance. In jobs that require considerable interaction among group members, group acceptance is especially important.

---

[53] Loi Dene Williams, "Off to a Good Beginning," *Supervision,* 44 (October 1982), pp. 4–5.

Reorientation

While orientation programs are typically conducted for new employees, programs designed for employees who have been on the payroll for a longer period are also needed. Organizations are constantly changing. Different management styles may evolve, communication methods may be altered, and the structure of the organization itself may—and typically does—change frequently. Even the corporate culture may take on a new flavor over time. Changes in any of these conditions warrant reorientation. Without it, employees may find themselves in organizations that they don't even recognize.[54]

■ GLOBAL AND JOINT-VENTURE ORIENTATION

Orientation for new employees to the company, the job, and the work group varies in its degree of complexity, but global orientation will almost certainly be more complex than any domestic program. Because of the extreme cost of global staffing and the staggering cost of failed expatriate assignments, global orientation takes on increased importance.[55] Orientation for new global employees is critical. It must incorporate an introduction to the organizational (and perhaps national) cultures of all parties that the individual is likely to encounter. Such an introduction should also include an overview of the history, traditions, and corporate values of partners, if any. Then, it should include a description of the new venture, its organization, and its management structure, followed by an introduction of the employee to the manager, department, and coworkers.[56]

Orientation cannot be a sketchy overview of the basics. It should be an in-depth process that has been thoroughly planned in advance, taking a long-term approach that includes provisions for follow-up and evaluation. The benefits of such programs are just now beginning to become evident. Two years after developing such a system, Corning, Inc., showed a 69 percent reduction in voluntary turnover among new hires, a 8:1 benefit/cost ratio in the first year, and a 14:1 ratio annually thereafter.[57]

Both the General Motors–Toyota NUMMI joint venture and the Chrysler–Mitsubishi Diamond Star alliance made new employee orientation one of their first priorities. Each joint venture spent millions of dollars on orientation and training long before it formally started its manufacturing operations in the United States. The success of these companies suggests that international alliances should expend as much effort preparing new employees to deal with the social context of their

---

[54] Margaret Magnus, "Training Futures," *Personnel Journal,* 65 (May 1986), p. 63.

[55] Mike Fergus, "Employees on the Move," *HRMagazine,* 36 (May 1990), p. 45.

[56] Wayne F. Cascio and Manuel G. Serapio, Jr., "Human Resources Systems in an International Alliance: The Undoing of a Done Deal?" *Organizational Dynamics,* 19 (Winter 1991), p. 68.

[57] *Ibid.*

jobs (and to cope with the insecurities and frustrations of a new learning situation) as they do developing the technical skills that employees need to perform effectively.[58]

---

[58] *Ibid.,* p. 69.

SUMMARY

Change involves moving from one condition to another and affects individuals, groups, and even entire organizations. If change is to be successfully implemented, it must be approached systematically. A crucial aspect of the change process involves reducing resistance to change. Change can be accomplished more readily if those involved want it and believe that it is needed. The most successful approach to changing attitudes is to create trust and confidence between those proposing the change and those affected by it. The change sequence does not end with implementation. A new and flexible position capable of dealing with present requirements and adapting to further change must be developed. The final phase of the change sequence involves evaluating the effectiveness of the change process.

Human resource development (HRD) is planned, continuous effort by management to improve employee competency levels and organizational performance through training, education, and development programs. The purpose of training is to improve an individual's performance on a currently held job or one related to it. The purpose of education is to improve the overall competence of an individual in a specific direction and beyond the current job. The purpose of development is to nurture the individual's growth but not with regard to any specific job.

Following recognition that change is needed, the process of determining training, education, and development needs (objectives) begins. Two questions must be answered: "What are our training needs?" and "What do we want to accomplish through our HRD efforts?"

Several factors can greatly influence a training and development program's effectiveness. First and foremost, training and development must have top management's full support. In addition, the HRD process must have the commitment of other managers, both generalists and HRD specialists. A firm's employee relations efforts and the firm's emphasis on employee health and safety can also influence the HRD process.

Management development provides learning experiences for the purpose of upgrading the skills and knowledge required for managerial positions. Coaching is an on-the-job approach to management development in which the manager is given an opportunity to teach on a one-to-one basis. Simulations that represent actual business situations are referred to as business games. The case study is a training method that utilizes simulated business problems for trainees to solve. The conference, or discussion, method brings together individuals with common interests to discuss and attempt to solve problems. Behavior modeling utilizes videotapes prepared specifically to illustrate how managers function in various situations and to develop interpersonal skills. In-basket training simulates business papers, such as memoranda, reports, and telephone messages, that a manager would typically receive and address. In an internship program, university students divide their time between attending classes and working for an organization. In role playing, participants "act out" responses to specific situations without the benefit of either a script or rehearsal. Job rotation moves employees from one job to another to broaden their experience. A teaching method that provides instruction without the intervention of an instructor is called programmed instruction (PI). Computer-based training takes advantage of the speed, memory, and data manipulation capabilities of the computer for greater flexibility. The classroom lecture is effective for certain types of employee training.

Training of operative employees includes on-the-job training (OJT), in which the person learns job tasks by actually performing them. Apprenticeship training combines classroom instruction with on-the-job training. Simulators are training devices of varying degrees of complexity that model the real world. Vestibule training takes place away from the production area on equipment that closely resembles the equipment actually used on the job.

Many organizations utilize various media to enhance training programs. As used in this context, media are special methods used in training and development to communicate ideas and concepts. These media include videotapes, films, closed-circuit television, slide projectors, overhead projectors, flip charts, and chalkboards.

A perfectly conceived training program can fail if the participants are not convinced that it has merit. They must believe that the program is valuable and can help them achieve their personal and professional goals. The credibility of HRD specialists may depend on a successful series of programs.

Organizations take several approaches to determining the worth of specific HRD programs, including evaluations of (1) the participants' opinions of the program, (2) the extent to which the participants learned the material, (3) the participants' ability to apply the new knowledge, and (4) whether the stated training objectives have been achieved. In evaluating HRD programs, managers should determine whether the programs were effective and document their findings.

The initial HRD effort designed for employees is orientation. Orientation introduces new employees to the company, the job, and the work group. The three primary purposes of orientation are: easing the new employee's adjustment to the organization, providing information concerning tasks and performance expectations, and creating a favorable impression.

Questions for Review

1. What can the manager do to reduce resistance to change?
2. Define and explain the scope of human resource development.
3. What are the general purposes of HRD?
4. Describe the HRD process.
5. Define *management development*. Why is it important?
6. List and describe the primary methods used in management development.
7. What methods are used primarily to train operative employees?
8. Describe the major factors that should be considered in the implementation of human resource development programs.
9. What are some of the means of evaluating HRD programs? Discuss.
10. Define *orientation* and explain the importance of employee orientation to a firm.

Terms for Review

Human resource development (HRD)
Training
Education
Development
Management development
Coaching
Mentoring
Business games
Case study
Conference method
Behavior modeling
In-basket training

Role playing
Job rotation
Programmed instruction (PI)
Computer-based training
On-the-job training (OJT)
Apprenticeship training
Simulators
Vestibule training
Job Training Partnership Act (JTPA)
Media
Teletraining
Orientation

INCIDENT 1   ▪   What to Do?   ▪

"I'm a little discouraged," said Susan Matthews to the training officer. "I keep making mistakes running the new printing press. It's a lot more complicated than the one I operated before, and I just can't seem to get the hang of it." "Well, Susan," responded George Duncan, "maybe you're just not cut out for the job. You know that we sent you to the two-week refresher course in Atlanta to get you more familiar with the new equipment."

"Yes," said Susan, "they had modern equipment at the school, but it wasn't anything like this machine." "What about the factory rep?" asked George. "Didn't he spend some time with you?" "No, I was on vacation at that time," said Susan.

George responded, "Have you asked your boss to get him back for a day or two?" "I asked him," said Susan, "but he said training was your responsibility. That's why I'm here." After she was gone, George got a yellow legal pad and began writing a letter to the printing press manufacturer.

Questions

1. What steps in the HRD process has the company neglected?
2. Is George taking the proper action? What would you do?

INCIDENT 2   ▪   Management Support of HRD?   ▪

As the initial training session began, John Robertson, the hospital administrator, spoke of the tremendous benefits he expected from the management development program the hospital was starting. He also complimented Brenda Short, the human resource director, for her efforts in arranging the program. As he finished his five-minute talk, he said, "I'm not sure what Brenda has in store for you, but I know that management development is important, and I'll expect each of you to put forth your best efforts to make it work." Mr. Robertson then excused himself from the meeting and turned the program over to Brenda.

For several years Brenda had been trying to convince Mr. Robertson that the supervisors could benefit from a management development program. She believed that many problems within the hospital were management related. Reluctantly, Mr. Robertson had agreed to authorize funds to employ a consultant. Through employee interviews and a self-administered questionnaire completed by the supervisors, the consultant attempted to iden-

tify development needs. The consultant recommended twelve 4-hour sessions emphasizing communication, leadership, and motivation. Each session was to be repeated once so that supervisors who missed it the first time could attend the second offering.

Mr. Robertson had signed the memo that Brenda had prepared, directing all supervisors to support the management development program. There was considerable grumbling, but all the supervisors agreed to attend. As Brenda replaced Mr. Robertson at the podium, she could sense the lack of interest in the room.

Questions

1. Have any serious errors been made so far in the management development program? What would you have done differently?
2. What advice do you have for Brenda at this point to help make the program effective?

DEVELOPING HRM SKILLS

Human resource development (HRD) is very important to any organization as it faces change and for the continual development of employees. Training, an integral part of the HRD process, can often be used to improve employee productivity. However, effective training cannot occur in a vacuum; therefore, training requires the support and understanding of the entire organization.

This day will be a training day, with the training specialist from the main office attempting to train an unwilling supervisor. The training specialist has almost completed this very difficult task and is looking forward to the last training session. All of the supervisors in this training session have risen through the ranks and have a definite dislike of college graduates. In addition, they all believe that they are experts on training in their areas. The training specialist wants to just get through this last briefing. As with the other supervisors, he'll show this supervisor the basics, and then go back to the main office where people are more receptive. As with the others, if no in-depth questions are asked, he'll provide no additional details. He really

doubts if the main office really expects improvement anyway. This operation seems to be going OK as it is.

The supervisor involved in this training session is really opposed to the training specialist trying to tell the supervisors how to train. It really grinds on this individual's nerves that since the company was bought out, the supervisors must do things their way. This person is scheduled to meet with the training specialist to learn how to train. The rumor mill has it that the training specialist is some 21-year-old college grad. According to this supervisor, "I was training my people before this person was born. All of a sudden, we can't do anything right. I look forward to my private session with that individual. I'm going to reeducate the college grad on training."

Two individuals will play roles in this exercise: one to serve as the training specialist and the other to play the supervisor. Each participant should carefully follow his or her role. All students not playing roles should carefully observe the behavior of both participants. Your instructor will provide the participants with additional information necessary to complete the exercise.

REFERENCES

Ackerman, Leonard. "Whose Ox Is Being Gored?" *HRMagazine,* 36 (February 1991), p. 96.

Asgar, Jack. "Give Me Relevance or Give Me Nothing." *Training,* 27 (July 1990), pp. 49–51.

Barnes, Don. "What's This Thing Called Mentoring?" *National Underwriters,* 22 (May 1990), p. 9.

Bettman, Ralph B. "Manage the Change Reaction." *Personnel Journal,* 68 (November 1989), pp. 60–67.

Cocheu, Ted. "Training from the Start." *Training and Development Journal,* 44 (October 1990), pp. 22–27.

Elliott, Ronald D. "The Challenge of Managing Change." *Personnel Journal,* 69 (March 1990), pp. 40–49.

Geber, Beverly. "Glory Days." *Training,* 27 (June 1990), p. 8.

Geber, Beverly. "Industry Report—Who, How, & What." *Training,* 26 (October 1989), pp. 49–63.

Gordon, Jack. "Where the Training Goes." *Training,* 27 (October 1990), pp. 51–69.

Giusti, Joseph P., David R. Baker, and Peter J. Graybash. "Satellites Dish Out Global Training." *Personnel Journal,* 70 (June 1991), pp. 80–84.

Halatin, Theodore J., and Rose E. Knotts. "Becoming a Mentor: Are the Risks Worth the Rewards?" *The AMA Handbook of Supervisory Management* (1989), pp. 520–521.

Hanlin, James R., and Nancy J. Johns. "Championship Training." *Training and Development Journal,* 45 (February 1991), pp. 56–62.

Harris, Thomas E. "A Partnership for Change." *Management World,* 18 (July–August 1989), pp. 15–16.

Kaul, Pamela A. "First Impressions Last." *Association Management,* 41 (May 1989), pp. 29–31.

Kizilos, Peter. "Take My Mentor, Please!" *Training,* 27 (April 1990), pp. 49–55.

Kleiman, Marcia. "Ease the Stress of Change." *Personnel Journal,* 68 (September 1989), pp. 106–110, 112.

Lawrie, John. "The ABCs of Change Management." *Training and Development Journal,* 44 (March 1990), pp. 87–89.

Lord, Virginia M., and Frank P. Louchheim. "Recruiting Strategies for the 1990s." *Employment Relations Today,* 16 (Autumn 1989), pp. 227–234.

McKenna, Joseph F. "Welcome Aboard!" *Industry Week,* 238 (November 6, 1989), pp. 31–38.

Mann, Robert W. "A Building-Blocks Approach to Strategic Change." *Training and Development Journal,* 44 (August 1990), pp. 23–25.

Moravec, Milan, and Kevin Wheeler. "Speed New Hires into Success." *Personnel Journal,* 68 (March 1989), pp. 74–75.

Moravec, Milan, Kevin Wheeler, and Brandon Hall. "Getting College Hires on Track Fast." *Personnel,* 66 (May 1989), pp. 56–59.

Nilson, Carolyn. "How to Use Peer Training." *Supervisory Management,* 35 (June 1990), p. 8.

Nowack, Kenneth M. "A True Training Needs Analysis." *Training and Development Journal,* 45 (April 1991), pp. 69–73.

Oberle, Joseph. "Training's 1989 Salary Survey." *Training: The Magazine of Human Resource Development,* 26 (November 1989), pp. 23–33.

Stahl, Diana, Terry O'Grady, and Dick Schaaf. "How Trainees Interact with Interactive Video." *Training: The Magazine of Human Resources Development,* 21 (April 1987), pp. 98–99.

Straub, Joseph T. "Diagnose Turnover Ills with an Exit Interview." *Training,* 26 (April 1989), p. 66.

Thornburg, Linda. "Creating a Commitment to Change." *HRMagazine,* 36 (January 1991), pp. 54–56.

Walker, James W. "What's New in HR Development?" *Personnel,* 67 (July 1990), pp. 38–42.

Wilhelm, Paul G. "Employment at Will Harms Productivity." *HRMagazine,* 35 (September 1990), p. 88.

Zemke, Ron. "Employee Orientation: A Process, Not a Program." *Training,* 26 (August 1989), pp. 33–38.

CHAPTER 9

CORPORATE CULTURE
AND ORGANIZATION
DEVELOPMENT

CHAPTER OBJECTIVES

1. Define *corporate culture,* describe the factors that interact to affect corporate culture, and explain the various types of cultures.
2. Define *organization development* and explain the organization development methods of total quality management, survey feedback, team building, and quality circles.
3. Describe the organization development methods of management by objectives, job enrichment, transactional analysis, quality of work life, and sensitivity training.
4. Explain the use of consultants in organization development and state the ways managers can evaluate OD programs.

During the past four years, the profits of International Motor Corporation have declined sharply. Teddy McCoy, International's CEO, is especially concerned about the results of an attitude survey, which revealed that 60 percent of International's employees were dissatisfied with their jobs. Teddy felt certain that this condition was directly related to an excessive number of product recalls and employee turnover. In a recent board meeting he asserted, "With competition from both domestic and foreign corporations increasing, broad changes are needed throughout the firm if International is to survive and prosper. If we maintain the status quo, we may go under."

In all likelihood, International Motor Corporation requires an organization-wide human resource development program. In this chapter, we first define *corporate culture* and then present factors that determine corporate culture. Next, we describe types of cultures and the participative culture. We then discuss organization development methods and illustrate them with an example of organization development. The last two topics that we cover in this chapter are the use of consultants and organization development evaluation.

■ CORPORATE CULTURE DEFINED

When beginning a new job, an employee may soon hear, "This is the way to do things around here." This bit of informal communication refers to something more formally known as corporate culture.[1] **Corporate culture** is the system of shared values, beliefs, and habits within an organization that interacts with the formal structure to produce behavioral norms.[2] Corporate culture embodies the values and standards that guide people's behavior. It determines the organization's overall direction. Corporate culture governs what the company stands for, how it allocates resources, its organizational structure, the systems it uses, the people it hires, the fit between jobs and people, the results it recognizes and rewards, and what it defines as problems and opportunities and how it deals with them.[3]

Corporate culture is similar in concept to meteorological climate. Just as the weather is described by variables such as temperature, humidity, and precipitation, corporate culture reflects characteristics such as friendliness, supportiveness, and risk taking. Each individual forms perceptions of the job and organization over a period of time as he or she works under the general guidance of a superior and a set of organizational policies. A firm's culture has an impact on employee job satisfaction as well as on the level and quality of employee performance. However, each employee may assess the nature of an organization's culture differently. One person may perceive the culture negatively, and another may view it positively. Employees who are quite dissatisfied may even leave an organization in the hope of finding a more compatible culture.

According to Anthony Jay, an eminent researcher in the field of corporate culture, "It has been known for some time that corporations are social institutions with customs and taboos, status groups, and pecking orders. But they are also political institutions, autocratic and democratic, peaceful and warlike, liberal and paternalistic."[4] What Jay was writing about, although the term had not then achieved broad usage, was *corporate culture*. In the early 1980s, several best-selling books on corporate culture appeared, including *In Search of Excellence, Theory Z: How American Business Can Meet the Japanese Challenge,* and *Corporate Cultures.*[5] In 1981, Harvard University introduced its first corporate culture course. By the mid-1980s the term was regularly used by those in both the business and academic communities.

---

[1] Arthur Sharplin, *Strategic Management* (New York: McGraw-Hill, 1985), p. 102.

[2] Jane C. Linder, "Computers, Corporate Culture and Change," *Personnel Journal,* 64 (September 1985), pp. 49–55.

[3] Frank Petrock, "Corporate Culture Enhances Profits," *HRMagazine,* 35 (November 1990), pp. 64–66.

[4] Anthony Jay, *Management and Machiavelli* (New York: Holt, Rinehart and Winston, 1967), p. 231.

[5] Thomas J. Peters and Robert H. Waterman, Jr., *In Search of Excellence: Lessons from America's Best Run Companies* (New York: Harper & Row, 1982); William G. Ouchi, *Theory Z: How American Business Can Meet the Japanese Challenge* (New York: Avon Books, 1987); and Terrence E. Deal and Allan A. Kennedy, *Corporate Culture* (Reading Mass.: Addison-Wesley, 1981).

Businesses are being forced to make many changes to stay competitive. They must find ways to improve quality, increase speed of operations, and adopt a customer orientation. These changes are so fundamental that they must take root in a company's very essence, which means in its culture.[6] Corporate culture is an integral part of accomplishing an organization's mission and objectives; therefore, the factors that determine corporate culture are also crucial to success.

■ FACTORS THAT DETERMINE CORPORATE CULTURE

The culture of a corporation evolves from the examples set by top management. It stems largely from what these executives do, not what they say.[7] In addition, other factors can interact to shape the culture of a firm. We emphasize three of them—communication, motivation, and leadership—because of the special impact they have on a firm's psychological environment. Other factors that can interact to determine corporate culture include organizational characteristics, administrative processes, organizational structure, and management style.

Communication

Communication is the transfer of information, ideas, understanding, and feelings between people. All managers must communicate effectively if they are to be successful. Moreover, effective organizational communication has a positive influence on corporate culture. By communicating effectively within the organization, management can accomplish its objectives more readily, helping ensure the firm's success.

Managers in progressive firms realize the importance of effective communication. According to one chief executive, "We have our communication department, with a full-time group working to refine communication with our people. They're going out on the plant floor to ask questions and get opinions."[8] To reinforce successful communication, this firm created a position of corporate director of communication that reports directly to the president.

Many other companies recognize that communication can break down in a multitude of ways. Fortunately, the ability to communicate effectively can be learned, and many communication breakdowns can be avoided. Individuals who are willing to make the effort to improve their ability to communicate can benefit both themselves and the organization.

---

[6] Brian Dumaine, "Creating a New Company Culture," *Fortune,* 121 (January 15, 1990), p. 127.

[7] Peter C. Reynolds, "Imposing a Corporate Culture," *Psychology Today,* 21 (March 1987), pp. 32–38.

[8] Keith W. Bennett, "Communication and Costs Can Alter the Bottom Line," *Iron Age* (June 26, 1978), p. 28.

In the global environment, communication problems are intensified by language barriers. Faced with the ongoing globalization of business, an increasing number of U.S. executives are learning a second language. Du Pont Chief Executive Edgar S. Woolard, Jr., learned Japanese. Other Du Pont managers are also cramming to learn second languages. Their counterparts at Eastman Kodak, Citicorp, General Electric's Medical Systems division, and other corporations are doing the same thing.[9]

Most big companies sign up with 111-year-old Berlitz International to teach executives to speak another language. Berlitz is the leading language school worldwide, operating 267 centers in 25 countries and teaching 50 languages. According to Berlitz marketing director Patricia Sze, "There's been a steady upswing in corporate clients over the past four years." Enrollment in the company's corporate-oriented total language immersion program and other classes increased more than 50 percent. As may be seen in Figure 9-1, French and German are among the most popular languages for Americans attending Berlitz classes, and enrollment in Japanese classes is rapidly increasing.[10]

Because many international companies have declared English as their official language, English classes account for 64 percent of Berlitz's business internationally. Since language proficiency tends to make employees more effective communicators, the trend toward learning a second language is likely to continue.[11]

Motivation

Motivation is the willingness to put forth effort in pursuit of organizational goals. Managers do not actually motivate their employees because motivation is internal to each individual. Motivation cannot be viewed directly; as with the wind, only the results are observable. Management's job is to provide an organizational culture that encourages positive employee behaviors.

Management traditionally has relied on the use of rewards—such as increased pay, job security, and good working conditions—or punishments—such as dismissal, demotions, or withholding rewards—to encourage worker motivation. Management in today's environment, however, cannot rely on the manipulation of pay, benefits, or working conditions to stimulate workers to perform effectively. Motivation is a much more complicated process.

Managers need to understand the forces that energize workers' behaviors. A manager's major motivational task is to develop and maintain an environment in which workers will want to be productive, contributing members of the organization. Today's human resource management profes-

---

[9] Richard S. Teitelbaum, "Language: One Way to Think Globally," *Fortune,* 120 (December 4, 1989), p. 11.

[10] *Ibid.,* p. 11.

[11] *Ibid.,* p. 12.

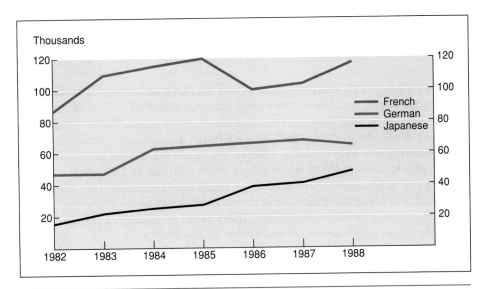

FIGURE 9-1 | Learning a Second Language: Berlitz Lessons Given Annually

Source: Richard S. Teitelbaum, "Language: One Way to Think Globally,"
Fortune, 120 (December 4, 1989), p. 11, © 1989 The Time Inc. Magazine
Company. All rights reserved.

sionals recognize that in order to achieve a corporate culture that fosters
improved productivity, employees' personal needs must be reasonably well
satisfied.

Leadership

Leadership is influencing others to do what the leader wants them to do.
The manner in which different managers attempt to persuade their employees may vary greatly and can affect the organization's culture in different ways. In the following discussion, we concentrate on the practical
aspects of choosing effective leadership styles.

Factors Related to the Manager. Self-knowledge is important to effective leadership. Leaders have different abilities and goals, and they also
have had different experiences. Through such experiences, managers develop basic beliefs about people. Some believe that people must be threatened before they will perform. Others believe in encouraging employees and
rewarding them for performance. Managers must be flexible in their choice
of leadership styles, and they usually perform better if they use a style that
is consistent with their personal beliefs and appropriate for a given
situation.

A manager's professional and technical competence also affects leadership style. Not only are competent managers more confident, but workers
are also less likely to challenge or question them. This would seem to allow

the manager to be more autocratic. In fact, it permits managers more flexibility in establishing appropriate leadership styles that are effective in meeting a variety of challenges within a company.

Factors Related to Employees. When deciding on a specific leadership style, a manager must also take into account characteristics of subordinates. One important consideration is their work ethic. Some employees feel that work, in and of itself, is satisfying, pleasurable, and fulfilling. Such workers are easy to lead. Others see work merely as an unpleasant way to obtain money. Such workers are more difficult to influence.

Workers' attitudes toward authority must also be considered. Some believe that the job of the manager is to tell them what to do. They don't want to be involved in decision making. Others want to make all the decisions, and they resist any exercise of authority by the leader.

The maturity level of subordinates influences the manager's leadership style. Some workers approach their work maturely. They take the initiative not only in doing their jobs but also in self-development. Others may have to be watched quite closely to obtain even minimal performance. However, a worker may handle one aspect of the job adequately but not other aspects of it.

Another factor is the experience level and skills of subordinates. The leadership style used with a trainee may be different from that used with an experienced craftsperson. A more directive style may prove best for the trainee, while the craftsperson may need no direction at all. For some employees an autocratic style works best. This may be particularly true in extremely favorable or extremely unfavorable situations. However, employees generally respond better to a participative approach.

Factors Related to the Situation. The situation that managers confront can also have a significant effect on the type of leadership style that will prove most effective. Many factors in the external and internal environments may cause a leader to alter his or her style. For instance, a firm's policies or pressures to produce may encourage an autocratic managerial style.

Leadership styles may vary within a firm for a number of reasons. An organization's overall leadership approach must of necessity be stated in broad terms. Thus in a firm that generally exhibits autocratic leadership, there may be some managers whose leadership style is highly participative. At the same time, an individual manager's leadership style isn't monolithic; it has various aspects, although there is usually a dominant one. A manager may, for example, normally stress employee participation. However, when the building is on fire, he or she may issue an order, "Get out of here now through exit number 2!" The leader does not consult anyone about this decision, and no committees are formed to study the problem. The situation required that the leader respond quickly, and the leader simply reverted to a more autocratic style. In organizations, there are many "fires"; that is, situations that require immediate and decisive action. Leaders who develop a high degree of mutual trust and confidence within their work groups will be able to adjust their leadership styles to differing situations and have them more readily accepted by everyone involved.

Organizational Characteristics

Organizational characteristics also affect corporate culture. The size and complexity of organizations vary. Large organizations tend to have more specialization and be less personal. Labor unions often find that large firms are easier to organize than small ones because small firms tend to have closer and more informal relationships between employees and management. Complex organizations tend to employ a greater number of professionals and specialists, which alters the general approach to solving problems. The degree to which organizations use written communications and attempt to program behavior through rules, procedures, and regulations varies widely. The degree to which organizations decentralize their decision-making authority also differs, which affects employee autonomy, freedom, and responsibility.

Administrative Processes

Administrative processes can also affect corporate culture. Firms that can develop a direct link between performance and rewards tend to create cultures that foster achievement. Communication systems that are open and free-flowing tend to promote participation and a creative atmosphere. General attitudes about the handling of risk and the tolerance of conflict will, in turn, have considerable impact on the type and amount of teamwork, organizational innovation, and creativity generated.

Organizational Structure

Organizational structure is the purposeful way in which the human resources of the firm are related or arranged. An organization's structure may be rigid or flexible, depending on managerial style or how rapidly its environment is changing. In some companies, all significant decisions are made by top management. In other firms, lower level managers are permitted to make important decisions. Lincoln Electric Company, a highly successful maker of welding products, is one such company. Richard Sabo, an executive with this firm, says, "Around here we give a high school graduate more authority than some companies give their mid-level managers." Yet another important characteristic of organizational structure is the number of managerial levels—whether the structure is tall (many managerial levels) or flat (few managerial levels). The manager's job is very different in a flexible and flat organization than in an inflexible one that has more managerial levels.

Management Style of Upper Management

The attitudes and preferences of middle and top management constrain first-line managers in somewhat the same way that the attitudes and preferences of shareholders constrain top managers. This is why it is important for organizations to have a consistent policy about the amount of openness and participation to be encouraged.

At times, the managerial style of upper management is different from that of subordinate managers. For example, an executive manager may believe in simply giving orders and having them followed. A middle manager who works for the executive may prefer involving supervisors and employees in decision making and give them a relatively large amount of freedom. This difference in approach may lead to conflict, especially if the executive believes that the middle manager's approach indicates a lack of toughness or decisiveness. Subordinate managers should attempt to follow their own individual management styles, and at the same time, work to limit overt conflicts with the styles of their superiors.

■ TYPES OF CULTURES

At times an organization must alter its culture in order to succeed or influence events just to survive. This was necessary at IBM when the computer industry changed so drastically in the early 1980s. However, alterations made to the corporate culture should always improve the current situation.

Management must be aware of the types of corporate culture that a firm may wish to emulate—and why one particular culture may prove superior to another. Most behavioralists advocate an open and participative culture. Some go so far as to contend that such a culture is best for all situations. This type of culture is characterized by the following characteristics:

Trust in subordinates

Open communication

Considerate and supportive leadership

Group problem solving

Worker autonomy

Information sharing

High output goals

Many U.S. businesses are culturally permissive and therefore embrace behavioralist principles. They have been guided by the philosophy that organization members who are free to choose among alternatives make the soundest decisions. When employees are asked to give up some of their individuality for the common good, the end result is often reinforcement of the status quo.[12]

The opposite of the open and participative culture is a closed and autocratic one. It, too, may be characterized by high output goals. But such goals are more likely to be declared and imposed on the organization by autocratic and threatening leaders. The greater rigidity in this culture results from strict adherence to a formal chain of command, narrower spans of management, and stricter individual accountability. The emphasis is on the individual rather than on teamwork. Employees often simply go through the motions and do as they are told.

■ GLOBAL BLENDING OF CULTURES AND MANAGEMENT STYLES

Often when a U.S. corporation goes global, it forms an alliance with a company in the host country. Once an alliance is formed it is essential that the cultures and management styles of the partners blend together as quickly as possible.[13] Alliances are useful for all partners because collaboration makes it possible to share the costs and risks of doing business, and it enables companies to share financial resources, technology, production facilities, marketing expertise, and, of course, human resources.

The AT&T alliance with Olivetti was plagued with difficulties because of a failure to blend the partners' divergent cultures and management styles. Robert Kravner, an AT&T senior executive, blames the problems on differences in these areas. Kravner has said, "I don't think we or Olivetti spent enough time understanding the behavior of the other partner. We knew that our cultures were different but we never really penetrated. We would get angry and they would get upset."[14] Problems may occur in international alliances when people from different organizations and national cultures work together. Such problems can often be traced to cultural differences. Overcoming such problems requires both parties to invest considerable time and effort in understanding each other's culture, on team-building efforts, and on continually improving two-way communication.[15]

For instance, when General Motors (GM) and the Fanuc Company of Japan formed the joint venture GMF Robotics Corporation, their management styles were quite different. Fanuc's managers operated with more autonomy than did GM managers. Yet despite this and other differences, GM and Fanuc were able to arrange a workable alliance. During the negotiation stage and the early years of the venture, both parent companies

---

[12] Richard Pascale, "The Paradox of Corporate Culture: Reconciling Ourselves to Socialization," *California Management Review,* 27 (Winter 1985), p. 28.

[13] Wayne F. Cascio and Manuel G. Serapio, Jr., "Human Resources Systems in an International Alliance: The Undoing of a Done Deal?" *Organizational Dynamics,* 19 (Winter 1991), p. 65.

[14] *Ibid.,* pp. 67–68.

[15] *Ibid.,* p. 68.

focused their efforts on building trust and on understanding each other's operations. In order to build trust, both avoided conflict and acceded to each other's demands during the formative stage of the joint venture. Today, GMF Robotics Corporation holds the dominant share of the heavy robotics market in the United States.[16]

■ THE PARTICIPATIVE CULTURE

The prevailing managerial approach in many organizations is highly structured. Consequently, most attempts to alter organizational culture have been directed toward opening it up and making it more participative. The theme of participation developed by McGregor, Herzberg, and Maslow, among others, relates primarily to self-actualization, consultative and democratic leadership, job enrichment, and management by objectives.

Values of Participation

The value of involving more people in the decision-making process relates primarily to productivity and morale. Increased productivity can result from the stimulation of ideas and encouragement of a greater cooperative effort. Psychologically involved employees will often respond to shared problems with innovative suggestions and unusually productive effort.

Open and participative cultures are often used to improve employee morale and satisfaction. Specific benefits to be derived include the following:

Increased acceptability of management's ideas

Increased cooperation between management and staff

Reduced turnover

Reduced absenteeism

Reduced complaints and grievances

Greater acceptance of changes

Improved attitudes toward the job and the organization

In general, greater employee participation seems to have a direct and immediate effect on employee morale. Employees take more interest in the job and the organization. They tend to accept—and sometimes initiate—change not only because they understand the necessity for it, but also because they are more secure as a result of knowing more about the change. Most experience and research indicates a positive relationship between employee participation and measures of morale, turnover, and absenteeism. However, little evidence has been presented that suggests a positive

---

[16] *Ibid.*

relationship between job satisfaction and productivity. Therefore, if productivity is not adversely affected by participation, the supplementary benefits alone may make participation worthwhile. However, if productivity actually fell, management would have to carefully scrutinize its organizational and managerial approach.

Limitations of Participation

Despite its benefits, the participative approach to decision making has certain prerequisites and limitations. The requirements for greater participation in decision making are: (1) sufficient time, (2) adequate ability and interest on the part of the participants, and (3) restrictions generated by the present structure and system.

If immediate decisions are required, time may not be available for group participation. The manager may be forced to decide what to do and issue directives accordingly. Participation calls for some measure of self-discipline instead of leaning on others. In addition, participation requires that the subordinate learn to handle freedom and the supervisor learn to trust the subordinate.

Whether greater involvement in decision making can be developed depends largely on the abilities and interests of the participants, both subordinates and managers. Obviously, if the subordinate knows or cares nothing about a subject, there is little reason to consult that person. As organizations and technology become increasingly complex, and as management becomes more professional, employee participation will likely involve more cooperation seeking and information sharing. However, not all employees want to participate in decisions about their work. Managers must face the fact that some workers do not seek and won't accept more job responsibility and involvement.

■ CHANGING THE CORPORATE CULTURE

Environmental factors such as governmental action and foreign competition often require a firm to change its culture and even make a clean break with the past. For example, the culture of AT&T is distinctly different from that of just a few years ago when it virtually monopolized its industry. After being dismantled by the government, the firm has had to deal with aggressive competitors and in doing so develop a new modus operandi.

Few firms have escaped the competitive pressure from foreign firms. This pressure has greatly increased the need for improved quality, competitive pricing, and better customer service. Since these critical factors are so dependent upon a firm's culture, the culture itself must be changed if the firm is to survive, much less prosper.

In changing a firm's culture, as much of the organization should be involved as possible. The chief executive officer should be proactively involved. The necessity of the change, along with the goals sought, should be clearly communicated to all organizational members. They too, should be involved either directly or indirectly.[17] Change of this magnitude is often called organization development. This topic is discussed in the next section.

■ ORGANIZATION DEVELOPMENT

We have examined various factors that affect employees' behavior on the job. To bring about desired changes in these factors and behavior, organizations must be transformed into market-driven, innovative, and adaptive systems if they are to survive and prosper in the highly competitive global environment of the next decade. Many firms are beginning to face this urgent need by practicing organization development, an HRD approach that involves the entire firm.[18] **Organization development (OD)** is an organization-wide application of behavioral science knowledge to the planned development and reinforcement of a firm's strategies, structures, and processes for improving its effectiveness.[19]

Organization development applies to an entire system, such as a company or a plant. Based on behavioral science knowledge, OD emphasizes personal needs. Although it doesn't produce a blueprint for how things should be done, OD does provide an adaptive strategy for planning and implementing change. In addition, OD ensures a long-term reinforcement of change. Organization development involves both changes in the grouping of people (structure) and changes in the methods of communication (process).[20]

In order for the International Motor Corporation (referred to at the beginning of the chapter) to overcome substantial problems, it must alter its corporate culture significantly. A special HRD program here and a management development session there may not be sufficient. In fact, some advocates of OD view traditional management development as an antiquated idea. The essential problem with traditional HRD programs is that they usually address organizational change in an environment away from the job. Individual managers are often provided with a good educational experience, but when the development program ends and they return to their firms, they find it very difficult to apply their new skills and knowledge. To avoid this problem, OD practitioners focus on changing organizational conditions that regulate individual behavior. The best training in the world could be offered and the participants could recite verbatim what they learned; however, if inappropriate behavior is not punished and appropriate behavior is not rewarded in the workplace, no form or amount of training will yield the desired results.[21]

---

[17] Paul E. O'Neill, "Transforming Managers for Organizational Change," *Training and Development Journal,* 44 (July 1990), pp. 87–90.

[18] Ralph H. Killmann, "A Completely Integrated Program for Creating and Maintaining Organizational Success," *Organizational Dynamics,* 18 (Summer 1989), p. 5.

[19] Edgar F. Huse and Thomas G. Cummings, *Organization Development and Change,* 3rd ed. (St. Paul, Minn.: West, 1985), p. 2.

[20] *Ibid.*

[21] Stephen B. Wehrenberg, "The Vicious Circle of Training and Organizational Development," *Personnel Journal,* 65 (July 1986), p. 98.

Some commonly used OD approaches include total quality management, survey feedback, team building, quality circles, management by objectives, job enrichment, transactional analysis, quality of work life, and sensitivity training. From a practical standpoint, some of these techniques may be combined to provide a strategic approach to organization development.

Total Quality Management (TQM)[22]

Total quality management (TQM) is a top management philosophy that emphasizes the continuous improvement of the processes which result in goods or services. Its ultimate goal is customer satisfaction. Instead of being content with the status quo, employees at all levels continually seek alternative methods or technologies that will improve existing processes. TQM provides a strategy for reducing the causes of poor quality and thereby increasing productivity. Its principles are as relevant to HRM and other staff activities as they are to those of the factory floor.

TQM originated in the 1930s with the pioneering work of Walter A. Shewart, who acted as a mentor to W. Edwards Deming. Deming applied Shewart's principles of statistical process control in Japan following World War II. He convinced the Japanese to do more than merely monitor the quality level of their manufacturing systems. He worked with their scientists, engineers, and managers to identify and remove the causes of variation. As we know, the Japanese were able to improve quality and productivity, capture world market share, add jobs, and improve the standard of living in their country. In a matter of forty years, the Japanese rose from the ashes of World War II to become a powerful economic force throughout the world. As you might expect, Deming is a hero in Japan. Today, Deming is over 90 years old, and he remains the dean of total quality management.[23]

While statistical process control was not new in the United States, its focus had been to monitor rather than improve manufacturing systems. It had become normal to expect and even accept a certain percentage of defective products. This attitude necessitated conducting extensive inspection testing in order to identify the defects and either remove or rework them. All of this added to manufacturing costs, did little to improve quality, and lessened America's competitive position in world markets. U.S. businesspeople assumed, incorrectly, that the quality was satisfactory if products were not being returned, if complaints were not received, and if the price/performance ratio for the customer was improved.[24]

---

[22] The Total Quality Management section was written by Robert M. Seay, Department of Marketing and Management, East Texas State University.

[23] Ellis Pines, "The Gurus of TQM," *Aviation Week and Space Technology,* 132 (May 21, 1990), p. S29.

[24] Fred G. Steingraber, "Total Quality Management," *Vital Speeches of the Day,* 57 (April 15, 1991), p. 415.

As world market share shifted away from U.S. producers, forward-thinking American managers recognized the necessity for change. Since 1960, more than half of the U.S. world market share was lost to other international producers in a number of product lines. These lines included athletic equipment, automobiles, cameras, computer chips, industrial robots, medical equipment, optical equipment, radial tires, stereos, and television sets.

The TQM approach focuses on continuously improving process quality over the long run. In the short run, once each of the linked processes within a firm is operating at or above a desired level of quality, reliance on costly inspection practices can be reduced or eliminated altogether. Attention can then be turned to monitoring the overall process to determine the sources of variation still present. If these sources are also eliminated, then the process can be more precise and fewer defects or errors produced. In the view of the ultimate customer, quality will have exceeded the expected level. The customer will be more satisfied and will probably continue to buy the firm's products.

The increased employee participation required by TQM creates a new role for all organizational members. Top management, middle managers, and first-level supervisors must embrace the philosophy and work to ensure its acceptance throughout the organization. Operative employees are consulted for assistance in determining and analyzing sources of process variation. They are also relied on to develop proposals for reducing or eliminating them.

Cultural change must precede or accompany the introduction of any new management approach. And, the organizational culture required to support the concepts of TQM is not likely to be changed quickly. Five to ten years is generally needed for such changes in top management's value system to permeate the organization. TQM is not a body of regulations and cannot be forced on employees. Since a company's culture is largely a product of positively reinforced behavior, the route to change almost always includes education and training.[25] In addition to training and development activities, employee selection practices will be a central component in implementing the TQM philosophy.

Several factors favor the growth of TQM in the United States. First, and perhaps most important, is that TQM companies are successfully taking world market share away from traditionally managed organizations. Second, consumers are no longer satisfied with lower quality levels even if the products or services are "Made in America." Third, national trade policy is decidedly against imposing trade restrictions of any kind to protect U.S. producers from international competitors.

A fourth factor, and a fairly new one, is the support and encouragement of the U.S. government for the TQM movement. The Japanese created a national award for high-quality firms, the Deming Award, and the Department of Commerce has created a similar honor, the Malcolm Baldrige

---

[25] Ellis Pines, "TQM Training: A New Culture Sparks Change at Every Level," *Aviation Week and Space Technology,* 132 (May 21, 1990), p. S38.

National Quality Award. This award recognizes outstanding firms in both the manufacturing and service sectors for their quality management programs. In addition, the federal government is now requiring contractors to provide evidence of the statistical control of their processes as a part of the bidding process. These contractors are likewise requiring similar evidence from their subcontractors.

The TQM movement began just over a decade ago in this country. However, many firms including Motorola, Ford Motor Company, Florida Power and Light, and Federal Express have demonstrated a long history of commitment toward improving quality. These firms have been recognized here and abroad for their efforts. The decade of the 1990s may well be remembered as the time American industry reversed its general decline in world markets. This goal can be achieved if managers and employees join together to become world-class competitors by continuously improving the processes that produce goods and services. As Robert Costello, former undersecretary of defense for acquisition, stated, "The ultimate goal is to ingrain basic cultural change to a depth where the slogan TQM will fade and, in its wake, the principles and practices of TQM will remain as a permanent, normal way of conducting business in the United States."[26]

Survey Feedback

Survey feedback consists of collecting information about the organization and making the data available to employees so that they can diagnose problems and develop action plans to solve them. It is probably the most popular OD method.[27]

Survey feedback involves three essential steps, as Figure 9-2 shows (see page 334). In the first step, a consultant collects data from employees, normally using questionnaires that the employees answer anonymously. The survey probably should cover only those areas in which management is willing to make changes. Otherwise, there is the possibility of raising employee expectations but not fulfilling them, which could result in even greater dissatisfaction.[28] The second step involves presenting the results of the study in the form of feedback to the participants. In the third step, employees analyze the data, which reveal problem areas, and make action decisions. These decisions are directed at improving relationships in the organization. The consultants act as facilitators to help the employees deal with the problems and make decisions through straightforward discussions.

An example of a management survey feedback instrument is provided in Figure 9-3 on page 335. This chart is used to analyze management performance in leadership, motivation, communication, decision making, goals,

---

[26] Ellis Pines, "From Top Secret to Top Priority: The Story of TQM," *Aviation Week and Space Technology,* 132 (May 21, 1990), p. S24.

[27] Edgar F. Huse and Thomas G. Cummings, *Organization Development and Change,* p. 129.

[28] Don Hellriegel, John W. Slocum, and Richard W. Woodman, *Organizational Behavior,* 4th ed. (St. Paul, Minn.: West, 1986), p. 610.

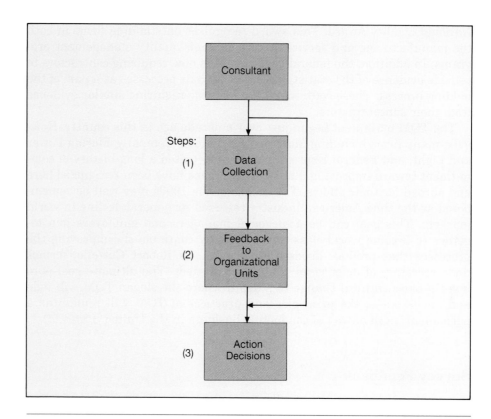

FIGURE 9-2 | The Survey Feedback Method

Source: Adapted by permission of the publisher, from *Organization Development for Operating Managers* by Michael E. McGill, p. 66. Copyright © 1977 by AMACOM, a division of American Management Association, New York. All rights reserved.

control, and other areas. Employees are asked to check—along a continuum—the point that best describes their organization. They are also asked to indicate their views of a desired state. Averaging the responses and charting them gives an organizational profile. Referring again to Figure 9-3, note that the present state of leadership is perceived as being quite negative. The employees surveyed apparently felt that their company's leadership was "condescending." The consensus was that the leader should show "substantial" confidence in subordinates (the desired state).

Team Building and Self-Directed Teams

A conscious effort to develop effective work groups throughout the organization is referred to as **team building.** Team building utilizes self-directed teams, each composed of a small group of employees responsible for an entire work process or segment. Team members work together to improve their operation or product, plan and control their work, and handle day-to-

		Present State		Desired State	
LEADERSHIP	How much confidence is shown in subordinates?	None	Condescending	Substantial	Complete
	How free do they feel to talk to superiors about job?	Not at All	Not Very	Rather	Fully
	Are subordinates' ideas sought and used, if worthy?	Seldom	Sometimes	Usually	Always
MOTIVATION	Is predominant use made of (1) fear, (2) threats, (3) punishment, (4) rewards, (5) involvement?	1, 2, 3 Occasionally 4	4, Some 3	4, Some 3 and 5	5, 4, based on group-set goals
	Where is responsibility felt for achieving organization's goals?	Mostly at Top	Top and Middle	Fairly General	All Levels
COMMUNICATION	How much communication is aimed at achieving organization's objectives?	Very Little	Little	Quite a Bit	A Great Deal
	What is the direction of information flow?	Downward	Mostly Downward	Down and Up	Down, Up and Sideways
	How is downward communication accepted?	With Suspicion	Possibly with Suspicion	With Caution	With an Open Mind
	How accurate is upward communication?	Often Wrong	Censored for the Boss	Limited Accuracy	Accurate
	How well do superiors know problems faced by subordinates?	Know Little	Some Knowledge	Quite Well	Very Well
DECISIONS	At what level are decisions formally made?	Mostly at Top	Policy at Top, Some Delegation	Broad Policy at Top, More Delegation	Throughout but **Well Integrated**
	What is the origin of technical and professional knowledge used in decision making?	Top Management	Upper and Middle	To a Certain Extent Throughout	To a Great Extent Throughout
	Are subordinates involved in decisions related to their work?	Not at all	Occasionally Consulted	Generally Consulted	Fully Involved
	What does the decision making process contribute to motivation?	Nothing, **Often Weakens It**	Relatively Little	Some Contribution	Substantial Contribution
GOALS	How are organizational goals established?	Orders Issued	Orders, Some Comment Invited	After Discussion, by Orders	By Group Action (Except in Crisis)
	How much covert resistance to goals is present?	Strong Resistance	Moderate Resistance	Some Resistance at Times	Little or None
CONTROL	How concentrated are review and control functions?	Highly at Top	Relatively Highly at Top	Moderate Delegation to Lower Levels	Quite Widely Shared
	Is there an informal organization resisting the formal one?	Yes	Usually	Sometimes	No—Same Goals as Formal
	Where are cost, productivity and other control data used for?	Policing, Punishment	Reward and Punishment	Reward, Some Self-Guidance	Self-Guidance Problem Solving

FIGURE 9-3 | An Example of a Survey Feedback Questionnaire

Source: Adapted by permission of the publisher, from *Organization Development for Operating Managers* by Michael E. McGill, p. 232. Copyright © 1977 by AMACOM, a division of American Management Association, New York. All rights reserved.

day problems. They may even become involved in broader, company-wide issues, such as vendor quality, safety, and business planning.[29] Team building is one of the more popular approaches to OD.[30]

Douglas McGregor has identified several characteristics of effective management teams (see Table 9-1). His version of an effective group emphasizes an informal organizational culture that is relatively free from tension. The group's decision-making process involves much discussion and broad participation. Communications are open, with listening to the views of others emphasized. Members feel free to disagree but do so in an atmosphere of acceptance. The effective group works as a team in pursuing goals that its members understand and accept.

Effective work groups focus on solving actual problems while building efficient management teams. The team-building process begins when the team leader defines a problem that requires organizational change (see Figure 9-4 on page 338). The group diagnoses the problem to determine the underlying causes. These causes may be related to breakdowns in communication, inappropriate leadership styles, deficiencies in the organizational structure, or other factors. The group then considers alternative solutions and selects the most appropriate one. The result of open and frank discussions is likely to be commitment to the proposed course of action. The interpersonal relations developed by group members improve the chances for implementing the change.[31]

The American Society for Training and Development (ASTD) recently conducted a survey that asked for the areas most improved through the use of trained self-directed teams. The factors that had noticeably or significantly improved are in the following list. The figure in parentheses indicates the percentage of respondents who felt the factor had improved.[32]

- Productivity (77%)
- Quality (72%)
- Job Satisfaction (65%)
- Customer Service (57%)
- Waste Reduction (55%)

Quality Circles

Another OD approach is the use of quality circles. **Quality circles** are groups of employees who meet regularly with their supervisors to identify production problems and recommend solutions. These recommendations are then presented to higher level management for review, and the approved actions are implemented with employee participation.

---

[29] Richard Wellins and Jill George, "The Key to Self-Directed Teams," *Training and Development Journal,* 45 (April 1991), p. 27.

[30] Bert A. Spector, "From Bogged Down to Fired Up: Inspiring Organizational Change," *Sloan Management Review,* 30 (Summer 1989), p. 31.

[31] Michael A. Hitt, R. Dennis Middlemist, and Robert L. Mathis, *Management: Concepts and Effective Practice* (St. Paul, Minn.: West, 1983), p. 394.

[32] Richard Wellins and Jill George, "The Key to Self-Directed Teams," p. 27.

TABLE 9-1 | Characteristics of Effective Groups

1. The atmosphere, which can be sensed in a few minutes of observation, tends to be informal, comfortable, and relaxed. There are no obvious tensions.

2. There is a lot of discussion in which virtually everyone participates, but it remains pertinent to the task of the group.

3. The task or the objective of the group is well understood and accepted by the members.

4. The members listen to each other! The discussion does not have the quality of jumping from one idea to another unrelated one. Every idea is given a hearing. People are not afraid of seeming foolish by expressing a creative thought even if it seems fairly extreme.

5. There is disagreement. The group is comfortable with this and shows no signs of having to avoid conflict or to keep everything light and on a plane of sweetness. Disagreements are not suppressed or overridden by premature group action. Individuals who disagree do not appear to be trying to dominate the group or to express hostility. Their disagreement is an expression of a genuine difference of opinion, and they expect a hearing in order to find a solution.

6. Most decisions are reached by a kind of consensus in which it is clear that everybody is in general agreement and willing to go along.

7. Criticism is frequent, frank, and relatively comfortable. There is little evidence of personal attack, either open or hidden. The criticism has a constructive flavor in that it is oriented toward removing an obstacle that prevents the group from getting the job done.

8. People freely express their feelings as well as their ideas on both the problem and the group's operation. There is little pussyfooting; there are few hidden agendas. Everybody appears to know quite well how everybody else feels about any matter under discussion.

9. When action is taken, clear assignments are made and accepted.

10. The chairperson of the group does not dominate it, nor to the contrary, does the group defer unduly to him or her. In fact, the leadership shifts from time to time, depending on the circumstances. At various times different members, because of their knowledge or experience, are in a position to act as "resources" for the group. The members utilize them in this fashion and they occupy leadership roles while they are thus being used. There is little evidence of a struggle for power as the group operates. The issue is not who controls but how to get the job done.

11. The group is conscious of its own operations. Frequently, it will stop to examine how well it is doing or what may be interfering with its operation. The problem may be a matter of procedure, or it may be that an individual's behavior is interfering with the accomplishment of the group's objectives. Whatever the problem, it is openly discussed until a solution is found.

Source: Adapted from Douglas McGregor, *The Human Side of Management* (New York: McGraw-Hill, 1960), pp. 232–235. Reprinted by permission of the McGraw-Hill Book Company.

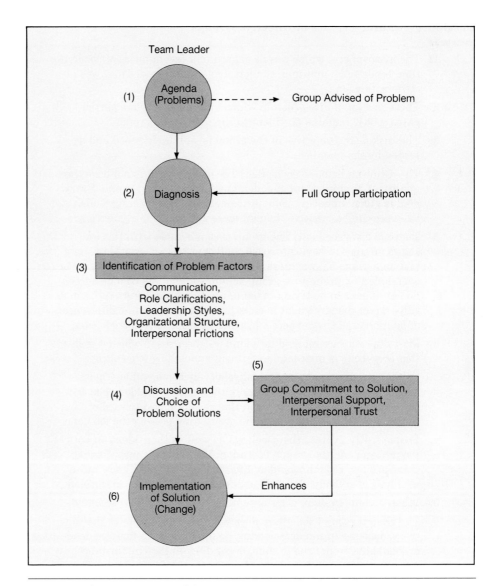

FIGURE 9-4 | The Team-Building Process

In Japan, more than ten million workers participate in quality circles, which results in annual savings of $20–$25 billion.[33] Even though the corporate culture in the United States is different, an increasing number of

---

[33] Sud Ingle, "How to Avoid Quality Circle Failure in Your Company," *Training and Development Journal,* 36 (June 1982), p. 59.

firms are adapting the quality circle concept to their operations. To illustrate, according to the International Association of Quality Circles, more than 100 U.S. firms are now using quality circles, including thirty of the fifty largest companies surveyed. Westinghouse alone has more than 700 quality circles.[34]

The decade of the 1980s saw a dramatic increase in the use of quality circles in all sectors of the U.S. economy. One study of the perceived effectiveness of quality circles concluded that member training was the most important factor. Apparently a few hours of specific training gives team members the confidence to handle challenges, solve difficult problems, and overcome constraints in the problem-solving process.[35]

However, quality circles are not a panacea for HRD and productivity problems. In fact, the concept has not worked at all for some firms.[36] In order to implement a successful quality circle program, the following actions should be taken:

- Establish clear goals for the program.
- Obtain top management's support.
- Create a corporate culture that accepts the idea of participative management.
- Select an enthusiastic and capable manager for the program.
- Communicate the goals and nature of the program to all employees.
- For the initial effort, select an area of the firm in which cooperation and enthusiasm from participants can be expected.
- Keep the program strictly voluntary.
- Give participants adequate training in the operation of quality circles.
- Start the program slowly and then let it proceed gradually but steadily.[37]

Management by Objectives

Consider the following scenario:

> Eileen Murphy, human resource manager for Red River Wholesale Company, stopped by Michael Willis's office to discuss a vacancy in her department. While she was waiting for Michael to return from lunch, she noticed that one of his employees appeared to be very busy. His desk was cluttered, and he was filling out forms and talking on the phone at the same time. When Michael returned, Eileen mentioned this extremely busy person. "Yes," said Michael, "He's always very active. The only problem is that he's one of my least effective employees. He has

---

[34] Roy G. Folz, "QWL's Effect on Productivity," *Personnel Administrator,* 27 (May 1982), p. 20.

[35] Alan Honeycutt, "The Key to Effective Quality Circles," *Training and Development Journal,* 43 (May 1989), pp. 81–84.

[36] Sud Ingle, "How to Avoid Quality Circle Failure," p. 54.

[37] *Ibid.,* pp. 57–59.

so many projects going at one time that nothing seems to get accomplished. He's very active, yes. But highly productive, no!"

Michael Willis is keenly aware that activity is not necessarily a measure of productivity. He also believes that random, ineffective behavior may result from a lack of clearly defined objectives. **Management by objectives (MBO)** is a philosophy of management that emphasizes the setting of agreed-on objectives by superior and subordinate managers and using these objectives as the primary basis for motivation, evaluation, and self-control. As a management approach that encourages managers to anticipate and plan for the future, MBO directs efforts toward attainable goals. It deemphasizes guessing or making decisions based on hunches. Knowledge of MBO is especially important to the human resource manager because that department is often responsible for overseeing the entire company's MBO program.

Since MBO emphasizes participative management approaches, it has been called a philosophy of management. Within this broader context, MBO becomes an important method of organization development. It focuses on the achievement of individual and organizational goals. The participation of individuals in setting goals and the emphasis on self-control promote not only personal development but also organizational development.

Management by objectives is a dynamic process that must be continuously reviewed, modified, and updated. Top management must both initiate the MBO process by establishing long-range goals (see Figure 9-5) and support the process. For example, the president and vice-president of human resources (superior and subordinate) may jointly establish the firm's HRM long-range goals and intermediate and short-range objectives. At this point, the president and vice-president mutually agree on the subordinate's performance objectives and action plans, which outline how the objectives will be achieved. The subordinate proceeds to work toward his or her goals. At the end of the appraisal period, both parties review the subordinate's performance and determine what can be done to overcome any problems encountered. Goals are then established for the next period, and the process is repeated.

From an organization development standpoint, MBO offers numerous potential benefits. It does the following:

- Provides an opportunity for development of managers and employees.
- Increases the firm's ability to change.
- Provides a more objective and tangible basis for performance appraisal and salary decisions.
- Results in better overall management and higher performance levels.
- Provides an effective overall planning system.
- Forces managers to establish priorities and measurable targets or standards of performance.
- Clarifies the specific roles, responsibilities, and authority of employees.
- Encourages the joint participation of employees and managers in establishing objectives.

- Promotes accountability.
- Lets individuals know clearly what is expected of them.
- Improves communication within the organization.
- Helps identify promotable managers and employees.
- Increases employee motivation and commitment.

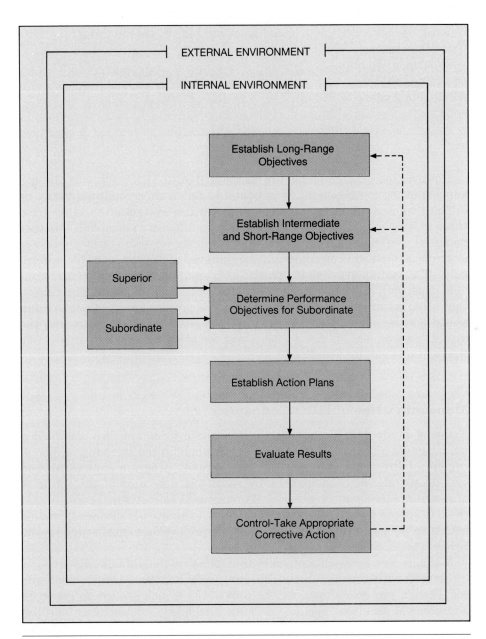

FIGURE 9-5 | The MBO Process

HRM In Action

"Charlie," said Bryan Atrip, president of Sharpco Industries, to Charlie Wallace, the human resource manager, "I've been reading and hearing a lot about management by objectives. Sounds like something that we need to get into. Work up a procedure to get it started at Sharpco. I'll inform the vice-presidents at next month's executive council meeting that this is the thing for us."

If you were Charlie, how would you respond?

However, certain problems are associated with MBO. Without the full support of top management, it is bound to fail. This commitment may be difficult to obtain because implementing such a system often takes from three to five years. In addition, goals may be difficult to establish. Another potential weakness is a tendency to concentrate on short-term plans. For example, short-term objectives may be achieved at the expense of long-term goals. The system also has the potential to create a seemingly insurmountable paper mill if it isn't closely monitored. Finally, some managers believe that MBO is excessively time consuming. The process forces people to think ahead and be capable of seeing how their goals and actions fit into the overall picture. This is not an easy task for some managers, but it is one that can prove quite beneficial.

Monsanto's Use of MBO Concepts

Utilizing many MBO concepts, the Monsanto Company has installed a management by results (MBR) program throughout the company. Although the initial direction came from top management, program implementation was decentralized. Management by results is now part of the fabric of Monsanto's management process. Its purpose is to motivate people, assist them in setting unit and personal directions, evaluate performance, provide equitable compensation, and ensure employee development throughout the firm.

Management by results ensures that plans of individuals are properly integrated with those of their reporting unit and that involvement and cooperation are encouraged as the unit seeks to achieve group goals. In addition, Monsanto's system permits flexibility by focusing not on subordinates' specific and immediate activities, but rather on their broader and longer-term progress. By emphasizing results for one year or longer, employees are encouraged to avoid short-term gains at the expense of longer-term results.

One mechanism for achieving these ends is the job results analysis/goals form—the basic document in the direction-setting phase of Monsanto's system. The corporate guidelines for preparing this document are broad and flexible. They emphasize that managers and units should exercise their best judgment when using the form. The first four sections constitute the job results analysis and center on the job's longer-term definition and direction. The last five sections, the goals document, deal with coming-year expectations and performance (see Figure 9-6).

The following briefly describes each section:

1. **General conditions.** In this section, employees state their assumptions about the environment in which they plan to operate for the coming year. For example, a salesperson would consider the growth rate of industries to be served and make projections about the health of the economy. If those assumptions later turn out to be off the mark, the supervisor and subordinate are encouraged to review the document for a possible change in overall direction or level of expectation.

FIGURE 9-6 | Monsanto's Job Results Analysis/Goals Form

2. **Principal thrust.** The most important thing to be done during the next year is stated in this section. It serves as a good check on the goals set later.
3. **Results sought.** Here, employees identify the areas of longer-term accomplishment that are important to the job and the unit.
4. **Major results.** An X is placed in this column to identify the most important results, which helps to establish priorities.
5. **Goals.** Here, the most important accomplishments for the coming year are identified. Goals are considered milestones toward longer-term results. Normally, a Monsanto employee has from three to five goals for the year.
6. **Joint accountability.** The purpose of this section is to identify and gain commitment from those individuals—other than the supervisor or subordinates—who give or receive help in achieving each goal. Employees are encouraged to discuss their goals with others from whom support is required.
7. **Range.** The range of performance for each goal is established and stated in this portion of the form. As an example, suppose that a goal was established "to achieve new customer sales of $1,000,000 (expected)." In this case, $500,000 might be entered in the basic column and perhaps $2,000,000 in the outstanding column.
8. **Weight.** The entries in this column establish goal priorities for the coming year. The weight established indicates priority—not the amount of time to be spent on each goal. To accomplish this ranking process, 100 points may be allocated among the goals, or the goals may be numerically ranked.
9. **Goals represent ____% of total performance.** The purpose of this entry is to show the relative importance of the stated goals to the entire job.

Monsanto's MBR program ensures continuous employee training and development. This approach integrates training and development into the overall Monsanto management process.

Job Enrichment

As defined in Chapter 4, job enrichment is the deliberate restructuring of a job to make it more challenging, meaningful, and interesting. It emphasizes accomplishing significant tasks so that the employee can feel a sense of achievement. Job enrichment takes an optimistic view of employee capabilities. Its use presumes that individuals have the ability to perform more difficult and responsible tasks than they are currently performing. Furthermore, it assumes that most people will respond favorably if given the opportunity to accomplish challenging tasks and will also be motivated to be more productive. When job enrichment is applied on a broad scale, it becomes an important OD method.

The use of job enrichment is illustrated by a department of the First National Bank of Chicago in which 110 employees worked on a "paperwork assembly line." [38] The primary responsibility of the department was to issue letters of credit. The work consisted of fragmented tasks that prevented employees from fully grasping the overall meaning of their work. The unit's productivity was less than that desired by management.

After a survey indicated an 80 percent dissatisfaction rate, the bank initiated a program whereby employees redesigned their work with the assistance of an OD specialist. Discrete tasks were consolidated into complete jobs that required broadly trained professionals performing in a more responsible, highly paid job classification. As a result, profitability, productivity, customer satisfaction, and staff morale increased sharply.

A less recent but more highly publicized experience with job enrichment involved Sweden's leading car manufacturer, A. B. Volvo. Pehr Gyllenhammar introduced a drastic alternative to the traditional assembly line soon after assuming the presidency in 1971. Work at the Kalmar plant was arranged so that groups of about twenty employees could assemble complete car components. This work arrangement permitted them to personally identify with their product. Gyllenhammar wanted his production employees to see a Volvo being driven down the street and say, "I made that car." [39]

When jobs are restructured to increase responsibility and challenge, employees continually develop while performing them. The nature of these jobs actually requires that employees keep their skills up to date.

Transactional Analysis[40]

It isn't clear how widespread the use of transactional analysis is as an OD method. However, it has been used for a number of years as a technique for teaching behavioral principles to individuals and small groups in training and development programs. **Transactional analysis (TA)** is a method that considers each individual's three ego states—the Parent, the Adult, and the Child—in helping people understand interpersonal relations. It provides a system for forming a mental image of the emotions and thought processes used by people interacting in either a social or business setting. It can be most useful in permitting an employee to understand where a customer or fellow employee "is coming from" and to respond appropriately.[41]

The attitudes, beliefs, and values learned from authority figures early in each person's life are stored in the Parent ego state. Everything seen or

---

[38] F. K. Plous, Jr., "Redesigning Work," *Personnel Administrator,* 32 (March 1987), p. 99.

[39] "Lessons from the Volvo Experience," *International Management,* 33 (February 1978), p. 42.

[40] The material on transactional analysis in this section is abridged and adapted from Thomas A. Harris, M.D., *"I'm O.K.—You're O.K."* Copyright © 1967, 1968, and 1969 by Thomas A. Harris, M.D. Reprinted by permission of Harper & Row Publishers, Inc.

[41] David J. Lill and John T. Rose, "Transactional Analysis and Personal Selling: A Primer for Banks," *Journal of Commercial Bank Lending,* 70 (February 1988), p. 57.

heard is recorded, as on tape, and these messages influence current behavior. The Parent ego state may reflect nurturing behavior that is sympathetic, protective, and instructive, or critical behavior that is punitive, prejudicial, and judgmental. The boss who comes on as a critical parent tends to find fault excessively and to punish, rather than to guide and develop subordinates.

The Adult ego state, on the other hand, is the objective part of each person. Through the Adult, data are analyzed, permitting each person to make independent, logical judgments. The Adult serves as an internal computer, and behavioral changes occur through this ego state.

The emotional side of individual behavior stems from the Child ego state. This state may take on different qualities—the Natural Child, the Little Professor, or the Adaptive Child. When the Natural Child dominates, the individual is expressive, self-centered, impulsive, and curious. The Little Professor centers around being intuitive, manipulative, and creative. The manner in which the Adaptive Child behaves is determined by the parental figures with whom the individual was associated.

The interaction of ego states can have a significant impact on behavior in organizations. If organizational members are able to recognize the ego state affecting a given communication, they may be able to respond appropriately. Various situations that a person may confront are presented in Figures 9-7 through 9-9. In Figure 9-7, Frank's three ego states are shown on the left and John's are shown on the right. The two have engaged in an adult-to-adult transaction. It is a complementary transaction because Frank's message gets the expected response. When this occurs, communication remains open, and there is no conflict or difficulty between the two.

A different situation is presented in Figure 9-8 on page 348. Here, Frank speaks from his Parent ego state to John's Child state. This also illustrates a complementary transaction. The lines of communication are open at the moment, but condescending behavior of this sort may have negative long-term consequences.

Crossed transactions occur when the message sent gets an unexpected response. Note in Figure 9-9 on page 349 that Frank delivers a message from his Parent ego state intended for John's Child state: "I don't ever want you to interrupt me again like you did in that meeting yesterday." Instead, John replies from his Parent state: "Who the hell are you to hog the whole conversation?" Frank expected an apologetic response but instead received one that was unexpected. Here, the transaction was crossed. These types of transactions are generally unproductive and represent a breakdown in communication. While individuals should use all their ego states, the Adult should remain in charge. As previously mentioned, it is through this state that behavioral changes occur.

At Bristol-Myers Products, a development program uses transactional analysis as the model. Since its inception, this program has reached more than 1,000 managers, supervisors, professionals, and sales representatives. As a Bristol-Myers HRM executive puts it, "The model is unique in that it teaches basic behavioral principles and does so in a down-to-earth, practi-

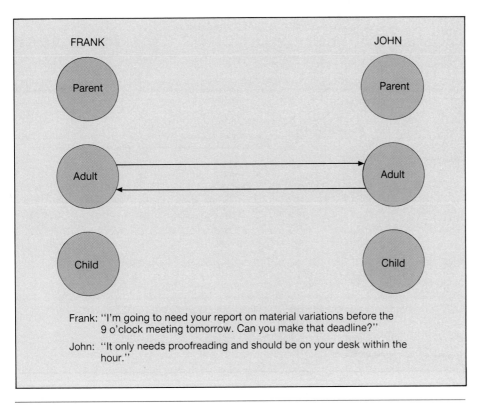

FRANK

Parent

Adult

Child

JOHN

Parent

Adult

Child

Frank: "I'm going to need your report on material variations before the 9 o'clock meeting tomorrow. Can you make that deadline?"

John: "It only needs proofreading and should be on your desk within the hour."

FIGURE 9-7 | A Complementary Transaction

Source: Used with the permission of Bristol-Myers Products, A Division of Bristol-Myers Company.

cal manner, using words that all people know and understand. It can be successfully employed at all levels in the organization." The executive added that the program was developed because "it was clear to me, as a human resource executive, that the poor handling of people (self and others) was the primary reason for the failure of managers." As individuals in a firm learn to analyze their own social interactions, better communication and greater organizational effectiveness can follow.

Quality of Work Life

A concept that has many implications for employee participation is called **quality of work life (QWL).** QWL is the degree to which members of a work organization are able to satisfy their most important personal needs through organizational experiences. QWL programs encompass many strategies, including job redesign, autonomous work groups, and worker participation in decision making. A basic assumption is that such programs

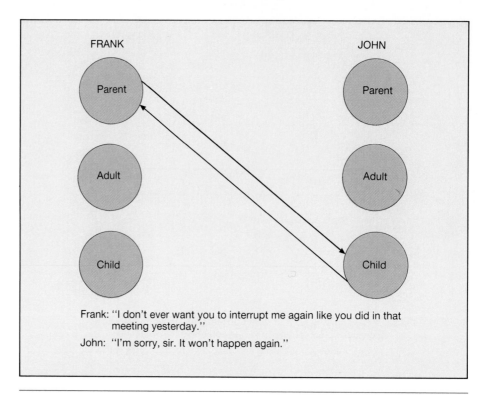

FRANK

JOHN

Frank: "I don't ever want you to interrupt me again like you did in that meeting yesterday."

John: "I'm sorry, sir. It won't happen again."

FIGURE 9-8 | A Complementary Transaction Involving Parent and Child Ego States

Source: Used with the permission of Bristol-Myers Products, A Division of Bristol-Myers Company.

will increase job satisfaction and worker motivation, which in turn will lead to increased productivity.[42]

Any firm that wants to develop a QWL program must first determine the goals it wants to achieve with the program. Therefore citing a list of appropriate activities (as is done with MBO programs) is difficult. The goals and actions undertaken are the joint responsibility of management, the union, and other members of the organization.

However, certain guidelines may be helpful in initiating QWL efforts. Generally, QWL improvement efforts call for the following:

- An understanding that they are not short-term, quick-fix programs that should be undertaken lightly.
- Organizations to forge new definitions of "how we work in this organization" when initiating QWL efforts.

---

[42] Barbara Mandell, "Does a Better Worklife Boost Productivity?" *Personnel,* 66 (October 1989), p. 49.

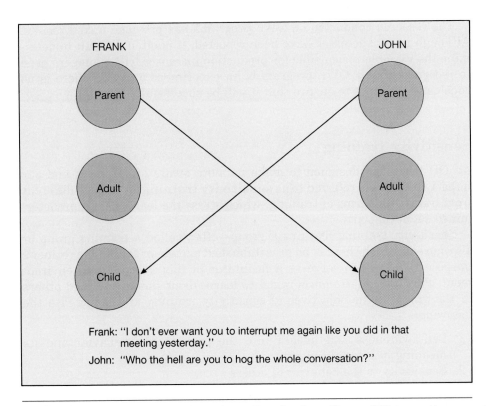

FIGURE 9-9 | An Unexpected Response Results in a Crossed Transaction

Source: Used with the permission of Bristol-Myers Products, A Division of
Bristol-Myers Company.

- The willing participation of people at all levels of the organization.
- A commitment from the organization's leaders that goes beyond the rhetoric of endorsement and support and that must be demonstrated daily.
- Organizations to communicate and integrate their strategic goals into the day-to-day business operations.
- Management and labor leaders to work with their constituencies to examine and resolve internal issues before moving on to cooperative problem solving in joint committees. (Management's demonstrated commitment in addressing its own issues and barriers can contribute substantially to supportive and responsible behaviors and actions on the part of others within the organization.)
- New approaches and processes in most organizations. (These processes are never static and require constant attentiveness and responsiveness to developments as they occur.[43])

---

[43] *Ibid.,* p. 27.

The research conducted on QWL programs has provided mixed results. Although many successes have been reported, it is often difficult to determine the variable responsible for production increases. HR managers need to recognize that a QWL program is an experiment and that there is no conclusive evidence to ensure that it will be successful.[44]

Sensitivity Training

An OD technique designed to make us more aware of ourselves and our impact on others is referred to as **sensitivity training.** It is quite different from traditional forms of training, which stress the learning of a predetermined set of concepts.[45]

Sensitivity training features a group—often called a training group or T-group—in which there is no preestablished agenda or focus. The trainer's purpose is merely to serve as a facilitator in this unstructured environment. Participants are encouraged to learn about themselves and others in the group. Some objectives of sensitivity training are to increase the following:

1. Self-awareness and insight into the participant's behavior and its meaning in a social context.
2. Sensitivity to the behavior of others.
3. Awareness and understanding of the types of processes that facilitate or inhibit group functioning and the interactions between different groups.
4. Diagnostic skills in social, interpersonal, and intergroup situations.
5. The participant's ability to intervene successfully in intergroup or intragroup situations so as to increase member satisfaction, effectiveness, and output.
6. The participant's ability to analyze continually his or her own interpersonal behavior in order to achieve more effective and satisfying interpersonal relationships.[46]

When sensitivity training begins, there is no agenda—and no leaders, no authority, and no power positions. Essentially, a vacuum exists until participants begin to talk. Through dialogue people begin to learn about themselves and others. Participants are encouraged to look at themselves as others see them. Then, if they want to change, they can attempt to do so.

Although the purpose of sensitivity training (to assist individuals to learn more about how they relate to other people) cannot be questioned, the technique has been roundly criticized. It is clear that sensitivity training

---

[44] *Ibid.,* p. 49.

[45] James L. Gibson and John M. Ivancevich, *Organizations: Behavior, Structure, Processes,* 4th ed. (Plano, Texas: Business Publications, 1982), pp. 580–581.

[46] John P. Campbell and Marvin D. Dunnette, "Effectiveness of T-Group Experiences in Managerial Training and Development," *Psychological Bulletin,* 70, no. 2, (August 1968), pp. 23–104. Copyright © 1968 by the American Psychological Association. Reprinted by permission.

often involves anxiety-provoking situations as stimulants for learning. In addition, some critics believe that it is one matter for participants to express true feelings in the psychological safety of the laboratory but quite another to face their coworkers back on the job.[47] Information learned in a sensitivity group may prove to be irrelevant or even damaging unless the participant returns to an organizational environment that supports the use of that knowledge.[48] Individuals may be encouraged to be more open and supportive in the T-group, but when they return to their jobs, they often have not really changed. In addition, participants often undergo severe emotional stress during training.

Sensitivity training flourished in the 1970s. Use of poorly trained, uncertified trainers may be the primary reason for the decline in popularity of this method.[49]

■ ORGANIZATIONAL DEVELOPMENT: AN EXAMPLE

Ronald C. Pilenzo, former president of the Society for Human Resource Management, tells of a major change he was involved in at International Multifoods Corporation. The company was confronted with the challenge of integrating women into its management ranks. The organization was very conservative and did not wish to create special opportunities (jobs) for women. It was seeking a way to (1) sensitize men holding managerial positions; (2) create an awareness in women employees of job opportunities and their individual responsibilities for self-determination and self-development; and (3) achieve affirmative action goals.

After conducting extensive research on the subject, discussing the challenge with consultants and women who were experts in the field, and reviewing existing programs, Pilenzo made the following proposal to top management:

1. Design a program to fit the "organizational personality" of the company and its unique needs.
2. Offer the program on a voluntary basis to *all* women, regardless of position and rank, and on a mandatory basis to men holding managerial positions.
3. Obtain full top-management support and participation.
4. Design and install a skills inventory system to identify available skills of both men and women employees nationwide to support the program.

The program was accepted by top management. Over a two-year period, more than 700 women employees and 250 executives attended sessions

---

[47] Irwin L. Goldstein, *Training in Organizations: Needs Assessment, Development, and Evaluation,* 2nd ed. (Monterey, Calif.: Brooks/Cole Publishing Company, 1986), p. 243.

[48] Frank E. Saal and Patrick A. Knight, *Industrial/Organizational Psychology: Science and Practice* (Pacific Grove, Calif.: Brooks/Cole Publishing Company, 1988), pp. 245–246.

[49] Raymond S. Ross and Jean Ricky Ross, *Small Groups in Organizational Settings* (Englewood Cliffs, N.J.: Prentice-Hall, 1989), p. 79.

designed for each group. The president of the company personally introduced the first four meetings to emphasize the company's commitment and goals. During the course of the program, fifteen to twenty high-potential women candidates were identified for top management positions. Another group of women began self-development programs. The financial cost of the program was significantly less than comparable programs in other companies, primarily because of the use of existing company resources and available talent.

■ USE OF CONSULTANTS

Organization development efforts rely heavily on the use of qualified consultants who work with teams from the firm's management and work groups. These teams come from throughout the organization, from top management to the shop floor.[50] The consultant—a facilitator—assists both types of groups in identifying goals and solving problems that interfere with goal achievement. The consultant is also responsible for helping guide implementation of planned change.

A consultant may come from within the organization or from the outside. The role of the consultant is to utilize his or her specialized knowledge in making proposals for intervention in the organization's activities. Consultants assist managers in bringing about change in areas such as communication, leadership styles, and motivational techniques.

Management frequently believes that an outside expert brings objectivity to a situation and obtains acceptance and trust from organizational members more easily. However, another popular approach is to utilize internal consultants (employees of the firm) as effective change agents. Proponents of this tactic believe that the internal consultant, who knows both the formal and informal nature of the organization, can often produce desired results at a lower cost.

In practice, most OD approaches focus on behaviorally based change. Structural and technological change methods are largely overlooked. This is perhaps due to the behavioral training of most OD change agents.[51]

■ ORGANIZATION DEVELOPMENT PROGRAM EVALUATION

When an OD effort has been implemented, the following question must be asked: "Did anything happen as a result of this experience?" All too often the answer is: "We don't know." Evaluation of an OD effort is more difficult than determining whether an employee has learned to operate a particular

---

[50] Fred E. Fiedler and Joseph E. Garcia, "Comparing Organization Development and Management Training," *Personnel Administrator,* 30 (March 1985), p. 35.

[51] Joseph E. Garcia and Carla Haggith, "OD Interventions that Work," *Personnel Administrator* 34 (June 1989), p. 91.

piece of equipment. Nevertheless, management should evaluate the effort. The company has probably invested a considerable amount of time and money in the program and deserves to know whether it has produced tangible benefits.

One means of measuring program effectiveness is to assess changes in meeting performance criteria.[52] Some of the factors to be measured might include (1) productivity, (2) absenteeism rate, (3) turnover rate, (4) accident rate, (5) costs, and (6) scrap. An improvement in these and other areas may mean that the OD yielded desired results. For instance, a lower turnover rate might mean that workers are more satisfied with their work and have chosen to remain with the firm. Lower costs per unit produced suggests that workers may be paying more attention to their work. Although such evaluative data are useful, they probably will not provide the entire answer.

An excellent means of determining the extent of change in employee attitudes is through the use of a survey questionnaire. This survey is administered to employees prior to OD efforts and after implementation of the change program. A measurable difference in total employee satisfaction may well suggest that the effort was effective.

Effectiveness should not be measured only when the program has been completed. Rather, questionnaires should be administered periodically over an extended period of time. Evaluation is a continuous process in which performance criteria are considered in order to measure the effect of the change effort. As early as the 1950s, OD was identified as a promising and effective approach to organizational change. This appraisal has been proven accurate by the successful utilization of OD by many organizations.[53]

---

[52] James L. Gibson and John M. Ivancevich, *Organizations: Behavior, Structure, Processes,* pp. 541–548.

[53] Fred E. Fiedler and Joseph E. Garcia, "Comparing Organization Development and Management Training," p. 36.

SUMMARY

Corporate culture is the system of shared values, beliefs, and habits within an organization that interacts with the formal structure to produce behavioral norms. The organization's reward system identifies the types of behavior and attitudes that are important for success.

Corporate culture evolves from the examples of top management, stemming largely from what they do, not what they say. Other factors also interact to shape the culture of a firm. Three of them—communication, motivation, and leadership—have a special impact on a firm's psychological environment. Organizational characteristics, administrative processes, organizational structure, and management style help shape corporate culture.

Most behavioralists advocate an open and participative culture. Some contend that such a culture is best for all situations. The opposite of the open and participative culture is a closed and autocratic one. This culture's greater rigidity results from strict adherence to a formal chain of command, a narrower span of control, and stricter individual accountability.

The prevailing managerial approach in many organizations is highly structured. Consequently, most attempts to alter organizational culture have been directed at creating a culture that is more open and participative. Open and participative cultures often improve employee morale and satisfaction.

Despite the benefits of a participative approach, greater employee participation in decision making involves certain prerequisites and limitations. The requirements for greater participation in decision making are (1) sufficient time, (2) adequate ability and interest on the part of the participants, and (3) restrictions generated by the present structure and system.

Organization development (OD) applies behavioral science knowledge to an organization-wide effort to improve effectiveness. Some common OD techniques include total quality management, survey feedback, team building, quality circles, management by objectives, job enrichment, transactional analysis, quality of work life, and sensitivity training. Some of these techniques may be combined to provide a strategic approach to organization development. Total quality management programs strive to instill in all employees the desire to make continuous efforts to improve the quality of their products and services. In survey feedback, information about the organization is collected and made available to employees so that they can diagnose problems and develop action plans to solve them. A conscious effort to develop effective work groups throughout the organization is known as team building. Quality circles are groups of employees who meet regularly with their supervisors to identify production problems and recommend actions for solutions. Management by objectives (MBO) is a philosophy of management that emphasizes joint setting of objectives by superior and subordinate and using these objectives as the primary basis for motivation, evaluation, and self-control. Job enrichment is the deliberate restructuring of a job to make it more challenging, meaningful, and interesting. Transactional analysis (TA) considers each individual's three ego states—the Parent, the Adult, and the Child—in helping people understand interpersonal relations. Quality of work life (QWL) is the extent to which employees satisfy significant personal needs through their organizational experiences. An OD technique designed to make us aware of ourselves and our impact on others is sensitivity training.

Organization development efforts rely heavily on the use of qualified consultants who work with groups of managers and workers from throughout the organization. The consultant is a facilitator who helps the groups identify goals and solve problems that interfere with goal achievement. The consultant may also be responsible for helping guide implementation of planned change.

One method of measuring program effectiveness is to assess changes in meeting performance criteria. Some of the factors measured might include

(1) productivity, (2) absenteeism rate, (3) turnover rate, (4) accident rate, (5) costs, and (6) scrap. An improvement in these and other areas may mean that the OD effort has led to improvements. An excellent way to determine the extent of change in employee attitudes is through the use of a survey questionnaire.

Questions for Review

1. Define *corporate culture*. What factors determine corporate culture?
2. Does a participative culture improve productivity? Defend your answer.
3. What are the values of an open and participative culture?
4. What are the limitations of participation?
5. Define each of the following terms:
   a. Organization development
   b. Survey feedback
   c. Team building
   d. Quality circles
   e. Job enrichment
   f. Quality of work life
   g. Transactional analysis
   h. Sensitivity training
6. How can organization development programs be evaluated?
7. Explain the use of consultants in organization development.

Terms for Review

Corporate culture
Communication
Motivation
Leadership
Organizational structure
Organization development (OD)
Total quality management (TQM)

Survey feedback
Team building
Quality circles
Management by objectives (MBO)
Transactional analysis (TA)
Quality of work life (QWL)
Sensitivity training

INCIDENT 1 ▪ Implementing MBO ▪

When Bruce McDaniel retired because of ill health in 1991, he appointed his 26-year-old son, Jim, president of the family firm. The company, McDaniel Corporation of Marietta, Georgia, marketed a line of hospital beds. The company manufactured the metal frames for the beds and purchased hydraulic items, springs, and certain other parts. The company also sold hospital furniture items and maintained a crew to repair the McDaniel beds. Employment at the firm totaled about 500.

With an MBA degree from Georgia State University and two years of experience with the company, Jim was eager to take over. He believed that his college training and work experience had prepared him well. One of the first things Jim wanted to do was to give decision-making authority to the managers. He remarked, "I felt this would let me pay attention to the big picture while the day-to-day problems were solved lower in the organization." He felt that one effective tool for helping him shift more authority downward in the organization would be an MBO program.

Bruce McDaniel had been president and owner of McDaniel Corporation for thirty years. During that time the firm had grown from a small hospital supply company with three employees to its present size. Bruce had been a hard worker, often putting in fifteen hours a day. Jim said that his dad was a "pleasant autocrat" because he insisted on making every important decision, but Bruce had such an affable personality that no one objected.

For a while, Jim tried to behave pretty much as his father had, giving managers firm decisions on matters they brought to him. But about a month after his father's retirement, Jim called a meeting to tell the managers that the firm was going to implement an MBO program. He made a brief presentation to them about how the system would work. He especially emphasized that they would have more responsibility in their areas and that he expected MBO principles to be applied down to the supervisory level.

Questions

1. Explain the process Jim should follow in implementing MBO. Is he on the right track?
2. Discuss any likely pitfalls.

INCIDENT 2   ▪ Close to the Vest ▪

For the past few years, sales at Glenco Manufacturing had been falling, reflecting an industry-wide decline. During this time, Glenco had actually been able to increase its share of the market slightly. Although forecasts indicated that demand for its products would improve in the future, Joe Goddard, the company president, believed that something needed to be done immediately to help the firm survive this temporary slump. As a first step he employed a consulting firm to determine whether reorganization might be helpful.

A team of five consultants arrived at the firm. They told Mr. Goddard that they first had to gain a thorough understanding of the current situation before they could make any recommendations. Mr. Goddard assured them that the company was open to them. They could ask any questions that they thought were necessary.

The grapevine was full of rumors virtually from the day the consulting group arrived. One employee was heard to say, "If they shut down the company, I don't know if I could take care of my family." Another worker said, "If they move me away from my friends, I'm going to quit."

When workers questioned their supervisors, they received no explanations. No one had told the supervisors what was going on, either. The climate began to change to one of fear. Rather than being concerned about their daily work, employees worried about what was going to happen to the company and their jobs. As a result, productivity dropped drastically.

A month after the consultants departed, an informational memorandum was circulated throughout the company. It stated that the consultants had recommended a slight modification in the top levels of the organization to achieve greater efficiency. No one would be terminated. Any reductions would be the result of normal attrition. By this time, however, some of the best workers had already found other jobs, and company operations were severely disrupted for several months.

Questions

1. Why did the employees tend to assume the worst about what was happening?
2. How could this difficulty have been avoided?

DEVELOPING HRM SKILLS

This exercise provides students with further insight into management by objectives (MBO). MBO is a philosophy of management that emphasizes the setting of agreed-on objectives by superior and subordinate managers and using these objectives as the primary basis for motivation, evaluation, and self-control. It facilitates achievement of results by directing efforts toward attainable goals. MBO is a management approach that encourages managers to anticipate and plan for the future. It deemphasizes guessing or making decisions based on hunches.

Patsy Olson is the controller for Multifoods International, and three supervisors of various specialties report directly to her. Today she must meet with her supervisors in order to put in place management's latest directive—management by objective (MBO). As Patsy prepares for her meeting, she thinks, "I am sure that not every supervisor is in total agreement as to the appropriateness of MBO. I've got to tell them exactly how to apply MBO, as much in line with their management styles as possible. I have been in various management positions for the past 20 years, and I have seen management policies and practices come and go. Now I must make sure that each of the supervisors involved understands how to apply the new system. I wonder how Nita, Robert, and Doug will react."

Nita Dickey has been in various management positions for the past fifteen years, and she has also seen management policies and practices come and go. She is ready to find out exactly how to implement management's latest miracle—MBO. Nita is sure that this is just another experiment in futility, but she will go along. After all, what is the harm of letting the people upstairs experiment as long as it doesn't stay in place very long?

Robert Zackery has been out of college for six years, and he is eager to see how MBO actually works in practice. He is anxious to get this experiment under way. This could be just the way to make some sorely needed changes.

Doug Warner has a degree in industrial psychology and is very excited about MBO. He believes that the primary emphasis of an organization should be on the employee. He is also eager to get this organizational change under way. For some time Doug has been bothered by the lack of emphasis on the human element by some of the less progressive supervisors.

Once these supervisors get together, the result will probably be less than total agreement. If you enjoy such situations, you should volunteer to participate. This exercise will require four students, who will play the roles of Patsy, Nita, Robert, and Doug. Those who are not lucky enough to participate should observe carefully. Additional instructions will be provided by your instructor.

REFERENCES

Block, Barbara. "Creating a Culture All Employees Can Accept." *Management Review,* 78 (July 1989), pp. 41–45.

Dumaine, Brian. "Creating a New Company Culture." *Fortune,* 121 (January 15, 1990), pp. 127–128, 130–131.

Elliott, Ronald D. "The Challenge of Managing Change." *Personnel Journal,* 69 (March 1990), pp. 40–49.

Garcia, Joseph E., and Carla Haggith. "OD Interventions That Work." *Personnel Administrator,* 34 (June 1989), pp. 90–92, 94.

Hellriegel, Don, John W. Slocum, and Richard W. Woodman. *Organizational Behavior,* 5th ed. (St. Paul, Minn.: West Publishing Company, 1989).

Honeycutt, Alan. "The Key to Effective Quality Circles." *Training and Development,* 43 (May 1989), pp. 81–84.

Killman, Ralph H. "A Completely Integrated Program for Creating and Maintaining Organizational Success." *Organizational Dynamics,* 18 (Summer 1989), pp. 5–19.

Lei, David, John W. Slocum, Jr., and Robert W. Slater. "Global Strategy and Reward Systems: The Key Roles of Management Development and Corporate Culture." *Organizational Dynamics,* 19 (Autumn 1990), pp. 35–39.

"Lessons from the Volvo Experience." *International Management,* 33 (February 1978), pp. 42–46.

Magnet, Myron. "The Decline and Fall of Business Ethics." *Fortune* (December 8, 1986), pp. 65ff.

Mandell, Barbara. "Does a Better Worklife Boost Productivity?" *Personnel,* 66 (October 1989), pp. 48–50, 52.

Meares, Larry B. "A Model for Changing Organizational Culture." *Personnel,* 63 (July 1986), pp. 38–42.

Melum, Mara Minerva. "Total Quality Management: Steps to Success." *Hospitals,* 64 (December 5, 1990), pp. 42–44.

Noel, Rita Thomas. "Manager's Toolbox: Five Tools for Better Management." *Supervisory Management,* 35 (September 1990), pp. 4–5.

O'Neill, Paul E. "Transforming Managers for Organizational Change." *Training and Development Journal,* 44 (July 1990), pp. 87–90.

Petrock, Frank. "Corporate Culture Enhances Profits." *HRMagazine,* 35 (November 1990), pp. 64–66.

Pines, Ellis. "From Top Secret to Top Priority: The Story of TQM." *Aviation Week & Space Technology,* 132 (May 21, 1990), pp. S5–S24.

Redecker, James R. "Code of Conduct as Corporate Culture." *HRMagazine,* 35 (July 1990), pp. 83–84, 86–87.

Reynolds, Peter C. "Imposing a Corporate Culture." *Psychology Today,* 21 (March 1987), pp. 32–38.

Richardson, Peter R. "The Challenge of Strategic Change." *Canadian Business Review,* 13 (August 1986), pp. 29–32.

Sheridan, John H. "A Philosophy for Commitment." *Industry Week,* 24 (February 4, 1991), pp. 11–13.

Spector, Bert A. "From Bogged Down to Fired Up: Inspiring Organizational Change." *Sloan Management Review,* 30 (Summer 1989), pp. 29–34.

Steingraber, Fred G. "Total Quality Management." *Vital Speeches of The Day,* 57 (April 15, 1991), pp. 415–416.

Ulrich, Dave, Wayne Brockbank, and Arthur Young. "HR Competencies in the 1990s." *Personnel Administrator,* 34 (November 1989), pp. 91–93.

Wellins, Richard, and Jill George. "The Key to Self-Directed Teams." *Training and Development Journal,* 45 (April 1991), pp. 26–31.

Wilkinson, Roderick. "Should You Run a Meeting—Or Forget It?" *Supervision,* 50 (October 1989), pp. 9–11.

Wilmot, Richard E., and Valorie McClelland. "How to Run a Reality Check." *Training,* 27 (May 1990), pp. 66, 68, 71–72.

CHAPTER 10

CAREER PLANNING AND DEVELOPMENT

CHAPTER OBJECTIVES

1. Define *career planning* and *career development* and describe factors affecting career planning.
2. Explain the importance of individual career planning and how a thorough self-assessment is crucial to career planning.
3. Explain the nature of career planning, discuss career paths, and identify methods of organizational career planning and development.
4. Describe career development and describe the avenues available for beginning a career in human resources.

Bob Allen and Thelma Gowen, both supervisors in the trust department of American Bank of New York, were in the employee lounge having a cup of coffee and discussing a point of mutual concern. Bob said, "I'm beginning to get frustrated. When I joined American four years ago, I really felt that I could make a career here. Now I'm not so sure. I spoke with the boss last week about where I might be in the next few years and all she kept saying was, 'There are all kinds of possibilities.' I need more than that. I'd like to know what specific opportunities might be available if I continue to do a good job. I'm not sure if I want to spend my career in the trust department. There may be better chances for advancement in other areas. This is a big bank."

Thelma replied, "I'm having the same trouble. She told me that 'the sky's the limit.' I'd also like to know where I might progress if I decide to stay with American. I wonder what 'the limit' means to her."

Obviously, American Bank has no career planning and development program. Bob is frustrated, and Thelma wants to know what career avenues are available to her. Lacking this knowledge, they may decide not to remain with the bank. Career planning and development are also important to the company because they ensure that people with the necessary skills and experience will be available when needed. According to an American Management Association study, promoting career development is the hallmark of a superior manager.[1]

In this chapter, we first discuss the concept of career planning and development. Next, we identify several factors that affect career planning and then discuss the nature of career planning. Then we address individual career planning and the

---

[1] Robert W. Goddard, "Building Careers for Your Employees," *Management World,* 14 (June 1985), p. 13.

reasons that organizations get involved in career planning. We then describe types of career planning that organizations conduct and follow that with a section on methods used in career planning and development. We devote the last part of the chapter to how a person might begin a career in human resources.

■ CAREER PLANNING AND DEVELOPMENT DEFINED

A **career** is a general course that a person chooses to pursue throughout his or her working life. **Career planning** is a process whereby an individual sets career goals and identifies the means to achieve them. The major focus of career planning should be on matching personal goals and opportunities that are realistically available. Career planning should not concentrate only on advancement opportunities. From a practical standpoint, there are not enough high-level positions to make upward mobility a reality for everyone. A tight market became even tighter during the 1980s and into the 1990s, as many organizations trimmed the number of management positions, especially middle-management positions. At some point, career planning needs to focus on achieving psychological successes that do not necessarily entail promotions.

Individual and organizational careers are not separate and distinct. A person whose individual career plan cannot be followed within the organization will probably leave the firm sooner or later. Thus organizations should assist employees in career planning so that both can satisfy their needs. A **career path** is a flexible line of progression through which an employee typically moves during employment with a company. Following an established career path, the employee can undertake career development with the firm's assistance. **Career development** is a formal approach taken by the organization to ensure that people with the proper qualifications and experience are available when needed.[2] Career planning and development benefit both the individual and the organization.

■ FACTORS AFFECTING CAREER PLANNING

Several factors affect a person's view of a career. The individual should recognize and consider the most important factors when planning a career. We describe two such factors, life stages and career anchors, in this section.

---

[2] Tom Jackson and Alan Vitberg, "Career Development, Part 3: Challenges for the Individual," *Personnel,* 64 (April 1987), p. 54.

Life Stages

People change constantly and thus view their careers differently at various stages of their lives. Some of these changes result from the aging process and others from opportunities for growth and status. The basic life stages are shown in Figure 10-1.

The first stage is that of establishing identity. A person typically reaches this stage between the ages of 10 and 20. The individual explores career alternatives and begins to move into the adult world. Stage two involves growing and getting established in a career. This stage typically lasts from ages 20 to 40. During this stage, a person chooses an occupation and establishes a career path. The third stage, self-maintenance and self-adjustment, generally lasts to age 50 and beyond. At this point, a person either accepts life as it is or makes adjustments. Career change and divorce occur during this phase because people seriously question the quality of their lives. The final stage is that of decline. Diminishing physical and mental capabilities may accelerate this stage. A person may have lower aspirations and less motivation during the decline stage, resulting in additional career adjustments.

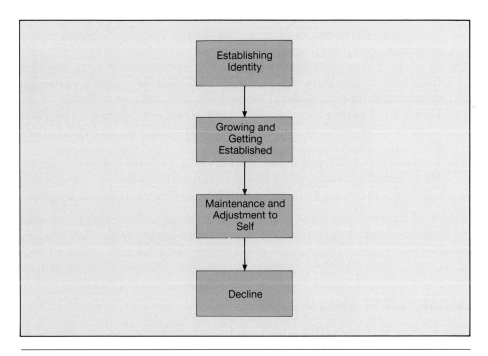

FIGURE 10-1 | Life Stages

Source: Adapted from James W. Walker, *Human Resource Planning.* (New York: McGraw-Hill Book Company, 1980.) Used with permission of the McGraw-Hill Book Company.

Even though most individuals have career development needs throughout their working lives, the majority of developmental activities are directed at new, younger workers. Since passage of the last amendment to the Age Discrimination in Employment Act, there has been no mandatory retirement age and therefore, the self-maintenance and self-adjustment stage is likely to be extended.[3] Consequently, future employees will probably need career development as much in later years as they do in the initial years of their working lives.

Career Anchors

All of us have different aspirations, backgrounds, and experiences. Our personalities are molded, to a certain extent, by the results of our interactions with our environments. Edgar Schein's research identified five different motives that account for the way people select and prepare for a career. He called them **career anchors.**[4]

1. *Managerial Competence.* The career goal of managers is to develop qualities of interpersonal, analytical, and emotional competence. People using this anchor want to manage people.
2. *Technical/Functional Competence.* The anchor for technicians is the continuous development of technical talent. These individuals do not seek managerial positions.
3. *Security.* The anchor for security-conscious individuals is to stabilize their career situations. They often see themselves tied to a particular organization or geographical location.
4. *Creativity.* Creative individuals are somewhat entrepreneurial in their attitude. They want to create or build something that is entirely their own.
5. *Autonomy and Independence.* The career anchor for independent people is a desire to be free from organizational constraints. They value autonomy and want to be their own boss and work at their own pace.

One of the implications of these career anchors is that companies must be flexible enough to provide alternative paths to satisfy people's varying needs.

■ CAREER PLANNING

The process by which individuals plan their life's work is referred to as career planning. Through career planning, a person evaluates his or her own abilities and interests, considers alternative career opportunities, establishes career goals, and plans practical development activities.

---

[3] James W. Walker, *Human Resource Planning* (New York: McGraw-Hill, 1980), pp. 331–332.
[4] Edgar Schein, "How 'Career Anchors' Hold Executives to Their Career Paths," *Personnel,* 52 (May–June 1975), pp. 11–24.

In addition to a self-assessment, an individual should also make a corporate opportunity assessment, asking questions such as the following:

1. What are the prospects for promotion or transfer from my present job?
2. What percentage of employees reach a certain target level within this organization?
3. What are the pay ranges for various job levels?
4. Where is the fastest growth and therefore the best promotion opportunity in the company?
5. If I have reached a dead end, what other paths are available so that I can move up in the organization?[5]

Career planning should begin with a person's placement in an entry-level job and initial orientation. Management will observe the employee's job performance and compare it with job standards. At this stage, management will note strengths and weaknesses, enabling them to assist the employee in making a tentative career decision. Naturally, this decision can be altered later as the process continues. This tentative career decision is based on a number of factors, including personal needs, abilities and aspirations, and the organization's needs. Management can then schedule human resource development programs that relate to the employee's specific needs. For instance, a person who wants a career in human resources may require some legal training.

Remember that career planning is an ongoing process. It takes into consideration the changes that occur in people and organizations. This type of flexibility is absolutely necessary in today's dynamic organizational environment. Not only do the firm's requirements change, but individuals may choose to revise their career expectations. An employee might believe, for instance, that he or she could be more productive in human resources than in marketing or vice versa. Rather than lose a valued employee, the firm may attempt to accommodate the employee.

Individual Career Planning

Career planning begins with self-understanding, which helps a person to see which career anchor may be predominant. Then, the person is in a position to establish realistic goals and determine what to do to achieve these goals. This action also lets the person know whether his or her goals are realistic.

Learning about oneself is referred to as **self-assessment.** Anything that could affect one's performance in a future job should be considered.[6] Realistic self-assessment may help a person avoid mistakes that could affect his or her entire career progression. Often an individual accepts a job without considering whether it matches his or her interests and abilities. This

---

[5] Marilyn A. Morgan, Douglas T. Hall, and Alison Martier, "Career Development Strategies in Industry: Where Are We and Where Should We Be?" *Personnel,* 56 (March/April 1979), p. 14.

[6] Paul Frichtl, "Keep Score," *Industrial Distribution,* 75 (August 1986), p. 37.

approach often results in failure. A thorough self-assessment will go a long way toward helping match an individual's specific qualities and goals with the right job or profession.

Some useful tools include a strength/weakness balance sheet and a likes and dislikes survey. However, any reasonable approach that assists self-understanding is helpful.

Strength/Weakness Balance Sheet. A self-evaluation procedure, developed originally by Benjamin Franklin, that assists people in becoming aware of their strengths and weaknesses is called a **strength/weakness balance sheet.** Employees who understand their strengths can use them to maximum advantage. By recognizing their weaknesses, they avoid having to utilize those qualities or skills. Furthermore, by recognizing weaknesses, they are in a better position to overcome them. This attitude is summed up by the statement "If you have a weakness, understand it and make it work for you as a strength; if you have a strength, do not abuse it to the point where it becomes a weakness." The first step in self-assessment is to recognize your strengths and weaknesses.

To use a strength/weakness balance sheet, the individual lists strengths and weaknesses as he or she perceives them. This is quite important because believing, for example, that a weakness exists can equate to a real weakness. Thus a person who believes that he or she will make a poor first impression when meeting someone will probably make a poor impression. The perception of a weakness often becomes a self-fulfilling prophesy.

The mechanics for preparing the balance sheet are quite simple. To begin, draw a line down the middle of a sheet of paper. Label the left side "strengths" and the right side "weaknesses." Record all perceived strengths and weaknesses. You may find it difficult to write about yourself. Remember, however, that no one else need see the results. The primary consideration is complete honesty.

Figure 10-2 shows an example of a strength/weakness balance sheet. Obviously Wayne (the person who wrote the sheet) did a lot of soul-searching in making these evaluations. Typically, a person's weaknesses will outnumber strengths in the first few iterations. However, as the individual repeats the process, some items which first appeared to be weaknesses may eventually be recognized as strengths and should then be moved from one column to the other. A person should devote sufficient time to the project to obtain a fairly clear understanding of his or her strengths and weaknesses. Typically, the process should take a minimum of one week. The balance sheet will not provide all the answers regarding a person's strengths and weaknesses, but many people have gained a better understanding of themselves by completing it.

Likes and Dislikes Survey. An individual should also consider likes and dislikes as part of a self-assessment. A **likes and dislikes survey** assists individuals in recognizing restrictions they place on themselves. For instance, some people aren't willing to live in certain parts of the country and such feelings should be noted as a constraint. Some positions require a

Strengths	Weaknesses
Work well with people.	Get very close to few people.
Like to be given a task and get it done in my own way.	Do not like constant supervision.
Good manager of people.	Don't make friends very easily with individuals classified as my superiors.
Hard worker.	
Lead by example.	Am extremely high-strung.
People respect me as being fair and impartial.	Often say things without realizing consequences.
Tremendous amount of energy.	Cannot stand to look busy when there is no work to be done.
Function well in an active environment.	Cannot stand to be inactive. Must be on the go constantly.
Relatively open-minded.	Cannot stand to sit at a desk all the time.
Feel comfortable in dealing with high-level businesspersons.	
Like to play politics. (This may be a weakness.)	Basically a rebel at heart but have portrayed myself as just the opposite. My conservatism has gotten me jobs that I emotionally do not want.
Get the job done when it is defined.	
Excellent at organizing other people's time. Can get the most out of people who are working for me.	Am sometimes nervous in an unfamiliar environment.
	Make very few true friends.
Have an outgoing personality—not shy.	Not a conformist but appear to be.
Take care of those who take care of me. (This could be a weakness.)	Interest level hits peaks and valleys.
	Many people look on me as being unstable. Perhaps I am. Believe not.
Have a great amount of empathy.	
Work extremely well through other people.	Divorced.
	Not a tremendous planner for short range. Long-range planning is better.
	Impatient—want to have things happen fast.
	Do not like details.
	Do not work well in an environment where I am the only party involved.

FIGURE 10-2 | Strength/Weakness Balance Sheet

Source: Wayne Sanders.

person to spend a considerable amount of time traveling. Thus an estimate of the amount of time a person is willing to travel would also be helpful. Recognition of such self-imposed restrictions may reduce future career problems.

Another limitation is the type of firm an individual will consider working for. The size of the firm might also be important. Some like a major organization whose products are well known. Others prefer a smaller organization, believing that the opportunities for advancement may be greater or that the environment is better suited to their tastes. All factors that could affect an individual's work performance should be listed in the likes and dislikes survey. An example of this type of survey is shown in Figure 10-3.

A self-assessment such as this one helps a person understand his or her basic motives, setting the stage for pursuing a management career or seeking further technical competence. A person with little desire for management responsibilities should probably not accept a promotion to supervisor or enter management training. People who know themselves can more easily make the decisions necessary for successful career planning. Many people get sidetracked because they choose careers based on haphazard plans or the wishes of others rather than on what they believe to be best for themselves.

Getting to know oneself is not a singular event. As individuals progress through life, priorities change. Individuals may think that they know themselves quite well at one stage of life and later begin to see themselves quite differently. Therefore self-assessment should be viewed as a continuous process. Career-minded individuals must heed the Red Queen's admonition to Alice: "It takes all the running you can do, to keep in the same place." [7]

Organizational Career Planning

The primary responsibility for career planning rests with the individual. [8] However, organizations should actively assist in the process. From the organization's viewpoint, career planning involves a conscious attempt to maximize a person's potential contributions. Firms that promote career planning programs for their employees reap many benefits. As Hendy Stewart MacKenzie Burns, an internationally known Shell Oil Company executive, said, "Good managers are people who aren't worried about their own careers, but rather the careers of those who work for them. My advice: Don't worry about yourself. Take care of those who work for you, and you'll float to greatness on their achievements." [9]

The process of establishing career paths within a firm is referred to as **organizational career planning.** Firms should undertake organizational

---

[7] Lewis Carroll, *Through the Looking Glass* (New York: Norton, 1971), p. 127.

[8] Lewis Newman, "Career Management Starts with Goals," *Personnel Journal,* 68 (April 1989), p. 91.

[9] Robert W. Goddard, "Building Careers for Your Employees," p. 12.

Likes	Dislikes
Like to travel.	Do not want to work for a large firm.
Would like to live in the East.	
Enjoy being my own boss.	Will not work in a large city.
Would like to live in a medium-size city.	Do not like to work behind a desk all day.
Enjoy watching football and baseball.	Do not like to wear suits all the time.
Enjoy playing racquetball.	

FIGURE 10-3 | Likes and Dislikes Survey

Source: Wayne Sanders.

career planning programs only when the programs contribute to achieving basic organizational goals. Therefore the rationale and approach to career planning programs vary among firms. In most organizations, career planning programs are expected to achieve one or more of the following objectives:

- *More effective development of available talent.* Individuals are more likely to be committed to development that is part of a specific career plan. This way, they can better understand the purpose of development.
- *Self-appraisal opportunities for employees considering new or nontraditional career paths.* Some excellent workers do not view the traditional upward mobility as an optimum career path. Other workers see themselves in dead-end jobs and seek relief. Rather than lose these workers, a firm can offer career planning to help them identify new and different career paths.
- *More efficient development of human resources within and among divisions and/or geographic locations.* If the traditional progression of workers has been upward within a division, career paths should be developed that cut across divisions and geographic locations.
- *A demonstration of a tangible commitment to EEO and affirmative action.* Adverse impact can occur at virtually any level in an organization. Firms that are totally committed to reducing adverse impact often cannot find qualified women and minorities to fill vacant positions. One means of overcoming this problem is an effective career planning and development program. Frequently, AAPs require companies to set up career development programs for women and minorities.
- *Satisfaction of employees' personal development needs.* Individuals who see their personal development needs being met tend to be more satisfied with their jobs and the organization.

HRM In Action

Fred, since you work in human resources, maybe you can explain why we hired Mary Moore," Sam Hakala asked of the human resource manager, Fred McCord. "What's the problem with Mary, Sam?" "Well, I went in to see Mary and asked her to develop a career plan for me. I wanted to know how long it will take me to advance up the corporate ladder. She obviously doesn't know much about career planning." "What did she do, Sam?" Fred asked. "Well, instead of outlining a career plan, she said that I would need to first gain some self-insight. I've been here five years, and now she says I don't have enough self-insight, can you believe that? She wants me to do her job for her. In my opinion, someone should clean house in that department."

How would you respond?

- *Improvement of performance through on-the-job training experiences provided by horizontal and vertical career moves.* The job itself is the most important influence on career development. Each job can provide different challenges and experiences.
- *Increased employee loyalty and motivation, leading to decreased turnover.* Individuals who believe that the firm is interested in their career planning will be more likely to remain with the organization.
- A *method of determining training and development needs.* If a person desires a certain career path and does not presently have the proper qualifications, this fact identifies a training and development need.[10]

All these objectives may be desirable. But successful career planning depends on a firm's ability to satisfy those that it considers most crucial to employee development and the achievement of organizational goals.

As Figure 10-4 shows, a career planning program may prompt some employees to develop more realistic expectations. This ultimately leads to enhanced performance, improved retention, and better utilization of talent. Although certain benefits are associated with career planning, risks are also involved. Difficulties occur when the career planning program raises employee expectations to unrealistic levels. When this occurs, organizational disruption, diminished performance, and higher turnover may result. Therefore a career planning program should be based on developing realistic expectations.[11]

---

[10] Milan Moravec, "A Cost-Effective Career Planning Program Requires a Strategy," *Personnel Administrator,* 27 (January 1982), p. 29.

[11] James W. Walker, *Human Resource Planning,* p. 3.

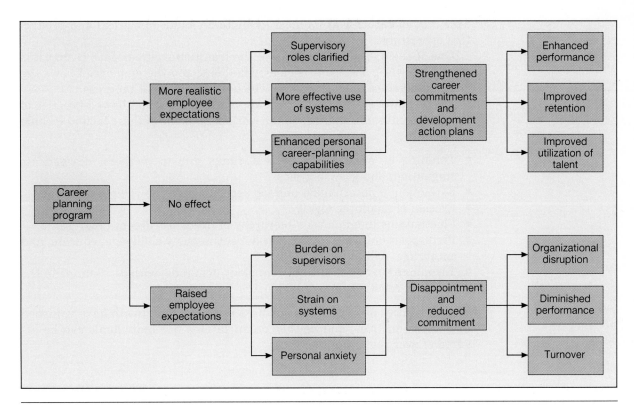

FIGURE 10-4 | The Effects of Career Planning

Source: James W. Walker, "Does Career Planning Rock the Boat?" *Human Resource Management,* 17 (Spring 1978), p. 3. Used with the permission of Human Resource Management, University of Michigan, Ann Arbor, Mich.

■ CAREER PATHS

Recall that a career path is a flexible line of progression through which an employee typically moves during employment with a company. Career paths usually have focused on upward mobility within a particular occupation. One of three types of career paths may be used: traditional, network, and dual.

Traditional Career Path

The **traditional career path** is one wherein an employee progresses vertically upward in the organization from one specific job to the next. The assumption is that each preceding job is essential preparation for the next higher level job. Therefore, an employee must move, step by step, from one job to the next to gain needed experience and preparation.

This type of career path is most likely to be found in clerical and production operations.

One of the biggest advantages of the traditional career path is that it is straightforward. The path is clearly laid out, and the employee knows the specific sequence of jobs through which he or she must progress.

Today, however, the traditional approach has become flawed because of business trends and changes in the workforce. Some of these factors include the following:

- Thinning of middle-management ranks due to mergers, downsizing, stagnation, and growth cycles.
- Extinction of paternalism and job security.
- Erosion of employee loyalty.
- Fluctuations in employees' hierarchy of needs as careers progress.
- Predisposition to assignments that continuously challenge, educate, and encourage skill expansion.
- Turbulence in business and technology demands, with oscillations in the skill mix requirements of employers.[12]

The certainties of yesterday's business methods and growth have vanished in many industries, and neither organizations nor individuals can be assured of ever regaining them.

Network Career Path

The **network career path** contains both a vertical sequence of jobs and a series of horizontal opportunities. The network career path recognizes the interchangeability of experience at certain levels and the need to broaden experience at one level before promotion to a higher level. This approach more realistically represents opportunities for employee development in an organization than does the traditional career path. The vertical and horizontal options lessen the probability of blockage. One disadvantage of this type of career path is that it is more difficult to explain to employees the specific route their careers may take for a given line of work.

Dual Career Path

The dual career path was originally developed to deal with the problem of technically trained employees who had no desire to move into management—the normal procedure for upward mobility in an organization. The **dual career path** recognizes that technical specialists can—and should be allowed to—contribute their expertise to a company without having to become managers. In organizations such as National Semiconductor, a

---

[12] Mike Hawkins and Milan Moravec, "Career Paths Discourage Innovation and Deflate Motivation," *Personnel Administrator,* 34 (October 1989), p. 112.

high-tech worldwide firm headquartered in Santa Clara, California, a dual career approach was set up to encourage and motivate individual contributors in engineering, sales, marketing, finance, human resources, and other areas.[13] Individuals in these fields can increase their specialized knowledge, make contributions to their firms, and be rewarded without entering management. Whether on the management or technical side of the path, compensation would be comparable at each level.

The dual career path is becoming increasingly popular. In our high-tech world, specialized knowledge is often as important as managerial skill. Rather than creating poor managers out of competent technical specialists, the dual career path permits an organization to retain both highly skilled managers and highly skilled technical people.[14]

Dow Corning has created what they describe as multiple ladders. As may be seen in Figure 10-5 on page 374, individuals can progress upward in research, technical service and development, and process engineering without being forced into management roles.

Career Path Information

Information regarding career options and opportunities must be available before individuals can begin to set realistic career objectives. One way to provide this information is to develop career path data for each job. This information can be developed from job descriptions, based on historical trends within the organization, or based on similarities to other jobs in the same job family. A small sample of job titles with related career guidance information is shown in Table 10-1 on page 375. Career path information is particularly useful because it does the following:

1. Shows each employee how his or her job relates to other jobs.
2. Presents career alternatives.
3. Describes educational and experience requirements for a career change.
4. Points out the orientations of other jobs.[15]

■ PLATEAUING

A problem that many individuals who aspire to move upward in an organization are now experiencing is plateauing. **Plateauing** occurs when an employee's job functions and work content remain the same because of a

---

[13] Milan Moravec and Beverly McKee, "Designing Dual Career Paths and Compensation," *Personnel,* 67 (August 1990), p. 5.

[14] Donald L. Caruth, Robert M. Noe III, and R. Wayne Mondy, *Staffing the Contemporary Organization* (New York: Praeger Publishers, 1990), pp. 253–254.

[15] *Ibid.,* p. 42.

Level	Managerial	Research	Technical Service and Development	Process Engineering
	Vice-President, R&D Director			
VIII	Manager	Senior Research Scientist	Senior Development Scientist	Senior Process Engineering Scientist
VII	Manager	Research Scientist	Development Scientist	Process Engineering Scientist
VI	Section Manager	Associate Research Scientist	Associate Development Scientist	Associate Process Engineering Scientist
V	Group Leader	Senior Research Specialist	Senior TS&D Specialist	Senior Engineering Specialist
IV		Research Specialist	TS&D Specialist	Senior Project Engineer
III		Project Chemist	TS&D Representative	Project Engineer
II		Associate Project Chemist	TS&D Engineer	Development Engineer
I		Chemist	Engineer	Engineer

FIGURE 10-5 | Multiple Ladders at Dow Corning

Source: Charles W. Lentz, "Dual Ladders Become Multiple Ladders at Dow Corning," *Research Technology Management,* 33 (May–June 1990), p. 28.

lack of promotional opportunities within the firm.[16] Plateauing has become more common recently because many organizations are reducing the number of management positions, developing a "lean, mean" management team. International competition has also slowed the growth of firms that might otherwise have needed more management positions. In addition, women and minorities are now competing for positions that once were not available to them.

Between 1950 and 1976, many companies offered extraordinary opportunities for advancement. However, the picture today is quite different, as a large number of people with similar educational backgrounds compete for fewer promotions. In our society, promotion has always been an important measure of success. Thus plateauing will present new challenges for those involved with career planning and development.

Several approaches have been suggested to deal with this problem.[17] One possibility is to move individuals laterally within the organization. Although status or pay may remain unchanged, the employee is given the opportunity to develop new skills. Firms that want to encourage lateral

---

[16] Geraldine Spruell, "Say So Long to Promotions," *Training and Development Journal,* 39 (May 1985), pp. 70–74.

[17] Beverly Kaye and Kathryn McKee, "New Compensation Strategies for New Career Patterns," *Personnel Administrator,* 31 (March 1986), pp. 61–68.

TABLE 10-1 | Sample Job Titles and Related Career Guidance Information

Conventional Investigative Job Family		Prerequisites			Career Path	
Job title	Division	Supervisory	Educational level	Years of experience	From	To
Senior Staff Accountant	Accounting	No	B.A. or B.S.	3–4	Staff Accountant Supervisor—Accounts Receivable Provider Auditor	Cost Analysis Coordinator Credit and Collection Coordinator Supervising Senior Staff Accountant
Cost Production Supervisor	Accounting	Yes	Some college	2–3	Supervisor—Cash Receipts Staff Accountant—Payroll	Supervisor—Government Reporting Assistant Manager—Payroll Accounts Payable Cost Production Coordinator
Cost Analyst	Controller	Yes	B.A. or B.S.	4–5	Senior Financial Analyst Cost Analyst Senior Staff Accountant	Manager—Cost Management and Investments Manager—Budget Administration Manager—Corporate Reporting and Business Analysis
Reports Analyst	Accounting	No	Some college	1–2	Payroll Processor Statistical Clerk IV Report Specialist	Management Information Coordinator Staff Accountant—Payroll

Source: Reprinted from Dennis J. Kravetz and Stephanie E. Derderian, "Developing a Career Guidance Program Through the Job Family Concept," from the October 1980 issue of *Personnel Administrator*, copyright © 1980. Reprinted with the permission from *HRMagazine* (formerly *Personnel Administrator*) published by the Society for Human Resource Management, Alexandria, Virginia.

movement may choose to pay a transfer bonus or utilize a skill-based pay system that rewards individuals for the type and number of skills they possess. Another approach, which we've already discussed, is job enrichment. This approach rewards (without promoting) an employee by increasing the challenge of the job, giving it more meaning and the employee a greater sense of accomplishment.

Exploratory career development is yet another way of dealing with plateauing. It gives an employee the opportunity to test ideas in another field without committing to an actual move. Demotions have long been associated with failure, but limited promotional opportunities in the future may make them more legitimate career options. If the stigma of demotion can be removed, more employees—especially older workers—might choose to make such a move. In certain instances this approach might open up a clogged promotional path and, at the same time, permit a senior employee to escape unwanted stress without being thought a failure.

■ CAREER DEVELOPMENT

Career development includes any and all activities that prepare a person for progression along a designated career path. Essentially everyone in the company could be involved.[18] Career development usually involves both formal and informal means. Career development programs may be conducted in-house or by outside sources, such as professional organizations or colleges and universities.

In-house programs are usually planned and implemented by a training and development unit within the firm's human resource department. Line managers are also frequently utilized to conduct program segments. Outside the company, organizations such as the Society for Human Resource Management and the American Management Association are active in conducting conferences, seminars, and other types of career development programs.

Certain principles should be observed with regard to career development. First, the job itself has the greatest influence on career development. When each day presents a different challenge, what is learned on the job may be far more important than formally planned development activities. Second, the type of developmental skills that will be needed is determined by specific job demands. The skills needed to become a first-line supervisor will likely differ from those needed to become a middle manager. Third, development will occur only when a person has not yet obtained the skills demanded by a particular job. If the purpose of a transfer is to further develop an employee—and the individual already possesses the necessary

---

[18] Zandby B. Leibowitz and Sherry H. Mosley, "Career Development Works Overtime at Corning, Inc.," *Personnel*, 67 (April 1990), p. 38.

skills for the new job—little or no learning will take place. Finally, the time required to develop the necessary skills can be reduced by identifying a rational sequence of job assignments for a person.

Responsibility for Career Development

Many key individuals must work together if an organization is to have an effective career development program. Management must first make a commitment to support the program through policy decisions and allocating resources to the program. Human resource professionals are then responsible for implementing it by providing the necessary information, tools, guidance, and program liaison with top management.

The worker's immediate supervisor is responsible for providing support, advice, and feedback. Through the supervisor, a worker can find out how supportive of career development the organization actually is. Finally, individual employees are ultimately responsible for developing their own careers.[19] "You can lead a horse to water but you can't make it drink" is an appropriate analogy for career development.

Unrealistic expectations on the part of participants are a major problem associated with career development programs. Employees often see the opportunity for promotion as the major outcome of their participation. If no positions are available, individuals often become disappointed and frustrated.

■ METHODS OF ORGANIZATION CAREER PLANNING AND DEVELOPMENT

Organizations can assist individuals in career planning and development in numerous ways. Some currently utilized methods, most of which are used in various combinations, are listed here.

- *Management by Objectives (MBO)*. MBO provides an excellent means of assisting in career planning and development. Recall that the superior and subordinate jointly agree on job objectives that can be accomplished during a certain period of time. The resources made available to achieve these objectives may well include development programs. In addition, failure to achieve objectives may assist in planning for future developmental needs.
- *Career Counseling*. Persons either inside or outside the organization may counsel employees in career planning and development. Human resource professionals are often called on for assistance, as are

---

[19] Loretta D. Foxman and Walter L. Polsky, "Aid in Employee Career Development," *Personnel Journal,* 69 (January 1990), p. 22.

psychologists and guidance counselors. Colleges and universities often provide such services.

- *Company Material.* Some firms provide material specifically developed to assist their workers in career planning and development. Such material is tailored to the firm's special needs.
- *Performance Appraisal System.* The firm's performance appraisal system can also be a valuable tool in career planning. Noting and discussing an employee's weaknesses can uncover development needs. If overcoming a particular weakness seems difficult or even impossible, an alternate career path may be the solution.
- *Workshops.* Some organizations conduct workshops lasting two or three days for the purpose of helping workers develop careers within the company. Employees define and match their specific career objectives with the needs of the company.

In addition to these methods, companies often use other techniques for developing high-potential employees, as shown in Figure 10-6.

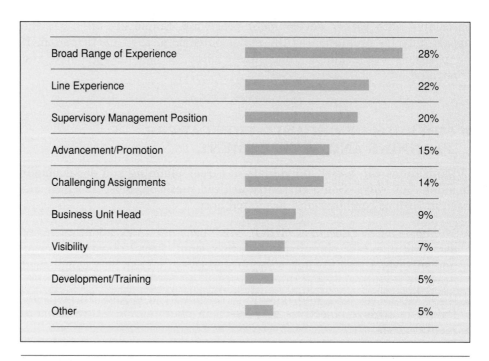

FIGURE 10-6 | Ways to Get Ahead

Note: Percentages total more than 100% because many respondents mentioned more than one opportunity.

Source: Michelle Neely Martinez, "The High Potential Woman," *HRMagazine,* 36 (June 1991), p. 50. Adapted from *HRMagazine,* © 1991, by permission of Catalyst, 250 Park Avenue South, New York, NY 10003.

Career Development Program: An Example

Realizing that highly skilled employees hold the key to corporate growth, Detroit Edison designed an Initial Professional Development Program (IPDP). The program helps build individual careers, and in so doing, ensures the development of employees to satisfy future human resource needs.

Detroit Edison's program is available to most entry-level professionals who possess a bachelor's degree and have less than three years of experience related to their major field of study. If selected for the program, participants assume the primary responsibility for their professional growth and are expected to take advantage of various opportunities provided.

The IPDP takes place over a three-year period and involves a number of specific developmental activities (see Figure 10-7 on page 380). The major activities include rotating work assignments and participation in company seminars. Work assignments involve the participants in stimulating and productive projects. Assistance is given by seasoned professionals who answer questions and provide guidance. Attendance at three formal seminars gives trainees the opportunity to expand skills and interact with employees from other functional areas of the company.

Additional development opportunities are provided in-house through courses covering such subjects as communication skills, power systems engineering, economic analysis, and problems and challenges faced by public utilities. Also, although not required, program participants are encouraged to take advantage of educational opportunities at local colleges and universities. Many employees have earned advanced degrees with the aid of Detroit Edison's educational assistance program.

■ PREPARATION FOR THE GLOBAL CAREER

It is estimated that 20 percent of the personnel sent abroad return prematurely; many others endure global assignments but are ineffective in their jobs and social lives, and often must endure broken marriages. The main reason this occurs is culture shock. Culture shock results in anxieties regarding customs and security that appear when an individual deals with a foreign culture. Culture shock is often accompanied by medical and personal problems, often continuing after the employee returns home. Returning employees nearly always experience less decision-making ability, autonomy, and pay, and fewer perks. It is also estimated that about one-quarter of all American expatriates do not ever regain a position in the firm upon returning from foreign assignments. Others leave the company immediately, take demotions, or relocate.[20]

---

[20] Mark E. Mendenhall and Gary Oddon, "The Overseas Assignment: A Practical Look," *Business Horizons,* 31 (Sept./Oct. 1988), pp. 78–79.

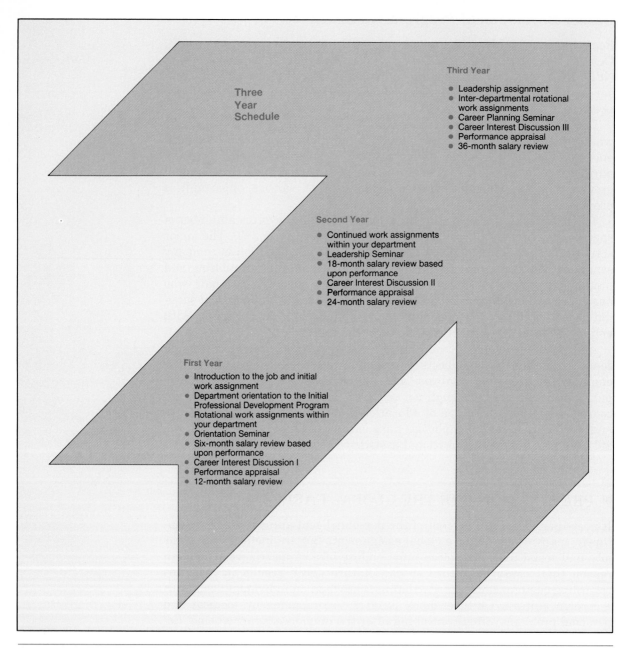

Three Year Schedule

Third Year
- Leadership assignment
- Inter-departmental rotational work assignments
- Career Planning Seminar
- Career Interest Discussion III
- Performance appraisal
- 36-month salary review

Second Year
- Continued work assignments within your department
- Leadership Seminar
- 18-month salary review based upon performance
- Career Interest Discussion II
- Performance appraisal
- 24-month salary review

First Year
- Introduction to the job and initial work assignment
- Department orientation to the Initial Professional Development Program
- Rotational work assignments within your department
- Orientation Seminar
- Six-month salary review based upon performance
- Career Interest Discussion I
- Performance appraisal
- 12-month salary review

FIGURE 10-7 | Detroit Edison's Initial Professional Development Program

Source: Used with the permission of Detroit Edison.

Many of these consequences result because of the failure of the organization to properly prepare the person with appropriate cross-cultural adaptation skills. Research indicates that success in overseas work assignments depends on the possession of personal skills, people skills, and perceptual skills. Personal skills are those techniques and attributes that facilitate the expatriate's mental and emotional well-being. They include means of finding solitude such as meditation, prayer, and physical exercise routines that tend to decrease the employee's stress level. One's abilities to manage time, delegate, and manage responsibilities are also essential personal skills.[21]

People skills are necessary to effectively interact with others, particularly with foreigners. Executives who desire or need to communicate with others should be willing to try to speak the foreign language (even when not necessary) and not worry about making linguistic mistakes. Such individuals are much more likely to be successful than those who are introverted, self-conscious, or otherwise uncomfortable when interacting with foreigners.[22]

Perceptual skills deal with the cognitive processes that help employees understand why foreigners behave as they do. The willingness to make tentative conclusions from the first observation of different actions or attitudes is an important cognitive dimension. Managers should be taught to size things up quickly and to make equally quick decisions. Perceptual skills also relate to one's consciousness of social cues and behaviors, one's attentiveness to them, and one's ability to imitate what is perceived. Preparing adequately for overseas assignments affords individuals the best opportunity to succeed, and may even help them excel to the point of using an overseas assignment as a springboard to career growth within the firm.[23]

■ BEGINNING A CAREER IN HUMAN RESOURCES

Individuals desiring a career in human resources may enter the field in one of two basic ways: They may go to work in another field and later transfer to human resources; or they may obtain an entry-level position in human resources. In order to assist in solving this dilemma, we asked human resource practitioners in various firms the following questions:

1. Which entry-level position in your firm would be most helpful if a person desires to progress into human resources?
2. What types of education or experience are most desirable for these entry-level positions?
3. Which human resource entry-level position would best assist a person's career progression in your firm?

As you can see in Table 10-2 on pages 382–383, the responses to these questions weren't consistent. Some firms clearly stress work in other

---

[21] *Ibid.*

[22] *Ibid.*

[23] *Ibid.*, p. 80.

TABLE 10-2 | Careers in Human Resource Management

Company	Entry-Level Position	Education/Experience
A. B. Dick Company	*Assistant Hourly Employment Manager Shop Foreman Assistant Salary Administrator	Bachelor's degree for all positions
Bristol-Myers Products	Human Resource Assistant	Bachelor's degree with two or three years' experience in general human resource work
Conoco, Inc.	*Human Resource Trainee Any position with Conoco	Bachelor's or master's degree in human resource administration, industrial relations, organizational development, business, or engineering
Denny's, Inc.	*Interviewer	Bachelor's degree in business or two years in human resource interviewing
	Wage and Salary Analyst	Bachelor's degree and one year of experience in human resources, preferably with compensation experience
	Human Resource Administrator	Bachelor's degree and/or two years' experience in human resources
GAF Corporation	*Production Supervisor Industrial Engineer Wage and Salary Analyst Safety Specialist	B.S.I.E., B.S.M.E., B.B.A. B.A. with relevant coursework B.S. with relevant coursework
General Cable Technologies	Assistant Plant Industrial Relations Manager Compensation Analyst	B.S. in industrial relations B.S. in industrial relations
Gerber Products Company	*Supervisor Trainee *Administrative Trainee	Four years of college Four years of college
Grumman Corporation	*Salary Analyst Employment Interviewer Career Development Analyst	Bachelor's degree in any of a variety of concentrations including psychology, business, and data processing
Hartmarx	Human Resource Assistant Compensation Assistant Employee Relations Assistant Human Resource Director (small plant or store)	Bachelor's or master's degree in business, human resources, or employee relations

*Indicates best entry-level position.

Company	Entry-Level Position	Education/Experience
International Paper Company	*Supervisor—Employee Relations Administrator—Industrial Relations Entry-level specialist assigned to the Corporate Human Resources Department	B.S. or B.A. in human resource or industrial management B.S. or B.A. in industrial labor relations, or B.S. in industrial management
Manville Corporation	*Employee Relations Supervisor *Plant Supervisor *Benefits Clerk	Bachelor's degree and some plant experience desirable
Motorola, Inc.	*Employment Interviewer	B.S. or B.A.; no experience
Nabisco Brands, Inc.	*Human Resource Assistant (Field)	Bachelor's degree in such fields as business or psychology
Rockwell International Corporation	Supervisory Trainee (Field) Industrial Relations Trainee	M.B.A. in human resources or industrial relations
Shell Oil Company	Employee Relations Analyst	Bachelor's or master's degree in human resources or industrial relations preferred
Squibb Corporation	Human Resource Assistant (nonexempt recruiting)	Two or three years' experience in human resource related activities preferred
Stokely-Van Camp, Inc.	Employee Relations— Management Trainee	Master's degree (preferably in human resources)
Teledyne, Inc.	*Wage and Salary Representative Labor Relations Representative	B.A. or human resource or financial administrative experience B.A. or general plant or human resource administrative experience
Trans World Airlines	Reservation Sales Agent	High school diploma, customer contact, and sales experience
USX	Labor Relations Trainee Employee Relations Trainee Line Operations Management Trainee	Law degree Master's degree, certification, experience Technical degree plus leadership
Walt Disney Productions	Human Resource Interviewer Human Resource Assistant Wage and Salary Analyst	People skills; B.A. and/or equivalent People skills; B.A. and/or equivalent Salaried experience and statistical orientation

functional areas before an employee moves into human resources, whereas others believe in direct entry into the human resource area.

Entry-Level Positions in Other Fields

Executives in numerous firms believe that an employee should gain experience in another field before moving into human resources. They believe that potential human resource professionals need varied exposure in the company to be effective in human resource positions. That is, they feel that such exposure can increase the person's credibility in dealing with other managers. Trans World Airlines, for one, selects human resource specialists from among their experienced reservation sales agents.

Entry-Level Positions in Human Resources

Not all firms require broad-based experience for those entering human resources. In fact, the number of individuals entering the human resource field directly appears to be increasing. This trend may be the result, in part, of specialized knowledge currently expected of human resource professionals. Firms that need people who can be productive very quickly in human resources do not feel that basic training time is available.

Several firms believe that the compensation specialty provides excellent entry-level positions. For example, the Grumman Corporation identifies salary administration as the best entry-level position "because it affects almost every aspect of human resource work and company operations." Management of Teledyne, Inc., believes that "starting in wage and salary provides an individual with exposure to relationships of job classifications throughout the company," and that this background is helpful to the human resource practitioner.

The nature of the firm's business may also affect the best human resource entry-level position. Labor-intensive organizations—those that have high labor costs relative to total operating costs—appear to emphasize staffing and recruitment positions in which interviewing skills are important. For instance, Denny's, Inc., lists the "interviewer" as being the best human resource entry-level position. Walt Disney Productions also identifies the "human resource interviewer" position as one of the best.

Entry-Level Positions: An Overview

Practitioners do not agree as to the most appropriate entry-level position for individuals aspiring to a job in human resources. A position considered best by one firm may not be viewed the same way by another. The nature of the firm's business or top management's human resource philosophy may account for these differences. Some firms stress the need for operating experience before entering human resources. Others believe that direct entry into human resources provides a more suitable beginning. People with ability who truly desire a position in human resources will likely be given the opportunity. It is no longer sufficient or desirable for organizations to employ human resource people who desire a career in human resources simply because they "like people" and enjoy "helping others." In fact, people who see this as their primary role are usually unsuccessful as professional human resource managers.

SUMMARY

A career is a general course a person chooses to pursue throughout his or her working life. Career planning is a process whereby the individual sets career objectives and identifies the means to achieve them. Career paths are flexible lines of progression though which people typically move during their employment with a company. Career development is an organization's formal approach to ensuring that people with the proper qualifications and experience are available when needed.

People change constantly and thus view their careers differently at various stages of their lives. The first stage is that of establishing identity, typically between the ages of 10 and 20. During this stage, a person explores career alternatives and begins to move into the adult world. Stage two involves growing and getting established in a career, which typically lasts from ages 20 to 40. During this stage a person chooses an occupation and establishes a career path. The third stage, self-maintenance and self-adjustment, generally lasts to age 50 and beyond. A person either accepts life as it is or makes adjustments. The final stage is that of decline. Diminishing physical and mental capabilities may bring on this stage. A person may come to terms with lowered aspirations and motivations, resulting in career changes.

Edgar Schein's research identified five different motives that account for the way people select and prepare for a career, which he called career anchors: managerial competence, technical/functional competence, security, creativity, and autonomy and independence. One of the implications of these career anchors is that companies must be flexible enough to provide alternative paths to satisfy people's varying needs.

Learning about oneself is referred to as self-assessment. Two useful tools in this endeavor include a strength/weakness balance sheet and a likes and dislikes survey.

The process by which individuals plan their life's work is referred to as career planning. It involves evaluating abilities and interests, considering alternative career opportunities, establishing career goals, and planning practical development activities. Career planning is a continuous process, which begins with a person's employment and initial orientation. Job performance is observed and compared with job standards. Strengths and weaknesses will be noted, enabling management to assist the employee in making a tentative career decision. This tentative career decision is based on a number of factors, including personal needs, abilities, and aspirations, as well as the needs of the organization. Management can then schedule training and development programs that relate to the employee's specific needs.

Depending on the organization and the nature of the jobs involved, one of three types of career paths may be used—traditional, network, or dual. In the traditional career path, an employee progresses vertically upward in the organization from one specific job to the next. The network career path contains both a vertical sequence of jobs and a series of horizontal opportunities. The dual career path recognizes that technical specialists can and should be allowed to continue to contribute without having to become managers. Plateauing is a career condition that occurs when job functions and work content remain the same because of a lack of promotional opportunities within the firm.

Organizations can assist individuals in numerous ways with their career planning and development. Some currently used methods, most of which are used in various combinations, are management by objectives (MBO), career counseling, company materials, performance appraisal systems, and workshops.

For individuals desiring a career in human resources, there are two basic ways of entering the field: from another field or directly into an entry-level position in human resources. Practitioners don't agree as to the best way to obtain an entry-level human resource position. However, people with ability who truly desire to obtain a position in human resources will likely be given the opportunity.

Questions for Review

1. Define the following terms:
   a. Career
   b. Career planning
   c. Career path
   d. Career development
2. Identify and discuss the basic life stages that people pass through.
3. List and briefly define the five types of career anchors.
4. How should a strength/weakness balance sheet and a likes and dislikes survey be prepared?
5. What kind of questions should a person involved in career planning attempt to answer?
6. Describe the stages in the organizational career planning process.
7. Why is it important for firms to engage in organizational career planning?
8. What are three types of career paths? Briefly describe each.
9. Define *plateauing*. How does plateauing affect human resource management?
10. Identify and describe some of the methods of organizational career planning.
11. What are the two basic means for entering the field of human resources? Why might a firm favor one means over the other?

Terms for Review

Career
Career planning
Career path
Career development
Career anchors
Self-assessment
Strength/weakness balance sheet

Likes and dislikes survey
Organizational career planning
Traditional career path
Network career path
Dual career path
Plateauing

INCIDENT 1   ■   In the Dark   ■

"Could you come to my office for a minute, Bob?" asked Terry Geech, the plant manager. "Sure, be right there," said Bob Glemson. Bob was the plant's quality control director. He had been with the company for four years. After completing his degree in mechanical engineering, he worked as a production supervisor and then as maintenance supervisor, prior to moving to his present job. Bob thought he knew what the call was about.

"Your letter of resignation catches me by surprise," began Terry. "I know that Wilson Products will be getting a good person, but we sure need you here, too." "I thought about it a lot," said Bob, "but there just doesn't seem to be a future for me here." "Why do you say that?" asked Terry. "Well," replied Bob, "the next position above mine is yours. With you being only 39, I don't think it's likely that you'll be leaving soon." "The fact is that I am leaving soon," said Terry. "That's why it's even more of a shock to learn that you're resigning. I think I'll be moving to the corporate office in June of next year. Besides, the company has several plants that are larger than this one, and we need good people in those plants from time to time, both in quality control and in general management." "Well, I heard about an opening in the Cincinnati plant last year," said Bob, "but by the time I checked, the job had already been filled. We never know about opportunities in the other plants until we read about the incumbent in the company paper."

"All this is beside the point now. What would it take to get you to change your mind?" asked Terry. "I don't think I will change my mind now," replied Bob, "because I've given my word that I am going to join them."

Questions

1. Evaluate the career planning and development program at this company.
2. What actions might have prevented Bob's resignation?

INCIDENT 2 ▪ Decisions, Decisions ▪

A nervous Jerry Fox was ushered into the Levitt Corporation president's office by the secretary. In the office he encountered Allen Anderson, the human resource manager, and Mr. Gorman, the vice-president. Jerry was flattered when Mr. Gorman stood to shake his hand.

"I'll make this short and sweet," Mr. Gorman said. "You probably have heard that Allen plans to retire at the end of next year. In preparing for the staff changes, we would like to move you in as his assistant to get some cross-training experience." Jerry responded, "Why me, Mr. Gorman? I'm a purchasing coordinator; I've never even worked in the human resource area."

"Well," replied Mr. Gorman, "we've been watching you carefully. I have personally reviewed your qualifications. From the company's standpoint, we know you can do the job. We need people who have been out in the company and can bring fresh perspectives to the human resource area." Mr. Gorman instructed Jerry to discuss the idea with Allen. Then he said he had to leave for another meeting. As he shook Jerry's hand, he said, "We would like to coordinate your transition from the purchasing department to make it as smooth as possible for everyone, and I know you're involved in some priority projects over there. Allen will get back with me on a time frame after you and he talk."

Jerry was 32 and he had been with Levitt for seven years. His business administration degree, from Arizona State, had included a heavy concentration in behavioral science courses, and he thought that probably was a factor in his selection. But he had worked only in purchasing. After three successful years as a buyer, he had been promoted to purchasing coordinator, with responsibility for supervising eight buyers and a small clerical staff.

He knew that he was respected throughout the company. This was especially true in the production department, which had a great deal of interaction with purchasing. The production manager made no secret of his high regard for Jerry. Jerry also had taken time to get to know members of the finance and research department. His purpose in pursuing all of these relationships, though, was to help him do his purchasing job better. He had no idea at all that he would be considered for a job in the human resource department.

Questions

1. How should Jerry respond to the new assignment? Discuss.
2. What are the main qualifications for a senior human resource manager? Discuss Jerry's apparent qualifications for such a job.

DEVELOPING HRM SKILLS

Career planning and development is extremely important to many individuals. Workers want to know how they fit into the future of the organization. Employees who believe that they have a future with the company are often more productive than those who don't. This exercise is designed to assist in understanding what it takes for a certain human resource professional to climb the organizational ladder. This climb is partially dependent on the individual's self-perceptions and perceptions of past experiences with the company. This exercise provides one method of individual career planning for the human resource manager described in the scenario below.

The individual being evaluated is 35 years old and is at a career crossroads. Upon self-reflection and appraisal at a birthday party, the person realizes that while only moderate success in ten years with the organization has been achieved, few others in the organization of comparable age and experience have any more "book or commonsense intelligence." In fact, the company is inundated with middle- and upper-level managers who are much older and often less intelligent, and who seem to spend an inordinate amount of time at the country club.

Assume that you are this person and have set your sights on an important human resource middle-management position in the next five to seven years, and a top management position with your organization in the next ten to fifteen years. You have figured out that there are twenty factors that determine upward movement in your organization. You are now trying to decide which are most important for survival and success, and which are least important. This decision will determine whether you take the career crossroad to organizational survival and success, or the crossroad to career failure and stagnation.

Each student will be given a list of twenty factors. You will rank the importance of each factor for your survival and success in the organization. Write the number "1" beside the **most important factor,** the number "2" beside the **second most important factor,** and so on through the number "20," the **least important factor.**

Everyone in the class can participate in this exercise. Each student will complete Exhibit 1, "Business Survival and Success Factors," as he or she believes the individual described in the scenario would. Your instructor will provide the participants with additional information necessary to complete the exercise.

REFERENCES

Archer, Mary Ann and Barbara Lea. "Canada Housing and Mortgage Surmounts Plateauing." *Personnel Journal,* 69 (April 1990), pp. 141–142.

Bratkovich, Jerrold R. "Developing New Career Management Strategies." *Personnel Journal,* 69 (September 1990), pp. 98–108.

"Career Tips for the Class of '94." *Fortune,* 122 (September 24, 1990), pp. 8–9.

Cohn, Mike. "Showing Commitment." *Nation's Business,* 78 (March 1990), p. 75.

Cooper, James C., and Kathleen Madigan. "If You're Not Nervous Yet, Take a Good Look at the Job Markets." *Business Week* (July 23, 1990), pp. 21–22.

Cooper, James C., and Kathleen Madigan. "The Job Numbers Paint a Picture—And It Isn't Pretty." *Business Week* (April 23, 1990), pp. 25–26.

Deutschman, Alan. "Pioneers of the New Balance." *Fortune,* 123 (May 20, 1991), pp. 60–68.

Dunn, Don. "Sitting Down with the Boss to Find Out Where You Stand." *Business Week,* (March 12, 1990), p. 134.

Eubanks, Paula. "Don't Rest When You Come to a Career Plateau." *Hospitals,* 64 (December 20, 1990), p. 56.

Fergus, Mike. "Employees on the Move." *HRMagazine,* 36 (May 1990), pp. 44–46.

Fierman, Jaclyn. "Why Women Still Don't Hit the Top." *Fortune,* 122 (July 30, 1990), pp. 40–62.

Filipowski, Diane. "Just the Fax, Ma'am." *Personnel Journal,* 70 (April 1991), p. 26.

Fitz-enz, Jac. "Getting—and Keeping—Good Employees." *Personnel,* 67 (August 1990), pp. 25–28.

Foxman, Loretta D., and Walter L. Polsky. "Aid in Employee Career Development." *Personnel Journal,* 69 (January 1990), pp. 22–24.

Hawkins, Mike, and Milan Moravec. "Career Paths Discourage Innovation and Deflate Motivation." *Personnel Administrator,* 34 (October 1989), pp. 112+.

Hoerr, John. "Sharpening Minds for a Competitive Edge." *Business Week* (December 17, 1990), pp. 72–78.

Kaye, Kenneth, and Roderick W. Correll. "Facing Up to Taking Action." *Nation's Business,* 78 (May 1990), p. 39.

Keenan, William, Jr. "The Nagging Problem of the Plateaued Salesperson." *Sales & Marketing Management,* 141 (March 1989), pp. 36–41.

Kirkpatrick, David. "Is Your Career on Track?" *Fortune,* 122 (July 2, 1990), pp. 38–48.

Koretz, Gene. "Women Still Earn Less, But They've Come a Long Way." *Business Week* (December 24, 1990), p. 14.

Leibowitz, Zandy B., Barbara H. Feldman, and Sherry H. Mosley. "Career Development Works Overtime at Corning, Inc." *Personnel,* 67 (April 1990), pp. 38–46.

Lentz, Charles W. "Dual Ladders Become Multiple Ladders at Dow Corning." *Research Technology Management,* 33 (May–June 1990), pp. 28–34.

McGregor, Elizabeth. "Emerging Careers." *Occupational Outlook Quarterly,* 34 (Fall 1990), pp. 22–23.

Mackay, Harvey. "A Career Roadmap: Getting Started." *Modern Office Technology,* 35 (June 1990), pp. 12–14.

Mackay, Harvey. "A Career Roadmap: Running the Show." *Modern Office Technology,* 35 (July 1990), p. 12.

Martinez, Michelle Neely. "Making Room for Work/Family Positions." *HRMagazine,* 35 (August 1990), pp. 45–47.

Morris, Michelle. "15 Fast-Track Careers." *Money,* 19 (June 1990), pp. 108–126.

Newman, Lewis. "Career Management: Start with Goals." *Personnel Journal,* 68 (April 1989), pp. 91–92.

Reynolds, Calvin, and Rita Bennett. "The Career Couple Challenge." *Personnel Journal,* 70 (March 1991), pp. 46–48.

Rich, Joseph R., and Beth C. Florin-Thuma. "Rewarding Employees in an Environment of Fewer Promotions." *Pension World,* 26 (November 1990), pp. 16–17.

Wolff, Michael F. "Building Careers at Procter & Gamble." *Research Technology Management,* 33 (September–October 1990), pp. 9–11.

CHAPTER 11 PERFORMANCE APPRAISAL

CHAPTER OBJECTIVES

1. Define *performance appraisal,* identify its basic objectives, and describe the performance appraisal process.
2. Identify who is usually responsible for performance appraisal, typical appraisal periods, and various methods used.
3. List the problems that have been associated with performance appraisal, and describe the importance of the appraisal interview.
4. Explain the characteristics of an effective performance appraisal system, and describe how assessment centers are used to assess an employee's management potential.

"Tim, we must increase our productivity," exclaimed Doug Parsley, vice-president of production for Black and Decker. "If we don't, the foreign competition is 'going to eat our lunch.' Worker productivity hasn't declined, but they seem to have little incentive to increase it."

"I agree with you Doug," said Tim Overbeck, vice-president for human resources. "We really don't have a good system for differentiating various performance levels. There is no incentive for a superior worker to do any more work than anyone else. We need a better system—one that rewards employees for what they do. Maybe that would give them a desire to work harder."

Doug Parsley was beginning to realize a need for identifying his top producers. All managers need to be able to recognize differences in job performance. Employees can then be rewarded on the basis of their contributions toward achieving organizational goals. The appraisal method used must be perceived as being fair and equitable, and it should also serve to identify employee development needs.

We begin this chapter by defining *performance appraisal* and describing its uses. We then explain the performance appraisal process and responsibility for appraisal. We follow this with a discussion of the performance appraisal period, methods, and problems. Next, we describe the characteristics of an effective appraisal system, legal implications, and the appraisal interview. The final portion of the chapter is devoted to assessment centers and human resource development for multinational corporations. The overall purpose of this chapter is to emphasize the importance of performance appraisal as it relates to human resource management and its special implications for development of the firm's human resources.

■ PERFORMANCE APPRAISAL DEFINED

Nothing is more discouraging for a top producer in a work group than to receive the same pay increase as a marginal employee. A major incentive to do superior work is destroyed. It is vital for managers to realize that employee evaluation is a continuous process rather than an event that happens once a year.[1] **Performance appraisal (PA)** is a formal system of periodic review and evaluation of an individual's job performance.[2,3]

Developing an effective performance appraisal system is most difficult. A survey of 3,500 organizations revealed that managers' major human resource concern was the PA system used in their firms.[4] The evidence suggests that many managers are not pleased with their appraisal efforts. For example, one study of more than 290 organizations found widespread dissatisfaction with appraisal systems. This attitude was prevalent despite the fact that over half of the responding firms had developed new systems within the three years preceding the study.[5] Another study involving 92 Ohio firms with a performance appraisal system in place revealed that approximately 65 percent were in some way dissatisfied with their system. Developing an effective performance appraisal system has been, and will continue to be, a high priority of human resource management. In this effort, it must be remembered that performance appraisal is not an end in itself but rather the means to achieve a higher performance level. Approached in this manner, it has the best chance for successful implementation.[6]

■ USES OF PERFORMANCE APPRAISAL

Managers must keep in mind that the primary goal of an appraisal system is to improve performance. A system that is properly designed and communicated helps achieve organizational objectives and motivates employee performance.[7] One survey identified the areas in which businesses actually use appraisal information. The results indicate that at least 50 percent of

---

[1] Peter M. Tafti, "Face to Face," *Training and Development Journal,* 44 (November 1990), p. 68.

[2] Thomas N. Baylie, Carl J. Kujawski, and Drew M. Young, "Appraisals of 'People' Resources," In Dale Yoder and Herbert G. Heneman, Jr. (eds.) *ASPA Handbook of Personnel and Industrial Relations, Staffing Policies and Strategies,* Vol. 1. (Washington, D.C.: The Bureau of National Affairs, 1974), pp. 4–168.

[3] R. Wayne Mondy, Robert M. Noe III, and Robert E. Edwards, "What the Staffing Function Entails," *Personnel,* 63 (April 1986), p. 55.

[4] Douglas B. Gehrman, "Beyond Today's Compensation and Performance Appraisal Systems," *Personnel Administrator,* 29 (March 1984), p. 21.

[5] William M. Fox, "Consentient Merit Rating: A Critical Incident Approach," *Personnel,* 58 (July–August 1981), p. 70.

[6] Charles Lee, "Smoothing Out Appraisal Systems," *HRMagazine,* 35 (March 1991), pp. 72, 76.

[7] Robert J. Sahl, "Design Effective Performance Appraisals," *Personnel Journal,* 69 (October 1990), p. 60.

those who responded use the appraisal process in areas related to compensation (merit pay increases), communication (feedback), human resource planning (performance potential, succession planning), career planning, and internal employee administration.[8]

Human Resource Planning

In assessing a firm's human resources, data must be available that describe the promotability and potential of all employees, especially key executives. Management succession planning is a key concern for all firms, and PA yields essential data for this activity. A well-designed appraisal system provides a profile of the organization's human resource strengths and weaknesses.[9]

Recruitment and Selection

Performance evaluation ratings may be helpful in predicting the future performance of job applicants. For example, a significant number of successful managers may have received their training from certain schools or majored in particular fields. This type of knowledge could certainly influence a firm's approach to recruitment. Also, in validating selection tests, employee ratings may be used as the variable against which test scores are compared. In this instance, correct determination of the selection test's validity would depend largely on the accuracy of appraisal results.

Human Resource Development

A performance appraisal should point out an employee's specific needs for training, education, and development. For instance, if Mary Jones receives a marginal evaluation on writing skills, additional training in written communication may be needed. If the human resource manager finds that a number of first-line supervisors rate low in verbal skills, training sessions in spoken communication may be required. By identifying these deficiencies, the human resource manager is able to develop HRD programs that permit individuals to build on their strengths and minimize their deficiencies. An appraisal system does not guarantee that employees will be properly trained and developed. However, the task of determining training and development needs is simplified when appraisal data are available.

---

[8] Charles J. Fombrun and Robert J. Laud, "Strategic Issues in Performance Appraisal: Theory and Practice," *Personnel,* 60 (November–December 1983), p. 26.

[9] *Ibid.,* p. 24.

Career Planning and Development

Career planning and development may be viewed from either an individual or organizational viewpoint. In either case, PA data are essential in assessing an employee's strengths and weaknesses and in determining potential. Managers may use such information to counsel subordinates and assist them in developing and implementing their career plans.

Compensation Programs

Performance appraisal results provide a basis for decisions regarding pay increases. Most managers believe that outstanding job performance should be rewarded tangibly with raises. They believe that "what you reward is what you get." This may be a basic problem with the compensation practice described at the beginning of the chapter by Doug Parsley, the production vice-president. He has discovered that a system is needed to encourage people to produce at their highest level of efficiency over the long run. He also realizes that the same rewards for poor performers and top producers will likely lead to marginal performance even from the previously productive employees. To encourage good performance, a firm should design and implement a fair performance appraisal system and then reward the most productive workers accordingly.

Internal Employee Relations

Performance appraisal data are also frequently used for decisions in several areas of internal employee relations, including promotion, demotion, termination, layoff, and transfer. For example, an employee's mastery of certain tasks may become apparent, as may areas in which development is required.

An employee's performance in one job may be useful in determining his or her ability to perform another job on the same level, as is required in the consideration of transfers. Or when the performance level is unacceptable, demotion or termination may be appropriate. When employees working under a labor agreement are involved, employee layoff is typically based on seniority. However, when management has more flexibility, an employee's performance record may be a more significant criterion.

Assessment of Employee Potential

Some organizations attempt to assess employee potential as they appraise job performance. It has been said that the best predictors of future behavior are past behaviors. However, an employee's past performance in a job may not accurately indicate future performance in a higher level or different position. The best salesperson in the company may not have what it takes to become a successful district sales manager. The best computer programmer may, if promoted, be a disaster as a data processing manager. Over-emphasizing technical skills and ignoring other equally important skills is a common error in promoting employees into management jobs. Recognition of this problem has led some firms to separate the appraisal of performance, which focuses on past behavior, from the assessment of potential, which is future oriented. These firms have established "assessment centers," which we discuss in a later section.

While PA systems have the potential to serve many critical areas, such systems are not an annual activity in all firms. In one nationwide survey, 45 percent of the respondents replied that their employer does not give a formal job performance appraisal or review each year.[10]

■ THE PERFORMANCE APPRAISAL PROCESS

Many of the external and internal environmental factors discussed in Chapter 2 can influence the appraisal process. Legislation, for example, requires that appraisal systems be nondiscriminatory. In the 1977 case of *Mistretta v. Sandia Corporation* (a subsidiary of Western Electric Company, Inc.), a Federal District Court judge ruled against the company, stating that "there is sufficient circumstantial evidence to indicate that age bias and age based policies appear throughout the performance rating process to the detriment of the protected age group." The *Albermarle Paper v. Moody* case supported validation requirements for performance appraisals, as well as for selection tests. Organizations should avoid using any appraisal method that results in a disproportionately negative impact on a protected class.[11] For example, are women consistently being rated lower than men? If so, their promotion potential would also be affected.

The labor union is another external factor that might affect a firm's appraisal process. Unions have traditionally stressed seniority as the basis for promotions and pay increases. They may vigorously oppose the use of a management-designed performance appraisal system that would be used for these purposes.

Factors within the internal environment can also affect the performance appraisal process. For instance, the type of corporate culture can serve to assist or hinder the process. In today's highly complex organizations, employees must often rely on coworkers in performing their tasks. A closed, nontrusting culture may discourage the cooperation needed to perform a job. In such an environment, performance may suffer even though an individual worker tries to do a good job. Recognizing the true contributions of an individual worker in such an environment may be quite difficult.

Identification of specific goals is the starting point for the PA process (see Figure 11-1 on page 398). An appraisal system may be unable to effectively serve all the purposes desired, so management should select those specific

---

[10] "What Does Your Boss Really Think of You?" *Supervision,* 51 (December 1990), p. 10.

[11] Robert V. Romberg, "Performance Appraisal, 1: Risks and Rewards," *Personnel,* 63 (August 1986), p. 20.

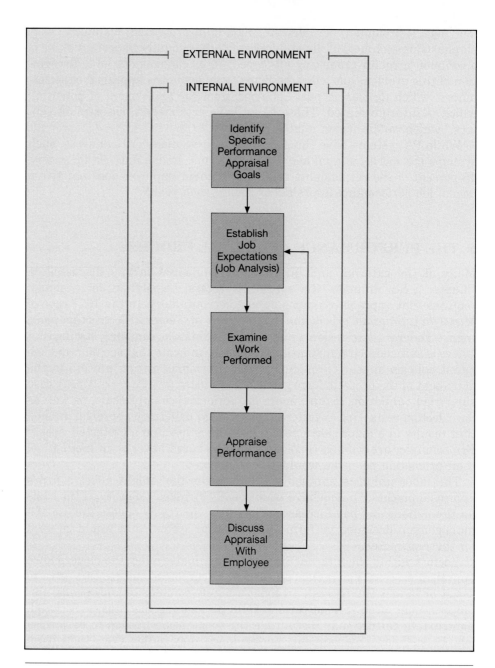

FIGURE 11-1 | The Performance Appraisal Process

PA goals that it believes to be most important and can be realistically achieved. For example, some firms may want to stress employee development, whereas other organizations may want to focus on administrative decisions, such as pay adjustments. Too many performance appraisal systems are poorly designed because management hasn't established clear objectives. In these instances, managers haven't determined specifically what they want the system to accomplish, often anticipating too much from one system.

After specific appraisal goals have been established, workers must understand what is expected from them in their jobs. It is helpful when their supervisors review with them the major duties determined through job analysis and contained in the job description. In fact, informing employees of what is expected of them may be a manager's most important employee-relation task.[12]

The supervisor then observes work performance, evaluates it against established job performance standards, and communicates the evaluation results to the worker. The performance evaluation discussion with the supervisor serves to reestablish job requirements in the employee's mind.

■ GLOBAL PERFORMANCE APPRAISAL

A performance appraisal system mandates a formal periodic review and evaluation of an employee's job performance. The development of an appropriate global performance appraisal system will undoubtedly be a complex process, but an effective global system is essential for credible employee evaluations.[13] Valid performance appraisal is difficult enough to achieve in the United States; evaluating overseas employees makes a normally complex problem nearly impossible. What usually works in one culture might not work in another.[14] What is a strength in one culture might be considered a weakness in another. When performance appraisals are done overseas, the issue of what performance standards to use comes into question. Differences in performance appraisal practices are almost always necessary. An improper performance appraisal system can create a great deal of misunderstanding and personal offense.[15]

Such problems can be partially avoided if HRM professionals take the following actions. First, managers determine the purpose of the appraisal—whether it is to enhance administrative decision making or to enhance the personal development of the employee. Second, whenever possible, performance objectives for job assignments or tasks should be developed. Third, managers must allow more time to achieve results in an overseas assignment. Finally, the objectives of the appraisal system should be flexible and

---

[12] J. Kenneth Matejka and Richard J. Dunsing, "Great Expectations," *Management World,* 16 (January 1987), p. 16.

[13] Wayne F. Cascio and Manuel G. Serapio, Jr., "Human Resources Systems in an International Alliance: The Undoing of a Done Deal?" *Organizational Dynamics,* 19 (Winter 1991), p. 70.

[14] Mark E. Mendenhall and Gary Oddon, "The Overseas Assignment: A Practical Look," *Business Horizons,* 31 (Sept./Oct. 1988), p. 81.

[15] *Ibid.,* p. 70.

responsive to potential markets and environmental contingencies. As with a domestic performance appraisal system, a global one should result in a realistic review and evaluation of the employee's job performance.[16]

■ RESPONSIBILITY FOR APPRAISAL

In most organizations, the human resource department is responsible for designing and overseeing performance appraisal programs. Responsibility for actually conducting the appraisals varies from company to company. However, line management must directly participate in the program if it is to succeed. Several possibilities exist as to who will actually rate the employee, some of which we present next.

Immediate Supervisor

An employee's immediate supervisor is the most common choice for evaluating performance. In fact, in one study, 96 percent of the respondents revealed that in their firms, appraisals were conducted by the employee's immediate supervisor.[17] There are several valid reasons for this approach. In the first place, the supervisor is usually in an excellent position to observe the employee's job performance. Another reason is that the supervisor has the responsibility for managing a particular unit. When the task of evaluating subordinates is given to someone else, the supervisor's authority may be seriously undermined. Finally, subordinate training and development is an important element in every manager's job and—as previously mentioned—appraisal programs and employee development are often closely related.

On the negative side, the immediate supervisor may emphasize certain aspects of employee performance and neglect others. Also, managers have been known to manipulate evaluations to justify their pay increase and promotion decisions. However, the immediate supervisor will probably continue to be the person most likely to evaluate employee performance. Organizations will seek alternatives, however, because of the weaknesses mentioned and a desire to broaden the perspective of the appraisal.

Subordinates

Some managers have concluded that evaluation of managers by subordinates is feasible. They reason that subordinates are in an excellent position to view their superior's managerial effectiveness. Advocates of this approach believe that supervisors will become especially conscious of the work

---

[16] Ibid.

[17] Charles J. Fombrun and Robert J. Laud, "Strategic Issues," p. 27.

group's needs and will do a better job of managing. In the academic environment, faculty members are often provided the opportunity of evaluating department heads and deans.

Peers

Another possibility is to have peers evaluate each other. Proponents of this approach believe that it need not result in popularity contests. Peer appraisal, they feel, may be reliable if the work group is stable over a reasonably long period of time and performs tasks that require considerable interaction. However, the use of peer evaluation has not been generally accepted.

Group Appraisal

Group appraisal involves the use of two or more managers who are familiar with the employee's performance to evaluate it as a team. For instance, if a person regularly works with the data processing manager and the financial manager, these two individuals might jointly make the evaluation. An advantage of this approach is that it injects a degree of objectivity by utilizing "outside parties." A disadvantage is that it diminishes the role of the immediate supervisor. Also, it may be difficult to get managers together for a group appraisal because of other demands on their time.

Self-Appraisal

At one small firm, 300 wage earners evaluate themselves using a rating scale with seventeen specific factors. Each employee's tutor also evaluates the employee, and the two are then required to reconcile significant differences.[18] If employees understand the objectives they are expected to achieve and the standards by which they are to be evaluated, they are—to a great extent—in the best position to appraise their own performance. Also, because employee development is self-development, employees who appraise their own performance may become more highly motivated. Self-appraisal has great appeal to managers who are primarily concerned with employee participation and development.

Combinations

When trying to decide who should evaluate an employee, one must recognize that these approaches are not mutually exclusive. In fact, many are used in combination. For example, in order to minimize subjectivity, a

---

[18] "How Johnsonville Shares Profits on the Basis of Performance," *Harvard Business Review*, 68 (November–December 1990), p. 74.

manager may be rated separately by a group of fellow workers, including the immediate superior, two or three higher level managers, two or three peers, and workers in lower positions. The combined use of several methods may provide greater insight into an individual's actual performance.

■ THE APPRAISAL PERIOD

Performance evaluations are usually prepared at specific intervals. In most organizations, they are made either annually or semiannually. Individuals are often evaluated just before the end of the probationary period. Evaluating new employees several times during their first year of employment is also a common practice. The following are the evaluation periods for three companies:

- The New York Times Company evaluates all its guild and nonunion employees annually. Craft unions are not included in this process.
- Cessna Aircraft Company appraises all monthly salaried employees and all weekly salaried supervisors approximately once a year.
- General Mills, Inc., evaluates all employees annually, except for operative, nonexempt employees, who are evaluated each six months.

The appraisal period may begin with each employee's date of hire, or all employees may be evaluated at the same time. Although both practices have advantages, staggered appraisals seem to have greater merit. There may not be sufficient time to evaluate each employee adequately if all appraisals are conducted at the same time. The problem would be especially acute in large departments.

■ PERFORMANCE APPRAISAL METHODS

Managers may choose from among several appraisal methods. The type of performance appraisal system utilized depends on its purpose. If the major emphasis is on selecting people for promotion, training, and merit pay increases, a traditional method such as rating scales may be most appropriate. Collaborative methods, such as MBO, are designed to assist employees in developing and becoming more effective.[19]

Rating Scales

A widely used appraisal method, which rates employees according to defined factors, is called the **rating scales method.** Using this approach, judgments about performance are recorded on a scale. The scale is divided into categories—normally 5–7 in number—which are often defined by ad-

---

[19] Robert L. Taylor and Robert A. Zawaki, "Trends in Performance Appraisal: Guidelines for Managers," *Personnel Administrator,* 29 (March 1984), p. 71.

jectives such as *outstanding, average,* or *unsatisfactory.* While an overall rating may be provided, the method generally allows for the use of more than one performance criterion. One reason for the popularity of the rating scales method is its simplicity, which permits many employees to be evaluated quickly.

The factors chosen for evaluation are typically of two types: job-related and personal characteristics. Note that in Figure 11-2 job-related factors include quantity and quality of work, whereas personal factors include such attributes as dependability, initiative, adaptability, and cooperation.[20] The rater (evaluator) completes the form by indicating the degree of each factor that is most descriptive of the employee and his or her performance.

Some firms provide space for the rater to comment on the evaluation given for each factor. This practice may be especially encouraged, or even required, when the rater gives either the highest or lowest rating. For instance, if an employee is rated *unsatisfactory* on initiative, the rater provides written justification for this low evaluation. The purpose of this type of requirement is to avoid arbitrary and hastily made judgments.

As you can see in Figure 11-2 on page 404, each factor and each degree have been defined. In order to receive an *exceptional* rating for the factor *quality of work,* a person must consistently exceed the prescribed work requirements. The more precisely the various factors and degrees are defined, the better the rater can evaluate worker performance. Evaluation agreement throughout the organization is achieved when each rater interprets the factors and degrees in the same way.

Many rating scale performance appraisal forms also provide for an assessment of the employee's growth potential. The form shown in Figure 11-2 contains four categories relating to a person's potential for future growth and development. They range from "now at or near maximum performance in present job" to "no apparent limitations." Although there are drawbacks in attempting to evaluate both past performance and future potential at the same time, this practice is often followed.

The Use of Rating Scales at the Southland Corporation

At the Southland Corporation, immediate supervisors are required to conduct a written performance review of nonexempt and exempt employees at least annually. An example of the form used to appraise nonexempt employees is shown in Figure 11-3 on pages 406–410. The appraisal system involves seven steps:

- Select key job parts
- Describe employee performance
- Rate employee performance

---

[20] Because the system depicted makes liberal use of personal factors that may not be job related, it has been described by one reviewer as "a good example of a poor method."

Employee's Name _____

Job Title _____

Department _____

Supervisor _____

Evaluation Period:
From _____ to _____

Instructions for Evaluation:
1. Consider only one factor at a time. Do not permit rating given for one factor to affect decision for others.
2. Consider performance for entire evaluation period. Avoid concentration on recent events or isolated incidents.
3. Remember that the average employee performs duties in a satisfactory manner. An above average or exceptional rating indicates that the employee has clearly distinguished himself or herself from the average employee.

EVALUATION FACTORS	Unsatisfactory. Does not meet requirements.	Below average. Needs improvement. Requirements occasionally not met.	Average. Consistently meets requirements.	Good. Frequently exceeds requirements.	Exceptional. Consistently exceeds requirements.
QUANTITY OF WORK: Consider the volume of work achieved. Is productivity at an acceptable level?					
QUALITY OF WORK: Consider accuracy, precision, neatness, and completeness in handling assigned duties.					
DEPENDABILITY: Consider degree to which employee can be relied on to meet work commitments.					
INITIATIVE: Consider self-reliance, resourcefulness, and willingness to accept responsibility.					
ADAPTABILITY: Consider ability to respond to changing requirements and conditions.					
COOPERATION: Consider ability to work for and with others. Are assignments, including overtime, willingly accepted?					

POTENTIAL FOR FUTURE GROWTH AND DEVELOPMENT:
☐ Now at or near maximum performance in present job.
☐ Now at or near maximum performance in this job, but has potential for improvement in another job, such as:

_____

☐ Capable of progressing after further training and experience.
☐ No apparent limitations.

EMPLOYEE STATEMENT: I agree ☐　　Disagree ☐　with this evaluation
Comments:

_____

Employee _____ Date _____

Supervisor _____ Date _____

Reviewing Manager _____ Date _____

FIGURE 11-2 | Rating Scales Method of Performance Appraisal

- Determine overall efficiency
- Prepare for the performance appraisal discussion
- Present results and (an optional step) prepare a performance development plan
- Obtain necessary signatures

Key job parts are aspects of the job such as duties, responsibilities, and assignments that are so important that their performance affects overall success or failure. Key job parts are determined by job analysis for each job family. The rating supervisor selects those that are most relevant to the job of the employee being evaluated. Normally, six to eight job parts are utilized. Again referring to Figure 11-3, note that the supervisor evaluates performance on a five-point scale. The factors used, however, are not nebulous personality traits, which are so often used. Rather, they are job-related factors. This approach not only conforms to requirements of the *Uniform Guidelines* but also places the rating supervisor's task of evaluating performance on a solid foundation.

Critical Incidents

The **critical incident method** requires that written records be kept of highly favorable and highly unfavorable work actions. When such an action affects the department's effectiveness significantly—either positively or negatively—the manager writes it down. It is called a critical incident. At the end of the appraisal period, the rater uses these records along with other data to evaluate employee performance. With this method, the appraisal is more likely to cover the entire evaluation period and not, for example, focus on the last few weeks or months. However, if a supervisor has many employees to rate, the time required for recording behaviors may become excessive.

Essay

In the **essay method,** the rater simply writes a brief narrative describing the employee's performance. This method tends to focus on extreme behavior in the employee's work rather than routine day-to-day performance. Ratings of this type depend heavily on the evaluator's writing ability. As the evaluations are reviewed, a positive evaluation may be negatively received if the evaluator misspells words or cannot write a good paragraph. Some supervisors, because of their excellent writing ability, can make even a marginal worker sound like a top performer. Comparing evaluations might be difficult because no common criteria exist. However, some managers believe that the essay method is the best approach to employee evaluation.

KEY JOB PARTS	PERFORMANCE DESCRIPTION	PERFORMANCE RATING*
1. Typing ■ Typing from handwritten draft ■ Typing information on forms ■ Statistical or financial typing ■ Typing from recorded dictation		(N/A) 1 2 3 4 5
2. Maintaining and ordering supplies ■ Checking supply levels ■ Ordering and picking up supplies	Employee needs to work with forms order and inventories more to gain more experience in this area. Make sure letters are prepared for checks taken from area.	N/A 1 2 (3) 4 5
3. Copying and recording information ■ Making routine entries in files, books, or on forms ■ Keeping tallies or lists	Employee does well making entries in check logs and on transmittals.	N/A 1 2 (3) 4 5
4. Making job-related decisions ■ Setting priorities for own work ■ Deciding the best way to complete an assignment ■ Reading and interpreting policies, rules, and procedures ■ Doing limited research (calling, looking things up in manuals, etc.) to resolve a problem or question ■ Conducting research or analyzing information	Employee has improved in limited research and writing Request for Assistance. Still needs to review all possibilities when researching missing reports.	N/A 1 2 (3) 4 5

Location _____

Period of Evaluation __2/88__ to __2/89__

Date of Last Review __2/88__

Supervisor's Name __Harry Hines__

Supervisor's Title __MIS Supply Supervisor__

Type of Review _____

Refer to the *Performance Appraisal System Reference Guide* before completing this form.

Employee Name __John Jacobs__

Employee Title __MIS Supply Clerk__

Employee Social Security Number __450-30-2641__

*Ratings are defined in *Reference Guide* and range from "well below performance requirements (1)" to "well above performance requirements (5)."

FIGURE 11-3 | Performance Appraisal System for Nonexempt Employees

KEY JOB PARTS	PERFORMANCE DESCRIPTION	PERFORMANCE RATING*
5. Processing requests ■ Receiving and reviewing incoming correspondence, telephone calls, or other requests ■ Deciding what the problem or inquiry is ■ Preparing responses to inquiries ■ Persuading others to take action or change their opinions ■ Responding to telephone inquiries		(N/A) 1 2 3 4 5
6. Proofreading and checking work ■ Reviewing forms, reports, correspondence for completeness and accuracy ■ Checking material for errors in typing, spelling, punctuation, grammar, capitalization or word usage ■ Checking work done by others to make sure procedures and/or instructions have been followed	Employee does well in checking the completeness of production output. Has improved in locating one-page reports attached to multipage reports.	N/A 1 2 3 (4) 5
7. Performing routine calculations ■ Adding, subtracting, multiplying, or dividing ■ Computing wages, taxes, commissions, etc. ■ Determining rates, discounts, etc. by referring to tables		(N/A) 1 2 3 4 5
8. Sorting, filing, or retrieving information ■ Sorting information ■ Filing or retrieving information (in an existing filing system) ■ Developing new filing or cross-index systems ■ Searching for missing files, forms, orders, etc.		(N/A) 1 2 3 4 5
9. Preparing written reports ■ Writing reports which summarize available information ■ Writing short, routine reports ■ Writing long or complicated reports ■ Preparing financial statements or numerical or statistical reports ■ Composing or initiating correspondence	Prepares precise transmittals and Request for Assistance.	N/A 1 2 (3) 4 5

FIGURE 11-3 | *Continued*

Task	Comments	Rating
10. Performing receptionist duties ■ Answering and routing telephone calls ■ Taking and distributing messages ■ Greeting visitors		(N/A) 1 2 3 4 5
11. Scheduling ■ Contacting individuals to schedule meetings ■ Making travel arrangements ■ Reserving meeting facilities		(N/A) 1 2 3 4 5
12. Performing data entry and retrieval tasks ■ Operating a key punch, data entry terminal, or verifier ■ Look up information using CRT		(N/A) 1 2 3 4 5
13. Performing accounting functions ■ Posting to ledgers ■ Receiving, counting, or paying out checks or cash ■ Balancing receipts ■ Debiting/crediting accounts		(N/A) 1 2 3 4 5
14. Operating and maintaining office machines ■ Setting up and adjusting machines (such as an offset press) ■ Cleaning or performing simple repairs on office machines ■ Operating simple office machines such as copying machines	Continues to do a good job operating all machines in distribution. He is an excellent operator of the burster.	N/A 1 2 3 (4) 5
15. Distributing material ■ Picking up or distributing materials ■ Preparing materials for mailing or shipping	Does well at preparing materials for mailing or shipping.	N/A 1 2 3 (4) 5
16. Performing supervisory duties ■ Making work assignments ■ Conducting employee evaluations ■ Coordinating activities of assigned employees ■ Resolving conflicts or problems among assigned employees		(N/A) 1 2 3 4 5
17. Computer operations ■ Operating Central Processing Unit ■ Operating a high-speed printer (on-line to CPU) ■ Operating tape drives		(N/A) 1 2 3 4 5

*Ratings are defined in *Reference Guide*

FIGURE 11-3   *Continued*

KEY JOB PARTS	PERFORMANCE DESCRIPTION	PERFORMANCE RATING*
18. Word Processing ■ Operating a word processor using a terminal or printer ■ Inputting and manipulating statistical data ■ Inputting and formatting text		(N/A) 1 2 3 4 5
19. Operating a Personal Computer ■ Creating simple programs ■ Performing sort, math and merge functions		(N/A) 1 2 3 4 5
20. Computer Knowledge ■ Input Documents	Employee has a good knowledge of distribution area. Needs to expand his knowledge of Data Control—Input, UCC7, Schedule.	N/A 1 2 (3) 4 5
21. General ■ Quality Control ■ Unsupervised Work ■ Attendance	Employee is very dependable and has an excellent attitude. He is very responsible and needs very little supervision. Employee continues to improve.	N/A 1 2 3 (4) 5
22. Attitude		N/A 1 2 3 (4) 5

*Ratings are defined in *Reference Guide.*

OVERALL PERFORMANCE DESCRIPTION

Well below performance requirements.	Below performance requirements.	Meets performance requirements.	Above performance requirements.	Well above performance requirements.
☐1	☐2	☐3	(☐4)	☐5

Refer to the *Guide to Developing Goals* before completing this section.

PERFORMANCE GOALS/RESULTS DESIRED	ACTION SUPERVISOR WILL TAKE TO HELP EMPLOYEE ACHIEVE GOALS	ACTION EMPLOYEE WILL TAKE TO ACHIEVE GOALS	TARGET DATE
1. Work with forms orders and inventories to gain more experience in this area. 2. Ensure that checks are accounted for with letters. 3. Improve research techniques. 4. Expand knowledge of UCC7 and scheduling.			

FIGURE 11-3 | *Continued*

EMPLOYEE COMMENTS:

Employee Signature _____   Date _____ 8/15/89

NOTE: Your signature does not necessarily signify your agreement with the appraisal; it simply means that the appraisal was discussed with you.

Reviewer's Signature _____   Date _____ 8/15/89

Second Level Reviewer's Signature _____   Date _____ 8/15/89

FIGURE 11-3 | *Continued*

Work Standards

The **work standards method** compares each employee's performance to a predetermined standard or expected level of output. Standards reflect the normal output of an average worker operating at a normal pace. Work standards may be applied to virtually all types of jobs, but they are most frequently used for production jobs. Several methods may be utilized in determining work standards, including time study and work sampling.

An obvious advantage of using standards as appraisal criteria is objectivity. However, in order for employees to perceive that the standards are objective, they should understand clearly how the standards were set. It follows that the rationale for any changes to the standards must also be carefully explained.

Ranking

In using the **ranking method,** the rater simply places all employees from a group in rank order of overall performance. For example, the best employee in the department is ranked highest, and the poorest is ranked lowest. A major difficulty occurs when individuals have performed at comparable levels.

Paired comparison is a variation of the ranking method in which the performance of each employee is compared with every other employee in the group. The comparison is often based on a single criterion, such as overall performance. The employee who receives the greatest number of favorable comparisons is ranked highest.

Some professionals in the field argue for use of a comparative approach—such as ranking—whenever human resource decisions are made. For example, they feel that employees are not promoted because they achieve their objectives but rather because they achieve them better than others in their work group. Such decisions do not involve a single individual and therefore should be considered on a broader basis.

Forced Distribution

In the **forced distribution method,** the rater is required to assign individuals in the work group to a limited number of categories similar to a normal frequency distribution. As an example, employees in the top 10 percent are placed in the highest group, the next 20 percent in the next group, the next 40 percent in the middle group, the next 20 percent in the next group, and the remaining 10 percent in the lowest category. This approach is based on the rather questionable assumption that all groups of employees will have the same distribution of excellent, average, and poor performers. If one department has all outstanding workers, the supervisor would likely be hard pressed to decide who should be placed in the lower categories.

Forced-Choice and Weighted Checklist Performance Reports

The **forced-choice performance report** requires that the appraiser choose from a series of statements about an individual those that are most or least descriptive of the employee. One difficulty with this method is that the descriptive statements may be virtually identical.

Using the **weighted checklist performance report,** the rater completes a form similar to the forced-choice performance report, but the various responses have been assigned different weights. The form includes questions related to the employee's behavior, and the evaluator answers each question either positively or negatively. The evaluator is not aware of each question's weight, however.

As with forced-choice performance reports, the weighted checklist is expensive to design. Both methods strive for objectivity, but the evaluator doesn't know which items contribute most to successful performance. Employee development, therefore, cannot result from this approach.

Behaviorally Anchored Rating Scales

The **behaviorally anchored rating scale (BARS) method** combines elements of the traditional rating scales and critical incidents methods. Using BARS, job behaviors derived from critical incidents—effective and ineffective behavior—are described more objectively. Individuals familiar with a particular job identify its major components. They then rank and validate specific behaviors for each of the components. Because BARS typically requires considerable employee participation, it may be accepted more readily by both supervisors and subordinates. Behaviorally anchored rating scales are potentially more reliable than graphic rating scales and, therefore, more defensible from a legal standpoint.[21]

In BARS, various performance levels are shown along a scale and described in terms of an employee's specific job behavior. Table 11-1 illustrates a portion of a BARS system that was developed to evaluate interviewers and claims deputies for the employment service of a state department of labor. Note that the factor *ability to absorb and interpret policies* (in the table's title) is job related and carefully defined. Instead of using adjectives at each scale point, BARS uses behavioral anchors related to the criterion being measured. This modification clarifies the meaning of each point on the scale. For example, instead of providing a box to be checked for a category such as *Very Positive* performance, the BARS method provides examples of such behavior. This approach facilitates discussion of the rating because specific behaviors can be addressed.[22] This method was

---

[21] Ronald G. Wells, "Guidelines for Effective and Defensible Performance Appraisal Systems," *Personnel Journal,* 61 (October 1982), p. 777.

[22] J. Peter Graves, "Let's Put Appraisal Back in Performance Appraisal: Part I," *Personnel Journal,* 61 (November 1982), pp. 848–849.

TABLE 11-1 | BARS for Factor: "Ability to Absorb and Interpret Policies"

Interviewers and claims deputies must keep abreast of current changes and interpret and apply new information. Some can absorb and interpret new policy guides and procedures quickly with a minimum of explanation. Others seem unable to learn even after repeated explanations and practice. They have difficulty learning and following new policies. When making this rating, disregard job knowledge and experience and evaluate ability to learn on the job.

Very Positive	9	This interviewer could be expected to serve as an information source concerning new and changed policies for others in the office.
	8	Could be expected to be aware quickly of program changes and explain these changes to employers.
	7	Could be expected to reconcile conflicting policies and procedures correctly to meet immediate job needs.
	6	Could be expected to recognize the need for additional information to gain better understanding of policy changes.
Neutral	5	After receiving instruction on completing ESAR forms, this interviewer could be expected to complete the forms correctly.
	4	Could be expected to require some help and practice in mastering new policies and procedures.
	3	Could be expected to know that there is a problem, but might go down many blind alleys before realizing they are wrong.
	2	Could be expected to incorrectly interpret program guidelines, thereby referring an unqualified person.
Very Negative	1	Even after repeated explanations, this interviewer could be expected to be unable to learn new procedures.

Source: Adapted from Cheedle W. Millard, Fred Luthans, and Robert
L. Ottemann, "A New Breakthrough for Performance Appraisal,"
Business Horizons, 19 (August 1976), p. 69. Copyright © 1976 by
the Foundation for the School of Business at Indiana University.
Reprinted by permission.

developed to overcome weaknesses in other evaluation methods. Reports on the effectiveness of BARS are mixed, and it does not seem to be superior to other methods in overcoming rater errors or in achieving psychometric soundness.[23] A specific deficiency is that the behaviors used are activity

---

[23] Stephen J. Carroll and Craig E. Schneier, *Performance Appraisal and Review Systems: The Identification, Measurement, and Development of Performance in Organizations* (Glenview, Ill.: Scott, Foresman, 1982), p. 117.

oriented rather than results oriented. This poses a potential problem for supervisors, because they must rate employees who are performing the activity but not accomplishing the desired goals.

Management By Objectives

As previously discussed, the MBO concept values and utilizes employee contributions. It is also an effective method of evaluating an employee's performance. In traditional approaches to performance appraisal, personal traits of employees are often used as criteria for evaluating performance. In addition, the role of the evaluating supervisor is similar to that of a judge. With MBO, the focus of the appraisal process shifts from the worker's personal attributes to job performance. The supervisor's role changes from that of an umpire to that of a counselor and facilitator. Also, the employee's function changes from that of passive bystander to that of active participant.

Individuals jointly establish objectives with their superiors, who then give them latitude in how to achieve the objectives. Jointly established goals make the employee an involved part of the process. This ownership of objectives increases the likelihood that they will be met.[24] At the end of the appraisal period, the employee and supervisor meet for an appraisal interview. They first review the extent to which the objectives have been achieved and then review the actions needed to solve remaining problems. Under MBO, the supervisor keeps communication channels open throughout the appraisal period. The problem-solving discussion during the appraisal interview is merely another conversation designed to assist the worker in progressing according to plan. At this time, objectives are established for the next evaluation period, and the process is repeated.

It should be obvious that not all leadership styles are compatible with the participative concept of MBO. It probably would not be successful in an organization run by highly autocratic managers. An attempt to implement an MBO appraisal system in such a setting would likely result in top management concluding that "MBO is okay in theory, but no good in practice." The theory *is* sound, but implementation problems often stem from the incompatibility of the theory with the organization's culture.

■ PROBLEMS IN PERFORMANCE APPRAISAL

Many performance appraisal methods have been severely criticized. The rating scales method seems to have received the greatest attention. In all fairness, many of the problems commonly mentioned are not inherent in

---

[24] Jay T. Knippen, "Boost Performance Through Appraisals," *Business Credit,* 92 (November–December 1990), p. 27.

the method but, rather, reflect improper usage. For example, raters may be inadequately trained, or the appraisal device actually used may not be job related.

Lack of Objectivity

A potential weakness of traditional performance appraisal methods is that they lack objectivity. In the rating scales method, for example, commonly used factors such as attitude, loyalty, and personality are difficult to measure. In addition, these factors may have little to do with an employee's job performance.

Some subjectivity will always exist in appraisal methods. However, the use of job-related factors does increase objectivity. Employee appraisal based primarily on personal characteristics may place the evaluator—and the company—in untenable positions with the employee and EEO guidelines. The firm would be hard pressed to show that these factors are job related.

Halo Error

Halo error occurs when the evaluator perceives one factor as having paramount importance and gives a good or bad overall rating to an employee based on this one factor. For example, David Edwards, accounting supervisor, placed a high value on "neatness," which was a factor used in the company's performance appraisal system. As David was evaluating the performance of his senior accounting clerk, Carl Curtis, he noted that Carl was not a very neat individual and gave him a low ranking on this factor. David also permitted, consciously or unconsciously, the low ranking on neatness to carry over to other factors, giving Carl undeserved low ratings on all factors. Of course, if Carl were very neat, the opposite could have occurred. Either way, the halo error does a disservice to the employee involved and the organization.

Leniency/Strictness

Leniency and strictness are often a major problem with regard to effective performance. Thomas M. Jordan, vice-president of human resources for Sea-Land Service, Inc., stated that one of the major problems encountered in his company's appraisal system is "getting managers to be objective and honest, especially where poor performance is involved." Giving undeserved high ratings is referred to as **leniency.** Often evaluations will be inflated if a supervisor is required to discuss them with employees. In many situations the evaluating supervisor simply gives the employee the benefit of the doubt. These actions are often motivated by a desire to avoid controversy over the appraisal. This practice is most prevalent for scenarios in which highly subjective factors are used as performance criteria.

Being unduly critical of an employee's work performance is referred to as **strictness.** While leniency is usually more prevalent than strictness, some managers apply an evaluation more rigorously than the company standard. When one manager is overly strict on an entire unit, workers in that unit suffer with regard to pay raises and promotion. Strictness typically occurs when managers do not have an accurate definition of the various evaluation factors.

A recent study revealed that over 70 percent of responding managers believe that inaccurate ratings are intentionally given to subordinates. Table 11-2 shows these managers' explanations for the rationale behind inaccurate ratings. These results could indicate that the reliability of many performance appraisal systems is flawed. The purposes of PA cannot be

TABLE 11-2 | Reasons for Intentionally Inflating or Lowering Ratings

Inflated Ratings

- The belief that accurate ratings would have a damaging effect on the subordinate's motivation and performance
- The desire to improve an employee's eligibility for merit raises
- The desire to avoid airing the department's dirty laundry
- The wish to avoid creating a negative permanent record of poor performance that might hound the employee in the future
- The need to protect good performers whose performance was suffering because of personal problems
- The wish to reward employees displaying great effort even when results are relatively low
- The need to avoid confrontation with certain hard-to-manage employees
- The desire to promote a poor or disliked employee up and out of the department

Lowered Ratings

- To scare better performance out of an employee
- To punish a difficult or rebellious employee
- To encourage a problem employee to quit
- To create a strong record to justify a planned firing
- To minimize the amount of the merit increase a subordinate receives
- To comply with an organizational edict that discourages managers from giving high ratings

Source: Clinton Longenecker and Dean Ludwig, "Ethical Dilemmas in Performance Appraisal Revisited," *Journal of Business Ethics,* 9 (December 1990), p. 963. Reprinted by permission of Kluwer Academic Publishers.

achieved when the system is misused. However, if this malpractice is brought to managers' attention, perhaps they will be encouraged to consider the negative consequences.

Central Tendency

Central tendency is a common error that occurs when employees are incorrectly rated near the average or middle of the scale. Some rating scale systems require the evaluator to justify in writing extremely high or extremely low ratings. In these instances, the rater may avoid possible controversy or criticism by giving only average ratings.

Recent Behavior Bias

Anyone who has observed the behavior of young children several weeks before Christmas can readily identify with the problem of recent behavior bias. All of a sudden, it seems, the wildest hellions in the neighborhood develop angelic personalities in anticipation of the rewards they expect to receive.

Individuals in the workforce are not children, but they are human. Almost every employee can tell a supervisor precisely when he or she is scheduled for a performance review. Although their actions may not be conscious, employee behavior often improves and productivity tends to rise several days or weeks before the scheduled evaluation. It is only natural to remember recent behavior more clearly than actions from the more distant past. However, performance appraisals generally cover a specified period of time, and an individual's performance should be considered for the entire period.

Personal Bias

Supervisors doing performance appraisals may have biases related to their employees' personal characteristics such as race, religion, gender, or age. While federal legislation protects such employees, discrimination continues to be an appraisal problem.

Discrimination in appraisal can be based on many factors in addition to those mentioned. For example, mild-mannered people may be appraised more harshly simply because they do not raise serious objections to the results. This type of behavior is in sharp contrast to the "hell raisers" who often confirm the adage, "the squeaking wheel gets the grease."

Judgmental Role of Evaluator

Supervisors conducting performance evaluations are at times accused of "playing God" with their employees. In some instances they control virtually every aspect of the process. Manipulation of evaluations by managers

HRM In Action

Bill, you're the human resource manager and I have a human resource problem that I need your advice on," said Marvin Alexander, production supervisor for Service International. "Tom has worked for me for four years. He is likable and never misses a day of work. However, he is strictly mediocre at his job, despite numerous retraining attempts, conferences, and even incentives. I hear that the company is preparing for a reduction in force. As I was working on Tom's appraisal this morning, he stuck his head in the door, handed me three cigars, and said that his wife had just had triplets. That sure puts pressure on me."

If you were Bill, how would you respond?

to justify their pay increase and promotion decisions is one example of how supervisors may abuse the system. They make decisions about the ratings and typically try to sell their version to the employees. The highly judgmental role of some evaluators often places employees on the defensive. Such relationships are hardly conducive to employee development, morale, and productivity.

■ CHARACTERISTICS OF AN EFFECTIVE APPRAISAL SYSTEM[25]

Validation studies of an appraisal system may be the most direct and certain approach to determining whether the system is satisfactory. However, such studies can be costly and time consuming. Also, many smaller firms will simply not have a sufficient number of positions to meet technical validation requirements.

It is unlikely that any appraisal system will be totally immune to legal challenge. However, systems that possess certain characteristics may be more legally defensible. And, at the same time, such systems can provide a more effective means for achieving performance appraisal goals.

---

[25] Portions of this section were adapted from Ronald G. Wells, "Guidelines for Effective and Defensible Performance Appraisal Systems," *Personnel Journal,* 61 (October 1982), pp. 776–782.

Job-Related Criteria

The criteria used for appraising employee performance must be job related. The *Uniform Guidelines* and court decisions are quite clear on this point. More specifically, job information should be determined through job analysis. Subjective factors, such as initiative, enthusiasm, loyalty, and cooperation, are obviously important. However, they virtually defy definition and measurement. Unless factors such as these can be clearly shown to be job related, they should not be used in formal evaluations.

Performance Expectations

Managers must clearly explain performance expectations to their subordinates in advance of the appraisal period. Otherwise, it isn't reasonable to evaluate employees using criteria that they know nothing about.

The establishment of highly objective work standards is relatively simple in many areas such as manufacturing, assembly, and sales. However, for many other types of jobs this task is more difficult. Still, evaluation must take place, and performance expectations, however elusive, should be defined in understandable terms.

Standardization

Employees in the same job category under the same supervisor should be appraised using the same evaluation instrument. In addition, the appraisals should cover similar periods of time. Feedback sessions and appraisal interviews should be regularly scheduled for all employees.

Another aspect of standardization is formal documentation. Records should include a description of employee responsibilities, expected performance results, and the way these data will be viewed in making appraisal decisions. However, smaller firms are not expected to maintain performance appraisal systems that are as formal as those used by large organizations. The courts reason that objective criteria are not as important in firms with fewer than thirty employees because a smaller firm's top managers are more familiar with their employees' work.[26]

Qualified Appraisers

Responsibility for evaluating employee performance should be assigned to the individual, or individuals, who directly observe at least a representative sample of job performance. Usually, this person is the employee's immediate supervisor.

---

[26] Barry J. Baroni, "The Legal Ramifications of Appraisal Systems," *Supervisory Management,* 27 (January 1982), pp. 41–42.

Situations that lessen the immediate supervisor's ability to appraise performance objectively include those found in matrix organizations. In these firms, certain employees may be formally assigned to a supervisor but actually work under various project managers. Also, a supervisor who is in a new position may have insufficient knowledge of employee performance initially. In such instances, multiple raters may be used.

In order to ensure consistency, appraisers must be well trained. Training should emphasize that performance appraisal is a significant component of every manager's job. Training should also stress that a primary task of the supervisor is to ensure that subordinates understand what is expected of them. In addition, training itself is an ongoing process. It responds to changes in the appraisal system and to the fact that supervisors, for various reasons, may deviate from established procedures. Training should cover how to rate employees and conduct appraisal interviews and should include written instructions. These instructions should be rather detailed and stress the importance of making objective and unbiased ratings.

It has been suggested that nonsupervisory employees should also receive a set of the performance appraisal instructions. The major benefits cited for this approach include not only the provision of a performance management and planning tool, but also a legal safeguard to deal with potentially disgruntled employees.[27]

Open Communication

Most employees have a strong need to know how well they are performing. A good appraisal system provides highly desired feedback on a continuing basis. A worthwhile goal is to avoid surprises during the appraisal interview. Even though the interview presents an excellent opportunity for both parties to exchange ideas, it should not serve as a substitute for day-to-day communication. On the other hand, a performance appraisal system should allow immediate access to information on key employees. The PA also alerts managers to individuals who may be risking termination if they do not improve their performance. The system permits HR professionals to take proactive measures, such as providing training or transfers to salvage those who are not performing satisfactorily.[28]

Employee Access to Results

Consider the following scenario:

> Now let's imagine you are in a bowling alley where drapes are hanging midway down the alley. You can't see the pins and you never know how many pins your ball knocked over. Your coach is

---

[27] Beverly L. Kaye and Shelley Krantz, "Preparing Employees: The Missing Link in Performance Appraisal Training," *Personnel*, 59 (May–June 1982), p. 24.

[28] Peter M. Tafti, "Face to Face," p. 71.

standing behind you saying, "You're doing fine, just keep bowling." You keep rolling the balls and the coach keeps encouraging
you. But, you don't know the score. You don't really know how
well you are doing. At the end of the game, the scorekeeper
informs you that you have set a new record—for low score. You
are flabbergasted and disappointed. You're out. You are off the
team. Tough luck.[29]

Obviously, this anecdote does not describe the best way to manage a
bowling team or, for that matter, any other type of organization. Yet, in too
many instances the same kinds of mistakes are made when employees are
not fully informed of the rules of the game and are not provided adequate
feedback on their performance. Such a situation is uncomfortable at best
and, at worst, totally demoralizing and defeating.

As a result of the Federal Privacy Act of 1974, employees of the federal
government and federal contractors must be given access to their employment files, which may include performance appraisal data. While this
requirement does not currently apply to all employees in the private sector,
there are good reasons—aside from the threat of broader legislative coverage—for allowing such access. Most importantly, employees will not trust
a system they don't understand. Secrecy will invariably breed suspicion and
thereby thwart efforts to obtain employee participation.

For the many appraisal systems that are designed to improve performance, withholding appraisal results would be unthinkable. Employees
simply could not perform better without having access to this information.
Also, permitting employees to review appraisal results allows them to
detect any errors that may have been made. Or the employee may simply
disagree with the evaluation and may want to challenge it formally.

Due Process

In connection with a formal challenge, ensuring due process is vital. A
formal procedure should be developed—if one doesn't exist—to permit employees to appeal appraisal results that they consider inaccurate or unfair.
They must have a procedure for pursuing their grievances and having them
addressed objectively.

A review of court cases makes it clear that perfect appraisals are not
expected from employers. Nor is it anticipated that supervisory discretion
should be removed from the process. However, the courts normally require
the following four conditions:

1. *Either the absence of adverse impact on members of certain groups or
   validation of the process.* As with the selection process, an unvali-
   dated performance appraisal system has the potential to have a negative impact on members of certain groups.

---

[29] Largent Parks, Jr., "Appraising Personnel Appraisals," *National Underwriters* (August 27,
1983), p. 13.

2. *A review process that prevents one manager from directing or controlling a subordinate's career.* The performance appraisal should be reviewed and approved by someone or some group higher in the organization.
3. *The rater must have personal knowledge and contact with the employee's job performance.* This requirement may appear to be too obvious, but there are instances in which the rater does not have an adequate opportunity to observe employee performance. When this type of situation exists, the chances of a valid appraisal are virtually nonexistent.
4. *The use of formal appraisal criteria that limit the manager's discretion.* A system is needed that forces managers to base evaluations on certain preestablished criteria.

■ LEGAL IMPLICATIONS

An estimated 30 million workers had their performance formally appraised during a single year in the 1980s. Thus appraisals are widely used in industry and government. Yet, the process still contains many potential sources for error.[30] Mistakes in appraising performance can have serious repercussions in various areas of human resource management, such as the improper allocation of money for merit increases. In addition, mistakes can result in costly legal action brought against a firm. In settling cases, courts have held employers liable for back pay, court costs, and other costs related to training and promoting certain group members. The four most common forms of human resource actions that lead to Age Discrimination in Employment Act (ADEA) complaints are promotions, layoffs, retirements, and discharges. A study that analyzed 26 ADEA cases decided in federal courts (in which employee appraisal had been a determinative factor) found that employers with formal appraisal systems were successful 73 percent of the time. However, employers who did not use a formal system were successful defendants only 40 percent of the time.[31]

The courts continue to emphasize the requirement of specifically relating performance appraisal factors to actual job content. In *Wade v. Mississippi Cooperative Extension Service,* the 5th Circuit Court ruled that in a performance appraisal system, general characteristics such as "leadership, public acceptance, attitude toward people, appearance and grooming, personal conduct, outlook on life, ethical habits, resourcefulness, capacity for growth, mental alertness, and loyalty to organization" are "susceptible to partiality and to the personal taste, whim, or fancy of the evaluator." The court also held that such characteristics are "patently subjective in form and obviously susceptible to completely subjective treatment" by those

---

[30] N. B. Winstanley, William H. Holley, and Hubert S. Field, "Will Your Performance Appraisal System Hold Up in Court?" *Personnel,* 59 (January–February 1982), pp. 59–64.

[31] Michael H. Schuster and Christopher S. Miller, "Performance Appraisal and the Age Discrimination in Employment Act," *Personnel Administrator,* 29 (March 1984), pp. 48–57.

conducting the appraisals. The key point in this decision is that the trait rating systems are generally suspect because they have no job-content basis. The burden of proof for demonstrating the relationship between a performance appraisal system and actual job content rests entirely with the employer.[32] One survey, however, indicated that fewer than 50 percent of the companies responding considered the *Uniform Guidelines* when designing their performance appraisal systems.[33]

While it is unlikely that any appraisal system will be totally immune to legal challenge, systems that possess the characteristics previously discussed are apparently more legally defensible. At the same time, they can provide a more effective means for achieving performance appraisal goals.

■ THE APPRAISAL INTERVIEW

The Achilles' heel of the entire evaluation process is the appraisal interview itself.[34] In spite of the problems involved, supervisors usually conduct a formal appraisal interview at the end of an employee's appraisal period. This interview is essential if employee development is to be achieved. However, effective performance appraisal systems require more than this single interview. Rather, the supervisor should continually discuss with the employee his or her responsibility for development and improvement and emphasize the manager's supportive role.

A successful appraisal interview requires structure so that both the supervisor and the subordinate will view it as a problem-solving rather than a fault-finding session. The supervisor should consider three basic purposes when planning an appraisal interview: discussing the employee's performance, assisting the employee in setting objectives, and suggesting means for achieving them.[35] For instance, a supervisor might rate a worker as average on the factor "quality of production." In the interview, the supervisor should discuss what reasonable improvement during the next appraisal period means. In suggesting ways to achieve a higher level objective, the supervisor might recommend specific methods. The interview should be scheduled soon after the end of the appraisal period. Employees usually know when their interview should take place, and their anxiety tends to increase when it is delayed. Interviews with top performers are often pleasant experiences. However, many supervisors are reluctant to meet face-to-face with poor performers. They tend to postpone these anxiety-provoking interviews.

The amount of time devoted to an appraisal interview varies considerably with company policy and the position of the evaluated employee.

---

[32] Donald L. Caruth, Robert M. Noe III, and R. Wayne Mondy, *Staffing the Contemporary Organization* (New York: Praeger Publishers, 1990) p. 58.

[33] Charles J. Fombrun and Robert J. Laud, "Strategic Issues," p. 27.

[34] C. O. Colvin, "Everything You Always Wanted to Know about Appraisal Discrimination," *Personnel Journal*, 60 (October 1981), pp. 758–759.

[35] Randall Brett and Alan J. Fredian, "Performance Appraisal: The System Is Not the Solution," *Personnel Administrator*, 26 (December 1981), p. 62.

Although costs must be considered, there is merit in conducting separate interviews for discussing (1) employee performance and development, and (2) pay increases. Many managers have learned that as soon as pay is mentioned in an interview it tends to dominate the conversation. For this reason, a rather common practice is to defer pay discussions. A brief interview for this purpose should be held within one or two weeks after the appraisal interview.

Conducting an appraisal interview is often one of management's more difficult tasks. It requires tact and patience on the part of the supervisor. Praise should be provided when warranted, but it can have only limited value if not clearly deserved. Criticism is especially difficult to give. So-called constructive criticism is often not perceived that way by the employee. Yet, it is difficult for a manager at any level to avoid criticism when conducting appraisal interviews. The supervisor should realize that all individuals have some deficiencies that may not be changed easily, if at all. Continued criticism may lead to frustration and have a damaging effect on employee development. Again, this possibility should not allow undesirable employee behavior to go unnoticed. However, discussions of sensitive issues should focus on the deficiency, not the person. Threats to the employee's self-esteem should be minimized whenever possible.[36]

A serious error that a supervisor sometimes makes is to surprise the subordinate by bringing up some past mistake or problem. For example, if an incident had not been previously discussed, it would be most inappropriate for the supervisor to state, "Two months ago, you failed to properly coordinate your plans for implementing the new accounts receivable procedure." Good management practice and common sense dictate that such situations be dealt with when they occur and not be saved for the appraisal interview.

The entire performance appraisal process should be a positive experience for the employee. In practice, however, it often is not. Negative feelings can often be traced to the appraisal interview and the manner in which it was conducted by the supervisor. Ideally, employees will leave the interview with positive feelings about the supervisor, the company, the job, and themselves. The prospects for improved performance will be bleak if the employee's ego is deflated. Past behavior can't be changed, but future performance can. Specific plans for the employee's development should be clearly outlined and mutually agreed on. Cessna Aircraft Company has developed several hints for supervisors that have been helpful in conducting appraisal interviews (see Figure 11-4).

■ ASSESSMENT CENTERS

Many employee performance appraisal systems evaluate an individual's past performance and at the same time attempt to assess his or her potential for advancement. Other organizations have developed a separate

---

[36] Donald Caruth, Bill Middlebrook, and Frank Rachel, "Performance Appraisals: Much More Than a Once-A-Year Task," *Supervisory Management,* 27 (September 1982), p. 33.

1. Give the employee a few days' notice of the discussion and its purpose. Encourage the employee to give some preparatory thought to his or her job performance and development plans. In some cases, have employees read their written performance evaluation prior to the meeting.

2. Prepare notes and use the completed performance appraisal form as a discussion guide so that each important topic will be covered. Be ready to answer questions employees may ask about why you appraised them as you did. Encourage your employees to ask questions.

3. Be ready to suggest specific developmental activities suitable to each employee's needs. When there are specific performance problems, remember to "attack the problem, not the person."

4. Establish a friendly, helpful, and purposeful tone at the outset of the discussion. Recognize that it is not unusual for you and your employee to be nervous about the discussion, and use suitable techniques to put you both more at ease.

5. Assure your employee that everyone on Cessna's management team is being evaluated so that opportunities for improvement and development will not be overlooked and each person's performance will be fully recognized.

6. Make sure that the session is truly a discussion. Encourage employees to talk about how they feel they are doing on the job, how they might improve, and what developmental activities they might undertake. Often an employee's viewpoints on these matters will be quite close to your own.

7. When your appraisal differs from the employee's, discuss these differences. Sometimes employees have hidden reasons for performing in a certain manner or using certain methods. This is an opportunity to find out if such reasons exist.

8. These discussions should contain both constructive compliments and constructive criticism. Be sure to discuss the employee's strengths as well as weaknesses. Your employees should have clear pictures of how you view their performance when the discussions are concluded.

9. Occasionally the appraisal interview will uncover strong emotions. This is one of the values of regular appraisals; they can bring out bothersome feelings so they can be dealt with honestly. The emotional dimension of managing is very important. Ignoring it can lead to poor performance. Deal with emotional issues when they arise because they block a person's ability to concentrate on other issues. Consult Personnel for help when especially strong emotions are uncovered.

10. Make certain that your employees fully understand your appraisal of their performance. Sometimes it helps to have an employee orally summarize the appraisal as he or she understands it. If there are any misunderstandings, they can be cleared up on the spot. Ask questions to make sure you have been fully understood.

11. Discuss the future as well as the past. Plan with the employee specific changes in performance or specific developmental activities that will allow fuller use of potential. Ask what you can do to help.

12. End the discussion on a positive, future-improvement-oriented note. You and your employee are a team, working toward the development of everyone involved.

FIGURE 11-4 | Suggestions for Conducting Appraisal Interviews

Source: Used with the permission of Cessna Aircraft Company.

approach for assessing potential. This process often takes place in what is appropriately referred to as an assessment center.

An **assessment center** requires employees to perform activities similar to those they might encounter in an actual job. These situational activity exercises are based on a thorough job analysis. The assessors usually observe the employees somewhere other than their normal workplace, over a certain period of time. The assessors selected are typically experienced managers who both participate in the exercises and evaluate performance. Assessment centers are used increasingly to (1) identify employees who have higher level management potential, (2) select first-line supervisors, and (3) determine employee developmental needs. Assessment centers are used by more than 1,000 organizations,[37] including small firms and large corporations, such as General Electric Company, J. C. Penney Company, Ford Motor Company, and AT&T. A typical schedule for G.E.'s supervisory assessment center (SAC) is shown in Table 11-3. The SAC program is used for selecting new employees and assessing the management potential of current employees. Note the number of exercises that are utilized in evaluating a participant's behavior.

An evaluation of the General Electric SAC process revealed the following:

> The SAC was based on a job analysis of a supervisor's job and is considered to have content validity.[38] The SAC provides all candidates an equal opportunity to demonstrate their skills and does not discriminate against any employee group. For example, a study of more than 1,000 candidates from fourteen company locations showed that the success ratios were acceptable for caucasians, minorities, and women. Those individuals who scored highest in the SAC are the same individuals who have subsequently received the greatest number of job promotions. Thus one area of predictive validity of the SAC was demonstrated.

As many as half a dozen assessors may evaluate each participant, as at General Electric. The participant's position in the organization often determines the amount of time spent in the center. First-line supervisory candidates may only spend a day or two, whereas more time may be needed for those being considered for middle-management and executive jobs. After the session is over, the participants return to their jobs, and the assessors prepare their evaluations. Interestingly, because the assessors are often not full-time members of the human resource development staff, they frequently gain further insight into how managers in their organization should function. And even though a primary purpose of assessment centers is to identify management potential, the J. C. Penney experience indicates that the "participants gain valuable insights into their own strengths,

---

[37] *General Electric Assessment Center Manual,* General Electric Company.

[38] Content validity is inherent in the assessment center process when the exercises developed are based on job analysis. This type of validity is acceptable according to the *Uniform Guidelines.*

TABLE 11-3 | Typical Schedule for General Electric Company's Supervisory Assessment Center

Day 1
Approximately four hours per candidate are required for the background interview and an in-basket exercise. The interview covers such traditional areas as work experience, educational background, and leadership experience. The in-basket exercise provides an opportunity for the individual to demonstrate how he or she would handle administrative problems including day-to-day "fire-fighting." All Day 1 activities are scheduled on an individual basis and are typically administered by persons in Employee Relations.
Day 2
An additional four hours are devoted to group and individual exercises. Group exercises related to reallocation of resources allow an individual's performance to be observed as the candidate solves problems in peer group situations. In the individual exercises each candidate assumes the role of a supervisor to handle four typical work-related problems. Six operating managers serve as the SAC staff for Day 2 activities. They observe and evaluate the performance of six candidates. The staff completes structured rating forms on each candidate's performance immediately following each exercise. After all exercises have been completed and the candidates dismissed, the staff conducts an overall evaluation of each individual's potential for a supervisory position. Over fifty pieces of data from each candidate's performance are reviewed along with information obtained from the interview. The staff then arrives at a consensus decision and a recommended course of action for each candidate.

Source: Used with permission of the General Electric Company.

weaknesses, and interests." These insights permit management and the individual to make plans for the employee's development.

Accurately assessing potential and evaluating performance are critical to productivity. Yet, systems poorly conceived or improperly implemented can actually impair employee performance. PA definitely presents management with a double-edged sword. However, as long as productivity must be improved and decisions made in such areas as pay increases, promotions, and transfers, organizations must strive for the best system possible.[39]

---

[39] Gary English, "Tuning Up for Performance Management," *Training and Development Journal,* 45 (April 1991), p. 56.

■ HUMAN RESOURCE DEVELOPMENT IN MULTINATIONAL CORPORATIONS

As we mentioned earlier, a key purpose of employee performance appraisal is human resource development. A firm's success and even survival depend on having competent and well-trained employees at every level of the organization. Performance appraisal systems serve the function of pointing out specific areas where training and development are needed. This role assumes even greater importance in the international arena. For example, human resource development needs are often quite different for multinational corporations. Career development is helped or hindered by the internal and external factors affecting the firm. The performance appraisal process should reflect the unique culture of the host country as well as the needs of the firm.

Human Resource Development

Only a few multinational corporations offer formal training programs to prepare people to live and work overseas. People who were regarded as superior employees have often failed because they were ill-equipped to cope with the complexities and dangers of intercultural management.[40] A review of placement decisions of some American multinational corporations found that they reported 30 percent of their placements to be mistakes—primarily because of the employees' failure to adjust properly to a new culture.[41] Companies that do offer training to expatriate employees generally provide training that is not comprehensive.[42] The duration of cross-cultural training programs tends to be relatively short, considering the amount of knowledge and skills that need to be taught. Also, spouses tend to be left out of whatever training is offered by the company. However, multinational corporations are beginning to study how different cultures communicate and work with each other.[43]

A major objective of intercultural training is to help people cope with unexpected events in a new culture. It is essential that the person chosen is suitable for cross-cultural work. The person with the most seniority or the person with the most technical competence may not have such skills.[44] An individual overwhelmed by a new culture will be unable to perform effectively. Moreover, someone who is poorly prepared may inadvertently

---

[40] Michael Berger, "Building Bridges Over the Cultural Rivers," *International Management,* 42 (July–August 1987), p. 61.

[41] P. Christopher Earley, "Intercultural Training for Managers: A Comparison of Documentary and Interpersonal Methods," *Academy of Management Journal,* 30, no. 4 (December 1987), p. 685.

[42] Mark E. Mendenhall, Edward Dunbar, and Gary R. Oddou, "Expatriate Selection, Training and Career-Pathing: A Review and Critique," *Human Resource Management,* 26 (Fall 1987), pp. 331–345.

[43] Michael Berger, "Building Bridges," p. 61.

[44] Prabhu Guptara, "Searching the Organization for the Cross-Cultural Operators," *International Management,* 41 (August 1986), p. 40.

offend or alienate a foreign host and perhaps jeopardize existing long-term relations with a host country.[45] Training should be sufficient to permit the person selected (and spouse) to understand the new culture and adapt to anticipated roles.[46]

Career Development

Foreign assignments have often been thought of as providing career advancement opportunities. However, the relationship between expatriation and career development and advancement is often unclear. The impetus for overseas assignment seems to come more from meeting immediate human resource needs than creating an integrated career development strategy for future corporate executives.[47]

Whatever the case, without generous support during the overseas assignment, employees can become demoralized, frustrated, and anxious.[48] Despite a company's intention to provide career advancement opportunities, skilled managers assigned to foreign operations may ultimately perceive that their careers have suffered. Some managers have returned from foreign assignments to find no job available, or they have been given jobs that do not utilize the skills they obtained overseas. To solve this problem, a "godfather" system has been set up in companies such as Control Data Corporation.[49] Before someone leaves on assignment, a specific executive is appointed as the godfather to look after the person's interests while he or she is in a foreign country and to help the person achieve a smooth transition upon returning home. A repatriation plan is worked out, including the duration of the assignment and the job to which the appointee will return. Ordinarily the godfather is the person's future boss. During the overseas assignment, the individual is kept informed of major events occurring in the unit that he or she will be assigned to in the future. Not only is a logical career plan worked out, there is no feeling of being lost in the vast international shuffle of the company.

Some repatriated managers say that the overseas assignment is a haphazard, ill-planned affair that usually accompanies vertical advancement. Yet upon return, many have difficulty readjusting to domestic operations, have less self-esteem, and, on occasion, have to look for a new job. Human resource professionals who are unaware of the challenges facing the repatriated manager may unknowingly allow career obstacles to persist for the expatriate.

---

[45] P. Christopher Earley, "Intercultural Training for Managers," p. 685.

[46] *Ibid.*

[47] Mark E. Mendenhall, Edward Dunbar, and Gary R. Oddou, "Expatriate Selection, Training and Career-Pathing," p. 331.

[48] Phillip R. Harris, "Employees Abroad: Maintain the Corporate Connection," *Personnel Journal,* 65 (August 1986), p. 108.

[49] David M. Noer, "Integrating Foreign Service Employees to Home Organization: The Godfather Approach," *Personnel Journal,* 53 (January 1974), pp. 45–50.

There is a need to assist the expatriate manager in career development. By putting in place policies and procedures toward that end, an organization can (1) more efficiently manage human resources globally and (2) encourage more employees to accept foreign assignments. The fundamental nature of such a system must be comprehensive; that is, the emphasis should not be solely on predeparture activities. The ideal international career management program should assess (and give feedback on and preparation for) career and skill issues prior to departure, during the assignment, and subsequent to repatriation.[50]

Performance Appraisal

Failure to develop highly flexible standards for performance evaluations of the expatriate manager may result in the manager viewing his or her role as undefined and dysfunctional. Present performance evaluations focus on personality traits, communication skills, belief in mission, and organizational structure, but fail to focus on the overall performance of an expatriate manager after arrival in a host country.[51] The performance evaluation system may need to be completely rethought and rewritten with regard to individuals working for multinational corporations.

SUMMARY

Performance appraisal is a system that provides a periodic review and evaluation of an individual's job performance. The overriding purpose of performance appraisal is to improve the organization's effectiveness. Identification of specific objectives provides the starting point for the performance appraisal process. Because an appraisal system cannot serve all purposes, a firm should select those specific objectives it desires to achieve. Next, workers must understand what is expected of them on the job. Supervisors normally discuss with employees the major duties contained in their job descriptions.

Work performance is observed and periodically evaluated against previously established job performance standards. The results of the evaluation are then discussed with the workers. The performance evaluation interview serves to reestablish job requirements in the employee's mind. The process is dynamic and ongoing. The human resource department is responsible for designing and overseeing the performance appraisal pro-

---

[50] Mark E. Mendenhall, Edward Dunbar, and Gary R. Oddou, "Expatriate Selection, Training and Career-Pathing," p. 331.

[51] Gurudutt M. Baliga and James C. Baker, "Multinational Corporate Policies for Expatriate Managers: Selection, Training, Evaluation," *SAM Advanced Management Journal,* 50 (Autumn 1985), p. 36.

cess. The person who actually conducts performance appraisals varies from company to company. However, direct participation by line management is necessary for success. The actual rating of the employee may be done by the immediate supervisor (most commonly), subordinates, peers, a group, the employee (self-appraisal), or a combination of these methods.

Performance appraisal methods include (1) rating scales, (2) critical incidents, (3) essay, (4) work standards, (5) ranking, (6) forced distribution, (7) forced-choice and weighted checklist performance reports, (8) behaviorally anchored rating scales, and (9) management by objectives. Problems associated with these performance appraisal methods include lack of objectivity, halo error, leniency, strictness, central tendency, recent behavior bias, personal bias, and the judgmental role of the evaluator ("playing God").

At the end of the appraisal period, the evaluator usually conducts a formal appraisal interview with the employee. The key to a successful interview is to structure it so that both the manager and subordinate will approach it as a problem-solving, rather than a fault-finding, session. This interview is essential for achieving employee development.

Certain appraisal system practices have successfully withstood legal challenges. Because improperly constituted systems can result in costly legal action against a firm, appraisal systems should be based on job content.

Many employee performance appraisal systems evaluate past performance and at the same time attempt to assess potential for advancement. Other organizations have developed a separate approach for assessing potential—the assessment center. An assessment center requires employees to perform activities similar to those that they might confront in an actual job. Assessment centers are being used increasingly for (1) identifying employees who have higher level management potential, (2) selecting first-line supervisors, and (3) determining employees' developmental needs.

Human resource development requirements are somewhat different for multinational corporations. Training and development, career development, and performance appraisal needs must be carefully evaluated to ensure proper reentry into the domestic workforce.

Questions for Review

1. State and briefly discuss the basic purposes of performance appraisal.
2. What are the basic steps in the performance appraisal process?
3. Many different people can conduct performance appraisals. Briefly describe the various alternatives.
4. Briefly describe each of the following methods of performance appraisal:
   a. Rating scales
   b. Critical incidents
   c. Essay
   d. Work standards
   e. Ranking
   f. Forced distribution
   g. Forced-choice and weighted checklist performance reports
   h. Behaviorally anchored rating scales
   i. Management by objectives
5. What are the various problems associated with performance appraisal? Briefly describe each.
6. Why should employee performance and development be discussed separately from pay increases?
7. Describe how an assessment center could be used as a means of performance appraisal.
8. What are the characteristics of an effective appraisal system?

Terms for Review

Performance appraisal (PA)
Group appraisal
Rating scales method
Critical incident method
Essay method
Work standards method
Ranking method
Paired comparison
Forced distribution method
Forced-choice performance report

Weighted checklist performance report
Behaviorally anchored rating scale (BARS) method
Halo error
Leniency
Strictness
Central tendency
Assessment center

INCIDENT 1   ▪ Objectives? ▪

It was performance appraisal time again and Alex Funderburk knew that he would receive a low evaluation. Janet Stevens, Alex's boss, opened the appraisal interview with the comment, "The sales department had a good increase this quarter. Also, departmental expenses are down considerably. But, we are nowhere near accomplishing the ambitious objectives you and I set last quarter."

"I know," said Alex. "I thought we were going to make it, though. We would have, too, if we had received that big Simpson order, and if I could have gotten us on the computer a little earlier in the quarter."

"I agree with you, Alex," said Janet. "Do you think we were just too ambitious or do you think there was some way we could have made the Simpson sale and speeded up the computerization process?" "Yes," replied Alex, "we could have received the Simpson order this quarter. I just made a couple of concessions to Simpson, and their purchasing manager tells me he can issue the order next week. The delay with the computer was caused by a thoughtless mistake I made. I won't let that happen again."

The discussion continued for about thirty minutes longer. Alex discovered that Janet was going to mark him very high in all areas despite his failure to accomplish the goals they had set.

Prior to the meeting, Janet had planned to suggest that the unattained goals for last period be set as the new objectives for the coming quarter. After she and Alex had discussed matters, however, they both decided to establish new, somewhat higher objectives. As he was about to leave the meeting, Alex said, "Janet, I feel good about these objectives, but I don't believe we have more than a 50 percent chance of accomplishing them." "I believe you can do it," replied Janet. She continued, "If you knew for sure that you could achieve these goals, then they wouldn't be high enough." "I see what you mean," said Alex, as he left the office.

Questions

1. What was wrong or right with Janet's appraisal of Alex's performance?
2. Should the new objectives be higher or lower than they are? Explain.

INCIDENT 2   ▪   Performance Appraisal?   ▪

As the production supervisor for Sweeny Electronics, Mike Mahoney was generally well regarded by most of his subordinates. Mike was an easygoing individual who tried to help his employees any way he could. If a worker needed a small loan until payday, he would dig into his pocket with no questions asked. Should an employee need some time off to attend to a personal problem, he would not dock the individual's pay; rather, he would take up the slack himself until the worker returned.

Everything had been going smoothly, at least until the last performance appraisal period. One of Mike's workers, Bill Overstreet, had been experiencing a large number of personal problems for the past year. Bill's wife had been sick much of the time and her medical expenses were high. Bill's son had a speech impediment and the doctors had recommended a special clinic. Bill, who had already borrowed the limit the bank would loan, had become upset and despondent over his general circumstances.

When it was time for Bill's annual performance appraisal, Mike decided he was going to do as much as possible to help him. Although Bill could not be considered more than an average worker, Mike rated him outstanding in virtually every category. Because the firm's compensation system was tied heavily to the performance appraisal, Bill would be eligible for a merit increase of 10 percent in addition to a regular cost of living raise.

Mike explained to Bill why he was giving him such high ratings, and Bill acknowledged that his performance had really been no better than average. Bill was very grateful and expressed this to Mike. As Bill left the office he was excitedly looking forward to telling his friends about what a wonderful boss he had. Seeing Bill smile as he left gave Mike a warm feeling.

Questions

1. From Sweeny Electronics' standpoint, what difficulties might Mike Mahoney's performance appraisal practices create?
2. What can Mike do now to diminish the negative impact of his evaluation of Bill?

DEVELOPING HRM SKILLS

Performance appraisal (PA) is an essential aspect of human resource management. It is a formal system that provides a periodic review and evaluation of an individual's job performance. Developing an effective performance appraisal system is difficult. However, some managers do not take PA as seriously as they should. Such attitudes are counterproductive, and they frequently lower individual and group productivity.

Larry Beavers, supervisor of the electrical department, has a busy day scheduled, but he needs to squeeze in the last of his performance appraisals. They are due today, and he has only got one more signature to get. Upon arriving for work he thinks, "I hate doing performance appraisals. It is the worst part of a supervisor's job. But, it does allow me to point out deficiencies that the workers must be aware of if they are to improve their performance. The guy I'm appraising today has always exceeded his quotas, he is very helpful to the workers he likes, and he is excellent on the new computerized production setup; but if he wants to advance he will need to change his behavior. He seems to have problems working with the females on the line, and he doesn't seem to be very open-minded. Also, on September 23 he failed to secure his work area. This guy really

has problems. Maybe our talk will do some good; either way I need to get this done. On the positive side, this is the last performance appraisal until next year."

Today is the day that Alex Martin gets his performance appraisal, and he is excited about it. Before the meeting with Larry, his supervisor, he thinks, "I've been very good on the new computerized setup, and very helpful to my friends on the line, and this will help me get my promotion. I expect that the boss saved my performance appraisal for last to praise my performance and recommend me for that promotion that I've been deserving for some time. I've been passed over for promotion for too long, this has been a great year for me, and this will cap off a year of excellent performance."

When these two get together it will be a meeting of two quite different minds, and in all likelihood the meeting will be filled with disagreement, dissatisfaction, and maybe even hard feelings. This exercise will require two of you to actively participate. One person will play the supervisor conducting the performance appraisal and the other will be the evaluated employee. Only two can play; the rest of you should observe carefully. Your instructor will provide the participants with additional information necessary to complete the exercise.

REFERENCES

Caruth, Donald L., Robert M. Noe III, and R. Wayne Mondy. *Staffing the Contemporary Organization.* (New York: Praeger Publishers, 1990).

English, Gary. "Tuning Up for Performance Management." *Training and Development Journal,* 45 (April 1991), pp. 56–60.

Fox, William M. "Improving Performance Appraisal Systems." *National Productivity Review,* 7 (Winter 1987–88), pp. 20–27.

Harris, Phillip R. "Employees Abroad: Maintain the Corporate Connection." *Personnel Journal,* 86 (August 1986), pp. 108–110.

Holley, William H., and Hubert S. Field. "Will Your Performance Appraisal System Hold Up in Court?" *Personnel,* 59 (January–February 1982), pp. 59–64.

"How Johnsonville Shares Profits on the Basis of Performance." *Harvard Business Review,* 68 (November–December 1990), p. 74.

Knippen, Jay T., and Thad B. Green. "Boost Performance Through Appraisals." *Business Credit,* 92 (November–December 1990), p. 27.

Lee, C. "Increasing Performance Appraisal Effectiveness: Matching Task Types, Appraisal Process, and Rater Training." *Academy of Management Review,* 10 (April 1985), pp. 322–331.

Lee, Charles. "Smoothing Out Appraisal Systems." *HRMagazine,* 35 (March 1990), pp. 72–74, 76.

Longenecker, Clinton, and Dean Ludwig. "Ethical Dilemmas in Performance Appraisal Revisited." *Journal of Business Ethics,* 9 (December 1990), pp. 961–969.

Matejka, J. Kenneth, and Richard J. Dunsing. "Great Expectations." *Management World,* 16 (January 1987), pp. 16–19.

Mendenhall, Mark E., Edward Dunbar, and Gary R. Oddou. "Expatriate Selection, Training and Career-Pathing: A Review and Critique." *Human Resource Management,* 26 (Fall 1987), pp. 331–345.

Miller, Christopher S., Joan A. Kaspin, and Michael H. Schuster. "The Impact of Performance Appraisal Methods on Age Discrimination in Employment Act Cases." *Personnel Psychology,* 43 (Autumn 1990), pp. 555–578.

Mondy, R. Wayne, Robert M. Noe III, and Robert E. Edwards. "What the Staffing Function Entails." *Personnel,* 63 (April 1986), pp. 55–58.

Odiorne, George S. "The Trend Toward the Quarterly Performance Review." *Business Horizons,* 33 (July–August 1990), pp. 38–41.

Rich, Joseph R. and Beth C. Florin-Thuma. "Rewarding Employees in an Environment of Fewer Promotions." *Pension World,* 26 (November 1990), pp. 16–17.

Sahl, Robert J. "Design Effective Performance Appraisals." *Personnel Journal,* 69 (October 1990), pp. 53–54, 56, 58, 60.

Segal, Jonathan A. "Could Peer Review Have Saved Marie Antoinette's Head?" *Personnel Administrator,* 34 (June 1989), pp. 172, 174, 176, 178, 180.

Tafti, Peter M. "Face to Face." *Training and Development Journal,* 44 (November 1990), pp. 66–71.

Weekley, Jeff A., and Joseph A. Gier. "Ceilings in the Reliability and Validity of Performance Ratings: The Case of Expert Raters." *Academy of Management Journal,* 32 (March 1989), pp. 213–222.

"What Does Your Boss Really Think of You?" *Supervision,* 51 (December 1990), p. 10.

P·A·R·T T·H·R·E·E

CASE III

Parma Cycle Company: Training the Workforce

As the September 1992 date for the new plant opening drew near, Mary Higgins, director of employee development at Parma Cycle Company in Parma, Ohio, grew increasingly nervous. With only six months to train the workforce for the new Clarksdale, Mississippi, plant, Mary knew that there was little room for error.

Mary had already arranged to lease a building near the Clarksdale factory site, and some of the machinery for the new plant was being installed in that building for training purposes. Most of the machinery was similar to that already being used at Parma, and Mary had selected trainers from among the supervisory staff at the Parma plant. One machine, however, a robotized frame assembler, was entirely new. The assembler was being purchased from a Japanese firm. Mary had sent two operators to train in the Japanese factory, and they were both back.

In connection with all this activity, Mary had personally made two trips to Clarksdale. She had also retained a training consultant, a management professor from the University of Mississippi. The training consultant had agreed to help Mary plan the training program and to evaluate the program as it went along. It was at the consultant's suggestion that Mary decided to use a combination of vestibule training and classroom lectures in developing a trained workforce prior to factory start-up time. In the past, Parma Cycle had used on-the-job training almost exclusively. This approach wasn't feasible, she felt, at the new plant.

As Mary was thinking about how short the time was, the phone rang. It was the human resource director, Jesse Heard, telling her that he was ready for their meeting. When she got to his office, she found him studying a training report she had prepared a few days earlier. "Mary," said Jesse, "It looks like you have things well under control for the Clarksdale plant. But I don't see anything here about training the workers who are going to be transferred down from this plant." "Well," said Mary, "they have all been working in bicycle manufacture for quite a while. I thought it might not be necessary to have any formal training for them." "That's true," said Jesse, "but most of them will be taking different jobs when they move to Clarksdale." "I'll get on it right away," said Mary.

"What are we going to do about supervisory training at the Clarksdale plant?" asked Jesse. Mary replied, "I think we'll use the same system we use here for the long haul. We'll bring our supervisors up through the ranks and have quarterly off-site seminars. To start, the supervisors who move down from Parma can help train the others." Jesse asked, "What do you think about bringing the supervisors hired in Clarksdale up here for a few days to help them learn how we do things?" "That's a good idea," said Mary. "We can pair them off with some of our better people at Parma."

"That won't help us with performance evaluations, Mary," said Jesse. "You know we're going to use a different system down there. We've decided to use management by objectives down to the supervisory level and a new three-item rating scale for the workers." "I know," answered Mary. "I'd planned classroom training on that beginning the month after start-up at the Clarksdale plant. I'm going to conduct those sessions myself. Because the performance scores will be used to allocate incentive bonuses, I want to make sure they are consistently assigned."

"Mary," said Jesse, "I'm really impressed with the way you are taking charge of our training effort for the Clarksdale plant. Just keep up the good work." "Thank you, Jesse," said Mary. "I'll get back to you next week on the training I recommend for the workers who will transfer down from Parma."

Questions

1. Describe how an untrained person hired in Clarksdale could become a competent machine operator by the time the new plant opens.
2. Do you think Mary needed the training consultant? Why or why not?
3. What do you think of Mary's idea to have the supervisors for the new plant trained by those transferred from Ohio? Explain your answer.

P·A·R·T F·O·U·R

COMPENSATION AND BENEFITS

Human Resource
Research

Human Resource
Planning,
Recruitment, and
Selection

Human Resource
Development

Human
Resource
Management

Employee and
Labor Relations

Safety and
Health

Compensation
and Benefits

CHAPTER 12

FINANCIAL COMPENSATION

CHAPTER OBJECTIVES

1. Define *compensation* and explain the concept of compensation equity.
2. Describe the organization and the labor market as determinants of financial compensation.
3. Define *job evaluation* and describe the basic job evaluation methods.
4. Describe the employee as a determinant of financial compensation and explain the factors associated with job pricing.
5. Describe the compensation issues of comparable worth, pay secrecy, and pay compression.

Earl Lewis and his wife are full of excitement and anticipation as they leave their home for a shopping trip. Earl recently found a job after several weeks of unemployment, and the paycheck he received today will enable them to make a down payment on a much needed refrigerator.

Inez Scoggin's anxiety over scheduled minor surgery was somewhat relieved. Her supervisor has assured her that 80 percent of her medical and hospitalization costs will be covered by her firm's health insurance plan.

Trig Ekeland, executive director of the local YMCA, returns home dead tired from his job each evening no earlier than six o'clock. His salary is small compared to the salaries of many other local managers who have similar responsibilities. Yet, Trig is an exceptionally happy person who believes that his work with youth, civic leaders, and other members of the community is extremely important and worthwhile.

Joanne Abrahamson has been employed by a large manufacturing firm for eight years. Although her pay is not what she would like it to be, her job in the accounts payable department enables her to have contact with some of her best friends. She likes her supervisor and considers the overall working environment to be great. Joanne would not trade jobs with anyone she knows.

Compensation and benefits are obviously important to Earl Lewis and Inez Scoggin, as they are to most employees. However, for Trig and Joanne, other factors in a total compensation package assume even greater importance. These components include a pleasant work environment and job satisfaction. Because it has many elements, compensation administration is one of the most difficult and challenging areas confronting human resource professionals.

We begin this chapter with an overview of compensation and an explanation of compensation equity. Next, we discuss determinants of individual financial compensation. We then present the organization, the labor market, and the job as determinants of financial compensation. Next, we address job evaluation and the employee as determinants of financial compensation. We devote the final portion of the chapter to job pricing and other compensation issues. We will discuss benefits, as well as nonfinancial factors, in Chapter 13.

■ COMPENSATION: AN OVERVIEW

Compensation refers to every type of reward that individuals receive in return for their labor. The components of a total compensation program are shown in Figure 12-1. **Direct financial compensation** consists of the pay that a person receives in the form of wages, salaries, bonuses, and commissions. Earl Lewis has just received direct financial compensation in the form of his paycheck. **Indirect financial compensation** (benefits) includes all financial rewards that are not included in direct compensation. Inez Scoggin will receive indirect financial compensation because her company provides for 80 percent of all medical and hospital costs. As you can see in Figure 12-1, this form of compensation includes a wide variety of rewards that are normally received indirectly by the employee.

Nonfinancial compensation consists of the satisfaction that a person receives from the job itself or from the psychological and/or physical environment in which the person works. Trig Ekeland and Joanne Abrahamson are receiving important forms of nonfinancial compensation. Trig is extremely satisfied with the job he performs. This type of nonfinancial compensation consists of the satisfaction received from performing meaningful job-related tasks. Joanne's job permits her to have contact with close friends. This form of nonfinancial compensation involves the psychological and/or physical environment in which the person works.

All such rewards comprise a total compensation program. People have different reasons for working, and the most appropriate compensation package depends on those reasons. When individuals are responsible for providing food, shelter, and clothing for their families, money may well be the most important reward. However, some people work many hours each day, receive little pay, and yet love their work. To a large degree, adequate compensation is in the mind of the receiver. It is often more than the financial compensation received in the form of a paycheck.

■ COMPENSATION EQUITY

Organizations must attract, motivate, and retain competent employees. In doing so, firms strive for equity in their compensation systems. **Equity** is workers' perceptions that they are being treated fairly. Compensation must

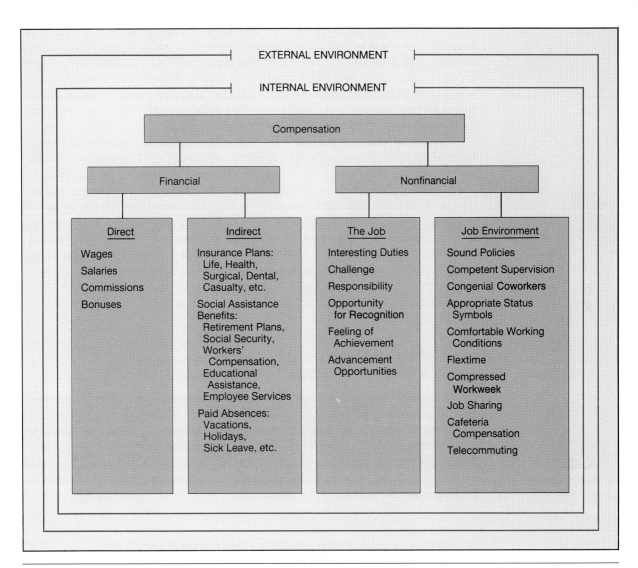

FIGURE 12-1 | Components of a Total Compensation Program

be fair to all parties concerned and be perceived as fair.[1] When chief executives are paid in excess of $26 million in one year[2] and receive huge bonuses along with "golden parachutes," serious questions arise as to what constitutes fairness within an organization.

External equity exists when a firm's employees are paid comparably to workers who perform similar jobs in other firms. Compensation surveys

---

[1] Thomas R. Horton, "80s Style Compensation," *Credit and Financial Management,* 89 (November 1987), p. 10.

[2] "Who Made the Most—and Why," *Business Week* (May 2, 1988), p. 51.

enable organizations to determine the extent to which external equity is present. **Internal equity** exists when employees are paid according to the relative value of their jobs within an organization. Job evaluation is a primary means for determining internal equity. **Employee equity** exists when individuals performing similar jobs for the same firm are paid according to factors unique to the employee. The most common factor is employee performance, as determined by performance appraisal.

Inequity in any category can be the source of severe morale problems. Regarding employee equity, for example, suppose that two workers in the same firm are performing similar jobs and one employee is far superior to the other in performance. If both workers receive equal raises, employee equity does not exist and the more productive employee is likely to be unhappy. Many workers are very concerned with pay equity, both internal and external. From an employee relations perspective, internal pay equity is more important than external equity. Employees simply have more information in this area, which they use to form perceptions of equity.[3] However, if an organization is to remain viable, it must be competitive in the labor market, and external equity must be a prominent consideration.

■ DETERMINANTS OF INDIVIDUAL FINANCIAL COMPENSATION

Compensation theory has never been able to provide a completely satisfactory answer to what an individual is worth. While there is no scientific approach available, a number of relevant factors are typically used to determine individual pay. These determinants are shown in Figure 12-2. The organization, the labor market, the job, and the employee all have an impact on job pricing and the ultimate determination of an individual's financial compensation.[4]

■ THE ORGANIZATION AS A DETERMINANT OF FINANCIAL COMPENSATION

Managers tend to view financial compensation as both an expense and an asset. It is an expense in the sense that it reflects the cost of labor. In service industries, for example, labor costs account for more than 50 percent of all expenses. However, financial compensation is an asset when it induces employees to put forth their best efforts and to remain in their jobs. Compensation programs have the potential to influence employee work behavior, encouraging workers to be more productive.[5] Improved perfor-

---

[3] George J. Meng, "Link Pay to Job Evaluation," *Personnel Journal,* 69 (March 1990), p. 104.

[4] Edward J. Giblin, Geoffrey A. Wiegman, and Frank Sanfilippo, "Bringing Pay Up To Date," *Personnel,* 67 (November 1990), p. 17.

[5] George T. Milkovich and Jerry M. Newman, *Compensation,* 3rd ed. (Homewood, Ill.: Richard D. Irwin, Inc., 1990), p. 3.

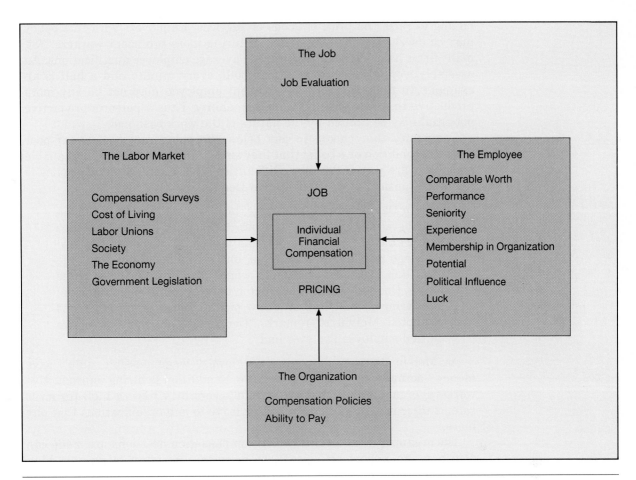

FIGURE 12-2 | Primary Determinants of Individual Financial Compensation

mance, increased productivity, and lower turnover are sought by all managers, which accounts for the serious attention compensation receives from top management.

Corporate culture has a major influence on an individual's financial compensation. An organization often establishes—formally or informally—compensation policies that determine whether it will be a pay leader or a pay follower, or strive for an average position in the labor market. **Pay leaders** are those organizations that pay higher wages and salaries than competing firms. Such organizations expect to have lower per unit labor costs. They feel that they will be able to attract high-quality, productive employees. Higher paying firms usually attract more and better qualified applicants than do lower paying companies in the same industry.

The **going rate** is the average pay that most employers provide for the same job in a particular area or industry. Many organizations have a policy that calls for paying the going rate. In such firms, management believes that it can employ qualified people and still remain competitive by not having to raise the price of goods or services. Employers with this policy may be overlooking the possibility of hiring more proficient workers. Yet, many firms have jobs that require only average employee qualifications. An assembly worker who tightens four bolts every minute and a half is an example. In this situation, an excellent employee may not be any more productive than one with only average ability. Thus a person's productive potential may be limited by the nature of the work assigned.

Companies that choose to pay below the going rate because of poor financial condition or a belief that they simply do not require highly capable employees are **pay followers.** Difficulties often occur when this policy is followed. Consider the case of Melvin Denney.

> Melvin Denney managed a large, but financially strapped farming operation in the Southwest. Although no formal policies had been established, Melvin had a practice of paying the lowest wage possible. For example, one of his farmhands, George McMillan, was paid minimum wage. During a period of three weeks, George wrecked the tractor, severely damaged a combine, and stripped the gears in a new pickup truck. George's actions prompted Melvin to remark, "George is the most expensive darned employee I've ever had."

As Melvin discovered, paying the lowest wage possible didn't save money—actually, it was quite expensive. In addition to hiring unproductive workers, organizations that are pay followers may have a high turnover rate as their most qualified employees leave to join organizations that pay more.

The organizational level in which compensation decisions are made can also have an impact on pay. These decisions are often made at a high management level to ensure consistency. However, there are advantages to making pay decisions at lower levels where better information may exist regarding employee performance. Top-level executives err when they make decisions that should be handled at lower levels.

An organization's assessment of its ability to pay is also an important factor in determining pay levels. Financially successful firms tend to provide higher than average compensation.[6] However, an organization's financial strength establishes only the upper limit of what it will pay. To arrive at a specific pay level, management must consider other factors.

■ THE LABOR MARKET AS A DETERMINANT OF FINANCIAL COMPENSATION

Potential employees located within the geographical area from which employees are recruited comprise the **labor market.** Labor markets for some jobs extend far beyond the locality of a firm's operations. Human resource

---

[6] David W. Belcher and Thomas J. Atchison, *Compensation Administration,* 2nd ed. (Englewood Cliffs, N.J.: Prentice-Hall, 1987), p. 127.

management of an aerospace firm in Seattle, for example, may be concerned about the labor market for engineers in Wichita or Orlando. Managerial and professional employees are often recruited from a wide geographical area. In fact, nationwide recruitment isn't unusual for certain skills.

Moreover, pay for jobs within these markets may vary considerably. Secretarial jobs, for example, may carry an average salary of $26,000 per year in a large, urban community but only $16,000 or less in a small, rural town. Compensation managers must be aware of these differences in order to compete successfully for employees. The going wage, or prevailing rate, is an important guide in determining pay. Many employees view it as the standard for judging the fairness of their firm's compensation practices.

Compensation Survey

Large organizations routinely conduct compensation surveys to determine prevailing pay rates within labor markets. These surveys provide the low, high, and average salaries for a given position. They give a good sense of what other companies are paying employees in various jobs. A Bureau of National Affairs study found that 93 percent of employers used salary surveys to determine pay levels; 55 percent of the respondents believed them to be essential or absolutely necessary.[7]

Compensation surveys provide information for establishing both direct and indirect compensation. The decisions that must be made prior to conducting a compensation survey include determining (1) the geographic area of the survey, (2) the specific firms to contact, and (3) the jobs to include. The geographic area to be included in the survey is often determined from employment records. Data from this source may indicate maximum distance or time that employees are willing to travel to work. Also, the firms to be contacted in the survey are often from the same industry but may also include others—regardless of industry—that compete for the same skills. Because obtaining data on all jobs in the organization may not be feasible, the human resource department often surveys only key jobs. A **key job** is one that is well known in the company and industry and that can be easily defined.

The primary difficulty in conducting a compensation survey involves determining comparable jobs. Recall that organizing work and designing jobs can be done in many different ways. A job in one company may only roughly resemble a job with a similar title in another. For this reason, job titles have little value in compensation surveys. Instead, the analyst must use well-written job descriptions when requesting compensation data.

There are other ways to obtain compensation data in a given labor market. Some professional organizations periodically conduct surveys. The U.S. Bureau of Labor Statistics also makes yearly surveys and provides

---

[7] Joseph E. McKendrick, Jr., "Salary Surveys: Roadmaps for the Volatile Employment Scene of the 1990s," *Management World,* 19 (March–April 1990), pp. 18–20.

data by area, industry, and job type. In addition, a number of journals, such as *Compensation Review* and *Hospital Administration,* report compensation information periodically. Some organizations choose to use other sources, even though they are large enough to afford surveys. Several life insurance companies, for example, use compensation data provided by the Life Office Management Association. They may supplement these data with survey information supplied by other organizations such as Hay Associates, the Society for Human Resource Management, and American Management Association.

Cost of Living

The logic for using cost of living as a pay determinant is simple: When prices rise over a period of time and pay does not, "real pay" is actually lowered. A pay increase must be roughly equivalent to the increased cost of living if a person is to maintain a previous level of real wages. For instance, if someone earns $24,000 during a year in which the average rate of inflation is 5 percent, a $100 per month pay increase will be necessary merely to maintain that person's standard of living.

People living on fixed incomes (primarily the elderly and the poor) are especially hard hit by inflation. But they are not alone; most employees also suffer financially. Recognizing this problem, some firms index pay increases to the inflation rate. Some firms will sacrifice "merit money" to provide across-the-board increases designed to offset the results of inflation.

Labor Unions

An excerpt from the Wagner Act, which is discussed in Chapter 15, prescribes the areas of mandatory collective bargaining between management and unions as "wages, hours, and other terms and conditions of employment." These broad bargaining areas obviously have great potential impact on compensation decisions. The union affects company compensation policies in three important areas: (1) the standards used in making compensation decisions, (2) wage differentials, and (3) payment methods.[8]

When a union uses comparable pay as a standard in making compensation demands, the employer must obtain accurate labor market data. When a union emphasizes cost of living, management may be persuaded to include a **cost-of-living allowance (COLA).** This is an escalator clause in the labor agreement that automatically increases wages as the U.S. Bureau of Labor Statistics cost of living index rises.

Unions may also attempt to create, preserve, or even destroy pay differentials between wages for craft workers and unskilled workers. The politics

---

[8] Cyril C. Ling, *The Management of Personnel Relations* (Homewood, Ill.: Richard D. Irwin, 1965), pp. 146–151.

of a given situation will determine the direction taken. For instance, if the unskilled workers have the strongest membership, an attempt may be made to eliminate pay differentials.

Management may want to use incentive plans to encourage greater productivity. However, decisions to implement such plans may be scrapped if the union strongly opposes this approach. Employee acceptance of such a plan is essential for successful implementation, and union opposition may make it unworkable.

Society

Compensation paid to employees often affects a firm's pricing of its goods or services. For this reason, consumers may also be interested in compensation decisions. At times in the past, the government has responded to public opinion and stepped in to encourage business to hold down wages and prices. The process of "jawboning" initiated by President John F. Kennedy in the early 1960s, involved using the prestige of the presidency to informally pressure large companies and unions to "hold the line."

Businesses in a given labor market are also concerned with the pay practices of competitors. For instance, when the management of a large electronics firm announced plans to locate a branch plant in a relatively small community, it was confronted by local civic leaders. Their questions largely concerned the wage and salary rates that would be paid. Subtle pressure was applied to keep the company's wages in line with other wages in the community. The electronics firm agreed to begin operations with initial compensation at a lower level than it usually paid. But the firm's management made it clear that a series of pay increases would be given over a period of two years to maintain its own "pay leader" policy.

The Economy

The economy definitely affects financial compensation decisions. For example, a depressed economy generally increases the labor supply. This, in turn, serves to lower the going wage rate. In most cases, the cost of living will rise in an expanding economy. Because the cost of living is commonly used as a pay standard, the economy's health exerts a major impact on pay decisions. Labor unions, government, and society are all less likely to press for pay increases in a depressed economy, but attitudes change as conditions improve.

Legislation

Federal and state laws can also affect the amount of compensation a person receives. We next describe some of the more significant pieces of federal legislation in this area.

Davis-Bacon Act of 1931. The Davis-Bacon Act of 1931 was the first national law to deal with minimum wages. It requires federal construction contractors with projects valued in excess of $2,000 to pay at least the prevailing wages in the area. The Secretary of Labor has the authority to make this determination, and the prevailing wage is often the average local union rate. Davis-Bacon has come under fire, with critics claiming that it has resulted in construction cost overruns approaching 20 percent. Critics have also charged that the act is inflationary and obstructs minority hiring because of its limitation of one apprentice for every three full-time journeymen on a job.

Social Security Act of 1935, as Amended. The Social Security Act established a federal payroll tax to fund unemployment and retirement benefits. The act also set up the Social Security Administration. Employers were required to share equally with employees the cost of old-age, survivors, and disability insurance. Employers were required to pay the full cost of unemployment insurance. Unemployment benefits are paid through agencies in each of the fifty states for a minimum period of twenty-six weeks.

Walsh-Healy Act of 1936. The Walsh-Healy Act of 1936 requires companies with federal supply contracts exceeding $10,000 to pay prevailing wages. The act differs from the Fair Labor Standards Act in that overtime payment is required for hours worked over forty per week or eight per day.

Fair Labor Standards Act of 1938, as Amended. The most significant law affecting compensation is the Fair Labor Standards Act of 1938 (FLSA). It establishes a minimum wage, requires overtime pay, and provides standards for child labor. This act is administered by the Wage and Hour Division of the U.S. Department of Labor. The basic requirements of the act apply to employees engaged in interstate commerce.[9]

As of April 1991, the act provided for a minimum wage of not less than $4.25 an hour. It also required overtime payment at the rate of one and one-half times the employee's regular rate after forty hours of work in a 168-hour period. Although most organizations and employees are covered by the act, certain classes of employees are specifically exempt from overtime provisions. However, nonexempt employees, many of whom are paid salaries, must receive overtime pay.

Exempt employees are categorized as executive, administrative, and professional employees and outside salespersons. An executive employee is essentially a manager (such as a production manager) with broad authority over subordinates. An administrative employee, while not a manager, occupies an important staff position in an organization and might have a title such as systems analyst or assistant to the president. A professional employee performs work requiring advanced knowledge in a field of learning, normally acquired through a prolonged course of specialized instruction.

---

[9] *Employment Relations Under the Fair Labor Standards Act* (Washington, D.C.: U.S. Department of Labor, Employment Standards Administration, Wage and Hour Division, WH Publication 1297; revised May 1980, reprinted August 1985).

This type of employee might have a title such as company physician, legal counsel, or senior statistician. Outside salespeople sell tangible or intangible items away from the employer's place of business. Employees in jobs not conforming to these definitions are considered nonexempt.

During one year alone in the 1980s, the Wage and Hour Division received over 46,000 wage complaints and conducted more than 68,000 investigations. The agency recovered $745 million in unpaid overtime wages owed to 291,000 employees. An employer must be aware of the minimum wage level, maintain accurate payroll records, and accurately identify workers covered by the act.

Equal Pay Act of 1963. The Equal Pay Act of 1963 (an amendment to the FLSA) has also influenced the field of compensation. In 1972, amendments expanded the act to cover employees in executive, administrative, professional, and outside sales force categories as well as employees in most state and local governments, hospitals, and schools. The purpose of this legislation is to prohibit discrimination in pay on the basis of gender. The act has teeth, as evidenced by the millions of dollars paid to women employees to compensate them for past discriminatory pay policies.

The act applies to all organizations and employees covered by the FLSA, including the exempt categories. The act requires equal pay for equal work for both men and women. Equal work is defined as work requiring equal skill, effort, and responsibility that is performed under the same or similar working conditions. The act doesn't prohibit the establishment of different wage rates based on seniority or a merit system. Also permitted are pay systems that are based on the quantity or quality of production and differentials based on any factor other than gender. In recent years, the act's effect has been less significant because a violation of the Equal Pay Act may also be a violation of Title VII of the Civil Rights Act.

Employee Retirement Income Security Act of 1974. Passed in 1974, the Employee Retirement Income Security Act (ERISA) is one of the most complex pieces of federal compensation legislation ever to be passed. The purpose of the act is described as follows:

> It is hereby declared to be the policy of this Act to protect . . . the interests of participants in employee benefit plans and their beneficiaries . . . by establishing standards of conduct, responsibility and obligations for fiduciaries of employee benefit plans, and by providing for appropriate remedies, sanctions, and ready access to the federal courts.[10]

Note that the word *protect* is used here because the act does not force employers to create employee benefit plans. It does set standards in the areas of participation, vesting of benefits, and funding for existing and new plans. Numerous existing retirement plans have been altered in order to conform to this legislation.

[10] *U.S. Statutes at Large 88,* Part I, 93rd Congress, 2nd Session, 1974, p. 833.

Consolidated Omnibus Budget Reconciliation Act of 1985 (COBRA).
COBRA requires employers to continue specified health insurance coverage
at group rates for certain employees and their families following termination of employment. Traditionally, employers receive a tax deduction for
expenses paid or incurred for any group health plan. The act doesn't allow
such deductions unless each "qualified beneficiary" under the group health
plan who would lose coverage as a result of a "qualifying event" is entitled
to elect continuation coverage under the plan within the election period. A
qualifying event is (1) termination of the covered employee (except in cases
of gross misconduct), (2) reduction of hours of the covered employee, (3) the
death of the covered employee, (4) the divorce or legal separation of the
covered employee from his or her spouse, (5) eligibility of the covered
employee for Medicare benefits, and (6) a child ceasing to be a dependent.
The requirements of COBRA do not apply to a group health plan for any
calendar year in which employers employed less than 20 employees on a
typical business day.

■ THE JOB AS A DETERMINANT OF FINANCIAL COMPENSATION

The jobs people are given to do are a major determinant of the amount of
financial compensation they will receive. Organizations pay for the value they
attach to certain duties, responsibilities, and other job-related factors (such as
working conditions). Management techniques utilized for determining a job's
relative worth include job analysis, job descriptions, and job evaluation.

Job Analysis and Descriptions

Before an organization can determine the relative difficulty or value of its
jobs, it must first define their content, which it normally does by analyzing
jobs. Recall from Chapter 4 that job analysis is the systematic process of
determining the skills and knowledge required for performing jobs. Recall,
also, that the job description is the primary by-product of job analysis,
consisting of a written document that describes job duties and responsibilities. Job descriptions are used for many different purposes, including job
evaluation. Job descriptions are essential to all job evaluation methods, the
success of which depends largely on their accuracy and clarity.

Job Evaluation

Job evaluation is that part of a compensation system in which a firm
determines the relative value of one job in relation to another.[11] The basic
purpose of job evaluation is to eliminate internal pay inequities that exist

---

[11] Richard I. Henderson, *Compensation Management*, 5th ed. (Englewood Cliffs, N.J.: Prentice-
Hall, 1989), p. 169.

because of illogical pay structures. For example, a pay inequity exists if the mailroom supervisor earns more money than the accounting supervisor.

More specifically, job evaluation has the potential to do the following:

- Identify the organization's job structure.
- Bring equity and order to the relationships among jobs.
- Develop a hierarchy of job value that can be used to create a pay structure.
- Achieve a consensus among managers and employees regarding jobs and pay within the firm.[12]

The concept of internal pay equity previously discussed is closely related to the purposes of job evaluation. It refers to the relationship between the pay that employees believe they should receive and that which they actually receive. Although individuals may be concerned with external equity, they basically believe that their pay should be related to their contributions to the firm. They quickly become unhappy when they perceive that someone in the organization receives more pay for performing the same or lower level work.

At the Bendix Corporation, the precise method of implementing job evaluation programs is left to the discretion of individual business groups and divisions. However, corporate philosophy serves as a basic guide to these operating units. This philosophy includes the belief that the job evaluation process is the foundation of a sound compensation system. Thus the job evaluation process must satisfy the following requirements:

- Provide a consistent measure of job worth that can be easily understood by everyone concerned.
- Involve managers from its inception through its administration and subsequent revision.
- Protect employees from favoritism, bias, and resultant internal pay inequities.
- Measure the job and not the performance of the employees doing the job.
- Apply to broad job clusters within functional groups.

The human resource department is usually responsible for administering job evaluation programs. However, actual job evaluation is typically done by committee. The committee often consists of managers from different functional areas. A typical committee might include the human resource director as chairperson and the vice-presidents for finance, production, and marketing. However, the composition of the committee usually depends on the type and level of the jobs that are being evaluated. In all instances, it is important for the committee to keep personalities out of the evaluation process. As the Bendix approach indicates, it is the job that should be evaluated, not the person(s) performing the job.

Small- and medium-sized organizations often lack job evaluation expertise and may elect to use an outside consultant. When employing a qualified consultant, management should require that the consultant develop an

---

[12] Roger J. Plachy, "The Case for Effective Point-Factor Job Evaluation, Viewpoint I," *Personnel,* 64 (April 1987), p. 31.

internal job evaluation program and train company employees to administer it properly.

Organizations use four basic job evaluation methods: ranking, classification, factor comparison, and point.[13] A firm should choose one method and
modify that method to its particular needs. The ranking and classification
methods are nonquantitative, whereas the factor comparison and point
methods are quantitative approaches.

Ranking Method. The simplest of the four job evaluation methods is the
ranking method. In the **ranking method,** the raters examine the description of each job being evaluated and arrange the jobs in order according to
their value to the company. The procedure is essentially the same as that
discussed in Chapter 11 regarding the ranking method for performance
appraisal. The only difference is that jobs, not people, are being evaluated.
The first step in this method—as with all the methods—is conducting job
analysis and writing job descriptions.

Classification Method. The **classification method** involves defining a
number of classes or grades to describe a group of jobs. In evaluating jobs
by the classification method, the raters compare the job description with
the class description. The class description that most closely agrees with
the job description determines the classification for that job. For example,
in evaluating the job of word processing clerk, the description might include
these duties:

1. Data enter letters from prepared drafts.
2. Address envelopes.
3. Deliver completed correspondence to unit supervisor.

Assuming that the remainder of the job description includes similar routine
work, this job would most likely be placed in the lowest job class.

The best-known example of this method is the federal government's Civil
Service System. This system has eighteen grades (GS-1 to GS-18). At the
bottom of the scale (GS-1), the nature and typical duties of the job are very
simple and routine. Jobs become progressively more difficult through GS-
18, which involves high-level executive tasks. However, clearly defining
grade descriptions for many diverse jobs is difficult. For this reason, the
federal government has now implemented a Factor Evaluation System
(FES). This system combines three methods of job evaluation: ranking,
factor comparison, and point. However, the FES is not the only job evaluation plan used within the federal government. As with private industry, the
government's approach is to select and adapt systems according to specific
needs.[14]

Factor Comparison Method. The basic version of the factor comparison
method was developed by Eugene Benge and is somewhat more complex

---

[13] George T. Milkovich and Jerry M. Newman, *Compensation,* p. 106.
[14] *Ibid.,* p. 112.

than the two previously discussed qualitative methods. In the **factor comparison method,** raters need not keep the entire job in mind as they evaluate; instead, they make decisions on separate aspects, or factors, of the job. A basic underlying assumption is that there are five universal job factors:

- Mental requirements, which reflect mental traits such as intelligence, reasoning, and imagination.
- Skill, which pertains to facility in muscular coordination and training in the interpretation of sensory impressions.
- Physical requirements, which involve sitting, standing, walking, lifting, etc.
- Responsibilities, which cover areas such as raw materials, money, records, and supervision.
- Working conditions, which reflect the environmental influences of noise, illumination, ventilation, hazards, and hours.[15]

The committee first ranks the relative degree of difficulty of each of the five factors for the selected key jobs. Job descriptions serve as a basis for making these decisions. An example of this initial ranking (average of all raters on the committee) is shown in Table 12-1. Note that the jobs are first ranked according to mental requirements. The systems analyst job ranked highest, followed by programmer (2), console operator (3), and data entry clerk (4). The same ranking procedure was used for the other four factors.

The committee next allocates pay rates for each job to each factor. This allocation is based on the importance of the respective factor to the job. For example, allocating the systems analyst's average pay rate ($12.00 per hour) to each of the five factors is shown in Table 12-2 on page 456. This step is probably the most difficult to explain satisfactorily to employees because the decision is highly subjective.

---

[15] John A. Patton, C. L. Littlefield, and Stanley A. Self, *Job Evaluation: Text and Cases,* 3rd ed. (Homewood, Ill.: Richard D. Irwin, 1964), p. 115.

TABLE 12-1 | Average Ranks of Factor Difficulty for Key Jobs

Job	Mental	Skill	Physical	Responsibility	Working Conditions*
Systems analyst	1	4	2	1	3
Data entry clerk	4	1	1	4	1
Programmer	2	3	3	2	4
Console operator	3	2	4	3	2

*The poorer the working conditions, the higher the rating. (The highest rating is 1.)

TABLE 12-2 | Allocation of Pay to Factors

Job: Systems analyst	Mental	$4.00
Average pay per hour: $12.00	Skill	2.00
	Physical	0.80
	Responsibility	4.00
	Working conditions	1.20

After assigning pay rates to each factor for each job, the committee places the results in a format similar to that shown in Table 12-3. This procedure results in a ranking of jobs within each factor on the basis of pay rates. (Rank order is shown in parentheses.)

By comparing the ranking of factor difficulty (DR) with the ranking of factor pay (PR), one can determine the committee's consistency. The two separate rankings are shown side-by-side in Table 12-4. Note that no differences exist. If there had been a ranking inconsistency, the jobs affected would not have been used in the next step.

A job comparison scale consisting of the five universal factors is developed next (see Figure 12-3). This scale is used to rate other jobs in the group being evaluated. The raters compare each job, factor by factor, with those appearing on the job comparison scale. They then place them on the chart in an appropriate position. For example, assume that the committee is evaluating the job of programmer analyst (which was not used as a key job). The committee determines that this job has fewer mental requirements than that of systems analyst but more than those of programmer. The job would then be placed on this chart between these two jobs at a point agreed on by the committee. In this example, the committee evaluated the mental requirements factor at $3.80. The committee repeats this procedure for the remaining four factors and for all jobs to be evaluated.

TABLE 12-3 | Average Ranks of Pay Rates by Factor for Key Jobs

Job	Mental	Skill	Physical	Responsibility	Working conditions	Pay rate
Systems analyst	$4.00(1)	$2.00(4)	$0.80(2)	$4.00(1)	$1.20(3)	$12.00
Data entry clerk	1.50(4)	2.70(1)	1.00(1)	1.30(4)	1.40(1)	7.90
Programmer	3.40(2)	2.50(3)	0.70(3)	3.00(2)	1.00(4)	10.60
Console operator	2.30(3)	2.60(2)	0.60(4)	1.80(3)	1.30(2)	8.60

TABLE 12-4 | Comparison of Difficulty Ranking (DR) and Pay Ranking (PR) by Factor

	Factor									
	Mental		Skill		Physical		Responsibility		Working conditions	
Job	DR	PR	DR	PR	DR	PR	DR	PR	DR	PR
Systems analyst	1	1	4	4	2	2	1	1	3	3
Data entry clerk	4	4	1	1	1	1	4	4	1	1
Programmer	2	2	3	3	3	3	2	2	4	4
Console operator	3	3	2	2	4	4	3	3	2	2

FIGURE 12-3 | Job Comparison Scale

The factor comparison method provides a systematic approach to job evaluation. However, at least two problems with it should be noted. The assumption that the five factors are universal has been questioned because certain factors may be more appropriate to some job groups than others. Also, while the steps are not overly complicated, they are somewhat detailed and may be difficult to explain.

Point Method. In the **point method,** raters assign numerical values to specific job components, and the sum of these values provides a quantitative assessment of a job's relative worth.[16] Most job evaluation plans in use today are some variation of the point method.[17] Some 95 percent of the major corporations in the United States are thought to use some variation of this method to evaluate jobs.[18] Point method plans are also used by many small companies. Their use has been encouraged by associations such as the National Electrical Manufacturers' Association, the Life Office Management Association, and the Administrative Management Society.

The point method requires selection of job factors according to the nature of the specific group of jobs being evaluated. Normally, organizations develop a separate plan for each group of similar jobs (job clusters) in the company. Shop jobs, clerical jobs, and sales jobs are examples of job clusters. The procedure for establishing a point method is illustrated in Figure 12-4. After determining the group of jobs to be studied, analysts conduct job analysis and write job descriptions. The job evaluation committee will later use these descriptions as the basis for making evaluation decisions.

Next, the analysts select and define the factors to be used in measuring job value. These factors become the standards used for the evaluation of jobs. They can best be identified by individuals who are thoroughly familiar with the content of the jobs under consideration. Education, experience, job knowledge, mental effort, physical effort, responsibility, and working conditions are examples of factors typically used. Each factor should be significant in helping to differentiate jobs. Factors that exist in equal amounts in all jobs obviously would not serve this purpose. As an example, in evaluating a company's clerical jobs, the working conditions factor would be of little value in differentiating jobs if all jobs in the cluster had approximately the same working conditions. The number of factors used varies, with the average being approximately eleven.[19]

The committee must establish factor weights according to their relative importance in the jobs to be evaluated. For example, if experience is considered quite important for a particular job cluster, this factor might be

---

[16] Donald L. Caruth, *Compensation Management for Banks* (Boston: Bankers Publishing Company, 1986), p. 65.

[17] Leonard R. Burgess, *Wage and Salary Administration* (Columbus, Ohio: Charles E. Merrill, 1984), p. 93.

[18] Edward E. Lawler III, "What's Wrong with Point-Factor Job Evaluation," *Personnel,* 64 (January 1987), p. 38.

[19] See David W. Belcher and Thomas J. Atchison, *Compensation Administration,* for a detailed discussion of compensable factors.

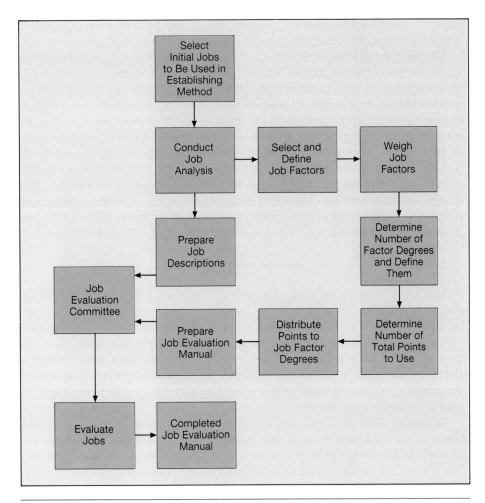

FIGURE 12-4 | Procedure for Establishing the Point Method of Job Evaluation

weighted as much as 35 percent. Physical effort (if used at all as a factor in an office cluster) would likely be low—perhaps less than 10 percent.

The next consideration is to determine the number of degrees for each job factor and define each degree. Degrees represent the number of distinct levels associated with a particular factor. The number of degrees needed for each factor depends on job requirements. If a particular cluster required virtually the same level of formal education (a high school diploma, for example), fewer degrees would be appropriate than if some jobs in the cluster required advanced degrees.

The committee then determines the total number of points to be used in the plan. The number may vary, but 500 or 1,000 points may work well. The use of a smaller number of points (for example, 50) would not likely provide the proper distinctions among jobs, whereas a larger number (such as

50,000) would be unnecessarily cumbersome. The total number of points in a plan indicates the maximum points that any job could receive.

The next step is to distribute point values to job factor degrees (see Table 12-5). As you can see, factor 1 (Education) has five degrees, factor 2 (Responsibility) has four, factor 3 (Physical effort) has five, and factor 4 (Working conditions) has three. Maximum points are easily calculated by multiplying the maximum points in the system by the assigned weights. For Education, the maximum points would be 250 (50 percent weight multiplied by 500 points). Points for the minimum degree correspond to the percentage weight assigned to the factor. (For Education, the percentage weight is 50 percent, so the minimum number of points is also 50.) The degree interval may be calculated by subtracting the minimum number of points from the maximum number, and dividing by the number of degrees used minus 1. For example, the interval for factor 1 (Education) is:

$$\text{Interval} = \frac{250 - 50}{5 - 1} = 50$$

As you can see in Table 12-5, the interval between each degree for Education is 50.

This approach to determining the number of points for each degree is referred to as arithmetic progression. An arithmetic progression is simple to understand and explain to employees. The factors have been defined so that the intervals between the degrees are equal. However, a geometric progression is just as valid when it conforms to the manner in which the degrees have been defined.[20]

The next step involves preparing a job evaluation manual. Although there is no standard format, the manual often contains an introductory section, factor and degree definitions, and job descriptions. As a final step, the job evaluation committee then evaluates jobs in each cluster by compar-

---

[20] Other alternatives, such as geometric progression and irregular progression, exist. For a detailed discussion of methods of progression, see John A. Patton et al., *Job Evaluation: Text and Cases,* pp. 153–154.

TABLE 12-5 | Overview of the Point System (500-Point System)

Job Factor	Weight	Degree of Factor				
		1	2	3	4	5
1. Education	50%	50	100	150	200	250
2. Responsibility	30%	30	70	110	150	
3. Physical effort	12%	12	24	36	48	60
4. Working conditions	8%	8	24	40		

ing each job description with the factors in the job evaluation manual. A portion of a large appliance manufacturer's job evaluation manual is shown in Figure 12-5. Assume that the job of human resource interviewer is being evaluated. After studying the job description, the evaluation committee decides that the job requirements closely match degree IV of the factor "contacts." The job receives 80 points for this factor. After determining the point values of all factors, the committee totals them to obtain the numerical value of the human resource interviewer job. The committee determines the values of all other jobs in each cluster in the same manner.

FACTOR: CONTACTS

This factor considers the responsibility for working with other people to get results, either interdepartmentally or outside the plant. In the lower degrees, it is largely a matter of giving or getting information or instructions. In the higher degrees, the factor involves dealing with or influencing other persons. In rating this factor, consider how the contacts are made, the duration of the contacts, and their purposes.

Level (Degree)		Points
IV	Usual purposes of the contacts are to discuss problems and possible solutions, to secure cooperation or coordination of efforts, and to get agreement and action; more than ordinary tact and persuasiveness required.	80
III	Usual purposes of the contacts are to exchange information and settle specific problems encountered in the course of daily work.	40
II	Contacts may be repetitive but usually are brief and with little or no continuity.	20
I	Contacts normally extend to persons in the immediate work unit only.	10

FACTOR: COMPLEXITY OF DUTIES

This factor considers the complexity of duties in terms of the character of the tasks to be performed, the scope of independent action allowed, and the exercise of perception and judgment required.

Level (Degree)		Points
IV	Performs work where only general methods are available. Independent action and judgment are required regularly to analyze facts, evaluate situations, draw conclusions, make decisions, and take or recommend action.	60
III	Performs duties working from standard procedures or generally understood methods. Some independent action and judgment are required to decide what to do, determine permissible variations from standard procedures, review facts in situations, and determine action to be taken, within limits prescribed.	80
II	Standard procedure limits independent action and judgment to decisions not difficult to make since choices are limited. Duties require deciding when to ask for assistance.	40
I	Little or no independent action or judgment. Duties are so standardized and simple as to involve little choice as to how to do them.	20

FIGURE 12-5 | Point Method of Job Evaluation (Example of Two Factors)

Point plans have been criticized for the amount of time and effort required to design them and for supporting traditional bureaucratic management.[21] However, a redeeming feature of the method is that, once developed, the plan may be used over a long period of time. The procedure for using an established point method is presented in Figure 12-6. As new jobs are created and the contents of old jobs substantially changed, job analysis must be conducted and job descriptions rewritten. The job evaluation committee evaluates the jobs and updates the manual. Only when job factors change, or for some reason the weights assigned become inappropriate, does the plan become obsolete.

The Hay Guide Chart-Profile Method (Hay Plan).[22]   A highly refined version of the point method is the **Hay guide chart-profile method.** The Hay Plan uses the factors of know-how, problem solving, accountability, and, where appropriate, working conditions. Point values are assigned to these factors to determine the final point profile for any job.

Know-how is the total of all knowledge and skills needed for satisfactory job performance. It has three dimensions: the amount of practical, specialized, or scientific knowledge required; the ability to coordinate many functions; and the ability to effectively deal with and motivate people.

Problem solving is the degree of original thinking required by the job for analyzing, evaluating, creating, reasoning, and making conclusions. Problem solving has two dimensions: the thinking environment in which problems are solved (from strict routine to abstractly defined); and the thinking challenge presented by the problems (from repetitive to uncharted). Problem solving is expressed as a percentage of know-how since people use what they know to think and make decisions.

Accountability is the responsibility for action and accompanying consequences. The three dimensions of accountability are the degree of freedom the job incumbent has to act, the job impact on end results, and the extent of the monetary impact of the job.

The Hay Plan is an extremely popular approach to determining compensation. It is used by some 4,000 employers worldwide.[23] The popularity of the Hay Plan gives it an important advantage: It facilitates job comparison between firms. Thus the method serves to determine both internal and external equity.

■ THE EMPLOYEE AS A DETERMINANT OF FINANCIAL COMPENSATION

In addition to the organization, the labor market, and the job, factors related to the employee are also essential in determining pay equity. We discuss each of these factors in this section.

---

[21] Edward E. Lawler III, "What's Wrong with Point-Factor Job Evaluation," pp. 39–40.

[22] George T. Milkovich and Jerry M. Newman, *Compensation,* pp. 576–578.

[23] Richard I. Henderson, *Compensation Management,* p. 196.

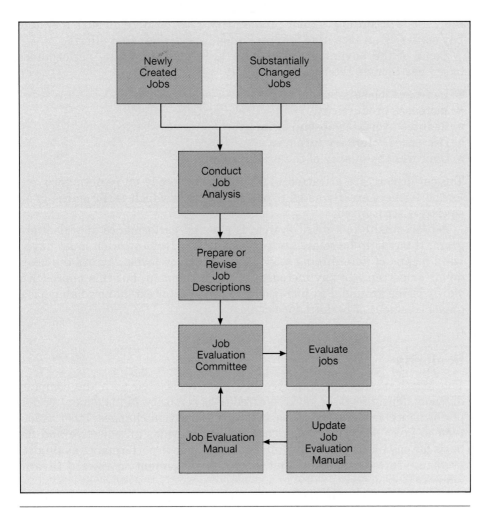

FIGURE 12-6 | Procedure for Using an Established Point Method of Job Evaluation

Performance

Rewarded behavior tends to be repeated. What you reward is generally what you get. It has been stated that the greatest obstacle to the success of today's organizations is that firms are not rewarding the behavior they need.[24] With increasing domestic and international competition, a high level of performance from each employee is essential. If pay can serve as a motivator of behavior, it follows that it should be tied to performance. Nothing is more demoralizing to outstanding employees than to be paid the same as less productive workers. Therefore management generally prefers a pay system based on employee performance. Such an approach rewards

---

[24] Tom Brown, "Does Compensation Add Up?" *Industry Week,* 239 (August 20, 1990), p. 13.

individuals according to their productivity. Furthermore, in such a system, pay serves as an incentive for employees to give their best efforts.

Some of the advantages that have been cited for using performance-based pay include the following[25]:

- Increases job satisfaction.
- Increases productivity.
- Reduces avoidable absenteeism.
- Decreases voluntary turnover.
- Improves the quality of the employee mix.

Top performers are attracted to firms that base pay on performance, and low performers are attracted to organizations in which performance is not so closely scrutinized.

A prerequisite to a merit system is a sound performance appraisal program. If pay is to be related to performance, an organization must have a valid means of determining varying performance levels. Across-the-board dollar or percentage pay increases are still common, but this approach is slowly losing ground. Pay increases are to a greater extent now being based on achievement of performance goals.[26]

Seniority

The length of time an employee has been associated with the company, division, department, or job is referred to as seniority. Management prefers performance as the primary basis for compensation changes; labor unions tend to favor seniority, which they believe provides an objective and fair basis for pay increases. Many union leaders believe performance evaluation systems are too subjective and permit management to reward favorite employees arbitrarily.

An acceptable performance-seniority compromise might be to permit employees to receive pay increases to the midpoints of their pay grades on the basis of seniority. The rationale is that workers performing at an acceptable level should eventually receive the average wage or salary of their pay grades. However, progression beyond the midpoint should be based on performance. This practice would permit only the outstanding performers to reach the maximum rate for the grade, and it reflects the initial rationale for rate ranges.

Skill-Based Pay

Most compensation systems focus on the value of jobs that have been evaluated to determine their relative worth to the organization so they can be priced accordingly. Skill-based pay, or pay for knowledge, is a system

---

[25] John A. Parnell, "Five Reasons Why Pay Must Be Based on Performance," *Supervision,* 52 (February 1991), p. 7.

[26] "Compensation Currents," *Compensation Review,* 17 (First Quarter 1985), p. 2.

that compensates employees on the basis of job-related skills and knowledge they possess.[27] The purpose of this approach is to encourage employees to gain additional skills, which will increase their value to the organization. The departments they serve are then provided with a greater degree of versatility in dealing with absenteeism and turnover. Employees benefit from the system by acquiring additional security and mobility. The flexibility they gain is derived from being able to handle different tasks or even different jobs. It also allows them the opportunity to increase their earnings without being moved permanently to a higher level job. This factor gains additional importance in a highly competitive environment in which promotional opportunities are limited.

Skill-based pay is often used with autonomous work groups or other job enrichment programs. A high commitment to human resource development is necessary to successfully implement such a program. In addition, employees involved must have the desire to grow and increase their knowledge and skills.

While skill-based pay appears to have advantages for both employer and employee, there are some potential problems. For example, the system normally results in above-average pay and higher training and development costs. Also, employees with newly acquired skills might become restless and want to move prematurely from job to job. There is also the danger that too many skills will be permitted, resulting in plans that are difficult to manage.[28]

Experience

Regardless of the nature of the task, very few factors have a more significant impact on performance than experience. "Experience has taught our best racquetball players how to really play the game," the director of a state university's recreational facility recently exclaimed. This statement, no doubt, was true. But, as someone else put it, "Experience has also taught our worst racquetball players how to play." The point is that while experience is invaluable, not all experience is good experience. A person can play golf for ten years (without lessons from a pro, of course), have a hook that almost returns to the tee box, and be further away than ever from being a good golfer.

Although not always realized in business circles, the same is true of management experience. How much ahead of the game is the manager who has been a poor manager for two decades? Managers who comment, with considerable confidence and pleasure, that they have had twenty years of management experience may actually have much less because of the duplication involved. Nevertheless, experience is often indispensable and, in many cases, management does indeed compensate employees on this basis.

---

[27] Fred Luthans and Marilyn L. Fox, "Update on Skill-Based Pay," *Personnel*, 21 (July–August 1989), p. 62.

[28] *Ibid.*, pp. 63–64.

Sometimes the practice is justified because of the valuable insights that can only be acquired through experience on the job. Occasionally, however, experience may be rewarded even though it is irrelevant.

Membership in the Organization

Some components of individual financial compensation are given to employees without regard to the particular job they perform or their level of productivity. These rewards are provided to all employees simply because they are members of the organization. For example, an average performer occupying a job in pay grade 1 may receive the same number of vacation days, the same amount of group life insurance, and the same reimbursement for educational expenses as a superior employee working in a job classified in pay grade 10. In fact, the worker in pay grade 1 may get more vacation time if he or she has been with the firm longer. Rewards based on organizational membership are intended to maintain a high degree of stability in the workforce and to recognize loyalty.

Potential

Potential is useless if it is never realized. Yet, organizations do pay some individuals based on their potential. In order to attract talented young people to the firm, the overall compensation program must appeal to the person with no experience or any immediate ability to perform difficult tasks. Many young employees are paid well because they have the potential to become a first-line supervisor, manager of compensation, vice-president of marketing, or possibly even CEO.

College graduates typically do not have significant business experience for employment managers to examine. Lacking such a record, organizations turn elsewhere for factors to predict the success of the graduate. Grades in college are often considered. Although the relationship between grades and job performance is arguable, human resource recruiters and line managers often have no alternative but to emphasize a student's academic success. Of course, other factors might indicate potential, so questions asked of college prospects often include the following:

- What percentage of your school expenses did you pay?
- What class offices did you hold?
- To what professional student associations did you belong, such as Society for Human Resource Management, Society for Advancement of Management, Pi Sigma Epsilon, Delta Sigma Pi, or Alpha Kappa Psi? Did you hold offices in any of these organizations?
- Were you a member of a social sorority or fraternity or a club of any kind? What leadership positions did you occupy?

These and many other questions may not relate directly to the job but are nevertheless asked as organizations attempt to identify individuals who can provide future leadership. The people sought are those with potential.

Political Influence

Political influence is a factor that obviously should not be used to determine financial compensation. However, to deny that it exists would be unrealistic. It is disheartening to hear someone say, "It's not what you know, it's who you know." Yet, there is an unfortunate element of truth in that statement. To varying degrees in business, government, and not-for-profit organizations, a person's "pull" or political influence may sway pay and promotion decisions. It may be natural for a manager to favor a friend or relative in granting a pay increase or promotion. Whether it is natural or not, if the person receiving the reward is not truly deserving, this fact will soon become known throughout the work group. This practice can have a devastating impact on employee morale. Employees want—and are demanding—equitable treatment. However, there is nothing equitable about a person receiving a promotion and/or pay increase based strictly on politics. The practice should be strictly avoided.

Luck

You've undoubtedly heard the expression, "It certainly helps to be in the right place at the right time." There is more than a little truth in this statement as it relates to a person's compensation. Positions are continually coming open in firms. Realistically, there is no way for managers to foresee many of the changes that occur. For instance, who could have known that the purchasing agent, Joe Flynch, an apparently healthy middle-aged man, would suddenly die of a heart attack? Although the company may have been grooming several managers for Joe's position, none may be capable of immediately assuming the increased responsibility. The most experienced person, Tommy Loy, has been with the company only six months. Tommy had been an assistant buyer for a competitor for four years. Because of his experience, Tommy receives the promotion and the increased financial compensation. Tommy Loy was in the right place at the right time.

When asked to explain their most important reasons for success and effectiveness as managers, two chief executives responded candidly. One said, "Success is being at the right place at the right time and being recognized as having the ability to make timely decisions. It also depends on having good rapport with people, a good operating background, and the knowledge of how to develop people." The other replied, "My present position was attained by being in the right place at the right time with a history of getting the job done." Both executives recognize the significance of luck combined with the ability to perform. Their experiences lend support to the idea that luck works primarily for the efficient employee.

■ JOB PRICING

The primary considerations in pricing jobs are the organization's policies, the labor market, and the job itself. If allowances are to be made for individual factors, they too must be considered. Recall that the process of job evaluation results in a job hierarchy. It might reveal, for example, that the job of senior accountant is more valuable than the job of computer operator, which in turn is more valuable than the job of senior invoice clerk. At this point, the relative value of these jobs to the company is known but their absolute value isn't. Placing a dollar value on the worth of a job is called **job pricing.** It takes place after the job has been evaluated and the relative value of each job in the organization has been determined. However, as shown in Figure 12-2 on page 445, additional factors should be considered in determining the job's absolute value. Firms often use pay grades and pay ranges in the job pricing process.

Pay Grades

A **pay grade** is the grouping of similar jobs to simplify the job pricing process. It is much more convenient for organizations to price fifteen pay grades rather than 200 separate jobs. The simplicity of this approach is similar to a college or university's practice of grouping grades of 90 to 100 into an "A" category, grades of 80 to 89 into a "B," etc. A false implication of preciseness is also avoided. While job evaluation plans may be systematic, none is scientific.

Plotting jobs on a scatter diagram is often useful in determining the appropriate number of pay grades. In Figure 12-7, each dot on the scatter diagram represents one job as it relates to pay and evaluated points, which reflect its worth. By following this procedure, it is likely that a certain point spread will work satisfactorily (100 points used in this illustration). Each dot represents one job but may involve dozens of individuals who fill that one job. The large dot at the lower left represents the job of data entry clerk, which was evaluated at 75 points. The data entry clerk's hourly rate of $7.90 represents either the average wage currently being paid for the job or its market rate. This decision depends on how management wants to price its jobs.

A **wage curve** (or pay curve) is the fitting of plotted points in order to create a smooth progression between pay grades. The line that is drawn to minimize the distance between all dots and the line—a line of best fit—may be straight or curved. However, when the point system is used (normally considering only one job cluster), a straight line is the usual result, as in Figure 12-7. Two approaches used in drawing this wage line are the least squares line (a statistical version) and the less sophisticated "eyeball" approach. Some compensation specialists use the latter because it's simpler.

Pay Ranges

The next decision is whether all individuals performing the same job will receive equal pay or whether pay ranges will be used. A **pay range** includes a minimum and maximum pay rate with enough variance between the two to allow for significant pay difference. Pay ranges are generally preferred because they allow employees to be paid according to length of service and performance. Pay then serves as a positive incentive. When pay ranges are

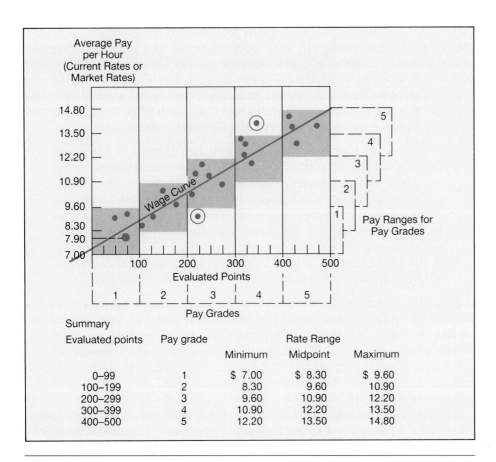

FIGURE 12-7 | Scatter Diagram of Evaluated Jobs Illustrating the Wage Curve, Pay Grades, and Rating Ranges

used, a method must be developed to advance individuals through the range. Although many organizations grant pay increases based on seniority, others hold the view that only outstanding performers should be allowed to advance to the top of their pay ranges. This philosophy also dictates that any discrepancy between where a person is in the pay range and where he or she could be—based on performance—should be corrected within a reasonable amount of time. This approach would necessitate larger pay increases for outstanding performers who are being paid at or near the bottom of their pay ranges.[29]

Referring again to Figure 12-7, note that anyone can readily determine the minimum, midpoint, and maximum pay rates per hour for each of the five pay grades. For example, for pay grade 5, the minimum rate is $12.20, the midpoint is $13.50, and the maximum is $14.80. The minimum rate is normally the "hiring in" rate that a person receives when joining the firm. The maximum pay rate represents the maximum that an employee can

---

[29] Graef S. Crystal, "Outlook on Compensation and Benefits: To the Rescue of Pay for Performance," *Personnel,* 62 (January 1985), p. 9.

receive for that job, regardless of how well the job is performed. A person at the top of a pay grade will have to be promoted to a job in a higher pay grade in order to receive a pay increase unless (1) an across-the-board adjustment is made, or (2) the job is reevaluated and placed in a higher pay grade. This situation has caused numerous managers anguish as they attempt to explain the pay system to an employee who is doing a tremendous job but is at the top of a pay grade. Consider this situation:

> Everyone in the department realized that Martha Wilson was the best secretary in the company. At times she appeared to do the job of three secretaries. Bill Merideth, Martha's supervisor, was especially impressed. Recently he had a discussion with the human resource manager to see what could be done to get a raise for Martha. After Bill described the situation, the human resource manager's only reply was, "Sorry, Bill. Martha is already at the top of her pay grade. There is nothing you can do except have her job upgraded or promote her to another position."

Situations such as Martha's present human resource managers with a perplexing problem. Many would be inclined to make an exception to the system and give Martha a salary increase. However, this action would violate a basic principle, which holds that every job in the organization has a maximum value, regardless of how well it is performed. In addition, making exceptions to the compensation plan could soon result in widespread pay inequities.

The rate ranges established should be large enough to provide an incentive to do a better job. At times, pay differentials may need to be greater to be meaningful, especially at higher levels. There may be logic in having the rate range become increasingly wide at each consecutive level (see Figure 12-8). Consider, for example, what a $50 per month salary increase would mean to a file clerk earning $600 per month (an 8.3 percent increase) and to a senior cost accountant earning $1,500 per month (a 3.3 percent increase). Assuming an inflation rate of 8 percent, the file clerk would be able to stay even, while the cost accountant would obviously fall behind.

Some workplace conditions do not favor pay ranges. For instance, in a situation in which all or most jobs are routine, with little opportunity for employees to vary their productivity, a single, or fixed, rate system may be more appropriate. When single rates are used, everyone working the same job receives the same pay, regardless of seniority or productivity.

Adjusting Pay Rates

When pay ranges have been determined and jobs assigned to pay grades, it may become obvious that some jobs are overpaid and others underpaid. Underpaid jobs are normally brought to the minimum of the pay range as soon as possible. Referring again to Figure 12-7, you can see that a job evaluated at about 225 points and having a rate of $9.00 per hour is represented by a circled dot immediately below pay grade 3. The job was determined to be difficult enough to fall in pay grade 3 (200–299 points).

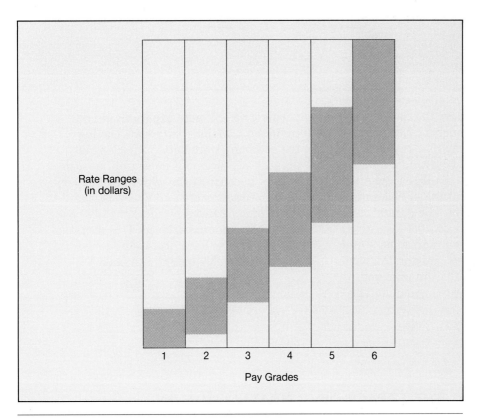

FIGURE 12-8 | Rate Ranges on Percentage Spreads

However, employees working in the job are being paid 60 cents per hour less than the minimum for the pay grade ($9.60 per hour). Some jobs in pay grade 2 and even in pay grade 1 are paid more. Good management practice would be to correct this inequity as rapidly as possible by placing the job in the proper pay grade and increasing the pay of those who work that job.

Overpaid jobs present more of a problem. An overpaid job for pay grade 4 is illustrated in Figure 12-7 (note the circled dot above pay grade 4). Employees in this job earn $14.00 per hour, or 50 cents more than the maximum for the pay grade. This type of overpayment (and underpayment as well) is referred to as a red circle rate.

An ideal solution to the problem of an overpaid job is to promote the employee. This might be a reasonable approach if the employee is qualified for a higher rated job and a job opening is available. Another possibility would be to bring the job rate and employee pay into line through a pay cut. This type of action may appear logical, but it isn't consistent with good management practice. This action would punish employees for a situation they did not create. Somewhere between these two possible solutions is a third: to freeze the rate until across-the-board pay increases bring the job into line. If the past few decades are an indication of the future, rising pay levels will eventually solve this problem.

HRM In Action

Lynn Marlow, the data processing manager for National Insurance Company, was perplexed as she spoke to Graham Johnston, the human resource manager. Lynn said, "I have trouble recruiting programmers and systems analysts. The data processing center employs a total of forty-five people, including ten programmers and four systems analysts. During the past six months, seven programmers and three systems analysts have quit. The people who left were experienced and competent. Major reasons for leaving the company were better salaries and greater advancement opportunities elsewhere. Because of the shortage of experienced programmers and analysts, the replacements hired by the company possess little prior experience. This situation has caused the data processing center to run continuously behind schedule."

How should Graham respond?

■ THE IMPACT OF GLOBALIZATION ON FINANCIAL COMPENSATION

Several questions arise when considering compensation levels for global employees. In the case of alliances, should the compensation system of the partners be linked, or will they be synthesized into a common system? Will compensation rates be adjusted for local markets or tied to similar jobs in the partner's home country? Often each partner in a venture has an established pay policy and those policies differ. At the very least, partners in such ventures should reach an agreement on the broad objectives of a compensation program for employees.[30]

Global compensation programs should be designed to establish and maintain a consistent relationship between the compensation of employees in all international alliances. The programs should also maintain compensation levels that are reasonable in relation to the practices of leading competitors. Failure to establish a uniform compensation policy can result in predictably adverse results, especially for employees doing the same jobs. Such compensation systems will inevitably lead to low morale, motivational problems, and less productive employees.[31]

---

[30] Wayne F. Cascio and Manuel G. Serapio, Jr., "Human Resources Systems in an International Alliance: The Undoing of a Done Deal?" *Organizational Dynamics,* 19 (Winter 1991), p. 70.

[31] *Ibid.,* p. 71.

■ OTHER COMPENSATION ISSUES

Several issues that affect compensation deserve special mention. They include comparable worth, pay secrecy, and pay compression. We will examine these issues next.

Comparable Worth

The comparable worth theory extends the concept of the Equal Pay Act, and it has become an important political and social issue.[32] The act requires equal pay for equal work, but advocates of comparable worth prefer a broader interpretation: requiring equal pay for comparable worth. **Comparable worth** requires the value for dissimilar jobs (e.g., company nurse and welder) to be compared under some form of job evaluation and pay rates to be assigned according to their evaluated worth. Because of the widespread support for this theory, it isn't likely to fade quickly.[33]

The basic premise of comparable worth is that jobs traditionally held by women are paid less than those traditionally held by men, even though both types may make equal contributions to the organization's goals.[34] Specifically, for the first quarter of 1984, the median weekly earnings of full-time women employees was 65 percent of that of men.[35] Jobs that have historically been filled by women pay less, and when employers use market data for establishing pay rates, the pay differentials are perpetuated.

Many business managers and business groups oppose comparable worth. However, some human resource executives believe that pay systems based on the comparable worth concept are fairer than those that rely on market pricing. Opponents of comparable worth contend that the earnings gap reflects an overall statistic and does not compare the earnings of two people performing the same job. They state that the gender difference is explainable by the large number of young women who have recently entered the workforce at entry-level pay rates. They also point out that a substantial number of women are employed in low-paying industries. Another point frequently made is that women often voluntarily leave the workforce to raise a family, while men continue with the job and receive promotions and pay increases.

Comparable worth detractors often state that the real problem in pay gap is gender segregation in jobs rather than either the underpayment of jobs traditionally filled by women or the overpayment of jobs traditionally

---

[32] John F. Sullivan, "Comparable Worth and the Statistical Audit of Pay Programs for Illegal Systematic Discrimination," *Personnel Administrator,* 30 (March 1985), p. 10.

[33] Lawrence Z. Lorber, J. Robert Kirk, Stephen L. Samuels, and David J. Spellman III, *Sex and Salary: A Legal and Personnel Analysis of Comparable Worth* (Alexandria, Va.: The ASPA Foundation, 1985), p. 51.

[34] Doug Grider and Mike Shurden, "The Gathering Storm of Comparable Worth," *Business Horizons,* 30 (July–August 1987), pp. 81–82.

[35] "Twenty Questions on Comparable Worth," The Equal Employment Advisory Council, 1984. Reprinted in *Personnel Administrator,* 30 (April 1985), p. 65.

filled by men.[36] Furthermore, they note that existing law prohibits employers from paying a woman at a lower rate than a man for doing the same work. A more effective solution, they suggest, would be to continue to enforce equal opportunity and equal pay laws. In addition, women should be encouraged to enter nontraditional occupations and be provided with equal access to education, training programs, and employment. Also, efforts should be continued to promote a nondiscriminatory socialization process for children. This view holds that these alternatives, rather than artificially raising the price of labor for special groups, will address the problem of gender discrimination.[37]

Perhaps the greatest fear of implementing comparable worth standards is the cost of replacing market forces of supply and demand with a government-imposed system of job evaluation. One source estimated that closing the earnings gap would cost $320 billion a year.[38] Proponents of comparable worth reject market pricing of jobs because they believe that markets reflect bias against occupations traditionally held by women.[39]

The Washington state case is perhaps the best known example of comparable worth in action. In 1982, the state was sued by the American Federation of State, County, and Municipal Employees (AFSCME). The union charged that women employees of the state were being discriminated against. In fact, some jobs traditionally filled by women had been evaluated at a higher level under the state's job evaluation plan, but the pay rates were less than for jobs traditionally filled by men. The discrimination charge was upheld in U.S. District Court and the judge's order required the state immediately to bring all workers in the job categories filled predominantly with women up to their evaluated rates. The U.S. Court of Appeals for the Ninth Circuit overturned this decision. However, propelled by political forces, the state negotiated an agreement with the union calling for broad implementation of comparable worth.[40] The issue will probably be decided finally by the U.S. Supreme Court.

In addition to Washington, a number of other states are obviously taking comparable worth seriously. Eleven states have completed a comparable worth study and have begun to implement wage adjustments. Several states have made pay adjustments for predominantly female jobs without having conducted a study. Ten states have conducted studies but have not implemented them. Twenty state governments have not engaged in any significant comparable worth activity although some have endorsed the concept.[41] The goal of nondiscriminatory pay practices is one that every organization should seek to achieve for ethical and legal reasons. Whether comparable worth is an appropriate solution remains to be seen.

---

[36] John F. Sullivan, "Comparable Worth and the Statistical Audit," p. 103.

[37] Julie M. Buchanan, "Comparable Worth: Where Is It Headed?" *Human Resources: Journal of the International Association for Personnel Women,* 2 (Summer 1985), p. 12.

[38] "Twenty Questions on Comparable Worth," p. 65.

[39] June O'Neill, Michael Brien, and James Cunningham, "Effects of Comparable Worth Policy: Evidence from Washington State," *American Economic Review,* 79 (May 1989), p. 305.

[40] *Ibid.*

[41] *Ibid.*

Pay Secrecy

Organizations tend to keep their pay rates secret for various reasons. If a firm's compensation plan is illogical, secrecy may indeed be appropriate because only a well-designed system can stand careful scrutiny.[42] An open system would almost certainly require managers to explain the rationale for pay decisions to subordinates.

Secrecy can have odd results, however. For example, managers who are unaware of pay rates in their firm tend to overestimate the pay of managers around them and to underestimate what higher level managers make. Such perceptions destroy much of the motivation intended in a differential pay system and indirectly contribute to turnover.[43]

Ideally, a firm will strive to develop a logical pay system, which reflects both internal and external equity. Employees in the process should participate to the greatest extent feasible. Compensation managers should take the lead in ensuring that employees understand the bases for their pay. Obviously, management cannot make all employees happy. The dissatisfaction and costs associated with a secret pay system, however, seem to make it a highly questionable practice.

Pay Compression

Organizations normally strive for both internal and external pay equity. In practice, however, this is often difficult or even impossible to accomplish. For example, in order to attract an engineer to a firm, an unusually high salary may have to be paid. Individuals possessing the skills needed to perform this job are in short supply relative to the demand for their services. Therefore these workers, and others in similar situations, are able to command high salaries (and in the process experience external pay equity).[44]

But how does the hiring of this type of employee affect internal equity? Other jobs within the firm may have greater value to the firm—as determined by job evaluation—but are now paid less than the engineers. In this instance, the firm sacrificed internal equity because it had little choice in the matter, assuming that it had to fill the engineer job.

Situations of this type may also result in a troublesome problem called pay compression. **Pay compression** occurs when workers perceive that the pay differential between their pay and that of employees in jobs above or below them is too small. It can be created in several ways, including the hiring of new employees at pay rates comparable to those of current employees who have been with the firm for several years. Making pay adjustments at the lower end of the job hierarchy without commensurate adjustments at the top is also a common cause of pay compression.

---

[42] Donald L. Caruth, *Compensation Management for Banks,* p. 244.

[43] Edward E. Lawler III, *Pay and Organizational Effectiveness: A Psychological View* (New York: McGraw-Hill, 1971), pp. 174–175, 196–197.

[44] William S. Hubbartt, "The Ten Commandments of Salary Administration," *Administrative Management,* 43 (April 1982), p. 24.

Pay compression may also result from granting pay increases on a flat cents-per-hour basis over a long period of time. Percentage increases, on the other hand, maintain relative differences in pay rates. The result of compression is usually dissatisfaction on the part of employees in higher level jobs. With a flattened pay curve, there is less financial incentive for employees to strive for promotion.

SUMMARY

Compensation refers to the rewards that individuals receive in return for their labor. Direct financial compensation consists of the pay that a person receives in the form of wages, salary, bonuses, and commissions. Indirect financial compensation (benefits) includes all financial rewards that are not included in direct compensation. Nonfinancial compensation is the satisfaction a person receives directly from the job or from the psychological and/or physical job environment. All these types of compensation comprise a total compensation program.

Equity refers to the perception by workers that they are being treated fairly. External equity exists when employees performing jobs within a firm are paid at levels comparable to those paid for similar jobs in other firms. Internal equity exists when employees are paid according to the relative value of their jobs within the organization. Job evaluation is a primary means for determining internal equity. Employee equity exists when individuals performing similar jobs in the same firm are paid according to factors unique to the employee, such as productivity.

Many factors interact with and affect compensation. The organization, the labor market, the job, and the employee all have an impact on determining the individual's financial compensation.

Before a company can determine the relative difficulty or value of its jobs, it must first define their content. This is normally achieved through job analysis. Job evaluation is that part of a compensation system that a firm uses to determine the relative values of its jobs. The basic purpose of job evaluation is to eliminate internal pay inequities that exist because of illogical pay structures. Organizations use four basic job evaluation methods: ranking, classification, factor comparison, and point. The ranking and classification methods are qualitative, whereas the factor comparison and point methods are quantitative approaches.

In the ranking method, raters examine the description of each job being evaluated and arrange the jobs in order according to their value to the company. The classification method defines a number of classes, or grades, of jobs. The factor comparison method is based on the assumption that five universal job factors exist; raters need not keep the entire job in mind as they evaluate, and they make decisions on separate aspects, or factors, of the job. In the point method, numerical values are assigned to specific job components and the sum of these values represents a job's relative worth.

Placing a dollar value on the worth of a job is called job pricing. Jobs are priced after they have been evaluated and the relative value of each job in the organization has been determined. A pay grade is the grouping of similar jobs to simplify the job pricing process. A pay range includes a minimum and maximum pay rate, with enough variance between the two to allow for significant pay difference. Pay ranges allow employees to be paid according to length of service and performance levels. When pay ranges are used, a method must be developed to advance individuals through the range. Global compensation issues include—in the case of alliances—how the pay systems of partners are to be related. In these situations, an agreement should be reached concerning the broad objectives of the compensation system.

Several issues that affect compensation deserve special mention, including comparable worth, pay secrecy, and pay compression. Comparable worth requires the value for dissimilar jobs (e.g., company nurse and welder) to be compared under some form of job evaluation and pay rates to be assigned according to their evaluated worth. The basic premise of comparable worth is that jobs traditionally held by women are paid less than those traditionally held by men, even though both types of jobs may contribute equally to achieving the organization's goals.

Organizations tend to keep their pay rates secret for various reasons. If a firm's compensation plan is illogical, secrecy may indeed be appropriate because only a well-designed system can stand careful scrutiny.

Pay compression occurs when workers perceive that the differential between their pay and that of employees in jobs above or below them is too small. It can be created in several ways, including hiring new employees at pay rates comparable to those of current employees who have been with the firm for several years. Making pay adjustments at the lower end of the job hierarchy without commensurate adjustments at the top is also a common cause of pay compression.

Questions for Review

1. Define each of the following terms:
   a. Compensation
   b. Direct financial compensation
   c. Indirect financial compensation
   d. Nonfinancial compensation
2. Distinguish among external equity, internal equity, and employee equity.
3. What are the primary determinants of financial compensation? Briefly describe each.
4. Distinguish among a pay follower, a pay leader, and a going-rate organization.
5. How has government legislation affected compensation?
6. Give the primary purpose of job evaluation.

7. Distinguish among the four basic methods of job evaluation: ranking, classification, factor comparison, and point.
8. What is the purpose of job pricing? Discuss this briefly.
9. State the basic procedure for determining pay grades.
10. What is the purpose of establishing pay ranges?
11. Describe the various factors relating to the employee in determining pay and benefits.
12. Describe each of the following concepts:
    a. Comparable worth
    b. Pay secrecy
    c. Pay compression

Terms for Review

Compensation	Exempt employees
Direct financial compensation	Job evaluation
Indirect financial compensation	Ranking method
Nonfinancial compensation	Classification method
Equity	Factor comparison method
External equity	Point method
Internal equity	Hay guide chart-profile method
Employee equity	Job pricing
Pay leaders	Pay grade
Going rate	Wage curve
Pay followers	Pay range
Labor market	Comparable worth
Key job	Pay compression
Cost-of-living allowance (COLA)	

INCIDENT 1   ▪ It's Just Not Fair! ▪

During a Saturday afternoon golf game with his friend Randy Dean, Harry Neil discovered that his department had hired a recent university grad as a systems analyst—at a starting salary almost as high as Harry's. Although Harry was good natured, he was bewildered and upset. It had taken him five years to become a senior systems analyst and attain his current salary level at Trimark Data Systems, Inc. He had been generally pleased with the company and thoroughly enjoyed his job.

The following Monday morning Harry confronted Dave Edwards, the human resource director, and asked if what he had heard was true. Dave apologetically admitted that it was and attempted to explain the company's situation: "Harry, the market for systems analysts is very tight and in order for the company to attract qualified prospects, we have to offer a premium starting salary. We desperately needed another analyst and this was the only way we could get one."

Harry asked Dave if his salary would be adjusted accordingly. Dave answered, "Your salary will be reevaluated at the regular time. You're doing a great job, though, and I'm sure the boss will recommend a raise." Harry thanked Dave for his time but left the office shaking his head and wondering about his future.

Questions

1. Do you think Dave's explanation was satisfactory? Discuss.
2. What action do you believe the company should have taken with regard to Harry?

INCIDENT 2   ■   Job Evaluation: Who or What?   ■

David Rhine, compensation manager for Farrington Lingerie Company, was generally relaxed and good natured. Although he was a no-nonsense, competent executive, David was one of the most popular managers in the company. This Friday morning, however, David was not his usual self. As chairperson of the company's job evaluation committee, he had called a late morning meeting at which several jobs were to be considered for reevaluation. The jobs had already been rated and assigned to pay grade 3. But the office manager, Ben Butler, was upset that one was not rated higher. To press the issue, Ben had taken his case to two executives who were also members of the job evaluation committee. The two executives (production manager Bill Nelson and general marketing manager Betty Anderson) then requested that the job ratings be reviewed. Bill and Betty supported Ben's side of the dispute, and David was not looking forward to the confrontation that was almost certain to occur.

The controversial job was that of receptionist. There was only one receptionist position in the company and it was held by Beth Smithers. Beth had been with the firm twelve years—longer than any of the committee members. She was extremely efficient, and virtually all the executives in the company, including the president, had noticed and commented on her outstanding work. Bill Nelson and Betty Anderson were particularly pleased with Beth because of the cordial manner in which she greeted and accommodated

Farrington's customers and vendors, who frequently visited the plant. They felt that Beth projected a positive image of the company.

When the meeting began, Dave said, "Good morning. I know that you're busy so let's get the show on the road. We have several jobs to evaluate this morning and I suggest we begin—." Before he could finish his sentence, Bill interrupted, "I suggest we start with Beth." Betty nodded in agreement. When David regained his composure, he quietly but firmly asserted, "Bill, we are not here today to evaluate Beth. Her supervisor does that at performance appraisal time. We're meeting to evaluate jobs based on job content. In order to do this fairly with regard to other jobs in the company, we must leave personalities out of our evaluation." David then proceeded to pass out copies of the receptionist job description to Bill and Betty, who were very irritated.

Questions

1. Do you feel that David was justified in insisting that the job, not the person, be evaluated? Discuss.
2. Do you believe that there is a maximum rate of pay for every job in an organization, regardless of how well the job is being performed? Justify your position.
3. Assuming that Beth is earning the maximum of the range for her pay grade, in what ways can she obtain a salary increase?

DEVELOPING HRM SKILLS

I n the future, one of the key issues concerning pay will be comparable worth. If comparable worth becomes law, organizations will have to base salaries and wages on job evaluation scores. They will be determined by the requirements of the job itself—skills required, knowledge required, effort required, working conditions, and responsibilities—rather than the workings of the labor market. Then equal pay for different jobs of the same value will have to be determined not by looking at the "going rate" in the marketplace, but rather at the job's difficulty, importance, and the training required to properly perform it. This exercise has been developed to impart an understanding and appreciation of the concept of comparable worth.

The concept of comparable worth is based on three premises:

1. That it is possible to compare different jobs and establish a "correct pay" relationship for them.

2. That the pay established by the supply and demand of the job market is often inequitable and discriminatory, especially with regard to pay for women.

3. That the government and the courts must intervene to ensure that pay relationships are corrected and made equitable.

Everyone will be given a copy of Exhibit 1, and based on these three premises determine the following:

1. Which of the following jobs would you consider "comparable"? (Select a job from the second list and write it beside the job on the first list to which you feel it "compares.")

2. What average monthly salary would you assign to each position?

After ten minutes everyone will sign their Exhibits and turn them in. Then, three participants with dissimilar comparisons will list their comparisons and salaries on the chalkboard and debriefing will begin.

REFERENCES

Beatty, Kate. "What's Driving Your Pay?" *HRMagazine,* 35 (July 1990), pp. 45–48.

Belcher, David W., and Thomas J. Atchison. *Compensation Administration,* 2nd ed. (Englewood Cliffs, N.J.: Prentice-Hall, 1987).

Brown, Tom. "Does Compensation Add Up?" *Industry Week,* 239 (August 20, 1990), p. 13.

Buchanan, Julie M. "Comparable Worth: Where Is It Headed?" *Human Resources,* 2 (Summer 1985), p. 12.

Candall, Lin D., and Mark I. Phelps. "Pay for a Global Work Force." *Personnel Journal,* 70 (February 1991), pp. 28–33.

Cissell, Michael J. "Designing Effective Reward Systems." *Compensation and Benefits Review,* 19 (November–December 1987), pp. 19–25.

Collins, Gail. "Wages and Sin." *Working Woman,* 16 (March 1991), p. 134.

Davis, K. R., Jr., et al. "What College Graduates Want in a Compensation Package." *Compensation Review,* 17 (1985), pp. 42–53.

Ellig, Bruce R. "Strategic Pay Planning." *Compensation and Benefit Review,* 19 (July–August 1987), p. 28.

Esquibel, Orlando, Jack Ning, and John Sugg. "New Salary System Supports Changing Culture." *HRMagazine,* 35 (October 1990), pp. 43–48.

Feuer, Dale. "Paying for Knowledge." *Training: The Magazine of Human Resources Development,* 21 (May 1987), p. 57–64.

Filipowski, Diane. "Is Pay Linked to Performance?" *Personnel Journal,* 70 (May 1991), p. 39.

Giblin, Edward J., Geoffrey A. Wiegman, and Frank Sanfilippo. "Bringing Pay Up To Date." *Personnel,* 67 (November 1990), pp. 17–18.

Ginsburg, Sigmund G. "Motivating with Money." *American School and University,* 59 (July 1987), p. 11.

Kuhne, R. J., and B. Toyne. "Who Manages the International Compensation and Benefits Program?" *Compensation Review,* 17 (1985), pp. 34–41.

Langer, Steven. "What You Earn—and Why." *Personnel Journal,* 70 (January 1991), p. 25–27.

Lawler, Edward E. III. "What's Wrong with Point-Factor Evaluation." *Personnel,* 64 (January 1987), p. 38.

Luthans, Fred, and Marilyn L. Fox. "Update on Skill-Based Pay." *Compensation and Benefits Review,* 21 (July–August 1989), pp. 62–67.

McKendrick, Joseph E., Jr. "Salary Surveys—Roadmaps for the Volatile Employment Scene of the 1990s." *Management World,* 19 (March–April 1990), pp. 18–20.

Manter, Marcia A., and Janice Y. Benjamin. "How to Hold On to First Careerist." *Personnel Administrator,* 34 (September 1989), pp. 44–52.

Meehan, Robert H., and G. V. Lemises. "Compensation Plan Analysis." *HRMagazine,* 35 (February 1990), pp. 69–72.

Meng, George J. "All the Parts of Comparable Worth." *Personnel Journal,* 69 (November 1990), pp. 99, 101–102, 104.

Meng, George J. "Link Pay to Job Evaluation." *Personnel Journal,* 69 (March 1990), pp. 98–104.

Mickler, Mary Louise. "Merit Pay: Boon or Boondoggle?" *Clearing House,* 61 (November 1987), pp. 137–141.

O'Neill, June, Michael Brien, and James Cunningham. "Effects of Comparable Worth Policy: Evidence from Washington State." *American Economic Review,* 79 (May 1989), pp. 305–309.

Parnell, John A. "Five Reasons Why Pay Must Be Based on Performance." *Supervision,* 52 (February 1991), pp. 6–8.

Plachy, Roger J. "The Case for Effective Point-Factor Job Evaluation, Viewpoint I." *Personnel,* 64 (April 1987), p. 31.

Schraeder, Terry E., and Mark D. Dore. "Compensation a Pay Formula for the '90s." *Personnel Journal,* 69 (October 1990), pp. 46–47.

CHAPTER 13

BENEFITS AND OTHER COMPENSATION ISSUES

Chapter Objectives

1. Define *benefits* and describe their importance to the total compensation program.
2. Explain the various incentive compensation programs that are available.
3. Describe how compensation for managers, professionals, and sales representatives is determined.
4. Explain the many forms of nonfinancial compensation that employees are beginning to expect.
5. Describe factors that affect compensation in multinational corporations.

John Hicks, a college dropout, is a senior credit clerk at Ajax Manufacturing Company. A bright young man, John has been with Ajax for four years. He had received excellent performance ratings in each of the several positions he had held with the firm. However, during his last appraisal interview, John's supervisor implied that promotion to a higher level job would require additional formal education. Because John appeared to be receptive to the idea, his supervisor suggested that he check with human resources to learn the details of Ajax's educational assistance policy.

Arnold Anderson, Bob Minnis, and Mason Kearby are all employed as shipping clerks for Mainstreet Furniture Company. Arnold and Bob are energetic young people who consistently work hard each day. Both earn about $8.50 per hour. Mason is a "good ole boy" who spends most of his time flipping quarters with dock workers and talking with anyone who will listen. Yesterday, work was piling up in the department and Arnold and Bob were working furiously to keep up. Mason was nowhere to be found. "Arnold," Bob said disgustedly, "the pay here just isn't fair. We do twice as much work as Mason, yet he makes as much as we do." "I know," Arnold acknowledged, "but we all punch in and out at the same time."

Liz Nichols is a divorcée and the mother of three elementary school children. She works as an illustrator for Busiform Company to support her family. Her normal working hours are from 8:00 A.M. to 5:00 P.M., Monday through Friday. The children's school begins each weekday morning at 9:00 A.M. and ends at 3:30 P.M. Satisfactory arrangements had been made for the children after school. However, she faced an almost impossible task of transporting them to school in the morning and arriving at her job on time. The school's principal permitted the children to enter the building at 7:45 each morning to wait until classes began, but Liz was afraid that she couldn't count on this practice to continue indefinitely. When Busiform management announced implementation of a new system of flexible working hours, Liz was delighted.

Although these anecdotes may seem to have little in common, each relates to the broad area of compensation. John is investigating the possibility of continuing his education through his company's educational assistance program. Arnold and Bob are angry because a less productive worker makes as much money as they do. Liz believes that the new flexible working hours will solve a difficult problem in caring for her children.

We begin the chapter with a discussion of benefits, both mandated and voluntary. Next, we present various types of incentive compensation systems, followed by a discussion of special pay considerations that are provided to managers, professionals, and sales representatives. Then we describe nonfinancial compensation that stems from the job itself and the job environment. In the final section we deal with the unique aspects of compensation in multinational corporations. The overall purpose of this chapter is to emphasize the significance of benefits in a total compensation system and provide an overview of other important issues associated with compensation programs.

■ BENEFITS (INDIRECT FINANCIAL COMPENSATION)

Most organizations recognize that they have a responsibility to their employees by providing insurance and other programs for their health, safety, security, and general welfare (see Figure 13-1). These programs are called **benefits** and include all financial rewards that generally are not paid directly to the employee. Benefits cost the firm money, but employees usually receive them indirectly. For example, an organization may spend $2,700 a year as a contribution to the health insurance premiums for each nonexempt employee. The employee does not receive money but does obtain the benefit of health insurance coverage. This type of compensation has two distinct advantages: (1) it is generally nontaxable to the employee; and (2) in the case of insurance, the premium rates are much less for large groups of employees than for individual policies.

Generally speaking, benefits are provided to employees because of their membership in the organization. They are typically not related to employee productivity and therefore do not serve as motivation for improved performance. However, an attractive benefit package can assist in the recruitment and retention of a qualified workforce.

The cost of benefits is high and is growing rapidly, costing employers some $350 billion a year. Between 1965 and 1985, costs rose from 24.7 percent to 37.7 percent of total financial costs. Most of the increase is attributable to escalations in social security taxes and group health plan costs.[1] In 1986, the average cost of benefits in all industries, as a percentage of total financial costs, was over 38 percent. The average annual benefits costs per employee ranged from $13,450 in the rubber, leather, and plastic industries to $5,102 for department stores.[2] A typical worker who earns

---

[1] Robert M. McCaffery, "Organizational Performance and the Strategic Allocation of Indirect Compensation," *Human Resource Planning,* 12, no. 3 (1989), p. 229.

[2] Albert G. Holzinger, "The Real Costs of Benefits," *Nation's Business,* 76 (February 1988), p. 30.

```
                    ┌─────────────────── EXTERNAL ENVIRONMENT ───────────────────┐

                        ┌─────────────── INTERNAL ENVIRONMENT ───────────────┐

                              ┌─────────────────────────────────────┐
                              │            Compensation             │
                              └─────────────────────────────────────┘

                    ┌──────────────────────┐          ┌──────────────────────┐
                    │       Financial      │          │     Nonfinancial     │
                    └──────────────────────┘          └──────────────────────┘

         ┌─────────────┐  ┌─────────────────┐   ┌─────────────┐  ┌─────────────────┐
         │   Direct    │  │    Indirect     │   │   The job   │  │ Job Environment │
         │             │  │                 │   │             │  │                 │
         │             │  │ Insurance Plans:│   │             │  │                 │
         │             │  │   Life, Health, │   │             │  │                 │
         │             │  │   Surgical,     │   │             │  │                 │
         │             │  │   Dental,       │   │             │  │                 │
         │             │  │   Casualty, etc.│   │             │  │                 │
         │             │  │ Social Assistance│  │             │  │                 │
         │             │  │ Benefits:       │   │             │  │                 │
         │             │  │   Retirement    │   │             │  │                 │
         │             │  │   Plans,        │   │             │  │                 │
         │             │  │   Social        │   │             │  │                 │
         │             │  │   Security,     │   │             │  │                 │
         │             │  │   Workers'      │   │             │  │                 │
         │             │  │   Compensation, │   │             │  │                 │
         │             │  │   Educational   │   │             │  │                 │
         │             │  │   Assistance,   │   │             │  │                 │
         │             │  │   Employee      │   │             │  │                 │
         │             │  │   Services      │   │             │  │                 │
         │             │  │ Paid Absences:  │   │             │  │                 │
         │             │  │   Vacations,    │   │             │  │                 │
         │             │  │   Holidays,     │   │             │  │                 │
         │             │  │   Sick Leave,   │   │             │  │                 │
         │             │  │   etc.          │   │             │  │                 │
         └─────────────┘  └─────────────────┘   └─────────────┘  └─────────────────┘
```

FIGURE 13-1 | Typical Benefits in a Total Compensation Program

$24,800 per year receives approximately $9,424 more, indirectly, in the form of benefits. This proportion no doubt accounts for the much less frequent use of the term *fringe* benefits. In fact, the benefits that employees receive today are significantly different from those of just ten years ago.

Legally Required Benefits

While most employee benefits are provided at the employer's discretion, others are required by law. These benefits currently account for about 9 percent of total compensation costs. They are, in order of relative costs, social security, workers' compensation, and unemployment insurance. The future comparative importance of these benefits will depend on how our nation deals with rising health care costs and with long-term custodial care for elderly citizens.[3]

Social Security. The Social Security Act of 1935 created a system of retirement benefits. Subsequent amendments to the act added other forms of protection, such as disability insurance, survivors benefits, and, most recently, medicare. Today, approximately nine out of ten employees in the United States are covered by social security. Disability insurance protects employees against loss of earnings resulting from total disability. Survivors benefits are provided to certain members of an employee's family when he or she dies. These benefits are paid to the widow or widower and unmarried children of the deceased employee. Unmarried children may be eligible for survivors benefits until they are 18 years old. In some cases, students retain eligibility until they are 19. Medicare provides hospital and medical insurance protection for individuals 65 years of age and older and for those who have become disabled.

While employees must pay a portion of the cost, the employer makes an equal contribution for social security coverage. It is the employer's part that is considered a benefit. As Table 13-1 shows, in 1937 workers paid 1 percent of the first $3,000 they earned—a maximum of $30. At that time, only 40 percent of American workers were covered. During the first forty years of its existence, the maximum tax increased to $965.25. From 1977 to 1987, the maximum tax almost tripled and projections indicate steady increases in the future. In 1991, a dual tax rate was imposed for the first time. As shown in Table 13-1, the tax rate of 7.65 percent applied to a maximum taxable wage of $53,400. The rate for hospitalization insurance, 1.45 percent, applied to earnings exceeding $53,400, up to a maximum of $125,000. The same format was also in effect in 1992 and will most likely continue as a result of escalating hospitalization costs. Today, approximately 95 percent of the workers in this country pay into and may draw social security benefits.

The normal retirement age under social security will be increased after the turn of the century. Beginning with employees who reach age 62 in the year 2000, the retirement age will be increased gradually until 2009, when it reaches age 66. After stabilizing at this age for a period of time, it will again increase in 2027 when it reaches age 67. These changes will not affect medicare, with full eligibility under this program holding at age 65.

Unemployment Compensation. An individual laid off by an organization covered by the Social Security Act may receive unemployment compensation for up to twenty-six weeks. While the federal government provides certain guidelines, unemployment compensation programs are administered by the states and the benefits vary by state. A payroll tax paid by employers funds the unemployment compensation program.

Workers' Compensation. Workers' compensation benefits provide a degree of financial protection for employees who incur expenses resulting

---

[3] George L. Stelluto and Deborah P. Klein, "Compensation Trends into the 21st Century," *Monthly Labor Review,* 113 (February 1990), p. 44.

TABLE 13-1 | Social Security Taxes, 1937–1992

| Year | Tax Rate for Employee and Employer (Each) | | | Maximum Taxable Wage | Maximum Tax |
	For cash benefits	For hospitalization insurance	Total		
1937	— %	— %	1.00%	$ 3,000	$ 30.00
1977	—	—	5.85	16,500	965.25
1984	5.70	1.30	7.00	37,800	2,646.00
1985	5.70	1.35	7.05	39,600	2,791.80
1986	5.70	1.45	7.15	42,000	3,003.00
1987	5.70	1.45	7.15	43,800	3,131.70
1988	6.06	1.45	7.51	45,000	3,379.50
1989	6.06	1.45	7.51	48,000	3,604.80
1990	6.20	1.45	7.65	51,300	3,924.45
1991	6.20	1.45	7.65	53,400* 125,000**	5,123.30
1992	6.20	1.45	7.65	55,500* 130,200**	5,328.90

*The total tax rate of 7.65 percent is applied to the first figure—
$53,400 in 1991 and $55,500 in 1992.

**The 1.45 percent rate for hospitalization insurance applies to
earnings over $53,400, up to a maximum of $125,000, for 1991;
for 1992, it applies to earnings over $55,500, up to a maximum
of $130,200.

Sources: Your Social Security (Washington, D.C.: U.S. Government
Printing Office), January 1986 and 1987 editions; *Social Security '88*
(Madison, Conn.: Business and Legal Reports), p. 1; and SSA Annual
Changes Reference Chart, Dallas Region, December 1991.

from job-related accidents or illnesses. As with unemployment compensation, the various states administer individual programs, which are subject to federal regulations. Employers pay the entire cost of workers' compensation insurance. Their premium expense is directly tied to their past experience with job-related accidents and illnesses. This situation should encourage employers to actively pursue health and safety programs, which are topics discussed in Chapter 14.

Voluntary Benefits

Organizations voluntarily provide a seemingly endless number of benefits. These benefits may be classified as (1) payment for time not worked, (2) employee health and security benefits, (3) services to employees, and (4) premium pay. Generally speaking, such benefits are not legally required. They are provided voluntarily by some firms and as a result of union-management negotiations in others.

Payment for Time Not Worked. In providing payment for time not worked, employers recognize that employees need time away from the job. For instance, paid vacations provide workers with an opportunity to rest and become rejuvenated, while also encouraging them to remain with the firm. Paid vacation time typically increases with seniority. For example, employees with six-months' service may receive one week of vacation; employees with one year of service, two weeks; ten-years' service, three weeks; and fifteen-years' service, four weeks.

A senior executive with a month of vacation and an annual salary of $96,000 would receive approximately $8,000 each year while not working. A junior employee earning $24,000 a year might receive two weeks of vacation time worth about $1,000.

Each year many firms allocate to each employee a certain number of days of sick leave, which they can use when ill. Employees who are too ill to report to work continue to receive their pay up to the maximum number of days accumulated. As with vacation pay, the number of sick leave days typically depends on seniority. However, some sick leave programs have been severely criticized. At times they have been abused by individuals calling in sick when all they really wanted was additional paid vacation. In order to counter this situation, some firms require a doctor's statement after a certain number of sick leave days have been taken.

Employees are also paid at other times, even though they aren't working. Holidays, coffee breaks, rest periods, jury duty service, voting time, clean-up time, and bereavement time are all in this category.

Employee Welfare. Benefits that provide for general employee welfare may be of several kinds. Health insurance typically includes hospital room and board costs, service charges, and surgical fees. This increasingly costly benefit is often paid in part, or totally, by the employer. Many plans provide for major medical benefits to cover extraordinary expenses. The use of "deductibles" is a common feature of major medical benefits. For example, the employee may have to pay the first $200 of medical bills before the insurance takes over payment. In order to control health care costs, a number of firms have increased the amount of deductibles and at times have even reduced the scope of insurance coverage.

In some firms, health insurance premiums alone amount to almost 10 percent of the total payroll. In an attempt to control medical costs, some 30 percent of the businesses that provide medical benefits now use some type of utilization review service. **Utilization review** is a process that scrutinizes medical diagnoses, hospitalization, surgery, and other medical treatment and care prescribed by doctors. The reviewer, often a registered nurse, explores alternatives to the treatment provided, such as outpatient treatment or admission on the day of surgery. The objective of this process is, of course, to hold down the costs of businesses' portion of the nearly $400 billion Americans spend annually on medical care.[4]

---

[4] Ellen Paris, "Hold That Scalpel?" *Forbes* (May 6, 1985), pp. 35–36.

Wellness is a concept that focuses on the prevention of illness and diseases. It is also an approach to health care that offers great promise in stemming the tide of increasing treatment costs. Heavy smoking, poor nutrition, and undue stress are life-style and personal habit patterns that wellness programs strive to change. It is important that the programs succeed because these patterns contribute to diseases that account for a large share of health care expenditures.

There is considerable evidence that wellness programs work. For example, New York Telephone estimates annual savings of more than $2 million in reduced absenteeism and lowered medical costs from its stop-smoking program. Kennecott Corporation has reduced its medical care costs by more than 50 percent for the 12,000 employees participating in its wellness program.[5] We discuss topics related to wellness, such as stress and physical fitness, in Chapter 14.

Group life insurance is a benefit commonly provided to protect the employee's family in the event of his or her death. The cost of group life insurance is low. Some plans call for the employee to pay part of the premium. Coverage may be a flat amount (for instance, $10,000) or based on the employee's annual earnings. For example, a worker earning $20,000 per year may have $40,000 worth of group life coverage. Typically, members of group plans do not have to show evidence of insurability. This provision is especially important to older employees and those with physical problems. Many of these employees may find the cost of individual insurance to be prohibitive.

Private retirement plans provide income for employees who retire after reaching a certain age or having served the firm for a specific period of time. Pension plans are vitally important to employees because social security was not designed to provide complete retirement income. Over the next thirty years, the U.S. population will be dominated by older people who are either retired or approaching retirement. Therefore, retirement financing will become a primary issue for individuals, employers, and governments.[6] The Employee Retirement Income Security Act of 1974 (ERISA) was passed to strengthen existing and future retirement programs. The act also ensures that retired employees will receive deserved pensions.

In 1984, ten years after ERISA became law, a major amendment, the Retirement Equity Act (REACT), was enacted. The purpose of this act is to provide greater equity in private pension plans for covered workers and their spouses. Changes were made in some of ERISA's rules, which originally tended to penalize working women. These modifications increase the likelihood that women will actually receive benefits on the basis of their participation in the workforce or as a surviving spouse.[7] Key features of REACT include the following:

---

[5] Robert D. Kilpatrick, "Increasing the Wellness Effort," *Industry Week* (February 4, 1985), p. 14.

[6] "Visions: Funding Retiree Benefits," *HRMagazine,* 36 (February 1991), p. 87.

[7] Jack H. Schechter, "The Retirement Equity Act: Meeting Women's Pension Needs," *Compensation Review,* 17 (First Quarter 1985), pp. 13–21.

- Pension plans must pay benefits as a qualified joining-and-survivor annuity when a participant retires, unless the employee's spouse consigns the benefit election form in which some other option is chosen.
- The qualified joint-and-survivor annuity requirement now also applies to defined-contribution pension plans other than employee stock ownership plans (ESOPs).
- Pension and profit-sharing plans must pay a survivor benefit to the widow or widower of any vested participant who dies before retirement, not just those of active employees who are 55 and older.
- Plans are allowed to honor state law alimony awards and other support orders if the order meets uniform basic standards, which may include an order to pay a benefit to the ex-spouse, even if the covered employee has not retired.
- Employees who are absent from work because of pregnancy, childbirth, adoption, or infant care are protected against break-in-service penalties for up to a year.
- A nonvested employee who leaves the employer's service and then comes back within five years will be entitled to credit for that earlier service, even if it was for less than five years.
- The minimum age for plan participation and benefit accrual cannot be higher than 21, and the minimum age for vesting service cannot be higher than 18.
- Service pensions and other subsidized retirement benefits—as well as optional payment forms—can only be dropped from a plan with respect to benefits that are earned after the plan is amended to make the change.
- Plans can cash out benefits worth up to $3,500 without the recipient's consent (the amount previously was $1,750).[8]

Another piece of legislation that has an important effect on retired employees is the Comprehensive Omnibus Budget Reconciliation Act (COBRA). This act became law in 1986 and requires, among other things, that most employers in the private sector make available to terminated or retired employees and their families continued health benefits for a period of time, usually eighteen months. The cost of these benefits, however, must be borne by the former employee.

It is not yet clear how many individuals will take advantage of the benefits provided by COBRA. In many instances, employees will utilize coverage from their next employer or their spouse's employer. In either case, the cost will almost always be less.[9]

Supplemental unemployment benefits (SUB) first appeared in auto industry labor agreements in 1955. They are designed to provide additional income for employees receiving unemployment insurance benefits. These plans have spread to many other industries and are usually financed by the company. They tend to benefit newer employees because layoffs are nor-

---

[8] Judith F. Mazo, "Another Compliance Challenge for Employers: The Retirement Equity Act," *Personnel*, 62 (February 1985), p. 43.

[9] Joan C. Szabo, "The Bite of COBRA," *Nation's Business*, 74 (December 1986), p. 54.

mally determined by seniority. For this reason, employees with considerable seniority are often not enthusiastic about SUB.

Employee Services. Organizations offer a variety of benefits that can be termed employee services. These include company-subsidized food services, financial assistance for employee-operated credit unions, legal and income tax aid, club memberships, athletic and recreational programs, discounts on company products, moving expenses, parking spaces, and tuition rebates on educational expenses. Such benefits can greatly enhance the employment relationship.

Premium Pay. Premium pay is compensation paid to employees for working long periods of time or working under dangerous or undesirable conditions. As we mentioned in Chapter 12, payment for overtime is required for nonexempt employees who work beyond forty hours in a given week. However, some firms pay overtime for hours worked beyond eight in a given day and pay double time—or even more—for work on Sundays and holidays.

Additional pay provided to employees who work under extremely dangerous conditions is called **hazard pay.** A window washer for skyscrapers in New York City might well be given extra compensation because of dangerous working conditions. Military pilots receive extra money in the form of flight pay because of the hazards involved.

A **shift differential** is paid to employees for the inconvenience of working undesirable hours. This type of pay may be provided on the basis of additional cents per hour. For example, employees who work the second shift ("swing" shift) from 4:00 P.M. until midnight might receive $0.35 per hour above the base rate for that job. The third shift ("graveyard" shift) often warrants an even greater differential. For example, an extra $0.42 per hour may be paid for the same job. Shift differentials are sometimes based on a percentage of the employee's base rate.

A Comprehensive Voluntary Benefits Program

International Business Machines Corporation offers a comprehensive voluntary benefits program. The program is noncontributory; that is, the company bears the full cost of the benefits. The growth of the IBM benefits program is shown in Figure 13-2 on page 492. Note that since its inception, the program has improved and has been enlarged to meet changing employee needs. Three of IBM's programs are particularly interesting: the Adoption Assistance Plan, the Retirement Education Assistance Plan, and the Elder Care Referral Service (ECRS).

Under the Adoption Assistance Plan, IBM reimburses employees for 80 percent of eligible charges up to a maximum of $1,750 for each adoption. Eligible charges include the following:

- Adoption agency fees
- Placement fees

- Lawyers' fees and other required legal fees
- Maternity fees (child's natural mother)
- Temporary foster care charges (immediately preceding placement of the child with the adopting family)

The IBM Retirement Education Assistance Plan is designed to help employees and their spouses prepare for activities and personal fulfillment in their retirement years. Under this plan, IBM will reimburse tuition costs for retirement courses—up to $2,500 per individual—upon evidence of course completion. This plan covers any course offered by nationally accredited colleges and postsecondary schools, as well as adult continuing-education courses conducted by state certified schools or educational organizations. Other courses that appear to meet the intent of the plan are also considered for reimbursement. An employee's eligibility in this plan begins five years before he or she is eligible to retire and continues until two years after the actual date of retirement.

The IBM Elder Care Referral Service is the first nationwide corporate program of its kind designed to provide consultation and referrals to em-

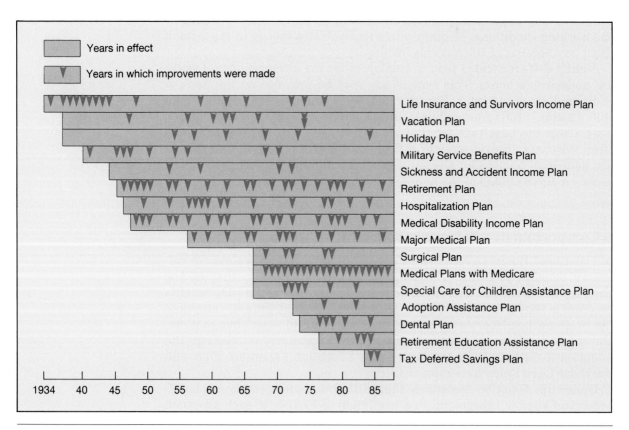

FIGURE 13-2 | IBM Benefits: Growth History

Source: Reprinted courtesy of International Business Machines Corporation.

ployees seeking care and services for elderly relatives. This service was introduced in 1988 to respond to a growing need among IBM employees that relates to the fact that people over 65 now represent the fastest growing segment of our population. ECRS is a program designed to clarify employee concerns and identify resources to assist in the care of relatives age 60 and over. The service is provided through a nationwide network of approximately 200 community-based consultation and referral organizations. These organizations provide personalized consultation, consumer information, and assistance in determining the type of elder care needed, along with referrals to the organizations best suited to provide such care. IBM will pay all costs for consultation and referrals, and employees or their older relatives are responsible for paying the fees to agencies furnishing the care. All regular IBM employees, retirees under the retirement plan, individuals receiving benefits under the medical disability income plan, spouses of these individuals, and surviving spouses who are eligible for IBM medical benefits may use the service.

Other Benefits

Several new benefits have recently appeared on the scene in addition to those included in IBM's innovative plan. One such benefit is subsidized day-care centers; the firm provides facilities for young children of employees for a modest fee. Parents typically transport the children to and from the center. While there, the children engage in supervised play and receive meals. This benefit is an effective recruitment aid and helps to reduce absenteeism. The need for such programs is emphasized by the fact that in 1950, only 12 percent of women with children under age 6 were in the labor force. That figure has now risen to almost 60 percent.[10] Although relatively few companies provide substantial child-care assistance, the number is growing rapidly. According to the U.S. Department of Health and Human Services, almost 600 firms provided this type of benefit in 1983, compared to only 100 five years earlier.[11]

In an attempt to conserve energy and relieve traffic congestion, some firms have begun transporting workers to and from work. Participating employees pay a portion of the cost and ride in company vans or buses. Some employees find this service a very convenient, attractive alternative to driving in heavy traffic.

Massachusetts Mutual Life Insurance Company has initiated two new health care benefits.[12] One of these programs serves to detect and treat high blood pressure. Once each year, all employees are offered a physical examination. When a case of high blood pressure is detected, the employee is

---

[10] Dan Cordtz, "Hire Me, Hire My Family," *Finance World,* 159 (September 18, 1990), p. 77.

[11] Carol Dilks, "Employers Who Help with the Kids," *Nation's Business,* 72 (February 1984), p. 59.

[12] "The New Corporate Goodies," *Dun's Review,* 18 (July 1981), p. 49.

referred to his or her own physician for further diagnosis and treatment. The company pays all medical costs for this treatment. The company and employees believe that this program literally saves lives, and, for this reason, it is a very popular benefit.

The other program encourages employees to stop smoking. The company will reimburse any person on the payroll who consults a hypnotist for treatment. At an early stage in the program, about half the participants had stopped smoking cigarettes.

Communicating Information about the Benefits Package

Employee benefits can help a firm recruit and retain a quality workforce. Management depends on an upward flow of information from employees in order to know when benefit changes are needed. In addition, because employee awareness of benefits is often severely limited, the program information must be communicated downward. Regardless of the technical soundness of a benefits program, a firm simply cannot get its money's worth if its employees do not know what they are receiving. Workers may even become resentful if they aren't frequently reminded of the value of the company's benefits. Employees may resent having to pay a portion of some benefits and overlook the larger picture of what they receive and the substantially greater costs borne by their employer.

The Employee Retirement Income Security Act provides still another reason for communicating information about a firm's benefits program. This act requires organizations with a pension or profit-sharing plan to provide employees with specific data at specified times. The act further mandates that the information be presented in an understandable manner and include the following details:

- The kind of plan.
- Eligibility requirements.
- Amount of benefits due at specific times and payment options.
- Surviving dependents' benefits.
- How the pension trust is invested.
- Who is responsible for managing the plan.[13]

Naturally, organizations can go beyond what is legally required. Many firms, such as the Southland Corporation, did so even before ERISA's enactment. Southland's report provides each employee with a compensation and benefits profile (see Figure 13-3 on pages 495–497). A summary of this type informs employees of their total compensation package and assists the firm in achieving its financial compensation and benefits objectives.

---

[13] Robert Krogman, "Is Your Company Getting the Most Out of Its Benefit Program?" *Personnel Administrator,* 25 (May 1980), pp. 45–46.

Prepared for: John Doe   Hire Date: 01/05/89
                 2828 N. Haskell Ave.   Employee #: 987654321
                 Dallas, TX 75204

COMPENSATION

Listed below is a schedule of compensation and benefits which Southland provided you either directly or indirectly for 1991:

Regular Earnings		$ 22,326.20
Profit Sharing Deferral	$1,665.90	
Earned Bonus		$ 2,679.14
F.I.C.A — Social Security		$ 1,662.83
Medical Expense Reimbursement		$ 282.71
Company Paid Medical Insurance Premium		$ 2,133.69
Profit Sharing Company Contribution		$ 883.01
Educational Reimbursement		$ 629.57
Vacation Days	10	
		$ 30,597.15

This Year 1992

Compensation:

Based on Your Present Annual Salary of	$ 25,260.00
and Including:	
Normal Bonus	$ 3,031.20
Your Estimated Compensation for 1992 Will Be	$ 28,291.20

Benefits

This benefits statement has been prepared for you based on information in Southland's records as of 02/19/92. Every effort has been made to assure the accuracy of the information reported; however, errors can occur. In all cases, actual benefits will be paid in accordance with the governing plan documents or insurance contracts. For more details on any of your benefits, refer to your plan booklets.

Benefits Package:
Protection for Today and Tomorrow . . .

Health Care

Hospital and Medical Benefits are provided for you by the Southland Corporation at no cost to you.

You have extended this benefit for 2 or more dependents at the cost of $14 per week. This premium is deducted from your check on a pre-tax basis.

Your medical plan reimburses 70% of all eligible hospital expenses after a $150 in-patient deductible (maximum $450 per year). With per-admission certification the hospital deductible is waived and hospital room and board charges are paid at 80%. Your medical plan reimburses 70% of eligible non-hospital expenses after a $200 deductible per year. After your out-of-pocket expenses in 1992 have reached $3,000 (not including hospital deductible) you will be reimbursed 100% for eligible medical expenses for the remainder of the year. The lifetime maximum for reimbursement per covered individual is $1,000,000

Dental Benefits

Your medical plan reimburses 70% of eligible dental expenses. Dental expenses are subject to the annual deductible. The maximum reimbursement for 1992 for each insured individual is . . . . $ 1,000

FIGURE 13-3 | The Southland Corporation Individual Employee Compensation and Benefits Profile

Source: Used with the permission of the Southland Corporation.

Disability Benefits

Your disability benefits are based on your average weekly earnings at the time this statement was prepared and are subject to change.

	Monthly	Benefits Period Annual	Total

Disability benefits are provided for you after 90 days of employment at no cost. Benefits are based on 75% of your weekly earnings for the first 26 weeks of disability—65% thereafter during the remainder of the disability, before applicable deductions. Your benefits for the first 26 weeks would be $384.67
Per week, benefits thereafter would be $333.38
Per week, and could be payable for a total of 51 weeks.

Life Insurance Benefits

Your life insurance benefits are based on your average weekly earnings at the time this statement was prepared and are subject to change.

At no cost to you, The Southland Corporation has provided term life insurance to your beneficiary or estate in the amount of . . . . $ 13,335.62

You have elected to increase the amount of your term life insurance by selecting:
    Additional life insurance payable to your beneficiary as a lump sum in the amount of . . . . $ 40,006.86
    Survivors' life insurance payable to your beneficiary as a lump sum in the amount of . . . . $ 40,006.86

The total life insurance benefit payable to your beneficiary in the event of your natural death is . . . . $ 80,013.72

Through the election of additional life insurance and survivors' life insurance, you have added:
    AD&D on yourself in the amount of . . . . $ 80,013.72
    Life insurance on your eligible spouse in the amount of $6,667.81
    Life insurance on each of your eligible dependent children in the amount of $3,333.90
The total life insurance benefit payable to your beneficiary in the event of your accidental death is $160,027.44

For more detailed information regarding other life insurance coverage, contact your division personnel manager or the group insurance department.

Employee Stock Ownership Plan

The employee stock ownership plan (ESOP) allows eligible employees to receive shares of the Southland Corporation common stock and participate in the growth of the company. If you were employed for one year or more on December 31, 1991, you will receive share allocations. These shares will be allocated to an account in your behalf. For 1990, Southland contributed in excess of $3,000,000
This amount was used to purchase shares of stock on behalf of eligible employees. Your account is paid to you if you retire or leave the company, or to your beneficiary in the event of your death. ESOP participants will receive their individual statements at the annual profit sharing meeting.

FIGURE 13-3 | *Continued*

Profit Sharing

The 1991 company contribution was in excess of $18,000,000

Your profit sharing account balance is payable to you at retirement. Payment may be made in a lump sum or on an installment schedule, whichever you select. Your account is payable to Jane Doe in the event of your death. Payment may be made in a lump sum or on an installment schedule, whichever your beneficiary elects. Your individual statement will be available to you at the annual profit sharing meeting.

The foundation of your retirement income will be your Southland profit sharing account along with social security. An individual retirement account (IRA) is another way to plan for your future and also provide tax advantages. IRA accounts are available through profit sharing, The Southland Credit Union, or other financial institutions. Consult with a savings/investment specialist to determine an approach that best suits your own savings ability and retirement goals.

Other Benefits

Social Security:

Southland matches your FICA payment for social security benefits. These benefits are provided to you by the United States government at age 65 or as early as age 62 at a reduced basis. Your spouse, age 65 or older, can receive additional social security payments equal to 40 to 50% of your benefit. In the event of your death or disability, benefits may be payable to your eligible dependents. For more detailed information, contact the Social Security Administration.

Credit Union:

You and your family members may join the credit union at any time after your employment. Secured and unsecured (signature) loans are available to credit union members at competitive rates. The credit union offers you the convenience of payroll deductions for savings, making loan payments, and for the direct deposit of your paycheck for those with checking accounts. The credit union also offers you many savings plans including regular shares (savings), checking (share draft) accounts, certificate accounts, individual retirement accounts (IRA), and an insured money management star account.

Workers' Compensation and Unemployment Compensation:

The Southland Corporation pays the required cost of federal and state mandated benefits such as workers' compensation, unemployment compensation, and disability benefits in some states.

Paid Time off for:

Vacation:
During 1991, you accrued 10 days of vacation time to be taken during 1992. This time may be adjusted if you were on a leave of absence during 1991.

Jury Duty:
Full pay for time served on jury duty.

Sick days:
Sick days vary by division as does eligibility.

Holidays:
Holidays vary by division as does eligibility.

Death in Family:
Full pay up to three days if there is a death in your immediate family.

In addition to all of the above, Southland provides numerous other valuable benefits which are significant and important to you:

Service Awards	Scholarships	Matching Gifts
Pre-Retirement Publications	Company Publications	Monthly Stock Investment
Leave of Absence	United States Auto Club	Holiday Gift Program
Discount Buying Service	Educational Reimbursement	Employee Assistance Program

FIGURE 13-3 | *Continued*

■ INCENTIVE COMPENSATION

One of the most significant U.S. economic problems in recent years has been its productivity growth rate relative to other nations. U.S. businesses must recognize that productivity growth can come not only from capital resources but also from the proper utilization of human resources. Pay for performance is one of the best means for motivating people and encouraging increased productivity.[14] While compensation is most often determined by how much time an employee spends at work, compensation programs that relate pay to productivity are referred to as **incentive compensation.** The basic purpose of all incentive plans is to improve employee productivity in order to gain a competitive advantage. To do this, the firm must utilize various rewards and focus on the needs of employees as well as the firm's business goals.[15] Productive workers, such as Arnold Anderson and Bob Minnis (mentioned at the beginning of the chapter), probably would prefer to be paid on the basis of their output. In fact, they may not maintain their high performance level for long if they are not paid in this way. Money can serve as an important motivator for those who value it—and many individuals do. However, a clear relationship must exist between performance and pay if money is to serve as an effective motivator.

Output standards must be established before any type of incentive system can be introduced. This standard is a measure of work that an average, well-trained employee, working at a normal pace, should be able to accomplish in a given period of time. For example, a firm may determine that employees in a particular department should be able to produce five finished parts per hour. The standard then becomes five. Time study specialists in industrial engineering or methods departments are often responsible for establishing work standards. A more direct approach to balancing pay and performance is to pay incentive compensation, which can be offered on an individual, group, or companywide basis.

Individual Incentive Plans

Many individual incentive plans have been used in an attempt to improve worker productivity and a firm's profitability. Under an incentive plan, if Arnold Anderson produces more than Mason Kearby (another employee performing the same job), he would be paid more for producing more.

A predetermined amount of money is paid for each unit produced under a **straight piecework plan.** The piece rate is calculated by dividing the standard hourly output into the job's pay rate. For example, if the standard output is 0.04 hour per unit, or 25 units per hour, and the job's pay rate is $5 per hour, the piece rate would be $0.20. Thus an employee who produced at the rate of 280 units per day would earn $56 in an eight-hour day. Most

---

[14] *Pay for Performance* (Chicago: Commerce Clearing House, Inc., 1990), p. 7.

[15] Michael Leibman and Harold P. Weinstein, "Money Isn't Everything," *HRMagazine,* 35 (November 1990), pp. 48–51.

incentive plans in use today have a guaranteed base. In this example, it would be the $5 per hour rate.

The straight piecework plan is the most commonly used incentive system.[16] It is simple and employees can easily understand it. One possible weakness (which is minimized by the use of computers) is that any change in the overall pay scale necessitates computing new piece rates for every job. The standard hour plan was devised to overcome this problem.

The **standard hour plan** is an individual incentive plan under which time allowances are calculated for each unit of output. Again, let's assume that 25 units per hour, or 0.04 hour per unit, is the standard output, $5 the hourly job rate, and eight hours the time worked per day. Under these assumptions, an employee would have an allowance of 0.04 hour per unit of output (instead of a piece rate of $0.20 per unit).

An employee producing at the rate of 280 units per day would receive an allowance of 0.04 hour per unit for all units produced in a day. Therefore, in an eight-hour day, this employee would earn 11.2 standard hours (280 units × 0.04 hour per unit). The pay for the day would be 11.2 standard hours × $5 per hour, or $56. The standard hour plan has the characteristics of the straight piecework plan; however, its advantage is that piece rates need not be recalculated for every pay rate change.

One potential problem with both the straight piecework plan and the standard hour plan is related to the output standard. Typically, industrial engineers establish the standard, which the workers may distrust. Employees may also view with considerable skepticism any change in the standard, although it may be justified in the eyes of management. Moreover, when individual output cannot be easily distinguished, group and companywide plans offer alternatives to individual incentive plans.

Group Incentive Plans

As we suggested earlier, paying individual incentives isn't always feasible. Work is often organized in such a manner that productivity results from group effort. It is then difficult, if not impossible, to determine each individual's contribution. In this event, if incentives are used, they must be provided to the group. For example, if the group produced 100 units over standard, each member would receive incentive compensation on a pro rata basis.

Group incentives have both advantages and disadvantages. For instance, in the assembly of electrical transformers, ten employees may be working on one phase of the operation. They must work together to successfully accomplish the overall task. If nine employees perform their tasks but one does not, the productivity of the entire group may suffer. However, the peer pressure exerted in such a situation can be so great that the affected individual will either conform to the group's standards or leave the group.

---

[16] George T. Milkovich and Jerry M. Newman, *Compensation,* 3rd ed. (Homewood, Ill.: Richard D. Irwin, Inc., 1990), p. 339.

Group incentive plans tend to foster teamwork and often encourage peers to serve as counselors and coaches for new members. Group members tend to lend a helping hand when it is needed.

Companywide Plans

In baseball, an outstanding pitcher or a great outfield isn't the standard by which a team is judged. The standard is the team's overall win-loss record. The criterion for success focuses on the team's performance, not the achievements of individuals. In business, companywide plans offer a feasible alternative to the incentive plans previously discussed. They may be based on the organization's productivity, cost savings, or profitability. To illustrate the concept of companywide plans, we discuss profit sharing, employee stock ownership, and the Scanlon Plan.

Profit Sharing. **Profit sharing** is a compensation plan that results in the distribution of a predetermined percentage of the firm's profits to employees. Many firms use this type of plan to integrate the employee's interests with those of the company. Profit-sharing plans can aid in recruiting, motivating, and retaining employees, which usually enhances productivity.

There are several variations of profit-sharing plans, but the three basic forms are current, deferred, and combination.[17]

- Current plans provide payment to employees in cash or stock as soon as profits have been determined.
- Deferred plans involve placing company contributions in an irrevocable trust to be credited to the account of individual employees. The funds are normally invested in securities, and become available to the employee (or his or her survivors) at retirement, termination, or death.
- Combination plans permit employees to receive payment of part of their share of profits on a current basis, while payment of part of their share is deferred.

Normally, most full-time employees are included in a company's profit-sharing plan after a specified waiting period. Vesting determines the amount of "profit" an employee actually owns in his or her account and is often established on a graduated basis. For example, an employee may become 25 percent vested after being in the plan for two years; 50 percent vested after three years; 75 percent vested after four years; and 100 percent vested after five years. This approach to vesting may tend to reduce turnover by encouraging employees to remain with the company.

Profit sharing tends to tie employees to the economic success of the firm. Reported results include increased efficiency and lower costs. However, in recent years the Employee Retirement Income Security Act and the intro-

[17] J. D. Dunn and Frank M. Rachel, *Salary Administration: Total Compensation Systems* (New York: McGraw-Hill, 1971), pp. 261–262.

HRM In Action

Did you realize that we spent over $70,000 on our incentive program last year?" asked Barry Cline, production manager. He was talking to the human resource manager, Elisia Chaumont. Barry continued, "For a company our size, we sure spend a lot of money for what we get. Frankly, I think the employees are paid too much. What do you think about upping the standards a bit for receiving incentive pay? It could save the company a lot of money."

If you were Elisia, how would you respond?

duction of employee thrift plans have slowed the growth of profit-sharing plans.[18] Also, variations in profits have had an impact. For example, if the company does not make sufficient profits for several years, employees may not benefit from the plan. This may be a special problem when employees have become accustomed to receiving added compensation from profit sharing, or when the plan itself represents a major part of the firm's benefits program.

Employee Stock Ownership Plan. A companywide incentive plan whereby the company provides its employees with common stock is called an **employee stock ownership plan (ESOP).** Currently, company contributions to ESOPs are tax deductible expenses.

Many of the benefits of profit-sharing plans have also been cited for ESOPs. Specifically, ESOP advocates have suggested that employees obtain a stake in the business and become more closely identified with the firm—a relationship that theoretically increases motivation. Finally, from a company viewpoint, when ESOPs borrow money to buy stock, tax benefits multiply for the sponsoring firm if the plan is used as a financing tool for anything from a stock buyout to a leveraged buyout.[19]

Although the potential advantages of ESOPs are impressive, critics point out the dangers of employees having "all their eggs in one basket." Employees would be in a vulnerable position should their company fail.

Scanlon Plan. The **Scanlon Plan** is a gain-sharing plan designed to bind employees to the firm's performance. It is the most popular plan of its type.[20] Gain-sharing plans (also known as productivity incentives, team

---

[18] David W. Belcher and Thomas J. Atchison, *Compensation Administration,* 2nd ed. (Englewood Cliffs, N.J.: Prentice Hall, 1987), p. 290.

[19] Laura Jereski, "Behind the ESOP Surge," *Forbes* (December 14, 1987), p. 140.

[20] David W. Belcher and Thomas J. Atchison, *Compensation Administration,* p. 289.

incentives, and performance sharing incentives) generally refer to incentive plans that involve many or all employees in a common effort to achieve a firm's productivity objectives.[21]

The Scanlon Plan was developed by Joseph Scanlon in 1937, and it continues to be a successful approach to group incentive, especially in smaller firms. Employees are financially rewarded for savings in labor costs that result from their suggestions. These suggestions are evaluated by employee-management committees. Savings are calculated as a ratio of payroll costs to the sales value of what that payroll produces. If the company is able to reduce payroll costs through increased operating efficiency, it shares the savings with its employees.

In reflecting on his company's experience with the Scanlon Plan, a vice-president of human resources for Midland-Ross stated: "American workers want and, in my judgement, are entitled to a piece of the action when, through their own efforts and ingenuity, they are able to help the company do better."[22]

■ COMPENSATION FOR MANAGERS

Managerial skill largely determines whether a firm will prosper, survive, or fail. Thus providing adequate compensation for managers is vital. A critical factor in attracting and retaining the best managers is a company's program for compensating executives.[23]

Determining Managerial Compensation

A survey of *Fortune* 200 companies indicated that these firms prefer to relate salary growth for the highest level executives to overall corporate performance. For the next management tier, they integrate overall corporate performance with market rates and internal considerations to come up with compensation factors. For lower level managers, they tend to determine salaries on the basis of market rates, internal pay relationships, and individual performance.[24]

In general, the higher the managerial position, the greater the flexibility managers have in designing their jobs. Management jobs are often difficult to define because of their complexity. And when they are defined, they are often described in terms of anticipated results rather than tasks or how the work is accomplished. Thus market pricing may be the best approach to use in determining managerial pay for several reasons. First, the jobs are very

---

[21] Barry W. Thomas and Madeline Hess Olsen, "Gain Sharing: The Design Guarantees Success," *Personnel Journal,* 67 (May 1988), p. 73.

[22] "Scanlon Plan Puts Everyone on the Team," *Iron Age* (August 9, 1976), p. 18.

[23] *Executive Compensation* (Chicago: Commerce Clearing House, Inc., 1990), p. 5.

[24] James T. Brinks, ADP, "Executive Compensation: Crossroads of the '80s," *Personnel Administrator,* 26 (December 1981), p. 23.

important to the organization, and the people involved are highly skilled and difficult to replace. Second, the firm often has a considerable investment in developing managers. Third, even though the market may support a high-wage decision, managers comprise a relatively small percentage of the total workforce, and the overall impact on total labor costs will be small. Finally, because of their outside contacts, managers are likely to know the going market rates.[25]

In using market pricing, organizations utilize compensation survey data to determine pay levels for a representative group of jobs. These data may be obtained from such sources as the American Management Association and Sibson & Company, Inc. Some organizations also adapt point and factor comparison methods of job evaluation to determine the relative value of management jobs.

Types of Managerial Compensation

Managers typically prefer to receive the bulk of their compensation in the form of salary because it determines their standard of living. Salary also provides the basis for other forms of compensation. An executive might receive life insurance protection at the rate of two and a half times his or her annual salary. Moreover, bonuses are often related to salary. These payments supplement salary and may be paid on a current or deferred basis. Payment of bonuses reflects a managerial belief in their incentive value. According to one report, 92 percent of executives in manufacturing and 81 percent in banking receive bonuses that are tied to base salary.[26]

The stock option is another form of compensation that is designed to further integrate the interests of management with those of the organization. Although various types of plans exist, the typical **stock option plan** gives the manager the option to buy a specified amount of stock in the future at or below the current market price. This form of compensation is advantageous when stock prices are rising. However, there are potential disadvantages to stock option plans. A manager may feel uncomfortable investing money in the same organization in which he or she is building a career. As with profit sharing, this method of compensation is popular when a firm is successful. But during periods of decline when stock prices fall, the participants may become disenchanted.

Deferred compensation—pay that is held in trust for a manager until retirement—is often used to provide a delayed reward for executives. This permits them to receive income when it is taxed at a lower rate.

An interesting, although extreme, case of executive compensation occurred a number of years ago. A large electronics firm supposedly lured a brilliant executive away from a competitor by offering him "everything but the kitchen sink." The following inducements apparently were offered: an

[25] David W. Belcher and Thomas J. Atchison, *Compensation Administration*, p. 377.

[26] George T. Milkovich and Jerry M. Newman, *Compensation*, p. 531.

annual salary of $120,000 (an increase of $30,000), an immediate payment of $250,000 or equivalent stock options, an option to buy 90,000 shares of company stock, and a loan at no interest for ten years of $5.4 million with which to exercise his stock option.[27]

That is obviously an extreme example of executive perks. **Perquisites (perks)** are any special benefits provided by a firm to a small group of key executives that are designed to give the executives something extra. In addition to status, these rewards either are not considered as earned income or are taxed at a lower level than ordinary income.[28] Some of the more common perks include the following:

- A company-provided car.
- Accessible, no cost, parking.
- Limousine service—the chauffeur may also serve as a bodyguard.
- Kidnap and ransom protection.
- Counseling service—including financial and legal services.
- Professional meetings and conferences.
- Spouse travel.
- Use of company plane and yacht.
- Home entertainment allowance.
- Special living accommodations away from home.
- Club memberships.
- Special dining privileges.
- Season tickets to entertainment events.
- Special relocation allowances.
- Use of company credit cards.
- Medical expense reimbursement—coverage for all medical costs.
- Reimbursement for children's college expenses.
- No- and low-interest loans.
- Professional journals and magazines.
- Assistance for personal services.[29]

A **"golden parachute" contract** protects executives in the event that their firm is acquired by another. The executives, if negatively affected, may receive maximum agreed-to payouts under both short- and long-term incentive plans.

Perquisites extend a firm's benefit program on an individual basis. For a reason not entirely clear, they seem to be more popular in smaller firms than in major organizations.

The high level of compensation for top executives has received increased attention in recent years. For example, Stephen Wolf, chief executive officer

---

[27] Reprinted with permission from *Electronics,* August 19, 1968, p. 47. Copyright © by McGraw-Hill, 1968. All rights reserved.

[28] Since the late 1970s, the IRS has required firms to place a value on more perks and has recognized them as imputed income.

[29] Richard I. Henderson, *Compensation Management: Rewarding Performance,* 5th ed. (Englewood Cliffs, N.J.: Prentice-Hall, 1989), pp. 448–449.

for UAL, received over $18 million in total pay for 1990. Although not the chief executive officer for his firm, John Shirley, president of Microsoft, earned $26 million.[30] Many lower level employees view compensation packages such as these as unjustified or downright obscene. However, the answer to the question "Are executives overpaid?" is difficult if not impossible to determine. One compensation expert, Robert Sibson, suggests that there may be some overpayment for mediocrity, but that there is at least an equivalent underpayment for high levels of business performance.[31]

■ COMPENSATION FOR PROFESSIONALS[32]

Professionals are initially paid for the knowledge they bring to the organization. Therefore, compensation programs for professionals are administered somewhat differently from those for managers. Many professional employees eventually become managers. However, for those who do not aspire to a management career, some organizations have created a dual compensation track. This approach provides a separate pay structure for professionals, which overlaps the managerial pay structure. With this system, high performing professionals are not required to enter management to obtain greater pay. Some firms face serious organizational problems when a highly competent and effective professional feels compelled to become a manager for more pay and is unable to perform well in this capacity.

Professional career curves, shown in Figure 13-4 on page 506, have been developed for determining compensation for professional jobs. They are based on the assumption that the more experience an individual has, the higher her earnings should be. However, as the figure shows, varying performance levels are also considered. For example, an individual with eight years' experience (see the boxed area) may earn from less than $3,300 per month to more than $5,925, depending on his performance appraisal rating (employee rating "E" being the highest and rating "A" the lowest). Career curves are similar to pay grades, which we discussed in Chapter 12.

■ SALES COMPENSATION

Because designing compensation programs for sales employees involves unique considerations, some executives assign this task to the sales staff rather than to human resources. Still, many general compensation practices apply to sales jobs. For example, job content, relative job worth, and job market value should be determined.

---

[30] John A. Byrne, "The Flap Over Executive Pay," *Business Week* (May 6, 1991), pp. 90–91.

[31] "In Practice: Overpaying Execs," *Training and Development Journal,* 39 (April 1985), p. 10.

[32] Adapted by permission of the publisher from *Compensation* by Robert E. Sibson, © 1990 AMACOM, a division of American Management Association, NY. All rights reserved.

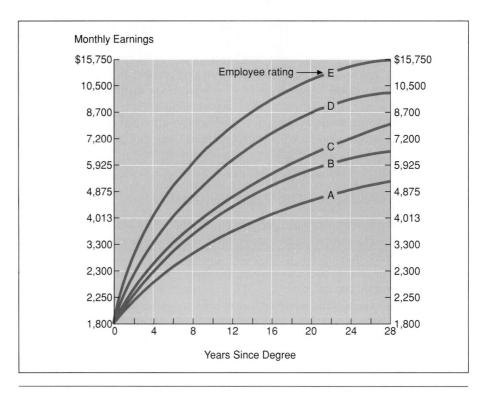

FIGURE 13-4 | Professional Career Curves

Source: Robert E. Sibson, *Compensation* 5th edition (New York: American Management Association, 1990) p. 279. Reprinted by permission of the publisher from *Compensation* by Robert E. Sibson, © 1990 AMACOM, a division of American Management Association, NY. All rights reserved.

The straight salary approach is at one extreme in sales compensation. In this method, salespersons receive a fixed salary regardless of their sales levels. Organizations use straight salary primarily when they stress continued product service after the sale. For instance, many sales representatives who deal largely with the federal government are compensated in this manner.

At the other extreme, the person whose pay is totally determined as a percentage of sales is on straight commission. An example of a salesperson in this category might be door-to-door salespersons. A director of compensation has stated that "the only 'pure' nondeferred compensation plan is the 100 percent sales commission plan. This type of pay is probably the most effective one to motivate salespeople. Unfortunately, straight commission is inappropriate for most of the selling that is done today."

Between these extremes is the endless variety of part-salary, part-commission combinations. The possibilities increase when various types of bonuses are added to the basic compensation package. The emphasis given to either commission or salary depends on several factors, including the organization's philosophy toward service, the nature of the product, and the amount of time required to close a sale.

In addition to salary, commissions, and bonuses, salespersons often receive other forms of compensation that are intended to serve as added incentives. Sales contests that offer television sets, refrigerators, or expense-paid vacations to exotic locations are common.

If any one feature sets sales compensation apart from other programs, it is the emphasis on incentives. The nature of sales work often simplifies the problem of determining individual output. Sales volume can usually be related to specific individuals, a situation that encourages payment of incentive compensation. Also, experience in sales compensation practices over the years has supported the concept of directly relating rewards to performance.

■ COMPENSATION IN GROWTH COMPANIES

The compensation approach for both executives and other employees in growth companies is basically different from average companies. Annual cash incentives are used but not as the primary inducement. The typical bonus for CEOs, as a percent of salary, is roughly the same as the traditional 40 to 50 percent. In growth companies, the primary incentive is through stock options. On the average, growth companies provide two to three times as many shares for their executive stock programs as nongrowth companies. In addition, growth companies share stock with essentially all employees, not just executives.[33]

The focus of growth companies' compensation packages is clearly on providing equity. They apparently want everyone in the organization to focus on building the company's financial strength and to share in the company's success. While causality between employee equity and growth has not been established, many entrepreneurial managers view it as an important factor in their firm's success.

■ NONFINANCIAL COMPENSATION

In recent years, many American workers have been able to satisfy their basic physiological and safety needs, so their interests have tended to shift somewhat away from money as the primary form of compensation. As employees receive sufficient cash to provide for basic necessities (and then stereos, color TVs, VCRs, and PCs), they tend to desire rewards that will satisfy higher order needs. Specifically, social, ego, and self-actualization needs are becoming more important. These needs may be satisfied through the job itself and/or the job environment. Figure 13-5 on page 508 shows the basic nonfinancial elements of the total compensation package.

---

[33] John D. McMillan and Chris Young, "Sweetening the Compensation Package," *HRMagazine*, 35 (October 1990), pp. 36–39.

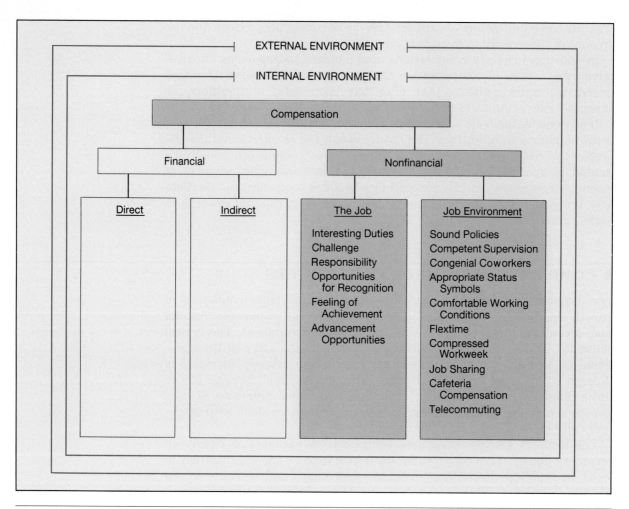

FIGURE 13-5 | Nonfinancial Elements of a Total Compensation Program

The Job

A major human resource management objective is to satisfactorily match job requirements with employee abilities and aspirations. Although the task of job design is typically performed by other organizational units, human resource management has a distinct responsibility for recruiting, selecting, and placing individuals in those jobs. Also, a good case could be made for directly involving human resources in the task of job design. Offering the employee a "good" job can be an important part of nonfinancial compensation. Because of this, a number of organizations have become actively engaged in job enrichment, which we discussed in Chapter 9.

The job is a central issue in many theories of motivation, and it is also a vital component of a total compensation program. Employees may receive important rewards by performing meaningful jobs. This type of reward is intrinsic in nature, but management determines job content and therefore the job's compensation possibilities are largely controlled by the organization. The selection and placement processes are extremely important in this context. A job that is challenging to one person may be quite boring to another, and failure to recognize this fact often leads to major problems.

The Job Environment

The job environment is also an important aspect of nonfinancial compensation. We discussed the significance of a warm, supportive corporate culture in Chapter 9. Many organizations have only "paid lip service" to making jobs more rewarding. However, others have made concerted efforts to improve many of the factors that surround the job.

Sound Policies. Human resource policies and practices expressing management's sincerity in its employee relationships can serve as positive rewards. For example, fostering stable employment reflects a company's respect for its employees, as IBM has done. Over a period of four decades, despite severe recessions and dramatic technological changes, no IBM employee has ever been laid off because of economic necessity. If a firm's policies show respect—rather than disrespect, fear, doubt, or lack of confidence—the result can be rewarding to both the employees and the organization.

Competent Supervision. Nothing in the job environment can be so demoralizing to employees as an incompetent supervisor. Successful organizations offer continuing programs that emphasize supervisory and executive development. These programs ensure, insofar as possible, the continuity of sound leadership and management.

Congenial Coworkers. Although a few individuals in this world may be quite self-sufficient and prefer to be left alone, this attitude is not prevalent. Most people possess, in varying degrees, a desire to be accepted by their work group. This acceptance helps them satisfy basic social needs. It is very important that management, in its staffing efforts, be concerned with developing compatible work groups.

Appropriate Status Symbols. At times, employees compare the size of their offices with those of peers or measure the distance from their offices to the CEO's. When such extreme behavior occurs, it is time to examine the firm's policy regarding status symbols. While these symbols may be appropriate in achieving certain purposes—such as providing incentives for employees to progress in the firm—management must take care not to overemphasize them. However, status symbols (such as office size, desk size and quality, other office furnishings, floor covering, office location, title, parking space, or make of company car) can serve as compensation because they often appeal to employees' ego needs. Some organizations tend to minimize the use of status symbols, but other firms use them liberally. A crucial point to remember in providing such rewards is to provide them equitably.

Comfortable Working Conditions. Good working conditions are taken for granted in many organizations today. However, a brief return to nonair-conditioned offices would quickly remind us of their importance. The view that working conditions can be a form of compensation is reinforced by pay plans that increase the financial reward for jobs that entail relatively poor working conditions.

Flextime. The practice of permitting employees to choose, with certain limitations, their own working hours is referred to as **flextime.** It was introduced in Germany in the late 1960s and has since spread throughout Europe and the United States. In a survey involving companies of all sizes, from all industries and from every region of the United States and Canada, flextime was reported being used by 30 percent of the responding firms. This was double the number reporting use of the system in 1977.[34]

In a flextime system, employees work the same number of hours per day as they would on a standard schedule. However, they are permitted to work these hours within what is called a *band width,* which is the maximum length of the work day (see Figure 13-6). Core time is that part of the day when all employees must be present. Flexible time is the time period within which employees may vary their schedules. A typical schedule permits employees to begin work between 6:00 A.M. and 9:00 A.M. and to complete their workday between 3:00 P.M. and 6:00 P.M.

Perhaps flextime's most important feature is that it allows employees to schedule their time to minimize conflicts between personal needs and job requirements. Remember the incident described at the beginning of the chapter involving Liz Nichols, who had scheduling problems. Flextime allows Liz to arrive at work later, after taking her children to school.

With flextime, personal needs can be accommodated without employees being tempted to illegitimately use sick leave. Flextime also permits employees to work at hours when they feel they can function best. It caters to those who are early risers or those who prefer to work later in the day. The public also seems to reap benefits from flextime. Transportation services, recreational facilities, medical clinics, and other services can be better utilized as a result of reduced competition for service at conventional peak times.

Flextime is not suitable for all types of organizations. Its use may be severely limited in assembly-line operations and companies utilizing multiple shifts. However, flextime is feasible in many situations, benefitting both the employee and the employer. Clearly, the use of plans such as flextime are compatible with the desire of employees (especially younger ones) to have greater control over their work situations.

---

[34] Joseph E. McKendrick, Jr., "Stretching Time in '89," *Management World,* 18 (July–August 1989), p. 10.

FIGURE 13-6 | Illustration of Flextime

The Compressed Workweek. Any arrangement of work hours that permits employees to fulfill their work obligation in fewer days than the typical five-day workweek is referred to as the **compressed workweek.** The most common compressed workweek is four ten-hour days. Working under this arrangement, employees have reported greater job satisfaction. In addition, the compressed workweek offers the potential for better use of leisure time for family life, personal business, and recreation. Employers in some instances have cited advantages such as increased productivity and reduced turnover and absenteeism.

However, work scheduling and employee fatigue problems have been encountered. In some cases, these problems have resulted in lower product quality and reduced customer service. Some firms have even reverted back to the conventional five-day week after experiencing problems with the compressed workweek. Apparently, overall acceptance of the compressed workweek is not as clear-cut as acceptance of flextime.

Job Sharing. A relatively new approach to work—job sharing—is attractive to people who want to work fewer than forty hours per week. In **job sharing,** two part-time people split the duties of one job in some agreed-on manner and are paid according to their contributions. From the employer's viewpoint, compensation is paid for only one job, but creativity is obtained from two employees. The total financial compensation cost may be greater because of the additional benefits provided; however, this expense may be offset by increased productivity. Job sharing may be especially attractive to individuals who have substantial family responsibilities and to older workers who wish to move gradually into retirement.

Flexible Compensation (Cafeteria Compensation). Flexible compensation plans permit employees to choose from among many alternatives in deciding how their financial compensation will be allocated. They are given considerable latitude in determining how much they will take in the form of salary, life insurance, pension contributions, and other benefits. Cafeteria plans permit flexibility in allowing each employee to determine the compensation package that best satisfies his or her particular needs.

Twenty years ago firms offered a uniform package that generally reflected a "typical" employee. The common prototype was a married male, 40 years old, with a nonworking wife, two dependent children, and a heavily mortgaged home. Today, the workforce has become considerably more heterogeneous, and this prototype is no longer typical.[35] A recent study of cafeteria compensation plans was conducted by the American Management Association and Noble Lowndes, an international employee benefits firm. The survey included more than 1,000 human resource executives. Of those surveyed, 70 percent said they currently sponsor some form of cafeteria plan. These executives considered their plans successful in meeting their firms' objectives, including developing greater employee appreciation for the company's benefit plan. Of the 30 percent who do not have such a plan, 10 percent indicated that they will adopt a plan within a year, and 45 percent are actively considering plans. Only 21 percent of the survey population currently have no plans regarding flexible compensation.[36]

The rationale behind cafeteria plans is that employees have individual needs and preferences. A 60-year-old man would probably not desire maternity benefits in an insurance plan. At the same time, a 25-year-old woman who regularly jogs three miles each day might not place a high value on a parking space near the firm's entrance. Some of the possible compensation vehicles utilized in a cafeteria approach are shown in Table 13-2.

Obviously, organizations cannot permit employees to select all their financial compensation vehicles. For one thing, benefits required by law must be provided. In addition, it is probably wise to require that each employee have core benefits, especially in areas such as retirement and medical insurance. Some guidelines would likely be helpful for most employees in the long run. However, the freedom to select highly desired benefits would seem to maximize the value of an individual's compensation. Involvement in the determination of tailored compensation plans should also effectively communicate the cost of benefits to employees.

TRW, Inc., has had a flexible compensation program since 1974. The program was inspired by a general belief that employees should have more flexibility and self-determination in shaping their compensation packages. The plan developed at TRW is based on the following principles:

- The core plan will be available to each employee at the company's expense.
- Plans that are better, but more costly than the current plan, will be developed and made available at the employee's expense.
- Plans that provide less coverage, and that are less costly than the current plan, will be developed and an employee given credit toward other benefits or given the difference in cash.
- The core plan will be reviewed annually and will be maintained at a competitive level.
- Additional choices will be added as experience is gained and as new elements of the total compensation package can be defined on a choice basis.

---

[35] Robert M. McCaffery, "Organizational Performance and the Strategic Allocation of Indirect Compensation," *Human Resource Planning,* 12, no. 3 (1989), p. 230.

[36] Aric T. Wilt, "Cafeteria Plans Help Meet Needs and Control Costs," *Management Review,* 79 (September 1990), p. 43.

TABLE 13-2 | Compensation Vehicles Utilized in a Cafeteria Compensation Approach

Accidental death, dismemberment insurance	Health maintenance organization fees
Birthdays (vacation)	Home health care
Bonus eligibility	Hospital-surgical-medical insurance
Business and professional membership	Incentive growth fund
Cash profit sharing	Interest-free loans
Club memberships	Long-term disability benefit
Commissions	Matching educational donations
Company medical assistance	Nurseries
Company provided automobile	Nursing-home care
Company provided housing	Outside medical services
Company provided or subsidized travel	Personal accident insurance
Day-care centers	Price discount plan
Deferred bonus	Recreation facilities
Deferred compensation plan	Resort facilities
Dental and eye care insurance	Sabbatical leaves
Discount on company products	Salary continuation
Education costs	Savings plan
Educational activities (time off)	Scholarships for dependents
Free checking account	Severance pay
Free or subsidized lunches	Sickness and accident insurance
Group automobile insurance	Stock appreciation rights
Group homeowners' insurance	Stock bonus plan
Group life insurance	Stock purchase plan

Choices in the current plan include health care, hospital, surgical, maternity, supplemental accident, and major medical benefits. Future possibilities for expanded areas of choice are retirement supplement, group auto and homeowners' insurance, and long-term disability compensation.

In spite of new legislative restrictions, the number of flexible compensation programs is increasing, primarily because such plans provide substantial advantages for both employer and employee.[37] For example, the employer can do the following:

- Improve its competitive position in the marketplace by appealing to individual needs.
- Provide a degree of cost control by shifting a portion of the costs to employees—but generally in ways that provide them with tax savings.
- Make employees more aware of the value of their compensation.
- Limit contributions to benefits programs without alienating employees.

Employees also receive highly valued advantages:

- Greater control over a significant aspect of their employment.
- Saving money by paying a portion of benefit costs with tax-deferred dollars.

---

[37] Susan J. Velleman, "Flexible Benefit Packages that Satisfy Employees and the IRS," *Personnel,* 62 (March 1985), p. 33.

United Hospitals, Inc., a health care system in the Philadelphia area, has realized many benefits from its flexible benefits program. The program was implemented in 1988 to control the escalation of health care costs. During the first three years of the plan, the firm avoided increases in health care costs of almost $8 million. The system also proved to be valuable in recruiting and retaining professional employees. In addition, the flexible program was acknowledged as a major factor in defeating a unionization attempt.[38]

While flexible compensation programs add to the organization's administrative burden, advantages seem to greatly outweigh shortcomings. Therefore, systems of this type will likely become more common in the future.

Telecommuting. Telecommuting allows employees to work at home, or at least in a location away from the office. They perform their work over data lines tied to a computer as if they were at the office. Telecommuters generally are information workers. They perform jobs that require, for example, analysis, research, writing, budgeting, data entry, or computer programming.[39]

In keeping with this concept and to combat the steady increase in employment costs, Control Data Corporation (CDC) developed a program it calls HOMEWORK. This innovative approach is a home-based training and employment program for persons seeking a nontraditional work environment.

Using a personal computer located in the employee's home and connected by telephone to CDC's computer network, both training and job duties are carried out without loss of efficiency and quality. An example of a HOME-WORK job is that of business application programmer. Initially, HOME-WORK was available only to a few severely disabled employees. It has now been expanded, and the program has great potential for many other employees. Additional HOMEWORK programs that have wide-ranging implications for other employers in both the private and public sectors are being developed by CDC. The following advantages have been cited for both employee and employer:

- Permits effective use of human resources.
- Eliminates the need for office space.
- Provides flexible working hours.
- Eliminates costs associated with travel to and from work.
- Enhances intellectual functioning.
- Helps establish strong bonds and company loyalty.
- Permits a higher level of self-care for severely disabled employees.
- Reduces costs of health care (CDC's costs decreased 50–75 percent for most of its participants).
- Increases employees' self-concept and confidence levels.
- Provides a means for reentering a traditional work environment.

---

[38] M. Michael Markowich, "Flex Still Works," *Personnel Journal,* 69 (December 1990), p. 62.

[39] Michael Alexander, "Travel-Free Commuting," *Nation's Business,* 78 (December 1990), p. 33.

As many as 100,000 people regularly work at home at least part-time, and more than 350 companies have some form of telecommuting program for their employees.[40] Some forecasters have predicted that 10 million Americans could be working at home within the next fifteen years.[41]

While telecommuting has many advantages, it also has some potential pitfalls. For example, ties between employees and their firms may be weakened, and successful programs will require a higher degree of trust between employees and their supervisors. However, one thing seems certain: The size of the workforce should increase with the ability of telecommuting to expand the utilization of handicapped workers and workers with small children.

■ COMPENSATION IN MULTINATIONAL CORPORATIONS

A major problem that confronts multinational corporations is deciding how to provide equitable compensation systems for workers given overseas assignments. Typically, employees from the parent country receive a salary, an overseas premium of up to 50 percent, relocation allowances, and living expense allowances. Normally, individuals from the parent country receive higher pay than workers from the host country. These differentials tend to create resentment and reduce cooperation. Many Americans have found that their standard of living and social class is considerably better in foreign countries than it had been at home. The drop in living standards when they return may create some difficulties. An important incentive for U.S. citizens to accept assignments in foreign countries is the opportunity to exclude a portion of their income earned in the foreign country from U.S. income taxes. Internal Revenue Service regulations allow a U.S. citizen to exclude certain income earned while working in a foreign country, provided that the individual resides in the foreign country twelve months or longer. The IRS issued a decision in 1985 on the taxation of U.S. citizens working abroad. In 1988, the exclusion was $85,000 and it reached a top of $95,000 in 1990. To qualify for this exclusion, a taxpayer must have a tax home in a foreign country for 330 days of foreign presence.[42]

Employee benefits often vary drastically from country to country or from industry to industry. In Europe, for instance, it is common for employees to receive added compensation in proportion to the number of their family members or the degree of their unpleasant working conditions. In Japan, a supervisor whose weekly salary is only $500 may also receive benefits that include family income allowances, housing or housing loans, subsidized vacations, year-end bonuses that can equal three months' pay, and profit sharing.[43]

[40] Karen A. Fortin and Shirley Dennis-Escottier, "Telecommuting Adds a New Dimension to Office in the Home," *The Woman CPA,* 48 (October 1986), p. 11.

[41] Carol-Ann Hamilton, "Telecommuting," *Personnel Journal,* 66 (April 1987), p. 91.

[42] Marion Gajek and Monica M. Sabo, "The Bottom Line: What HR Managers Need to Know about the New Expatriate Regulations," *Personnel Administrator,* 31 (February 1986), p. 87.

[43] Wayne F. Cascio and Manuel G. Serapio, Jr., "Human Resources Systems in an International Alliance: The Undoing of a Done Deal?" *Organizational Dynamics,* 19 (Winter 1991), p. 71.

Successful management of employee benefits in a multinational corporation depends on various factors. Perhaps the most important one is a corporate policy statement that outlines specific instructions for the development, approval, and administration of all benefits plans. This policy statement should clearly establish that no benefits plan is to be implemented or changed by a foreign subsidiary without prior approval of the corporate benefits department. Employee benefits covered by the policy statement should include any payment of company funds to employees other than base salary, such as pensions, medical and life insurance, vacations, and severance pay.[44]

In drafting the policy statement, two general objectives must be kept in mind. First, the organization's overall welfare must be given primary consideration. Second, employee benefits must be competitive on the international level if a multinational corporation is to attract and retain the dynamic, aggressive kind of leadership that is required to be successful.[45]

SUMMARY

Most organizations recognize a responsibility to their employees by providing programs covering their health, safety, security, and general welfare. These programs are called benefits and include all financial rewards that generally are not paid directly to the employee. Benefits cost the firm money, but employees usually receive them indirectly. This type of compensation has two distinct advantages. First, it is generally nontaxable to the employee. Second, in the case of insurance, the premium rates are much less for large groups of employees than for individual policies. Legally required benefits include social security, unemployment compensation, and workers' compensation.

A seemingly endless number of benefits are provided voluntarily by organizations. These benefits may be classified as (1) payment for time not worked, (2) employee health and security benefits, (3) services to employees, and (4) premium pay. Although they are provided voluntarily, some no doubt have resulted from union-management negotiations. Employee benefits can help a firm recruit and retain a quality workforce. Management depends on an upward flow of information from employees in order to know when benefit changes are needed. In addition, because employee awareness of benefits is often severely limited, information about benefits must also be communicated downward.

Compensation is most often determined by how much time an employee spends at work. Compensation programs that relate pay to productivity provide an incentive for greater individual and work group productivity. A

---

[44] Neil B. Krupp, "Managing Benefits in Multinational Organizations," *Personnel,* 63 (September 1986), p. 76.

[45] *Ibid.*

predetermined amount of money is paid for each unit produced under a straight piecework plan. The standard hour plan is an individual incentive plan whereby time allowances are calculated for each unit of output. However, work is often organized in such a manner that productivity results from group effort. Determining each individual's contribution is then difficult, if not impossible, and the group must be given the incentive—and the reward.

Companywide incentive plans include profit sharing, employee stock ownership plans (ESOP), and the Scanlon Plan. The latter is the most popular plan of its type.

Managerial skill significantly affects a firm's success. Managerial effectiveness and the firm's welfare are closely related. Therefore it isn't unusual for a large portion of management compensation—especially for top executives—to be linked to the company's performance. Managers typically receive the bulk of their compensation as salary, which provides the basis for other forms of compensation.

The stock option is designed to integrate the interests of management and the organization. Deferred compensation—pay that is held in trust for a manager until retirement—is often used because of its tax advantages. Perquisites (perks) are any special benefits provided by a firm to a small group of key executives to give them something extra.

Professionals are initially compensated primarily for the knowledge they bring to the organization. Many professional employees eventually become managers. For those who don't want to move into management, some organizations have created a dual compensation track. The dual track provides a separate pay structure for professionals, which may overlap a portion of the managerial pay structure.

Compensation programs for sales employees involve unique considerations, but general compensation practices such as job content, relative job worth, and job market value still apply to sales jobs. The straight salary approach is at one extreme in sales compensation. At the other extreme is the straight commission. There is an endless variety of part-salary, part-commission combinations between these extremes.

Compensation in growth companies is different from that of average firms. Growth companies use stock options as the primary incentive. In addition, the stock is shared with all employees, not just executives.

As employees receive sufficient cash to provide for basic necessities, they tend to want rewards that will satisfy higher order needs. Specifically, social, ego, and self-actualization needs become more important. These needs may be satisfied by the job itself and/or the job environment.

Permitting employees to choose, within certain limits, their own working hours is known as flextime. Any arrangement that permits employees to work full-time but in fewer days than the typical five-day workweek is called a compressed workweek. In job sharing, two part-time people split the duties of one job in some agreed-on manner and are paid according to their contributions. Flexible compensation plans permit employees to choose from among many alternatives in allocating their financial compensation. Telecommuting permits employees to work at home and communicate via computer and telephone.

A major problem confronting multinational corporations is equitable compensation for workers given overseas assignments. Typically, employees from the parent country receive a salary, an overseas premium of up to 50 percent, relocation allowances, and living expense allowances. Many Americans working abroad find that their standard of living and social status improve considerably over what they had been in the United States. The drop in living standards when they return may create some difficulties. An important incentive for U.S. citizens to accept overseas assignments is the opportunity to exclude a portion of their income earned in the foreign country from U.S. income taxes. Successful management of employee benefits depends primarily on a corporate policy statement that outlines specific instructions for the development, approval, and administration of all benefits plans.

Questions for Review

1. Define *benefits*. What are the general purposes of benefits?
2. Which benefits are required by law?
3. What are the basic categories of voluntary benefits? Give an example of each type.
4. Distinguish among premium pay, hazard pay, and shift differential pay.
5. What is meant by the term *incentive compensation*? When would an individual incentive plan, as opposed to a group incentive plan, be used?
6. Define the following terms:
   a. Straight piecework plan
   b. Standard hour plan
   c. Profit sharing
   d. Employee stock ownership plan
   e. Scanlon Plan
7. What are major determinants of compensation for managers? List and define the primary types of managerial compensation.
8. Why are nonfinancial compensation considerations becoming so important?
9. Distinguish between flextime and the compressed workweek.
10. What are some of the factors that affect compensation for individuals in multinational corporations?

Terms for Review

Benefits
Utilization review
Wellness
Premium pay
Hazard pay
Shift differential
Incentive compensation
Straight piecework plan
Standard hour plan
Profit sharing
Employee stock ownership plan (ESOP)

Scanlon Plan
Stock option plan
Deferred compensation
Perquisites (perks)
"Golden parachute" contract
Flextime
Compressed workweek
Job sharing
Flexible compensation plans
Telecommuting

INCIDENT 1   ▪   A Double-Edged Sword   ▪

The decline in oil prices during the mid-1980s adversely affected many industries. Profits were down for all major oil companies and many of their suppliers. Few new orders were received by the producers of drilling fluids, for example, and many existing orders were canceled or scaled back. As a supplier of drilling fluids, Beta Chemical Company's sales plummeted. Beta, located in Lafayette, Louisiana, supplies companies such as Texaco, Shell, and Pennzoil, as well as independent oil drillers, often called "wildcatters."

Beta had implemented a comprehensive profit-sharing plan in the 1970s, after several years of rapidly increasing sales and profits. The decision was based largely on an attitude survey of the employees at Beta, which showed that they strongly preferred profit sharing over other benefits.

In the late 1980s, the compensation plan at Beta provided for base wages about 20 percent below wage levels for similar jobs in Lafayette. But half of company profits were paid out each quarter as a fixed percentage of employee wages. Distributed profits averaged more than 50 percent of base wages. This caused average total compensation at Beta to be 20 percent above that of the area. Because of the high pay, Beta remained a popular employer, able to take its pick from a long waiting list of applicants.

Benefits were kept to a minimum at Beta. There was no retirement plan and a very limited medical plan designed to cover catastrophic illnesses only. Employees considered this a good bargain, though, in light of the above-average compensation.

Profits were down markedly in 1987, and the profit-sharing bonus was less than half the historical average. Earnings declined further for the first two quarters of 1988. By midyear, it was clear that the company would be in the red for the entire second half. A board meeting was called in late August to discuss the profit-sharing program. One director made it known that he felt the company should drop profit sharing. The human resource director, Vince Harwood, was asked to sit in at the board meeting and to make a presentation suggesting what the company should do about compensation.

Questions

1. Evaluate the compensation plan at Beta.
2. If you were Mr. Harwood, what would you recommend for the short term? For the long term?

INCIDENT 2   ▪ A Benefits Package Designed for Whom?   ▪

Wayne McGraw greeted Robert Peters, his next interviewee, warmly. Robert had an excellent academic record and appeared to be just the kind of person Wayne's company, Beco Electric, was seeking. Wayne is the university recruiter for Beco and had already interviewed six graduating seniors at Centenary College.

Based on the application form, Robert appeared to be the most promising candidate to be interviewed that day. He was 22 years old and had a 3.6 overall grade point average and a 4.0 in his major field, industrial management. He was the vice-president of the Student Government Association and was activities chairman for Kappa Alpha Psi, a social fraternity. The reference letters in Robert's file revealed that he was both very active socially and a rather intense and serious student. One of the letters, from Robert's employer the previous summer, expressed satisfaction with Robert's work habits.

Wayne knew that discussion of pay could be an important part of the recruiting interview. But he did not know which aspects of Beco's compensation and benefits program would appeal most to Robert. The company has an excellent profit-sharing plan, although 80 percent of profit distributions are deferred and included in each employee's retirement account. Health benefits are also good. The company's medical and dental plan pays almost 100 percent of costs. A company lunchroom provides meals at about 70 percent of outside prices, although few managers take advantage of this. Employees get one week of paid vacation after the first year and two weeks after two years with the company. In addition, there are twelve paid holidays each year. Finally, the company encourages advanced education, paying for tuition and books in full and often allowing time off to attend classes during the day.

Questions

1. What aspects of Beco's compensation and benefits program are likely to appeal to Robert? Explain.
2. Is the total compensation package likely to be attractive to Robert? Explain.

DEVELOPING HRM SKILLS

Due to a downward trend in business and resulting financial constraints over the last two years, Straight Manufacturing Company has been able to grant only cost-of-living increases to its employees. However, the firm has just signed a lucrative three-year contract with a major defense contractor. As a result, management has formed a salary review committee to award merit increases to deserving employees. Members of the salary review committee have only $13,500 of merit money and deciding who will receive merit increases will be difficult. Louis Convoy, Sharon Kubiak, J. Ward Archer, Ed Wilson, C. J. Sass, and John Passante have been recommended for raises.

Louis Convoy, financial analyst, has an undergraduate business degree and is currently working on an M.B.A. His previous work experience has allowed him to develop several outstanding financial contacts.

Sharon Kubiak, HRM administrative assistant, began as a secretary and after three years with the organization was promoted to her present position. Because her first position was that of secretary, her current salary is not at the range commensurate with her new position and responsibilities.

J. Ward Archer, assistant plant manager, worked three years as a production supervisor after obtaining his undergraduate degree in business. He then received an M.B.A. degree from Harvard two years ago. He is viewed by many as a "successful fast tracker."

Ed Wilson, production supervisor, has been with the organization for nine years; the last two years he has been a production supervisor. Last year he virtually single-handedly prevented a wildcat strike. To become a member of management as a production supervisor, Ed took a pay cut in comparison to his union wages.

C. J. Sass, director of computer services, has a doctoral degree in computer science and was hired away from a business college at a leading eastern university three years ago. Two and one-half years ago he introduced a corporatewide Human Resource Information System that has refined the internal recruiting and promotion policies of the organization.

John Passante, district sales manager, has been with the organization for twelve and one-half years. In his tenth year with the organization, John was promoted to his current position, and he has done a fine job.

Six students will serve on the salary review committee. While the committee would like to award significant merit increases to all those who have been recommended, there are limited funds available for raises. The committee must make a decision as to how the merit funds will be distributed. Your instructor will provide the participants with additional information necessary to complete the exercise.

REFERENCES

Adair, Donald R. "Golden Parachutes Can Be More than an Executive's Bailout." *Bottomline* (March 1987), p. 39.

Alexander, Michael. "Travel-Free Commuting." *Nation's Business,* 78 (December 1990), pp. 33, 36–37.

Anderson, Richard A. "Handling Health-Care Costs in the '90s." *HRMagazine,* 35 (June 1990), pp. 89–94.

Belcher, David W., and Thomas J. Atchison. *Compensation Administration,* 2nd ed. (Englewood Cliffs, N.J.: Prentice Hall, 1987), p. 290.

Borman, Melissa A. "What Do Women Get?" *Across the Board,* 21 (March 1987), pp. 19–21.

Byrne, John A. "The Flap Over Executive Pay." *Business Week* (May 6, 1991), pp. 90–103.

Candall, Lin D., and Mark I. Phelps. "Pay for a Global Work Force." *Personnel Journal,* 70 (February 1991), pp. 28–33.

Caruth, Donald L. *Compensation Management for Banks* (Boston: Bankers Publishing Company, 1986), pp. 152–177.

Cordtz, Dan. "Hire Me, Hire My Family." *Finance World,* 159 (September 18, 1990), pp. 76–79.

Deloux, Gene. "Is Your Maternity Policy Ready for the '90s?" *HRMagazine,* 35 (November 1990), pp. 57–59.

Executive Compensation (Chicago: Commerce Clearing House, Inc., 1989), pp. 5–6.

"Executive Perks: What's Out, What's In." *Dun's Business Month,* 129 (February 1987), pp. 75–77.

Garland, Susan B. "The Retiring Kind Are Getting Militant About Benefits." *Business Week* (May 28, 1990), p. 29.

Garland, Susan B., and Dean Foust. "Putting Pension Managers on a Short Leash." *Business Week* (March 26, 1990), p. 47.

"HR Professionals Sport More Hats than Ever Before." *Employee Benefits Journal,* 15 (September 1990), p. 9.

Koretz, Gene. "Health Care Keeps Taking Bigger Bites of the Economy." *Business Week* (February 19, 1990), p. 22.

Kuttner, Robert. "Health Care: Why Corporate America Is Paralyzed." *Business Week* (April 8, 1991), p. 14.

Leibman, Michael, and Harold P. Weinstein. "Money Isn't Everything." *HRMagazine,* 35 (November 1990), pp. 48–51.

McCaffery, Robert M. "Organizational Performance and the Strategic Allocation of Indirect Compensation." *Human Resource Planning,* 12 (1989), pp. 229–238.

McKendrick, Joseph E., Jr. "Stretching Time in '89." *Management World,* 18 (July–August 1989), pp. 10–11.

McMillan, John D., and Chris Young. "Sweetening the Compensation Package." *HRMagazine,* 35 (October 1990), pp. 36–39.

Milkovich, George T., and Jerry M. Newman. *Compensation,* 3rd ed. (Homewood, Ill.: Richard D. Irwin, Inc., 1990).

"More Employer-Supported Childcare Assistance Needed." *Management Review,* 76 (August 1987), pp. 10–11.

Murphy, Betty Southard, Wayne E. Barlow, and D. Diane Hatch. "Employee Benefit Plans Under ADEA." *Personnel Journal,* 68 (September 1989), pp. 22–23.

O'Dell, Carla, and Jerry McAdams. "The Revolution in Employee Rewards." *Management Review,* 76 (March 1987), pp. 30–31.

Olney, Peter B., Jr. "Meeting the Challenge of Comparable Worth: Part 2." *Compensation and Benefits Review,* 19 (May–June 1987), pp. 15–23.

Pay for Performance (Chicago: Commerce Clearing House, Inc., 1990), pp. 6–7.

Perkins, Robert E. "The Employer's Role in Benefits Evolution." *Personnel,* 64 (February 1987), p. 66.

Sibson, Robert E. *Compensation,* 5th ed. (New York: American Management Association, 1990).

Stelluto, George L., and Deborah P. Klein. "Compensation Trends into the 21st Century." *Monthly Labor Review,* 113 (February 1990), pp. 38–45.

Summers, Lawrence H. "Some Simple Economics of Mandated Benefits." *American Economics Review,* 79 (May 1989), pp. 177–183.

"Visions: Funding Retiree Benefits." *HRMagazine,* 36 (February 1991), pp. 87–88.

Weiss, Barbara. "Child Care: The Employee Benefit of the Future." *Drug Topics* (February 17, 1986), pp. 11–13.

Wilt, Aric T. "Cafeteria Plans Help Meet Needs & Control Costs." *Management Review,* 79 (September 1990), pp. 43–46.

P·A·R·T F·O·U·R

CASE IV

Parma Cycle Company: The Pay Plan

At Parma Cycle Company in Parma, Ohio, wage rates for hourly workers were established by a three-year labor-management agreement. The agreement provided for cost-of-living adjustments (COLA) based on changes in the U.S. Consumer Price Index. Wage rates varied according to job class and by seniority within each class. For example, a machine operator with two to four years' seniority earned $10.75 per hour. With four to eight years' seniority the rate increased to $12.60 an hour. A company-paid health plan provided medical and dental care for employees. The company contributed 6.5 percent of wages to a retirement plan administered by the machinists union.

Salaried workers at Parma Cycle were paid straight salaries based on a forty-hour workweek. For first- and second-level managers and clerical workers, work beyond forty hours in any week was compensated on a pro rata basis. Above the second management level there was no additional compensation for work after forty hours per week. COLA adjustments were made semiannually for all salaried employees.

Only in the sales department at Parma was any kind of incentive compensation program in effect. The sales representatives were paid a commission averaging about 2 percent of sales in addition to straight salary. The sales manager assigned the sales representatives to particular territories; they were generally given a choice of territories according to seniority. Once a sales representative had become accustomed to a given territory, however, requests to change were usually turned down. As older sales representatives left the company, some of the younger ones moved into the better sales areas. This caused some of the more senior sales representatives to insist upon changes in territory to increase their sales potential. This was done in a few cases, but no consistent policy was developed.

Parma Cycle Company was building a new plant in Clarksdale, Mississippi, in 1988. The new plant was to employ about 530 people, two-thirds the number working at the main plant in Parma, Ohio. Of course, the workforce would be smaller than that at first. About two months before the new plant was scheduled to open, Jesse Heard, the human resource director, was asked to meet with the president to discuss the compensation policies that would be followed in Clarksdale. Jesse knew that Jim Burgess, the president, tended to take a personal hand in matters relating to pay, so he prepared thoroughly for their meeting.

Mr. Burgess had a reputation for getting right to the heart of the matter. "I'm worried about the pay differentials that we are going to have between this plant and the one in Clarksdale," he began. "As I see it, some of the people down there won't be paid half as much as similar workers here."

"That's true," said Jesse. "That really is the main reason for the move to Clarksdale. Without the union and with the low wage rates in that area, we will be able to pay just what the market requires. Most of the helpers and trainees will be available, we think, at minimum wage." "How will the pay classifications down there compare to those up here?" asked Mr. Burgess.

"Well," said Jesse, "up here we have 'workers' and 'machine operators' and the pay within classes is by seniority. Down there we plan to have helpers/trainees, grades 1 and 2, and machine operators, grades 1, 2, and 3. Seniority won't count. We will promote workers based on the recommendations of their supervisors and their performance evaluation scores."

"I liked the incentive plan when you told me about it before, Jesse," said Mr. Burgess. "Let's go over it again. As I understand it, we are going to take 30 percent of the cost savings and pay it out as semiannual bonuses." "Yes," said Jesse. "To some degree, we modeled the plan after that at Lincoln Electric. [Lincoln is a Cleveland maker of electric welding products.] An individual's bonus will be a certain percentage of the gross wages paid during that period. But we will multiply that by the person's performance evaluation score." "Will the standard costs be the same as the ones we have here at the Parma plant?" asked Mr. Burgess. "Yes, they will," answered Jesse.

Mr. Burgess continued, "The last time we talked I think you said that we would save money in Clarksdale on the benefits package too." "Yes," replied Jesse. "For one thing, the tradition in that area is for the company to pay a health insurance premium for a worker and for the worker to pay the portion applicable to any dependents. Also, we don't have a dental plan down there, just medical. Finally, I don't think that we will even have a retirement program for those workers, at least not for a few years." "I think I know the answer," said Mr. Burgess, "but what about the ones who transfer down from Parma?"

"They'll have the same benefits they have here," replied Jesse. "We will continue to cover them under the same insurance plan and guarantee that their wages will keep pace with those of similar workers here at Parma."

Questions

1. What are the pros and cons of paying workers on the basis of seniority?
2. How do cost-of-living adjustments (COLA) work?
3. Is anything legally wrong with Parma's plan for paying salaried workers? Explain.
4. Are the pay and benefits differentials between the plants likely to create problems? Why? Why not?

P·A·R·T F·I·V·E

SAFETY AND HEALTH

Human Resource
Research

Human Resource
Planning,
Recruitment, and
Selection

Human Resource
Development

Human
Resource
Management

Employee and
Labor Relations

Safety and
Health

Compensation
and Benefits

CHAPTER 14

A SAFE AND HEALTHY WORK ENVIRONMENT

CHAPTER OBJECTIVES

1. Describe the Occupational Safety and Health Act and the importance of safety programs in business operations, and explain health and wellness programs.
2. State the nature of stress and the importance of stress management in business today, and describe why burnout is of major concern to management.
3. Describe physical fitness programs, alcohol abuse programs, drug abuse programs, and employee assistance programs.
4. Describe the possible impact of AIDS in the workplace.

Dionne Moore, safety engineer for Sather Manufacturing, was walking through the plant when she spotted a situation that immediately caught her attention. Someone had spilled a large quantity of oil on the floor and had not cleaned it up. Just at that moment, Ron Wade, one of the firm's employees, stepped on the oil. His feet went out from under him and the packages he was carrying scattered everywhere. Ron landed squarely on his back and for a moment didn't move. He got up slowly but it appeared that he was not injured. Dionne was relieved but became quite concerned when she realized the many possible consequences of the accident.

Bob Byrom, production foreman for King Electronics, is concerned about the health of one of his best workers, Cecil Weeks. For the past several months Cecil has been relatively ineffective on the job. He has been doing sloppy work and many of his coworkers have complained about his poor disposition. Recently, Bob observed Cecil at his locker during a work break drinking from a bottle in a brown bag. The odor on Cecil's breath suggested to Bob the cause of Cecil's changed work habits. Bob believes that Cecil may be an alcoholic. He wonders what should be done.

Dionne and Bob are each involved with but a few of the many critical areas related to employee safety and health. Dionne realizes that safety is a major concern in her organization and that she must constantly strive to minimize or eliminate accidents such as the one she just witnessed. Bob has just discovered that the poor performance of one of his employees may be caused by a drinking problem.

We begin this chapter with definitions of *safety* and *health* and an overview of the Occupational Safety and Health Act. We then discuss the following issues: safety programs; health and wellness programs; stress management; burnout; and programs for physical fitness, alcohol abuse, and drug abuse. Employee assistance programs are presented next, and the chapter ends with a discussion of AIDS in the workplace.

■ THE NATURE AND ROLE OF SAFETY AND HEALTH

In our discussion, **safety** involves protecting employees from injuries caused by work-related accidents. **Health** refers to employees' freedom from physical or emotional illness. The human resource professional is vitally concerned with these aspects of employment. Safety and health problems seriously affect both productivity and quality of work life. Employee accidents and illnesses can dramatically lower a firm's effectiveness and employee morale. Although line managers are primarily responsible for maintaining a safe and healthy work environment, human resource professionals provide staff expertise to help them deal with these issues. In addition, the human resource manager is frequently responsible for coordinating and monitoring specific safety and health programs.

■ THE OCCUPATIONAL SAFETY AND HEALTH ACT

For years, industrial safety has been a major problem that seemingly resists solution. Prior to 1971, it was regulated primarily by workers' compensation laws of the various states. When Congress passed the Occupational Safety and Health Act of 1970, it quickly became one of the most controversial laws affecting human resource management. There is little doubt that the act's intent is justified and that many businesses have long neglected safety and health. The act's basic requirements are summarized in Table 14-1.

The act's enforcement by the Occupational Safety and Health Administration (OSHA) dramatically altered management's role in the area of safety and health. Within OSHA, administrative changes have also been made to make the agency more responsive to valid criticism and to overcome the negative image that it originally had. At the same time, OSHA continues to take its inspection and enforcement responsibilities quite seriously. When appropriate, it seeks criminal sanctions against corporations or individuals. In one instance, a corporate safety director was sentenced to three months in jail and fined $10,000 for lying to an OSHA inspector. The agency is definitely alive and well. During a single year in the 1980s, OSHA conducted more than 71,000 inspections. It detected almost 120,000 violations and levied fines totaling $9 million. Less than 3 percent of the violations were contested. An amendment in the most recent federal budget authorizes OSHA to levy fines seven times higher than previously permitted. For example, the $1,000 maximum on serious violations is now $7,000, and the ceiling on willful violations has been increased from $10,000 to $70,000. Total penalties assessed in the fiscal year ending in September 1990 were over $89 million, up 30 percent from the previous year.[1]

---

[1] Brad Lee Thompson, "OSHA Bounces Back," *Training*, 28 (January 1991), p. 46.

TABLE 14-1 | Job Safety and Health Protection

The Occupational Safety and Health Act of 1970 provides job safety and health protection for workers through the promotion of safe and healthful working conditions throughout the nation. Requirements of the act include the following.

Employers

Each employer must furnish to each of his or her employees a place of employment free from recognized hazards that are causing or are likely to cause death or serious harm to employees; and shall comply with occupational safety and health standards issued under the act.

Employees

Each employee shall comply with all occupational safety and health standards, rules, regulations, and orders issued under the act that apply to his or her own actions and conduct on the job. The Occupational Safety and Health Administration (OSHA) of the Department of Labor has the primary responsibility for administering the act. OSHA issues occupational safety and health standards, and its Compliance Safety and Health Officers conduct job site inspection to ensure compliance with the act.

Inspection

The act requires that a representative of the employer and a representative authorized by the employees be given an opportunity to accompany the OSHA inspector for the purpose of aiding the inspection. Where there is no authorized employee representative, the OSHA Compliance Officer must consult with a reasonable number of employees concerning safety and health conditions in the workplace.

Complaint

Employees or their representatives have the right to file a complaint with the nearest OSHA office requesting an inspection if they believe unsafe or unhealthful conditions exist in their workplace. OSHA will withhold, on request, names of employees complaining. The act provides that employees may not be discharged or discriminated against in any way for filing safety and health complaints or otherwise exercising their rights under the act. An employee who believes he or she has been discriminated against may file a complaint with the nearest OSHA office within thirty days of the alleged discrimination.

Citation

If upon inspection OSHA believes an employer has violated the act, a citation alleging such violations will be issued to the employer. Each citation will specify a time period within which the alleged violation must be corrected. The OSHA citation must be prominently displayed at or near the place of alleged violation for three days, or until it is corrected, whichever is later, to warn employees of dangers that may exist there.

Proposed Penalty

The act provides for mandatory penalties against employers of up to $7,000 for each serious violation and for optional penalties of up to $1,000 for each nonserious violation. Penalties of up to $7,000 per day may be proposed for failure to correct violations within the proposed time period. Also, any employer who willfully or repeatedly violates the act may be assessed penalties of up to $70,000 for each such violation. Criminal penalties are also provided for in the act. Any willful violation resulting in death of an employee, upon conviction, is punishable by a fine of not more than $70,000 or by imprisonment for not more than six months, or by both. Conviction of an employer after a first conviction doubles these maximum penalties.

Continued on next page

TABLE 14-1 | *Continued*

Voluntary Activity

While providing penalties for violations, the act also encourages efforts by labor and management, before an OSHA inspection, to reduce injuries and illnesses arising out of employment. The Department of Labor encourages employers and employees to reduce workplace hazards voluntarily and to develop and improve safety and health programs in all workplaces and industries. Such cooperative action would initially focus on the identification and elimination of hazards that could cause death, injury, or illness to employees and supervisors. There are many public and private organizations that can provide information and assistance in this effort, if requested.

Source: *OSHA Bulletin* (poster) (Washington, D.C.: U.S. Department of Labor).

While attempting to tighten its procedures, OSHA is also emphasizing the preventive effect of its inspections.[2] For example, all companies employing more than ten workers are now required to maintain data regarding hazardous substances in the workplace. In addition, they must display warning labels when applicable.[3]

The agency is also concentrating on high-risk industries, such as ship building and meat packing, in which there is greater potential for reducing injuries and illnesses (see Table 14-2). Industries with lower accident and illness rates will not receive as much attention as before. Although it has emphasized safety in the past, OSHA has begun moving more into areas that affect health. Inspectors trained in this area are now being utilized.

Many of OSHA's rules have been simplified. For instance, instead of requiring that a fire extinguisher be a certain number of inches above the floor, the rule now states only that it has to be readily accessible. In addition, numerous inappropriate rules have been eliminated, a trend that is expected to continue. The agency's leaders are expected to maintain their pressure on businesses, but they appear to be taking a more positive and realistic approach than they did in the past.

■ SAFETY

Thousands of workers are killed or injured each year as a result of job-related accidents. The cost of these accidents is substantial— over $47 billion in 1988 alone—(see Table 14-3 on page 532). Unfortunately, the cost is often passed along to the consumer in the form of higher prices. Thus everyone is affected (directly or indirectly) by job-related accidents. Although many businesses had elaborate safety programs years

---

[2] B. S. Murphy et al., "OSHA: Alive and Well," *Personnel Journal,* 65 (June 1986), pp. 32–35.

[3] Hazel Bradford, "OSHA Orders Benzene Curb," *Engineering News Record,* 219 (September 10, 1987), p. 38.

TABLE 14-2 | Industries with the Highest Injury and Illness Incidence Rates in 1987 and 1988

Industry	1987		1988	
	Rank	Incidence rate*	Rank	Incidence rate*
Ship building and repairing	1	40.1	1	44.9
Meat packing plants	2	38.4	2	39.2
Special product sawmills, n.e.c.	9	26.4	3	31.0
Gray iron foundries	15	23.8	4	30.3
Automotive stampings	36	20.7	5	30.0
Primary aluminum	6	28.6	6	29.6
Mobile homes	5	28.9	7	28.7
Vitreous plumbing fixtures	14	25.1	8	28.4
Structural wood members, n.e.c.	12	25.6	9	28.3
Truck trailers	33	20.8	9	28.3
Motor vehicles and car bodies	220	12.8	11	28.0
Prefabricated wood buildings	4	31.5	12	27.9
Truck and bus bodies	18	23.0	13	27.5
Petroleum and coal products, n.e.c.	n.a.		14	26.5
Sausages and other prepared meats	24	22.2	15	25.5
Steel foundries, n.e.c.	40	20.3	16	25.4
Fabricated structural metal	21	22.6	17	25.2
Raw cane sugar	20	22.7	18	24.8
Flat glass	35	20.8	19	24.6
Household cooking equipment	34	20.8	20	24.5
Secondary nonferrous metals	42	20.1	21	24.2
Travel trailers and campers	17	23.5	22	24.1
Metal office furniture	47	19.8	23	24.0
Cold finishing of steel shapes	23	22.5	23	24.0
Canned and cured seafoods	9	26.4	25	23.8

*The incidence rate represents the number of injuries and illnesses per 100 full-time workers.

The abbreviation n.e.c. stands for *not elsewhere classified.*

The abbreviation n.a. stands for *not available.*

Source: Occupational Injuries and Illnesses in the United States by Industry, 1988 (Washington, D.C.: U.S. Department of Labor, Bureau of Labor Statistics, August 1990), Bulletin 2366, p. 2.

before the Occupational Safety and Health Act was passed, a large number of firms didn't establish formal safety programs until it was enacted.

The Focus of Safety Programs

Safety programs may be designed to accomplish their purposes in two primary ways. The first approach is to create a psychological environment and attitudes that promote safety. Accidents can be reduced when workers

TABLE 14-3 | Job-Related Accident Costs

The true cost to the nation, to employers, and to individuals of work related deaths and injuries is much greater than the cost of workers' compensation insurance alone. The figures presented below show the National Safety Council's estimates of the total costs of occupational deaths and injuries. Uninsured costs are estimated, conservatively, to be equal to insured costs. The Council recommends, however, that each organization establish its own ratio of uninsured to insured costs through a study of its own experience. Guidance for such a study is contained in the Council's *Accident Prevention Manual.*

TOTAL COST IN 1988 . . . . **$47.1 billion**

Includes wage losses of $7.9 billion, insurance administrative costs of $6.0 billion, and medical costs of $8.1 billion. Includes uninsured costs of $22.0 billion such as the money value of time lost by workers other than those with disabling injuries, who are directly or indirectly involved in accidents, and the cost of the time required to investigate accidents, write up accident reports, etc. Also includes fire losses of $3.1 billion, but excludes the cost of other property damage.

Cost per Worker **$410**

This figure indicates the value of goods or services each worker must produce to offset the cost of work injuries. It is *not* the average cost of a work injury.

Cost per Death **$550,000**

Cost per Disabling Injury **$16,800**

These figures include estimates of wage losses, medical expenses, insurance administration costs, and uninsured costs, and exclude any property damage costs.

Source: Accident Facts (Chicago, Ill.: National Safety Council, 1989), p. 34.

consciously or subconsciously think about safety. This attitude must permeate the firm's operations, and a strong company policy emphasizing safety and health is crucial. For example, a major chemical firm's policy states, "It is the policy of the company that every employee be assigned to a safe and healthful place to work. We strongly desire accident prevention in all phases of our operations. Toward this end, the full cooperation of all employees will be required." As the policy infers, no one person is assigned the task of making the workplace safe. It is everyone's job from top management to the lowest level employee, and everyone should be encouraged to come up with solutions to safety problems. Accident prevention requires a sustained effort by everyone, but unfortunately, the following adage applies to certain situations: "Everyone's responsibility often becomes no one's responsibility." Therefore, the firm's managers, who can authorize that the safety effort be carried out, must take the lead. The unique role of management is made clear by the fact that OSHA places the responsibility for employee safety primarily on the employer.[4]

The second approach to safety program design is to develop and maintain a safe working environment. Here, the physical work environment is altered to prevent accidents. Even if Joe, a machine operator, has been partying all night and can barely open his eyes, the safety devices on his machine will help keep him safe. It is in this area that OSHA has had its greatest influence. For instance, the agency's guidelines for power transmission apparatus are shown in Table 14-4 on page 534. Through procedures such as these and those developed by individual organizations, an attempt is made to create a physical environment in which accidents cannot occur.

Developing Safety Programs

Organizational safety programs require planning for prevention of workplace accidents. Plans may be relatively simple, as for a small retail store, or more complex and highly sophisticated, as for a large automobile assembly plant. Regardless of the organization's size, top management's support is essential if safety programs are to be effective. The top executives in a firm should be aware of the tremendous economic losses that can result from accidents.

Some of the reasons for top management's support of a safety program are listed in Table 14-5 on page 535. As you can see, the lost productivity of a single injured worker is not the only factor to consider. Every phase of human resource management is involved. For instance, the firm may have difficulty in recruitment if it gains a reputation for having hazardous working conditions. Employee relations may be seriously eroded if workers believe that management doesn't care enough about them to make their workplace safe. Compensation may also be affected if the firm must pay a premium to attract qualified applicants and retain valued employees. Maintaining a stable workforce may become very difficult if the workplace is perceived as hazardous.

The Superfund Amendments Reauthorization Act, Title III (SARA—the hazard communication standard), in addition to state laws, has required businesses to communicate more openly about the hazards associated with the materials they use and produce and the wastes they generate. Good "risk communication" entails getting people's attention when dangerous situations exist and they are not responding to them. It also involves calming employees down when they are unduly alarmed about an unimportant risk.[5]

Managers in unionized firms should recognize that a collective bargaining agreement—even if it contains both no-strike and grievance arbitration clauses—does not prohibit an employee walkout if objective evidence of

---

[4] Alton L. Thygerson, *Safety,* 2nd ed. (Englewood Cliffs, N.J.: Prentice-Hall, 1986), p. 258.

[5] John C. Bruening, "Risk Communication: A Two-Way Connection," *Occupational Hazards,* 52 (October 1990), p. 76.

abnormally dangerous working conditions exists. Managers in union-free firms should be aware that their employees' right to walk out when hazardous working conditions exist is also protected by the Labor Management Relations Act. Whether the firm is unionized or union-free, it is an unfair labor practice to interfere with workers' rights in regard to safe working conditions.

One way to strengthen a safety program is to include employee input, which provides workers with a sense of accomplishment. To prevent accidents, each worker must make a personal commitment to safe work practices. A team concept wherein employees watch out for each other as a moral obligation is a worthy goal. One way to develop this is to form safety committees. Participation in a committee helps form positive attitudes, and employees develop a sense of ownership of the program. The committee may become involved with not only safety issues but also with ways to

TABLE 14-4 | Office of Safety and Health Administration Guidelines for Power Transmission Apparatus

Power Transmission Apparatus
All belts, pulleys, shafts, flywheels, couplings, and other moving power transmission parts must be securely guarded.
A flywheel located so that any part is seven feet or less above a floor or platform must be guarded with an enclosure of sheet, perforated, or expanded metal, or woven wire. It must also be fenced in with guard rails.
All exposed parts of horizontal shafting must be enclosed in a metal or wire cage on a frame of angle iron or iron pipe securely fastened to the floor or frame of the machine. If wire mesh forms the enclosure, it should be the type in which the wires are strongly fastened at every cross point, either by welding, soldering, or galvanizing.
Projecting shaft ends must be guarded by nonrotating caps or safety sleeves.
Pulleys or sheaves seven feet or less from the floor must be guarded with metal or wire mesh enclosures.
Horizontal, vertical, and inclined belt, rope, and chain drives must be enclosed in metal or wire mesh cages. The same applies to chains, sprockets, couplings, and gears.
Guards for horizontal overhead belts must run the entire length of the belt and follow the line of the pulley to the ceiling. This also applies to overhead rope and chain drives.

Source: Essentials of Machine Guarding (Washington, D.C.: U.S. Department of Labor, Office of Safety and Health Administration, July 1975), OSHA no. 2227, pp. 10, 12.

TABLE 14-5 | Reasons for Management's Support of a Safety Program

- *Personal loss.* Most individuals strongly prefer not to be injured. The physical pain and mental anguish associated with injuries is always unpleasant and may even be traumatic. Of much greater concern is the possibility of permanent disablement or even death.
- *Financial loss to injured employees.* Most employees are covered by company insurance plans or personal accident insurance. However, an injury may result in financial losses not covered by the insurance.
- *Lost productivity.* When an employee is injured, there will be a loss of productivity to the firm. In addition to obvious losses, there are often hidden costs. For example, a replacement may need additional training to replace the injured employee. Even when a person can be moved into the injured employee's position, efficiency may suffer.
- *Higher insurance premiums.* Workers' compensation insurance premiums are based on the employer's history of insurance claims. The potential for savings related to employee safety provides a degree of incentive to establish formal programs.
- *Possibility of fines and imprisonment.* Since the enactment of the Occupational Safety and Health Act, a willful and repeated violation of its provisions may result in serious penalties.
- *Social responsibility.* Many executives feel responsible for the safety and health of their employees. A number of firms had excellent safety programs years before OSHA existed. They understand that safety is in the best interest of the firm.

improve productivity. Employee feedback is essential, and good safety performance must be rewarded.[6]

Companies with effective safety programs work to involve virtually everyone in the firm. Line managers are normally responsible for controlling conditions that cause accidents. As part of this responsibility, they must set the proper safety example for other employees. If a supervisor fails to use safety devices when demonstrating use of the equipment, subordinates may feel that the devices aren't really necessary. The line manager's attitude can also affect a worker's attitude toward safety training. Comments such as "Let's go to that boring safety meeting" aren't likely to elicit enthusiastic support from subordinates. The supervisor can show support for the safety program by conscientiously enforcing safety rules and cooperating with those who monitor the program.

---

[6] Dean W. Chappell, "How to Involve Employees in Safety Management," *Safety and Health,* 142 (October 1990), pp. 52–53.

In many companies, one staff member coordinates the overall safety program. Some major corporations have risk management departments, which anticipate losses associated with safety factors and prepare legal defenses in the event of lawsuits. Titles such as safety director and safety engineer are common. One of the safety director's primary tasks is to provide safety training for company employees. This involves educating line managers about the merits of safety and recognizing and eliminating unsafe situations. Although the safety director operates essentially in an advisory capacity, a well-informed and assertive director may have considerable power in the organization.

Accident Investigation

Accidents can happen even in the most safety-conscious firms. Each accident, whether or not it results in an injury, should be carefully evaluated to ensure that it doesn't recur. The safety engineer and the line manager jointly investigate accidents. One of the responsibilities of any supervisor is to prevent accidents. To do so, the supervisor must learn—through active participation in the safety program—why accidents occur, how they occur, where they occur, and who is involved. Supervisors gain a great deal of knowledge about accident prevention by helping prepare accident reports.

Safety should also be emphasized during the training and orientation of new employees. The early months of employment are often critical because, as Table 14-6 shows, work injuries decrease substantially with length of service.[7] Note that the pattern is consistent for both men and women. This knowledge should lead supervisors to stress safety as they train new employees.

Evaluation of Safety Programs

Perhaps the best indicator that a safety program is succeeding is a reduction in the number and severity of accidents. Thus program evaluation involves more than counting the number of accidents; it must also consider their severity. Statistics such as frequency and severity rates are often used in program evaluation. The **frequency rate** is expressed by the following formula, which yields the number of lost-time accidents per million person-hours worked:

$$\text{Frequency rate} = \frac{\text{Number of lost-time accidents} \times 1,000,000}{\text{Number of person-hours worked during the period}}$$

---

[7] Norman Root and Michael Hoefer, "The First Work-Injury Data Available from New BLS Study," *Monthly Labor Review,* 102 (January 1979), p. 77.

TABLE 14-6 | Accident Rates by Length of Service

Length of Service	Men*	Women*
1 month	10.64	8.78
2–3 months	5.90	5.47
4–6 months	3.41	3.31
7–12 months	1.72	1.84
2–3 years	0.84	0.95
4–5 years	0.43	0.46
6–10 years	0.21	0.23
11–25 years	0.06	0.05
26–35 years	0.02	0.01

*Rates are expressed as the average percentage per month of work injuries, by length of service, for 218,446 men and 52,136 women in ten states, 1976–1977.

Source: Norman Root and Michael Hoefer, "The First Work-Injury Data Available from New BLS Study," *Monthly Labor Review,* 102 (January 1979), p. 77. Reprinted by permission.

Although this formula is often used, OSHA has developed one that is conceptually different.[8] The agency's formula follows:

$$\text{Incident rate} = \frac{\text{Number of injuries and/or illnesses}}{\text{Total hours worked by all employees during reference year}} \times 200,000$$

In this formula the constant (200,000) represents the base for 100 full-time equivalent workers at 40 hours per week, 50 weeks per year. The major differences between this formula and the first one are that both injuries and illnesses are considered and that the base for reporting injury frequency rates is 100 full-time employees (as opposed to 1 million person-hours).

The **severity rate** indicates the number of days lost because of accidents per million person-hours worked. It is expressed by the following formula:

$$\text{Severity rate} = \frac{\text{Number of person-days lost} \times 1,000,000}{\text{Number of person-hours worked during the period}}$$

In addition to program evaluation criteria, an effective reporting system is needed to ensure that accidents are recorded. When a new safety program is initiated, the number of accidents may decline significantly. However, some supervisors may be failing to report certain accidents to make the statistics for their units look better. Proper evaluation of a safety program depends on the accurate reporting and recording of data.

---

[8] Lyne R. Schauer and Thomas S. Ryder, "New Approach to Occupational Safety and Health Statistics," *Monthly Labor Review,* 95 (March 1972), pp. 18–19.

To be of value, the conclusions derived from an evaluation must be used to improve the safety program. Gathering data and permitting them to collect dust on the safety director's desk will not solve problems or prevent accidents. The results of the evaluation must be transmitted upward to top management and downward to line managers in order to generate improvements.

Safety and Health Trends

According to recent reports, organizations are spending an increasing amount of money on safety. There are a number of reasons for this direction:[9]

- *Profitability.* Employees can only produce while they are on the job. In addition to reducing payouts related to rising medical costs, other factors, such as lost production, recruiting, and training, add to a firm's expenses.
- *Employee Relations.* Firms with good safety records have an effective vehicle for attracting and retaining good employees.
- *Reduced Liability.* An effective safety program can reduce corporate and executive liability for charges when their employees are injured.
- *Marketing.* A good safety record may well provide companies with a competitive edge. Recruiting of employees may be facilitated, and the winning of contracts may also be aided.
- *Productivity.* An effective safety program may boost morale and productivity while simultaneously reducing rising costs.

There is a payoff for sound safety and health programs. According to Jan Williams, deputy assistant secretary of the Occupational Safety and Health Administration, worksites with excellent safety and health programs can expect lost workday rates to run between 20 and 40 percent of the industry average.[10]

One specific safety and health approach that seems destined to become more common is the increased use of ergonomics. **Ergonomics** is the study of equipment design that reduces operator fatigue and discomfort. The Bureau of Labor Statistics reports that more than 50 percent of all occupational illnesses reported in 1990 were related to repetitive trauma, which may result in repetitive-motion disorders such as back injuries and upper extremity problems. Many of these medical problems involved the use of computers. It has been estimated that by the year 2000, 75 percent of all jobs will involve the use of computers. Another factor that may contribute to the increase of repetitive trauma relates to aging of the workforce. By the year 2050, at least one-third of the U.S. population will be 55 years old or older. Since older workers have decreased muscle performance, flexibil-

---

[9] Robert Pater, "Safety Leadership Cuts Costs," *HRMagazine,* 35 (November 1990), p. 46.

[10] "To OSHA, 'Workplace Safety Is Good Business,'" *Risk Management,* 36 (October 1989), p. 172.

ity, and joint mobility, repetitive-motion disorders could reasonably be expected to increase. In dealing with this problem, the Occupational Safety and Health Administration has increased its budget and staff to concentrate on ergonomics issues. Ergonomics standards are being established for all industries.[11]

■ HEALTH AND WELLNESS PROGRAMS

The reason for a firm to be concerned about its employees' health becomes obvious when employee worth is calculated. For instance, how valuable is a highly qualified executive who has developed and implemented a new marketing program? What is the worth of a skilled engineer trained by the firm for five years? Consider, for example, the bright, 40-year old executive who succumbs to alcoholism because of job stress; the machinist, who because of job boredom, turns to drugs to brighten the day; or the designer who pushes herself so hard that she dies of cardiac arrest while driving to work. Health problems not only affect individuals but also an organization's profitability.

In addition to management and government initiatives, union support has also hastened the establishment of more effective health programs. Unions are placing industrial health issues high on their list of demands in collective bargaining. Rather than concentrating on pay, unions now seek gains in such areas as health care and recreational facilities.

Environmental factors play a major role in the development of physical and mental disorders. The traditional view that health is dependent on medical care and is simply the absence of disease is changing. Today, many individuals perceive that optimal health can be achieved through environmental safety, organizational changes, and different life-styles. Infectious diseases, over which the individual has little control, are not the problem they once were. For example, from 1900 to 1970 the death rate from major infectious diseases dropped dramatically. Yet, the death rate from major chronic diseases such as heart disease, cancer, and stroke increased by more than 250 percent.[12] Although chronic life-style diseases are much more prevalent today, people have a great deal of control over many of them. These are the health problems related to smoking, undue stress, lack of exercise, obesity, and alcohol and drug abuse.

A formal company wellness program involves more than merely dispensing aspirin and bandages. As with a safety program, it should reflect a company philosophy that emphasizes the value of its human assets. Many of the procedures used in establishing an effective safety program are also applicable to a company wellness program. A firm with the reputation of having a healthy work environment is in a stronger position to achieve

---

[11] Marilyn Joyce, "Ergonomics Will Take Center Stage During '90s and into New Century," *Occupational Health and Safety,* 60 (January 1991), pp. 31–32.

[12] Cathy J. Brumback, "EAPs–Bringing Health and Productivity to the Workplace," *Business,* 37 (April–June 1987), p. 42.

many other human resource objectives. For instance, recruitment may be easier because more people want to work for the company. Employee and management relations may also improve when workers believe that the company is genuinely concerned about them.

Back and neck injuries, sprains, and strains are among the most common and costly problems in industry. For this reason, many wellness programs began with a focus on physical fitness or were actually developed out of a company-sponsored physical fitness program. While physical fitness continues to be an important component of most major wellness programs, the movement is now toward a more holistic approach to improving health.[13] Another important element in wellness programs is stress management.

■ STRESS MANAGEMENT

A notable trend within U.S. industry is an increasing concern for employees' emotional well-being. Managers are becoming more aware that long-term productivity depends largely on the dedication and commitment of the company's employees. Another reason is that employees increasingly hold their employers liable for emotional problems they claim are work related. In fact, during the past few years, stress-related mental disorders have become the fastest growing occupational disease. Stress claims now account for almost 14 percent of occupational disease claims, up from 5 percent less than a decade ago.[14] It is interesting to note that among the most frequently used drugs in the United States are tranquilizers, hypertension drugs, and ulcer medication. For various reasons, programs dealing with stress and its related problems are becoming increasingly popular.

Stress is the body's reaction to any demand made on it. It is therefore a highly individual condition. Certain events may be quite stressful to one person but not to another. Moreover, the effect of stress is not always negative. For example, mild stress actually improves productivity, and it can be helpful in developing creative ideas. In fact, the only people who do not experience stress are those who are dead.[15] Although everyone lives under a certain amount of stress, if it is severe enough and persists long enough, it can be harmful. In fact, stress can be as disruptive to an individual as any accident. It can result in poor attendance, excessive use of alcohol or other drugs, poor job performance, or even overall poor health. There is increasing evidence indicating that undue stress is related to the diseases that are leading causes of death—coronary heart disease, stroke, hypertension, cancer, emphysema, diabetes, and cirrhosis; stress may even

---

[13] R. Blake Smith, "Wellness Administrator Working to Prove Programs Cost Effective," *Occupational Health and Safety,* 59 (October 1990), pp. 103–104.

[14] Randall Poe, "Does Your Job Make You Sick?" *Across the Board,* 24 (January 1987), p. 3.

[15] Hans Selye, "Secret of Coping with Stress," *U.S. News and World Report,* 82 (March 21, 1977), p. 51.

lead to suicide.[16] Stress costs U.S. industry billions of dollars each year in lost wages and treatment of related disorders. It causes American workers to miss an average of sixteen days on the job each year.[17]

Aside from humanitarian reasons, the economic factor is sufficient to gain management's interest in helping employees manage stress. A legal factor may provide still another reason. One manager filed suit against his company, charging that his physical ailments (including a heart attack) were caused by the pressure of his job. The man won his case and the company was ordered to make a cash settlement.[18]

The National Institute for Occupational Safety and Health (NIOSH) is one organization that has studied stress as it relates to work. This organization's research indicates that some jobs are generally perceived as being more stressful than others. The twelve "most stressful" jobs are listed in Table 14-7 on page 542. The common factor among these jobs is lack of employee control over work. Workers in such jobs may feel trapped and that they are treated more like machines than people. Some of the less stressful jobs are held by workers who have more control over their jobs, such as college professors and master craftspersons.

The fact that certain jobs are being identified as more stressful than others has important managerial implications. Managers are responsible for recognizing significantly deviant behavior and referring employees to health professionals for diagnosis and treatment. (Refer to Figure 14-1 on page 542 for behavior that may indicate problems.) In addition, managers should monitor their employees' progress and provide them with the incentive to succeed. They should inform employees that there are rewards for life-style changes and that the advantages are greater than the costs involved. Stress may result in many complex problems, but it can generally be handled successfully. In the following section, we describe burnout, a condition that often results from organizational and individual failure to deal with stress effectively.

Burnout

Consider the following scenario:

> Cheryl Weaver supervises fifty people in the administrative department of a large insurance firm. She is normally a competent and conscientious manager with a reputation for doing things right and on time. Until recently, Cheryl had been strongly considered as a candidate for the position of vice-president of administration. However, things have changed. Cheryl behaves

---

[16] John M. Ivancevich and Michael T. Matteson, "Optimizing Human Resources: A Case for Preventive Health and Stress Management," *Organizational Dynamics,* 9 (Autumn 1980), p. 5.

[17] Janice Somerville, "Stress Treatment Costing Billions," *American Medical News,* 32 (November 1989), p. 17.

[18] John M. Ivancevich and Michael T. Matteson, "Optimizing Human Resources," p. 6.

TABLE 14-7 | Stressful Jobs

The twelve jobs with the most stress

1. Laborer	7. Manager/administrator
2. Secretary	8. Waitress/waiter
3. Inspector	9. Machine operator
4. Clinical lab technician	10. Farm owner
5. Office manager	11. Miner
6. Supervisor	12. Painter

Other high-stress jobs (in alphabetical order)

Bank teller	Nurses' aide
Clergy member	Plumber
Computer programmer	Policeperson
Dental assistant	Practical nurse
Electrician	Public relations worker
Fire fighter	Railroad switchperson
Guard	Registered nurse
Hairdresser	Sales manager
Health aide	Sales representative
Health technician	Social worker
Machinist	Structural-metal worker
Meatcutter	Teachers' aide
Mechanic	Telephone operator
Musician	Warehouse worker

Source: From a ranking of 130 occupations by the federal government's National Institute for Occupational Safety and Health.

- Reduced clarity of judgment and effectiveness
- Rigid behavior
- Medical problems
- Strained relationships with others due to irritability
- Increasing excessive absence
- Emerging addictive behaviors (e.g., drugs, alcohol, smoking)
- Expressions of inadequacy and low self-esteem
- Apathy or anger on the job

FIGURE 14-1 | Signs of Stress

Source: Michael Pesci, "Stress Management: Separating Myth from Reality." Reprinted from the January 1982 issue of *Personnel Administrator,* copyright © 1982. Reprinted with the permission from *HRMagazine* (formerly *Personnel Administrator*) published by the Society for Human Resource Management, Alexandria, Virginia.

differently. She can't seem to concentrate on her work and appears to be a victim of "battle fatigue." "Oh, Cheryl," a coworker advised, "you'll make it. You've always been so strong." But Cheryl surprised her associate when she responded, "I don't want to be told I'll make it on my own. I already know I can't."

Cheryl doesn't know exactly what has caused her run-down condition. She feels that she is at her wit's end and desperately needs assistance. Cheryl apparently is the victim of a stress-related phenomenon known as burnout. **Burnout** is a state of fatigue or frustration, which stems from devotion to a cause, way of life, or relationship that did not provide the expected reward. In essence, burnout is the perception that an individual is giving more than he or she is receiving—whether it is money, satisfaction, or praise.[19]

Burnout is often associated with a mid-life or mid-career crisis, but it can happen at different times to different people. A key factor in burnout is unrealistic expectations. When people strive excessively to achieve unfeasible goals, they may experience a feeling of helplessness—that no matter what they do they won't succeed. When this occurs, they may lose their motivation to perform. Although some employees try to hide their problems, there are some shifts in behavior that indicate dissatisfaction. They may start procrastinating or do the opposite extreme of taking on too many assignments. They may lose things and become increasingly scatterbrained. Individuals who are normally amiable may turn irritable. They may become cynical, irritable, or even pompous, or develop paranoia.[20]

Individuals in the helping professions, such as teachers and counselors, seem to be susceptible to burnout because of their jobs, whereas others may be vulnerable because of their upbringing, expectations, or personalities. Burnout is frequently associated with people whose jobs require working closely with others under stressful and tension-filled conditions. Any employee may experience this condition, and managers and executives are not exempt. The dangerous part of burnout is that it is contagious. A highly cynical and pessimistic burnout victim can quickly transform an entire group. Therefore, it is important that the problem be dealt with quickly. Once it has begun, it is difficult to stop.

Some of the symptoms of burnout include (1) chronic fatigue; (2) anger at those making demands; (3) self-criticism for putting up with demands; (4) cynicism, negativism, and irritability; (5) a sense of being besieged; and (6) hair-trigger display of emotions.[21] Other symptoms might include recurring health problems, such as ulcers, back pain, or frequent headaches. The burnout victim is often unable to maintain an even balance of emotions; unwarranted hostility may occur in totally inappropriate situations.

---

[19] Hugh F. Stallworth, "Realistic Goals Help Avoid Burnout," *HRMagazine,* 35 (June 1990), p. 1.

[20] Patti Watts, "Are Your Employees Burnout-Proof?" *Personnel,* 67 (September 1990), p. 12–13, 20.

[21] Harry Levinson, "When Executives Burn Out," *Harvard Business Review,* 59 (May–June 1981), p. 76.

Burnout is a problem that should be dealt with before it occurs. In order to do so, managers must be aware of potential sources of stress. These sources exist both within and outside the organization.

Sources of Stress

Regardless of its origin, stress possesses devastating potential. While some factors are controllable to varying degrees, others are not. In the following paragraphs, we discuss some of the primary sources of stress.

The Family. Although a frequent source of happiness and security, the family can also be a significant stressor. As a result, nearly one half of all marriages end in divorce, which is often quite stressful. When divorce leads to single parenthood, the difficulties may be compounded.

Children are one of life's great sources of happiness. Yet, consider the effect of an infant awakening parents in the middle of the night with a severe asthmatic attack! This type of incident would certainly cause anxiety levels to rise significantly. Academic or extreme social adjustment problems for a teenager can also create much anguish for the entire family.

A relatively recent phenomenon is the dual-career family. When both husband and wife have job and family responsibilities, traditional roles are altered. What happens when one partner is completely content with a job and the other is offered a desired promotion requiring transfer to a distant city? At best, these circumstances are beset with difficulties.

Financial Problems. Problems with finances may place an unbearable strain on the employee. For some, these problems are persistent and never quite resolved. Unpaid bills and bill collectors can create great tension and play a role in divorce or poor work performance.

Living Conditions. Stress levels may be higher for people who live in densely populated areas. These people face longer lines, endure more hectic traffic jams, and contend with higher levels of air and noise pollution. Urban life has many advantages, but the benefits are not without costs—often in the form of stress.

Life Changes. Life change events, such as divorce, have been weighted according to the stress they produce and assigned life change unit (LCU) values. As Table 14-8 shows, the most stressful life event is the death of a spouse. One study determined that 70 percent of the persons who experienced events totaling more than 300 LCUs in a year had an illness during the following year. It was also noted that these people tended to have multiple illnesses.[22]

---

[22] E. K. Erich Gunderson and Richard H. Rahe (eds.), *Life Stress and Illness* (Springfield, Ill.: Charles C. Thomas, 1974), p. 62.

TABLE 14-8 | Life Change Events

Type of Event		LCU Values
Family	Death of a spouse	100
	Divorce	73
	Marital separation	65
	Death of close family member	63
	Marriage	50
	Marital reconciliation	45
	Major change in health of family member	44
	Pregnancy	40
	Addition of new family member	39
	Major change in arguments with spouse	35
	Son or daughter leaving home	29
	In-law troubles	29
	Spouse starting or ending work	26
	Major change in family get-togethers	15
Personal	Detention in jail	63
	Major personal injury or illness	53
	Sexual difficulties	39
	Death of a close friend	37
	Outstanding personal achievement	28
	Start or end of formal schooling	26
	Major change in living conditions	25
	Major revision of personal habits	24
	Changing to a new school	20
	Change in residence	20
	Major change in recreation	19
	Major change in church activities	19
	Major change in social activities	18
	Major change in sleeping habits	16
	Major change in eating habits	15
	Vacation	13
	Christmas	12
	Minor violations of the law	11
Work	Being fired from work	47
	Retirement from work	45
	Major business adjustment	39
	Changing to different line of work	36
	Major change in work responsibilities	29
	Trouble with boss	23
	Major change in working conditions	20
Financial	Major change in financial state	38
	Mortgage or loan over $10,000	31
	Mortgage foreclosure	30
	Mortgage or loan less than $10,000	17

Source: Reprinted from E. K. Eric Gunderson and Richard H. Rahe (eds.), *Life Stress and Illness* (Springfield, Ill.: Charles C. Thomas, 1974), by courtesy of the publisher.

Corporate Culture. Generally speaking, corporate culture has a lot to do with stress. The CEO's leadership style often sets the tone. An autocratic CEO who permits little input from subordinates may create a stressful environment. However, a weak CEO may encourage subordinates to compete for power, resulting in internal conflicts. Certain firms have even been considered stressful because the chief executive insists on superior performance.

Even in the healthiest corporate culture, stressful relationships among employees can occur. Employee personality types vary and, combined with differing values and belief systems, they may so impair communication that stress is inevitable. Also, competition encouraged by the organization's reward system for promotion, pay increases, and status may add to the problem.

Role Ambiguity. Role ambiguity exists when an employee doesn't understand the content of the job. The employee may feel stress when he or she doesn't perform certain duties expected by the supervisor, even though the employee didn't know to do them. An employee may also feel pressure from above when he or she mistakenly, although innocently, attempts to perform tasks that are part of someone else's job. These situations often result from role ambiguity, a condition that can be quite threatening to an employee and produce feelings of insecurity.

Role Conflict. Role conflict occurs when an individual is placed in the position of having to pursue opposing goals. For example, a manager may be expected to increase production while having to decrease the size of the workforce. Attaining both goals may be impossible, and stress is likely to result. A nationwide survey identified the extent of such problems. It revealed that 35 percent of the respondents had complaints about role ambiguity, and 48 percent felt that they were victims of role conflict.[23]

Job Overload. When employees are given more work than they can reasonably handle, they become victims of **job overload.** A critical aspect of this problem is that the best performers in the firm are often the ones so affected. These individuals have proven that they can perform more, so they are given more to do. At its extreme, work overload results in burnout.

Working Conditions. The physical characteristics of the workplace, including the machines and tools used, can create stress. Overcrowding, excessive noise, poor lighting, and poorly maintained work stations and equipment can all adversely affect employee morale and increase stress. Something as apparently benign as an antiquated photocopier that doesn't always work properly can create great stress when an important report must be assembled and sent to the CEO first thing in the morning.

---

[23] Peter J. Frost, Vance F. Mitchell, and Walter R. Nord, *Organizational Reality: Reports from the Firing Line,* 2nd ed. (Glenview, Ill.: Scott, Foresman, 1982), p. 4.

Managerial Work. The nature of managerial work may itself be a source of stress. According to one management consultant, as many as half of today's business managers may suffer undue stress on the job.[24] Responsibility for people, conducting performance appraisals, coordinating and communicating layoffs, and conducting outplacement counseling can create a great deal of stress.

A recent study of human resource executives in the Southwest did not reveal that these individuals were in a highly stressful profession. It did determine, however, that female HR professionals felt significantly more stress as a result of organizational politics. This was the only significant difference found in sources of stress for men and women. The reason for this phenomenon could relate to the exclusion of many women from political networks.[25]

It is important for managers to be aware of sources of stress. It is equally important that they implement programs to deal with stress effectively.

Coping with Stress

A number of programs and techniques may effectively prevent or relieve excessive stress. General organizational programs, while not specifically designed to cope with stress, may nevertheless play a major role. The programs and techniques listed in Table 14-9 are discussed in the chapters of this text as indicated (see page 548). Their effective implementation will achieve these results:

- A corporate culture that holds anxiety and tension to an acceptable level is created. Employee inputs are sought and valued, employees are given greater control over their work, and communication is emphasized.
- Each person's role is defined, yet care is taken not to discourage risk-takers and those who want to assume greater responsibility.
- Individuals are given the training and development they need to successfully perform current and future jobs. Equal consideration is given to achieving personal and organizational goals. Individuals are trained to work as effective team members and to develop an awareness of how they and their work relate to others.
- Employees are assisted in planning for career progression.
- Employees participate in making decisions that affect them. They know what is going on in the firm, what their particular roles are, and how well they are performing their jobs.
- Employee needs, financial and nonfinancial, are met through an equitable reward system.

---

[24] "Half of Managers Suffer Work Stress," *Supervision,* 51 (July 1990), p. 10.

[25] Debra L. Nelson, James C. Quick, and Michael A. Hitt, "What Stresses HR Professionals?" *Personnel,* 67 (August 1990), pp. 36–39.

TABLE 14-9 | Organizational Programs and Techniques That Can Be Effective in Coping with Stress

General Organizational Programs	Chapter
Job analysis	4
Human resource development	8
Effective communication, motivation, and leadership styles (corporate culture)	9
Organization development	9
Career planning and development	10
Performance appraisal	11
Compensation	12, 13
Specific Techniques	
Hypnosis, transcendental meditation, and biofeedback	14
Specific Organizational Programs	
Physical fitness, alcohol and drug abuse, and employee assistance programs	14

Table 14-9 also identifies several specific techniques that individuals can utilize to deal with stress. These methods include hypnosis, biofeedback, and transcendental meditation.

Hypnosis is an altered state of consciousness that is artificially induced and characterized by increased receptiveness to suggestions. A person in a hypnotic state may therefore respond to the hypnotist's suggestion to relax.[26] Hypnosis can help many people cope with stress. The serenity achieved through dissipation of anxieties and fears can restore an individual's confidence. A principal benefit of hypnotherapy is that peace of mind continues after the person awakens from a hypnotic state. This tranquility continues to grow, especially when the person has been trained in self-hypnosis.

Biofeedback is a method that can be used to control involuntary bodily processes, such as blood pressure or heart rate. For example, using equipment to provide a visual display of blood pressure, individuals may learn to lower their systolic blood pressure levels.

Transcendental meditation (TM) is a stress-reduction technique whereby a secret word or phrase (mantra) provided by a trained instructor is mentally repeated while an individual is comfortably seated. Repeating the mantra over and over helps prevent distracting thoughts. It has successfully produced the following physiologic changes: decreased oxygen

---

[26] Herbert Benson, *The Relaxation Response* (New York: William Morrow, 1975), p. 72.

consumption, decreased carbon dioxide elimination, and decreased breathing rate. Transcendental meditation results in a decreased metabolic rate and a restful state.[27]

Table 14-9 also lists organizational programs that are designed specifically to deal with stress and related problems. These include physical fitness, alcohol and drug abuse, and employee assistance programs, which will be discussed later in this chapter.

■ CULTURE SHOCK—THE ULTIMATE STRESSOR

The international movement of employees can be a major stressor for expatriates.[28] It is vitally important that human resource professionals properly prepare employees to cope with the stress they will encounter because of global assignments. Expatriates often experience stress from the moment they learn of global assignments until well after returning home.

Stress is evident in almost any work environment, but it is usually quite high in the global arena. Inappropriately addressing global stressors can result in failure and a disinterested employee. Culture shock is the main stressor, resulting in maladies such as poor job performance, unhappy social lives, broken marriages, change in sex drives, eating binges, bouts with depression, nervousness, anger and aggression, substance abuse, homesickness, impatience with family members, and insomnia.[29]

Human resource professionals should work to limit the impact of culture shock by properly preparing individuals for overseas assignments. Global assignments for those who are unprepared are costly to the individual involved and quite costly to the organization. The Employee Relocation Council (ERC) reports that the average annual cost to send an employee overseas for a year or two is between $200,000 and $250,000. One executive estimates the cost to the multinational firm of a failed expatriate assignment is three times the individual's salary, not including the price of lost productivity.[30] This could account for the recent findings by Organization Resources Counselors, Inc., that the number of U.S. expatriates per company continues to decrease. The trend is toward a lower number of U.S. expatriates per company. Often, those who are sent abroad are selected for global assignments because they are the most qualified and best choice.[31] Basically, human resource professionals should help assure that these individuals have the personal skills, people skills, and perceptual skills needed to cope with the global environment they will encounter.

---

[27] *Ibid.,* pp. 60–62.

[28] Mike Fergus, "Employees on the Move," *HRMagazine,* 36 (May 1990), p. 45.

[29] Mark E. Mendenhall and Gary Oddon, "The Overseas Assignment: A Practical Look," *Business Horizons,* 31 (Sept./Oct. 1988), pp. 78–79.

[30] Mike Fergus, "Employees on the Move," p. 45.

[31] Calvin Reynolds, "U.S. Expatriates' Numbers Continue to Decline," *HR News International HR* (March 1991), Section C, p. 2.

■ PHYSICAL FITNESS PROGRAMS

Although few organizations have fully staffed facilities, thousands of U.S. business firms have exercise programs designed to help keep their workers physically fit. From management's viewpoint, this effort makes a lot of sense. Loss of productivity resulting from coronary heart disease costs U.S. businesses billions of dollars annually. The total cost to society is even higher because of lost tax revenue, health care costs, and the expense involved in finding and training replacements. Company-sponsored fitness programs often reduce absenteeism, accidents, and sick pay. There is increasing evidence that if employees stick to company fitness programs, they will experience better health and the firm will have lower costs. Table 14-10 lists some positive effects that resulted from physical fitness and wellness programs.

The Xerox Program

Xerox Corporation currently has nine in-house physical fitness centers at locations throughout the United States. The Xerox programs are designed to help employees avoid coronary heart disease and other degenerative disorders. A fitness program, carefully designed for each individual, helps people feel and look better. As an added benefit, it also enhances their self-concept. A program manager of executive fitness at Xerox has stated, "We are concerned about the ever-increasing costs of medical and insurance premiums, but beyond that, we have an obligation to our people as people."

The Xerox executive fitness program emphasizes four areas: (1) cardiovascular fitness, (2) flexibility, (3) relaxation by means of biofeedback, and (4) weight conditioning. In the cardiovascular training program, the motorized treadmill is the primary tool. The bicycle ergometer is also used, along with biofeedback training. Biofeedback, which was mentioned earlier, is a process whereby an individual monitors his or her own physiological states (such as pulse rate, skin temperature, blood pressure, muscular tension, and brain waves) through the use of bioinstruments. Electrodes placed over selected muscles during exercise indicate the level of muscular tension. By listening to an audio tone, individuals can actually measure and then relax the tension existing in a specific muscle.

Flexibility (the range of movement in a joint or joints) is achieved by using static methods. Static stretching holds muscles and connective tissues at their greatest length, thus helping to relax them. Joint flexibility helps prevent the aches and pains that are common with aging.

Relaxation by means of biofeedback is also an important aspect of the exercise program. Appropriate exercise has been shown to have a greater effect on relaxation than the use of tranquilizers.

Xerox's weight conditioning program is used to strengthen major muscle groups and joints. The lifting of heavy weights, especially for middle-aged individuals, is carefully avoided; relatively light weights and frequent repetition are emphasized.

TABLE 14-10 | Examples of Benefits of Physical Fitness and
Wellness Programs

- At DuPont, heart attacks dropped from 6.47 per 1,000 persons in 1957 to 2.83 in 1983.

- In San Diego, the health care expenses for school employees and fire fighters average $548 less for fitness program participants.

- The fitness program at SpeedCall Corporation resulted in a 65 percent decline in smoking and a 50 percent drop in the number of insurance claims filed by those who quit smoking.

- Weyerhaeuser Company claimed savings of about $8 million in two years through a program designed to enhance employee health.

- At Control Data Corporation, nonexercisers cost the company an additional $115 per year each in health care costs.

- Dallas school teachers involved in a fitness program took an average of three fewer sick days per year. This saved almost $500,000 a year in substitute teacher pay alone.

- At Tenneco, the average insurance claim for exercising women was less than half that for nonexercising women ($639.07 vs. $1,535.83). Similar statistics exist for men.

- At Tenneco, a high percentage of excellent performers are also exercisers; a large number of low performers are nonexercisers.

- Lockheed Missiles and Space Company estimates that it saved $1 million in life insurance costs over a five-year period through its wellness programs.

- Absenteeism at Lockheed was 60 percent lower for exercisers than for nonexercisers.

- The turnover rate at Lockheed is 13 percent lower among regular exercisers.

Source: Otto H. Chang and Cynthia Boyle, "Fitness Programs: Hefty Expense or Wise Investment?" *Management Accounting,* 20 (January 1989), p. 47. Reprinted by permission. Published by Institute of Management Accountants (formerly National Association of Accountants), 10 Paragon Drive, Montvale, N.J. 07645.

Programs at Kimberly-Clark and Tenneco

At Kimberly-Clark Corporation, approximately 1,200 employees participate in a health management program. A staff of twenty-three full-time health care professionals administers this program, utilizing a $2.5 million facility. Prior to admission, employees undergo a physical and medical history exam. Each employee then receives an individualized health prescription. The program at Kimberly-Clark began after its top management made a commitment to reduce health care costs.[32]

---

[32] John M. Ivancevich and Michael T. Matteson, "Optimizing Human Resources," p. 6.

Tenneco's 100,000 square-foot facility in Houston cost $11 million. The facility includes racquetball courts, dressing rooms, exercise equipment, a sauna, and a whirlpool bath. It also features indoor gardens, employee dining rooms, and a conference and training center for 264 people.[33]

Smaller companies often avoid large construction costs by converting unused rooms into aerobic centers. The price of a well-rounded facility of this type ranges from around $3,500 to $10,000. Other firms choose to join a commercial fitness center, which may charge, for example, an initial fee of $4,000 and annual dues of $1,000.[34]

The Future of Fitness and Wellness Programs

The number of programs such as those at Xerox, Kimberly-Clark, and Tenneco is expected to increase dramatically in the future. Firms now recognize that healthy workers contribute directly to the profitability of the organization. Summing up the rationale for fitness programs, one corporate president stated the following:

> Companies will continue to invest in the health and well-being of their employees, and not just to keep health care costs down. They are now starting to see that there is a direct productivity-related benefit to keeping people healthy. Also, people like to be in a situation where management says: Sure you can jog—there is a jogging track, and here is counseling for how to quit smoking, or whatever. So, the absorption by employers of more health care costs, mostly resulting from making available more health care benefits, is going to rise—not because it's a social requirement but because it makes good business sense.[35]

■ ALCOHOL ABUSE PROGRAMS

Alcoholism is a disease characterized by uncontrolled and compulsive drinking that interferes with normal living patterns. It is a significant problem and can both result from and cause excessive stress. Although our society attaches a stigma to the disease, in 1956 the American Medical Association described it as treatable.

An individual may feel that drinking improves his or her ability to cope. However, alcohol rarely improves performance; to the contrary, it almost always impairs performance. As a person starts to drink excessively, the drinking itself results in greater stress. This increased stress is dealt with

---

[33] Otto H. Chang and Cynthia Boyle, "Fitness Programs: Hefty Expense or Wise Investment?" *Management Accounting,* 20 (January 1989), p. 46.

[34] *Ibid.*

[35] "Today's Trends Suggest Revolutionary Changes for Business in the Future," *Personnel Administrator,* 30 (February 1985), pp. 70–71.

by more drinking, creating a vicious cycle. Alcohol abuse affects people at every level of society, from top-level managers to vagrants. It is also one of the most difficult conditions to detect. Sometimes a person progresses to advanced stages of alcohol abuse before perceiving that he or she may actually be an alcoholic. By then, the person's career may be on the verge of destruction. Early signs of alcohol abuse are especially difficult to identify. Often the symptoms are nothing more than an increasing number of absences from work. Over a period of time, productivity may begin to decline, or accidents may occur more frequently. A normally pleasant person can become highly disagreeable. Although alcohol abuse poses many problems for all concerned, no longer does it result in automatic termination. In fact, an increasing number of firms are establishing alcohol abuse programs, and supervisors are now being trained to cope with this health problem. In many instances, alcohol abuse programs are combined with those focusing on other drugs.

■ DRUG ABUSE PROGRAMS

As with alcohol, cocaine, heroin, PCP, THC, crack, and numerous other mind-altering substances have definitely found their way into the workplace. In fact, 65 percent of employees entering the full-time workforce for the first time have used drugs illegally.[36] As you see in Table 14-11 on page 554, chemically dependent employees exhibit behaviors that distinguish them from drug-free workers. Any one of these behaviors taken individually doesn't necessarily suggest that an individual is on drugs. It is when the behaviors are observed as a pattern that drug abuse may exist.

Numerous firms have recognized that drug problems pervade our society, and have taken positive action to deal with them. One such formal program is illustrated in Figure 14-2 on page 554. The program includes (1) safeguards that identify drug problems or prevent them from occurring, and (2) mechanisms that lead to discharge of drug abusers from the firm.

A major purpose of the program is to ensure that drug abusers are not hired. However, if a person becomes an abuser after employment, a supervisor may be forced to resort to discipline for work-related irregularities such as absenteeism and low productivity. All supervisors should be trained to look for signs of drug abuse. And if there is evidence that it does exist, the employee should be required to report to the medical department, where a bona fide attempt will be made to salvage the person. However, failure to comply with the supervisor's direction should reasonably result in discharge.

The medical department works with employees or refers them to appropriate agencies for treatment. If an employee assistance program exists, it may be able to deal with the problem. In either event, there should be an ongoing educational program that constantly reminds employees of the dangers of drug abuse.

---

[36] Russell Harris, "Cover Your Assets," *American Printer,* 205 (July 1990), p. 48.

TABLE 14-11 | Warning Signs of Substance Abuse

The behavior of chemically dependent employees is distinct in a number of ways from drug-free workers. For example, chemically dependent employees are:

- More than two times as likely to ask to leave work early or to have time off.
- Two and a half times more likely to be absent eight days or more.
- Three times more likely to report to work late.
- Over three and a half times more likely to injure themselves or another person on the job.
- Five times more likely to be involved in an off-job accident.
- Five times more likely to file a workers' compensation claim.
- Seven times more likely to have their wages garnished.

Source: Russell Harris, "Cover Your Assets," *American Printer,* 205 (July 1990), p. 48. Reprinted by permission.

	Safeguards which identify a drug problem or prevent it from occurring	Mechanisms that eliminate drug users from the firm
EXTERNAL LABOR SUPPLY (APPLICANTS)	Selection screening techniques suggest evidence of drug use ⟶	Applicant not hired
PRESENT WORKFORCE OF FIRM	Supervisory detection of drug-related work irregularities: absenteeism, low productivity, etc. ⟶	Progressive discipline culminating in discharge for specific irregularities
	Supervisory detection of alleged drug usage and orders for employee to go to medical department	Employee discharged for insubordination if he/she repeatedly refuses to go to medical department
	Voluntary employee referral to medical department ⟶	Medical department determines rehabilitation is appropriate
	All employees involved in semi-continuous drug abuse education program ⟵	Employee returns either during or after rehabilitation process

FIGURE 14-2 | Safeguards and Mechanisms Used to Eliminate Employee Drug Use

Source: Ken Jennings, "The Problem of Employee Drug Use and Remedial Alternatives," *Personnel Journal* (November 1977), p. 556. Copyright © 1977. Reprinted with permission.

Texas Instruments has recently implemented a comprehensive drug-free policy. The policy is simple: "There will be no use of any illegal drug. There will be no illicit use of a legal drug." The difficult part is not formulating the policy but rather implementing it. This aspect has four standards:

- Implementation of the policy must be unbiased. All employees will be treated the same way.
- Policy implementation must assure accuracy. It must contain a system of checks and balances that prevents or detects errors.
- Employees must understand the policy. They must realize the rationale behind the policy.
- Employees must be able to explain the policy. This assures not only understanding of the policy but elicits their support of it.[37]

The Alcohol, Drug Abuse, and Mental Health Administration (ADAMHA) estimated that annual productivity losses from drug and alcohol abuse cost employers almost $100 billion in 1986. This is an increase from $60 billion in 1983 and $46 billion in 1979. In the 1990s, the cost could reach $200 billion.[38]

Effective drug and alcohol abuse policies may help alleviate this trend, however. For example, several years ago, Better-Bilt Aluminum Company, Inc., implemented a drug and alcohol abuse policy. OSHA recordable accidents dropped by 51 percent in 1987 and 44 percent in 1988.[39]

■ EMPLOYEE ASSISTANCE PROGRAMS

Chief executive officers are fond of saying, "Employees are our most important asset." Actions speak louder than words, however, and a president and CEO of the American Management Association once stated that the most useful approach in dealing with impaired workers is through an employee assistance program.[40]

An **employee assistance program (EAP)** is a comprehensive approach that many organizations have taken to deal with burnout, alcohol and drug abuse, and other emotional disturbances. In an EAP, a firm either provides in-house professional counselors or refers employees to an appropriate community social service agency. Typically, most or all of the costs—up to a predetermined amount—are borne by the employer. The EAP concept includes a response to personal psychological problems that interfere with both an employee's well-being and overall productivity. The purpose of EAPs is to provide emotionally troubled employees with the same consideration and assistance given employees having physical illnesses.

---

[37] Bill Oliver, "Do You Drug Test Your Employees?" *HRMagazine,* 35 (October 1990), p. 57.

[38] Cheryl Thieme, "Better-Bilt Builds a Substance Abuse Program That Works," *Personnel Journal,* 69 (August 1990), p. 52.

[39] *Ibid.*

[40] Thomas R. Horton, "Drugs in the Workplace," *Management Review,* 76 (February 1987), p. 5.

HRM In Action

I just don't know what to do about Robert Lewis," said the production supervisor, Marty Fagetti, to Eli Richard, the human resource manager. "Lately I've noticed that Robert has missed work frequently. Even when he shows up, he is usually late. His eyes are always bloodshot, and he seems to move in slow motion. He also doesn't hang around with the "old gang" anymore. Again, today, he didn't show up for work. I just received a call from the police saying he was in the detoxification center and wanted us to be called."

If you were Eli, what action would you suggest?

There are at least 10,000 EAPs in the United States today.[41] Nearly 80 percent of the *Fortune* 500 companies have introduced EAPs.[42] They are being set up primarily to increase worker productivity and reduce costs. For example, an executive of a national benefits consulting firm states that investments in EAPs are returned many times over in the form of increased productivity and decreased health care claims.[43]

The American Coil Spring Company has implemented an effective EAP. The purpose of the program has been described as follows:

> Its intent is to help employees whose personal problems are affecting their work. Frequently, drinking, drugs, impending divorce, finances, etc., will adversely affect a person's attendance, productivity, or relationship with fellow employees. Often they result in disciplinary action and ultimately termination. The intent of the EAP is to catch these problems early on and refer the employee to counseling before his or her job is in jeopardy.

The Kemper Group also has a successful EAP. At Kemper, the following principles guide administration of the program:

1. We believe that alcoholism, drug addiction, and emotional disturbances are illnesses and should be treated as such.
2. We believe the majority of employees who develop alcoholism, other drug addiction, or emotional illness can be helped to recover, and the company should offer appropriate assistance.

---

[41] Patricia Galagan, "Here's the Situation," *Training and Development Journal,* 41 (July 1987), p. 21.

[42] Tom Pope, "EAPs: Good Idea, But What's the Cost?" *Management Review,* (August 1990), p. 50.

[43] Kay Wyrtzen, "Employee Assistance Programs," *Supervision,* 46 (May 1985), pp. 6–7.

3. We believe the decision to seek diagnosis and accept treatment for any suspected illness is the responsibility of the employee. However, continued refusal of an employee to seek treatment when it appears that substandard performance may be caused by any illness is not tolerated. We believe that alcoholism, or drug addiction, or emotional illness should not be made an exception to this commonly accepted principle.

4. We believe that it is in the best interest of employees and the company that when alcoholism, other drug addiction, or emotional illness is present, it should be diagnosed and treated at the earliest possible date.

5. We believe that the company's concern for individual alcohol consumption, drug use, and behavioral habits begins only when they result in unsatisfactory job performance, poor attendance, or behavior detrimental to the good reputation of the company.

6. We believe that confidential handling of the diagnosis and treatment of alcoholism, or other drug addiction, or emotional illness is essential.

In emphasizing the potential benefits of EAPs, one major firm's EAP brochure cites the program's advantages:

- Early recognition and resolution of business and personal problems.
- Retention of valuable employees.
- Improved productivity and profits.
- Reduced absenteeism.
- Improved morale.[44]

Employee assistance programs are justified not only because they help improve the quality of life for employees, but also because they enhance an organization's performance. EAP advocates estimate savings of as much as $1.17 for every dollar spent. Improvements claimed are lower absenteeism, decreases in workers' compensation claims, and fewer accidents.[45]

To become even more effective, however, directors of EAPs need to reexamine the practice of waiting for supervisory referrals. Typically, problems are not dealt with until they have adversely affected job performance. Instead, EAPs should actively promote health improvement and disease prevention programs. Prevention of alcohol and drug abuse is more cost effective than treatment, which is the common EAP practice.[46]

Another problem relates to the need for supervisory training. Supervisors need specialized interpersonal skills for recognizing troubled employees and referring them to the firm's EAP. Addicted employees are often experts at deception and can fool even experienced counselors. The problem of making EAP referrals is further compounded because supervisors often identify more with their workers than with management and don't want their employees to think they are on a witch hunt. One study found that

---

[44] Hermine Zagat Levine, "Employee Assistance Programs," *Personnel,* 62 (April 1985), p. 14.

[45] "Employee Assistance Programs for Workers Boost Bottom Line," *Training and Development Journal,* 41 (June 1987), p. 20.

[46] Keith McClelland, "The Changing Nature of EAP Practice," *Personnel Administrator,* 30 (August 1985), p. 24.

typical supervisors in public and private-sector organizations covered up for troubled employees for from eight to twelve years.[47]

In the future, companies may have to expand their EAPs to deal with the AIDS issue. In order to effectively address this concern, human resource professionals must understand the nature and impact of this disease.

■ AIDS IN THE WORKPLACE

AIDS (acquired immune deficiency syndrome) is a disease that undermines the body's immune system, leaving the person susceptible to a wide range of fatal diseases. AIDS has become a worldwide epidemic with the potential to kill more people than the Black Plague did during the Middle Ages.[48]Approximately 32,000 cases were reported in the United States between 1981 and 1988, and more than half of those victims have died.[49]

Although AIDS has become more feared than cancer, a relatively small percentage of firms have established formal policies to deal with it. A 1989 survey of more than 300 business firms in the San Francisco Bay area found that only about 10 percent of the respondents had a formal written AIDS policy.[50] Since AIDS and HIV victims are protected by the Americans with Disabilities Act, business practices will undoubtedly change.

It is apparent that some firms historically did not want to treat AIDS differently from other major illnesses. In one important respect, however, AIDS does differ significantly from all other diseases: It is always fatal. This fact no doubt accounts for both rational and irrational fears. Employees often hesitate to work with someone they believe has the disease, in spite of the law and despite assurance from medical experts that the disease cannot be transmitted through casual contact. At this time, it seems that the most aggressive action being taken by businesses regarding AIDS is in developing information programs that emphasize how to avoid contracting the disease.

There are only two ways that an individual can contract AIDS. The first is through the exchange of body fluids during sexual activity. The second is through exposure to contaminated blood in a manner that permits it to enter one's bloodstream. Outside of health care, workplace exposure to blood is rare. Therefore, there is no rational reason for employees to fear working with someone who has AIDS or who has been exposed to the virus. The problem is that workers are not always rational. Their fear of the disease can result in the employer facing business interruption (if employees refuse to work with an AIDS victim) or unlawful discrimination (if the employer discharges the ill person).

---

[47] Mark Ralfs and John M. Morley, "Turning Employee Problems into Triumphs," *Training and Development Journal,* 44 (November 1990), p. 73.

[48] Throughout history there have been several major epidemics of bubonic plague. In the 1300s, the infamous Black Plague destroyed one-fourth of Europe's population.

[49] George E. Stevens, "Understanding AIDS," *Personnel Administrator,* 33 (August 1988), p. 84.

[50] John P. Kohl, Allan N. Miller, and David S. Hames, "AIDS in the Work Place," *Supervision,* 51 (November 1990), pp. 12–13.

The need for educating employees is obvious. They must understand how the AIDS virus is transmitted and that it is not transmitted through casual contact. Only then can employees be assured that they are protected from this awful disease. It is estimated that by 1995, 365,000 Americans will have AIDS and another 3 million will have been exposed to the virus. It is possible that every victim will die from the disease.[51]

Firms that do provide AIDS training sessions for their employees often use more than one technique. Among the methods used are seminars, workshops, discussion groups, articles in employee publications, videotapes, literature in the company library, and health fairs.[52] Providing training sessions is a commendable first step. However, it is quite clear that business organizations, in concert with the federal government, must soon deal more directly with this deadly disease. If human resources is truly the heart of the organization, as one HR executive stated, the chief human resource officer will be the catalyst in this effort.

---

[51] Jonathan A. Segal, "AIDS Education Is a Necessary High-Risk Activity," *HRMagazine,* 36 (February 1991), pp. 82–83.

[52] Hermine Zagat Levine, "AIDS in the Work Place," *Personnel,* 63 (March 1986), p. 57.

SUMMARY

Safety involves protecting employees from injuries caused by work-related accidents. Health refers to the employees' freedom from physical or emotional illness. For years, industrial safety has been a major problem that seemingly resists solution. Prior to 1971, safety was regulated primarily by the workers' compensation laws of the various states. When Congress passed the Occupational Safety and Health Act, it quickly became one of the most controversial laws affecting human resource management. It has dramatically altered management's role in the area of safety and health.

One approach to safety programs is to create a psychology of promoting safety. Another approach to safety programs is to develop and maintain a safe working environment. Evaluation of safety programs involves measuring both the frequency and severity of accidents. Promoting employee health has led many firms to develop wellness programs. They start with initial applicant screening and continue throughout workers' employment.

Stress is the body's reaction to any demand made on it. Everyone lives under some stress, which can be positive if not excessive but can be damaging when it is excessive. Burnout is a state of fatigue or frustration, which stems from devotion to a cause, way of life, or relationship that did not provide the expected reward. Burnout is often associated with a mid-life or mid-career crisis, but it can happen at different times to different people. Symptoms of burnout include (1) chronic fatigue; (2) anger at those making demands; (3) self-criticism for putting up with demands; (4) cynicism, negativism, and irritability; (5) a sense of being besieged; and (6) hair-trigger display of emotions. Stress can be managed, and firms are helping employees deal with it in various ways.

Although few organizations have fully staffed facilities, thousands of U.S. business firms have exercise programs designed to help keep their workers physically fit. Company-sponsored fitness programs often reduce absenteeism, accidents, and sick pay. Employees who are physically fit are more alert and productive, and their morale is higher.

Alcoholism is a disease characterized by uncontrolled and compulsive drinking that interferes with normal living patterns. It is a significant problem and can both result from and cause excessive stress. In 1956, the American Medical Association described it as treatable.

Cocaine, heroin, PCP, THC, crack, and numerous other mind-altering substances have found their way into the workplace. Numerous firms have recognized that drug problems exist and have taken positive action to deal with them.

An employee assistance program (EAP) is a comprehensive approach that many organizations have taken to deal with burnout, alcohol and drug abuse, and other emotional disturbances. In an EAP, a firm either provides in-house professional counselors or refers employees to an appropriate community social service agency. The EAP concept includes a response to personal psychological problems that interfere with both an employee's well-being and overall productivity. The purpose of EAPs is to provide emotionally troubled employees with the same consideration and assistance given employees having physical illnesses.

AIDS (acquired immune deficiency syndrome) is a disease that destroys the body's immune system, leaving the person susceptible to a wide range of fatal diseases. AIDS has become a worldwide epidemic, but so far, most firms have not established formal policies to directly deal with the AIDS problem. It is the human resource professional's responsibility to lead the firm in taking more aggressive action in response to this deadly disease.

Questions for Review

1. Distinguish between safety and health.
2. What are the primary ways in which safety programs are designed? Discuss.
3. What are some measurements that would suggest the success of a firm's safety program?
4. What are the purposes of health and wellness programs?
5. Why should a firm attempt to identify stressful jobs? What could an organization do to reduce the stress associated with a job?
6. Why should a firm be concerned with employee burnout?
7. What are some signs that a supervisor might look for in identifying alcohol abuse?
8. Explain why employee assistance programs are being established.
9. What concerns should a manager have regarding AIDS in the workplace?

Terms for Review

Safety	Job overload
Health	Hypnosis
Frequency rate	Biofeedback
Severity rate	Transcendental meditation (TM)
Ergonomics	Alcoholism
Stress	Employee assistance program
Burnout	(EAP)
Role ambiguity	AIDS (acquired immune
Role conflict	deficiency syndrome)

INCIDENT 1   ▪   To Test or Not to Test   ▪

John Hicks, human resource manager of Miller Chemical Company, had just read a report of a case filed in district court against a large neighboring company. One of that company's truck drivers had been involved in an accident in which two people were killed. The driver was tested by the police and evidence of cocaine use was found.

John discussed the matter with the company president, Patsy Swain, who was familiar with the case. "Ms. Swain," he said, "I think we should adopt a policy of drug screening as part of all pre-employment physicals." She replied, "I'm not sure that the testing requirement could be defended if we ever had a serious legal complaint. But the company could be in trouble if employee drug use led to negligence in some of these plant jobs." John asked, "What about the testing program for current employees? Should it be made a part of the annual physicals? Annual physicals aren't really mandatory now, but we can make them so."

Questions

1. What is the primary purpose of a testing program such as the one John wants to establish?
2. What would Miller Chemical do if an employee became a drug abuser after employment?

INCIDENT 2   ▪   A Star Is Falling   ▪

"Just leave me alone and let me do my job," said Manuel Gomez. Dumbfounded, Bill Brown, Manuel's supervisor, decided to count to ten and not respond to Manuel's comment. As he walked back to his office, Bill thought about how Manuel had changed over the past few months. He had been a hard worker and extremely cooperative when he came to work for Bill two years earlier. The company had sent Manuel to two training schools and had received glowing reports about his performance in each of them.

Until about a year ago, Manuel had a perfect attendance record and was an ideal employee. At about that time, however, he began to have personal problems, which resulted in a divorce six months later. Manuel had requested a day off several times to take care of personal business. Bill had attempted to help in every way he could without getting directly involved in Manuel's personal affairs. But Bill was aware of the strain Manuel must have experienced as his marriage broke up and he and his wife engaged in the inevitable disputes over child custody, alimony payments, and property.

During the same time period, top management initiated a push for improving productivity. Bill found it necessary to put additional pressure on all his workers, including Manuel.

He tried to be considerate, but he had to become much more performance-oriented, insisting on increased output from every worker. As time went on, Manuel began to show up late for work and actually missed two days without calling Bill in advance. Bill attributed Manuel's behavior to extreme stress. Because Manuel had been such a good worker for so long, Bill excused the tardiness and absences, only gently suggesting that Manuel should try to do better.

Sitting at his desk, Bill thought about what might have caused Manuel's outburst a few minutes earlier. Bill had simply suggested to Manuel that he shut down the machine he was operating and clean up the surrounding area. This was a normal part of Manuel's job and something he had been careful to do in the past. Bill thought that the disorder around Manuel's machine might account for the increasing number of defects in the parts he was making. "This is a tough one. I think I'll talk to the boss about it," thought Bill.

Questions

1. What do you think is likely to be Manuel's problem? Discuss.
2. If you were Bill's boss, what would you recommend that he do?

DEVELOPING HRM SKILLS

At times, workers have personal problems that negatively influence their work and that may make the workplace unsafe. When this occurs, both managers and human resource professionals may be required to become involved to maintain a safe and healthy work environment. Dealing with one's own personal problems is often difficult, and assisting employees in dealing with their personal problems can be even more taxing on managers. However, since a problem employee can have a negative effect on workforce productivity, this situation must be addressed by individuals involved in human resource management. This exercise should provide a better understanding of how to handle a most difficult issue—that of resolving employee problems.

"I am going to do it, and I am going to do it today. This has gone on long enough!" thought Annette Dommert, the data processing manager. "I can't put it off any longer. I realize that Walter has been with the company for fourteen years, and with this department for eleven of those years, but this drinking thing is out of hand. Lately the problem is affecting other members of the work group. His friends are covering up pretty well for him, but that is causing their productivity to go down. Evidently Walter is

not going to be able to work things out, and the situation will only get worse. We are going to meet today and resolve this matter one way or the other; he's dry or he's out! I am not a villain, and I really want him to work things out, but this is causing the department problems."

Walter Hollingsworth, a programmer in the data processing department, was concerned. He thought, "I heard from a friend in the boss's office that I am going to get chewed out about my drinking. I have always gotten my work done, but I guess I've let things slip lately. I know I can lick this problem. I'm going to straighten myself out, and when I meet with the boss I'll admit that I drink too much sometimes; everybody does. Drinking has only recently affected my work. I'll do better in the future. I've been with the company for fourteen years, and with this division for eleven of those years. One problem in all those years makes me a good risk. I can do it, and I deserve a chance. The boss should be compassionate."

If you are a sensitive person, you may want to play a role in this exercise. Two students will actively participate. One will play Annette and one will play Walter. The rest of you should observe carefully. Your instructor will provide any additional information necessary to participate.

REFERENCES

Axline, Larry L. "Identifying and Helping the Troubled Executive." *Personnel*, 61 (November 1987), pp. 10–18.

Binion, Janet. "One More Safety Meeting! Safety Meetings Should Be Fun, Not Boring." *Safety & Health*, 142 (October 1990), pp. 82, 84.

Borowka, Harry. "Healthy Profits Through Safety Planning." *Risk Management*, 36 (April 1989), pp. 36–38, 42, 44.

Bruening, John C. "Risk Communication: A Two-Way Connection." *Occupational Hazards*, 52 (October 1990), pp. 76–80.

Brumback, Cathy J. "EPAs—Bringing Health and Productivity to the Workplace." *Business*, 37 (April-June 1987), p. 12.

Chappell, Dean W. "How to Involve Employees in Safety Management." *Safety & Health*, 142 (October 1990), pp. 52–55.

Goldbeck, Willis B. "AIDS and the Workplace: Business Fights the Epidemic." *Futuristic*, 22 (March-April 1988), pp. 18–19.

"Half of Managers Suffer Work Stress." *Supervision*, 51 (July 1990), p. 10.

Harrington, Harry, and Nancy Richardson. "Retiree Wellness Plan Cuts Health Costs." *Personnel Journal*, 69 (August 1990), pp. 60, 62.

Ivancevich, John M., Michael T. Matteson, and Cynthia Preston. "Occupational Stress, Type A Behavior, and Physical Well-Being." *Academy of Management*, 25 (September 1987), p. 68.

Joyce, Marilyn. "Ergonomics Will Take Center Stage During '90s and into New Century." *Occupational Health and Safety*, 60 (January 1991), pp. 31–32, 34, 37.

Kohl, John P., Alan N. Miller, and David S. Hames. "AIDS in the Work Place." *Supervision*, 51 (November 1990), pp. 11–13.

Nelson, Debra L., James Campbell Quick, and Michael A. Hitt. "What Stresses HR Professionals?" *Personnel*, 67 (August 1990), pp. 36–39.

Oliver, Bill. "Do You Drug Test Your Employees?" *HRMagazine*, 35 (October 1990), p. 57.

Pater, Robert. "Safety Leadership Cuts Costs." *HRMagazine*, 35 (November 1990), pp. 46–47.

Pope, Tom. "EAPs: Good Idea, But What's the Cost?" *Management Review*, 79 (August 1990), pp. 50–53.

Ralfs, Mark, and John Morley. "Turning Employee Problems into Triumphs." *Training and Development Journal*, 44 (November 1990), pp. 73–76.

Ralston, David A. "How Flextime Eases Work/Family Tensions." *Personnel*, 67 (August 1990), pp. 45–48.

Segal, Jonathan A. "AIDS Education Is a Necessary High-Risk Activity." *HRMagazine*, 36 (February 1991), pp. 82–85.

Smith, R. Blake. "Wellness Administrators Working to Prove Programs Cost-Effective." *Occupational Health & Safety*, 59 (October 1990), pp. 100, 102–104.

Stallworth, Hugh F. "Realistic Goals Help Avoid Burnout." *HRMagazine*, 35 (June 1990), pp. 169, 171.

Thieme, Cheryl. "Better-Bilt Builds a Substance Abuse Program That Works." *Personnel Journal*, 69 (August 1990), pp. 52, 54, 57–58.

Thompson, Brad Lee. "OSHA Bounces Back." *Training*, 28 (January 1991), pp. 45–46, 48, 50–51, 53.

"To OSHA, 'Workplace Safety is Good Business.'" *Risk Management*, 36 (October 1989), p. 72.

Watts, Patti. "Are Your Employees Burnout-Proof?" *Personnel*, 67 (September 1990), pp. 12–14.

Yehay, Stephen C., and Garon E. Dodge. "Criminal Prosecutions for Occupational Injuries: An Issue of Growing Concern." *Employee Relations Law Journal*, 13 (August 1987), pp. 197+.

P·A·R·T F·I·V·E

CASE V

Parma Cycle Company: Safety and Health at the New Plant

"I want the new plant to be a model of safety and health," said Mr. Burgess, the president of Parma Cycle Company in Parma, Ohio. "I do too," said Jesse Heard, the human resource director, "but you have to be aware that it's going to cost a lot." "Remember now, Jesse," the president replied, "we're putting the plant in Clarksdale, Mississippi, primarily to reduce costs. I believe that the main thing we can do for safety is to train our workers to be safety-oriented. That doesn't cost much." "That's the main thing, I know," said Jesse, "but we'll also have to spend some money. There are several areas where safety can be improved by install-ing handrails. Also, a good number of the ma-chines will come in without chain belt guards. We'll have to have those fabricated." "Well," said Mr. Burgess, "let's just try to meet the OSHA requirements on those kinds of things. I'd like to see a cost-benefit analysis of any-thing that goes beyond the OSHA standards." Mr. Burgess was referring to the U.S. Occupa-tional Safety and Health Administration.

At about that time, Cliff Brubaker, the chief engineer at Parma, who had also been sum-moned to the meeting, came in. After a few niceties, Cliff asked, "Mr. Burgess, making sure that all the machinery and the machine layouts meet OSHA requirements made engi-neering the new plant a lot more difficult. We won't be able to use our floor space nearly as efficiently at Clarksdale as we do here at Parma. Also, the work flow is going to be less efficient because I had to separate machines to keep the area noise level below the maxi-mum standard. Don't you think we could fudge a little on some of this? The Parma plant doesn't come close to meeting OSHA

requirements, and we have only had one fine since I've been here."

"I don't think you can trade off personal safety against a few dollars of cost savings," Jesse said. "You remember when Joe Blum lost his arm last year? The company came out okay on that because Joe didn't sue us. But what about Joe? How much was his arm worth?" "Don't get upset, Jesse," said Cliff. "I know what you mean and I really feel the same way. But we can go to extremes."

Mr. Burgess spoke up, adding, "I don't think that meeting OSHA standards is going to extremes. Besides, if companies like Parma Cycle don't take some initiative in protecting workers, we're going to see even more enforce-ment efforts in the future. I want to make sure that you both understand my position. Everything in the plant at Clarksdale is to meet OSHA requirements for safety and health as a minimum. If the requirements can be exceeded with no additional costs, I want to opt for maximum safety. If you have to spend extra money to improve safety or health at the Clarksdale plant, I want to see a benefit-cost analysis on each item." "I think that that's clear enough," said Jesse. "Me too," said Cliff, "but, I'll have to get back with you on a number of the modifications we had planned."

Questions

1. What do you think of Mr. Burgess's insis-tence on meeting OSHA standards at the Clarksdale plant?
2. Do you agree with Jesse that a firm should not "trade off personal safety against a few dollars of cost savings"?

P·A·R·T S·I·X

EMPLOYEE AND
LABOR
RELATIONS

Human Resource
Research

Human Resource
Planning,
Recruitment, and
Selection

Human Resource
Development

Human
Resource
Management

Employee and
Labor Relations

Compensation
and Benefits

Safety and
Health

CHAPTER OBJECTIVES

1. Describe the history of the labor movement.
2. Explain the most significant union objectives, identify the reasons why employees join unions, and describe the basic structure of the union.
3. Explain what is involved in establishing the collective bargaining relationship, and relate the future of unionism and collective bargaining in a global economy.
4. Explain the various strategies that a union may use to gain bargaining unit recognition, describe signs of a troubled labor movement, and discuss why there is a growing legalistic approach to collective bargaining.

Robert Sweeney, president of United Technologies, was disturbed and disappointed. He had just been informed by the National Labor Relations Board that a majority of his employees had voted to have the union represent them. The past months had been difficult ones, with charges and countercharges being made by both management and labor. The vote had been close, with only a few votes tipping the scales in favor of labor.

He looked at the human resource manager, Marthanne Bello, and said, "I don't know what to do. The union will demand so much we can't possibly be competitive."

Marthanne replied, "Just because the union has won the right to be represented doesn't mean that we have to accept all their terms. I believe that a reasonable contract can be negotiated. I know many of those guys and I am sure that we can work out a contract that will be fair to both sides."

Robert Sweeney is not only troubled, but he is also misinformed as to the necessary impact of collective bargaining. Employees have decided to unionize, but that in no way mandates management acceptance of contractual terms that would adversely impact the health and profitability of the company. We begin this chapter with a history of the labor movement in the United States and the legislation relating to it. Next, we discuss the objectives of unions, the reasons why employees join unions, and the multilevel organizational structure of unions. Then we address the steps taken to establish a collective bargaining relationship and some union strategies used to obtain recognition. Finally, we review the issue of collective bargaining and unionism in a global economy, the signs of a troubled labor movement, and the growing legalistic approach to collective bargaining.

■ THE LABOR MOVEMENT BEFORE 1930

Unions are not a recent development in American history. The earliest unions originated toward the end of the eighteenth century about the time of the American Revolution. Although these early associations had few characteristics of present-day labor unions, they did bring workers in craft- or guild-related occupations together to consider problems of mutual concern. These early unions were local in nature and usually existed for only a short time.[1]

Development of the labor movement has been neither simple nor straightforward; it has experienced as much failure as success. Employer opposition, the impact of the business cycle, the growth of American industry, court rulings, and legislation have exerted their influence in varying degrees at different times. As a result, the history of the labor movement has somewhat resembled the swinging of a pendulum. At times, the pendulum has moved in favor of labor and, at other times, it has swung toward the advantage of management.

Prior to the 1930s, the trend definitely favored management. The courts strongly supported employers in their attempts to thwart the organized labor movement. This was first evidenced by the use of criminal and civil conspiracy doctrines derived from English common law. A **conspiracy,** generally defined, is the combination of two or more persons who band together to prejudice the rights of others or of society (e.g., by refusing to work or demanding higher wages). An important feature of the conspiracy doctrine is that an action by one person, though legal, may become illegal when carried out by a group.[2] In 1806, the year in which the conspiracy doctrine was first applied to labor unions, the courts began to influence the field of labor relations.[3] From 1806 to 1842, seventeen cases went to trial charging labor unions with conspiracies. These cases resulted in the demise of several unions and certainly discouraged other union activities. The conspiracy doctrine was softened considerably by the decision in the landmark case *Commonwealth v. Hunt* in 1842. In that case, Chief Justice Shaw of the Supreme Judicial Court of Massachusetts contended that labor organizations were legal. Thus in order for a union to be convicted under the conspiracy doctrine, it had to be shown that the union's objectives were unlawful or the means employed to gain a legal end were unlawful. To this day the courts continue to exert a profound influence on both the direction and character of labor relations.

Other tactics used by employers to stifle union growth were injunctions and yellow-dog contracts. An **injunction** is a prohibiting legal procedure that was used by employers to prevent certain union activities, such as strikes and unionization attempts. A **yellow-dog contract** was a written agreement between the employee and the company made at the time of

---

[1] *Brief History of the American Labor Movement* (Washington, D.C.: U.S. Department of Labor Statistics, Bulletin 1000, 1970), p. 1.

[2] Benjamin J. Taylor and Fred Witney, *Labor Relations Law,* 5th ed. (Englewood Cliffs, N.J.: Prentice-Hall, 1987), pp. 12–13.

[3] *Ibid.,* pp. 14–18.

employment, prohibiting a worker from joining a union or engaging in union activities. Each of these defensive tactics, used by management and supported by the courts, severely limited union growth.

In the latter half of the nineteenth century the American industrial system started to grow and prosper. Factory production began to displace handicraft forms of manufacturing. The Civil War gave the factory system a great boost. Goods were demanded in quantities that only mass production methods could supply. The railroads developed new networks of routes spanning the continent and knitting the country into an economic whole. Employment was high and unions sought to organize workers in both new and expanding enterprises. Most unions during this time were small and rather weak, and many did not survive the economic recession of the 1870s. Union membership rose to 300,000 by 1872 and then dropped to 50,000 by 1878.[4] This period also marked the rise of radical labor activity and increased industrial strife as unions struggled for recognition and survival.[5]

Out of the turbulence of the 1870s emerged the most substantial labor organization that had yet appeared in the United States. The Noble Order of the Knights of Labor was founded in 1869 as a secret society of the Philadelphia garment workers. After its secrecy was abandoned and workers in other areas were invited to join, it grew rapidly, reaching a membership of more than 700,000 by the mid-1880s. Internal conflict among the Knights' leadership in 1881 gave rise to the nucleus of a new organization that would soon replace it on the labor scene.[6] That organization was the American Federation of Labor (AFL).

Devoted to what is referred to as either "pure and simple unionism," or "business unionism," Samuel Gompers of the Cigarmakers Union led some twenty-five labor groups representing skilled trades to found the American Federation of Labor in 1886. Gompers was elected the first president of the AFL, a position he held until his death in 1924 (except for one year, 1894–1895, when he adamantly opposed tangible support for the strikers of the Pullman group). He is probably the single most important individual in American trade union history. The AFL began with a membership of some 138,000 and doubled that number during the next twelve years.[7]

In 1890, Congress passed the Sherman Anti-Trust Act. This marked the entrance of the federal government into the statutory regulation of labor organizations. Although the primary stimulus for this act came from public concern over business's monopoly power, court interpretations soon applied its provisions to organized labor. Later, in 1914, Congress passed the Clayton Act (an amendment to the Sherman Act), which, according to Samuel Gompers, was the Magna Carta of Labor. The intent of this act was to remove labor from the purview of the Sherman Act. Again, judicial interpretation nullified that intent and left labor even more exposed to

[4] *Brief History,* p. 9.

[5] Foster Rhea Dulles, *Labor in America,* 3rd ed. (New York: Crowell, 1966), pp. 114–125.

[6] *Ibid.,* pp. 126–149.

[7] *Brief History,* pp. 15–16.

lawsuits.[8] Nonetheless, as a result of industrial activity related to World War I, the AFL grew to almost five million members by 1920.[9]

During the 1920s, labor faced legal restrictions on union activity and unfavorable court decisions. The one exception to such repressive policies was the passage and approval of the Railway Labor Act of 1926. This was the first time that the government declared without qualification the right of private employees to join unions and bargain collectively through representatives of their own choosing without interference from their employers. It also set up special machinery for the settlement of labor disputes. Although the act covered only employees in the railroad industry (a later amendment extended coverage to the airline industry), it foreshadowed the extension of similar rights to other classes of employees in the 1930s.

■ THE LABOR MOVEMENT AFTER 1930

The 1930s found the United States in the midst of the worst depression in its history. The unemployment rate rose as high as 25 percent.[10] The sentiment of the country began to favor organized labor as many people blamed business for the agony that accompanied the Great Depression. The pendulum began to swing away from management and toward labor. This swing was assisted by several acts and actions that supported the cause of unionism.

Anti-Injunction Act (Norris-LaGuardia Act)—1932

The Great Depression caused a substantial change in the public's thinking about the role of unions in society. Congress reflected this thinking in 1932 with the passage of the Norris-LaGuardia Act. It affirms that U.S. public policy sanctions collective bargaining and approves the formation and effective operation of labor unions.[11] While this act did not outlaw the use of injunctions, it severely restricted the federal courts' authority to issue them in labor disputes. It also made yellow-dog contracts unenforceable in the federal courts.[12]

National Labor Relations Act (Wagner Act)—1935

In 1933, Congress made an abortive attempt to stimulate economic recovery by passing the National Industry Recovery Act (NIRA). Declared unconstitutional by the U.S. Supreme Court in 1935, the NIRA did provide the

---

[8] E. Edward Herman, Alfred Kuhn, and Ronald L. Seeber, *Collective Bargaining and Labor Relations* (Englewood Cliffs, N.J.: Prentice-Hall, 1987), pp. 32–34.

[9] *Brief History,* p. 27.

[10] *Historical Statistics of the United States, Colonial Times to 1970, Bicentennial Edition,* Part I (Washington, D.C.: U.S. Bureau of the Census, 1975), p. 126.

[11] Benjamin J. Taylor and Fred Witney, *Labor Relations Law,* pp. 78–81.

[12] *Ibid.,* pp. 81–85.

nucleus for legislation that followed it. Section 7a of the NIRA proclaimed the right of workers to organize and bargain collectively. Congress did not, however, provide procedures to enforce these rights.[13]

Undeterred by the Supreme Court decision and strongly supported by organized labor, Congress speedily enacted a comprehensive labor law, the National Labor Relations Act (Wagner Act). This act, approved by President Roosevelt on July 5, 1935, is one of the most significant labor-management relations statutes ever enacted. Drawing heavily on the experience of the Railway Labor Act of 1926 and Section 7a of the NIRA, the act declared legislative support, on a broad scale, of the right of employees to organize and engage in collective bargaining. The spirit of the Wagner Act is stated in Section 7, which defines the substantive rights of employees:

> Employees shall have the right to self-organization, to form, join, or assist labor organizations, to bargain collectively through representatives of their own choosing, and to engage in other concerted activities, for the purpose of collective bargaining or other mutual aid or protection.

The rights defined in Section 7 were protected against employer interference by Section 8, which detailed and prohibited five management practices deemed to be unfair to labor:

1. Interfering with or restraining or coercing employees in the exercise of their right to self-organization.
2. Dominating or interfering in the affairs of a union.
3. Discriminating in regard to hire or tenure or any condition of employment for the purpose of encouraging or discouraging union membership.
4. Discriminating against or discharging an employee who has filed charges or given testimony under the act.
5. Refusing to bargain with chosen representatives of employees.

The National Labor Relations Board (NLRB) was created by the National Labor Relations Act to administer and enforce the provisions of the act. The NLRB was given two principal functions: (1) to establish procedures for holding bargaining-unit elections and to monitor the election procedures; and (2) to investigate complaints and prevent unlawful acts involving unfair labor practices. However, current NLRB election procedures are often cumbersome because of technicalities employers can use to delay elections for years.[14] Much of the NLRB's work is delegated to thirty-three regional offices throughout the country.

In recent years, many labor leaders have expressed their dismay with the composition of the NLRB. Some feel the recent Republican administrations made it easier for employers to beat unions by changing the way labor law is interpreted and enforced. William Wynn, president of the United

---

[13] *Ibid.*, pp. 150–151.

[14] Sandra Atchison and Aaron Bernstein, "A Silver Bullet for the Union Drive at Coors?" *Business Week* (July 11, 1988), pp. 61–62.

Food and Commercial Workers, stated, "There has been a total breakdown in the system of law and order established for labor-management relations."[15] Evidently, Wynn believes that the labor-management relations system of law and order is unfair in terms of its treatment of labor.

Following passage of the Wagner Act, union membership increased from approximately three million to fifteen million between 1935 and 1947.[16] The increase was most conspicuous in industries utilizing mass production methods. New unions in these industries were organized on an industrial basis rather than a craft basis, and members were primarily unskilled or semiskilled workers. An internal struggle developed within the AFL over the question of whether unions should be organized to include all workers in an industry or strictly on a craft or occupational basis. In 1935, ten AFL-affiliated unions and the officers of two other AFL unions formed the Committee for Industrial Organization to promote the organization of workers in mass production and unorganized industries. The controversy grew to the point that in 1938 the AFL expelled all but one of the Committee for Industrial Organization unions. In November 1938, the expelled unions held their first convention in Pittsburgh and reorganized as a federation of unions under the name of Congress of Industrial Organizations (CIO). The new federation included the nine unions expelled from the AFL and thirty-two other groups established to recruit workers in various industries. John L. Lewis, president of the United Mine Workers, was elected the first president of the CIO.[17]

The rivalry generated by the two large federations stimulated union organizing efforts in both groups. With the ensuing growth, the labor movement gained considerable influence in the United States. However, many individuals and groups began to feel that the Wagner Act favored labor too much. This shift in public sentiment was in part related to a rash of costly strikes following World War II. Whether justified or not, much of the blame for these disruptions fell on the unions.

Labor Management Relations Act (Taft-Hartley Act)—1947

In 1947, with public pressure mounting, Congress overrode President Truman's veto and passed the Labor Management Relations Act (Taft-Hartley Act). The Taft-Hartley Act extensively revised the National Labor Relations Act and became Title I of that law. A new period in the evolution of public policy regarding labor began. The pendulum had begun to swing toward a more balanced position between labor and management.

Some of the important changes introduced by the Taft-Hartley Act included the following:

---

[15] Cary W. English, "Why Are Unions Running Scared?" *U.S. News & World Report* (September 10, 1984), pp. 62–65.

[16] *Brief History*, p. 65.

[17] *Ibid.*, pp. 29–33.

1. Modifying Section 7 to include the right of employees to refrain from union activity as well as engage in it.
2. Prohibiting the closed shop (the arrangement requiring that all workers be union members at the time they are hired) and narrowing the freedom of the parties to authorize the union shop (the situation in which the employer may hire anyone he or she chooses, but all new workers must join the union after a stipulated period of time).
3. Broadening the employer's right of free speech.
4. Providing that employers need not recognize or bargain with unions formed by supervisory employees.
5. Giving employees the right to initiate decertification petitions.
6. Providing for government intervention in "national emergency strikes."

Another significant change extended the concept of unfair labor practices to unions. Labor organizations were to refrain from the following:

1. Restraining or coercing employees in the exercise of their guaranteed collective bargaining rights.
2. Causing an employer to discriminate in any way against an employee in order to encourage or discourage union membership.
3. Refusing to bargain in good faith with an employer regarding wages, hours, and other terms and conditions of employment.
4. Engaging in certain types of strikes and boycotts.
5. Requiring employees covered by union-shop contracts to pay initiation fees or dues "in an amount which the Board finds excessive or discriminatory under all circumstances."
6. "Featherbedding," that is, requiring that an employer pay for services not performed.

One of the most controversial elements of the Taft-Hartley Act is its Section 14b, which permits states to enact right-to-work legislation. **Right-to-work laws** are laws that prohibit management and unions from entering into agreements requiring union membership as a condition of employment. Twenty-one states, located primarily in the South and West, have adopted such laws, which are a continuing source of irritation between labor and management.[18] Much of the impetus behind the right-to-work movement is provided by the National Right to Work Committee, based in Springfield, Virginia.

For about ten years after the passage of the Taft-Hartley Act, union membership expanded at about the same rate as nonagricultural employment. But all was not well within the organized labor movement. Since the creation of the CIO, the two federations had engaged in a bitter and costly rivalry. Both the CIO and the AFL recognized the increasing need for cooperation and reunification. In 1955, following two years of intensive negotiations between the two organizations, a merger agreement was

---

[18] Right-to-work states include: Alabama, Arizona, Arkansas, Florida, Georgia, Idaho, Iowa, Kansas, Louisiana, Mississippi, Nebraska, Nevada, North Carolina, North Dakota, South Carolina, South Dakota, Tennessee, Texas, Utah, Virginia, and Wyoming.

ratified, the AFL-CIO became a reality, and George Meany was elected president. In the years following the merger, the labor movement faced some of its greatest challenges.

Labor-Management Reporting and Disclosure Act (Landrum-Griffin Act)—1959

Corruption had plagued organized labor since the early 1900s. Periodic revelations of graft, violence, extortion, racketeering, and other improper activities aroused public indignation and invited governmental investigation. Even though the number of unions involved was small, every disclosure undermined the public image of organized labor as a whole.[19] Corruption has been noted in the construction trades and the Laborers, Hotel and Restaurant, Carpenters, Painters, East Coast Longshoremen, and Boilermakers unions. The inability of the labor movement to deal with massive corruption and racketeering may be evidence of deep-seated union problems.[20] For example, the International Brotherhood of Teamsters faced a change of leadership in the late 1980s because of its alleged ties to organized crime.[21]

Scrutiny of union activities is a focal point in today's labor environment, but it began to intensify right after World War II. Ultimately, inappropriate union activities led to the creation in 1957 of the Senate Select Committee on Improper Activities in the Labor or Management Field, headed by Senator McClellan of Arkansas. Between 1957 and 1959, the McClellan Committee held a series of nationally televised public hearings that shocked and alarmed the entire country. As evidence of improper activities mounted—primarily against the Teamsters and Longshoremen/Maritime—the AFL-CIO took action.

In 1957, the AFL-CIO expelled three unions (representing approximately 1.6 million members) for their practices. One of them, the Teamsters, was the largest union in the country.

In 1959, largely as a result of the recommendations of the McClellan Committee, Congress enacted the Labor-Management Reporting and Disclosure Act (Landrum-Griffin Act). This act marked a significant turning point in the involvement of the federal government in internal union affairs. The Landrum-Griffin Act spelled out a "Bill of Rights of Members of Labor Organizations" designed to protect certain rights of individuals in their relationships with unions. The act requires extensive reporting on numerous internal union activities and contains severe penalties for violations. Employers are also required to file reports when they engage in activities or make expenditures that might undermine the collective bargaining process or interfere with protected employee rights. In addition, the

---

[19] Foster Rhea Dulles, *Labor in America,* pp. 382–383.

[20] Herman Benson, "Union Democracy," in *Unions in Transition* (San Francisco: ICS Press, 1988), p. 343.

[21] Harris Cooingwood, "The Teamsters' Vacuum at the Top," *Business Week* (July 25, 1988), p. 41.

act amended the Taft-Hartley Act by adding additional restrictions on picketing and secondary boycotts.[22]

In 1974, Congress extended coverage of the Taft-Hartley Act to private, not-for-profit hospitals. This amendment brought within the jurisdiction of the National Labor Relations Board some two million employees. Proprietary (profit-making) health care organizations were already under NLRB jurisdiction. The amendment does not cover government-operated hospitals; it applies only to the private sector.

Even though the AFL-CIO merger was completed in 1955, internal conflict remained. The Teamsters expulsion was followed in 1968 by the disaffiliation of the second largest union in the country, the United Automobile Workers (UAW). This split was caused primarily by personality and philosophical clashes between Walter Reuther, president of the UAW, and Meany. Shortly thereafter the UAW and the Teamsters formed the Alliance of Labor Action (ALA) with the possible aim of developing a rival federation.[23] The ALA lasted only until the untimely death of Walter Reuther in a plane crash in 1970. The UAW reaffiliated with the AFL-CIO in July 1981. The Teamsters Union was allowed to reaffiliate in October 1987, when it brought its members back into the AFL-CIO.[24]

Overall, the fall of "Big Labor" has been dramatic since 1970.[25] Despite the reaffiliation of the Teamsters with the AFL-CIO, union membership dropped from about one-third of the nonfarm workforce in 1950 to 16.4 percent in 1989.[26] As Figure 15-1 on page 578 shows, the unionized share of the private workforce shrunk to about 10 percent in 1989, which is less than one-third of its size in the mid-1950s.[27] Unions have also won fewer and fewer representation elections as collective bargaining agents in recent years. According to a study presented at a recent National Bureau of Economic Research conference, union membership in the private sector could drop below 5 percent by the year 2000 if present trends continue.[28]

■ THE PUBLIC SECTOR

Government (public-sector) employees are generally considered a class apart from private-sector workers. This is reflected in their exclusion from the coverage of general labor legislation.[29] However, like their counterparts in private industry, government employees have demonstrated a

---

[22] *Brief History,* pp. 58–61.

[23] *Ibid.,* p. 139.

[24] "The AFL-CIO: A Tougher Team with the Teamsters," *Business Week* (November 9, 1987), p. 110.

[25] Gene Koretz, "Why Unions Thrive Abroad—But Wither in the U.S." *Business Week* (September 10, 1990), p. 26.

[26] Gene Koretz and Celeste Whittaker, "More Picket Lines, Fewer Rank-And-Filers," *Business Week* (May 7, 1990), p. 24.

[27] *Ibid.*

[28] *Ibid.*

[29] Examples include the Social Security Act, Fair Labor Standards Act, and the National Labor Relations Act, as amended.

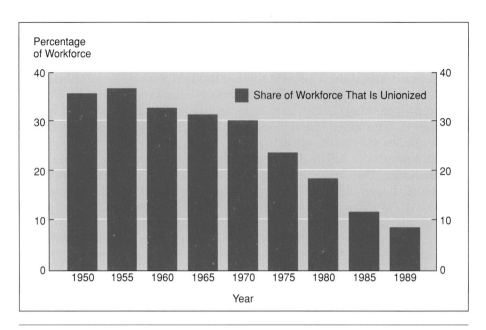

FIGURE 15-1 | Percentage of the Private Workforce That Is Unionized

Source: Labor Department

persistence in organizing in order to gain an effective voice in the terms and conditions of their employment. The unionized share of government workers is now approximately 37 percent.[30]

For many years the federal government had no well-defined policy on labor-management relations regarding its own employees. In order to address this situation, President Kennedy issued Executive Order 10988 in 1962. Section 1(a) of the order stated the following:

> Employees of the federal government shall have, and shall be protected in the exercise of, the right, freely and without fear of penalty or reprisal, to form, join and assist any employee organization or to refrain from any such activity.

For the first time in the history of the federal civil service, a uniform, comprehensive policy of cooperation between employee organizations and management in the executive branch of government was established. Employees were permitted to organize and negotiate human resource policies and practices and matters affecting working conditions that were within the administrative discretion of the agency officials concerned. However, Public Law 84-330, passed in 1955, made it a felony to strike against the U.S. government.[31]

---

[30] Gene Koretz, "Why Unions Thrive Abroad—But Wither in the U.S.," p. 26.

[31] Section 305 of the Labor Management Relations Act of 1947 also makes it unlawful for government employees to participate in any strike.

Executive Order 10988 established the basic framework for collective bargaining in federal government agencies. Subsequent EOs revised and improved this framework and brought about a new era of labor relations in the public sector.[32] In fact, the federal government codified the provisions of those executive orders and transferred them to Title VII of the Civil Service Reform Act of 1978. This act regulates most of the labor-management relations in the federal service. It establishes the Federal Labor Relations Authority (FLRA), which is modeled on the National Labor Relations Board. The intent of the FLRA is to bring the public sector model in line with that of the private sector. Requirements and mechanisms for recognition and elections, dealing with impasses, and handling grievances are covered in the act.

The U.S. Postal Service is not subject to Title VII of the Civil Service Reform Act of 1978. It was given independent government agency status by the Postal Reorganization Act of 1970. Postal employees were given collective bargaining rights comparable to those governing private industry. National Labor Relations Board rules and regulations controlling representation issues and elections are applicable to the postal service. Unfair labor practice provisions are also enforced by the NLRB. However, the right to strike is prohibited, and union-shop arrangements are not permitted.

Labor Relations and Bargaining Patterns

There is no uniform pattern to state and local labor relations and bargaining rights. Some states have no policy at all, whereas a haphazard mixture of statutes, resolutions, ordinances, and civil service procedures exists in others. However, public-employer legislation passed by state and local government accelerated noticeably after the issuance of EO 10988 in 1962.[33] By 1984, forty-one states and the District of Columbia had collective bargaining statutes covering all or some categories of public employees. By 1980, thirty-eight states had passed some form of legislation that obligates state agencies and local governments to permit their public employees to join unions and to recognize bona fide labor organizations. Prior to 1960, just a handful of states had such legislation. The diversity of state labor laws makes it difficult to generalize about the legal aspects of collective bargaining at the state and local levels.

Unilateral determination of the conditions of employment by public employers is increasingly being questioned. These decisions—made without worker input—are being questioned not only by government workers, but also by the unions and associations that represent them. Placed in the middle between their employees and the general public, state and local governments are being forced to specify in clearer terms the collective bargaining rights of workers.[34]

---

[32] They are Executive Order 11491 (effective January 1, 1970); EO 11616 (effective November 1971); EO 11636 (effective December 1971); and EO 11838 (effective May 1975).

[33] E. Edward Herman, Alfred Kuhn, and Ronald L. Seeber, *Collective Bargaining and Labor Relations,* p. 407.

[34] Benjamin J. Taylor and Fred Witney, *Labor Relations Law,* p.649.

Employee Associations

Membership in public-sector professional and state employee associations greatly exceeds private-sector unionization.[35] The largest of the employee associations, the National Education Association (NEA), has become the largest "union" in the United States.[36] In the past, employee associations were concerned primarily with the professional aspects of employment and avoided any semblance of unionism. In recent years, this approach has changed as public- and private-sector unions have actively organized both professional and government employees. Many employee associations now enthusiastically pursue collective bargaining relationships.

The greater public-sector penetration indicates that the process of unionization in the public sector differs from that in the private labor market. One factor that accounts for membership gains is clearly the role played by government employee associations, particularly at the state and local level. Challenged by established unions, the associations either merged with unions or transformed themselves into collective bargaining organizations. Many are becoming de facto unions, as with the NEA. Another reason that membership gains were made so quickly was the encouragement union organizations received from public-sector management.[37]

Next, we discuss the global sector.

■ THE GLOBAL SECTOR

Surprisingly, the future of unionism abroad seems much brighter than domestic unionism. According to economist Richard Freeman, unionism fell in some countries in the 1980s, but no country had the consistent abrupt drop experienced by U.S. unions. While unionism has waned in the United States, it is maintaining its strength abroad. Even though unions in all countries have been under increasing pressure in recent decades because of slowing productivity, lower economic growth, rapid technological change, and a shift toward a free market system, unionism in the United States has suffered the most.[38]

Freeman and fellow economist David Blanchflower believe that the critical difference between U.S. unions and their overseas counterparts is that U.S. unions have managed to win much higher wages than those received by nonunion workers. That gap is 20 to 25 percent in the United States compared with 10 percent or less abroad. This pronounced gap gives U.S. employers a major incentive to oppose unions and establish nonunion operations. In addition, foreign unions are generally less adversarial with

---

[35] Leo Troy, "The Rise and Fall of American Trade Unions: The Labor Movement from FDR to RR," in *Unions in Transition* (San Francisco: ICS Press, 1988), p. 85.

[36] Walter Galenson, "The Historical Role of American Trade Unionism," in *Unions in Transition* (San Francisco: ICS Press, 1988), p. 68.

[37] Leo Troy, "The Rise and Fall of American Trade Unions," p. 85.

[38] Gene Koretz, "Why Unions Thrive Abroad—But Wither in the U.S.," p. 26.

management, and less focused on wage gains. Instead, they concentrate on worker councils and participative decision making. Freeman and Blanchflower warn that domestic unions must change their direction of pursuing a "monopoly wage advantage" or their influence in the U.S. economy may be reduced even more.[39]

■ UNION OBJECTIVES

As previously indicated, the labor movement has a long history in the United States. Although each union is a unique organization seeking its own objectives, several broad objectives characterize the labor movement as a whole:

1. To secure and, if possible, improve the living standards and economic status of its members.
2. To enhance and, if possible, guarantee individual security against threats and contingencies that might result from market fluctuations, technological change, or management decisions.
3. To influence power relations in the social system in ways that favor and do not threaten union gains and goals.
4. To advance the welfare of all who work for a living, whether union members or not.[40]
5. To create mechanisms to guard against the use of arbitrary and capricious policies and practices in the workplace.

The underlying philosophy of the labor movement is that of organizational democracy and an atmosphere of social dignity for working men and women. In order to accomplish these objectives, most unions recognize that they must strive for continued growth and power. Although growth and power are related, we will discuss them separately to identify the impact of both factors on unionization.

Growth

To maximize its effectiveness, a union must strive for continual growth. Members pay dues, which are vital to promoting and achieving union objectives. Obviously, the more members the union enlists, the more dues they pay to support the union and the labor movement. Thus an overall goal of most unions is continued growth. But, as we previously mentioned, the percentage of union members in the workforce is declining. Most union leaders are concerned about this trend. Much of a union's ability to accomplish its objectives is derived from strength in numbers. For this reason, unions must continue to explore new sources of potential members. Unions

---

[39] *Ibid.*

[40] Edwin F. Beal and James P. Begin, *The Practice of Collective Bargaining,* 5th ed. (Homewood, Ill.: Richard D. Irwin, 1982), p. 91.

are now directing much of their attention to organizing the service industries, professional employees, and government employees.

Even with these efforts, union membership is expected to decline in the future, accompanied by a continual decline in labor's political and bargaining strength.[41] But, there is a glimmer of hope for unions. Some experts theorize that the stage will be set for a "mild" resurgence of unionism. A more demanding workforce and a federal administration whose policies toward unions are less aggressive may create favorable conditions for some growth in the ranks of organized labor.[42]

Power

According to one survey, "management continues to improve its power base in relation to organized labor."[43] Most observers agree that the power base of organized labor continues to erode. We define *power* here as the amount of external control that an organization is able to exert. As we mentioned previously, a union's power is influenced to a large extent by the size of its membership and the possibility of future growth. However, we also have to consider other factors when assessing the future power base of unions.

The importance of the jobs held by union members significantly affects union power. For instance, an entire plant may have to be shut down if unionized machinists performing critical jobs decide to strike. Thus a few strategically located union members may exert a disproportionate amount of power. A union's power can also be determined by the type of firm that is unionized. Unionization of truckers, steel workers, or farm workers can affect the entire country and subsequently enhance the union's power base. Through control of key industries, a union's power may extend to firms that are not unionized. For instance, in some areas of the country the power of the trucking unions extends well beyond firms that the truckers serve. Firms that depend on deliveries by the trucking industry may yield to union pressures in order to continue receiving services.

By achieving power, a union is capable of exerting its force in the political arena. The political arm of the AFL-CIO is the **Committee on Political Education (COPE).** Founded in 1955, its purpose is to support politicians who are friendly to the cause of organized labor. The union recommends and assists candidates who will best serve its interests. Union members also encourage their friends to support those candidates. The larger the voting membership, the greater the union's influence with politicians is. With "friends" in government, the union is in a stronger position to maneuver against management.

---

[41] *Ibid.,* pp. 20–22.

[42] Anne Ritter, "Are Unions Worth the Bargain?" *Personnel,* 67 (February 1990), p. 14.

[43] R. Wayne Mondy and Shane R. Premeaux, "The Labor/Movement Power Relationship Revisited," *Personnel Administrator,* 30 (May 1985), p. 52.

As reduced union strength contributes to weaker unions at the bargaining table, labor leaders will strive to increase their political clout. One of the most noteworthy features of labor's decline was reported by the Labor Department in 1985. According to this report, compensation gains for union workers slowed, rising only 2.6 percent compared to 4.6 percent for non-union workers.[44] This slowdown in union gains, coupled with declining union membership and organizing activities, caused unions to compensate by increasing their political activity.[45]

Even though unions have taken their political knocks over the past decade, they remain a fairly potent political force. The AFL-CIO and five of its largest affiliates spent more than $16.5 million, through political action committees, in previous national elections. Unions can provide many members to staff phone banks and organize campaigns. The unions' long association with such narrow issues as picketing rules and organizing regulations have given way to more popular campaigns for plant-closing legislation, child care, and family leave.[46] Unions' political activity will continue to parallel their changing philosophy toward a desire for "more government intervention" in the U.S. economy and society.[47]

As unions become more political, an internally explosive situation could be brewing because the overall goals of public- and private-sector unions are different. Over the long term, these goals may conflict. According to an AFL-CIO committee, "This is because private-sector unions, with the help of government intervention, want to raise members' income. To the extent they are successful, their members become subject to higher taxes, which their fellow public-sector unions will want to push even higher."[48] Regardless of the internal impact of an increased emphasis on political activities, the inevitability of union political involvement is a reality.[49]

■ WHY EMPLOYEES JOIN UNIONS

Individuals join unions for many different reasons, and these reasons tend to change over time. They may involve job, personal, social, or political considerations. It would be impossible to discuss them all, but the following are some of the major reasons: dissatisfaction with management, need for a social outlet, opportunity for leadership, forced unionization, and peer pressure.

---

[44] Clyde H. Farnsworth, "Wages and Benefit Costs Rose More Slowly in 1985," *The New York Times* (January 29, 1986), p. D1.

[45] Leo Troy, "The Rise and Fall of American Trade Unions," p. 104.

[46] Susan B. Garland, "Why Democrats Still Want to Wear the Union Label," *Business Week* (March 5, 1990), p. 37.

[47] Stan Crock, "The Duke Is Still Playing Hard-to-Get with Labor," *Business Week* (August 29, 1988), p. 39.

[48] "The Changing Situation of Workers and Their Unions," A Report by the AFL-CIO Committee on the Evolution of Work (Washington, D.C.: AFL-CIO, February 1985).

[49] *New Management Magazine* (Los Angeles: University of Southern California, Winter 1986), pp. 19–22.

Dissatisfaction with Management

Every job holds the potential for real dissatisfactions. Each individual has a boiling point that can trigger him or her to consider a union as a solution to real or perceived problems. Unions look for problems in organizations and then emphasize the advantages of union membership as a means of solving them. Some of the more common reasons for employee dissatisfaction are described in the following paragraphs.

Compensation. Employees want their compensation to be fair and equitable. Wages are important to them because they provide both the necessities and pleasures of life. If employees are dissatisfied with their wages, they may look to a union for assistance in improving their standard of living. However, the ability of the unions to make satisfactory gains in income has been severely hampered in the past few years. Of the contracts negotiated in 1990, the wage rate adjustment averaged only 3.3 percent annually over the life of the contract.[50]

An important psychological aspect of compensation involves the amount of pay an individual receives in relation to that of other workers performing similar work. If an employee perceives that management has shown favoritism by paying someone else more to perform the same or a lower level job, the employee will likely become dissatisfied. Union members know precisely the basis of their pay and how it compares with others. Therefore pay inequities, with seniority as the accepted criterion for fairness, are less likely to become a major problem area.

Two-Tier Wage System. The **two-tier wage system** is a wage structure that reflects lower pay rates for newly hired employees as compared to those received by established employees performing similar jobs. This system is one of the most controversial developments in collective bargaining. Several industries (airlines, trucking, supermarkets, aerospace, and ship building) are operating under such contracts. Under this system, newly hired workers are paid less than employees already on the payroll. While the two-tier system basically provides unequal pay for equal work, the system does save organizations a great deal of money in labor costs, and at the same time provides more jobs. The system has been accepted by unions in lieu of wage cuts in companies hit hard by deregulation, foreign competition, and aggressive nonunion competitors.

There are two basic types of two-tier scales: temporary and permanent. In a temporary system, the new employees are hired for less than those hired earlier, but they can advance to parity over time. In a permanent system, the new hires will never achieve parity. There are also variations and modifications of these basic types of scales, and some companies have even instituted a third (lower) tier.

---

[50] Fehmida Sleemi, Joan D. Borum, and Edward J. Wasilewski, Jr., "Collective Bargaining During 1991," *Monthly Labor Review,* 114 (January 1991), p. 4.

In recent years firms using the two-tier wage system have been phasing it out, especially in wholesale and retail trade contract negotiations. (The system has been found to cause high turnover and worker morale problems.) Thus the gaps in wages created by the system are expected to be narrowed in the future.[51]

Job Security. For a young employee, job security is often less important than it is for an older worker. The young employee may think, "If I lose this job, I can always get another." But, if employees see management consistently terminating older workers to make room for younger, more aggressive employees, they may begin to think about job security. If the firm doesn't provide its employees with a sense of job security, workers may turn to a union. Employees are more concerned than ever before about job security due to the decline in employment in such key industries as automobiles, rubber, and steel.

The United Automobile Workers (UAW) union now has one of the strongest systems of job security in industrial America: Job guarantees at the "Big Three" automakers protect workers with at least one year's seniority from everything but sales decline.[52] Also, in a recent three-year contract that Xerox signed with the Amalgamated Textile & Clothing Workers Union (ATCWU), the company promised not to lay off employees.[53] The concern over job security was translated into legislation in 1988, with enactment by Congress of a plant closing bill that requires employers to give advance notification prior to plant closings.

Management's Attitude. People like to feel that they are important. They do not like to be considered a commodity that can be bought and sold. Thus employees do not like to be subjected to arbitrary and capricious actions by management. In some firms, management is insensitive to the needs of its employees. When this situation occurs, employees may perceive that they have little or no influence in job-related matters. Workers who feel that they are not really part of an organization are prime targets for unionization.

Management's attitude may be reflected in such small actions as how bulletin board notices are written. Memos addressed "To All Employees" instead of "To Our Employees" may indicate managers that are indifferent to employee needs. Such attitudes likely stem from top management, but they are noticed initially by employees in the actions of first-line supervisors. Workers may notice that supervisors are judging people entirely on what they can do, how much they can do, and when they can do it. Employees may begin to feel that they are treated more

---

[51] Edward J. Wasilewski, Jr., "Collective Bargaining in 1992: Contract Talks and Other Activity," *Monthly Labor Review,* 115 (January 1992), p. 14.

[52] Wendy Zellner, "All the Ingredients for Disaster Are There," *Business Week* (April 16, 1990), p. 28.

[53] Anne Ritter, "Are Unions Worth the Bargain?" p. 13.

as machines than people. Supervisors may fail to give reasons for unusual assignments and may expect employees to dedicate their lives to the firm without providing adequate rewards. The prevailing philosophy may be: "If you don't like it here, leave." A management philosophy such as this, which does not consider the needs of employees as individuals, makes the firm ripe for unionization.

The Xerox Corporation appears to realize the importance of considering the needs of employees. Ron Blackwell of the ATCWU (which represents Xerox employees) commends the company's philosophy of cooperation. He comments, "Many companies talk about cooperation, but few are willing to take the steps to make it work. Xerox is a farsighted company in terms of the effective relationship unions and management can have when they cooperate." He says the firm realizes that in order to have employee cooperation, management has to give workers recognition as human beings.[54]

Management must keep in mind that unions would never have gained a foothold if management had not abused its power.[55]

A Social Outlet

By nature, many people have strong social needs. They generally enjoy being around others who have similar interests and desires. Some employees join a union for no other reason than to take advantage of union-sponsored recreational and social activities that members and their families find fulfilling. Some unions now offer day-care centers and other services that appeal to working men and women and increase their sense of solidarity with other union members. People who develop close personal relationships, in either a unionized or union-free organization, will likely stand together in difficult times.

Providing Opportunity for Leadership

Some individuals aspire to leadership roles, but it isn't always easy for an operative employee to progress into management. However, employees with leadership aspirations can often satisfy them through the union. As with the firm, the union also has a hierarchy of leadership, and individual members have the opportunity to work their way up through its various levels. Employers often notice employees who are leaders in the union, and it is not uncommon for them to promote such employees into managerial ranks as supervisors.

---

[54] *Ibid.*

[55] *Ibid.*, p. 14.

Forced Unionization

It is generally illegal to require that an individual join a union prior to employment. However, in the twenty-nine states without right-to-work laws, it is legal for an employer to agree with the union that a new employee must join the union after a certain period of time (generally thirty days) or be terminated. This is referred to as a union-shop agreement. However, data are not available to indicate the number of employees who become union members because of these compulsory agreements.

Peer Pressure

Many individuals will join a union simply because they are urged to do so by other members of the work group. Friends and associates may constantly remind an employee that he or she is not a member of the union. This social pressure from peers is difficult to resist. Failure to join the union may result in rejection of the employee by other workers. In extreme cases, union members threaten nonmembers with physical violence and sometimes carry out these threats.

■ UNION STRUCTURE

The labor movement has developed a multilevel organizational structure over time. This complex of organizations ranges from local unions to the principal federation, the AFL-CIO. Each level has its own officers and ways of managing its affairs. Many national unions have intermediate levels between the national and the local levels. In this section, however, we describe only the three basic elements of union organization: (1) the local union, (2) the national union, and (3) the federation, or AFL-CIO.

The Local Union

The basic element in the structure of the American labor movement is the **local union** (or simply, the local). To the individual union member, it is the most important level in the structure of organized labor. Through the local, the individual deals with the employer on a day-to-day basis. There are approximately 65,000 locals in the United States, most of which are affiliated with one of the 170 or so national or international unions. The latter are generally organized along industry or craft lines[56] and ninety-four are affiliated with the AFL-CIO.

---

[56] Daniel K. Benjamin, "Combination of Workmen: Trade Unions in the American Economy," in *Unions in Transition* (San Francisco: ICS Press, 1988), p. 104.

There are two basic kinds of local unions: craft and industrial. A **craft union,** such as the Carpenters and Joiners union, is typically composed of members of a particular trade or skill in a specific locality. Members usually acquire their job skills through an apprenticeship training program. An **industrial union** generally consists of all the workers in a particular plant or group of plants. The type of work they do and the level of skill they possess are not a condition for membership in the union. An example of an industrial union is the United Auto Workers.

The local union's functions are many and varied. Administering the collective bargaining agreement and representing workers in handling grievances are two quite important activities. Other functions include keeping the membership informed about labor issues, promoting increased membership, maintaining effective contact with the national union, and, when appropriate, negotiating with management at the local level.

The National (or International) Union

The most powerful level in the union structure is the national union. As we stated previously, most locals are affiliated with national unions. Some national unions are called *international* unions because they have affiliated locals in Canada.

A **national union** is composed of local unions, which it charters. As such, it is the parent organization to local unions. The local union—not the individual worker—holds membership in the national union. The national union is supported financially by each local union, whose contribution is based on its membership size.

The national union is governed by a national constitution and a national convention of local unions, which usually meets every two to five years. The day-to-day operation of the national is conducted by elected officers, aided by an administrative staff. The national union is active in organizing workers within its jurisdiction, engaging in collective bargaining at the national level, and assisting its locals in their negotiations. In addition, the national union may provide numerous educational and research services for its locals, dispense strike funds, publish the union newspaper, provide legal counsel, and actively lobby at national and state levels.

AFL-CIO

The American Federation of Labor and Congress of Industrial Organizations (AFL-CIO) is the central trade union federation in the United States. It represents the interests of labor and its member national unions at the highest level. The federation does not engage in collective bargaining; however, it provides the means by which member unions can cooperate to pursue common objectives and attempt to resolve internal problems faced by organized labor. The federation is financed by its member national unions and is governed by a national convention, which meets every two years.

As shown in Figure 15-2 on page 590, the structure of the AFL-CIO is complex. The federation has state bodies in all fifty states and Puerto Rico. Also, national unions can affiliate with one or more of the trade and industrial departments. These departments seek to promote the interests of specific groups of workers who are in different unions but who have common interests. The federation's major activities include the following:

1. Improving the image of organized labor.
2. Extensive lobbying on behalf of labor interests.
3. Political education through COPE.
4. Resolving disputes between national unions.
5. Policing internal affairs of member unions.

The AFL-CIO is a loosely knit organization of more than ninety national unions. It has little formal power or control. The member national unions remain completely autonomous and decide their own policies and programs. Not all national unions are members of the federation. In fact, one of the largest unions, the Teamsters, was expelled in 1957 and did not rejoin the AFL-CIO until October 1987. In the late 1970s affiliated unions represented approximately seventeen million members, or about 78 percent of all union members in the United States.[57] Currently, the AFL-CIO represents approximately fourteen million members.[58]

■ ESTABLISHING THE COLLECTIVE BARGAINING RELATIONSHIP

The primary law governing the relationship of companies and unions is the National Labor Relations Act, as amended.[59] Collective bargaining is one of the key parts of the act. Section 8(d) of the act defines **collective bargaining** as the following:

> The performance of the mutual obligation of the employer and the representative of the employees to meet at reasonable times and confer in good faith with respect to wages, hours, and other terms and conditions of employment, or the negotiation of an agreement, or any question arising thereunder, and the execution of a written contract incorporating any agreement reached if requested by either party, but such obligation does not compel either party to agree to a proposal or require the making of a concession.

---

[57] *Directory of National Unions and Employee Associations* (Washington, D.C.: U.S. Department of Labor, Bureau of Labor Statistics, Bulletin 2079, September 1980), p. 73.

[58] *Wall Street Journal,* 89 (April 14, 1992), p. 1.

[59] Other names for this act are the Labor Management Relations Act of 1947 and the Taft-Hartley Act.

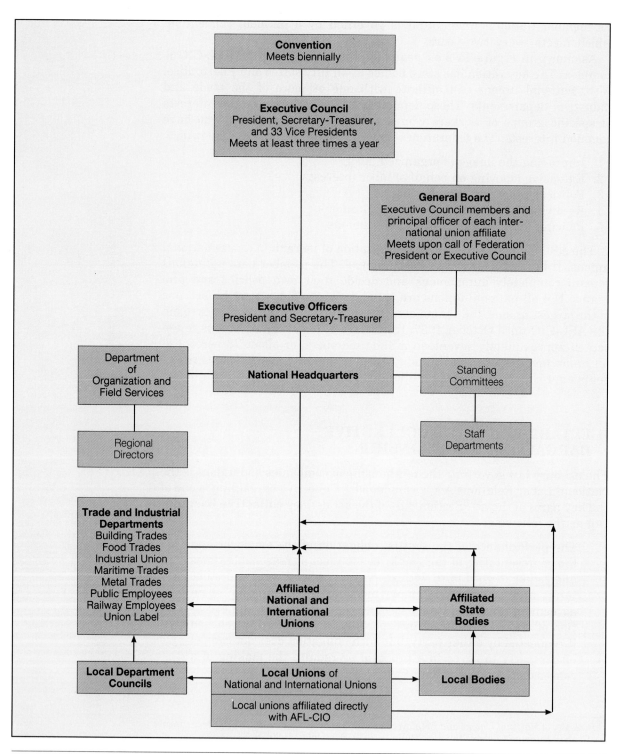

FIGURE 15-2 | The Structure of the AFL-CIO

Source: Bureau of Labor Statistics, *Directory of National Unions and Employee Associations,* 1980.

The act further provides that the designated representative of the employees shall be the exclusive representative for *all* the employees in the unit for purposes of collective bargaining. A **bargaining unit** consists of a group of employees, not necessarily union members, recognized by an employer or certified by an administrative agency as appropriate for representation by a labor organization for purposes of collective bargaining. A unit may cover the employees in one plant of an employer, or it may cover employees in two or more plants of the same employer. Although the act requires the representative to be selected by the employees, it does not require any particular procedure to be used, so long as the choice clearly reflects the desire of the majority of the employees in the bargaining unit. The employee representative is normally chosen in a secret ballot election conducted by the NLRB. When a union desires to become the bargaining representative for a group of employees, several steps leading to certification have to be taken (see Figure 15-3). External and internal factors can affect the process. The primary external factors are legislation and the union; the prevailing corporate culture can affect the internal environment.

Signing of Authorization Cards

A prerequisite to forming a recognized bargaining unit is to determine whether there is sufficient interest on the part of employees. Evidence of this interest is expressed when at least 30 percent of the employees in a work group sign an authorization card. The **authorization card** is a document indicating that an employee wants to be represented by a labor organization in collective bargaining. Most union organizers will not proceed unless at least 50 percent of the workers in the group sign cards. An authorization card used by the International Association of Machinists and Aerospace Workers is shown in Figure 15-4 on page 592.

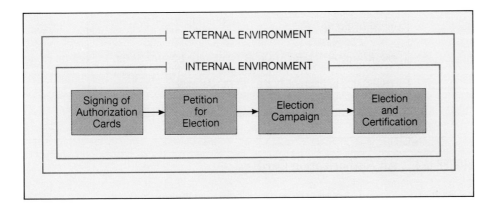

FIGURE 15-3 | The Steps That Lead to Forming a Bargaining Unit

Petition for Election

After the authorization cards have been signed, a petition for an election may be made to the appropriate regional office of the NLRB. When the petition is filed, the NLRB will conduct an investigation. The purpose of the investigation is to determine, among other things, the following:

1. Whether the Board has jurisdiction to conduct an election.
2. Whether there is a sufficient showing of employee interest to justify an election.
3. Whether a question of representation exists (for example, the employee representative has demanded recognition, which has been denied by the employer).
4. Whether the election will include appropriate employees in the bargaining unit (for instance, the Board is prohibited from including plant guards in the same unit with the other employees).

YES, I WANT THE IAM

I, the undersigned, an employee of

(Company) _____

hereby authorize the International Association of Machinists and Aerospace Workers (IAM) to act as my collective bargaining agent with the company for wages, hours and working conditions.

NAME (print) _____ DATE _____

ADDRESS (print) _____

CITY _____ STATE _____ ZIP _____

DEPT. _____ SHIFT _____ PHONE _____

Classification _____

SIGN HERE ✗ _____

NOTE: THIS AUTHORIZATION IS TO BE SIGNED AND DATED IN EMPLOYEE'S OWN HANDWRITING. YOUR RIGHT TO SIGN THIS CARD IS PROTECTED BY FEDERAL LAW.

FIGURE 15-4 | An Authorization Card

Source: The International Association of Machinists and Aerospace Workers.

5. Whether the representative named in the petition is qualified (for example, a supervisor or any other management representative may not be an employee representative).
6. Whether there are any barriers to an election in the form of existing contracts or prior elections held within the past twelve months.[60]

If these conditions have been met, the NLRB will ordinarily direct that an election be held within thirty days. Election details are left largely to the agency's regional director. Management is prohibited from making unusual concessions or promises that would encourage workers to vote against union recognition.

Election Campaign

When an election has been ordered, both union and management usually promote their causes actively. Unions will continue to encourage workers to join the union and management may begin a campaign to tell workers the benefits of remaining union-free. The supervisor's role during the campaign is crucial. Supervisors need to conduct themselves in a manner that avoids violating the law and committing unfair labor practices. Specifically, they should be aware of what can, and cannot, be done in the pre-election campaign period. In many cases it is not so much what is said by the supervisor as how it is said.[61] Human resource professionals can give them a lot of help in these matters. Throughout the campaign, they should keep upper management informed about employee attitudes.

Theoretically, both union and management are permitted to tell their stories without interference from the other side. At times, the campaign becomes quite intense. Election results will be declared invalid if the campaign was marked by conduct that the NLRB considers to have interfered with the employee's freedom of choice. Examples of such conduct follow:

- An employer or a union threatening loss of jobs or benefits to influence employees' votes or union activities.
- An employer or a union misstating important facts in the election campaign when the other party does not have a chance to reply.
- Either an employer or a union inciting racial or religious prejudice by inflammatory campaign appeals.
- An employer firing employees to discourage or encourage their union activities or a union causing an employer to take such an action.
- An employer or a union making campaign speeches to assembled groups of employees on company time within twenty-four hours of an election.

---

[60] *A Guide to Basic Law and Procedures Under the National Labor Relations Act* (Washington, D.C.: U.S. Government Printing Office, October 1978), pp. 11–13.

[61] Art Bethke, R. Wayne Mondy, and Shane R. Premeaux, "Decertification: The Role of the First-Line Supervisor," *Supervisory Management,* 31 (February 1986), pp. 21–23.

HRM In Action

Sandy Marshall, one of the workers in the plant, has just come to see the human resource manager, Lonnie Miller, for advice. Apparently a union organizer approached her yesterday and asked her to help with the union organizing effort. Lonnie knows that lately there have been growing tensions and a lot of talk about unions. He has even seen what appears to be authorization cards being passed about. Lonnie knows that if Sandy starts working for the union, she will have a lot of influence. She seems to be a natural leader, and Lonnie thinks she is supervisory material.

What advice should Lonnie give Sandy?

Election and Certification

The NLRB monitors the secret-ballot election on the date set. Its representatives are responsible for making sure that only eligible employees vote and for counting the votes. Following a valid election, the board will issue a certification of the results to the participants. If a union has been chosen by a majority of the employees voting in the bargaining unit, it will receive a certificate showing that it is now the official bargaining representative of the employees in the unit. However, the right to represent employees does not mean, as was assumed by Robert Sweeney in the scenario at the beginning of this chapter, the right to dictate terms to management that would adversely affect the organization. The bargaining process does not require either party to make concessions; it only compels them to bargain in good faith.

Union Strategies in Obtaining Bargaining Unit Recognition

Unions may use various strategies to obtain recognition by management. Unions generally try to make the first move because this places management in the position of having to react to union maneuvers. The search for groups of employees to organize involves a continuous effort by union leaders. To begin a drive, unions often look for disaffection. Union organizers recognize that if employees generally have an overall positive attitude toward management, organizing employees will be extremely difficult. Some situations indicate that employees are ripe for organizing:

- A history of unjustified and arbitrary treatment of employees.
- Compensation below the industry average.
- Lack of concern for employee welfare.

A union does not normally look at isolated conditions of employee unrest. Rather, it attempts to locate general patterns of employee dissatisfaction. Whatever the case, the union will probably not make a major attempt at organizing unless it believes that it has a good chance of success.

The union may take numerous approaches in getting authorization cards signed. One effective technique is to first identify workers who are not only dissatisfied but also influential in the firm's informal organization. These individuals can assist in developing an effective organizing campaign. Information is obtained through the grapevine regarding who was hired, who was fired, and management mistakes in general. Such information is beneficial to union organizers as they approach company employees. Statements such as this are common: "I hear Bill Adams was fired today. I also understand that he is well liked. No way that would have happened if you had a union."

Ultimately, the union must abandon its secret activities. Sooner or later, management will discover the organizing attempt. At this point, union organizers may station themselves and other supporters at company entrances and pass out "throwsheets" or campaign literature proclaiming the benefits of joining the union and emphasizing management weaknesses. They will talk to anyone who will listen in their attempt to identify union sympathizers. Employees who sign an authorization card are then encouraged to convince their friends to sign also. The effort often mushrooms, yielding a sufficient number of signed authorization cards before management has time to react.

Union efforts continue even after the election petition has been approved by the NLRB. Every attempt is made by the organizers to involve as many workers from the firm as possible. The outside organizers would like to take a back seat and let company employees convince their peers to join the union. Peer pressure typically has a much greater effect on convincing a person to join a union than outside influence does. Whenever possible, unions utilize peer pressure to encourage and expand unionization.

■ SIGNS OF A TROUBLED LABOR MOVEMENT

The labor movement appears to be in serious trouble. Overall union membership by occupation and by industry continues to decline.[62] As we have mentioned earlier in this chapter, the percentage of unionized

---

[62] Larry Reynolds, "Management-Labor Tensions Spell Union Busting," *Personnel,* 68 (March 1991), pp. 8–9.

workers in the private sector was a mere 10 percent in 1989, and union membership was down to 16.4 percent of the overall nonfarm workforce.[63] In 1990, the share of representation elections won by unions was 47.6 percent of the 3,424 NLRB representation elections, down from 49.8 percent in 1989. This was the smallest number of NLRB representation elections conducted since 1984.[64] The legacy of the Reagan administration, which created the perception that unions were weak, and encouraged the anti-labor environment of the 1980s, continues to linger.[65]

These are not encouraging signs for those who support unionism; however, according to Stephen J. Cabot, a management-labor attorney from Philadelphia, the perception of weak unions began to change with the Bush administration. In 1989, some significant events indicated that the tide might be turning. For example, in line with the contract that Xerox Corporation signed with the ATCWU, the company restored cost-of-living adjustments, increased profit-sharing percentages from 6.5 percent of profits to 10 percent before taxes, and promised not to lay off employees.[66] At AT&T, the Communications Workers of America negotiated a contract that had landmark dependent care provisions.[67] These "victories" are signs of what Cabot called a "mild union resurgence." According to Cabot, "The unions are more organized and their workers are better trained." These factors, coupled with increasing employee frustration over the economy, are expected to contribute to a rise in union popularity.[68] However, by 1992 unions at companies such as AT&T were losing clout and seeing some of their gains reversed.

Also, there appears to be a major threat to American unionism just across the border. Unions are bracing to absorb the shock that will result from the movement of major full-fledged manufacturing from the United States to Mexico. Many companies with unionized employees are carefully studying the feasibility of moving their manufacturing operations across the border. The Thompson Consumer Electronics firm already employs some 5,500 Mexican workers, and is considering moving production for its 20-inch television sets to Mexico from Bloomington, Indiana. The cost to organized labor will be the loss of 2,000 union jobs. According to a representative of the United Automobile Workers, movement to Mexico will place extreme downward pressure on wages. Representative Don J. Pease (D-Ohio), a member of the House Ways and Means Committee, summed up his view of the impact of the difference between wage scales this way: "I don't think there is any way our folks can compete with $1-an-hour Mexican

---

[63] Gene Koretz and Celeste Whittaker, "More Picket Lines, Fewer Rank-And-Filers," p. 24.

[64] "Unions Win Fewer Representation Votes," *HRNews,* 10 (July 1991), p. 11.

[65] Anne Ritter, "Are Unions Worth the Bargain?" p. 12.

[66] *Ibid.,* pp. 12–13.

[67] *Ibid.*

[68] *Ibid.*

workers."[69] Continued downward pressure on wages and additional losses in union membership are expected in the U.S. manufacturing sector.[70]

Currently, employers still have the upper hand when dealing with unions, but fading union strength will not enable management to deal with workers in a free and unrestricted manner. Some business leaders believe that they will get a union-free environment, but they may inherit a legalistic system instead. Unionism seems to be declining, but legalized worker protection is a growing trend.

■ THE GROWING LEGALISTIC APPROACH

Recent emergence of an employee rights movement has the potential to "forge revolutionary changes in the workplace and the way companies manage people."[71] As nonunion sentiment intensifies, the courts and state legislatures are becoming the most effective champions of employee rights. As union membership declines, so does union political and legal clout. However, according to Harvard labor law specialist Paul C. Weiler, employee rights will be protected by a legalistic system.[72] A web of legislation is growing at the national, state, and local levels and in all aspects of the work environment. Legislation has been developed with regard to the following: right-to-know laws; whistle-blower protection; prohibition against a mandatory retirement age; notice requirements of plant shutdowns; severance pay for workers affected by plant shutdowns; employee privacy protection; enhanced standards for a safe and healthful workplace; protection against discrimination in hiring, promotion, and discharge; prohibitions against sex discrimination in pay; retirement security protection; national minimum wage; and limitations on company ability to discharge and discipline employees for union activity.

This growing network of legal protection may eventually replace collective bargaining. However, top AFL-CIO officials refuse to accept legislation as an acceptable substitute for bargaining or the suggestion that unions are in permanent decline. Regardless of the state of unionism, the employee rights movement will continue to expand, providing employees with more influence in their work.[73] Companies and unions that fail to recognize this latest movement are ignoring what appears to be an inevitable part of future work environments.

---

[69] William J. Holstein, David Woodruff, and Amy Borrus, "Is Free Trade with Mexico Good or Bad for the U.S.?" *Business Week* (November 12, 1990), p. 113.

[70] *Ibid.*

[71] John Hoerr et al., "Beyond Unions," *Business Week* (July 8, 1985), p. 72.

[72] *Ibid.*, p. 74.

[73] *Ibid.*, p. 77.

■ THE FUTURE OF UNIONISM AND COLLECTIVE BARGAINING IN A GLOBAL ECONOMY

The future of unionism is one of change; therefore, unionism and collective bargaining in the United States will not, in all likelihood, be as we know them today. Global competition will no longer allow highly structured bargaining that links wages and benefits to macroeconomic factors, rather than company-specific performance.[74] In the early days of the growth of the U.S. economy, the railroads developed new networks of routes spanning the continent and knitted the country into an economic whole. Similarly, the trading ties with other countries have united the world into an economic whole. No longer can the processes of collective bargaining and unionism be considered domestic issues; they must be considered in the global spectrum.

Recent developments such as the two-tier wage system, increased management flexibility, gain-sharing, and employee identification with productivity are necessary to compete effectively in a global environment. These factors must therefore be considered in many collective bargaining situations and will affect the future of unionism in the United States. The President's Commission on Industrial Competitiveness summarized changes needed to compete in the global economy:

- Labor-management cooperation is essential. The new cooperative relationships will maximize productivity by involving employees and their elected representatives in the decision-making process.
- Employee incentives must be strengthened to reward the efforts of individual employees and to emphasize the linkage between compensation and performance.
- Displaced workers must be handled in a more resourceful manner. Employers must be encouraged to strengthen their commitment to employee security and will be required to provide early notification of plant closings. All parties should work toward the goal of re-employment.
- Improved work skills must be developed by training employees to effectively compete in the job market. Specifically, employers should be encouraged to take a more systematic approach in their training activities.[75]

Obviously, times have changed and will continue to change, and labor and management must evolve to compete in the global economy. Neither labor nor management should attempt to hold on to the practices of the past because today's global economy will not tolerate such entrenched behavior.

---

[74] Alexander B. Trowbridge, "A Management Look at Labor Relations," in *Unions in Transition* (San Francisco: ICS Press, 1988), p. 417.

[75] "Global Competition: The New Reality," *Vol. 2, Report of the President's Commission on Industrial Competitiveness,* (Washington, D.C.: U.S. Government Printing Office, 1985), pp. 137–160.

SUMMARY

The labor movement has not enjoyed simple and straightforward progress. Prior to the 1930s, attitudes definitely favored management. This was first evidenced by the use of criminal and civil conspiracy doctrines derived from English common law. Other tactics used by employers to stifle union growth were injunctions and yellow-dog contracts. In 1890, Congress passed the Sherman Anti-Trust Act. This marked the entrance of the federal government into the statutory regulation of labor organizations. Later, in 1914, Congress passed the Clayton Act (an amendment to the Sherman Act). The intent of this act was to remove labor from the purview of the Sherman Act. During the 1920s labor faced legal restrictions on union activity and unfavorable court decisions. The one exception to such repressive policies was enactment of the Railway Labor Act of 1926.

The pendulum began to swing away from management and toward labor after 1930. Congress passed the Norris-LaGuardia Act in 1932, affirming the use of collective bargaining and approving the formation of labor unions. In 1933 Congress made an abortive attempt to stimulate economic recovery by passing the National Industry Recovery Act (NIRA). Undeterred by a Supreme Court decision and strongly supported by organized labor, Congress speedily enacted a comprehensive labor law, the National Labor Relations Act (Wagner Act), in 1935. Drawing heavily on the experience of the Railway Labor Act of 1926 and Section 7a of the NIRA, the act declared legislative support, on a broad scale, of the right of workers to organize and engage in collective bargaining. In 1947, with public pressure mounting, Congress overrode President Truman's veto and passed the Labor Management Relations Act (Taft-Hartley Act), which extensively revised the National Labor Relations Act. One of the most controversial elements of the Taft-Hartley Act permits states to enact right-to-work legislation. Right-to-work laws are laws that prohibit management and unions from agreements requiring union membership as a condition of employment. In 1959, Congress enacted the Labor-Management Reporting and Disclosure Act (Landrum-Griffin Act), which spelled out a "Bill of Rights of Members of Labor Organizations" designed to protect certain rights of individuals in their relationships with unions.

Government employees are generally considered a class apart from private-sector workers. This is reflected in their exclusion from the coverage of general labor legislation. However, like their counterparts in private industry, government employees have demonstrated a persistence in organizing in order to gain an effective voice concerning the terms and conditions of their employment. Membership in public-sector professional and state employee associations greatly exceeds private-sector unionization.

Most unions recognize that they must strive for continued growth and power. Members pay dues, which are essential for achieving union objectives. A union's power is influenced to a large extent by the size of its membership and the possibility of future growth. By achieving growth and power, a union is capable of exerting political force. The political arm of the AFL-CIO is the Committee on Political Education (COPE).

Individuals join unions for many different reasons, and these reasons tend to change over time. They may involve job, personal, social, or political considerations. Some of the major reasons are dissatisfaction with management, need for a social outlet, opportunity for leadership, forced unionization, and peer pressure.

The labor movement has developed a multilevel organizational structure that includes (1) the local union, (2) the national union, and (3) the federation, or AFL-CIO. The basic element in the structure of the American labor movement is the local union, of which there are two basic kinds: craft and industrial. A national union is composed of local unions, which it charters. The American Federation of Labor and Congress of Industrial Organizations (AFL-CIO) is the main trade union federation in the United States.

The primary law governing the relationship of companies and unions is the National Labor Relations Act, as amended. A bargaining unit consists of a group of employees recognized by an employer as appropriate for representation by a labor organization for purposes of collective bargaining. A prerequisite to forming a recognized bargaining unit is to determine whether there is sufficient interest on the part of employees. After authorization cards have been signed, a petition for an election may be made to the appropriate regional office of the National Labor Relations Board (NLRB). The NLRB monitors a secret-ballot election. Unions may use various strategies to obtain recognition by management. Unions generally try to make the first move because this places management in the position of having to react to union maneuvers.

Unionism and collective bargaining will change in the future. Global competition will no longer allow highly structured bargaining that links wages and benefits to macroeconomic factors rather than company-specific performance. Recent developments, such as the two-tier wage system, increased management flexibility, gain-sharing, and employee identification with productivity are necessary to compete effectively in a global environment.

Many signs point to serious trouble in the labor movement. Certain fundamental indicators of union growth and survival are declining. As anti-union sentiment grows, however, a legalistic approach to employee protection appears to be replacing collective bargaining.

Questions for Review

1. Describe the development of the labor movement in the United States.
2. List the unfair labor practices by management that were prohibited by the Wagner Act.
3. What union actions were prohibited by the Taft-Hartley Act?
4. In what way does unionization of the public sector differ from unionization of the private sector?
5. Why would unions strive for continued growth and power? Discuss.
6. What are the primary reasons for employees joining labor unions?
7. What steps must a union take in attempting to form a bargaining unit? Briefly describe each step.
8. Describe the ways unions might go about gaining bargaining unit recognition.
9. Discuss the signs of a troubled labor movement.
10. Describe the process of collective bargaining and unionism in a global economy.

Terms for Review

Conspiracy
Injunction
Yellow-dog contract
Right-to-work laws
Committee on Political Education (COPE)
Two-tier wage system

Local union
Craft union
Industrial union
National union
Collective bargaining
Bargaining unit
Authorization card

INCIDENT 1   ■   Work Rules   ■

Jerry Sharplin eagerly drove his new company pickup onto the construction site. He had just been assigned by his employer, Lurgi-Knost Construction Company, to supervise a crew of sixteen equipment operators, oilers, and mechanics. This was the first unionized crew Jerry had supervised, and he was unaware of the labor agreement in effect that carefully defined and limited the role of supervisors. As he approached his work area, he noticed one of the cherry pickers (a type of mobile crane with an extendable boom) standing idle with the operator beside it. Jerry pulled up beside the operator and asked, "What's going on here?"

"Out of gas," the operator said.

"Well, go and get some," Jerry said.

The operator reached to get his thermos jug out of the toolbox on the side of the crane and said, "The oiler's on break right now. He'll be back in a few minutes."

Jerry remembered that he had a five-gallon can of gasoline in the back of his pickup. So he quickly got the gasoline, climbed on the cherry picker, and started to pour it into the gas tank. As he did so, he heard the other machines shutting down in unison. He looked around and saw all the other operators climbing down from their equipment and standing to watch him pour the gasoline. A moment later, he saw the union steward approaching.

Questions

1. Why did all the operators shut down their machines?
2. If you were Jerry, what would you do now? Explain.

INCIDENT 2   ■   Union Appeal   ■

In late 1991, a vigorous union-organizing campaign was under way at Dodge Tube Company in Rochester, North Carolina. The management at Dodge was strongly anti-union and made no bones about it. Roger Verdon was a general supervisor at Dodge, with the responsibility for four supervisors and about eighty machine operators and helpers. Roger had become increasingly incensed as the union's organizing attempts became more apparent.

At first, fliers and other promotional literature had been handed out at the plant gates. There had been an increasing number of complaints, and Roger felt that many of them were caused by the union-organizing activity. The workers in general had become more belligerent, Roger thought, and he saw indications of more and more secret communication. Workers who had previously been his friends seemed to have pulled away. While they were not unfriendly, they typically limited their conversation with him to office matters.

Roger felt that Dodge was a good employer and treated its people fairly. Discipline was administered by supervisors on the spot. Helpers were paid minimum wage, but few stayed in that position very long. Most helpers were either fired or promoted to machine operator within about six months. The machine operators were placed in pay grade 1, 2, or 3 at the discretion of the supervisor. Supervisors were encouraged to base pay grade assignments only on job proficiency. Most of the supervisors were required to participate in the company's management training program. The ones who were not college graduates were required to complete a correspondence course in management from the University of Maryland during their first six months as supervisors.

The company had an aggressive health and safety program. Workers in noisy areas were required to wear earplugs, and a worker who failed to do so was immediately fired. The same was true of safety glasses in areas involving grinding, drilling, or chipping. The workers in and around the tube-cleaning area were required to wear respirators because an OSHA inspector had cited the company for the amount of particulate matter in the air.

One day in early December, Roger observed what he considered to be the "last straw." He saw a worker from another part of the plant walking through his area handing out cards to the workers. Bob asked to see one of the cards and realized that it was a union authorization card. He decided to have a meeting with his supervisors.

Questions

1. What factors could have produced union-organizing activity?
2. What can Roger do about it?

DEVELOPING HRM SKILLS

U nionization is often met with mixed feelings by all concerned. Management is usually opposed to such efforts. Beth Morrison, the production manager of the heavy motors division of MNP Corporation, knows that upper management does not care much for unions. They believe that this unionizing effort is not good for anybody involved with this company and that the union wants to turn the employees against them. Upper management also feels that a union will destroy the company's competitive edge—something that has happened to many other firms. The firm must do everything possible to circumvent this union-organizing effort, but it must do so in line with NLRB guidelines.

Beth thought, "I've got to meet with Ray Miller, the supervisor over in section 4, today. He is a little too eager about stopping the union. We don't want this union, but we also don't want the NLRB breathing down our necks. Indirect threats are okay, but direct threats can get us in trouble. Ray must understand the ground rules, and apply those rules to stop this union. Obviously, we don't want this union, but no supervisor can threaten loss of jobs or benefits, or fire anybody, at least until after the election. I'm going to tell Ray that if his employees ask his opinion, he should definitely discourage workers from unionizing."

If you are anti-union or pro-union, there is a role for you here. One of you will play the production manager and another will play the supervisor. The rest of you observe carefully. Your instructor will provide the participants with additional information.

REFERENCES

Benson, Herman. "Union Democracy." in *Unions in Transition* (San Francisco: ICS Press, 1988).

Bernstein, Aaron. "Bad Connection at AT&T." *Business Week* (April 22, 1991), pp. 32–33.

Bernstein, Aaron. "Been Down So Long . . . but Unions May Ride Out the Recession." *Business Week* (January 14, 1991), pp. 30–31.

Bernstein, Aaron. "Busting Unions Can Backfire on the Bottom Line." *Business Week* (March 18, 1991), p. 108.

Bernstein, Aaron. "The Teamsters and the Mob: It May Really Be Over." *Business Week* (June 17, 1991), pp. 102–103.

Bernstein, Aaron, and Jim Bartimo. "Wrong Time for Scare Tactics?" *Business Week* (April 16, 1990), pp. 27–28.

Bethke, Art, R. Wayne Mondy, and Shane R. Premeaux. "Decertification: The Role of the First-Line Supervisor." *Supervisory Management,* 31 (February 1986), pp. 21–23.

Caruth, Don, and Harry N. Mills. "Working Toward Better Union Relations." *Supervisory Management,* 30 (February 1985), pp. 7–13.

Colford, Steven W. "Unions Flock to TV Ads." *Advertising Age,* 61 (September 10, 1990), p. 82.

"Court Sides with Unions." *Personnel,* 67 (June 1990), pp. 6–7.

Eubanks, Paula. "Employee Grievance Policy: Don't Discourage Complaints." *Hospitals,* 64 (December 20, 1990), pp. 36–37.

Galand, Susan B. "Why Democrats Still Want to Wear the Union Label." *Business Week* (March 5, 1990), p. 37.

Hoerr, John. "What Should Unions Do?" *Harvard Business Review,* 69 (May–June 1991), pp. 30–45.

Kelly, Kevin, and Aaron Bernstein. "Why United Is Putting Pilots on the Gravy Train." *Business Week* (April 29, 1991), p. 32.

Kilgour, John G. "The Odds on White-Collar Organizing." *Personnel,* 67 (August 1990), pp. 29–35.

Kirkpatrick, David. "The Union's Role as Co-Manager." *Fortune,* 121 (March 26, 1990), p. 37.

Koretz, Gene, and Celeste Whittaker. "More Picket Lines, Fewer Rank-And-Filers." *Business Week* (May 7, 1990), p. 24.

Lissy, William E. "Election of 'Financial Core' Union Membership." *Supervision,* 51 (September 1990), pp. 22–23.

Lissy, William E. "Management-Sponsored Employees' Committee Not Illegal." *Supervision,* 51 (April 1990), pp. 17–19.

Mondy, R. Wayne, and Shane R. Premeaux. "The Labor/Management Power Relationship Revisited." *Personnel Administrator,* 30 (May 1985), pp. 52–57.

Premeaux, Shane R., R. Wayne Mondy, and Art L. Bethke. "The Two-Tier Wage System." *Personnel Administrator,* 31 (November 1986), pp. 92–100.

Reynolds, Larry. "Management and Labor Draw the Picket Line." *Personnel,* 68 (March 1991), p. 15.

Reynolds, Larry. "Management-Labor Tensions Spell Union Busting." *Personnel,* 68 (March 1991), pp. 7–9.

Ritter, Anne. "Are Unions Worth the Bargain?" *Personnel,* 67 (February 1990), pp. 12–14.

Ritter, Anne. "The UAW Strikes Out at Nissan." *Personnel,* 66 (November 1989), pp. 5–6.

Sanyal, Rajib N. "An Empirical Analysis of the Unionization of Foreign Manufacturing Firms in the U.S." *Journal of International Business Studies,* 21 (First Quarter 1990), pp. 119–132.

Solomon, Charlene Marmer. "Nightmare at Nordstrom." *Personnel Journal,* 69 (September 1990), pp. 76–83.

Tidwell, Gary L. "The Supervisor's Role in a Union Election." *Personnel Journal,* 62 (August 1983), pp. 640–645.

Troy, Leo. "The Rise and Fall of American Trade Unions: The Labor Movement from FDR to RR." in *Unions in Transition* (San Francisco: ICS Press, 1988).

Voos, Paula B. "Does It Pay to Organize? Estimating Costs to Unions." *Monthly Labor Review,* 107 (June 1984), pp. 43–44.

White, Rudolph A. "Union Membership Rates for Manufacturing Employees by State, 1985–1987." *Economic Development Review,* 7 (Winter 1989), pp. 67–70.

Zalusky, John. "Labor Seeks Security, Not Bonuses." *Personnel,* 68 (January 1991), p. 13.

CHAPTER 16

COLLECTIVE BARGAINING

Chapter Objectives

1. Discuss the collective bargaining process, describe the role of the human resource manager in it, and explain the psychological aspects of collective bargaining.
2. Describe what both labor and management do as they prepare for negotiations.
3. Explain typical bargaining issues and the process of negotiating.
4. Identify and describe ways to overcome breakdowns in negotiations, and describe what is involved in ratifying and administering the agreement.
5. Discuss the future of collective bargaining.

Barbara Washington, the chief union negotiator, was meeting with company representatives on a new contract. Both the union team and management had been preparing for this encounter for a long time. Barbara's deep concern was whether union members would support a strike vote if one were called. Sales for the industry were generally down because of imports. In fact, there had even been some layoffs at competing firms. The union members' attitude could be described as "Get what you can for us, but don't rock the boat." She hoped, however, that skillful negotiating could win concessions from management.

In the first session, Barbara's team presented its demands to management. The team had determined that pay was the main issue, and a 20 percent increase spread over three years was demanded. Management countered by saying that since sales were down it could not afford to provide any pay raises. After much heated discussion, both sides agreed to reevaluate their positions and meet again in two days.

Barbara met with her negotiating team in private, and it decided to decrease the salary demand slightly. The team felt that the least they could accept was a 15 percent raise.

At the next meeting, Barbara presented the revised demands to management. They were not well received. Bill Thompson, the director of industrial relations, began by saying, "We cannot afford a pay increase in this contract, but we will make every attempt to ensure that no layoffs occur. Increasing wages at this time will virtually guarantee a reduction in the workforce."

Barbara's confidence collapsed. She knew that there was no way that the general membership was willing to accept layoffs and that a strike vote would be virtually impossible to obtain. She asked for a recess to review the new proposal.

Barbara is experiencing the negotiating crunch that has existed for several years in the United States. The power pendulum has swung in favor of management, making it very difficult for union negotiators to effectively bargain with management on certain issues, including pay increases.

We devote the first part of this chapter to the collective bargaining process and the human resource manager's role in it. We then describe global labor-management relations, the psychological aspects of collective bargaining, and preparing for negotiations. Next, we address bargaining issues, negotiating, and overcoming breakdowns in negotiations. We then discuss ratifying and administration of the agreement. We conclude the chapter with a look at the future of collective bargaining.

■ THE COLLECTIVE BARGAINING PROCESS

The collective bargaining process is fundamental to management-labor relations in the United States. Extensive collective bargaining activity occurs each year. In 1992, major collective bargaining agreements for about 2.7 million workers under 679 collective bargaining agreements were set to expire or reopen. Such agreements covering 1,000 or more workers account for one-third of the workers under all major agreements. Approximately 1.9 million of these workers are in private industry. A large proportion of these workers are involved in construction and telephone communication.[1]

During the 1980s, management had the power advantage in collective bargaining, and this is not expected to change in the foreseeable future. Management appeared to have achieved their collective bargaining goals in the 1980s. Among the unusual features of collective bargaining settlements that indicated increased management clout were the large proportion of workers receiving no wage increase, the large number of performance-based contracts negotiated, the increasing importance of lump-sum payments, the large proportion of workers who were not covered by cost-of-living adjustments, and in some industries, the establishment of multi-tiered compensation systems.[2] The number of strikes has also sharply declined. Some workers believe that if harm is done to the employer, their job opportunities will be reduced. Other employees are avoiding strikes because they do not want to lose wages. Others fear that management will replace them with nonstriking employees.[3]

Even though collective bargaining is widely practiced, there is no precise format of what to do or how to do it. In fact, diversity is probably the most prominent characteristic of collective bargaining in the United States. The collective bargaining process, in general, is shown in Figure 16-1. As you can see, both external and internal environmental factors can influence the process. For instance, the form of the bargaining structure can affect the

[1] Edward J. Wasilewski, Jr., "Collective Bargaining in 1992: Contract Talks and Other Activity," *Monthly Labor Review,* 115 (January 1992), p. 3.

[2] Fehmida Sleemi, "Higher Settlements in 1989 End Innovative Decade," *Monthly Labor Review,* 113 (May 1990), p. 3–4.

[3] Edward J. Wasilewski, Jr., "Collective Bargaining in 1992," p. 5.

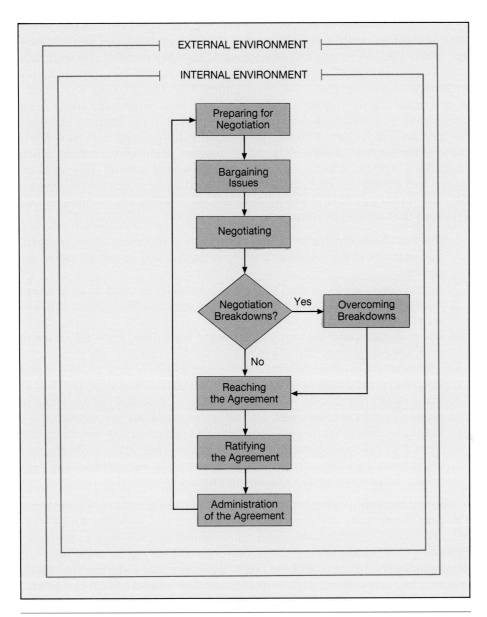

FIGURE 16-1 | The Collective Bargaining Process

conduct of collective bargaining. The four major types of structure are (1) one company dealing with a single union, (2) several companies dealing with a single union, (3) several unions dealing with a single company, and (4) several companies dealing with several unions. Most contract bargaining is carried out under the first type of structure. The process can become quite complicated when several companies and unions are involved in the same negotiations.

Another environmental factor influencing collective bargaining is the type of union-management relationship that exists. When a group of workers decide they want union representation, changes occur in the organization. In the absence of a union, management exercises virtually unlimited authority, except for the limitations imposed by the growing web of employee legal rights protection. As we noted in Chapter 15, these legal protections may well replace collective bargaining in the future.[4] However, for the present, when a union becomes the bargaining representative, management must change its style of decision making to include union bargaining agents. When employees take collective action, such as slowdowns and strikes, an adversarial relationship can be created, with varying degrees of conflict. Sloane and Witney list six types of union-management relations that may exist in an organization:

1. *Conflict.* Each challenges the other's actions and motivation; cooperation is nonexistent; uncompromising attitudes and union militancy are present.
2. *Armed truce.* Each views the other as antagonistic but tries to avoid head-on conflict; bargaining obligations and contract provisions are strictly interpreted.
3. *Power bargaining.* Management accepts the union; each side tries to gain advantage from the other.
4. *Accommodation.* Each tolerates the other in a "live and let live" atmosphere and attempts to reduce conflict without eliminating it.
5. *Cooperation.* Each side accepts the other, and both work together to resolve human resource and production problems as they occur.
6. *Collusion.* Both "cooperate" to the point of adversely affecting the legitimate interests of employees, other businesses in the industry, and the consuming public; this involves conniving to control markets, supplies, and prices illegally and/or unethically.[5]

The nature and quality of union-management relations vary over time. The first three types of relationships mentioned are generally unsatisfactory; collusion is unacceptable, and cooperation has been rare in the past. Typically, U.S. union-management relations appear to be some form of accommodation. In all likelihood, collective bargaining during the 1990s will be more cooperative, with joint economic survival being all important. Furthermore, a lessening of the adversarial relationships, and cooperation in areas never possible in the past is a real future prospect.[6]

The relationship between some companies and unions (such as Nissan and the UAW) is still quite adversarial, but more and more companies are forging cooperative relationships with their unions. Such a cooperative relationship exists between Xerox and the union. According to Arthur J. Zuckerman, manager of public relations programs, "Xerox has a partner-

[4] John Hoerr et al. "Beyond Unions," *Business Week* (July 8, 1985), p. 77.

[5] Arthur A. Sloane and Fred Witney, *Labor Relations,* 4th ed. (Englewood Cliffs, N.J.: Prentice-Hall, 1981), pp. 28–35.

[6] Abby Brown, "An Interview with Fritz Ihrig," *Personnel Administrator,* 31 (April 1986), p. 60.

ship with its unions. We are indivisible; they are not a separate part of the company." Approximately 3,000 manufacturing employees belong to the union at Xerox.[7] Ron Blackwell, the union representative for Xerox employees, commends the company's philosophy of cooperation. According to Blackwell, Xerox makes cooperation work. Management and employees at Xerox are bound together by a commitment to quality production. Xerox encourages employee participation in many ways. It solicits employee suggestions to uncover and solve problems and designs assembly lines so that individual employees can stop production without approval from a supervisor if they spot problems.[8]

In 1989, AT&T signed a contract with the union that was probably the most far-reaching and progressive one the company has ever had. Management was in favor of the spirit of the contract, which has dependent care as its central issue. The underlying principles of the contract are that women work as well as men, life exists before and after work hours, and employee families include children and older people who need help.[9] At the time, Burke Stinson, media relations manager at AT&T, stated that the company's willingness to listen to employees' concerns had positively affected employee-management relations. He believed that employees were more willing to listen to management because management was more willing to listen to them. However, recent contract negotiations between AT&T and the union could call into question management's commitment to its unionized employees.[10]

These practices empower employees, foster pride in them, and help assure joint economic survival. Since both groups agree that joint economic survival is most important, it is quite possible that past adversarial relationships will be replaced with cooperation. When both groups cooperate, everyone involved benefits.

Depending on the type of relationship encountered, the collective bargaining process may be relatively simple, or it may be a long, tense struggle. Veteran labor negotiator Robert J. Harding, a consulting firm executive, offers the following seven tips for successful collective bargaining:

1. Don't underestimate the importance of the first preparatory, non-adversarial meeting between labor and management representatives; use this opportunity to set the ground rules for future sessions.
2. Carefully document each meeting because accurate, well-organized notes can be quite useful in initial, and subsequent, contract negotiations.
3. If the CEO is well regarded by employees, consider including that person in the sessions.
4. Within the bounds of law and propriety, develop a personal profile of each member of the committee who will take part in the collective bargaining process.

---

[7] Anne Ritter, "Are Unions Worth the Bargain?" *Personnel,* 67 (February 1990), p. 14.

[8] *Ibid.,* p. 15.

[9] *Ibid.,* p. 14.

[10] *Ibid.,* p. 15.

5. Accept negotiators as peers; never underestimate them.
6. Maintain strong communications with those individuals who best know the people most affected by the contract and the issues being discussed.
7. If negotiations break down, consider federal mediation.[11]

Regardless of the complexity of the bargaining issues, the ability to reach agreement is the key to any successful negotiation. Success requires good communication skills and an understanding of these seven negotiation tips.

As we stated previously, the first step in the collective bargaining process is preparing for negotiations. This step is often extensive and ongoing for both union and management. After the issues to be negotiated have been determined, the two sides confer to reach a mutually acceptable contract. Although breakdowns in negotiations can occur, both labor and management have at their disposal tools and arguments that can be used to convince the other side to accept their views. Eventually, however, management and the union reach an agreement that defines the rules of the game for the duration of the contract. The next step is for the union membership to ratify the agreement.

Note the feedback loop from Administration of the Agreement to Preparing for Negotiation in Figure 16-1 on page 609. Collective bargaining is a continuous and dynamic process, and preparing for the next round of negotiations often begins the moment a contract is ratified.

■ THE HUMAN RESOURCE MANAGER'S ROLE

When a firm becomes unionized, the human resource manager's role tends to change rather significantly. In a unionized environment, the human resource manager must deal primarily with a union organizational structure consisting of union stewards and business agents rather than with individual workers. The human resource manager is the one who must live with the consequences of the contract, and therefore he or she should be an integral part of the ultimate resolution of contractual issues. According to veteran negotiator Fritz Ihrig, if the human resource manager is a strong and capable individual, that person should actually negotiate the contract.[12] Successful negotiators must have a thorough understanding of what is going on and an appreciation of the human element of the collective bargaining process.

Because the role of first-line supervisors is crucial, the human resource manager *must* maintain close contact with them before, during, and after collective bargaining. First-line supervisors administer the contract and know whether it is working well or if there are problems with it. Through an active and involved role, the human resource manager can limit prob-

---

[11] Abby Brown, "Labor Contract Negotiations: Behind the Scenes," *Labor Relations: Reports from the Firing Line* (Plano, Tex.: Business Publications, 1988), pp. 305–308.

[12] Abby Brown, "An Interview with Fritz Ihrig," p. 60.

lems such as animosity, fighting, games, role-playing, and a "stick it to them" mentality. Human resource managers who assume their proper roles in the collective bargaining process can make that process more beneficial to all concerned.

■ GLOBAL LABOR-MANAGEMENT RELATIONS

Before doing business in another country or entering into an international alliance, it is important to understand the characteristics of the industrial relations system in the country and for each partner. For example, contrast the following two situations: In the first situation, a German firm (where roughly 40 percent of the workforce is represented by unions domestically)[13] forms an alliance with a Swedish firm (where roughly 93 percent of the workforce is represented by a union domestically). Both partners are quite sympathetic to the workers' desires to be represented collectively; both partners accept the idea that the workers want to be associated with national or international unions. In the second situation, a Japanese firm (whose U.S. plant is nonunionized) forms an alliance with a U.S. company whose workers are members of a union. When asked for their most important concern about the partnership, the plant managers cited the fact that their alliance called for two companies with different industrial relations systems to work together.[14]

Obviously, the industrial relations issues that human resources professionals must address in these two situations are quite different. It is critically important to understand the implications of (and agree to abide by) a particular type of industrial relations system before consummating an international alliance. Regardless of the union or nonunion status of the country or alliance, it is imperative that the industrial relations issues that could decrease the productivity of the workforce be addressed prior to entering a country or forming an international alliance.[15]

■ PSYCHOLOGICAL ASPECTS OF COLLECTIVE BARGAINING

Prior to collective bargaining, both the management team and the union team have to prepare positions and accomplish certain tasks. Vitally important for those involved are the psychological aspects of collective bargaining. Psychologically, the collective bargaining process is often difficult because it is an adversarial situation and must be approached as such. It is

---

[13] Wayne F. Cascio and Manuel G. Serapio, Jr., "Human Resources Systems in an International Alliance: The Undoing of a Done Deal?" *Organizational Dynamics,* 19 (Winter 1991), pp. 72–73.

[14] *Ibid.*

[15] *Ibid.,* p. 73.

"a situation that is fundamental to law, politics, business, and government, because out of the clash of ideas, points of view, and interests come agreement, consensus, and justice."[16]

In effect, those involved in the collective bargaining process will be matching wits with the competition, will experience victory as well as defeat, and will ultimately resolve problems, resulting in a contract. The role of those who meet at the bargaining table "essentially involves the mobilization and management of aggression," in a manner that allows them to hammer out a collective bargaining agreement.[17] Because those involved must "mobilize and manage aggression" their personalities have a major impact on the negotiation process. The attitudes of those who will be negotiating have a direct effect on what can be accomplished and how quickly a mutually agreed-on contract can be finalized. Problems are compounded by differences in the experience and educational backgrounds of those involved in the negotiation process.[18] Finally, the longer, more involved, and intense the bargaining sessions are, the greater the psychological strain on all concerned will be.

Recent "scare tactics" have intensified the psychological pressures of collective bargaining. In order to break unions in the 1980s, management permanently replaced striking workers. In the past couple of years certain companies have placed advertisements and even hired permanent replacements during contract talks. According to a recent *Business Week* article by Bernstein and Bartimo, "This dramatically upped the ante, since employees knew that a decision to strike could cost them their jobs."[19] However, a recent NLRB ruling could limit the use of this tactic. In the past, employers replaced striking workers without taking a vote because the assumption was made that newly hired workers opposed the union. The NLRB recently ruled that replacement workers should be presumed to support the union.[20] If employers use a permanent-replacement threat and it does not work, it may become even harder for management to ease the tensions between labor and management.[21] Some unions, such as the UAW are reaching the bargaining table in a combative mood, all but stating that union members are quite willing to strike. One UAW negotiator viewed this approach as bringing all of the ingredients for disaster together.[22] As psychological pressures intensify, the gap between labor and management can easily widen, further compounding the problems of achieving mutual accommodation.

---

[16] Harry Levinson, "Stress at the Bargaining Table," *Labor Relations: Reports from the Firing Line* (Plano, Tex.: Business Publications, 1988), p. 310.

[17] *Ibid.*

[18] Gary N. Chaison and Mark S. Plovnick, "Is There a Collective Bargaining?" *California Management Review,* 28, no. 4, p. 116.

[19] Aaron Bernstein and Jim Bartimo, "Wrong Time for Scare Tactics?" *Business Week* (April 16, 1990), pp. 27–28.

[20] "HR Focus: Labor Relations: Court Sides with Unions," *Personnel,* 67 (June 1990), pp. 6–7.

[21] Aaron Bernstein and Jim Bartimo, "Wrong Time for Scare Tactics?" p. 28.

[22] Wendy Zellner, "All the Ingredients for Disaster Are There," *Business Week* (April 16, 1990), p. 28.

■ PREPARING FOR NEGOTIATIONS

Because of the complex issues facing labor and management today, the negotiating teams must carefully prepare for the bargaining sessions. Prior to meeting at the bargaining table, the negotiators should thoroughly know the culture, climate, history, present economic state, and wage and benefits structure of the organization and similar organizations.[23] Because the length of a typical labor agreement is three years, negotiators should develop a contract that is successful both now and in the future. This consideration should prevail for both management and labor, although it rarely does. During the term of an agreement, both sides usually discover contract provisions that need to be added, deleted, or modified. These items become proposals to be addressed in the next round of negotiations.

Bargaining issues can be divided into three categories: mandatory, permissive, and prohibited. **Mandatory bargaining issues** fall within the definition of wages, hours, and other terms and conditions of employment (see Table 16-1 on page 616). These issues generally have an immediate and direct effect on workers' jobs. A refusal to bargain in these areas is grounds for an unfair labor practice charge. **Permissive bargaining issues** may be raised, but neither side may insist that they be bargained over. For example, the union may want to bargain over health benefits for retired workers or union participation in establishing company pricing policies, which management may choose not to bargain over. **Prohibited bargaining issues** such as the closed shop are statutorily outlawed.

The union must continuously gather information regarding membership dissatisfaction. The union steward is normally in the best position to collect such data. Because stewards are usually elected by their peers, they should be well-informed regarding union members' attitudes. The union steward constantly funnels information up through the union's chain of command where the data are compiled and analyzed. Union leadership attempts to uncover any areas of dissatisfaction because the general union membership must approve any agreement before it becomes final. It would be foolish for union leaders to demand management concessions and have the members reject their proposals. Because they must be elected, union leaders will lose their positions if the demands they make of management do not represent the desires of the general membership.

Management also spends long hours preparing for negotiations. The many interrelated tasks that management must accomplish are presented in Figure 16-2 on page 617. In this example, the firm allows approximately six months to prepare for negotiations. All aspects of the current contracts are considered, including flaws that should be corrected. When preparing for negotiations, management should listen carefully to first-line supervisors. These individuals must administer the labor agreement on a daily basis and live with any error that management makes in negotiating the contract. An alert first-line supervisor is also able to inform upper management of the demands unions may plan to make during negotiations.

---

[23] Abby Brown, "An Interview with Fritz Ihrig," p. 56.

TABLE 16-1 | Mandatory Bargaining Issues

Wages	Price of meals provided by company
Hours	Group insurance—health, accident, life
Discharge	Promotions
Arbitration	Seniority
Paid holidays	Layoffs
Paid vacations	Transfers
Duration of agreement	Work assignments and transfers
Grievance procedure	No-strike clause
Layoff plan	Piece rates
Reinstatement of economic strikers	Stock purchase plan
Change of payment from hourly base to salary base	Workloads
Union security and checkoff of dues	Change of employee status to independent contractors
Work rules	Motor carrier—union agreement providing that carriers use own equipment before leasing outside equipment
Merit wage increase	
Work schedule	
Lunch periods	Overtime pay
Rest periods	Agency shop
Pension plan	Sick leave
Retirement age	Employer's insistence on clause giving arbitrator right to enforce award
Bonus payments	
Cancellation of seniority upon relocation of plant	Management rights clause
Discounts on company products	Plant closing
Shift differentials	Job posting procedures
Contract clause providing for supervisors keeping seniority in unit	Plant reopening
	Employee physical examination
Procedures for income tax withholding	Truck rentals—minimum rental to be paid by carriers to employee-owned vehicles
Severance pay	
Nondiscriminatory hiring hall	Arrangement for negotiation
Plant rules	Change in insurance carrier and benefits
Safety	Profit-sharing plan
Prohibition against supervisor doing unit work	Company houses
Superseniority for union stewards	Subcontracting
Partial plant closing	Production ceiling imposed by union
Hunting on employer's forest reserve where previously granted	
Plant closedown and relocation	
Change in operations resulting in reclassifying workers from incentive to straight time, or a cut in the workforce, or installation of cost-saving machinery	

Source: Reed Richardson, "Positive Collective Bargaining," Chapter 7.5 of *ASPA Handbook of Personnel and Industrial Relations,* pp. 7–121. Copyright © 1979 by The Bureau of National Affairs, Inc., Washington, D.C. Reprinted by permission.

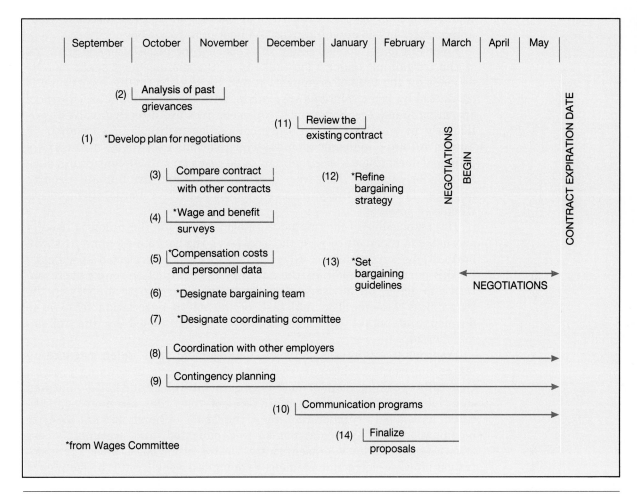

FIGURE 16-2 | An Example of Company Preparations for Negotiations

Source: Adapted from Ronald L. Miller, "Preparations for Negotiations,"
Personnel Journal, Vol. 57, p. 38. Copyright © January 1978. Reprinted with
permission.

Management also attempts periodically to obtain information regarding
employee attitudes. Surveys are often administered to workers to determine their feelings toward their jobs and job environment. When union and
management representatives sit down at the bargaining table, both sides
like to know as much as possible about employee attitudes.

Another part of preparation for negotiations involves identifying various
positions that both union and management will take as the negotiations
progress. Each usually takes an initial extreme position, representing the
conditions union or management would prefer. The two sides will likely
determine absolute limits to their offers or demands before a breakdown in
negotiations occurs. They also usually prepare fallback positions based on

combinations of issues. Preparations should be detailed because clear minds often do not prevail during the heat of negotiations.

Finally, a major consideration in preparing for negotiations is selection of the bargaining teams. The makeup of the management team usually depends on the type of organization and its size. Normally, bargaining is conducted by labor relations specialists, with the advice and assistance of operating managers. Sometimes, top executives are directly involved, particularly in smaller firms. Larger companies utilize staff specialists (a human resource manager or industrial relations executive), managers of principal operating divisions, and in some cases an outside consultant, such as a labor attorney. However, it is essential that the human resource manager become actively involved in the collective bargaining process whenever possible.

The responsibility for conducting negotiations for the union is usually entrusted to union officers. At the local level, the bargaining committee will normally be supplemented by rank-and-file members elected specifically for this purpose. In addition, the national union will often send a representative to act in an advisory capacity or even participate directly in the bargaining sessions. The real task of the union negotiating team is to develop and obtain solutions to the problems raised by the union's membership.

Traditional differences between management and union negotiating teams contribute additional friction to the collective bargaining process. Generally speaking, management negotiators are older and better educated than labor negotiators. From their point of view, they are more sophisticated, have a better understanding of the issues at hand, and are likely to be impatient with younger, not so well educated, and presumably less knowledgeable union representatives. On the other hand, labor representatives often perceive management as being less sensitive to the feelings of employees than to property rights and the realities of economic survival and future company growth.[24] As part of their preparation for collective bargaining, negotiators on both sides should fully appraise the makeup of the other team in terms of their strengths and weaknesses and bring this information to bear in the negotiations.

■ BARGAINING ISSUES

The document that emerges from the collective bargaining process is known as a labor agreement or contract. It regulates the relationship between employer and employees for a specified period of time. Each agreement is unique, and there is no standard or universal model. Despite many dissimilarities, certain topics are included in virtually all labor agreements. These include recognition, management rights, union security, compensation and benefits, grievance procedure, employee security, and job-related factors.

---

[24] Harry Levinson, "Stress at the Bargaining Table," p. 312.

Recognition

This section usually appears at the beginning of the labor agreement. Its purpose is to identify the union that is recognized as the bargaining representative and to describe the bargaining unit—that is, the employees for whom the union speaks. A typical recognition section might read as follows:

> The XYZ Company recognizes the ABC Union as the sole and exclusive representative of the bargaining unit employees for the purpose of collective bargaining with regard to wages, hours, and other conditions of employment.

Management Rights

A section that is often, but not always, written into the labor agreement spells out the rights of management. If no such section is included, management may reason that it retains control of all topics not described as bargainable in the contract. The precise content of the management rights section will vary by industry, company, and union. When included, management rights generally involve three areas:

1. Freedom to select the business objectives of the company.
2. Freedom to determine the uses to which the material assets of the enterprise will be devoted.
3. Power to discipline for cause.[25]

In a brochure it publishes for all its first-line supervisors, AT&T describes management's rights when dealing with the union, including the following:

> You should remember that management has all such rights except those restricted by law or by contract with the union. You either make these decisions or carry them out through contact with your people. Some examples of these decisions and actions are:
>
> - To determine what work is to be done and where, when, and how it is to be done.
> - To determine the number of employees who will do the work.
> - To supervise and instruct employees in doing the work.
> - To correct employees whose work performance or personal conduct fails to meet reasonable standards. This includes administering discipline.
> - To recommend hiring, dismissing, upgrading, or downgrading of employees.
> - To recommend employees for promotion to management.[26]

---

[25] Edwin F. Beal and James P. Begin, *The Practice of Collective Bargaining,* 6th ed. (Homewood, Ill.: Richard D. Irwin, 1982), pp. 295–298.

[26] *Management/Employee/Union Relations* (Dallas: Southwestern Bell Telephone Company, December 1971), p. 3.

Management rights in collective bargaining could be somewhat restricted by a June 16, 1991, ruling by the NLRB stating that companies must bargain with workers prior to relocating their business operations. The new standard directs employers to bargain over proposed relocations unless they can prove (1) that labor costs were not a factor in the relocation decision, or (2) that if labor costs were a consideration, other costs of staying were greater than any wage concessions the union could offer. If the union offered concessions that equaled the size of the financial gains of moving, employers have a bargaining obligation. However, if the relocation involves "a basic change in the nature of the employer's operation," employers do not have to bargain over relocation.[27]

Union Security

Union security is typically one of the first items negotiated in a collective bargaining agreement. The objective of union security provisions is to ensure that the union continues to exist and perform its functions. A strong union security provision makes it easier for the union to enroll and retain members. We describe some basic forms of union security clauses in the following paragraphs.

Closed Shop. A **closed shop** is an arrangement whereby union membership is a prerequisite to employment. Such provisions are generally illegal in the United States.

Union Shop. As we mentioned in Chapter 15, a **union shop** arrangement requires that all employees become members of the union after a specified period of employment (the legal minimum is thirty days) or after a union shop provision has been negotiated. Employees must remain members of the union as a condition of employment. The union shop is generally legal in the United States, except in states that have right-to-work laws.

Maintenance of Membership. Employees who are members of the union at the time the labor agreement is signed or who later voluntarily join must continue their memberships until the termination of the agreement, as a condition of employment. This form of recognition is also prohibited in most states that have right-to-work laws.

Agency Shop. An **agency shop** provision does not require employees to join the union; however, the labor agreement requires, as a condition of employment, that each nonunion member of the bargaining unit "pay the union the equivalent of membership dues as a kind of tax, or service charge,

---

[27] "NLRB Requires Firms to Bargain Before Relocating," *The Wall Street Journal* (June 17, 1991), p. A12.

in return for the union acting as the bargaining agent." [28] The agency shop is outlawed in most states that have right-to-work laws.

Exclusive Bargaining Shop. Thirteen of the twenty-one states having right-to-work laws allow only exclusive bargaining shop provisions. Under this form of recognition, the company is legally bound to deal with the union that has achieved recognition, but employees are not obligated to join or maintain membership in the union or to financially contribute to it.

Open Shop. An open shop describes the absence of union security rather than its presence. The **open shop,** strictly defined, is employment that has equal terms for union members and nonmembers alike. Under this arrangement, no employee is required to join or financially contribute to the union.

Dues Checkoff. Another type of security that unions attempt to achieve is the checkoff of dues. A checkoff agreement may be used in addition to any of the previously mentioned "shop" agreements. Under the **checkoff of dues** provision, the company agrees to withhold union dues from members' paychecks and to forward the money directly to the union. Because of provisions in the Taft-Hartley Act, each union member must voluntarily sign a statement authorizing this deduction. Dues checkoff is important to the union because it eliminates much of the expense, time, and hassle of collecting dues from each member every pay period or once a month.

Compensation and Benefits

This section typically constitutes a large portion of most labor agreements. The importance of compensation and benefits is illustrated in a survey of union members. Those surveyed ranked pay, pensions, and benefits as the second, third, and fifth most important compensation-related items.[29] Virtually any item that can affect compensation and benefits may be included in labor agreements. Some of the items frequently covered include the following:

- *Wage rate schedule.* The base rates to be paid each year of the contract for each job are included in this section. Figure 16-3 on page 622 illustrates the average annual wage adjustments provided by major collective bargaining agreements in private industry from 1980 to 1989. The figure shows the first-year average increase and the average increase over the life of the contract.[30] At times, unions are able to obtain a cost-of-living allowance (COLA) or escalator clause in the contract in order to protect

---

[28] Edwin F. Beal and James P. Begin, *The Practice of Collective Bargaining,* p. 286.

[29] Shane R. Premeaux, R. Wayne Mondy, and Art L. Bethke, "Decertification: Fulfilling Unions' Destiny?" *Personnel Journal,* 32 (June 1987), p. 148.

[30] Fehmida Sleemi, "Higher Settlements in 1989 End Innovative Decade," pp. 3–4.

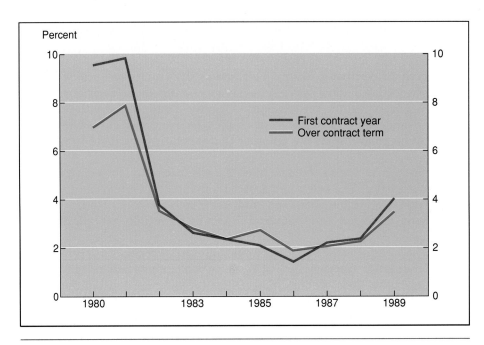

Percent

First contract year
Over contract term

FIGURE 16-3 | Average Annual Wage Rate Adjustments

Source: Fehmida Sleemi, "Higher Settlements in 1989 End Innovative Decade," *Monthly Labor Review,* 113 (May 1990), p. 4.

the purchasing power of employees' earnings. These clauses are generally related to the Consumer Price Index (CPI) prepared by the Bureau of Labor Statistics.

- *Overtime and premium pay.* Provisions covering hours of work, overtime, and premium pay, such as shift differentials, are included in this section.
- *Jury pay.* Some firms pay an employee's entire salary when he or she is serving jury duty. Others pay the difference between jury pay and the compensation that would have been earned. The procedure covering jury pay is typically stated in the contract.
- *Layoff or severance pay.* The amount that employees in various jobs and/or seniority levels will be paid if they are laid off or terminated is presented in this section.
- *Holidays.* The holidays to be recognized and the amount of pay that a worker will receive if he or she has to work on a holiday are specified. In addition, the pay procedure for times when a holiday falls on a worker's nominal day off is provided.
- *Vacation.* This section spells out the amount of vacation that a person may take, based on seniority. Any restrictions as to when the vacation may be taken are also stated.
- *Family care.* This is a benefit that has been included in recent collective bargaining agreements. As previously discussed, AT&T and the Communications Workers of America (CWA) negotiated a contract that had landmark family-care provisions.

Grievance Procedure

A portion of most labor agreements is devoted to a grievance procedure. It contains the means whereby employees can voice dissatisfaction with and appeal specific management actions. Also included in this section are the procedures for disciplinary action by management and the termination procedure that must be followed. We devote a portion of Chapter 18 to disciplinary action and the grievance process.

Employee Security

This section of the labor agreement establishes the procedures that cover job security for individual employees. According to a nationwide survey, employee security was the prime concern of union members.[31] Security continues to be a major concern for employees. Recent labor negotiations have dramatically focused on the security issue. As mentioned earlier, labor agreements with the "Big Three" automakers[32] and the Xerox Corporation included provisions to protect employee job security.[33] Seniority and grievance handling procedures are the key topics related to employee security. Seniority is determined by the amount of time that an employee has worked in various capacities with the firm. Seniority may be companywide, by division, by department, or by job. Agreement on seniority is important because the person with the most seniority, as defined in the labor agreement, is typically the last to be laid off and the first to be recalled. The seniority system also provides a basis for promotion decisions. When qualifications are met, employees with the greatest seniority will likely be considered first for promotion to higher level jobs.

Job-Related Factors

Many of the rules governing employee actions on the job are also included. Some of the more important factors are company work rules, work standards, and rules related to safety. This section varies, depending on the nature of the industry and the product manufactured. Work rules are vitally important to both employers and employees, but companies tend to desire less restrictive work rules.

■ NEGOTIATING THE AGREEMENT

There is no way to ensure speedy and mutually acceptable results from negotiations. At best, the parties can attempt to create an atmosphere that will lend itself to steady progress and productive results. For example, the

---

[31] Anne Ritter, "Are Unions Worth the Bargain?" p. 14.
[32] Wendy Zellner, "All the Ingredients for Disaster Are There," p. 28.
[33] Anne Ritter, "Are Unions Worth the Bargain?" p. 14.

two negotiating teams usually meet at an agreed-on neutral site, such as a hotel. It is generally important that a favorable relationship be established early in order to avoid "eleventh hour" bargaining.[34] It is equally important that union and management negotiators strive to develop and maintain clear and open lines of communication. Collective bargaining is a problem-solving activity, so good communication is essential to its success. Negotiations should be conducted in the privacy of the conference room, not in the news media. If the negotiators feel that publicity is necessary, joint releases to the media may avoid unnecessary conflict.

The negotiating phase of collective bargaining begins with each side presenting its initial demands. Because a collective bargaining settlement can be expensive for a firm, the cost of various proposals should be estimated as accurately as possible. Some changes can be quite expensive, and others cost little or nothing, but the cost of the various proposals being considered must always be carefully deliberated. The term *negotiating* suggests a certain amount of give-and-take, the purpose of which is to lower the other side's expectations. The union will bargain to upgrade their members' economic and working conditions. The company will negotiate to maintain or enhance profitability. One of the most costly components of any collective bargaining agreement is a wage increase provision. An example of the negotiation of a wage increase is shown in Figure 16-4.

In this example, labor initially demands a $0.40 per hour increase. Management counters with an offer of only $0.10 per hour. Both labor and management—as expected—reject each other's demand. Plan B calls for labor to lower its demand to a $0.30 per hour increase. Management counters with an offer of $0.20. The positions in Plan B are feasible to both sides, as both groups are in the bargaining zone. Wages within the bargaining zone are those that management and labor can both accept—in this case, an increase of between $0.20 and $0.30 per hour. The exact amount will be determined by the power of the bargaining unit and the skills of the negotiators.

The realities of negotiations are not for the weak of heart and at times are similar to a high-stakes poker game. A certain amount of bluffing and raising of the ante takes place in many negotiations. The ultimate bluff for the union would be when a negotiator says, "If our demands are not met, we are prepared to strike." Management's version of this bluff would be to threaten a lockout. We will discuss each of these tactics later; utilizing them is a form of power politics. The party with the greater leverage can expect to extract the most concessions. In recent years, management has gained negotiating power, with 84 percent of union members surveyed believing that management now has the upper hand in labor negotiations.[35]

Even though one party in the negotiating process may appear to possess the greater power, negotiators often take care to keep the other

---

[34] Eleventh hour bargaining refers to last-minute settlement attempts just prior to the expiration date of an existing agreement. Failure to reach agreement in this manner frequently results in a strike.

[35] R. Wayne Mondy and Shane R. Premeaux, "The Labor/Management Power Relationship Revisited," *Personnel Administrator,* 30 (May 1985), p. 55.

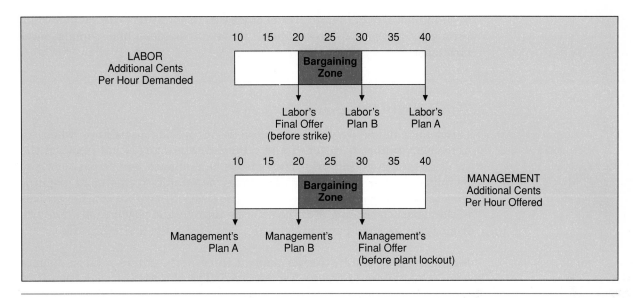

FIGURE 16-4 | An Example of Negotiating a Wage Increase

side from losing face. They recognize that the balance of power may switch rapidly. By the time the next round of negotiations occurs, the pendulum may be swinging back in favor of the other side. Even when management appears to have the upper hand, it may make minor concessions that will allow the labor leader to claim gains for the union. Management may demand that workers pay for grease rags that are lost (assuming that the loss of these rags has become excessive). In order to obtain labor's agreement to this demand, management may agree to provide new uniforms for the workers if the cost of these uniforms would be less than the cost of lost rags. Thus labor leaders, although forced to concede to management's demand, could show the workers that they have obtained a concession from management.

As we mentioned previously, each side usually does not expect to obtain all the demands presented in its first proposal. However, management must remember that a concession may be difficult to reverse in future negotiations. For instance, if management agreed to provide dental benefits, withdrawing these benefits in the next round of negotiations would be difficult. Labor, on the other hand, can lose a demand and continue to bring it up in the future. Demands that the union does not expect to receive when they are first made are known as **beachhead demands.**

■ BREAKDOWNS IN NEGOTIATIONS

At times negotiations break down, even though both labor and management may sincerely want to arrive at an equitable contract settlement. Several means of removing roadblocks may be used in order to get negotiations moving again. Breakdowns in negotiations can be overcome through third-party intervention, union strategies, and management strategies.

Third-Party Intervention

Often an outside person can intervene to provide assistance when an agreement cannot be reached and a breakdown occurs—that is, when the two sides reach an impasse. The reasons behind each party's position may be quite rational. Or the breakdown may be related to emotional disputes that tend to become distorted during the heat of negotiations. Regardless of the cause, something must be done to continue the negotiations. The two basic types of third-party intervention are mediation and arbitration.

Mediation. In **mediation,** a neutral third party enters a labor dispute when a bargaining impasse has occurred. The objective of mediation is to persuade the parties to resume negotiations and reach a settlement. A mediator has no power to force a settlement but can help in the search for solutions, make recommendations, and work to open blocked channels of communication. Successful mediation depends to a substantial degree on the tact, diplomacy, patience, and perseverance of the mediator. The mediator's fresh insights are used to get discussions going again.

Arbitration. In **arbitration,** a dispute is submitted to an impartial third party for a binding decision. Arbitration is very much a part of many human resource managers' jobs. There are two principal types of union-management disputes: rights disputes and interests disputes. Those that involve disputes over the interpretation and application of the various provisions of an existing contract are referred to as rights arbitration. This type of arbitration is used in settling grievances. Grievance arbitration is common in the United States and is discussed in Chapter 18. The other type of arbitration, interest arbitration, involves disputes over the terms of proposed collective bargaining agreements. In the private sector, the use of interest arbitration as an alternative procedure for impasse resolution is not a common practice. Unions and employers rarely agree to submit the basic terms of a contract (such as wages, hours, and working conditions) to a neutral party for disposition. They prefer to rely on collective bargaining and the threat of economic pressure (such as strikes and lockouts) to decide these issues.[36]

In the public sector, most governmental jurisdictions prohibit their employees from striking. As a result, interest arbitration is used to a greater extent than in the private sector. Although there is no uniform application of this method, fourteen states have legislation permitting the use of interest arbitration to settle unresolved issues for public employees. In a num-

---

[36] Raymond A. Smardon, "Arbitration Is No Bargain," *Nation's Business* (October 1974), pp. 80–83.

ber of states, compulsory arbitration of interest items is required at various jurisdictional levels.[37] A procedure used in the public sector is final-offer arbitration, which has two basic forms: package selection and issue-by-issue selection. In package selection, the arbitrator must select one party's entire offer on all issues in dispute. In issue-by-issue selection, the arbitrator examines each issue separately and chooses one or the other party's final offer on each issue.[38]

Sources of Mediators and Arbitrators

The principal organization involved in mediation efforts, other than some state and local agencies, is the Federal Mediation and Conciliation Service (FMCS). The FMCS was established as an independent agency by the Taft-Hartley Act in 1947. Either or both parties involved in negotiations can seek the assistance of the FMCS, or the agency can offer its help if it feels that the situation warrants this. Federal law requires that the party wishing to change a contract must give notice of this intention to the other party sixty days prior to the expiration of a contract. If no agreement has been reached thirty days prior to the expiration date, the FMCS must be notified.

In arbitration, the disputants are free to select any person as their arbitrator, so long as they agree on the selection. Most commonly, however, they make a request for an arbitrator to either the American Arbitration Association (AAA) or the FMCS. The AAA is a nonprofit organization with offices in many cities. Both the AAA and the FMCS maintain lists of arbitrators. Only people who can show, through references, experience in labor-management relations and acceptance by both labor and management as neutrals are selected for inclusion on these lists.[39]

Union Strategies for Overcoming Negotiation Breakdowns

There are times when a union believes that it must exert extreme pressure to get management to agree to its bargaining demands. Strikes and boycotts are the primary means that the union may use to overcome breakdowns in negotiations.

Strikes. When union members refuse to work in order to exert pressure on management in negotiations, their action is referred to as a **strike.** A strike halts production, resulting in lost customers and revenue, which the union hopes will force management to submit to its terms.

---

[37] Benjamin J. Taylor and Fred Witney, *Labor Relations Law,* 4th ed. (Englewood Cliffs, N.J.: Prentice-Hall, 1983), pp. 652–653.

[38] Robert E. Allen and Timothy J. Keaveny, *Contemporary Labor Relations* (Reading, Mass.: Addison-Wesley, 1983), pp. 558–559.

[39] Donald Austin Woolf, "Arbitration in One Easy Lesson: A Review of Criteria Used in Arbitration Awards," *Personnel,* 55 (September–October 1978), p. 76.

The timing of a strike is important in determining its effectiveness. An excellent time is when business is thriving and the demand for the firm's goods or services is expanding. However, the union might be hard-pressed to obtain major concessions from a strike if the firm's sales are down and it has built up a large inventory. In this instance, the company would not be severely damaged.

Contrary to many opinions, unions prefer to use the strike only as a last resort. In recent years, many union members have been even more reluctant to strike because of the fear of being replaced. The Supreme Court ruled in 1989 that when a union goes on strike and the company hires replacements, they do not have to lay off these individuals at the end of the strike. Even with the threat of replacement looming and union membership declining, organized labor was involved in fifty-one major strikes in 1989, up from a record low in 1988 of only forty strikes.[40]

Strikes are extremely expensive not only for the employer, but also for the union and its members. A union's treasury is often depleted by payment of strike benefits to its members. In addition, members suffer because they aren't receiving their nominal pay. Although strike benefits help, union members certainly cannot maintain a normal standard of living on them because they are minimal. Sometimes during negotiations (especially at the beginning) the union may want to strengthen its negotiating position by taking a strike vote. Members often give overwhelming approval to a strike. This vote does not necessarily mean that there will be a strike, only that the union leaders now have the authority to call one if negotiations reach an impasse. A favorable strike vote can add a sense of urgency to efforts to reach an agreement.[41]

Successful passage of a strike vote has additional implications for union members. Virtually every national union's constitution contains a clause requiring the members to support and participate in a strike if one is called. If a union member fails to comply with this requirement, he or she can be fined. Thus union members place themselves in jeopardy if they cross a picket line without the consent of the union. Fines may be as high as 100 percent of wages for as long as union pickets remain outside the company. However, the Supreme Court has ruled that an employee on strike may resign from the union during a strike and avoid being punished by the union. More subtle measures, such as sickouts and work slowdowns, have been used successfully by union members in order to avoid the impact of a strike on the membership and still bring pressure on the company to meet union demands.

Boycotts. The boycott is another of labor's weapons to get management to agree to its demands. A **boycott** involves an agreement by union members to refuse to use or buy the firm's products. A boycott

---

[40] Gene Koretz and Celeste Whittaker, "More Picket Lines, Fewer Rank-And-Filers," *Business Week* (May 7, 1990), p. 24.

[41] Edwin F. Beal and James P. Begin, *The Practice of Collective Bargaining,* pp. 221–222.

exerts economic pressure on management, and the effect often lasts much longer than that of a strike. Once shoppers change buying habits, their behavior will likely continue long after the boycott has ended. At times, significant pressures can be exerted on a business when union members, their families, and friends refuse to purchase the firm's products and encourage the public not to patronize the firm. This approach is especially effective when the products are sold at retail outlets and are easily identifiable by brand name. For instance, the decade-old boycott against Adolph Coors Company, which ended in the summer of 1987, was effective because the product, beer, was directly associated with the company.[42] The practice of a union attempting to encourage third parties (such as suppliers and customers) to stop doing business with the firm is known as a **secondary boycott.** This type of boycott was declared illegal by the Taft-Hartley Act.

Management's Strategies for Overcoming Negotiation Breakdowns

Management may also use various strategies to encourage unions to come back to the bargaining table. One form of action that is somewhat analogous to a strike is called a lockout. In a **lockout,** management keeps employees out of the workplace and may run the operation with management personnel and/or temporary replacements. Unable to work, the employees do not get paid. Although the lockout is used rather infrequently, the fear of a lockout may bring labor back to the bargaining table. A lockout is particularly effective when management is dealing with a weak union, when the union treasury is depleted, or when the business has excessive inventories.

Another course of action that a company can take if the union goes on strike is to operate the firm by placing management and nonunion workers in the striking workers' jobs. The type of industry involved has considerable effect on the impact of this maneuver. If the firm is not labor intensive and if maintenance demands are not high, as at a petroleum refinery or a chemical plant, this practice may be quite effective. When it is utilized, management will likely attempt to show how production actually increases with the use of nonunion employees. For example, unionized employees at Southwestern Bell Telephone Company went on strike, and the company continued to provide virtually uninterrupted service to consumers. At times management personnel will actually live in the plant and have food and other necessities delivered to them.

Another way management can continue operating a firm during a strike is to hire replacements for the strikers. Hiring replacements on either a temporary or a permanent basis is legal when the employees are engaged in an economic strike—that is, one that is part of a collective bargaining

---

[42] Sandra Atchison and Aaron Bernstein, "A Silver Bullet for the Union Drive at Coors?" *Business Week* (July 11, 1988), p. 61.

dispute. However, a company that takes these courses of action risks inviting violence and creating bitterness among its employees, which may adversely affect the firm's performance long after the strike has ended.

■ RATIFYING THE AGREEMENT

Most collective bargaining leads to an agreement without a breakdown in negotiations or disruptive actions. Typically, agreement is reached before the current contract expires. After the negotiators have reached a tentative agreement on all contract terms, they prepare a written agreement covering those terms, complete with the effective and termination dates. The approval process for management is often easier than for labor. The president or CEO has usually been briefed regularly on the progress of negotiations. Any difficulty that might have stood in the way of obtaining approval has probably already been resolved with top management by the negotiators.

However, the approval process is more complex for the union. Until a majority of members voting in a ratification election approve it, the proposed agreement is not final. At times, union members reject the proposal and a new round of negotiations must begin. In recent years, approximately 10 percent of all tentative agreements have been rejected when presented to the union membership. Many of these rejections might not have occurred if union negotiators had been better informed of the desires of the membership.

■ ADMINISTRATION OF THE AGREEMENT

Negotiating, as it relates to the total collective bargaining process, may be likened to the tip of an iceberg. It is the visible phase, the part that makes the news. The larger and perhaps more important part of collective bargaining is administration of the agreement, which is seldom viewed by the public.[43] The agreement establishes the union-management relationship for the duration of the contract. Usually, neither party can change the contract's language until the expiration date, except by mutual consent. However, the main problem encountered in contract administration is uniform interpretation and application of the contract's terms. Administering the contract is a day-to-day activity. Ideally, the aim of both management and the union is to make the agreement work to the benefit of all concerned. Often, this is not an easy task.

Management is primarily responsible for explaining and implementing the agreement. This process should begin with meetings or training sessions not only to point out significant features but also to provide a clause-by-clause analysis of the contract. First-line supervisors in particular need to know their responsibilities and what to do when disagreements arise.

---

[43] Harold W. Davey, *Contemporary Collective Bargaining,* 3rd ed. (Englewood Cliffs, N.J.: Prentice-Hall, 1972), p. 141.

Additionally, supervisors and middle managers should be encouraged to notify top management of any contract modifications or new provisions required for the next round of negotiations.

The human resource manager plays a key role in the day-to-day administration of the contract. He or she gives advice on matters of discipline, works to resolve grievances, and helps first-line supervisors establish good working relationships within the terms of the agreement. As we mentioned previously, when a firm is unionized, the HRM function tends to change rather significantly, and it may even be divided into separate human resource and industrial relations departments. The Bendix Corporation provides an excellent example of this separation of activities. The company has both a vice-president of human resources and a vice-president of industrial relations (see Figure 16-5 below and Figure 16-6 on page 632). In situations such as this, the vice-president of human resources may perform all human resource management tasks with the exception of industrial relations. The vice-president of industrial relations would most likely deal with all union-related matters. As one vice-president of industrial relations stated:

> My first challenge is, wherever possible, to keep the company union-free and the control of its operations in the hands of corporate management at all levels. Where unions represent our employees, the problem becomes one of negotiating collective bargaining agreements which our company can live with, administering these labor agreements with the company's interests paramount

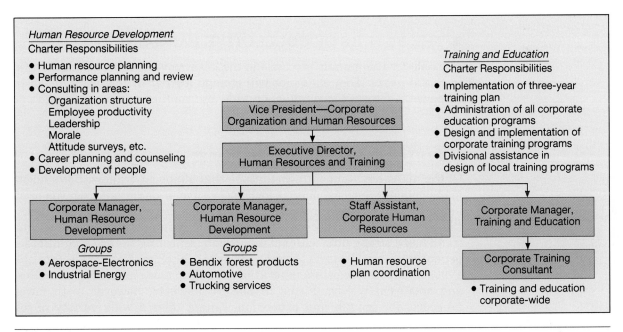

FIGURE 16-5 | The Organization of the Human Resource Department at Bendix Corporation

Source: Bendix Corporation.

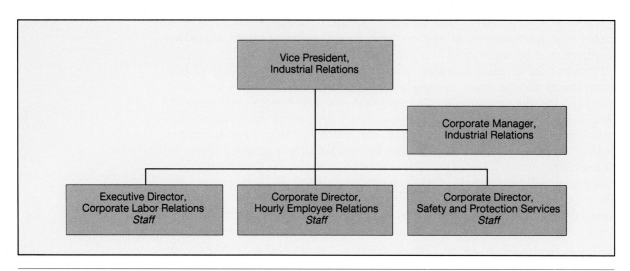

FIGURE 16-6 | The Corporate Industrial Relations Department at Bendix Corporation by Functional Responsibility

Source: Bendix Corporation.

(consistent with good employee relations), and trying to solve all grievances arising under the labor agreement short of their going to arbitration, without giving away the store.

■ THE FUTURE OF COLLECTIVE BARGAINING

The collective bargaining process and the labor movement have both changed in recent years. They no doubt will change further in the years ahead in response to forces of varying magnitude and conflicting perspectives.

Industrial and Occupational Change

Of the many environmental conditions that shape an organization's labor-management relations, none is more pervasive or dominant than the market for the firm's goods or services and its own labor market.[44] In the 1980s, the trend was toward increased competition within product markets. This trend has a strong international dimension, reflecting the growing interdependence of world markets and will, in all likelihood, continue into the 1990s. Competition fosters innovation, opens up new market opportunities, and creates new jobs. Firms in mature markets, however, with fewer prospects for growth and expansion, cannot offer a wide variety of job

---

[44] Thomas A. Kochan and Thomas A. Barocci, *Human Resource Management and Labor Relations* (Boston: Little, Brown, 1985), pp. 528–529.

HRM In Action

I think I might have messed up this morning," said the maintenance supervisor, Carlos Chavez, to Doug Williams, the industrial relations manager. "One of the workers in my section wasn't doing the job exactly according to specs, and I blew up and told him to hit the road. Five minutes later the union steward was in the office reading me the riot act. She said something like situations such as this are covered in our contract and that I was violating it. I had never spoken to the worker before about that particular offense, and the steward said the contract called for both oral and written warnings before termination."

How would you respond?

opportunities. In such situations, employers and employees alike need to concern themselves with career transitions, job losses, and organizational restructuring.

Historically, unions have had their greatest success in the manufacturing, mining, transportation, and construction industries. With the relative decline in importance of these industries and the relative growth in importance of service industries, union membership has decreased. Major increases in employment have taken place in wholesale and retail trades; finance and insurance; general service industries; and federal, state, and local government. However, with the exception of government, these industries have had low union membership in the past.[45]

The pattern of employment by occupation has also changed markedly over time. Major changes in white-collar occupations include increases in the number of professional and clerical employees. In blue-collar occupations, the proportion of operative employees increased through 1950; then a long-term decline in the use of laborers and an increase in service occupations occurred.[46] It is also interesting to note that between 1955 and 1984 a larger proportion of industrial workers were assigned to nonproduction jobs.[47] The shift toward more professional, service, and white-collar occupations suggests that future employees may well have different expectations of their work. Not only may labor need to rethink its organizing strategy, but management also needs to sharpen its managerial skills in negotiating and team building.

---

[45] David A. Dilts and Clarence R. Deitsch, *Labor Relations* (New York: Macmillan, 1983), p. 363.

[46] John A. Fossum, *Labor Relations,* 3rd ed. (Plano, Tex.: Business Publications, 1985), pp. 472–473.

[47] *Ibid.,* pp. 475–477.

In addition, the composition of the labor force will change dramatically in the future. New entrants in the labor force from 1985 to the year 2000 are expected to be 15 percent U.S. born white men, 42 percent U.S. born white women, 7 percent U.S. born nonwhite men, 13 percent U.S. born non-white women, 13 percent immigrant men, and 10 percent immigrant women.[48] Union leadership will need to redefine organizing strategies to attract those who will account for future growth in the U.S. employment sector.

Multinational Corporations and Foreign Competition

Unions often point to multinational corporations as an important cause of U.S. economic problems, especially unemployment. Many companies have located part or all of their operations outside the United States to take advantage of lower labor and material costs and favorable tax laws. Investment funds have been diverted to foreign operations, costing the U.S. economy jobs.[49] However, Japanese and European firms have invested significantly in U.S. marketing and manufacturing, which has created new jobs here in the United States. As these firms hire American workers, some interesting collective bargaining situations will likely be created.

Foreign competition has had major impacts on employment in several U.S. industries already. The shoe, apparel, auto, steel, and rubber industries have lost jobs, and their remaining employees have also felt the effects at the bargaining table in terms of wage and work-rule concessions.[50]

If predictions are accurate, Mexico will dramatically alter the nature of business in North America. Thousands of American producers, from small manufacturers to global giants like the Eastman Kodak Company, are pouring into Mexico for low-cost labor.[51] In the near future, Mexico may become the most popular location for U.S. manufacturers who are faced with global competition and pricing pressures. One of the major reasons for the move across the border is Mexico's wage structure. Figure 16-7 compares Mexico's wages to those of Singapore, South Korea, Taiwan, and the United States.

It is evident from the information in this figure that wages in Mexico are extremely low. Cheap labor, combined with open markets and a government that seems capable of delivering both political and economic security, could mean that Mexico will be one of the world's best places to do business. According to Kodak President Donald F. Spielex, "By 2000, I see Mexico as being a Korea, but with an even wider industrial base."[52] These changes in Mexico may dramatically impact domestic unionism and the nature of collective bargaining in the United States.

---

[48] Bruce Nussbaum, "Needed: Human Capital," *Business Week* (September 19, 1988), p. 103.

[49] David A. Dilts and Clarence R. Deitsch, *Labor Relations,* pp. 364–365.

[50] John A. Fossum, *Labor Relations,* pp. 472–473.

[51] Stephen Baker, Elizabeth Weener, and Amy Borrus, "Mexico: A New Economic Era," *Business Week* (November 12, 1990), p. 103.

[52] *Ibid,* p. 104.

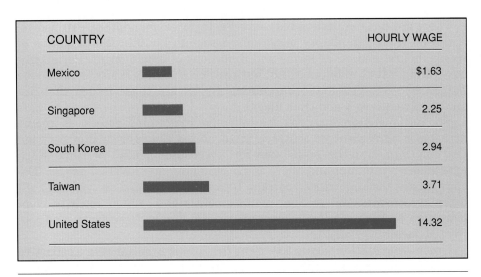

COUNTRY	HOURLY WAGE
Mexico	$1.63
Singapore	2.25
South Korea	2.94
Taiwan	3.71
United States	14.32

FIGURE 16-7 | International Hourly Wages

Source: Bureau of Labor Statistics.

SUMMARY

Collective bargaining is fundamental to management-labor relations in the United States. Labor and management go through periods in which one has the power to dictate the majority of terms to the other party. During the foreseeable future, management is expected to maintain the power advantage in collective bargaining.

The structure of collective bargaining can affect how it is conducted. The four major types of structure are (1) one company dealing with a single union, (2) several companies dealing with a single union, (3) several unions dealing with a single company, and (4) several companies dealing with several unions. Another environmental factor influencing collective bargaining is the current union-management relationship. It may allow the collective bargaining process to be relatively simple, or it may cause a long, tense struggle.

When a firm becomes unionized, the role of human resource management tends to change rather significantly. In major corporations in which the large majority of the operative employees belong to unions, the HRM function may even be divided into separate human resource and industrial relations departments. The human resource manager must maintain contact with first-line managers before, during, and after collective bargaining. These supervisors administer the contract and know whether or not it is working.

There are three collective bargaining categories: mandatory, permissive, and prohibited. Mandatory bargaining issues fall within the definition of wages, hours, and other terms and conditions of employment. Permissive bargaining issues may be raised, but neither side may insist that they be bargained over. Prohibited bargaining issues are those issues that are statutorily outlawed and thus illegal.

The document produced by the collective bargaining process is known as a labor agreement or contract. It regulates the relationship between the employer and the employees for a specified period of time. Each agreement is unique, and there is no standard or universal model. Despite many dissimilarities, certain topics are included in virtually all labor agreements: recognition, management rights, union security, compensation and benefits, grievance procedure, employee security, and job-related factors.

Union security is typically one of the first items negotiated in a collective bargaining agreement. This section could specify a closed shop, a union shop, an exclusive bargaining shop, or an open shop. Under a checkoff of dues provision, the company agrees to withhold union dues from members' checks and to forward the money directly to the union.

At times negotiations break down, even though both labor and management may sincerely want to arrive at an equitable contract settlement. Several means of removing roadblocks may be used in order to get negotiations moving again, including third-party intervention, union strategies, and management strategies.

The two basic types of third-party intervention are mediation and arbitration. Strikes and boycotts are the primary means that the union may use to overcome a breakdown in negotiations. When union members refuse to work in order to exert pressure on management in negotiations, their action is referred to as a strike. A boycott involves an agreement by union members to refuse to use or buy the firm's products.

Management may also use various strategies to encourage unions to resume negotiations. In a lockout, management keeps employees out of the workplace and may run the operation with management personnel and/or temporary replacements. Management can continue operations during a strike by utilizing management personnel and hiring nonunion replacements for the strikers.

Unions often point to multinational corporations as an important cause of U.S. economic problems, especially unemployment. Foreign competition has had a major impact on employment in several U.S. industries already. The shoe, apparel, auto, steel, and rubber industries have lost jobs, and their remaining employees have also felt the effects at the bargaining table in terms of wage and work-rule concessions.

Questions for Review

1. Describe the basic steps involved in the collective bargaining process.
2. Distinguish among mandatory, permissive, and prohibited bargaining issues.
3. Why is it said that "at times negotiations are similar to a high-stakes poker game?"
4. Define each of the following:
   a. Closed shop
   b. Union shop
   c. Agency shop
   d. Maintenance of membership
   e. Checkoff of dues
5. What are the primary means by which breakdowns in negotiations may be overcome? Briefly describe each.
6. What is the human resource manager's role in the collective bargaining process?
7. What is involved in the administration of a labor agreement?
8. What appears to be the future of collective bargaining?

Terms for Review

Mandatory bargaining issues
Permissive bargaining issues
Prohibited bargaining issues
Closed shop
Union shop
Agency shop
Open shop
Checkoff of dues

Beachhead demands
Mediation
Arbitration
Strike
Boycott
Secondary boycott
Lockout

INCIDENT 1   ■   Maybe I Will, and Maybe I Won't   ■

Yesterday Bill Brown was offered a job as an operator trainee with Gem Manufacturing. He had recently graduated from Milford High School in a small town in the Midwest. Bill had no college aspirations, so upon graduation, he moved to Chicago to look for a job.

Bill's immediate supervisor spent only a short time with him and then turned him over to Gaylord Rader, an experienced operator, for training. After they had talked for a short time, Gaylord asked, "Have you given any thought to joining our union? You'll like all of our members."

Bill had not considered this. Moreover, he had never associated with union members, and his parents had never been members either. At Milford High his teachers had never really talked about unions. The fact that this union operated as an open shop meant nothing to him. Bill replied, "I don't know. Maybe. Maybe not."

The day progressed much the same way, with several people asking Bill virtually the same question. They were all friendly, but there seemed to be a barrier that separated Bill from the other workers. One worker looked Bill right in the eyes and said, "You're going to join, aren't you?" Bill still did not know, but he was beginning to lean in that direction.

After the buzzer rang to end the shift, Bill went to the washroom. Just as he entered, David Clements, the union steward, also walked in. After they exchanged greetings, David said, "I hear that you're not sure about wanting to join our union. You and everyone else reaps the benefits of the work we've done in the past. It doesn't seem fair for you to be rewarded for what others have done. Tell you what, why don't you join us down at the union hall tonight for our beer bust? We'll discuss it more then."

Bill nodded yes and finished cleaning up. "That might be fun," he thought.

Questions

1. Why does Bill have the option of joining or not joining the union?
2. How are the other workers likely to react toward Bill if he chooses not to join? Discuss.

INCIDENT 2 ■ What's Causing the Turnover? ■

Alonzo Alexander, human resource manager for Hyatt Manufacturing, had a problem that he did not know how to handle. His firm was unionized, and the relationship between management and the union had generally been good. The firm also had a strong affirmative action program, which required Alonzo to recruit women for jobs which had traditionally been filled by men. Hyatt had made major strides in implementing this program throughout the firm, with the notable exception of the machine department. There were only two women among the thirty-three operators in that department, both of whom had been hired within the past two months.

Alonzo had continued to locate numerous women applicants for the machine operator jobs. Some had trained at the local trade school and were obviously well qualified. A reasonable percentage of women were hired but they never stayed long. Reviewing records of exit interviews with women who had quit the machine department, Alonzo categorized the main reasons given for leaving as follows: to take a better job (10 responses); pay not high enough (5); personal and family obligations (3); personal relationships on the job (12); and supervision (2).

When Alonzo interviewed coworkers of women who had quit, he felt that he got little cooperation. Typical comments were "They just had their feelings hurt too easily," and "They were treated like any other worker; if they couldn't hack it maybe they didn't belong here." At one point the union steward told Alonzo that the continued questioning of workers could be considered harassment.

Questions

1. What action would you suggest that Alonzo take? Discuss.
2. How might the union be involved in helping Alonzo solve the problem?

DEVELOPING HRM SKILLS

A major part of the human resource manager's job is to advise managers at all levels regarding human resource matters. The human resource manager's knowledge and experience are often required in dealing with union matters, especially in handling situations that have an impact on future unionization. This exercise provides additional insight into the importance of properly handling employee problems in a unionized environment.

The human resource manager, Gregory Menchew, works very closely with all the managers and employees in an attempt to settle problems before they become critical. Today, one of the union stewards, Eugene Wilson, called for an appointment and said he had a complaint. The manager agreed to talk to Eugene, but prior to that conversation he wants to talk to the supervisor, Larry Bradley. That way Gregory can get both sides of the story. Gregory really hopes this is not a major problem, since it appears that the company is moving toward union decertification, and problems now might derail the decertification effort.

Larry Bradley has been with the company for twelve years, the last four as a supervisor. He is a very safety-conscious supervisor with a reputation for strictly enforcing the rules. In Larry's opinion, because of this safety-consciousness, there has not been a lost-time accident in the division since he became the supervisor. There is a rule in the plant, well known to everyone, that every intersection is a "four-way stop" for forklift trucks. According to the labor-management agreement, even minor safety violations justify a three-day suspension and a written warning. Larry saw a forklift truck, with Charlie Fox at the wheel, come around a corner at a high speed and not stop at an intersection. Virtually no one except Charlie Fox and Larry were at the plant, but Larry suspended Charlie for three days and placed a written warning in his personnel folder.

Eugene Wilson was elected union steward last year. There have been few grievances since the election, and therefore Eugene has done little as union steward. A couple of workers have brought complaints, but management was correct in each case and workers were told so. Eugene likes being the union steward and believes that it might be tough to be reelected unless he can make a "show." In Eugene's opinion, Charlie Fox was improperly suspended for three days. Eugene has found his reelection platform.

Three individuals will participate in this exercise: one to serve as the human resource manager, one to serve as the supervisor, and another to play the role of union steward. Your instructor will provide the participants with additional information necessary to complete the exercise.

REFERENCES

Anderson, Kay E., Philip M. Doyle, and Albert E. Schwenk. "Measuring Union-Nonunion Earnings Differences." *Monthly Labor Review,* 113 (June 1990), pp. 26–38.

Barbush, Jack. "Do We Really Want Labor on the Ropes? We're Entering a New Era of Industrial Relations and That's Cause for Concern." *Harvard Business Review,* 63 (July–August 1985), pp. 10–16.

Bauman, Alvin. "A New Measure of Compensation Cost Adjustments." *Monthly Labor Review,* 113 (August 1990), pp. 11–18.

Bernstein, Aaron. "Bad Connection at AT&T." *Business Week* (April 22, 1991), pp. 32–33.

Bernstein, Aaron. "Been Down So Long . . . But Unions May Ride Out the Recession." *Business Week* (January 14, 1991), pp. 30–31.

Bernstein, Aaron. "Busting Unions Can Backfire on the Bottom Line." *Business Week* (March 18, 1991), p. 108.

Bernstein, Aaron. "The Teamsters and The Mob: It May Really Be Over." *Business Week* (June 17, 1991), pp. 102–103.

Bernstein, Aaron, and Jim Bartimo. "Wrong Time for Scare Tactics?" *Business Week* (April 16, 1990), pp. 27–28.

Brown, Marlene. "I'm Overqualified, Bored and Quitting!" *Management World* 19 (March–April 1990), pp. 14–15.

Cimin, Michael. "Collective Bargaining in 1990: Search for Solutions Continues." *Monthly Labor Review,* 114 (January 1991), pp. 19–33.

Colford, Steven W. "Unions Flock to TV Ads." *Advertising Age,* 61 (September 10, 1990), p. 82.

"Court Sides With Unions." *Personnel,* 67 (June 1990), pp. 6–7.

Eubanks, Paula. "Employee Grievance Policy: Don't Discourage Complaints." *Hospitals,* 64 (December 20, 1990), pp. 36–37.

Freedman, Audrey, and William E. Fulmer. "Last Rites for Pattern Bargaining." *Harvard Business Review,* 60 (March–April), pp. 39–42ff.

Garland, Susan B. "Why Democrats Still Want to Wear the Union Label." *Business Week* (March 5, 1990), p. 37.

Hoerr, John. "What Should Unions Do?" *Harvard Business Review,* 69 (May–June 1991), pp. 30–45.

Kelly, Kevin, and Aaron Bernstein. "Why United Is Putting Pilots on the Gravy Train." *Business Week* (April 29, 1991), p. 32.

Kilgour, John G. "The Odds on White-Collar Organizing." *Personnel,* 67 (August 1990), pp. 29–35.

Kirkpatrick, David. "The Union's Role as Co-Manager." *Fortune,* 121 (March 26, 1990), p. 37.

Kochan, T. A. et al. "U.S. Industrial Relations in Transition." *Monthly Labor Review,* 108 (May 1985), pp. 28–29.

Kohl, J. P., and D. B. Stephens. "On Strike: Legal Development in Labor-Management Relations." *Cornell Hotel / Restaurant Administration Quarterly,* 25 (February 1985), pp. 71–75.

Koretz, Gene, and Celeste Whittaker. "More Picket Lines, Fewer Rank-And-Filers." *Business Week* (May 7, 1990), p. 24.

Koretz, Gene. "Why Unions Thrive Abroad—But Wither in the U.S." *Business Week* (September 10, 1990), p. 26.

Lissy, William E. "Election of 'Financial Core' Union Membership." *Supervision,* 51 (September 1990), pp. 22–23.

Lissy, William E. "Management-Sponsored Employees' Committee Not Illegal." *Supervision,* 51 (April 1990), pp. 17–19.

McDonough, Paul S. "Maintain a Union-Free Status." *Personnel Journal,* 69 (April 1990), pp. 108–114.

Premeaux, Shane R., R. Wayne Mondy, and Art L. Bethke. "Decertification: Fulfilling Unions' Destiny?" *Personnel Journal,* 32 (June 1987), pp. 144–148.

Reynolds, Larry. "Management and Labor Draw the Picket Line." *Personnel,* 68 (March 1991), p. 15.

Reynolds, Larry. "Management-Labor Tensions Spell Union Busting." *Personnel,* 68 (March 1991), pp. 7–9.

Ritter, Anne. "Are Unions Worth the Bargain?" *Personnel,* 67 (February 1990), pp. 12–14.

Ritter, Anne. "The UAW Strikes Out at Nissan." *Personnel,* 66 (November 1989), pp. 5–6.

Sanyal, Rajib N. "An Empirical Analysis of the Unionization of Foreign Manufacturing Firms in the U.S." *Journal of International Business Studies,* 21 (First Quarter 1990), pp. 119–132.

Schiffman, Barry. "Tougher Tactics to Keep Out Unions: Consultants Give Employers a New Bag of Tricks." *The New York Times,* 140 (March 3, 1991), sec. 3, F8 (N), col 1.

Solomon, Charlene Marmer. "Nightmare at Nordstrom." *Personnel Journal,* 69 (September 1990), pp. 76–83.

Zalusky, John. "Labor Seeks Security, Not Bonuses." *Personnel,* 68 (January 1991), p. 13.

CHAPTER 17

UNION-FREE ORGANIZATIONS

CHAPTER OBJECTIVES

1. Explain why employees choose not to join a union, and describe both the costs and benefits of unionization.
2. List and describe the various strategies and tactics a firm might use to maintain its union-free status.
3. Explain union decertification and describe the role of the human resource manager in a union-free organization.

Wayne Roberts recently joined Royal Airlines as a reservation agent in Dallas. Prior to this job he had been employed by Muse Airline of New York. When that airline went out of business recently, he was offered a job with Royal. The pay wasn't as good, and he seemed to be working harder, but he needed the job.

During his first week on the job, he was talking with several workers on his shift: "I don't see why we don't have a union here. Who's going to represent us when management puts the screws on?" Wayne's conversation was quickly cut off by one of the other workers, who replied, "We don't believe in unions at Royal. Management has done a good job. If you believe you need a union to represent you, maybe you don't need to work here." Wayne nodded his head to indicate his understanding and did not mention his feelings about wanting a union again.

In an unrelated incident, Brad Carpet, general manager for Royal, was visibly upset. He had just walked through the Royal terminal and accidentally heard one of the supervisors severely reprimanding an employee in front of coworkers. Brad called the supervisor aside and said, "We're a union-free organization and hope to remain that way. What you just did is one of the fastest ways to create a feeling among our employees that they need a union."

These incidents describe some employee and management attitudes in union-free firms. Wayne Roberts discovered that many of his fellow employees feel they do not need to be represented by a union. On the other hand, Brad Carpet is quite concerned that the actions of one of his supervisors may create an atmosphere in which employees believe they do need a union. Employees of union-free firms comprise a major part of the labor force in the United States. Remaining union-free is the obvious choice of management. However, continuation of a union-free environment can be threatened by many work-related factors of which management must be acutely aware.

We begin this chapter with a discussion of the reasons that employees avoid joining unions. We then present a cost/benefit analysis of unionization. Next, we describe strategies and tactics for maintaining a union-free status. We devote the final portion of the chapter to union decertification and the role of the human resource manager in a union-free organization.

■ WHY EMPLOYEES AVOID JOINING UNIONS

Most employees in the United States do not belong to unions. Basically, employees avoid unions when the human resource system deals directly and effectively with employees and their needs.[1] Maintaining a union-free organization requires sustaining an environment in which labor cannot successfully organize. The old saying that "management gets what it deserves" is never more true than when a union successfully organizes a group of employees.[2] After the union arrives and successfully organizes, management usually recognizes the avoidable mistakes that led to unionization. However, a well-conceived and implemented employee relations system could substantially reduce the likelihood of unionization.[3] Employees don't join unions for several reasons, some of which are shown in Figure 17-1.

In the first place, it costs money to be a union member. Typically, there is an initiation fee followed by dues that must be paid regularly. From time to time, there may also be special assessments. Although dues typically do not amount to more than 2 percent of before-tax pay, many individuals would rather use this money in other ways. A worker who makes $24,000 annually would pay dues of approximately $40 per month, in addition to the initiation fee and any special assessments.

Also, many employees think that unions are unnecessary. They believe that they shouldn't have to depend on a third party to help satisfy their job-related needs. These individuals feel that their value to the organization should be judged on an individual basis; if their performance is superior, the rewards should be appropriate and direct. Joining a union, they believe, is an admission that others control their destiny, limiting opportunities to maximize rewards.

In addition, just as there may be peer pressure in some firms to encourage employees to join the union, in other instances there may be as much pressure against union affiliation. Even if an individual might desire to join a union, the informal work group may be powerful enough to stop the individual from joining. As Wayne Roberts discovered in the incident at the beginning of the chapter, the prevailing attitude of his coworkers to maintain a union-free status created extreme peer pressure on him to conform.

---

[1] Alexander B. Trowbridge, "A Management Look at Labor Relations," in *Unions in Transition* (San Francisco: ICS Press, 1988), p. 415.

[2] John P. Bucalo, Jr., "Successful Employee Relations," *Personnel Administrator,* 31 (April 1986), p. 63.

[3] Paul S. McDonough, "Maintaining a Union-Free Status," *Personnel Journal,* 69 (April 1990), p. 108.

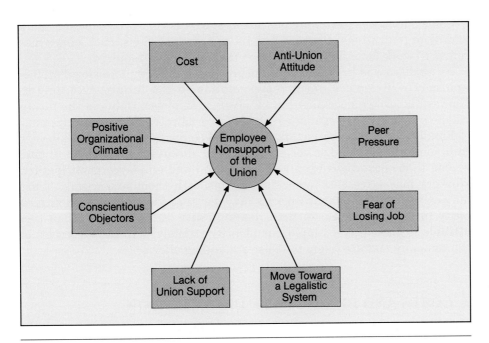

FIGURE 17-1 | Why Employees Don't Join Unions

Reprisals for union activities are illegal in the United States. Even so, some employees would feel insecure about their jobs if they engaged in union activities. Perhaps they have seen workers who supported a union receive what they perceive as unfair treatment from the employer. A worker who can be easily replaced may decide not to take a chance on losing his or her job by supporting union activities.

Establishing a union is much like starting a business. The cost of starting and maintaining a union must be evaluated in relation to the revenue and other benefits to be gained. Under certain circumstances a union may decide to expend little or no effort to create a new bargaining unit. For instance, a union would tend to favor organizing a unit of five hundred skilled workers rather than a group of fifty semiskilled employees. Although the union might like to help the fifty employees, the cost of organizing and supporting their demands might be excessive.

Unions also recognize that there are certain industries, firms, and locations in the country with a tradition of resisting unions. For instance, in the Sunbelt states unions commonly experience organizing difficulties. Also, a union may believe that additional attempts to unionize an organization, such as IBM Corporation, are a waste of money, because previous efforts proved fruitless. According to the *Daily Labor Report,* a "union's campaign to organize IBM is a task likened to putting a man on the moon."[4]

---

[4] "Unions Launch Campaign to Organize IBM; Task Likened to Putting 'Man on the Moon,'" *Daily Labor Record* (Washington, D.C.: The Bureau of National Affairs, January 22, 1987), p. A-1.

Some employees have religious or moral beliefs that preclude them from joining organizations. Because unions are organizations, such employees refuse to work for a firm where union membership is required.

As we discussed in Chapter 15, the growing web of employee legal protection may well replace union representation in the future. According to Harvard labor law specialist Paul C. Weiler, employee rights in the future will be protected by a legalistic rather than a collective bargaining system.[5]

Finally, there may be factors within the company that keep employees from joining a union. The corporate culture (discussed in Chapter 9) may be one that encourages open communication and employee participation. Workers may have excellent relationships with their supervisors. Trust may exist to the point that workers may feel that they do not need a third party to represent them in their dealings with management. When this attitude is present, the employees identify strongly with the objectives of the company and are likely to resist organizing efforts.

■ COSTS AND BENEFITS OF UNIONIZATION

Valid reasons exist for management's acceptance or rejection of unionization, as shown in Figure 17-2. We discuss the rationales for both philosophies next.

Acceptance of Unionization Attempts

There may be times when resisting unionizing attempts is not advantageous. In such situations, management must set aside personal feelings and make decisions that are in the firm's best interest. For example, in certain areas of the United States, the maritime and construction unions often provide a ready source of labor from their hiring halls. A firm operating in one of these industries in an area that is strongly unionized may find it advantageous to accept unionization in order to obtain qualified workers.

In addition, there are situations in which union-management relationships are quite good and well established. In such instances, it may be prudent to keep that union. Otherwise, a more demanding union may take its place. Thus management rationalizes that it can work within the present system, whereas the future, with a different union, may be uncertain.

Management may also desire unionization of competing firms. If a competitor attempts to enter the industry by paying lower nonunion wages, the established firms will likely desire unionization of the new firm. Costs to all firms producing similar products remain relatively constant when all are unionized. An additional factor determining whether a firm should resist unionization attempts involves a realistic appraisal of whether it can remain union-free. In some cases, the firm would have little hope of staying union-free. For example, a maritime company located in New York City

---

[5] John Hoerr et al., "Beyond Unions," *Business Week* (July 8, 1985), p. 74.

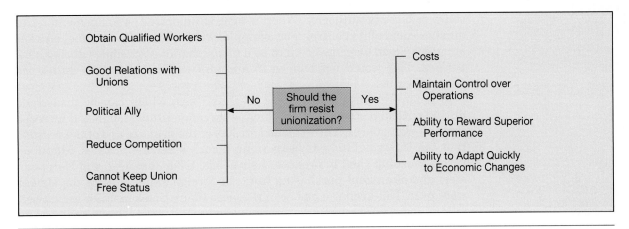

FIGURE 17-2 | Should the Organization Resist Unionization?

would have little chance of remaining union-free. In such cases it would probably be in the firm's best interest to begin developing a strategy for working with a union.

Resistance to Unionization Attempts

Although there may be valid reasons for a firm to accept unionization, a large majority of executives would prefer that their companies remain union-free. In fact, that is a major goal for many organizations. We describe some of the reasons for remaining union-free next.

Costs. The compensation paid to union members is generally higher than that for nonunion workers. However, firms realize that they must remain competitive in order to survive. Delta Air Lines, a union-free organization, has had considerable success in comparison to its unionized competitors because of employees' desire for jobs and security.

In general, unionization increases labor costs.[6] Factors that contribute to these costs include: "the high cost of complex, payroll-padding work rules; work stoppages, strikes and slowdowns; lengthy negotiations and the grind of arbitration cases; and layoff by seniority."[7] The type of working relationship between labor and management will have a considerable impact on costs.

Maintaining Control over Operations. Management typically wants to operate without restrictive union work rules and other provisions that

---

[6] Jerry Eisen, "Don't Be Complacent About Union Organizing," *Personnel Administrator,* 30 (August 1985), p. 122.

[7] Wiley I. Beavers, "Employee Relations Without a Union." In Dale Yoder and Herbert G. Heneman, Jr. (eds.), *ASPA Handbook of Personnel and Industrial Relations: Employee and Labor Relations,* Vol. III (Washington, D.C.: The Bureau of National Affairs, 1976), pp. 7–82.

could reduce its authority. When a firm is unionized, management relinquishes some of its control. For example, with a union-free airline, a ticket agent may load baggage or fill in as a dispatcher or a scheduler during slow periods. This would not happen in a unionized firm where job duties are often inflexible.

A union-free firm doesn't face costly strikes, which can be disastrous during critical periods. It avoids having its competitors step in and increase their market shares. The extended strikes of the past are one of the reasons that the U.S. steel industry experienced such a decline in sales. Manufacturers, needing steel to produce their goods, tried Japanese and European steel and often kept purchasing from the foreign supplier after the strikes were over. This scenario has been repeated many times in other industries.

Ability to Reward Superior Performance.   Rewarding superior performance in a union-free organization is often much easier. A study involving twenty-six nonunion firms revealed that "company executives believe they achieve higher productivity than they would if they were organized."[8] In union-free organizations, promotions and salary increases may be based solely on performance instead of seniority. In a unionized organization, the compensation paid each worker is specified by the agreement, not based on performance.

Ability to Adapt Quickly.   Most organizations experience fluctuations in demand for their products. Some firms undergo severe business downturns before the cycle reverses. Union-free firms are typically able to respond more easily to changing conditions. If wages must be reduced to remain competitive, the union-free firm can generally adjust them rapidly. The unionized firm is bound by the labor agreement and cannot lower wages unless the union agrees to a contract change. When the automobile industry was in severe difficulty because foreign products were less expensive and of better quality, management could not quickly lower wages to be competitive. Any wage concessions had to be negotiated. Often these negotiations were unsuccessful, partially resulting in the severe slump in the sale of U.S.-made automobiles throughout most of the 1980s.

When workers must be laid off as a result of declining demand, management in a union-free firm is able to lay off marginally productive employees. The seniority system determines who will be laid off in a unionized company, further diminishing management's ability to raise productivity.

■ BUSTING UNIONS CAN NEGATIVELY IMPACT PROFITABILITY

A union-free organization is often viewed by management as the best environment in which to do business. However, should a company "bust" a union to become union-free? Is it better to break a union or to

---

[8] Fred K. Foulkes, "How Top Nonunion Companies Manage Employees," *Harvard Business Review,* 59 (September–October 1981), p. 90.

encourage cooperation between labor and management? Evidence is surfacing that supports the notion of cooperation. According to Conference Board labor economist Audrey Freedman, "Over the long haul, moderate behavior [by management when dealing with unions] is probably more efficient."[9]

Industrial relations professor William N. Cooke surveyed fifty-six unionized manufacturers that either ousted unions or developed cooperative relations with them. After adjusting for factors such as changing market conditions, Cooke and a collaborator reached an unexpected conclusion. Employers that tried teamwork reported a 19 percent increase over the course of a decade in value added per employee, but combative employers experienced a 15 percent decline. *Value added* was defined as operating income plus inventory divided by the number of workers. Companies who experienced a decline eventually recovered from the decline, which was apparently caused by the huge cost of withstanding a union-busting strike. However, according to Cooke, "Our evidence suggests that cooperation seems to pay off the best, at least so far." It is unlikely that after many years of significant power over unions that management will embrace unions and attempt to bring them into the fold (as the Japanese did at their Bridgestone tire plant in Warren County, Tennessee). Yet, this certainly should be one strategy that is considered.[10]

■ STRATEGIES AND TACTICS FOR REMAINING UNION-FREE

Some managers believe that the presence of a union is evidence of management's failure to treat employees fairly.[11] The factors that the AFL-CIO believes will significantly reduce chances of unionizing are listed in Table 17-1 on page 650. According to a report published in *Unions in Transition,* certain similar characteristics help organizations remain union-free: competitive pay and strong benefits, a team environment, open communication, a pleasant work environment, and the avoidance of layoffs.[12]

If a firm's goal is to remain union-free, it must establish its strategy long before a union-organizing attempt begins. The development of long-term strategies and effective tactics for the purpose of remaining union-free is crucial because the employees' decision to consider forming a union is usually not made overnight. Negative attitudes regarding the company are typically formed over a period of time and well in advance of any attempt at unionization.

If a firm desires to remain union-free, it must borrow some of the union's philosophy. Basically, management must be able to offer workers equal or better conditions than they could expect with a union. Weakness in any

---

[9] Aaron Bernstein, "Busting Unions Can Backfire on the Bottom Line," *Business Week* (March 18, 1991), p. 108.

[10] *Ibid.*

[11] Wiley I. Beavers, "Employee Relations Without a Union," pp. 7–83.

[12] Alexander B. Trowbridge, "A Management Look at Labor Relations," pp. 415–416.

TABLE 17-1 | AFL-CIO: Factors That Reduce the Chances for
Union Organizing

1. A conviction by employees that the boss is not taking advantage of them.
2. Employees who have pride in their work.
3. Good performance records kept by the company. Employees feel more secure on their jobs when they know their efforts are recognized and appreciated.
4. No claims of high-handed treatment. Employees respect firm but fair discipline.
5. No claim of favoritism that's not earned through work performance.
6. Supervisors who have good relationships with subordinates. The AFL-CIO maintains that this relationship of supervisors with people under them—above all—stifles organizing attempts.

Source: "What to Do When the Union Knocks," *Nation's Business,* 54 (November 1966), p. 107. Copyright © 1977 by *Nation's Business.* Reprinted by permission.

critical area may be an open invitation to a union.[13] As shown in Figure 17-3, all aspects of an organization's operations are involved in maintaining its union-free status.

Effective First-Line Supervisors

Extremely important to an organization's ability to remain union-free is the overall effectiveness of its management, particularly its first-line supervisors. These supervisors represent the first line of defense against unionization. Their supervisory ability often determines whether unionization will be successful. The supervisor assigns work, evaluates each individual's performance, and provides praise and punishment. The manner in which he or she communicates with the employee in these and other matters can affect the individual's attitude toward the firm. Even though the first-line supervisor is the lowest level of management, in the workplace this individual usually has more influence over employees than any other manager.

The supervisor also must communicate information about the firm to employees. Information regarding profits, sales, how the firm's products compare to competitors', and the like are important. The grapevine may reveal that sales are declining, which would likely disturb many workers. If the supervisor explains that sales are down across the industry but are expected to return to normal in the next quarter, employees might be less anxious.

In order for a supervisor to communicate effectively with employees, he or she must possess timely and accurate information. If an employee is

---

[13] *Ibid.,* p. 417.

aware of company plans before the supervisor, the supervisor loses credibility. For instance, if top management changes a company policy regarding safety hats in a particular area and the supervisor is not told of the change, the supervisor might continue to tell employees to adhere to the old policy. Any disciplinary action resulting from such a situation would embarrass the supervisor.

The supervisor must also be adept at interpreting the signals of nonverbal communication. A well-trained supervisor can identify symptoms of unrest among employees. For instance, increasing signs of resentment, where there were none before, may indicate union activity. Emerging informal groups may also indicate unrest. The supervisor might notice that workers may stop talking or change the subject when he or she approaches. A competent supervisor will notice these signs and report them immediately to upper level management. There may be patterns of similar activities in other departments, suggesting an attempt at unionization. This knowledge can assist management in developing appropriate strategies and tactics.

One of the fastest ways to convert a nonunion person into a union advocate is to allow favoritism. To the worker, favoritism is equivalent to discrimination. The supervisor must establish an atmosphere in which the worker believes that he or she can receive fair treatment and equitable rewards.

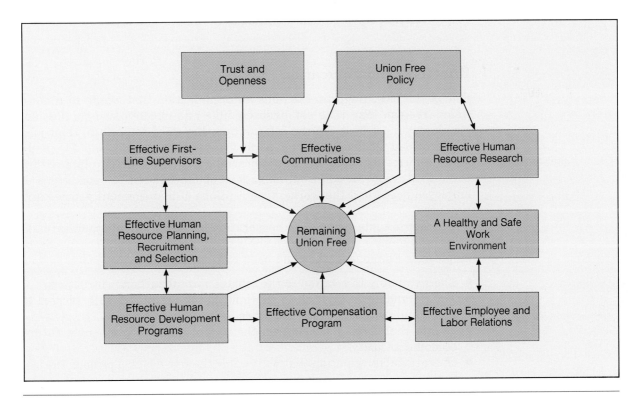

FIGURE 17-3 | Factors Involved in Maintaining a Union-Free Status

Union-Free Policy

The fact that the organization's goal is to remain union-free should be clearly and forcefully communicated to all its members. Such a policy statement might read as follows:

> Our success as a company is founded on the skill and efforts of our employees. Our policy is to deal with employees as effectively as possible, respecting and recognizing each of them as individuals.
>
> In our opinion, unionization would interfere with the individual treatment, respect, and recognition the company offers. Consequently, we believe a union-free environment is in the employees' best interest, the company's best interest, and the interest of the people served by the corporation.[14]

This type of policy evolves into a philosophy that affects everyone in the organization. All employees, from the lowest paid worker to top management, must understand it. No major human resource-related decision should be made without asking, "How will this affect our union-free status?" The union-free policy should be repeatedly communicated to every worker. Workers must be told why the company advocates the policy and how it affects them. This involves much more than sending a memo each year to all employees stating that the company's goal is to remain union-free. Every means of effective communication may be needed to convince employees that the organization intends to remain union-free.

Effective Communication

One of the most important actions an organization that wants to remain union-free can take is to establish credible and effective communication. Employees must be given the information they need to perform their jobs and provided feedback on their performance. Management should openly share information with workers concerning activities taking place within the organization. In addition, management must listen to expressions of employee needs and the workers' perceptions of management policies and practices.

In order to sustain employee cooperation in the pursuit of organizational goals and remain union-free, management must consider the needs of employees. Employees want and need to know the following:

- Their standing in relation to the official, formal authority structure.
- Their standing in relation to the informal organization with respect to individual status, power, acceptance, and so on.
- Events that have a bearing on their own, and the company's, future economic security.
- Operational information that will enable them to develop pride in the job.

---

[14] James F. Rand, "Preventive-Maintenance Techniques for Staying Union-Free," *Personnel Journal,* 59 (June 1980), p. 497.

HRM In Action

 As Allen Fender, human resource director for Service Industries, rounded the corner in the mixing department he heard the supervisor, Judy Morgan, reprimanding one of her employees in front of five other workers. It was obvious that the worker was very embarrassed and wanted to get back to work, but Judy continued to press the issue. Service Industries had recently been experiencing some worker unrest, and there were rumblings of a unionization attempt.

What actions should Allen take?

One approach taken to encourage open communication is the open-door policy. The **open-door policy** gives employees the right to take any grievance to the person next in the chain of command if the problem cannot be resolved by the immediate supervisor. Delta Air Lines is well known for its open-door policy, which enables employees to express their grievances. An effective open-door policy represents an attitude of openness and trust among people within the organization. It is counterproductive to state that an open-door policy exists and then punish an employee for bypassing his or her immediate supervisor. The employee must not fear that talking to the manager next in line will be detrimental to his or her career. Although it might seem that an open-door policy would result in wasted time for upper and middle managers, in most instances this has not proven to be the case. The mere knowledge that an employee can move up the chain of command with a complaint without fear of retribution often encourages the immediate supervisor and the employee to work out their differences.

Trust and Openness

Openness and trust on the part of managers and employees alike are important in order to remain union-free. The old expression "actions speak louder than words" is certainly valid for an organization that desires to remain union-free. Credibility, based on trust, must exist between labor and management, and this trust develops only over time. If employees perceive that the manager is being open and receptive to ideas, feedback is encouraged. Managers need this feedback to do their jobs effectively. However, if managers give the impression that their directives should never be questioned, communication will be stifled and credibility lost.

One of the major factors in the success of Japanese businesses is said to be that managers trust not only their workers, but also their peers and superiors. As a result, a simpler organizational structure than that generally used in the United States is possible. More levels of management result in higher overhead costs and more time-consuming decision making. Japanese firms assume that workers at all levels are competent and trustworthy. As a result, they do not have to employ highly paid executives to review the work of other highly paid executives.[15]

Effective Human Resource Planning, Recruitment, and Selection

A firm's ability to remain union-free relates closely to its human resource planning, recruitment, and selection practices. For instance, if a firm used only word-of-mouth from current employees as a recruiting source, a very homogeneous workforce of friends and relatives could develop. Such a workforce would likely have strong interpersonal relationships. However, should management take action against any worker, the work group might perceive this as an action against them all. For this reason, and others discussed in Chapter 6, the human resource manager recruits from a wide variety of sources.

The method of human resource planning used can have a major impact on the organization's susceptibility to unionization. If it is constantly hiring and terminating employees in reaction to fluctuating demand for its products, the firm may face unionization. However, a firm can often maintain stable employment with adequate planning.

Effective Human Resource Development Programs

Many employees want the opportunity to grow and advance within the organization. Employees can often attain these goals through training and development. A philosophy that is genuinely supportive of HRD would extend from top management to the lowest-level employee. As we discussed in Chapter 8, the success of any companywide training and development program depends on the support and interest shown by top management. Management support is crucial because management attitudes will filter down and influence employees at other levels of the organization.

One important requirement of human resource development is that employees have a genuine desire for self-improvement. Some employees are content in their present positions, while others desire to develop their potential. More employees will wish to improve their skills if they are able to see a relationship between increased training and higher pay and other rewards. An organization takes a giant step toward remaining union-free when it provides avenues for advancement in skill and status. The seniority system often denies union employees these opportunities.

Supervisors also need training to prepare them to deal with organizing attempts. If the union knows that supervisors have been thoroughly trained in the tactics of dealing with unionizing efforts, it may decide

---

[15] "Trust: The New Ingredient of Management," *Business Week* (July 6, 1981), p. 104.

against organizing attempts. This type of training will also assist in preventing costly mistakes that could lead to charges of unfair labor practices during an organizing campaign. Training is necessary because the supervisor's actions can actually bind the employer. Ignorance on the part of the supervisor is no excuse for inappropriate behavior.

Effective Compensation Programs

The financial compensation that employees receive is the most tangible measure they have of their worth to the organization. If an individual's pay is substantially below that provided for similar work in the area, the employee will soon become dissatisfied. Compensation must remain relatively competitive if the organization expects to remain union-free.[16]

The compensation program should be intelligently planned and communicated to all employees. They must understand what they are being compensated for and how the system works. If employees perceive the system as being unfair, they are ripe for unionizing activities.

The same approach should be followed with regard to benefits. The organization need not have the best benefits in a geographic area or an industry to protect its union-free status. However, the benefits package must be competitive. Employees must know what benefits they are actually receiving. Too often, management doesn't adequately inform employees about their benefits. When such a situation exists, the organization is wasting financial resources and jeopardizing its union-free status.

A Healthy and Safe Work Environment

An organization that gains a reputation for failing to maintain a safe and healthy work environment leaves itself wide open for unionization. For years unions have campaigned successfully by convincing workers that the union will provide them with a safer work environment. In fact, labor organizations were leading advocates of the Occupational Safety and Health Act, and they continue to support this type of legislation.

Effective Employee Relations

No organization is free from employee disagreements and dissatisfaction. Therefore, a means of resolving employee complaints, whether actual or perceived, should be available. The **grievance procedure** is a formal process that permits employees to complain about matters affecting them. Most labor-management agreements contain formal grievance procedures, and union members regard handling grievances as one of the most important functions of a labor union. Until the early 1980s, grievance procedures

---

[16] James F. Rand, "Preventive-Maintenance Techniques," p. 498.

were not so common in union-free organizations. However, since that time many nonunion firms have started grievance procedure programs. When employees do not have ways to voice their complaints and have them resolved, even small gripes may grow into major problems.

The grievance procedure is a way of keeping problems from becoming serious. Total commitment to such a policy needs to start with top management and be instilled in every manager. Supervisors should develop an attitude of wanting to resolve problems before they become formal complaints.[17] Employees who believe that management is concerned with resolving problems lack a major reason for needing a union.

A means of resolving grievances in union-free organizations is through the use of ombudspersons. This approach has been used for some time in Europe, and the practice is becoming more popular in the United States. An **ombudsperson** is a complaint officer with access to top management, who hears employees' complaints, investigates them, and sometimes recommends appropriate action. Because of their access to top management, ombudspersons can often resolve problems swiftly. In many cases, they simply help employees locate people who can solve their problems. Sometimes, ombudspersons recommend specific action to managers. The Singer Company uses an ombudsperson system. This program is described in Figure 17-4.

In recent years the ombudsperson has assumed the additional duties of helping uncover scandals within organizations. Large defense contractors, such as McDonnell Douglas and General Electric, have used ombudspersons to respond to questions raised regarding product design safety or defense contract billings. Workers who believe that a problem exists can now bypass the supervisor and talk to the ombudsperson.[18]

Effective Human Resource Research

Human resource research can reveal changes in attitudes within the organization that could lead to unionization. One purpose of human resource research is the early identification of employee dissatisfaction. Corrective action should be taken before workers feel a need for a union to solve their problems. Ignored problems often encourage unionization.

Research may reveal symptoms of worker unrest. For instance, statistics that reveal an increase in the turnover rate may indicate growing employee dissatisfaction. Good exit interviews, as part of the research effort, can assist management in identifying the problems causing higher turnover before they become critical.[19]

Another indicator of employee dissatisfaction is the number of customer complaints received. For example, research that reveals increasing custo-

---

[17] George W. Bohlander and Harold C. White, "Building Bridges: Nonunion Employee Grievance Systems," *Personnel,* 65 (July 1988), p. 62.

[18] Michael Brody, "Listen to Your Whistleblower," *Fortune,* 24 (November 1986), pp. 77–78.

[19] Wanda R. Embrey, R. Wayne Mondy, and Robert M. Noe, "Exit Interview: A Tool for Personnel Development," *Personnel Administrator,* 24 (May 1979), p. 48.

In A Less Than Perfect Universe . . .

See the Ombudsperson

An employee is fired for cause, disciplined, or perceives himself or herself a victim of discrimination. To reverse the decision or remedy the situation, the employee tries normal channels—but remains dissatisfied with the results.

In many organizations, the story would end here. At Singer, because of the Corporate Ombudsperson program started in 1976, the story can have another chapter or two. And, although the story may not necessarily have a happy ending, employees are guaranteed that they won't be subjected to harassment or retribution for contacting the Ombudsperson.

A concept borrowed from Scandinavia, the Ombudsperson function entails an impartial investigation of and assistance in equitably settling complaints. At Singer this corporate-wide function is the responsibility of Harry P. Hancock, Jr., senior director, employee relations programs. "Because the program is informal rather than formal and the range of cases is varied," explains Mr. Hancock, "there is really no single modus operandi. I handle each case as it presents itself."

The range of cases includes grievances about performance appraisals, involuntary discharge, sexual harassment, sexual discrimination, denial of promotion, formal reprimand, and conflict with or unfair treatment by a supervisor.

For the purpose of illustrating the thoroughness of the Ombudsperson proceedings, Mr. Hancock describes how he might deal with a discharge-for-cause case brought to his attention by an employee who had exhausted all normal channels and remained dissatisfied.

"In the investigation and evaluation," he explains, "we rely heavily on the division personnel staff. Our objective is to make sure that:

- The rule or policy allegedly broken by the employee has been published, posted or otherwise made known to employees.
- The employee has been warned about any earlier infractions and given counseling.
- The employee has been given a reasonable length of time to improve performance.
- The proposed disciplinary action is appropriate to the infraction.
- Other employees charged with similar infractions have been treated in a similar manner."

If it is determined that the employee has been unfairly discharged, the case is discussed with the immediate supervisor who initiated the action. If the decision is not reversed or amended at this level—which it usually is—then the discussion is brought to successively higher levels. On the other hand, if it is judged that the decision was appropriate, the employee is so advised and the case is closed.

Most problems are resolved, of course, through Singer's normal channels. Resolving a problem via normal channels includes an initial discussion with the immediate supervisor. If the issue is not settled at that level, then the matter is taken to higher levels, in the specific unit. Equal Opportunity coordinators, industrial relations personnel and other employee relations specialists may become involved.

In cases of terminations of employees with more than ten years of continuous service, standard procedure requires that those terminations be approved by members of the Management Committee.

If employees, after having gone through normal channels, still believe that they have received unfair treatment then they can bring the matter to the attention of the Ombudsperson.

FIGURE 17-4 | Description of an Ombudsperson Program

Source: Used with permission of The Singer Company.

---

mer complaints because of lower quality might point to certain employees who have problems that need resolving. Accident frequency, maintenance costs, and theft are other indicators of employee dissatisfaction.[20]

---

[20] Wiley I. Beavers, "Employee Relations Without a Union," pp. 7-69–7-70.

■ UNION DECERTIFICATION

Until 1947, once a union was certified, it was certified forever.[21] However, the Taft-Hartley Act made it possible for employees to decertify a union. This action results in a union losing its right to act as the exclusive bargaining representative of a group of employees. **Decertification** is essentially the reverse of the process that employees must follow to be recognized as an official bargaining unit. In recent years, many decertification elections have been held.

The 1980s were not a good decade for labor unions in the United States. Organized labor lost 2.7 million members between 1980 and 1984. In addition, because this decline occurred while the nation's workforce increased, the proportion of those employed who were union members declined even more dramatically.

Union memberships are at the lowest levels in at least 50 years.[22] Also, a recent National Bureau of Economic Research report estimated that union membership in the private sector could drop below 5 percent by the year 2000 if present trends continue.[23] The two primary reasons for this decline are decertification and the U.S. economy's continuing shift to service industries.

In light of this significant reduction in union ranks, the outcome of certification and decertification elections are of increasing concern to unions. Unions are winning fewer certification elections and are losing the majority of their decertification elections.[24]

Some union leaders are concerned that the trend may even be spreading to larger firms. Should this occur, the foundation of the U.S. labor movement would be threatened. Not only would the total number of union members decline, but unions' hold on major domestic industries would be substantially reduced.[25] Decertification elections have been won in such well-known firms as Holiday Inn, Goodyear, Dow Chemical, and Sears. However, smaller firms appear to be achieving the greatest won-lost decertification record. Perhaps this is because it is easier for management to reestablish trust with employees in smaller firms.

Decertification Procedure

The rules established by the NLRB spell out the conditions for filing a decertification petition. At least 30 percent of the bargaining unit members must petition for an election. As might be expected, this task by itself may be difficult because union supporters are likely to strongly oppose the move.

---

[21] 93 Daily Congressional Record 3954 (23 April 1947).

[22] Gene Koretz, "Why Unions Thrive Abroad—But Wither in the U.S." *Business Week* (September 10, 1990), p. 26.

[23] Gene Koretz and Celeste Whittaker, "More Picket Lines, Fewer Rank-And-Filers," *Business Week* (May 7, 1990), p. 24.

[24] Woodruff Imberman, "How to Win a Decertification Election," *Management Review,* 66 (September 1977), p. 38.

[25] *Ibid.*

Although the petitioners' names are supposed to remain confidential, many union members are fearful that their signatures on the petition will be discovered.

Timing of the NLRB's receipt of the decertification petition is also critical. The petition must be submitted between sixty and ninety days prior to the expiration of the current contract. When all these conditions have been met, the NLRB regional director will schedule a decertification election by secret ballot.

The NLRB carefully monitors the events leading up to the election. Current employees must initiate the request for the election. If the NLRB determines that management initiated the action, it probably won't certify the election. After the petition has been accepted, however, management can support the decertification election attempt. If a majority of the votes cast are against the union, the employees will be free from that union. Strong union supporters are all likely to vote. Thus if a substantial number of employees are indifferent to the union and choose not to vote, decertification may not occur.

Management and Decertification

When management senses employee discontent with the union, it often does not know how to react. Many times, management decides to do nothing, reasoning that it is best not to get involved or that it may even be illegal to do so. But if it does want to get involved, management can use a variety of legal tactics. If management really wants the union decertified, it must learn how to be active rather than passive.

Meetings with union members to discuss the benefits of becoming union-free have proven beneficial. In fact, they are often cited as being the most effective campaign tactic. These meetings may be with individual employees, small groups, or even entire units. Management explains the benefits and answers employees' questions.

Management may also provide workers with legal assistance in preparing for decertification. Because the workers probably have never been through a decertification election, this type of assistance may prove invaluable. For example, the NLRB may not permit an election if the paperwork has not been properly completed. Management must always remember that it cannot initiate the decertification action; that is the workers' responsibility.

The most effective means of accomplishing decertification is to improve the corporate culture so that workers no longer feel the need to have a union. This cannot be done overnight, as mutual trust and confidence must be developed between workers and the employer.

If decertification is to succeed, management must eliminate the problems that initially led to unionization. Although many executives believe that pay and benefits are the primary reasons for union membership, these factors are probably not the real cause.[26] Failure to treat employees as individuals

---

[26] *Ibid.*

is often the primary reason for unionization. The real problems often stem from practices such as failing to listen to employees' opinions, dealing with workers unfairly and dishonestly, and treating employees as numbers and not as people. Many organizational attitudes and actions indicate to employees how the firm feels toward them, including the following:

- Poor housekeeping.
- Poor supervision.
- Inadequate wage differentials among various skill levels.
- Inadequate preventive maintenance.
- Arbitrary company policies.
- Unfair promotional policies.
- An ineffective complaint and discipline procedure.[27]

Such problems may have initially led to unionization. Even if an organization desires to become union-free, it cannot become so immediately. Unsatisfactory conditions must be eliminated, and this takes time.

■ THE ROLE OF THE HUMAN RESOURCE MANAGER

The human resource manager in a union-free firm has a somewhat different role than his or her counterpart in a unionized company. The tasks of the human resource manager in a unionized firm often revolve around contract negotiations and grievance handling. The human resource manager in a union-free firm must work toward creating an atmosphere in which workers do not feel the need for union representation. Human resource managers serve as the catalyst for developing and maintaining nonunion attitudes.

In the mid-1960s, many senior labor relations professionals gave primary attention to stabilizing collective bargaining relationships. At that time, the most important force for change was the rise of laws and governmental regulations mandating nondiscrimination and affirmative action in employment. Affirmative action brought about rational human resource policies and practices, which resulted in management focusing on better employment relationships.

The Conference Board survey on labor-management relations showed that preventing the spread of unionism and developing effective employee relations systems are more important to managers today than achieving sound collective bargaining results.[28] These changes in priority, along with the current emphasis on remaining or becoming union-free, have given human resource managers greater corporate power and importance.[29]

---

[27] *Ibid.*

[28] Alexander B. Trowbridge, "A Management Look at Labor Relations," p. 414.

[29] *Ibid.*

The desire for union-free operations, and the greater emphasis on employee oriented policies, has created a management perspective that emphasizes the individual employee over adversary labor relations. The union-free approach is basically a human resource system that bypasses the union and deals directly with the individual worker—and his or her needs. This human resource system matches compensation and benefits with worker performance, properly designs the organization and the workplace to enhance productivity and worker satisfaction, and involves employees in solving workplace problems and in making decisions.[30]

Remaining union-free requires a strong commitment by management at all levels, open communication, and trust. In many ways, the commitment necessary to maintain a union-free environment requires a much more demanding effort by the human resource professional. Some organizations may not maintain that commitment and therefore will become vulnerable to organizing efforts. The old maxim is still true: "Unions don't organize employees—managers do." They do this through mistakes, neglect, and (unfortunately) plain greed.[31] The human resource manager, therefore, must ensure that an employee relations system is created whereby employees are treated in a positive manner, allowing each individual to maintain his or her self-esteem and advance individually as the organization advances.

■ THE ROLE OF THE GLOBAL HUMAN RESOURCE MANAGER

Global human resource managers in union-free multinational organizations have much more difficult roles than their counterparts in union-free domestic companies. These managers must work even harder to create an atmosphere in which workers will not feel the need for union representation. The 1980s were a difficult decade for many workers in this country. Between 1969 and the 1980s, average weekly earnings declined by more than 30 percent. Dislocations became commonplace, and disgruntled employees filed a record number of wrongful discharge and job discrimination suits in the 1980s; unfair labor practice complaints also soared.[32] Even in these difficult times U.S. workers did not turn to unions. They apparently did not view union representation as a feasible solution to their problems. In such an environment, domestic human resource managers are under less pressure to create a human resource system that bypasses the union and deals directly with the needs of individual workers.[33]

---

[30] David C. Metz, "12 Key Factors in Staying Union Free—A Checklist for Employers," *CUE*, 30 (Washington, D.C., 1989), pp. 49–73.

[31] Alexander B. Trowbridge, "A Management Look at Labor Relations," p. 417.

[32] John Hoerr, "What Should Unions Do?" *Harvard Business Review*, 69 (May–June 1991), pp. 30–31.

[33] David C. Metz, "12 Key Factors in Staying Union Free," pp. 49–73.

However, the drastic decline in union membership in the United States during the past two decades appears to be a uniquely American phenomenon. Global workers are much more likely to turn to unions when the union-free environment is not worker oriented. In the past two decades, union membership in the United States has declined by nearly 50 percent, but in other industrialized countries it has declined only slightly. In the United Kingdom, union membership dropped from 58 to 50 percent, and in Japan it fell from 32 to 28 percent. Membership remained nearly the same in Germany at 43 percent and in Canada at 36 percent. In Sweden, union membership even increased from 79 to 96 percent.[34] Because of the relatively strong state of global unionization, a much more decisive effort by global human resource managers is needed to maintain a multinational's union-free status. Global organizations that do not maintain that commitment could become quite vulnerable to union-organizing efforts. Even more than their domestic counterparts, global human resource managers must ensure that effective employee relations systems are created whereby employees are treated in a positive manner.

SUMMARY

Most employees in the United States don't belong to unions. Their reasons for not joining are many and varied: It costs money to be a union member, many employees think that unions are unnecessary, and peer pressure against union affiliation may be exerted. Reprisals against employees for union activities are illegal in the United States. Even so, some employees would feel insecure about their jobs if they engaged in union activities. Certain employees have religious or moral beliefs that preclude them from joining organizations, including unions.

Under certain circumstances a union may decide to expend little or no effort to establish a new bargaining unit. Unions also recognize that there are certain industries, firms, and locations in the country with an anti-union tradition. Moreover, the growing web of employee legal protection may well take the place of union representation in the future.

Valid reasons exist for management's acceptance or rejection of a union. There may be times when resistance to organizing attempts isn't advantageous. In addition, there are situations in which the relationship between management and the union is quite good and well established. Management may also desire unionization of competing organizations.

---

[34] John Hoerr, "What Should Unions Do?" pp. 30–31.

Although there may be valid reasons for a firm to accept unionization, a large percentage of executives prefer that their companies remain union-free. In fact, that is a major goal for many organizations. Some reasons for remaining union-free are costs, maintaining control over operations, ability to reward superior performance, and ability to adapt quickly to changing conditions.

To remain union-free, an organization must establish its strategy and tactics long before a union-organizing attempt begins. This approach is crucial because the employees' decision to consider forming a union is usually not made overnight. Extremely important to remaining union-free is overall management effectiveness, particularly that of first-line supervisors. The fact that the organization's goal is to remain union-free should be clearly communicated to everyone in the organization. One of the most important considerations of remaining union-free is the establishment of credible communication. Openness and trust on the part of managers and employees are essential. The ability to remain union-free relates closely to the organization's human resource planning, recruitment, and selection practices. Lack of opportunity to grow and advance, inadequate or inequitable financial compensation, and a reputation for having an unsafe and unhealthy work environment leave an organization wide open to unionization. A means of resolving employee complaints should be available. Human resource research can reveal changes in attitudes within the organization that could lead to unionization.

Decertification means that a union has lost its right to act as the exclusive bargaining representative of a group of employees. The process is essentially the reverse of what a union must go through to be recognized as an official bargaining unit. In light of significant reductions in union ranks, the outcome of certification and decertification elections is of increasing concern to unions.

Rules established by the NLRB specify the procedures for filing a decertification petition and holding a decertification election. When all of the conditions have been met, the NLRB regional director will schedule a decertification election by secret ballot. The NLRB carefully monitors the events leading up to the election.

The most effective means to accomplish decertification is to improve the corporate culture so that workers no longer feel the need to have a union. This takes time because mutual trust and confidence must develop. If decertification is to succeed, management must eliminate the problems that initially led to unionization.

The human resource manager in a union-free firm has a somewhat different role from his or her counterpart in a unionized company. The tasks of the human resource manager in a unionized firm often revolve around contract negotiations and grievance handling. The human resource manager in a union-free firm must work toward creating an atmosphere in which workers do not feel the need for union representation. Human resource managers serve as the catalyst for developing and maintaining nonunion attitudes.

Questions for Review

1. What are the most important reasons for employees not joining unions? Discuss each of them.
2. What are the reasons both for and against a firm resisting unionization attempts?
3. Briefly describe the factors involved in maintaining a union-free status.
4. What role does the first-line supervisor play in helping a firm remain union-free?
5. Describe the process of decertification.
6. How might the role of a human resource manager change if he or she moves from a unionized firm to a union-free firm? Discuss.

Terms for Review

Open-door policy
Grievance procedure

Ombudsperson
Decertification

INCIDENT 1 ▪ Being Fair ▪

Ed Davis is a supervisor at the Paxma Manufacturing Company, a manufacturer of a special kind of filler material for packaging. Ed was transferred to his present job from another plant. He accepted the transfer because he felt it would provide a better opportunity for promotion. Ed's new section includes fifteen workers whose jobs are essentially identical. The workload of Paxma often fluctuates, requiring extensive use of overtime. This overtime is very popular among the workers, and Ed's predecessor had distributed it on a simple rotation basis.

When Ed took over, he felt that overtime should be a reward for excellent performance. He also felt that certain workers needed the overtime more than others. Ed did not discuss this with the workers but simply began to assign the overtime as he saw fit.

Everything seemed to be going well until the day Ed was called to the office of Mary Donnelly, the human resource manager. After a brief greeting Mary said, "Ed, I hear through the grapevine that there's a good deal of dissension in your crew. Some of the workers feel they're not being given their fair share of overtime." Ed replied, "I assign everybody their share. It's just not always an equal share." "That may be true, Ed," said Mary, "but at least a couple of the workers believe that most of the overtime has been going to the three new people you've hired." "Who told you that?" asked Ed. "I don't think that is important," Mary answered, "but you need to think about whether there's any substance to the impression your workers have." "You may be right," said Ed. He admitted, "I suppose I could have unconsciously favored the people I personally selected."

Questions

1. Was it appropriate for the human resource manager to get involved in the line function of assigning overtime? Explain.
2. What would you do if you were Ed?

INCIDENT 2 ▪ Open the Door! ▪

Barney Cline, the new human resource manager for Ampex Utilities, was just getting settled in his new office. He had recently moved from another firm to take his new job. Barney had been selected over several in-house candidates and numerous other applicants because of his record of getting things done. He had a good reputation for working through people to get the job accomplished.

Barney's phone rang. The person on the other end of the line asked, "Mr. Cline, could I set up an appointment to talk with you?" "Certainly," Barney said, "when do you want to get together?" "How about after work? It might be bad if certain people saw me speaking to anyone in management," said the caller.

Barney was a bit puzzled, but he set up an appointment for 5:30 P.M., when nearly everyone would be gone. At the designated time there was a knock on his door; it was Mark Johnson, a senior maintenance worker who had been with the firm for more than ten years.

After the initial welcome, Mark began by saying, "Mr. Cline, several of the workers asked me to talk to you. Rumor has it that you're a fair person. The company says it has an open-door policy, but we're afraid to use it. Roy Edwards, one of the best maintenance workers in our section, tried it several months ago. They hassled him so much that he quit last week. We just don't know what to do to get any problems solved. There have been talks of organizing a union. We really don't want that, but something has to give."

Barney thanked Mark for his honesty and promised not to reveal the conversation. In the weeks following the conversation with Mark, Barney was able to verify that the situation existed just as Mark had described it. There was considerable mistrust between managers and the operative employees.

Questions

1. What are the basic causes of the problems confronting Ampex Utilities?
2. How should Barney attempt to resolve this situation?

DEVELOPING HRM SKILLS

Union-organizing attempts are a real challenge to human resource managers and first-line supervisors. During a recent conference on maintaining a union-free status, the point was stressed that supervisors are the key to preventing companies from being organized. Therefore, those in human resource management should maintain direct and continual contact with supervisors. This exercise is designed to give participants an opportunity to experience what goes on when a union is being considered.

Two committees, one employee group and one supervisor group, will discuss the prospects of unionization. Each committee must come up with a recommendation for or against unionization and state its reasons for the recommendation. The spokesperson for the employee group is Bob Jones and the group members are Gerald Young, Julie Faire, and Tony Wells. Bob Jones is a very outspoken union advocate who has always believed this company should have a union. He believes wages are lower here than at unionized firms in the area and sees too much "brother-in-lawing" going on in the organization. He was also denied a raise recently and was told that the boss just did not "feel" he deserved one.

This is Gerald Young's first job, but his father is the union steward of another company. Gerald's dad often said, "What you guys need over there is a good union." Last month when production standards were raised, Gerald's piece-rate bonus was wiped out. His dad says they do not pull that in a unionized firm.

Julie Faire has been working here for several years, and the company has always been good to her. She had some family problems last year and her boss let her off for several days. She wonders if a union could be better than her understanding boss.

Tony Wells is an old hand here, and he has seen lots of things come and go over the years. Tony's experience has been that if employees have enough guts to go to their supervisors directly they can usually get satisfaction. It seems to Tony that too many people today are looking for a "free lunch."

The spokesperson for the supervisor group, Charlie Neal, is very anti-union. Charlie is really fed up with all this union talk and believes that these people do not seem to know when they are well off. Charlie has been with the company for nearly twenty years and does not intend to put up with a union now. He believes the company should "get tough." Charlie has a pretty good idea of who is leading the union advocates. Charlie thinks that if the other supervisors will listen, it will be easy to find reasons to get rid of the troublemakers.

Beverly Woods has been a supervisor for only a few years, but previously she was a supervisor in a unionized company. Beverly has a healthy respect for unions and some feeling for how they get their power. Beverly feels that this is a great opportunity for the supervisors to get together with the employees and solve the employees' legitimate complaints.

continued on next page

continued from previous page

She believes this would be all it would take to convince employees that they do not need a union.

Depending on what is determined in the conference, there may be an agreement proposed that will prevent unionizing, or will create a delaying action such as a joint committee. There may be hard lines drawn leading to a showdown, or even an immediate call for a union election. The groups will decide, and the spokespersons will report their decisions. Your instructor will provide the participants with additional information necessary to complete the exercise.

REFERENCES

Adams, C. T. "Changing Employment Patterns of Organized Workers." *Monthly Labor Review,* 108 (February 1985), pp. 25–31.

Anderson, Kay E., Philip M. Doyle, and Albert E. Schwenk. "Measuring Union-Nonunion Earnings Differences." *Monthly Labor Review,* 113 (June 1990), pp. 26–38.

Angle, Harold L., and James L. Perry. "Dual Commitment and Labor-Management Relationship Climates." *Academy of Management Journal,* 29 (March 1986), pp. 31–47.

Barbash, Jack. "Do We Really Want Labor on the Ropes?" *Harvard Business Review,* 63 (July–August 1985), pp. 10–16.

Bohlander, George W., and Harold C. White. "Building Bridges: Nonunion Employee Grievance Systems." *Personnel,* 65 (July 1988), pp. 62–67.

Clark, K. B. "Unionization and Firm Performance: The Impact on Profits, Growth, and Productivity." *American Economic Review,* 74 (December 1984), pp. 893–919.

Diaz, Edmund M., John W. Minton, and David M. Saunders. "A Fair Nonunion Grievance Procedure." *Personnel,* 64 (April 1987), pp. 13–18.

Eubanks, Paula. "Employee Grievance Policy: Don't Discourage Complaints." *Hospitals,* 64 (December 20, 1990), pp. 36–37.

Foulkes, Fred K. "How Top Nonunion Companies Manage Employees." *Harvard Business Review,* 59 (September–October 1981), pp. 90–96.

Hughes, Charles L. *Making Unions Unnecessary* (New York: Executive Enterprises, 1976).

Koretz, Gene. "Why Unions Thrive Abroad—But Wither in the U.S." *Business Week* (September 10, 1990), p. 26.

Lewis, Ephraim. "BW/Harris Poll: Confidence in Unions Is Crumbling." *Business Week* (July 8, 1985), p. 76.

Lissy, William E. "Election of 'Financial Core' Union Membership." *Supervision,* 51 (September 1990), pp. 22–23.

Lissy, William E. "Management-Sponsored Employees' Committee Not Illegal." *Supervision,* 51 (April 1990), pp. 17–19.

McCracken, P. W. "Giving Unions Their Due." *Across the Board,* 21 (November 1984), pp. 59–60.

McDonough, Paul S. "Maintain a Union-Free Status." *Personnel Journal,* 69 (April 1990), pp. 108–114.

Markham, S., and D. Scott. "Controlling Absenteeism: Union and Nonunion Differences." *Personnel Administrator,* 30 (February 1985), pp. 87–88ff.

Mulcahy, Robert W., and Jon E. Anderson. "The Bargaining Battleground Called Comparable Worth." *Public Personnel Management,* 15 (Fall 1986), pp. 233–245.

Premeaux, Shane R., R. Wayne Mondy, and Art L. Bethke. "The Two-Tier Wage System." *Personnel Administrator,* 31 (November 1986), pp. 92–100.

Ritter, Anne. "Are Unions Worth the Bargain?" *Personnel,* 67 (February 1990), pp. 12–14.

Ritter, Anne. "The UAW Strikes Out at Nissan." *Personnel,* 66 (November 1989), pp. 5–6.

Sanyal, Rajib N. "An Empirical Analysis of the Unionization of Foreign Manufacturing Firms in the U.S." *Journal of International Business Studies,* 21 (First Quarter 1990), pp. 119–132.

Schiffman, Barry. "Tougher Tactics to Keep Out Unions: Consultants Give Employers a New Bag of Tricks." *The New York Times,* 140 (March 3, 1991), sec. 3, F8(N), col 1.

Voos, P. B. "Trends in Union Organizing Expenditures." *Industrial Labor Relations Review,* 38 (October 1984), pp. 52–63.

CHAPTER **18**

INTERNAL EMPLOYEE RELATIONS

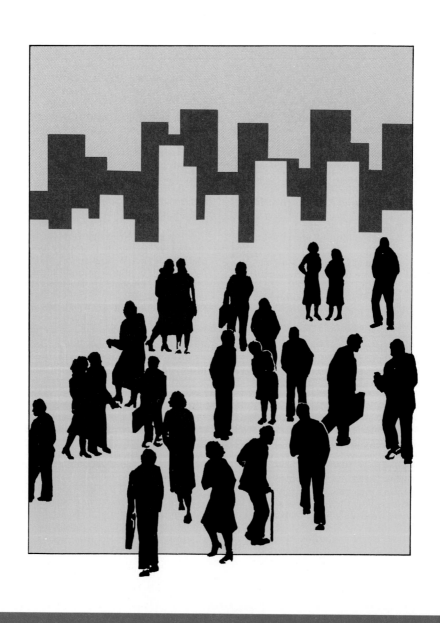

1. Distinguish between discipline and disciplinary action, identify and describe the steps involved in the disciplinary process, and describe the steps involved in progressive discipline.

2. Explain how grievance handling is typically conducted under a collective bargaining agreement and in union-free firms.

3. State how termination conditions may differ when operative employees, executives, managers, or professionals are involved, and explain the concept of employment at will.

4. Explain the role of internal employee relations with regard to resignations, demotions, layoffs, transfers, promotions, and retirements.

5. Discuss the legal implications of internal employee relations and how multinational corporations cope with internal employee relations.

■ Bob Halmes, the production supervisor for American Manufacturing, was mad at the world when he arrived at work. The automobile mechanic had not repaired his car on time the day before, so he had been forced to take a taxi to work this morning. No one was safe around Bob today, and it was not the time for Phillip Martin, a member of Local 264, to report for work late. Without hesitation, Bob said, "You know our company can't tolerate this type of behavior. I don't want to see you around here anymore. You're fired." Just as quickly, Phillip replied, "You're way off base. Our contract calls for three warnings for tardiness. My steward will hear about this."

■ Bill Morton, a ten-year employee at Ketro Productions, arrived at the office of the human resource manager to turn in his letter of resignation. Bill was very upset with his supervisor. When the human resource manager, Robert Noll, asked what was wrong, Bill replied, "Yesterday, I made a mistake and set my machine up wrong. It was the first time in years that I'd done that. My boss chewed me out in front of my friends. I wouldn't take that from the president, much less a two-bit supervisor!"

These scenarios represent only two of the many situations that human resource managers confront when dealing with internal employee relations. Bob Halmes has just been reminded that his power to fire Phillip Martin has limits. The resignation of Bill Morton might have been avoided if his supervisor had not shown poor judgment and disciplined him in front of his friends.

In this chapter, we first define *internal employee relations*. Next, we discuss the reasons for disciplinary action, the disciplinary action process, approaches to disciplinary action, and the administration of disciplinary action. We then describe grievance handling under a collective bargaining agreement and for nonunion employees. Next, we review termination, employment at will, resignation, demotion, layoff, transfer, promotion, and retirement. We devote the last portion of the chapter to legal implications of internal employee relations and internal employee relations in multinational corporations.

■ INTERNAL EMPLOYEE RELATIONS DEFINED

The status of most workers is not permanently fixed in an organization. Employees constantly move upward, laterally, downward, and out of the organization. In order to ensure that workers with the proper skills and experience are available at all levels, constant and concerted efforts are required to maintain good internal employee relations. A well-conceived and implemented employee relations program is very beneficial to both the organization and its employees. **Internal employee relations** consists of the human resource management activities associated with the movement of employees within the organization. These HRM activities include the actions of promotion, transfer, demotion, resignation, discharge, layoff, and retirement. Discipline and disciplinary action are also crucial aspects of internal employee relations.

Increasingly, management is patterning employee relations systems on models provided by such leaders as the Hewlett-Packard Company, which has been committed to good employee relations since its founding. Exemplary employee relations systems go beyond providing competitive salaries and benefits, involving workers in decision making, and treating employees fairly. Such systems also deal with matters such as establishing an employee grievance procedure and a no-layoff policy. The trend toward more responsible internal employee relations systems seems to spreading among industry leaders, which could usher in an era dedicated to sound and equitable employee relations.

■ DISCIPLINARY ACTION

Discipline is the state of employee self-control and orderly conduct and indicates the extent of genuine teamwork within an organization. **Disciplinary action** invokes a penalty against an employee who fails to meet established standards. Effective disciplinary action addresses the employee's wrongful behavior, not the employee as a person.[1] Incorrectly administered disciplinary action is destructive to both the employee and the organization. Thus disciplinary action should not be applied haphazardly.

A necessary but often trying aspect of internal employee relations is the application of disciplinary action. Disciplinary action is not usually management's initial response to a problem. Normally, there are more positive ways of convincing employees to adhere to company policies that

---

[1] Keith Davis, *Human Behavior at Work* (New York: McGraw-Hill, 1977), p. 261.

are necessary to accomplish organizational goals. However, managers must administer disciplinary action when company policies are violated. Disciplinary policies afford the organization the greatest opportunity to accomplish organizational goals, thereby benefiting both employees and the corporation. Not only is there a need for such policies, but a process should also exist to assist employees in appealing disciplinary actions. Because disciplinary action involves interaction between human beings, the process is sometimes biased and emotional, and therefore such actions are not always justified. Unjustified action is unfair to the employee involved, is counterproductive, and has contributed to the loss of union-free status by some firms. It has also resulted in wildcat strikes, walkouts, and slow-downs in unionized firms. Even if employees don't react overtly to unjustified disciplinary actions, morale will likely decline, which can negatively affect the firm.

Despite management's desire to solve employee problems in a positive manner, at times this is not possible. A major purpose of disciplinary action is to ensure that employee behavior is consistent with the firm's rules. Rules are established to further the organization's objectives. When a rule is violated, the effectiveness of the organization is diminished to some degree, depending on the severity of the infraction. For instance, if a worker is late to work once, the effect on the firm may be minimal. Consistently being late is another matter because it negatively affects both the productivity of the worker and the morale of other employees. Supervisors must realize that disciplinary action can be a positive force for the company when it is applied responsibly and equitably. The firm benefits from developing and implementing effective disciplinary policies. Without a healthy state of discipline, or the potential for disciplinary action, the firm's effectiveness may be severely limited.

Disciplinary action can also help the employee become more productive, thereby benefiting him or her in the long-run. For example, if a worker is disciplined because of failure to monitor the quality of his or her output—and quality improves after the disciplinary action—it has been useful in the worker's development. Because of improved performance, the individual may receive a promotion or pay increase. The employee is reminded of what is expected and fulfills these requirements better. Effective disciplinary action can thus encourage the individual to improve his or her performance, ultimately resulting in gain for that individual.

■ THE DISCIPLINARY ACTION PROCESS

The disciplinary action process is dynamic and ongoing. Because one person's actions can affect others in a work group, the proper application of disciplinary action fosters acceptable behavior by other group members. Conversely, unjustified or improperly administered disciplinary action can have a detrimental effect on other group members.

The disciplinary action process is shown in Figure 18-1 on page 672. The external environment affects every area of human resource management, including disciplinary policies and actions. Changes that happen in the

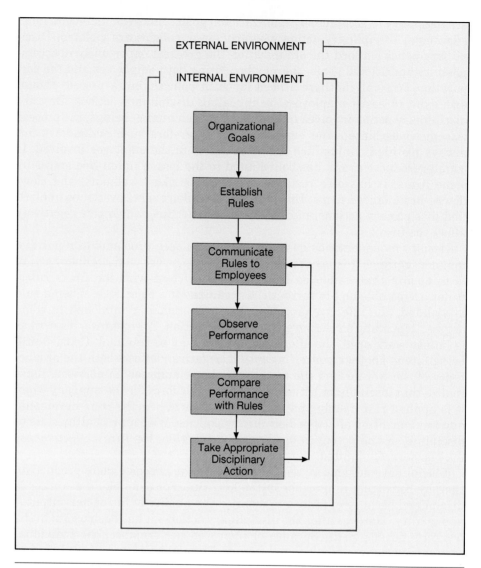

FIGURE 18-1 | The Disciplinary Action Process

external environment, such as technological innovations, may render a rule inappropriate; they may also necessitate new rules. Laws and government regulations that affect company policies and rules are also constantly changing. For instance, the Occupational Safety and Health Act has caused many firms to establish safety rules.

Unions are another external factor. Specific punishment for rule violations is subject to negotiation and inclusion in the agreement. For example, the union may negotiate for three written warnings for tardiness before a worker is suspended instead of the two warnings a present contract might require.

Changes in the internal environment of the firm can also alter the disciplinary process. Through organizational development, the firm may alter its culture. This change may result in first-line supervisors handling disciplinary action more positively. Organization policies can also have an impact on the disciplinary action process. For instance, a policy of treating employees as mature human beings would significantly affect the process.

The disciplinary action process deals largely with infractions of rules. Rules are specific guides to behavior on the job. The do's and don'ts associated with accomplishing tasks may be highly inflexible. For example, company rules may prohibit smoking in certain areas and require that hard hats be worn in hazardous areas for safety reasons.

After management has established rules, it must communicate these rules to employees. Individuals cannot obey a rule if they do not know it exists. So long as employee behavior doesn't vary from acceptable practices, there's no need for disciplinary action. But when an employee's behavior violates a rule, corrective action may be necessary. The purpose of this action is to alter the types of behavior that can have a negative impact on achievement of organizational objectives—not merely to chastise the violator.

Note that the process shown in Figure 18-1 includes feedback from the point of taking appropriate disciplinary action to communicating rules to employees. When appropriate disciplinary action is taken, employees should realize that certain behaviors are unacceptable and should not be repeated. However, if appropriate disciplinary action is not taken, employees may view the behavior as acceptable and repeat it.

■ APPROACHES TO DISCIPLINARY ACTION

Several concepts regarding the administration of disciplinary action have been developed. We discuss three of these concepts next: the hot stove rule, progressive disciplinary action, and disciplinary action without punishment.

The Hot Stove Rule

One approach to administering disciplinary action is referred to as the hot stove rule. According to this approach, disciplinary action should have the following consequences, which are analogous to touching a hot stove:

1. *Burns immediately.* If disciplinary action is to be taken, it must occur immediately so that the individual will understand the reason for it. With the passage of time, people have the tendency to convince themselves that they are not at fault, which tends to partially nullify later disciplinary effects.
2. *Provides warning.* It is also extremely important to provide advance warning that punishment will follow unacceptable behavior. As individuals move closer to a hot stove, they are warned by its heat that they will be burned if they touch it and thus have the opportunity to avoid the burn if they so choose.

3. *Gives consistent punishment.* Disciplinary action should also be consistent in that everyone who performs the same act will be punished accordingly. As with a hot stove, each person who touches it with the same degree of pressure, and for the same period of time, is burned to the same extent.

4. *Burns impersonally.* Disciplinary action should be impersonal. The hot stove burns anyone who touches it—without favoritism.

Although the hot stove approach has some merit, it also has weaknesses. If the circumstances surrounding all disciplinary situations were the same, there would be no problem with this approach. However, situations are often quite different, and many variables may be present in each individual disciplinary case. For instance, does the organization penalize a loyal, twenty-year employee the same as an individual who has been with the firm less than six weeks? Thus a supervisor often finds that he or she cannot be completely consistent and impersonal in taking disciplinary action. Because situations do vary, progressive disciplinary action may be more realistic—and more beneficial to both the employee and the organization.

Progressive Disciplinary Action

Progressive disciplinary action is intended to ensure that the minimum penalty appropriate to the offense is imposed. Its use involves answering a series of questions about the severity of the offense. The manager must ask these questions—in sequence—to determine the proper disciplinary action, as illustrated in Figure 18-2. After the manager has determined that disciplinary action is appropriate, the proper question is: "Does this violation warrant more than an oral warning?"[2] If the improper behavior is minor and has not previously occurred, perhaps only an oral warning will be sufficient. Also, an individual may receive several oral warnings before a "yes" answer applies. The manager follows the same procedure for each level of offense in the progressive disciplinary process. The manager does not consider termination until each lower level question is answered "yes." However, major violations, such as assaulting a supervisor or another worker, may justify immediate termination of the employee.

In order to assist managers in recognizing the proper level of disciplinary action, some firms have formalized the procedure. One approach is to establish progressive disciplinary action guidelines, as shown in Table 18-1 on page 676. In this example, a worker who is absent without authorization will receive an oral warning the first time it happens and a written warning the second time; the third time, the employee will be terminated. Fighting on the job is an offense that normally results in immediate termination. However, specific guidelines for various offenses should be developed to meet the needs of the organization. For example, smoking in an unauthorized area may be grounds for immediate dismissal in an explosives factory.

---

[2] Arthur R. Pell, "Effective Reprimanding," *Manager's Magazine,* 65 (August 1990), p. 26.

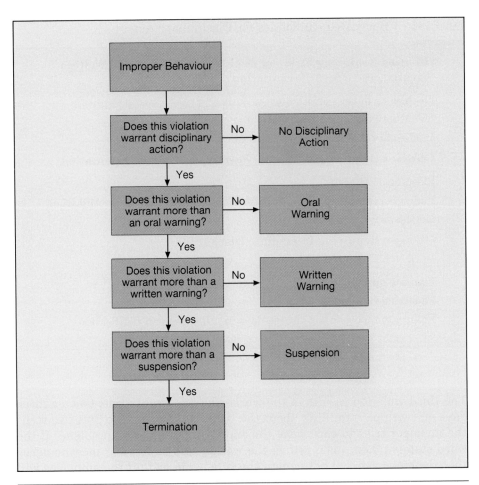

FIGURE 18-2 | The Progressive Disciplinary Approach

On the other hand, the same violation may be less serious in a plant producing concrete products. Basically, the penalty should be appropriate to address the severity of the violation, and no greater.[3]

Disciplinary Action Without Punishment

Disciplinary action without punishment gives a worker time off with pay to think about whether he or she really wants to follow the rules and continue working for the company.[4] When an employee violates a rule, the manager issues an oral "reminder." Repetition brings a written reminder.

---

[3] Robert N. Lussier, "16 Guidelines for Effective Discipline," *Supervisory Management,* 35 (March 1990), p. 10.

[4] Laurie Baum, "Punishing Workers with a Day Off," *Business Week* (June 16, 1986), p. 80.

TABLE 18-1 | Suggested Guidelines for Disciplinary Action

Offenses Requiring First, an Oral Warning, Second, a Written Warning, and Third, Termination

Negligence in the performance of duties

Unauthorized absence from job

Inefficiency in the performance of job

Offenses Requiring a Written Warning and Then Termination

Sleeping on the job

Failure to report to work one or two days in a row without notification

Negligent use of property

Offenses Requiring Immediate Discharge

Theft

Fighting on the job

Falsifying time cards

Failure to report to work three days in a row without notification

The third violation results in the worker having to take one, two, or three days off (with pay) to think about the situation. During the first two steps the manager tries to encourage the employee to solve the problem.[5] If the third step is taken, upon return the worker and supervisor meet to agree that the employee will not violate the rule again or that the employee will leave the firm. When disciplinary action without punishment is used, it is especially important that all rules be explicitly stated in writing. At the time of orientation, new workers should be told that repeated violations of different rules will be viewed in the same way as several violations of the same rule. This keeps workers from taking undue advantage of the process.

■ ADMINISTRATION OF DISCIPLINARY ACTION

As you might expect, disciplinary actions are not pleasant supervisory tasks. Many managers find them to be quite difficult. Reasons for managers wanting to avoid disciplinary action include the following:

1. *Lack of training.* The supervisor may not have the knowledge and skill necessary to handle disciplinary problems.
2. *Fear.* The supervisor may be concerned that top management will not support a disciplinary action.

---

[5] David N. Campbell, R. L. Fleming, and Richard C. Grote, "Discipline Without Punishment— At Last," *Harvard Business Review,* 63 (July–August 1985), p. 168.

3. *The only one.* The supervisor may think, "No one else is disciplining employees, so why should I?"
4. *Guilt.* The supervisor may think, "How can I discipline someone if I've done the same thing?"
5. *Loss of friendship.* The supervisor may believe that disciplinary action will damage friendship with an employee or the employee's associates.
6. *Time loss.* The supervisor may begrudge the valuable time that is required to administer and explain disciplinary action.
7. *Loss of temper.* The supervisor may be afraid of losing his or her temper when talking to an employee about a rule violation.
8. *Rationalization.* The supervisor may think, "The employee knows it was the wrong thing to do, so why do we need to talk about it?"[6]

These reasons apply to all forms of disciplinary action—from an oral warning to termination. However, we should mention some additional reasons regarding termination. Supervisors often avoid this form of disciplinary action, even when it is in the company's best interest. This reluctance often stems from breakdowns in other areas of the human resource management function. For instance, if a supervisor has consistently rated an employee high on annual performance appraisals, the supervisor's position for terminating a worker for poor performance would be weak. It is embarrassing to decide to fire a worker and then be asked why you rated this individual so high on the previous evaluation. It could be that the employee's productivity has actually dropped substantially. It could also be that the employee's productivity has always been low but that the supervisor has been reluctant to give the individual a low rating.

Another problem related to reluctance to fire employees for cause is poor record keeping. Without adequate documentation, the supervisor may have trouble justifying to upper level management that a person should be terminated. Rather than run the risk of a decision being overturned, the supervisor retains the ineffective worker.

Finally, some supervisors believe that even attempting to terminate women and minorities is useless. However, the statutes and subsequent court decisions associated with women and minorities in the workplace were not intended to protect nonproductive workers. Anyone whose performance is consistently below standard can, and should, be terminated after the supervisor has made reasonable attempts to salvage the employee.

A supervisor may be perfectly justified in administering disciplinary action, but there is usually a proper time and place for doing so. For example, disciplining a worker in the presence of others may embarrass the individual and actually defeat the purpose of the action. Even when they are wrong, employees resent disciplinary action administered in public. The scenario at the beginning of the chapter in which Bill Morton quit his job because he was disciplined in front of his peers provides an excellent illustration. By disciplining employees in private, supervisors prevent them from losing face with their peers.

---

[6] Wallace Wohlking, "Effective Discipline in Employee Relations," *Personnel Journal,* 54 (September 1975), p. 489.

In addition, many supervisors may be too lenient early in the disciplinary action process and too strict later. This lack of consistency doesn't give the worker a clear understanding of the penalty associated with the inappropriate action. As Robert F. Garrett, manager of labor relations for Georgia-Pacific Corporation, stated, "A supervisor will often endure an unacceptable situation for an extended period of time. Then, when the supervisor finally does take action, he or she is apt to overreact and come down excessively hard." However, consistency does not necessarily mean that the same penalty must be applied to two different workers for the same offense. For instance, employers would be consistent if they always considered the worker's past record and length of service. For a serious violation, a long-term employee might only receive a suspension, while a worker with only a few months' service might be terminated for the same act. This type of action could reasonably be viewed as being consistent.

In order to assist management in administering discipline properly, a *Code on Discipline Procedure* has been prepared by the Advisory, Conciliation and Arbitration Service. The purpose of the code is to give practical guidance on how to formulate disciplinary rules and procedures and use them effectively. The code recommends the actions shown in Table 18-2. As you can see, it stresses communication of rules, telling the employee of the complaint, conducting a full investigation, and giving the employee an opportunity to tell his or her side of the story.

TABLE 18-2 | Recommended Disciplinary Procedures

- All employees should be given a copy of the employer's rules on disciplinary procedures. The procedures should specify which employees they cover and what disciplinary actions may be taken, and should allow matters to be dealt with quickly.

- Employees should be told of complaints against them and given an opportunity to state their case. They should have the right to be accompanied by a trade union representative or fellow employee of their choice.

- Disciplinary action should not be taken until the case has been fully investigated. Immediate superiors should not have the power to dismiss without reference to senior management, and, except for gross misconduct, no employee should be dismissed for a first breach of discipline.

- Employees should be given an explanation for any penalty imposed, and they should have a right of appeal, with specified procedures to be followed.

- When disciplinary action other than summary dismissal is needed, supervisors should give a formal oral warning in the case of minor offenses, or a written warning in more serious cases.

Source: "Code on Discipline Procedure," *Industrial Management,* 7 (August 1977), p. 7. Used with permission.

HRM In Action

As Billy Bowen, a first-line supervisor for Kwik Corporation, entered the office of Sandra Findley, human resource director, he was obviously disturbed and wanted help. Billy started the conversation by saying, "Allen Smith, one of my employees, violated a serious company policy today by failing to wear his safety glasses on a very dangerous job. The company policy states that any employee who does not

follow the stated policy will receive a written reprimand on the first offense and will be terminated on the second violation. Allen has already received one reprimand and has just committed his second violation. However, he has been one of my best workers for over five years, and letting him go could have a really negative impact on productivity."

What advice should Sandra provide?

■ GRIEVANCE HANDLING UNDER A COLLECTIVE BARGAINING AGREEMENT

If employees in an organization are represented by a union, workers who believe that they have been disciplined or dealt with unjustly can appeal through the grievance and arbitration procedures of the collective bargaining agreement. The grievance procedure has been described as "one of the truly great accomplishments of the American industrial relations movement. For all its defects . . . it constitutes a social invention of great importance."[7] The grievance system encourages and facilitates the settlement of disputes between labor and management. A grievance procedure permits employees to express complaints without jeopardizing their jobs. It also assists management in seeking out the underlying causes and solutions to grievances.

The Grievance Procedure

Virtually all labor agreements include some form of grievance procedure. A **grievance** can be broadly defined as an employee's dissatisfaction or feeling of personal injustice relating to his or her employment. A grievance under a collective bargaining agreement is normally well defined. It is usually restricted to violations of the terms and conditions of the agreement. There are other conditions that may give rise to a grievance:

---

[7] Neil W. Chamberlain, *The Labor Sector* (New York: McGraw-Hill, 1955), p. 240.

- A violation of law.
- A violation of the intent of the parties as stipulated during contract negotiations.
- A violation of company rules.
- A change in working conditions or past company practices.
- A violation of health and/or safety standards.[8]

Grievance procedures have many common features. However, variations may reflect differences in organizational or decision-making structures or the size of a plant or company. Some general principles based on widespread practice can serve as useful guidelines for effective grievance administration:

- Grievances should be adjusted promptly.
- Procedures and forms used for airing grievances must be easy to utilize and well understood by employees and their supervisors.
- Direct and timely avenues of appeal from rulings of line supervision must exist.[9]

The multiple-step grievance procedure shown in Figure 18-3 is the most common type. In the first step, the employee usually presents the grievance orally and informally to the immediate supervisor in the presence of the union steward. This step offers the greatest potential for improved labor relations, and a large majority of grievances are settled here. The procedure ends if the grievance can be resolved at this first step. If it remains unresolved, the next step involves a meeting between the plant manager or human resource manager and higher union officials, such as the grievance committee or the business agent or manager. Prior to this meeting the grievance is written out, dated, and signed by the employee and the union steward. The written grievance states the events as the employee perceives them, cites the contract provision that allegedly has been violated, and indicates the settlement desired. If the grievance is not settled at this meeting, it is appealed to the third step. This step typically involves the firm's top labor representative (such as the vice-president of industrial relations) and high-level union officials. At times, depending on the severity of the grievance, the president may represent the firm. A grievance that remains unresolved at the conclusion of the third step may go to arbitration, if provided for in the agreement and the union decides to persevere.

Labor-relations problems can escalate when the supervisor is not equipped to handle grievances at the first step. Although the first step is usually handled informally by the union steward, the aggrieved party, and the supervisor, the supervisor must be fully prepared. The supervisor should obtain as many facts as possible before the meeting because the union steward is likely to have done his or her homework.

---

[8] K. L. Sovereign and Mario Bognanno, "Positive Contract Administration." In Dale Yoder and Herbert G. Heneman, Jr., (eds.), *ASPA Handbook of Personnel and Industrial Relations: Employee and Labor Relations,* Vol. III (Washington, D.C.: The Bureau of National Affairs, 1976), pp. 7-161–7-162.

[9] *Ibid.,* p. 7-164.

FIGURE 18-3 | A Multiple-Step Grievance Procedure

Source: Robert W. Eckles et al., *Essentials of Management for First-Line Supervision* (New York: John Wiley & Sons, 1974), p. 529. Reprinted by permission of John Wiley & Sons, Inc.

The supervisor needs to recognize that the grievance may not reflect the real problem. For instance, the employee might be mad at the company for modifying its pay policies, even though the change was agreed to by the union. In order to voice discontent, the worker might file a grievance for an unrelated, minor violation of the contract. The idea of hidden causes of grievances has been referred to as the "iceberg theory"[10] and must always be explored.

Arbitration

The grievance procedure has successfully and peacefully resolved many labor-management problems. The final step in most grievance procedures is arbitration. In arbitration, the parties submit their dispute to an impartial third party for resolution. Most agreements restrict the arbitrator's decision to application and interpretation of the agreement and make the decision final and binding on the parties. Although arbitration at times is used to settle contract negotiation conflicts, its primary use has been in settling grievances.

If the union decides in favor of arbitration, it notifies management. At this point, the union and the company select an arbitrator. Most agreements specify the selection method. It is usually made from a list supplied by the Federal Mediation and Conciliation Service (FMCS) or the American Arbitration Association (AAA), both of which were discussed in Chapter 16. When considering potential arbitrators, both management and labor will study the candidates' previous decisions in an attempt to detect any biases. Obviously, neither party wants to select an arbitrator who might tend to favor the other's position.

When arbitration is used to settle a grievance, a variety of factors may be used to evaluate the fairness of the management actions that caused the grievance. These factors include the following:

- Nature of the offense.
- Due process and procedural correctness.
- Double jeopardy.
- Grievant's past record.
- Length of service with the company.
- Knowledge of rules.
- Warnings.
- Lax enforcement of rules.
- Discriminatory treatment.

The large number of interacting variables in each case makes the arbitration process difficult. The arbitrator must possess exceptional patience and judgment in rendering a fair and impartial decision.

After the arbitrator has been selected—and has agreed to serve—a time and place for a hearing will be determined. The issue to be resolved will be

---

[10] *Ibid.,* p. 7-159.

presented to the arbitrator in a document that summarizes the question(s) to be decided. It will also point out any contract restrictions that prohibit the arbitrator from making an award that would change the terms of the contract.

At the hearing, each side presents its case. Arbitration is an adversarial proceeding, so a case may be lost because of poor preparation and presentation. The arbitrator may conduct the hearing much like a courtroom proceeding. Witnesses, cross-examination, transcripts, and legal counsel may all be used. The parties may also submit, or be asked by the arbitrator to submit, formal written statements. After the hearing, the arbitrator studies the material submitted and testimony given and reaches a decision within thirty to sixty days. The decision is usually accompanied by a written opinion giving reasons for the decision.

The courts will generally enforce an arbitrator's decision unless: (1) the arbitrator's decision is shown to be unreasonable or capricious in that it did not address the issues; (2) the arbitrator exceeded his or her authority; or (3) the award or decision violated a federal or state law.

Proof That Disciplinary Action Was Needed

Any disciplinary action administered may ultimately be taken to arbitration, when such a remedy is specified in the labor agreement. Employers have learned that they must prepare records that will constitute proof before an arbitrator.

The supervisor should document any employee behavior suggesting that disciplinary action may ultimately be required. The burden of proof is on the employer, so the supervisor should record information regarding events, circumstances, places, and witnesses. It is not sufficient for the employer to allege that the employee is incompetent; the arbitrator will demand clear proof.

Written warnings offer substantial proof of disciplinary action and the reasons for it. Although the format of a written warning may vary, the following information should be included:

1. Statement of facts concerning the offense.
2. Identification of the rule that was violated.
3. Statement of what resulted or could have resulted because of the violation.
4. Identification of any previous similar violations by the same individual.
5. Statement of possible future consequences should the violation occur again.
6. Signature and date.

An example of a written warning is shown in Figure 18-4 on page 684. In this instance, the worker has already received an oral reprimand. The individual is also warned that continued tardiness could lead to termination. It is important to document oral reprimands because they may be the first step in disciplinary action leading ultimately to arbitration.

DATE: August 1, 1992
TO: Shane Boudreaux
FROM: Wayne Goodson
SUBJECT: Written Warning

We are quite concerned because today you were thirty minutes late to work and offered no justification for this. According to our records, a similar offense occurred on July 25, 1992. At that time you were informed that failure to report to work on time is unacceptable. I am therefore notifying you in writing that you must report to work on time. It will be necessary to terminate your employment if this happens again.

Please sign this form to indicate that you have read and understand this warning. Signing is not an indication of agreement.

_____
Name

_____
Date

FIGURE 18-4 | An Example of a Written Warning

Weaknesses of Arbitration

Arbitration has achieved a certain degree of success in resolving grievances. However, it is not without weaknesses. Some practitioners claim that arbitration is losing its effectiveness because of the length of time between the first step of the grievance procedure and final settlement. Often, 100–250 days may elapse before a decision is made.[11] The reason for the initial filing of the grievance may actually be forgotten before it is finally settled.

Others object to the cost of arbitration, which has been rising at an alarming rate. The cost of settling even a simple arbitration case can be quite high, even though it is typically shared by labor and management. Forcing every grievance to arbitration could be used as a tactic to place either management or the union in a difficult financial position.

■ GRIEVANCE HANDLING IN UNION-FREE ORGANIZATIONS

As we mentioned in Chapter 17, until the early 1980s few union-free firms had formalized grievance procedures. In fact, a 1977 study found that only 11 percent of union-free firms (91 of 793) had any kind of

---

[11] Lawrence Stessin, "Expedited Arbitration: Less Grief Over Grievances," *Harvard Business Review,* 55 (January–February 1977), p. 129.

grievance procedure.[12] Today this is not the case, as more and more firms have established formal grievance procedures and encourage employees to use them.[13]

While the step-by-step procedure for handling union grievances is common practice, the means of resolving complaints in union-free firms varies. A well-designed grievance procedure ensures that the worker has ample opportunity to make complaints without fear of reprisal. If the system is to work, employees must be well informed about the program and convinced that management wants them to use it. Most employees are hesitant to formalize their complaints and must be constantly urged to avail themselves of the process.[14] The fact that a manager says, "Our workers must be happy because I have received no complaints" does not necessarily mean that employees have no grievances. In a closed, threatening corporate culture, workers may be reluctant to voice their dissatisfaction to management.

Typically, an employee initiates a complaint with his or her immediate supervisor. However, if the complaint involves the supervisor, the individual is permitted to bypass the immediate supervisor and proceed to the employee-relations specialist or the manager at the next higher level. The grievance ultimately may be taken to the organization's top executive for a final decision.

■ TERMINATION

Termination is the most severe penalty that an organization can impose on an employee. Therefore, it should be the most carefully considered disciplinary action. The experience of being terminated is traumatic for employees regardless of their position in the organization. Feelings of failure, fear, disappointment, and anger can occur. It is also a difficult time for the person making the termination decision. Knowing that termination may affect not only the employee but an entire family increases the trauma. Not knowing how the terminated employee will react also may create considerable anxiety for the manager who must do the firing. Regardless of the similarities in the termination of employees at various levels, distinct differences exist with regard to nonmanagerial/nonprofessional employees, executives, managers, and professionals. Termination is an extremely serious form of discipline, and must therefore always be carefully considered and appropriate. Furthermore, in today's business environment, companies need to be as concerned with the termination process as with the hiring process.[15] In a recent survey, company representatives were asked to rank

---

[12] William G. Scott, *The Management of Conflict: Appeal Systems in Organizations* (Homewood, Ill.: Richard D. Irwin, 1977), pp. 56–80.

[13] Paula Eubanks, "Employee Grievance Policy: Don't Discourage Complaints," *Hospitals,* 64 (December 20, 1990), p. 36.

[14] James P. Swann, Jr., "Formal Grievance Procedures in Non-Union Plants," *Personnel Administrator,* 26 (August 1981), p. 67.

[15] Elliot H. Shaller, "Avoid Pitfalls in Hiring, Firing," *Nation's Business,* 79 (February 1991), p. 53.

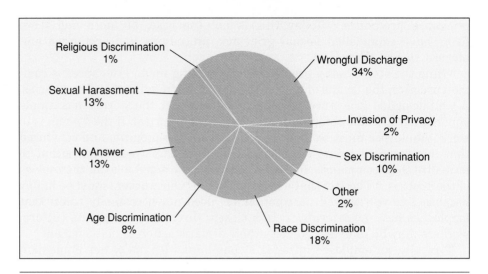

FIGURE 18-5 | Rank Order of EEO Issues Companies Said Were Most Serious

Source: Adapted from Richard T. Reminger, "At Risk," *Personnel Journal,* 70 (March 1991), pp. 51–54.

EEO issues according to their seriousness. As Figure 18-5 shows, 34 percent of the respondents ranked wrongful discharge as the most serious issue. (Note that 34 percent is about the same as the combination of the percentages for age, sex, and race discrimination combined.)[16]

Termination of Nonmanagerial/Nonprofessional Employees

Individuals in this category are neither managers nor professionally trained individuals, such as engineers or accountants. They generally include employees such as steel workers, secretaries, truck drivers, and waiters. If the firm is unionized, the termination procedure is typically well defined in the labor-management agreement. For example, drinking on the job might be identified as a reason for immediate termination. Excessive absences, on the other hand, may require three written warnings by the supervisor before termination action can be taken.

When the firm is union-free, these workers could generally be terminated more easily. A history of unjustified terminations within a firm, however, may provide an opportunity for unionization. In many union-free organizations, violations justifying termination are included in the firm's employee handbook. At times, especially in smaller organizations, the termination process is informal, with the first-line supervisor advising em-

---

[16] Richard T. Reminger, "At Risk," *Personnel Journal,* 70 (March 1991), p. 51.

ployees as to what actions warrant termination. Regardless of the size of the organization, employees should be informed by a representative of management of the actions that warrant termination.

Termination of Executives

Executive termination must be viewed from a different perspective. Executives usually have no formal appeal procedure. The decision to terminate an executive has probably been approved by the chief executive officer in the organization. In addition, the reasons for termination may not be as clear as for lower level employees. Some of the reasons include the following:

1. *Economic.* At times, business conditions may force a reduction in the number of executives.
2. *Reorganization.* In order to improve efficiency, a firm may reorganize, resulting in the elimination of some executive positions.
3. *Philosophical differences.* A difference in philosophy of conducting business may develop between an executive and other key company officials. In order to maintain consistency in management philosophy, the executive may be replaced.
4. *Decline in productivity.* The executive may have been capable of performing satisfactorily in the past, but, for various reasons, he or she can no longer perform the job as required.

This list does not include factors related to illegal activities or actions taken that are not in the best interests of the firm. Under those circumstances, the firm has no moral obligation to the terminated executive.

While an organization may derive positive benefits from terminating executives, they also present a potentially hazardous situation for the organization. Many corporations are concerned about developing a negative public image that reflects insensitivity to the needs of their employees. They fear that such a reputation would impede their efforts to recruit high-quality managers. Also, terminated executives have, at times, made public statements detrimental to the reputation of the firm.

Termination of Middle and Lower Level Managers and Professionals

In the past, the most vulnerable and perhaps the most neglected group of employees with regard to termination has been middle and lower level managers and professionals, who are generally not union members and thus not protected by a labor-management agreement. They also may not have the political clout that a terminated executive has. Termination may have been based on something as simple as the attitude or feelings of an immediate superior on a given day. Some firms have begun to provide outplacement services for these individuals.

Outplacement

Many organizations have established a systematic means of assisting terminated employees in locating jobs.[17] In **outplacement,** a terminated employee is given assistance in finding employment elsewhere. Through outplacement, the firm tries to soften the impact of termination, particularly for an employee who has been with the firm for a long time. Often an outside consultant is employed to aid the terminated employee in finding appropriate employment elsewhere. The reason for termination will probably determine the amount of effort devoted to outplacement assistance. If the individual was terminated because of a reduction in the workforce, more effort is likely than if the individual made a serious error in judgment that harmed the company.

The use of outplacement began at the executive level but has recently been used at other organizational levels. In executive termination, the use of outside consultants probably is superior to the use of in-house staff members. The released executive may not trust insiders and may be more open with an outsider. When executive outplacement is used, outplacement consultants provide the executive with a variety of services. Consultants may initially assist the executive in performing a thorough self-assessment to determine his or her future career interests. The consultant will also instruct the executive in proper interviewing techniques. Because the executive may not have had an interview in many years, the consultant can help the individual prepare for reentry into the job market. The outplacement consultant also may assist the executive in identifying firms that could best use his or her capabilities. At organizational levels lower than middle management, the outplacement consultant is often the human resource manager. Many of the same services may be provided to other terminated individuals.

■ EMPLOYMENT AT WILL

Approximately two of every three U.S. workers' jobs depend almost entirely on the continued goodwill of their employers. Individuals falling into this category are known as "at-will employees." Generally, the U.S. legal system presumes that the jobs of such employees may be terminated at the will of the employer and that these employees have a similar right to leave their jobs at any time.[18] **Employment at will** is an unwritten contract that is created when an employee agrees to work for an employer, but there is no agreement as to how long the parties expect the employment to last. Because of a century-old common law precedent in the United States,

---

[17] Loretta D. Foxman and Walter L. Polsky, "Outplacement Results in Success," *Personnel Journal,* 69 (February 1990), p. 30.

[18] Lawrence Z. Lorber, J. Robert Kirk, Kenneth H. Kirschner, and Charlene R. Handorf, *Fear of Firing: A Legal and Personal Analysis of Employment at Will* (Alexandria, Va.: The ASPA Foundation, 1984), p. 1.

employment of indefinite duration can, in general, be terminated at the whim of either party.

With the exception of a few states, the employment-at-will rule is the current standard everywhere in the country. However, some courts have decided that terminations of at-will employees are unlawful if they are contrary to general notions of acceptable "public policy" or if they are done in "bad faith."[19] Although the concept of employment at will remains strong, judges, legislators, and employees are increasingly willing to challenge rigid notions of unlimited employer discretion.

Employers can do certain things to protect themselves against litigation for wrongful discharge based on a breach of implied employment contract. In fact, in a recent survey 60 percent of the companies responding said that they included an employment-at-will statement on the application blank that applicants are required to sign.[20] Statements in documents such as employment applications and policy manuals that suggest job security or permanent employment should be avoided if employers want to minimize charges of wrongful discharge. Companies such as Sears Roebuck & Company have long been determined in protecting their right to terminate at will. Each job applicant signs a statement that he or she can be terminated at any time "with or without cause," which has helped Sears win court cases.

■ RESIGNATION

Even when an organization is totally committed to making its environment a good place to work, workers will still resign. Some employees cannot see promotional opportunities, or at least not enough, for themselves and will move on. A certain amount of turnover is healthy for an organization and is often necessary to afford employees the opportunity to fulfill career objectives. But when turnover becomes excessive, something must be done. The most qualified employees are often the ones who resign because they are more mobile. On the other hand, marginally qualified workers seemingly never leave. If excessive numbers of a firm's highly qualified and competent workers are leaving, means must be found to reverse the trend.

Analyzing Voluntary Resignations

A frequently given reason for resignation is to obtain a better salary and/or benefits. However, most firms conduct salary surveys or otherwise keep in touch with what competitors are paying. Research has shown that when workers mention pay as a reason for resigning, they often have other, deeper reasons for deciding to leave. The cause may be a department

---

[19] *Ibid.*

[20] Raymond L. Hilgert, "Employers Protected by At-Will Statements," *HRMagazine,* 36 (March 1991), p. 60.

manager with whom no one can work or a corporate culture that is stifling creative employees. Management should identify the causes and correct them as quickly as possible.

When a firm wants to determine the real reasons that individuals decide to leave, it can use the exit interview and/or the postexit questionnaire.[21] In a recent survey conducted by the *HRNews* and The Bureau of National Affairs, Inc., 96 percent of respondents indicated that their companies have some form of exit interview program.[22] The exit interview typically is the last major contact the employee has with the company. The exit interview encourages the employee to tell the reasons for resigning openly and freely. A human resource professional usually conducts this interview. An employee is not as likely to respond as freely during an interview with the supervisor, reasoning that he or she may need a letter of recommendation from the supervisor in the future. The typical exit interview involves the following:

- Establishment of rapport.
- Purpose of the interview.
- Attitudes regarding the old job.
- Exploration of reasons for leaving.
- Comparing the old and new jobs.
- Changes recommended.
- Conclusion.[23]

Specific topics that might be covered by the interviewer during the exit interview are listed in Figure 18-6. Note that the interviewer is focusing on job-related factors and is probing for the real reasons that the person is leaving. Over a period of time, properly conducted exit interviews can provide considerable insight into why employees are leaving. Patterns are often identified that uncover weaknesses in the firm's human resource management system. Knowledge of the problem permits corrective action to be taken.

The postexit questionnaire is sent to former employees several weeks after they leave the organization. Usually, they have already started work at their new company. The questionnaire is structured to draw out the real reason that the employee left. Ample blank space is also provided so that former employees can express their feelings about, and perceptions of, the job and the organization. One strength of this approach is that the individuals are no longer with the firm and may respond more freely to the questions. A weakness is that the interviewer is not present to interpret and probe for the real reasons for leaving.

---

[21] Lin Grensing, "Don't Let Them out the Door Without an Exit Interview," *Management World,* 19 (March–April 1990), p. 11.

[22] Robert Wolfe, "Most Employers Offer Exit Interviews," *HRNews,* 10 (June 1990), p. 2.

[23] Wanda R. Embrey, R. Wayne Mondy, and Robert M. Noe, "Exit Interview: A Tool for Personnel Development," *Personnel Administrator,* 24 (May 1979), p. 46.

1. Let's begin by your outlining briefly some of the duties of your job.

2. Of the duties you just outlined, tell me three or four that are crucial to the performance of your job.

3. Tell me about some of the duties you liked the most and what you liked about performing those duties.

4. Now, tell me about some of the duties you liked least and what you did not like about performing those duties.

5. Suppose you describe the amount of variety in your job.

6. Let's talk a little bit now about the amount of work assigned to you. For example, was the amount assigned not enough at times, perhaps too much at times, or was it fairly stable and even overall?

7. Suppose you give me an example of an incident that occurred on your job that was especially satisfying to you. What about an incident that was a little less satisfying?

8. Let's talk now about the extent to which you feel you were given the opportunity to use your educational background, skills, and abilities on your job.

9. Tell me how you would assess the quality of training on your job.

10. Suppose you describe the promotional opportunities open to you in your job.

FIGURE 18-6 | Questions Related to General Job Factors

Source: Wanda R. Embrey, R. Wayne Mondy, and Robert M. Noe, "Exit Interview: A Tool for Personnel Development." Reprinted from the May 1979 issue of *Personnel Administrator,* copyright © 1979. Reprinted with the permission from *HRMagazine* (formerly *Personnel Administrator*) published by the Society for Human Resource Management, Alexandria, Virginia.

Advance Notice of Resignation

Most firms would like to have at least two-weeks' notice of resignation from departing workers. However, a month's notice may be desired from professional and managerial employees who are leaving. When notice is desired by the firm, the policy should be clearly communicated to all employees. If they want departing employees to give advance notice, companies have certain obligations. For instance, suppose that a worker gives notice—then is terminated immediately. Word of this action will spread rapidly to other employees. Later, should they decide to resign, they will likely not give any advance notice.

However, permitting a resigned worker to remain on the job once a resignation has been submitted may create some problems. If bad feelings exist between the employee and the supervisor, or the company, the departing worker may be a disruptive force. On a selective basis, the firm may wish to pay the employee for the notice time and ask him or her to leave immediately. However, this action should not often be necessary.

■ DEMOTION AS AN ALTERNATIVE TO TERMINATION

Termination frequently is the solution used when a person isn't able to perform his or her job. At times, however, demotions are used as an alternative to discharge, especially when a long-term employee is involved. The worker may have performed satisfactorily for many years, but his or her productivity may then begin to decline for a variety of reasons. Perhaps the worker is just not physically capable of performing the job any longer. Or the individual may no longer be willing to work the long hours that the job requires. **Demotion** is the process of moving a worker to a lower level of duties and responsibilities, which typically involves a reduction in pay. Emotions often run high when an individual is demoted. The demoted person may feel betrayed, loss of respect from peers, embarrassment, anger, and disappointment. The employee's productivity may also decrease further. For these reasons, demotion should be used very cautiously.

One means of reducing the trauma associated with a demotion is to establish a probationary period in which a promoted worker is permitted to try out the new job. Should the person not work out, the individual will not view moving back to the old job so negatively.

If demotion is chosen over termination, efforts must be made to preserve the self-esteem of the individual. The person may be asked how he or she would like to handle the demotion announcement. A positive image of the worker's value to the company should be projected.

The handling of demotions in a unionized organization is usually spelled out clearly in the labor-management agreement. Should a decision be made to demote a worker for unsatisfactory performance, the union should be notified of this intent and given the specific reasons for the demotion. Often the demotion will be challenged and carried through the formal grievance procedure. Documentation is necessary for the demotion to be upheld. Even with the problems associated with demotion for cause, it is often easier to demote than to terminate an employee. In addition, demotion is often less devastating to the employee. For the organization, however, the opposite may be true if the demotion creates lingering ill will and an embittered employee.

■ LAYOFF

The economic well-being of many companies rises and falls in cycles. At times a firm's goods or services may be in great demand; at other times demand falls. Often when demand is low, the firm has no other choice but to lay off workers. Although being laid off is not the same thing as being fired, it has the same effect: The worker is unemployed. Downsizing has had a major impact on the number of layoffs that the country is encountering. In one survey, 35 percent of respondents said that their company had downsized during the previous twelve months.[24]

---

[24] Richard L. Bunning, "The Dynamics of Downsizing," *Personnel Journal,* 69 (September 1990), p. 69.

Being laid off can be worse psychologically than being terminated. With termination, the relationship with the firm is severed, and the former employee has no choice but to look for another job. This is not the case with a layoff because the worker still has some ties to the firm. In many cases, the laid-off worker does not even have a general idea of when he or she will be recalled, if ever. In the meantime, the worker's financial resources dwindle. The longer the layoff, the more frustrating it becomes. Life-styles may change, and tension increases.

Whether the firm is union-free or unionized, carefully constructed layoff/recall procedures should be developed.[25, 26] Workers should understand when they are hired how the system will work in the event of a layoff. When the firm is unionized, the layoff procedures are usually stated clearly in the labor-management agreement. Seniority usually is the basis for layoffs, with the least senior employees laid off first. The agreement may also have a clearly spelled-out *bumping* procedure. When senior-level positions are eliminated, the people occupying them have the right to bump workers from lower level positions, assuming that they have the proper qualifications for the lower level job. When bumping occurs, the composition of the workforce is altered.

Procedures for recalling laid-off employees are also usually spelled out in labor-management agreements. Again, seniority is typically the basis for worker recall, with the most senior employees being recalled first.

Some firms such as Delta Air Lines, Digital Equipment, and Hewlett-Packard have established no-layoff strategies.[27] Regardless of a union-free firm's current stand on the issue of layoffs, it should establish layoff procedures prior to facing one. In union-free firms also, seniority should be an integral part of any layoff procedure. But, frequently, other factors should be considered. Productivity of the employee is typically an important consideration. When productivity is a factor, management must be careful to see to it that productivity, not favoritism, is the actual basis. Workers generally have an accurate perception of their own productivity level and that of their fellow employees. Therefore, it is important to accurately define both seniority and productivity considerations well in advance of any layoffs.

■ TRANSFERS

The lateral movement of a worker within an organization is called a **transfer.** A transfer may be initiated by the firm or by an employee. They do not, and should not, imply that a person is being promoted or demoted.

---

[25] Michael Smith, "Help in Making Those Tough Layoff Decisions," *Supervisory Management,* 35 (January 1990), p. 3.

[26] Robert W. Keidel, "Layoffs Take Advance Preparation," *Management Review,* 80 (May 1991), p. 6.

[27] Mary Lord, "Where You Can't Get Fired," *U.S. News & World Report,* 110 (January 14, 1991), p. 48.

Transfers serve several purposes. First, firms often find it necessary to reorganize. Offices and departments are created and abolished in response to the company's needs. In order to fill positions created by reorganization, employee moves not entailing promotion may be necessary. The same is true when an office or department is closed. Rather than terminate valued employees, management may transfer them to other areas within the organization. These transfers may entail moving an employee to another desk in the same office or to a location halfway around the world.

A second reason for transfers is to make positions available in the primary promotion channels. Firms are typically organized into a hierarchical structure resembling a pyramid. Each succeeding promotion is more difficult to obtain because fewer positions exist. At times, very productive but unpromotable workers may clog promotion channels. Other qualified workers in the organization may find their opportunities for promotion blocked. When this happens, a firm's most capable future managers may seek employment elsewhere. In order to keep promotion channels open, the firm may decide to transfer employees who are unpromotable but productive at their present levels.

Another reason for transfers is to satisfy employees' personal desires. The reasons for wanting a transfer are numerous. An individual may need to work closer to home to care for aging parents. Or the worker may dislike the long commuting trips to and from work. Factors such as these may be of such importance that employees may resign if a requested transfer is not approved. Rather than risk losing a valued employee, the firm may agree to the transfer.

Transfers may also be an effective means of dealing with personality clashes. Some people just cannot get along with each other. Because each of the individuals may be a valued employee, transfer may be an appropriate solution to the problem. But human resource managers must be cautious regarding "the grass is always greener on the other side of the fence" syndrome. When some workers encounter a temporary setback, they immediately ask for a transfer—before they even attempt to work through the problem.

Finally, because of the downsizing of the management levels, it is becoming necessary to have a wide variety of experiences before achieving a promotion. It has been estimated that by the year 2000 the typical large corporation will have half the management levels and one-third the managers that it has today.[28] Individuals who desire upward mobility often explore possible lateral moves so that they can learn new skills.[29]

Before any worker's request for transfer is approved, it should be analyzed in terms of the best interests of both the firm and the individual. Disruptions may occur when the worker is transferred if, for

[28] David Kirkpatrick, "Is Your Career on Track?" *Fortune,* 122 (July 2, 1990), p. 39.

[29] Harvey Mackay, "A Career Roadmap: Getting Started," *Modern Office Technology,* 35 (June 1990), p. 12.

example, a qualified worker isn't available to step into the position being vacated.

Management should establish clear policies regarding transfers. Such policies let workers know in advance when a transfer request is likely to be approved and what its ramifications will be. For instance, if the transfer is for personal reasons, some firms do not pay moving costs. Whether the organization will or will not pay should be clearly spelled out.

■ PROMOTION

A **promotion** is the movement of a person to a higher level position in the organization. The term *promotion* is one of the most emotionally charged words in the field of human resource management. An individual who receives a promotion normally receives additional financial rewards and the ego boost associated with achievement and accomplishment. Most employees feel positively about being promoted. But for every individual who gains a promotion, there are probably others who were not selected. If these individuals wanted the promotion badly enough, they may slack off or even resign. If the consensus of employees directly involved is that the wrong person was promoted, considerable resentment may result.

Promotions in the future may not be as available as in the past.[30] For one thing, many firms are reducing the number of levels in their hierarchies. As the number of middle management positions declines, fewer promotional opportunities will be available. The effect of these changes is that more people will be striving for fewer promotion opportunities. Consequently, organizations must look for ways other than promotion to reward employees. One alternative is the dual-track system that we described in Chapter 10, whereby highly technical individuals can continue to receive financial rewards without progressing into management.

■ RETIREMENT

Most long-term employees leave an organization by retiring. Retirement plans may be based on a certain age or a certain number of years with the firm, or both. Upon retirement, former employees usually receive a pension each month for the remainder of their lives.

In the past there were far too many instances of retirement-plan failure. Many workers who retired believing that they would receive lifelong pensions were devastated to find that retirement programs had been insufficiently funded by their employers. In 1974, the Employee Retirement Income Security Act (ERISA) was passed for the purpose of protecting employees participating in company-sponsored retirement plans.

---

[30] Joseph R. Rich and Beth C. Florin-Thuma, "Rewarding Employees in an Environment of Fewer Promotions," *Pension World,* 26 (November 1990), p. 16.

Early Retirement

Sometimes employees will retire before reaching the organization's age or length of service requirement. Often, retirement pay is reduced for each year that the retirement date is advanced. From an organization's viewpoint, early employee retirement has both positive and negative aspects.

Because of the large number of staff reductions many firms are now encountering, early retirement is often viewed as an attractive solution.[31] If an extended layoff is expected, a product line is being discontinued, or a plant is being closed, early retirement may be a responsible solution to the problem of surplus employees.

From a negative viewpoint, valued employees may take advantage of the early retirement option and leave the organization. In addition, early retirement is often more expensive to the company than normal retirement. And, early retirement decisions are often made on short notice, resulting in some disruption of operations.

Retirement Planning

Strong emotions often accompany anticipation of retirement. As retirement approaches, the individual may be haunted by these and other questions: Do I have enough money? What will I do? Will I be able to adjust? Just as a well-planned orientation program eases the transition of a new hire into the organization, a company-sponsored retirement planning program eases the transition of long-term employees from work to leisure.

Often a firm devotes time, staff, and money to provide useful information to workers approaching retirement. Typically, such information relates to finances, housing, relocation, family relations, attitude adjustment, and legal affairs.[32]

Some firms have taken retirement planning a step further. At times firms consider both the social and psychological implications of the retirement process. Adaptation to retirement living is the focus of this form of planning. Individuals who have already retired are brought to meetings to speak and answer questions regarding retirement life. Managing the change in life-style is often a topic for discussion,[33] which is helpful to all those considering retirement. Retirement is a major event in an individual's life, and employers can often help to make the transition much smoother.

---

[31] Jeffrey S. Hoffman, "Sweetening Early-Retirement Programs," *Personnel,* 67 (March 1990), p. 18.

[32] Marilyn Merikangas, "Retirement Planning with a Difference," *Personnel Journal,* 62 (May 1983), p. 420.

[33] *Ibid.*

■ LEGAL IMPLICATIONS OF INTERNAL EMPLOYEE RELATIONS

Many people believe that equal employment opportunity legislation primarily affects individuals entering the company for the first time. Nothing could be further from the truth. Virtually all phases of internal employee relations are affected. Of special concern to the EEOC are decisions relating to promotion. The Household Finance Corporation was required to pay more than $125,000 to white-collar women employees who charged that they were denied promotion because of their gender. Under terms of a consent decree, the company also agreed to hire women for 20 percent of the branch representative openings (subject to availability) until women comprised 20 percent of such representatives. It also was required to hire 20 percent of its new employees from specified minority groups for clerical, credit, and branch representative jobs, until the total of such employees reached 65 percent of their population proportion in the labor area. Household Finance Corporation also agreed to train women and minority employees to help them qualify for better jobs where they are underrepresented.[34]

One of the largest payments ever made was under an agreement signed by AT&T with the EEOC and the Department of Labor. It provided for payment of approximately $15 million to employees allegedly discriminated against. The agreement also called for additional affirmative action and for an estimated $50 million in yearly payments for promotion and wage adjustments to minority and women employees.[35]

Termination of workers who have reached a certain age is a major concern in enforcement of the Age Discrimination Act. In *EEOC v. Liggett and Myers,* the commission alleged that age was a factor in the discharge of approximately 10 percent of the employees during a reduction in force. The court ruled against the company, and back-pay recovery was estimated at $20 million. In *Hagman and EEOC v. United Airlines,* a jury awarded $18.2 million to 112 pilots who had been forced to retire at age 60. In *EEOC v. Home Insurance Company,* an age discrimination case was won on behalf of 143 employees who had been forced to retire at age 62; back-pay recovery was estimated at $6–8 million.

In 1986, the Age Discrimination in Employment Act was further amended by removing the upper age ceiling for mandatory retirement. Employers who attempt to systematically retire workers for factors other than performance are coming under increased scrutiny by the EEOC. The problem in many cases is that for appraisal periods prior to termination, high-performance evaluations had often been given to the employees involved. These evaluations provided the terminated employees with the data

---

[34] *U.S. v. Household Finance Corporation,* 4 EPD para. 7680 (N.D. Ill., 1972)—Consent decree.

[35] U.S. Equal Employment Opportunity Commission, *Affirmative Action and Equal Employment: A Guidebook for Employers,* Vol. 1 (Washington, D.C.: U.S. Government Printing Office, January 1974), p. 10.

they needed to develop valid cases contending that the reason for termination was age, not declining performance.

Some firms have tried to open avenues for promotion of younger workers by offering early voluntary retirement. A potential problem with this option is whether the retirement is truly voluntary. Exerting pressure on employees to retire when they really do not want to is beginning to receive considerable EEOC attention.

The thrust of EEO legislation is that women and minorities should not receive unequal treatment, and internal employee relations should reflect this principle. For instance, are blacks being fired at a higher rate than whites? Are women not receiving promotional opportunities? The same questions may be asked about demotions and layoffs. As more women and minorities enter the workforce, EEO administration will likely focus increasingly on internal employee relations.

■ THE GLASS CEILING

A recent study indicates that the proportion of women managers has more than doubled since 1975 and is currently at 40 percent. However, the percentage of women who hold top-management positions is less than 3 percent.[36] A term that has become common in recent years is *glass ceiling*. It refers to an invisible barrier in organizations that prevents many women from achieving top-level management positions. Companies are discovering that the courts are being forceful in eliminating such barriers. In one instance, a highly rated female supervisor was denied a promotion because her boss said it would be easier for male workers to work with a man who was their "chum." The employer reasoned that when it came to working long hours, naturally the men would work better with the male worker who was promoted. The courts disagreed and called this action unlawful discrimination.[37] It is expected that this topic will be vigorously pursued in the future.

■ EMPLOYEE RELATIONS IN TIMES OF INTERNATIONAL CRISIS

Crises will occur regardless of whether the employee works in the domestic or global arena. According to Jay Hornsby, Dow Chemical Company's vice-president of human resources, "For an expatriate employee thousands of miles away from home, the company is the family." Therefore, the firm

---

[36] Gary N. Powell, "Upgrading Management Opportunities for Women," *HRMagazine,* 35 (November 1990), p. 67.

[37] Jack Raisner, "When Workplace Relationships Cause Discrimination," *HRMagazine,* 36 (January 1991), p. 75.

must provide support for the employee in times of crisis. Hornsby adds, "Whenever something goes wrong, and it will, he or she will naturally turn to the company for help." The key to maintaining good employee relations is for the company to be there when an expatriate employee needs help. Global human resource professionals have been called on to assist employees based abroad with a wide range of often difficult problems. Some of these problems include medical emergencies, natural disasters, revolutions and other international crises, and wars, such as the recent conflict in the Middle East.[38]

Medical emergencies occur fairly frequently. Ralph W. Stevens, vice-president of personnel and employee relations for Hamilton Oil Corporation, recalls the case of a high-ranking technical manager who suffered a stroke while on business in Korea, where the company maintains no office. Stevens managed to find a first-rate physician, set the employee up in a well-regarded hospital, and transfer sufficient funds to cover the medical bills, while comforting the manager's frantic family.[39]

Because of its extensive operations in Latin America, Ferro, a $1 billion international manufacturer, has long had contingency plans in place for another kind of emergency: a terrorist kidnapping. Nothing adverse has ever happened, but the company still strives to maintain a politically neutral and noncontroversial image when it operates in potentially dangerous international locations. Various contingency plans, including means and methods to evacuate workers if necessary, are in place for most U.S. companies currently operating in the Middle East. CPC International, Inc., for example, has a food processing plant in Saudi Arabia. Richard P. Bergeman, the company's vice-president of human resources, has stated, "Naturally we have contingency procedures approved and ready, although we would rather not discuss them."[40]

During its more than 100-year history, Fluor Daniel has had to deal with almost every kind of international crisis. "Earthquakes, hurricanes, uprisings—we've probably had employees caught in all of them," says Tom Blackburn, the company's director of international administration. To Blackburn, more difficult and wrenching than politically induced crises are instances when an expatriate employee dies abroad. He once had to coordinate the transport of a worker's coffin from an international site back to the United States, giving what solace he could to the man's grieving widow.[41] As this scenario illustrates, the ultimate test of a company's concern about positive employee relations comes in times of extreme crisis.

---

[38] Ellen Brandt, "Global HR," *Personnel Journal,* 70 (March 1991), p. 43.

[39] *Ibid.*

[40] *Ibid.*

[41] *Ibid.*

SUMMARY

A necessary but often difficult aspect of internal employee relations is disciplinary action. A major purpose of disciplinary action is to ensure that employee behavior is consistent with the firm's policies, rules, and regulations. Disciplinary action invokes a penalty against an employee who fails to meet company standards of behavior.

The disciplinary action process is dynamic and ongoing. Rules are established to facilitate the accomplishment of organizational objectives. These rules must be communicated to employees because they can't obey a rule if they don't know it exists. As long as employee behavior does not vary from acceptable practices, disciplinary action is not needed. But when an employee's behavior violates a rule, corrective action should be taken. The purpose of this action is to alter behavior that can have a negative impact on the organization. When the progressive disciplinary action approach is followed, an attempt is made to make the penalty appropriate to the violation (or accumulated violations).

If the employees in an organization are represented by a union, workers who believe that they have been disciplined or dealt with unjustly can appeal through the grievance procedure of the collective bargaining agreement. A grievance procedure permits employees to express complaints without jeopardizing their jobs. In arbitration, the parties submit a dispute to an impartial third party for resolution if it cannot otherwise be settled.

Termination is the most severe penalty that an organization can impose on an employee. The procedure used to terminate operative employees—and for them to appeal the decision—is usually well defined. However, executives do not have a formal appeals procedure. In the past, the most vulnerable and perhaps the most neglected groups of employees with regard to termination have been middle and lower level managers and professionals, who generally are not union members and thus not protected by a labor agreement.

Employment at will is created when an employee agrees to work for an employer but there is no agreement as to how long the parties expect the employment to last. In the United States, employment of indefinite duration can, in general, be terminated at the whim of either party.

Internal employee relations also pertain to resignation, demotion, layoff, transfer, promotion, and retirement. Even in the best organizations, some workers will still resign. Two techniques—the exit interview and the postexit questionnaire—may be used to help determine the real reasons that an individual has decided to leave the organization.

At times, demotion of an employee may be a better alternative than termination. Demotion involves moving a worker to a lower level of duties and responsibilities, and typically, less pay.

At times, a firm has no choice but to lay off employees. Although being laid off does not have the same negative connotation as being fired, it has the same short-term effect: The worker is unemployed.

A person can move laterally within the organization by transfer. A transfer may be initiated by the firm or by the employee. Transfers do not, and should not, imply a promotion.

The means by which long-term employees usually leave an organization is through retirement. Retirement may be based on a certain age, a certain number of years' service, or both.

Most people believe that equal employment opportunity legislation primarily affects individuals entering the company for the first time. Nothing could be further from the truth. Virtually all phases of internal employee relations are affected. Of special concern to the EEOC are decisions relating to promotion. A multinational corporation headquartered in the United States often must alter its approach to internal employee relations to address the problems associated with international crises.

Questions for Review

1. Distinguish between discipline and disciplinary action.
2. In progressive disciplinary action, what steps are involved before employee termination?
3. What are the steps that should typically be followed in handling a grievance under a collective bargaining agreement?
4. Why is arbitration often used in the settlement of grievances in a unionized firm?
5. How would grievances typically be handled in a union-free firm? Describe briefly.
6. How does termination often differ with regard to nonmanagerial/nonprofessional employees, executives, managers, and professionals?
7. What is meant by the phrase *employment at will*?
8. Briefly describe the techniques available to determine the real reasons that an individual decides to leave an organization.
9. Distinguish between demotions, transfers, and promotions.
10. What are some legal implications of internal employee relations?

Terms for Review

Internal employee relations
Discipline
Disciplinary action
Progressive disciplinary action
Disciplinary action without
    punishment

Grievance
Outplacement
Employment at will
Demotion
Transfer
Promotion

INCIDENT 1   ▪ Stepping Over the Line ▪

Quality Business Forms, Inc., has a policy stating that an employee should not be absent more than four days during a ninety-day work period without medical verification. If an employee does not have medical reasons for excessive absences, he or she may be subject to disciplinary action.

Ed Thompson has been employed by Quality for more than twenty-one years. In the past three years he has had an abnormal number of absences, which his supervisor chose to ignore because of Ed's long tenure with the company. When Ed's supervisor was transferred and another individual in the department, Alice Randall, assumed the supervisory position, she immediately advised Ed that his absenteeism was excessive and that it would have to cease or disciplinary action would be taken. Ed claimed that he had been injured on the job five years ago and that his absences were a result of that injury. Alice reviewed Ed's health records, which contained no report of such an injury.

Ed's attendance improved during the first six months under Alice's supervision but began to deteriorate during the latter part of the year. Ed, warned again about absenteeism, came back with his previous excuse. At this point, Alice contacted the human resource manager for assistance in dealing with Ed. She was told that further disciplinary steps should be taken, along with a complete physical evaluation by the corporate doctor. The physical exam was conducted immediately and no physical abnormalities were found.

The doctor gave Ed this information verbally, but Ed refused to accept the findings. He was then counseled by the human resource manager, his supervisor, and his department manager. Ed listened very intently to what was being said and took notes. He was told that the next step in the disciplinary procedure would be dismissal if his absenteeism continued. He said that he understood and would work when he felt good and would not work when he did not feel good.

Thirty days later, Ed and Alice were called in to the human resource office at 7:00 A.M., and Ed was terminated. Ed was shocked at actually being fired, since it was necessary for the president of the company to approve the termination of an employee with a long service record. A discrimination charge was filed but was dropped when no grounds could be established. A workers' compensation claim was received but could not be substantiated. And, finally, an unemployment claim was submitted, but it was dismissed.

Questions

1. Do you agree with the standards developed by the firm with regard to absenteeism?
2. What responsibilities does an employer have with regard to the termination of a long-term employee?

INCIDENT 2   ▪ Something Is Not Right ▪

As Norman Blankenship came into the office at Consolidated Coal Company's Rowland mine, near Clear Creek, West Virginia, he told the mine dispatcher not to tell anyone of his presence. Norman was the general superintendent of the Rowland operation. He had been with Consolidated for more than twenty-three years, having started out as a coal digger.

Norman had heard that one of his section bosses, Tom Serinsky, had been sleeping on the job. Tom had been hired two months earlier and assigned to the Rowland mine by the regional human resource office. He went to work as section boss, working the midnight to 8:00 A.M. shift. Because of his age and experience, he was the senior person in the mine on his shift.

Norman took one of the battery-operated jeeps used to transport workers and supplies in and out of the mine and proceeded to the area where Tom was assigned. Upon arriving, he saw Tom lying on an emergency stretcher. Norman stopped his jeep a few yards away from where Tom was sleeping and approached him. "Hey, you asleep?" Norman asked. Tom awakened with a start and said, "No, I wasn't sleeping."

Norman waited a moment for Tom to collect his senses and then said, "I could tell that you were sleeping. But that's beside the point. You weren't at your work station. You know that I have no choice but to fire you." After Tom had left, Norman called his mine supervisor, who had accompanied him to the dispatcher's office, and asked him to complete the remainder of Tom's shift.

The next morning, Norman had the mine human resource officer officially terminate Tom. As part of the standard procedure, the mine human resource officer notified the regional director that Tom had been fired and gave the reasons for firing him. The regional human resource director asked the mine human resource officer to put Norman on the line. When he did so, Norman was told, "You know that Tom is the brother-in-law of our regional vice-president, Bill Frederick?" "No, I didn't know that," replied Norman, "but it doesn't matter. The rules are clear, and I wouldn't care if he was the regional vice-president's son."

The next day, the regional human resource director showed up at the mine just as Norman was getting ready to make a routine tour of the mine. "I guess you know what I'm here for," said the human resource director. "Yeah, you're here to take away my authority," replied Norman. "No, I'm just here to investigate," said the human resource director.

When Norman returned to the mine office after his tour, the human resource director had finished his interviews. He told Norman, "I think we're going to have to put Tom back to work. If we decided to do that, can you let him work for you?" "No, absolutely not," said Norman. "In fact, if he works here, I go." A week later, Norman learned that Tom had gone back to work as section boss at another Consolidated coal mine in the region.

Questions

1. What would you do now if you were Norman?
2. Do you believe that the human resource director handled the matter in an ethical manner? Explain.

DEVELOPING HRM SKILLS

I sadore Lamansky is the manager of the machine tooling operations at Lone Star Industries and has five supervisors who report to him. One of his employees is Susie Canton, a supervisor in maintenance. As Isadore comes to work this morning, his thoughts focus on Susie: "Today is the day that I must talk to Susie. I sure hate to do it. I know she is going to take it the wrong way. Ever since Susie was promoted to Unit Supervisor she has had trouble maintaining discipline. She tries too hard to keep the men in line because she thinks they are continually trying to push her, and she lets the women get away with murder. Well, I guess I'll get this over with since that's what I get paid for."

The grapevine is strong at Lone Star Industries, and it didn't take long for Susie to hear rumors. She thinks, "The word is that old Isadore is going to come down on me. He recommended someone else for my job because he doesn't like women in charge. The reason it is so hard to maintain discipline is the fact that the men I supervise intentionally push me to see what I'll do. The women support me, and they are proud of me; the men just want me gone. He is probably going to dredge up some minor stuff to reprimand me about; we need more women in charge, and the boss will have to accept that I'm here for good!"

Who is right, and who is wrong? Can there be a reasonable solution to the problems that exist? This exercise will require two of you to participate. One person will play Susie and another person will play Isadore. All others should observe carefully. Your instructor will provide additional information to participants.

REFERENCES

Barnett, Timothy R., and Daniel S. Cochran. "Making Room for the Whistleblower." *HRMagazine,* 36 (January 1991), pp. 58–61.

Bunning, Richard L. "The Dynamics of Downsizing." *Personnel Journal,* 69 (September 1990), pp. 69–75.

Colon, Robert J. "Grievances Hinge on Poor Contract Language." *Personnel Journal,* 69 (September 1990), pp. 32–36.

Droste, Therese. "Announcing Your Retirement: Timing Is Crucial." *Hospitals,* 64 (March 5, 1990), p. 66.

Eubanks, Paula. "Employee Grievance Policy: Don't Discourage Complaints." *Hospitals,* 64 (December 20, 1990), pp. 36–37.

Fergus, Mike. "Employees on the Move." *HRMagazine,* 36 (May 1990), pp. 44–46.

Foxman, Loretta D., and Walter L. Polsky. "Outplacement Results in Success." *Personnel Journal,* 69 (February 1990), pp. 30–37.

Garland, Susan B. "The Retiring Kind Are Getting Militant About Benefits." *Business Week* (May 28, 1990), p. 29.

Grensing, Lin. "Don't Let Them out the Door Without an Exit Interview." *Management World,* 19 (March–April 1990), pp. 11–13.

Harris, Tim. "Relocation Trends: Hitting a Moving Target." *Sales and Marketing Management,* 142 (October 1990), pp. 54–60.

"Heirs and Races." *The Economist,* 318 (March 9, 1991), p. 69.

Hoffman, Jeffery S. "Sweetening Early-Retirement Programs." *Personnel,* 67 (March 1990), pp. 18–20.

Hukill, Craig. "Labor and the Supreme Court: Significant Issues of 1990–91." *Monthly Labor Review,* 114 (January 1991), pp. 34–40.

Karp, Robert E. "Ethical Values Underlying the Termination Process." *Business & Society,* 30 (Spring 1991), pp. 1–6.

Kiechel, Walter III. "How to Discipline in the Modern Age." *Fortune,* 121 (May 7, 1990), pp. 179–180.

Kohl, John P., and David B. Stephens. "Is Demotion a Four-Letter Word?" *Business Horizons,* 33 (March–April 1990), pp. 74–76.

Levy, Martin. "Discipline for Professional Employees." *Personnel Journal,* 69 (December 1990), pp. 27–28.

Lord, Mary. "Where You Can't Get Fired." *U.S. News & World Report,* 110 (January 14, 1991), pp. 46–48.

Lussier, Robert N. "A Discipline Model for Increasing Performance." *Supervisory Management,* 35 (August 1990), pp. 6–7.

Lussier, Robert N. "16 Guidelines for Effective Discipline." *Supervisory Management,* 35 (March 1990), p. 10.

McCormick, William. "You Can Avoid the Transfer Training Trap." *Sales and Marketing Management,* 142 (May 1990), pp. 84–88.

Matusewitch, Eric. "Retirement: An Executive Decision?" *Personnel Journal,* 68 (July 1989), pp. 86–89.

Pell, Arthur R. "Effective Reprimanding." *Manager's Magazine,* 65 (August 1990), pp. 26–27.

Raisner, Jack. "Relocate Without Making False Moves." *HRMagazine,* 36 (February 1991), pp. 46–50.

Reynolds, Calvin, and Rita Bennett. "The Career Couple Challenge." *Personnel Journal,* 70 (March 1991), pp. 46–48.

Rich, Joseph R., and Beth C. Florin-Thuma. "Rewarding Employees in an Environment of Fewer Promotions." *Pension World,* 26 (November 1990), pp. 16–17.

Saltzman, Amy, Anne K. Smith, and Francesca L. Kritz. "Girding for a Pink Slip." *U.S. News & World Report,* 110 (January 14, 1991), pp. 54–55.

Shaller, Elliot. "Avoid Pitfalls in Hiring, Firing." *Nation's Business,* 79 (February 1991), pp. 51–54.

Smith, Michael. "Help in Making Those Tough Layoff Decisions." *Supervisory Management,* 35 (January 1990), p. 3.

Stroh, Linda K., Anne H. Reilly, and Jeanne M. Brett. "New Trends in Relocation." *HRMagazine,* 35 (February 1990), pp. 42–44.

Touby, Laurel Allison. "How to Leave Without Burning Your Bridges." *Working Woman,* 16 (April 1991), p. 30.

Wilson, Steve. "Layoffs Take Advance Preparation." *Management Review,* 80 (May 1991), pp. 5–6.

P·A·R·T S·I·X

CASE VI

Parma Cycle Company: The Union-Organizing Effort

The Clarksdale, Mississippi, plant of Parma Cycle Company had been open for only six months in March 1989 when the first efforts at unionization became apparent. A known union organizer was in town and pro-union leaflets began to appear around the factory. The human resource director at Clarksdale, Edward Deal, had been expecting this to occur. He knew that the workers who had been brought down from the main plant in Parma, Ohio, had a strong union tradition. He also knew that the wage and benefits package at Clarksdale was far less liberal than that at the Ohio plant. So far, this hadn't created a major problem. Most of the workers recruited from the Clarksdale area felt that they were well paid in comparison to others in that area.

In the plant that same day, Janice Snively was thinking about whether she should talk to the human resource director. Janice had been hired by Parma two weeks prior to start-up. She had previously worked as a maintenance supervisor at a garment factory about sixty miles from Clarksdale. She had taken a slight pay cut in order to take what she thought would be a better job in the long run and to be closer to her family, who lived in Clarksdale.

Janice's crew of ten machine operators and two parts handlers was among the best in the plant. Janice had made friends with each of them, and they obviously respected her. She felt that one reason she was a good leader was her willingness to "get her hands dirty." Because of her experience in maintenance she was able to repair the machines herself when they broke down. When an operator was absent, she would simply take over that machine in order to keep the work flowing.

Lately she had noticed a change. The workers seemed to be shutting her out. In a couple of instances, when several of her crew were congregated at one table in the lunchroom, the conversation stopped as she approached and then awkwardly began again. The change of topic was obvious. For the first time, too, she began to hear complaints from the employees. For example, the operator of the cutoff machine, which cuts certain frame members to size, complained of the speed with which the machine operated. "I have less than one second to move the cutoff piece before the tubing feeds through to start another cut. I'll be lucky not to lose an arm," he said. There had been a number of similar complaints (many of them related to safety, some to working conditions), and a number of workers had asked about the date of their next raise.

Janice thought that handling these kinds of problems was part of the supervisor's job, so she wasn't too concerned. Because of something that had happened this morning, though, Janice decided it was time to talk to the human resource director.

Janice walked in as Ed was thinking about the advantages and disadvantages of having a union. "Ed," she said, "I want you to look at this. One of the workers gave it to me and asked if it is true. I didn't know how to answer." Janice handed Ed a photocopied sheet. After studying the sheet for a moment Ed said, "It's basically true, but I wish it weren't."

Here is a reproduction of the sheet:

DID YOU KNOW?

- Parma's workers in Ohio do not pay for their dependents' medical insurance. You do!

- Parma's employees in Ohio have dental insurance. You don't!

- Employees in Ohio have ten paid holidays. You have only eight.

- Trainees at the Ohio plant get $7.50 per hour. At Clarksdale, they get minimum wage.

- Senior machine operators in Ohio get $12.60 an hour. Here, they get $8.90 or less.

Questions

1. What do you think caused the unionizing attempt at Parma Cycle's Clarksdale plant?
2. What sequence of events is likely to occur before the Clarksdale plant becomes unionized?
3. Assuming that Parma Cycle wishes to prevent unionization of the Clarksdale plant, what might the union and management legally do before and after a union representation election is ordered by the NLRB?

P·A·R·T S·E·V·E·N

HUMAN RESOURCE RESEARCH

Human Resource
Research

Human Resource
Planning,
Recruitment, and
Selection

Human Resource
Development

Human
Resource
Management

Employee and
Labor Relations

Safety and
Health

Compensation
and Benefits

CHAPTER 19

HUMAN RESOURCE RESEARCH

CHAPTER OBJECTIVES

1. Explain the importance of research to human resource management.
2. Identify the basic methods of inquiry for research, and describe the steps in the research process.
3. Describe how quantitative methods may be used in human resource research, how the human resource function may be evaluated, and how technological advances can affect human resource management.

Annette Dommert, human resource manager for Saint Joseph Medical Center in Decatur, Illinois, was disturbed as she studied the list of workers who had resigned during the past month. For the sixth month in a row, the number of terminations had increased. To compound the problem, the terminations were in critical areas such as X-ray and laboratory. Quite a few RNs had also turned in their resignations. Annette had conducted exit interviews with many of the workers who had quit, and most had responded that they were leaving for "more money." However, Annette was well aware of the salary schedules of the other hospitals in the area. Saint Joseph's pay level was well in line overall and even higher in a few categories.

Annette knew that a continued exodus of qualified workers would have a serious impact on patient care at Saint Joseph. She decided to propose a confidential questionnaire to be administered to all employees in the hospital in an attempt to identify reasons for the excessive turnover.

Employee attitudes revealed through human resource research can be of tremendous benefit to managers such as Annette Dommert as they attempt to determine the real reasons for high turnover rates and other indicators of employee dissatisfaction. Without this information, a situation may continue to erode until the quality of goods and services seriously declines.

We begin this chapter by discussing the benefits of human resource research and methods of inquiry in human resource research. We then describe the research process and quantitative methods in human resource research. We end the chapter with sections on evaluating the human resource function and technological advances that affect human resource management.

■ BENEFITS OF HUMAN RESOURCE RESEARCH

The human resource manager's job, as we discussed in Chapter 1, is vastly different from only a few years ago. In order to contend with mounting responsibilities, the human resource manager has discovered that information derived from research is constantly required. **Human resource research** is the systematic study of a firm's human resources for the purpose of maximizing personal and organizational goal achievement.

Applications of human resource research are numerous and increasing rapidly. The potential benefits of sound human resource research also are numerous. Management has begun to realize the full significance of the human component on an organization's ability to achieve its goals. This enlightenment, however belated, has occurred at a time when the competitive nature of business makes it increasingly difficult to obtain and retain qualified individuals.

Specific applications of human resource research depend to a large extent on a firm's needs. As Table 19-1 shows, the type of research presently being conducted overlaps, but differences do exist. These variations reflect the size, goals, and specific problems of particular organizations.

Effective Management

Laws, government regulations, and judicial decisions have called into question many past human resource management practices. Managers must now be prepared to prove that their employment decisions are based on valid requirements. However, as Walter Tornow, vice-president of research and publication for The Center for Creative Leadership, states, "On the whole, government regulations have had a positive effect because they cause organizations to examine and document their practices in ways that heretofore were not deemed necessary for some."

Another reason for the increased need for human resource research relates to rapid changes in the composition of the workforce. Research is required to determine how the goals of these new workforce members can be integrated with those of the firm.

Largely because of increased educational opportunities, managers and nonmanagers alike have become more sophisticated in their employment expectations. To respond appropriately, managers may need to modify their approaches to HRM. Although a highly autocratic manager may have been successful in the past, a similar style today may quickly lead to resentment and lower productivity. Also, the organizational structure may need to be modified. The means of identifying appropriate managerial styles and organizational structure will continue to be a major task of human resource research.

The nature of work itself has also been changing rapidly. This has caused firms to continuously strive to upgrade their workforces. One of management's most difficult tasks is to get employees to accept change resulting from new technology. The use of robotics in automobile assembly plants has created a tremendous need for retraining. The General Motors Saturn

TABLE 19-1 | Uses of Human Resource Research

Company	Research Area
Atlantic Richfield Company	■ Selection test validation Assessment center validation Survey research
Fleming Companies, Inc.	■ Specific emphasis on turnover, turnover reasons, turnover costs Identification of high-potential employees for accelerated development Impact of union contracts on compensation Improving performance appraisal
Control Data Corporation	■ Staffing, compensation, interviewing, performance appraisal, management training, surveys of employee attitudes, productivity enhancement, employee development, selection
Ashland Oil, Inc.	■ Selection at both the exempt and nonexempt levels and also in the early identification of people with potential to become high-level managers
Ford Motor Company	■ Selection, opinion surveys, career progress, performance appraisal, quality motivation, management potential, organization

plant in Springhill, Tennessee, required many new employee skills. It isn't easy for people to accept the fact that their skills are no longer needed and that they must learn new skills. Research may indicate ways in which people may learn to accept change more readily and thereby continue to be productive members of the workforce.

Human Resource Planning, Recruitment, and Selection

Plans must be made to recruit, select, and retain productive employees. Each organization has a distinct personality, as does an individual. Thus organizations must seek to find the best match between their needs and those of their employees. Research can help explain why an individual may be an excellent worker in one firm and a poor worker in another, even though the jobs seem to be similar.

Recruitment research is directed toward determining how individuals with high potential can be encouraged to apply for jobs with the firm. Firms need to determine the most likely sources of qualified candidates for their jobs. It does little good to know the qualities that prospective employees should possess and not know where and how to recruit them.

The objective of employee selection research is to identify prospective employees with the greatest potential for success. As you might expect, the definition of a successful employee varies from organization to organization. This research often attempts to identify factors (such as background and experience, education, and test scores) that can be used to differentiate successful applicants from less successful ones.[1] Complicating these efforts are variations in the profiles of successful workers by geographic location and gender.

Human Resource Development

Research is also quite important in the area of human resource development. Studies may identify the employees who can benefit from training. For instance, a high error rate associated with certain employees might indicate the need for additional training.

Also, research into the usefulness of the training program may be needed: Are workers better prepared to do their jobs after training, or is the training an exercise in futility? Training and development is expensive and its costs must be justified.

In addition, the type of training and development that is needed may be identified through human resource research. The productivity of different departments may suggest that certain managers would benefit from communication training. Finally, an analysis of employee performance may suggest additional areas of training and development that are needed.

Compensation

Both actual and perceived inequities in the firm's compensation system can create problems. Managers must be able to identify actual inequities and correct them, as well as provide information to employees to help overcome misconceptions. In order to maintain a fair pay policy, many firms conduct extensive compensation surveys. In addition, in-house surveys are often conducted to determine employee attitudes regarding pay. Compensation research is widely used to identify potential problems before they get out of hand. For instance, if the supply and demand for skilled employees in the labor force is constantly changing, an organization's compensation program can rapidly become outdated and must therefore be closely monitored.

---

[1] R. Wayne Mondy, "Job Longevity Differs by Sex," *Convenience Store News* (May 2, 1975), p. 1.

Employee and Labor Relations

Research in the area of employee and labor relations focuses primarily on areas that affect individual job performance. Some of this research may be needed to identify factors that will permit the firm to remain union-free. Research may show that internal factors, such as working conditions, may have a detrimental effect on employee productivity and job satisfaction. This type of information can prompt actions that would help an organization remain union-free. When problems are left unsolved, the worker may believe that the only remedy to the situation is to join the union. Continually monitoring factors that affect employee and labor relations will probably always prove beneficial to both the employee and the organization.

Safety and Health

The primary task of research in health and safety relates to identification of potential problem areas. For instance, research may be conducted to determine the locations and causes of accidents. It also can be used to identify characteristics of workers having higher accident probabilities. Accident patterns may be identified and changes recommended to prevent their occurrence. Health and safety concerns increased during the 1980s and will probably be even more important in the future. Therefore, human resource managers must make every attempt to identify health and safety problems and solve them as quickly as possible.

■ MAJOR GLOBAL HUMAN RESOURCE MANAGEMENT PROBLEMS

Human resource research has expanded dramatically in the past few years. Recent research findings clearly indicate the main global human resource difficulties.[2] In a recent survey, company representatives were asked to name the "most important" issue related to global human resource management (see Table 19-2 on page 716). These twelve issues will probably be the primary focus of international human resource research in the future.

■ METHODS OF INQUIRY IN HUMAN RESOURCE RESEARCH

The type of problem and the particular needs of the organization determine, to a large extent, the method of inquiry that will be used. Specific research methods that are particularly useful include the case study, the survey feedback method, and the experiment.

---

[2] Spencer Hayden, "Our Foreign Legions Are Faltering," *Personnel,* 67 (August 1990), p. 42.

TABLE 19-2 | The Most Important Human Resource Issues

Human Resource Issue	Percentage of Respondents
Selecting and training local managers	70
Generating companywide loyalty and motivation	70
Speaking and understanding local language and culture	66
Appraising the performances of managers abroad	65
Planning systematic manager development and succession	59
Hiring indigenous sales personnel	57
Compensating foreign managers	54
Hiring/training foreign technical employees	52
Selecting/training U.S. managers overseas	48
Dealing with unions and labor laws abroad	44
Promoting and transferring foreign managers	42
Compensating U.S. nationals abroad	42

Note: The total sample was 95 companies (manufacturing: 51; non-manufacturing: 44; more profitable: 58; less profitable: 37).

Source: Adapted from Spencer Hayden, "Our Foreign Legions Are Faltering," *Personnel,* 67 (August 1990), p. 42. Used with the permission of The Spencer Hayden Co.

The Case Study

The **case study** is an investigation into the underlying causes of specific problems in a plant, a department, or a work group. The results of the research apply only to that particular set of problems and cannot be generalized. Typical problems that the case study method might be used to investigate include the following:

- An excessively high turnover rate at a particular plant.
- A high absenteeism rate in a specific department.
- A high accident rate at a certain building site.
- Low morale in a particular department.
- The low number of minority group members in a certain plant.
- The underlying reasons for a wildcat strike at a particular location.

Naturally, there are many more situations in which the case study method may be appropriate. Although the results can't be generalized, the results of such studies may suggest possible new management approaches. The human resource management example later in this chapter provides an illustration of a case study provided by an outside consultant for a regional medical center. In other situations, the firm's human resource manager or an HRM specialist will conduct the research.

The Survey Feedback Method

A major function of human resource research is to determine periodically the attitudes of employees toward their jobs, pay, and supervision. Typically, this is done by means of survey questionnaires. Responses to questions may also reveal ways to improve productivity. Recall that Annette Dommert, in the case at the beginning of the chapter, is proposing a confidential questionnaire to be administered to all employees in the hospital. In the **survey feedback method,** anonymous questionnaires are used to systematically collect and measure employee attitudes. The Ford Motor Company uses the survey method to obtain the opinions of its salaried workers every other year. The results are published in Ford's in-house publication *The American Road.*

Surveys may be either the objective multiple-choice type or the scaled-response type, which asks for degrees of agreement or disagreement (see Figure 19-1 on page 718). Objective analysis of survey results often requires a more detailed study. There are many possible bases for comparison of survey results:

1. Section or department.
2. Age.
3. Gender.
4. Seniority.
5. Job level or degree of responsibility.
6. Changes in attitudes from previous surveys.
7. Comparison with other divisions, departments, or work groups.
8. Comparison with a standardized score if a validated instrument is being used.

The data become more meaningful to management when analyzed by various subgroups. A major point to consider is that survey responses often identify symptoms rather than causes. For instance, even if the compensation and benefits program is quite competitive, a low evaluation in this area (symptom) may reflect general dissatisfaction with management style rather than an inadequate compensation system. When surveys are administered, the researcher should avoid concentrating on isolated responses. Instead, the data should be viewed from a broader perspective, which may uncover a pattern or general trend. Collectively, the responses will likely reflect this trend if there are difficulties throughout the organization.

When surveys are used to identify employee attitudes and opinions, confidentiality of responses must be ensured.[3] Employees must believe that their specific responses will not be communicated to management. For this reason, outside consultants are often employed to administer the questionnaire. Even if the human resource professionals are completely ethical, employees may still perceive them as a tool of management. Rightly or wrongly, employees may always wonder whether the human resource

---

[3] R. Wayne Mondy and Wallace F. Nelson, "Job Satisfaction Among Radiologic Technologies," *Applied Radiology,* 7, no. 4 (July–August 1978), p. 66.

Why did you decide to do what you are now doing?

a. Desire to aid or assist others
b. Influenced by another person or situation
c. Always wanted to be in this vocation
d. Lack of opportunity or interest in other vocational fields
e. Opportunities provided by this vocation
f. Personal satisfaction from doing this work

What do you like least about your job?

a. Nothing
b. Pay
c. Supervisor relations
d. Problems with fellow workers
e. Facilities
f. Paperwork and reports

Considering all aspects of your job, evaluate your compensation with regard to your contributions to the needs of the organization. Circle the number that best describes how you feel.

Pay Too Low		Pay Low		Pay Average		Pay Above Average		Pay Too High	
1	2	3	4	5	6	7	8	9	10

What are your feelings about overtime work requirements? Circle the number that best indicates how you feel.

Unnecessary				Necessary on Occasion			Necessary		
1	2	3	4	5	6	7	8	9	10

FIGURE 19-1 | Examples of Multiple-Choice and Scaled-Response Survey Questions

department will succumb to management pressure to reveal specific employee responses.

Confidentiality means more than merely omitting a worker's name on the questionnaire. Even in a large firm, numerous sections consist of only a small number of employees. Or in a large department, a characteristic of a particular worker may make identification easy. For instance, a department might have only one woman in it. Protection of such a person's confidentiality is crucial to obtaining accurate results. The researcher must constantly be alert to these situations and be prepared to consolidate groups when necessary to preserve anonymity.

Survey results must be communicated back to the affected groups. Employees need to see what their collective responses were. And if surveys are to be taken seriously, management must act on the results.

When survey results are communicated to management, it is often best for each department or section head to be contacted individually. For instance, if the survey suggests that problems exist in the marketing department, the department head will likely be more receptive to criticism if his or her peers are not listening. Just as workers do not like to be disciplined in the presence of their coworkers, managers do not like to receive survey results in the presence of others. Better results are typically obtained when the data are discussed with each person or group separately.

At times, surveying every employee is not feasible because of time or cost restraints. **Sampling** is the process in which only a portion of the total group is studied and conclusions are drawn for the entire group. For example, assume that the total number of workers in a firm is 5,000. The time, effort, and cost necessary to survey all 5,000 workers may be prohibitive. If so, the researcher will probably decide to survey a smaller sample group. For example, a sample size of 500 workers may be deemed representative of the entire group. Conclusions are based on the responses from the employees comprising the sample and then applied to the entire group of 5,000 employees.

The Experiment

A method of inquiry that involves the manipulation of certain variables while others are held constant is referred to as an **experiment.** This method utilizes a control group and an experimental group. The control group continues to operate as usual, whereas selected variables are manipulated for the experimental group. For instance, a manager may want to determine the effect that a new training program will have on productivity. The control group would continue to perform tasks in the conventional manner. The experimental group would receive the training. The assumption is that any change in productivity in the experimental group results from the training. On the surface, the experiment appears to be an excellent means of inquiry. Actually, isolating the many interrelated variables affecting people and their performance can be extremely difficult.

■ THE RESEARCH PROCESS

A systematic approach to human resource research is needed. The most fruitful research is accomplished by following a logical process, such as that shown in Figure 19-2 on page 720.

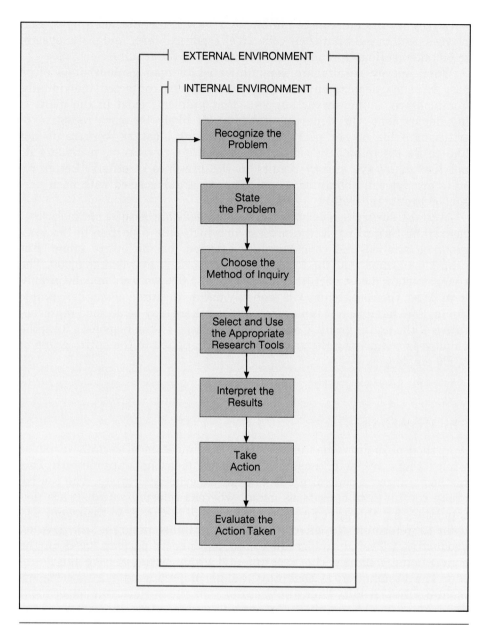

FIGURE 19-2 | The Human Resource Research Process

Recognize the Problem

One of the difficult tasks in the research process is to recognize that a problem exists. For instance, at what point does absenteeism or turnover become excessive? A certain amount of turnover may be healthy for an organization. However, explaining away a potential problem is often convenient. A manager may state, "Even though turnover is high, we really don't

HRM In Action

Bob Stephens, president of Queens Manufacturing Company, and Mary Bushnell, the company's human resource director, were engaged in a serious conversation that could have a major impact on the future of the firm. "Mary," said Bob, "I've been hearing rumblings of discontent throughout the organization. For some reason that I can't figure out, people at Queens just don't appear to be as happy as they have been in the past. And it isn't just isolated instances. There is a different attitude everywhere. Any ideas as to how we can determine what's going on so we can correct the problem?"

If you were Mary, how would you respond?

have a problem because those people didn't fit into the organization anyway." Such a comment would lead a researcher to suspect that this manager may not be open to problem recognition. In actuality, the problem may be caused by an inadequate selection process, insufficient managerial training, or any number of other reasons. Or, as the manager suggests, there might not be a problem. Regardless of the situation, openness on the part of the manager is the cornerstone of problem recognition.

State the Problem

The next step in the process is to clearly state the purpose of the research. The major hurdle to overcome is that the problem—not the symptoms—must be identified. As you might expect, this can be difficult. For instance, a manager might maintain that the cause of declining production is low pay when, in fact, the real reason is inadequate supervision or insufficient training. Research may determine that dictatorial supervisors have been exerting so much pressure on employees that they couldn't care less about productivity. If the manager attempted to solve the morale problem through means such as increasing benefits, it is unlikely that conditions would improve. A clear definition of the problem is essential for effective research.

Choose the Method of Inquiry

The method of inquiry chosen depends to a large extent on the nature of the research. The methods of inquiry previously described—the case study, the survey, and the experiment—are all valuable. However, most human resource research involves either the case method or the survey.

Select and Use the Appropriate Research Tools

Numerous quantitative tools are available for use by the human resource researcher. Managers do not have to be experts in mathematics and statistical theory in order to take advantage of their use; however, managers do need to know the following:

- Availability of quantitative tools.
- Circumstances under which these tools should be used.
- Strengths and weaknesses of each method.
- How to interpret the results.

The selection of a tool depends on the particular purpose for which the research is being conducted.

Interpret the Results

The person closest to the problem should participate in interpreting the results. When outsiders alone attempt to do this, they often arrive at strange conclusions. For instance, the survey may suggest that major dissatisfaction exists in the engineering department. A person not close to the situation might mistakenly identify the problem as one of inadequate supervision. Actually, the engineers may have voiced their dissatisfaction with the condition of their facilities.

Take Action

The most difficult phase of the research process is to take action based on research findings. The results may have identified areas in which changes need to be made. The human resource manager now becomes the catalyst to convince line management that a change is necessary. Many times, this task is quite difficult. Telling a manager that his or her managerial style is causing excessive turnover can be an awkward task. However, the benefits of research are realized only when action is being taken to resolve the problem that has been identified.

Evaluate the Action Taken

No research effort is complete until the action has been evaluated. Evaluation requires an objective assessment of whether the action has solved the problem and if so, how. Recall that Figure 19-2 on page 720 shows a feedback loop from evaluation to problem recognition. Determining whether the problem has been adequately solved will assist in future research efforts. Revisions may be needed or the entire research approach may need to be rethought, but the information gained through a well-conceived research project almost always proves useful.

■ QUANTITATIVE METHODS IN HUMAN RESOURCE RESEARCH

Numerous quantitative methods are available to those who conduct human resource research. Most of these tools are available on both mainframe and personal computers. Correlation analysis, regression analysis, discriminant analysis, and time series analysis are described here.

Correlation Analysis

Often a researcher would like to know the relative strength of the relationships between variables. **Correlation analysis** measures the degree of association that exists between two or more variables. For instance, is there a relationship between job satisfaction and employee absenteeism? Figure 19-3 shows a high *negative* relationship between job satisfaction and employee absenteeism: As job satisfaction goes down, absenteeism goes up. (Employees who have a low level of job satisfaction tend to be absent more often.) Figure 19-4 shows a high *positive* correlation between the level of employee education and productivity: The higher the education level is, the greater the productivity (see page 724). These correlations are based on data from one firm. They might not hold for another firm and thus cannot

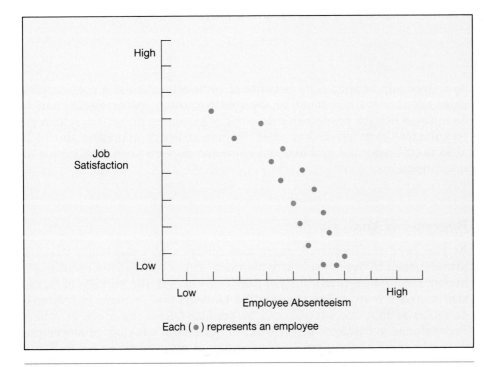

FIGURE 19-3 | The Negative Correlation Between Job Satisfaction and Employee Absenteeism at a Particular Firm

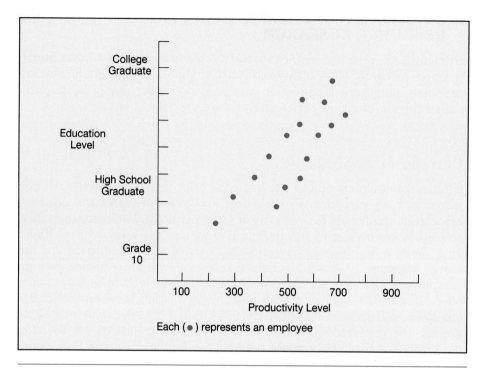

FIGURE 19-4 | The Positive Correlation Between Education Level and Level of Productivity at a Particular Firm

be universally applied. The benefits of correlation analysis are considerable, but this method must be used with caution. A correlation can be deceptive when the relationship does not reflect cause and effect. A high but meaningless correlation may exist. Human resource managers should be alert to this potential problem and not make decisions based on erroneous interpretations.

Regression Analysis

As discussed in Chapter 5, regression analysis is a technique that has proven useful in human resource planning. It has also proven beneficial in human resource research. As was previously stated, the purpose of regression analysis is to utilize the relation between two or more quantitative variables so that one variable can be predicted from the other, or others. For instance, a manager might want to determine whether employee productivity can be estimated from educational attainment (refer to Figure 19-4). In regression analysis terminology, the productivity level is referred to as the *dependent* variable. The education level used to estimate the level of productivity is called the *independent* variable. In this example, there is only one independent variable, so the process is referred to as *simple linear* regression. The use of two or more independent variables is termed *multiple* regression.

When regression analysis is used in human resource research, some possible dependent variables might be the following:

- Satisfaction level of employees.
- Length of employment of employees.
- Productivity level of employees.
- Accident rate of employees.

Employment data that might be used as the independent variable include these factors:

- Background and biographical data.
- Work history with the firm.
- Personal goals and aspirations.
- Test scores.

The researcher might attempt to determine through regression analysis which of the independent variables aid in differentiating more productive and less productive workers. The regression model developed using these variables may help the manager to identify prospective employees who are likely to become successful workers, thereby improving selection decisions. The model's accuracy must be validated through other statistical means; however, if the model proves appropriate, it can be very useful in the selection process.

Discriminant Analysis

The purpose of discriminant analysis is to identify factors that differentiate between two or more groups in a population. When two-group discriminant analysis is used, an attempt might be made to identify factors that differentiate these groups:

- Satisfied from less satisfied employees.
- Long-term from short-term employees.
- Productive from less productive employees.
- Accident-prone from less accident-prone employees.

Only the imagination of the researcher limits the factors that can be used. Some of the factors that the researcher might use to differentiate two groups include background and biographical data, work history with the firm, personal goals and aspirations, and test scores.

For instance, suppose the researcher were attempting to determine whether certain background or biographical factors differentiated satisfied from less satisfied workers. As with regression analysis, the level of satisfaction becomes the dependent variable. However, unlike regression analysis, individuals in the two groups are identified as either satisfied or less satisfied. Through the use of discriminant analysis, independent variables capable of distinguishing between the two selected groups are identified. The mechanics of discriminant analysis also permit the researcher to determine the reliability of the model developed.

Time Series Analysis

A technique that has proven quite helpful in making projections is time series analysis. Time series analysis is a variation of regression analysis in which the independent variable is expressed in units of time. As in regression analysis, both a dependent variable and an independent variable are required. However, the independent variable is now associated with time and the dependent variable is associated with demand. When the number of employees required in a company is closely associated with demand for the firm's product, time series analysis may prove useful in forecasting the organization's human resource needs. Using the same general mathematical procedure as in regression analysis, a time series equation can be derived and estimates of future demand calculated.

■ HUMAN RESOURCE RESEARCH: AN ILLUSTRATION

In order to illustrate how human resource research may be used in an organization, this section presents an actual example. At the firm's request, it will not be identified. The techniques used and the benefits achieved are factual. The organization, a regional medical center in the Southwest, had experienced rapid growth and the accompanying "growing pains." The human resource director and the hospital administrator recognized that problems were developing and called in an outside consultant. He was to work with them in identifying and solving those problems before they became critical.

The consultant first talked with numerous employees to get a general view of the situation. Hesitancy of employees to talk about certain subjects and their apparent nervousness during the informal interviews suggested the existence of problems.

The next phase of the research project involved developing a survey tailored specifically for the hospital. Sample questions, which are shown in Figure 19-5, were developed. As you can see, topics ranged from managerial style to compensation. Administration of the questionnaire to all hospital employees was a critical step, and maintaining each participant's confidentiality was crucial. The hospital administrator's role was to notify the employees of the survey. From that point on, the employees would have no further contact with any member of the administration regarding the survey.

Groups of employees met with the consultant in the room where the survey was to be administered. He first explained the survey's purpose and then assured the employees of confidentiality. Employees were told that summary results only would be provided to the administration. At

What do you like most about your job?
a. Helping or providing service for others
b. Learning opportunities
c. Personal satisfaction
d. Being around people
e. The work you perform at this hospital at this job
f. Nothing
g. Other (Specify)
h. Other (Specify)

What do you like least about your job?
a. Nothing
b. Pay
c. Supervisor relations
d. Problems with fellow workers
e. Facilities
f. Paperwork and reports
g. Patient-related problems
h. Doctor-related problems
i. Other (Specify)
j. Other (Specify)

How would you describe your overall working environment? Circle the number that best describes how you feel.

Extremely Frustrating		Frustrating		Acceptable		Above Average		Excellent	
1	2	3	4	5	6	7	8	9	10

What do you think of strikes in the health care field? Circle the number that indicates how you feel.

Strongly Favor		Favor		Neutral		Opposed		Strongly Opposed	
1	2	3	4	5	6	7	8	9	10

What do you think about the system of giving pay increases at this hospital? Circle the number that best describes how you feel.

Very Bad		Poor		Satisfied		Good		Excellent	
1	2	3	4	5	6	7	8	9	10

Considering all aspects of your job, evaluate your compensation with regard to your contributions to the needs of the hospital. Circle the number that best describes how you feel.

Pay Too Low		Pay Low		Pay Average		Pay Above Average		Pay Too High	
1	2	3	4	5	6	7	8	9	10

FIGURE 19-5 | Sample Survey Questions

this point it became even more obvious that problems did exist. Many employees wanted to know in detail the relationship between the consultant and the administration. Continuous assurances of confidentiality had to be given. Because of the nature of hospital work, the researcher had to administer the questionnaire over a forty-eight-hour period. To further ensure confidentiality, the respondents were told that they should put their completed questionnaires in blank envelopes so they could not be identified. Some employees even chose to mail their responses to the consultant rather than risk having the questionnaire get lost at the hospital.

The next phase entailed analyzing the results. Data from each employee were entered into a computer. The data were analyzed for the entire hospital and for each of its departments.

Statistics for the entire hospital proved inconclusive. However, when the survey results were evaluated by departments, some obvious problems began to surface. Employees in certain departments appeared to be much more unhappy than workers in other departments. For instance, the levels of satisfaction in the radiology and lab departments appeared to be consistently below the satisfaction level of the hospital in general. Although not as negative, job satisfaction among nurses and aides was also below the hospital average. Figure 19-6 shows the summary of responses by department regarding overall working environment.

At this point, however, only symptoms had been uncovered. The next phase entailed identification of specific problems. The results of the survey were presented to each department head individually. They reviewed the results, discussed what the symptoms revealed, and participated in the identification of problems.

The analysis of the radiology department provides an excellent illustration of the difference between the identification of symptoms and identification of problems. The hospital had experienced rapid growth during the past few years, and while other departments had increased staff to handle the increased workload, the radiology department had not. This placed considerable pressure on the employees in the department. A mistake made in this department could have serious consequences for patients. Also, questioning of workers revealed that the salary level of this department had not kept pace with radiology departments in nearby hospitals. The combination of these two factors—a department under pressure and an unreasonable salary level—resulted in considerable job dissatisfaction. The cause of the dissatisfaction had now been determined. The same procedure was used in the other departments in which employees had expressed low job satisfaction.

The consultant was now able to provide the hospital administrator with not only the survey results, but also some sound recommendations. Suggestions for improvement were made for each department, as well as for the entire hospital. They included these two steps:

1. Implementation of a management training program emphasizing communication skills, leadership, motivation, and other human relation techniques.
2. Reevaluation of the hospital's compensation program, including reacquainting employees with their benefits package, clarifying the method of granting pay increases, and evaluating new benefits.

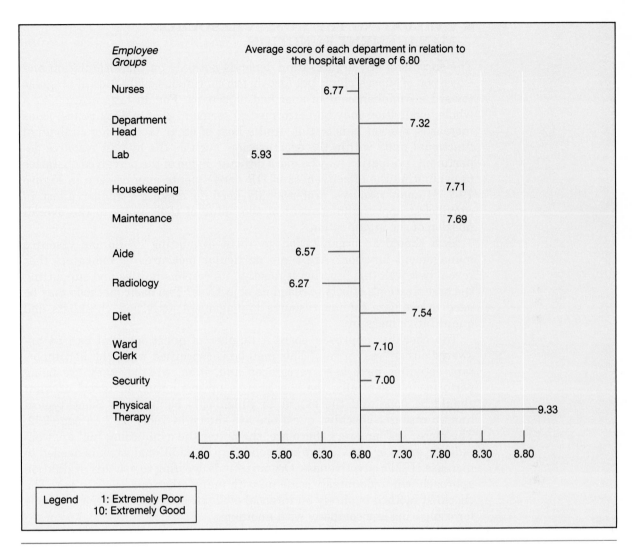

FIGURE 19-6 | Descriptions of Overall Working Environment

The timing of the research and resulting implementation of the recommendations later proved to be crucial. Within a year, a major attempt at unionizing the hospital was made, but it failed. The research study, which identified human resource problems and proposed solutions, was credited as the major factor in preparing the hospital for its successful efforts to remain union-free.[4]

---

[4] R. Wayne Mondy and Wallace F. Nelson, "Job Satisfaction Among Radiologic Technologies," *Applied Radiology*, 7, no. 4 (July–August 1978), pp. 65–67. Copyright © Barrington Publications, Inc., 825 S. Barrington Avenue, Los Angeles, CA 90049. Reprinted by permission.

■ EVALUATING THE HUMAN RESOURCE MANAGEMENT FUNCTION

The success of any organization depends not only on the formulation and execution of superb plans, but also on the continuous evaluation of progress toward accomplishment of specified objectives. For an organization as a whole, evaluation may be performed in terms of profitability ratios, sales increases, market penetration, and a host of other factors. For individual functional units within the organization, such as the human resource department, evaluation may be more difficult. Some of the perceived obstacles to evaluating the effectiveness of HR departments may be seen in Figure 19-7. Human resource professionals need to make a stronger effort in convincing upper management of the value of their units to the overall mission of the organization.[5]

How should an organization go about evaluating its human resource management function? Are there particular measures or indicators that reveal how well this function is meeting its responsibilities and supporting the organization's efforts to reach its objectives? Two basic methods may be used to evaluate human resource management activities: checklists and quantitative measures.

The checklist approach poses a number of questions that can be answered either "yes" or "no." This method is concerned with whether important activities have been recognized and, if so, whether they are being performed. Essentially, the checklist is an evaluation in terms of what should be done and the extent to which it is being done. Some typical human resource checklist questions are shown in Table 19-3 on page 732. The more "yes" answers there are, the better the evaluation; "no" answers indicate areas or activities where follow-up or additional work is needed to increase HRM's effectiveness. Organizations deciding to use this evaluation approach will undoubtedly come up with many other questions to ask. The checklist method is purely an internal evaluation device. It is not a vehicle for comparing one company with another.

The second method for evaluating the performance of human resource activities is a quantitative one. It relies on the accumulation of various types of numerical data and the calculation of certain ratios from them. Numerical data are useful primarily as an indicator of activity levels and trends. Ratios show results that are important in themselves but that also reveal (when maintained over a period of time) trends that may be even more important.

In some instances, quantitative measures may be used for external comparisons with other organizations. However, since very few performance standards exist for the HRM function, external comparisons should always be interpreted with care. For example, the area in which the amount of external comparative data is probably greatest is employee

---

[5] Margaret E. Cashman and James C. McElroy, "Evaluating the HR Function," *HRMagazine*, 36 (January 1991), p. 73.

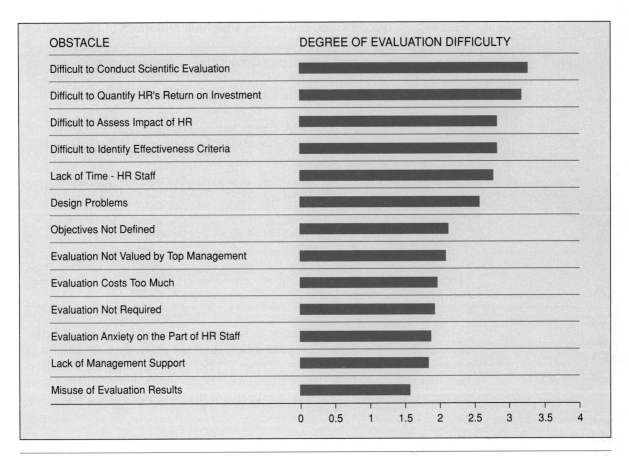

FIGURE 19-7 | Perceived Obstacles to Evaluating the Effectiveness of HR Departments

Note: 1 = little difficulty and 5 = extreme difficulty.

Source: Margaret E. Cashman and James C. McElroy, "Evaluating the HR Function," *HRMagazine,* 36 (January 1991), p. 73. Reprinted with the permission from *HRMagazine* (formerly *Personnel Administrator*) published by the Society for Human Resource Management, Alexandria, VA.

turnover. While it may be tempting to evaluate an organization's turnover in terms of the "industry average" or by size of workforce, such comparisons may be meaningless. There is just too much variation in the factors that affect a specific organization's turnover, such as the nature of the local labor market, the number of long-time employees, the ability of the firm to pay competitive rates, the company's reputation as an employer, and so on.

One measure that can truly be considered a standard is the four-fifths or 80–20 rule, which measures the selection rate of women and minorities against other employees. Generally this ratio should approximate 80 percent. But even so, there are exceptions to this standard because of the specific situations that organizations face.

TABLE 19-3 | Typical Human Resource Checklist Questions

- Are all legally mandated reports submitted to requiring agencies on time?
- Have formalized procedures and methods been developed for conducting job analysis?
- Are human resource requirements forecasts made at least annually?
- Is the recruiting process effectively integrated with human resource planning?
- Does the application form conform to applicable legal and affirmative action standards?
- Are all employees appraised at least annually?
- Are skills inventories maintained on all employees?
- Are career opportunities communicated clearly to all employees?

In short, although quantitative data may be somewhat useful for external comparisons with similar companies, they are probably most helpful in establishing internal baselines (frames of reference) and showing the direction of movement from those baselines.[6] Some examples of quantitative measures for human resource management are listed in Table 19-4.

■ TECHNOLOGY AFFECTING HUMAN RESOURCE MANAGEMENT[7]

Technological advances in computer hardware and software occur virtually every day. These developments can improve human resource management and raise employee productivity. It's impossible to foresee all the new uses for each technological breakthrough. The only certainty is that managers must be aware of these innovations and their capabilities. An executive for United Services Automobile Association (USAA) noted that even during tough economic times, technological changes must be tracked to maintain a competitive edge.[8] Failure to keep up with developments in this rapidly changing area can threaten a firm's competitive position and possibly even its survival. We next discuss some of the developments that most significantly affect human resource management.

---

[6] Donald L. Caruth, Robert M. Noe III, and R. Wayne Mondy, *Staffing the Contemporary Organization* (New York: Praeger Publishers, 1990), pp. 283–299.

[7] This section written by Dr. Judy A. Mondy, Department of Management and Marketing, McNeese State University.

[8] Alice Laplante, "The Needing Edge," *Computerworld,* 25, no. 11 (March 18, 1991), p. 65.

TABLE 19-4 | Examples of Quantitative Human Resource
Management Measures

- Women and minorities selection ratio
- Women and minorities promotion ratio
- Women and minorities termination ratio
- Minority and women hiring percentage
- Minority and women workforce percentage
- Requirements forecast compared to actual human resource needs
- Availability forecast compared to actual availability of human resources
- Average recruiting cost per applicant
- Average recruiting cost per employee hired
- Percentage of positions filled internally
- Average testing cost per applicant
- Percentage of required appraisals actually completed
- Percentage of employees rated in highest performance category
- Percentage of appraisals appealed
- Turnover percentage
- New hire retention percentage
- Percentage of new hires lost

Application and Communication Software

Several types of existing software continue to affect human resource management. This software includes data communication, word processing, computer graphics, spreadsheet programs, decision support systems, and database management.

Data Communication. The sending of computer data over some form of communication medium, such as phone lines, is referred to as **data communication**. This form of communication is becoming increasingly important in the business world. Caterpillar, Inc., owns its own communications satellite, and the firm places a heavy emphasis on advanced data communication to better serve its global market.[9] Human resource managers can transmit documents or messages over phone lines and eliminate wasted time and potential misunderstandings; thus, decision making is facilitated. For example, prior to a teleconference it is often useful to utilize

---

[9] Michael Fitzgerald, "IS Helps 'Cat' Stay on its Feet," *Computerworld Premier 100,* sec. 2 (October 9, 1990), p. 60.

electronic mail so that everyone involved can become familiar with the exact nature of the discussion before the conference begins.

Electronic mail users have the capability to schedule a meeting for an entire work group, automatically send messages to meeting attendees, and even check spelling.[10] The use of facsimile machines (fax) to copy a document and send it electronically to another location has been revitalized by faster, lower cost personal computer systems.[11] Cellular radio is another important communications medium for mobile voice as well as data communications.[12]

Word Processing. A computer application that permits an operator to create and edit written material is referred to as **word processing**. Word processing allows simplified editing of manuscripts and correspondence. For example, inserting a new paragraph at the beginning of a ten-page manuscript no longer requires retyping the entire document. Word processing allows managers to work more efficiently. For example, a manager can type out a memo, edit it on the screen, and with a few commands, print it out or route it to several recipients using electronic mail. Word processing has become one of today's most significant communication enhancement tools. It allows human resource managers to develop sensitive documents, such as workforce reduction plans or performance appraisal reports, without risking a breach of security.

Computer Graphics. "A picture is worth a thousand words." This adage is certainly applicable to the use of computer graphics. Managers can already use computer programs to produce various kinds of graphs and charts in both black and white and color. These graphics represent a large amount of data reduced to a single image.[13] Human resource managers frequently present data graphically because this method often illustrates the message much more effectively than simple text could.

Spreadsheet Programs. Spreadsheet programs provide a column-row matrix on which numbers or words can be entered, stored, and used for calculations. Predefined statistical, financial, and mathematical functions allow the user to quickly and easily answer "what if" questions.[14] Spreadsheet analysis is particularly beneficial in activities such as human resource planning.

Decision Support Systems. Computer departments are often backed up with demands for urgently needed information. To overcome this problem,

---

[10] Richard Brady, Rod Chapin, Steve Irvin, Patrick Lyons, and Sebastian Rupley, "Product Comparison: Meeting the Mail," *Infoworld,* 12 (October 29, 1990), p. 71.

[11] James A. O'Brien, *Introduction to Information Systems in Business Management,* 6th ed. (Homewood, Ill.: Richard D. Irwin, 1991), p. 257.

[12] *Ibid.*, p. 181.

[13] James A. Senn, *Information Systems in Management,* 4th ed. (Belmont, Cal.: Wadsworth Publishing Co., 1990), p. 265.

[14] *Ibid.*, p. 255.

a manager can acquire a **decision support system (DSS),** an information system that allows users to quickly process and retrieve information. Normally DSSs are sophisticated database systems capable of retrieving, displaying, and processing a wide variety of information. Graphics, simulation, modeling, and quantitative analysis are also typically available through the DSS. Obviously, decision support systems can be very useful in human resource planning.

Database Management. Information subsystems are commonly developed for accounting, office management, manufacturing, marketing, and human resource departments. Often the data and programs in these subsystems are considered to be separate and distinct, resulting in a tremendous amount of redundant data. For example, the accounting subsystem would normally contain the names and Social Security numbers of all employees—and so would the human resource files. The purpose of **database management** is to minimize such redundancies. The term thus refers to the integration of information subsystems in order to reduce the duplication of information, effort, and cost, and to provide controlled access to this information. When Toyota sought to staff its manufacturing plant in Georgetown, Kentucky, more than 60,000 people applied. An intensive eight-phase hiring process was used and monitored through a computer tracking system.[15]

Teleconferencing

Partly because of the high cost of business travel—in terms of both time and money—teleconferencing is becoming increasingly popular. **Teleconferencing** is a method of conducting or participating in multiparty discussions by telephone or videophone. Teleconferencing may become a major means of not only improving managerial communication and productivity, but also of lowering their cost. Such systems allow human resource managers to resolve many problems without ever meeting in person with other parties, thus saving both time and money.

Voice Mail

Voice mail records spoken messages electronically and stores them for delivery to the recipient at a later time. When a voice mail system is used, an individual gains access to his or her account by dialing a special telephone number and then providing a password and user-identification number. The user may then listen to any new messages, replay old messages, eliminate messages, and/or record messages for others. Managers can place confidential information in the system and know that the message will be

---

[15] Chuck Consentino, John Allen, and Richard Wellins, "Choosing the Right People," *HRMagazine,* 35 (March 1990), pp. 66–70.

received in the exact manner that it was sent. Voice mail is useful when human resource managers are dealing with sensitive matters, such as layoffs, and want to avoid phone conversations that could be overheard by others.

Telecommuting

As previously mentioned in Chapter 13, many firms have turned to telecommuting as a way of meeting particular human resource needs. Through telecommuting, employees work at home and transmit data over telephone lines tied to a computer. Working at home is not appropriate for every job, but writers, reservation agents, researchers, and computer programmers, for example, can often easily adapt to this style of work. One computer programmer quit his job in San Diego and moved to the island of St. John, agreeing to "help out" his former employer if needed. Within two weeks, the programmer had established a consulting firm and was working his own hours. Gil Gordon, editor of *Telecommuting Review,* described this exotic setup as "feasible only if the employee is highly trained, can do virtually all of the job long-distance and possesses a hard-to-find skill."[16] Telecommuters often have more productive time since there is no wasted travel time for them. Also, handicapped people who cannot easily get to an office find telecommuting an excellent alternative.

Although the concept of telecommuting has many positive aspects, managers often have difficulty coping with it in practice. The question they often ask is "How do I supervise a person that I never see?" Some workers dislike telecommuting because they miss the friendly association with coworkers. Pacific Bell has a systematic procedure for selecting the types of jobs and the types of people who would benefit from telecommuting. In 1991, an estimated 4.4 million people were working at home during normal business hours.[17] Certainly, human resource professionals must be prepared to deal with this alternative type of work.

Expert Systems

An **expert system** is a system that uses knowledge about a narrowly defined, complex area to act as a consultant to a human.[18] In some instances, an organization may rely significantly upon the knowledge of one or more

---

[16] Carol Hildebrand, "Give This Programmer Sun, Surf and Software," *Computerworld,* 25 (March 11, 1991), pp. 1–16.

[17] Mitch Betts, "Bush to Push Work-At-Home," *Computerworld,* 24 (November 26, 1990), p. 1.

[18] James A. O'Brien, *Introduction to Information Systems in Business Management,* p. 325.

individuals in particular areas that can be captured in an expert system.[19] This captured expertise may then be used for training or may be disseminated throughout the organization for other employees to use. Mrs. Fields Cookies, Inc., uses an expert system to develop a profile of prospective applicants that is compared with the desired employee profile, and reports the results to the store manager.[20] Other typical expert systems in the area of human resource management contain data associated with employee performance evaluation, education scheduling, and employee benefits.[21]

Graphical User Interfaces

Graphical user interfaces (GUIs) represent a significant advancement because they make software applications much easier to use. The user communicates with the computer program by touching or aiming at graphic figures (icons) or framed written commands. No longer are keys depressed on the keyboard. Popular GUIs include Microsoft Windows, the IBM/Microsoft Presentation Manager, Open Software Foundation's Motif, and the Macintosh GUI.[22]

Multimedia

Multimedia is a computer application that produces presentations combining automation, stereo sound, full-motion video, and graphics. Users are immediately drawn to these presentations, which makes multimedia very useful in sales presentations and in training and development. For example, American Airlines uses it to train thousands of employees annually. Human resource managers are able to incorporate photographs, voice, documents, and images into personnel database files. The manager can then access the employee's photograph, Social Security card, and signed year-end appraisals.[23]

---

[19] Fritz H. Grupe, "Planning Your Expert System Strategy," *Information Executive,* 4 (Winter 1991), p. 47.

[20] Michael Fitzgerald, "Cooking with Expert Systems," *Computerworld,* 24 (October 15, 1990), p. 45.

[21] James A. O'Brien, *Introduction to Information Systems in Business Management,* pp. 325–330.

[22] William A. Newman and Floyd J. Brock, "Moving into the Graphical Decade: Graphical User Interfaces in the '90's," *Information Executive,* 4 (Winter 1991), pp. 28–32.

[23] Robert Sadarini, "The Art of Imagineering," *Information Executive,* 4 (Summer 1991), pp. 6–7.

SUMMARY

Human resource research is aimed at maximizing personal and organizational goal achievement. Human resource research should be systematic, with specific applications depending to a large extent on a firm's particular needs. From time to time, all aspects of the HRM functions have needs for research.

The type of problem confronting the human resource manager determines, to a large extent, the method of inquiry that will be used. When called on to uncover the underlying reasons for a particular occurrence, the human resource manager often uses the case study. The survey feedback method is used to determine employee attitudes. A method of inquiry that involves the manipulation of certain variables while others are held constant is referred to as an experiment.

The seven basic steps in the research process are (1) recognizing the problem, (2) stating the problem, (3) choosing the method of inquiry, (4) selecting and using the appropriate research tools, (5) interpreting the results, (6) taking action, and (7) evaluating the action taken.

Numerous quantitative tools are available for use by human resource managers. The purpose of correlation analysis is to measure the degree of association between two or more variables. The purpose of regression analysis is to determine the relationship between two or more variables so that one variable can be predicted from the others. The purpose of discriminant analysis is to identify factors that differentiate two or more groups in a population. Time series analysis permits projections to be made over time.

Two basic methods may be used to evaluate human resource management activities: checklists and quantitative measures. The checklist approach poses a number of questions that can be answered with "yes" or "no." This method is concerned with whether important activities have been recognized and, if so, whether they are being performed. The quantitative method relies on accumulating numerical data and calculating various ratios from these data for comparative purposes.

Technological advances in computer hardware and software occur virtually every day. These developments can improve human resource management and raise employee productivity. Teleconferencing is a method of conducting or participating in multiparty discussions by telephone or videophone. Voice mail is electronic transmission and storage of spoken messages for delivery to the recipient at a later time. A computer application that permits an operator to create and edit written material is referred to as word processing. Spreadsheet programs provide a column-row matrix on which numbers or words can be entered, stored, and used for calculations. A decision support system (DSS) is an information system that allows users to interact directly with a mainframe computer to quickly process and retrieve information. The purpose of database management is to reduce data and programming redundancies as much as possible; the term thus refers to the integration of the various information subsystems in order to minimize duplication. The sending of computer data over some form of communication medium, such as telephone lines, is referred to as data communication. Through telecommuting, employees work at home and transmit data over telephone lines tied to a computer.

Questions for Review

1. Describe the general methods of inquiry available for use by the human resource researcher.
2. Why would the experiment rarely be used as a means of inquiry in human resource management?
3. Identify the basic steps of the research process.
4. Why has management begun to realize that organizations can benefit from effective human resource research?

5. Briefly define each of the following quantitative tools as they are used in human resources:
   a. Correlation analysis
   b. Regression analysis
   c. Discriminant analysis
   d. Time series analysis
6. Explain how the human resource management function may be evaluated.
7. Identify and define the technological advances affecting human resource management.

Terms for Review

Human resource research
Case study
Survey feedback method
Sampling
Experiment
Correlation analysis
Data communication

Word processing
Decision support system (DSS)
Database management
Teleconferencing
Voice mail
Expert system
Multimedia

INCIDENT 1   ▪ Best Not to Know ▪

Mike Manton was president of Sadler Federal Bank, a Muncie, Indiana, mortgage lender. The company had about 100 employees and assets totaling $250 million in 1992. Mike had managed the company since the mid-1950s. He became the principal owner in 1987, when he put together a group of investors to convert Sadler from a saver-owned savings and loan company to a federal bank. Mike had always taken pride in knowing every employee by name, both before and after the management-led buyout. He often remarked that his company was "just one big, happy family."

In 1991, however, Mike had sensed growing dissatisfaction. Turnover increased and the workers just didn't seem content anymore. When Mike mentioned this to his office manager, Jeffery Wilson, Jeffery agreed that there had been a change. "I don't know what has caused it," said Jeffery, "but I do know that things are getting worse." Jeffery suggested a professionally conducted attitude survey to identify the problem. Mike agreed, and the survey was conducted with the assistance of a professor from Indiana University. Employees were encouraged to give honest answers and were given the usual assurances of anonymity. They were told that the company management would receive only generalized summaries of the survey results.

Mike was shocked by the results. It was evident that a large number of his people were dissatisfied with various aspects of their jobs. Some thought the pay was too low. Others felt that supervision was inadequate or arbitrary. Many objected to harsh working conditions. A few even mentioned the "high and mighty" attitude of the "big boss." Mike told Jeffery, "I simply cannot believe that the people I trusted could be so unappreciative of the jobs Sadler has provided them over the years."

He called in his vice-presidents, three of whom were co-owners, to discuss the results of the survey. After describing the survey results, he remarked, "We've always provided good jobs for our people and respected their rights. But if I knew who the strongest dissenters were, I don't think we would want them around. If they aren't happy with this company, they can leave."

Questions

1. If you were one of the vice-presidents, how would you handle the situation?
2. Discuss Mike's attitude concerning the survey results.

INCIDENT 2   ▪ So What's the Problem? ▪

Isabelle Anderson is plant manager for Hall Manufacturing Company in Alexandria, Louisiana, a company that produces a line of relatively inexpensive painted wood furniture. Six months ago, Isabelle became concerned about the turnover rate among workers in the painting department. Manufacturing plant turnover rates in that part of the South generally averaged about 30 percent, and this was the case at Hall. The painting department, however, had experienced a turnover of nearly 200 percent in each of the last two years. Because of the limited number of skilled workers in the area, Hall had an extensive training program for new painters, and Isabelle knew that the high turnover rate was very costly.

Isabelle conducted exit interviews with many of the departing painters. Some of them said that they were leaving for more money, others mentioned better benefits, and most cited some kind of "personal reasons" for quitting. Isabelle checked and found that Hall's wages and benefits were competitive with, if not better than, those of other manufacturers in the area. She then called in Nelson Able, the painting supervisor, to discuss the problem. Nelson's response was, "You know how this younger generation is. They work to get enough money to live on for a few weeks and then quit. I don't worry about it. Our old-timers can take up the slack." "But Nelson,"

Isabelle replied, "we have to worry about the turnover rates. It's really costing the company a lot of money. I'm going to ask Joe Swan in the HR department to administer a survey to get to the bottom of this." Nelson replied, "Do whatever you think is right. I don't see any problem."

Questions

1. Do you agree that a survey of employees is the best way to identify the problem? Explain.
2. If you determine that a survey is needed, what kind of survey would you conduct, and how would you analyze the results?

REFERENCES

Bownas, D. A. "A Quantitative Approach to Evaluating Training Curriculum Content Sampling Adequacy." *Personnel Psychology,* 38 (Spring 1985), pp. 117–131.

Cashman, Margaret E., and James C. McElroy. "Evaluating the HR Function." *HRMagazine,* 36 (January 1991), pp. 70–73.

Cosgrove, Charles V. "How to Report Productivity: Linking Measurements to Bottom-Line Financial Results." *National Productivity Review,* 6 (Winter 1986), pp. 63–71.

Cox, Mark M. "Human Resources' Expanding Role in the Health Care Industry." *Personnel Journal,* 69 (May 1990), pp. 41–44.

Goodrich, Jonathan N. "Telecommuting in America." *Business Horizons,* 33 (July–August 1990), pp. 31–37.

Gow, Jack F. "Human Resources Managers Must Remember the Bottom Line." *Personnel Journal,* 64 (April 1985), pp. 30–33.

Herren, Laura M. "The New Game of HR: Playing to Win." *Personnel,* 66 (June 1989), pp. 19–22.

Keaton, Paul N., and Michael J. Semb. "Shaping Up the Bottom Line." *HRMagazine,* 35 (September 1990), pp. 81–86.

Knapp, Jeffrey. "Trends in HR Management Systems." *Personnel,* 67 (April 1990), pp. 56–61.

Koretz, Gene. "A Worker Exodus that Could Weaken Productivity." *Business Week* (July 2, 1990), p. 22.

Kossek, Ellen Ernst. "Why Many HR Programs Fail." *Personnel,* 67 (May 1990), pp. 50–53.

Kromling, Larry K. "Calcomp Reshapes HR for the Future." *Personnel Journal,* 69 (January 1990), pp. 57–63.

Layton, William G., and Eric J. Johnson. "Break the Mold: Strategies for Productivity." *Personnel Journal,* 66 (May 1987), pp. 74–78.

Likert, Rensis. *The Human Organization* (New York: McGraw-Hill, 1967).

Portwood, James D., and Robert W. Eichinger. "The Challenge of Human Resource Management: Adding Value." *Human Resource Planning,* 8 (December 1985), pp. 209–228.

Rollins, Thomas, and Jerrold R. Bratkovich. "Productivity's People Factor." *Personnel Administrator,* 33 (February 1988), pp. 50–63.

Sachs, Robert. "A Productive Workforce: The Final Frontier of Competitive Advantage?" *Business Forum,* 15 (Spring 1990), pp. 5–7.

Shetty, Y. K., and Paul F. Buller. "Regaining Competitiveness Requires HR Solutions." *Personnel,* 67 (July 1990), pp. 8–12.

DEVELOPING HRM SKILLS

After studying this textbook, students should have a much better appreciation of the type of work human resource managers are involved in. In this exercise, participants will attempt to develop a profile of the attributes a human resource manager should possess. Knowledge gained throughout the course should be used in identifying necessary attributes.

Participants will have a copy of Exhibits 1, 2, and 3. The attributes listed in Exhibit 1 may be more or less important for a human resource manager. Put this list into an order by assigning the letter "A" to the five attributes that you think are the most important for a human resource manager to have. Assign a "B" to the five attributes you think are the second most important; "C" to the five attributes third most important; and "D" to the five attributes that you feel are least important. Definitions of each of these attributes are listed in Exhibit 2. You will have ten minutes for this activity.

After doing your individual ranking of these attributes, all students, except six individuals, will be placed into either Group 1 or Group 2. The six individuals not assigned to Groups 1 or 2 will make up the Review Committee; these individu-als will sit together and reach a consensus on the attribute rankings. Groups 1 and 2 will review the individual rankings of each of their members, discuss them, and then agree on a group ranking for the attributes listed. Exhibit 3, a Group Summary Sheet, is provided for this purpose. You will have fifteen minutes for this activity.

After the completion of this exercise, the debriefing will begin with Groups 1 and 2 answering the questions "What are the top five qualities needed by human resource professionals? Why?"

Then, members of the Review Committee will answer the questions "Which group identified the most appropriate top five qualities needed by human resource professionals? Why?"

Next, both groups will be asked, "What were the least important qualities needed by human resource professionals? Why?"

Finally, members of the Review Committee will be asked, "Which group identified the most appropriate least important qualities needed by human resource professionals? Why?"

The result of this exercise should be a realistic profile of what attributes an effective human resource manager should possess.

CASE VII

Parma Cycle Company: Looking Ahead

Edward Deal was jubilant. He had just received notification from the National Labor Relations Board that the union representation election at Parma Cycle's Clarksdale, Mississippi, plant had gone against the union. The margin was small—only 53 percent to 47 percent—but Ed considered it a significant victory. As human resource director at Clarksdale, he had done everything within his power to prevent the plant from becoming unionized. For example, wages and benefits at Clarksdale had started far below those at the Parma, Ohio, plant. At Edward's insistence, the package had been made competitive in the labor market. His recommendation for this had not been approved until top management was convinced that a unionizing effort was under way at Clarksdale.

With the new wage and benefits package, Parma Cycle became the highest-paying employer in the Clarksdale area. From Ed's vantage point, morale seemed to be quite high in the plant. Jobs with Parma were highly sought after. An average day saw twenty or thirty new job applicants. In fact, the rush of job applicants had forced Edward to post a sign reading "No Jobs Available."

There were still a couple of things that concerned Edward, though. First, the representation election had been extremely close. Twenty-five more votes would have swung it in the union's favor. Ed thus felt a certain insecurity about the prospects for future unionizing attempts at the plant. He knew that the company would have to live up to workers' expectations in order to keep the union out. He was also concerned about the

qualifications of the workers he had hired. During the recruiting process, all that Ed had been able to offer to new trainees was minimum wage. The average wage for beginning workers at Parma's Clarksdale plant had been only $5.20 an hour. Consequently, only very young, mostly unskilled workers had applied. They had been trained to some degree but were certainly no match for the workforce at Parma's Ohio plant.

Ed decided to call Jesse Heard, his old boss and the human resource director at the Parma, Ohio, plant. After a friendly greeting, Ed got right to the point. "Jesse," he said, "I thought we were surely going to lose the representation election, and I'd have been thrilled to get even a 1 percent victory margin. But, let's not kid ourselves. If we don't do a super job of keeping our workers satisfied, the union will get those extra twenty-five votes next time." "You're right," replied Jesse, "and even if you do, the result might be the same in the long run." "Why is that?" asked Ed. Jesse answered, "There has been a good deal of pressure by the union up here for us to recognize a bargaining unit at Clarksdale. I don't know how long top management will have the will to resist." "You really know how to let the air out of a fella's balloon," said Ed. "I don't mean to do that," Jesse replied, "but I do think we need to take a realistic view."

"Speaking of being realistic," continued Ed, "let's face it. We started the plant in Clarksdale to reduce labor costs, and we hired a full workforce here at very low rates compared to those we are paying now. We have raised wages and we still have the same workers.

The only way we can really have lower costs now is if the workers here produce more than those in Ohio." "I see what you mean," said Jesse. "I'll be down for a visit in a couple of months. I don't know if I can help in any way, but we can sure talk about it."

A few weeks later Ed decided that it was time to find out a little more about his workforce. He called Jules Cagney, a professor of human resources at Memphis State University, and asked him to recommend a research design. "Professor Cagney," said Ed, "I am not as concerned about keeping the union out as I am about treating our people fairly and maintaining a high level of motivation. I mainly want to know what their attitudes and concerns are so that we can design the human resource program around that." "I'll think about that," said Jules, "and be back in touch with you within a day or two."

Questions

1. What kind of study should Professor Cagney recommend? Explain.
2. What are the trends in human resources that Ed should consider when designing or redesigning the human resource program at Clarksdale?

GLOSSARY

Accountability: The responsibility for action and accompanying consequences.

Adverse impact: A concept established by the *Uniform Guidelines;* occurs if women and minorities are not hired at the rate of at least 80 percent of the best-achieving group.

Advertising: A way of communicating the firm's employment needs to the public through media such as radio, newspaper, or industry publications.

Affirmative action: Stipulated by EO 11246, it requires employers to take positive steps to ensure employment of applicants and treatment of employees during employment without regard to race, creed, color, or national origin.

Affirmative action program (AAP): A program that an organization develops to employ women and minorities in proportion to their representation in the firm's labor market.

Agency shop: A labor agreement provision requiring, as a condition of employment, that each nonunion member of the bargaining unit pay the union the equivalent of membership dues as a service charge for the union acting as the bargaining agent.

AIDS (acquired immune deficiency syndrome): A disease that undermines the body's immune system, leaving the person susceptible to a wide range of fatal diseases.

Aiming: The ability to move the hands quickly and accurately from one spot to another, which is important in jobs such as electronic parts assembly.

Alcoholism: A treatable disease characterized by uncontrolled and compulsive drinking that interferes with normal living patterns.

Apprenticeship training: A combination of classroom and on-the-job training.

Arbitration: A process in which a dispute is submitted to an impartial third party for a binding decision.

Assessment center: An appraisal approach that requires employees to participate in a series of activities similar to those they might be expected to do in an actual job.

Authorization card: A document indicating that an employee wants to be represented by a labor organization in collective bargaining.

Availability forecast: Determining whether the firm will be able to secure employees with the necessary skills, and the sources of these individuals.

Bargaining unit: A group of employees, not necessarily union members, recognized by an employer or certified by an administrative agency as appropriate for representation by a labor organization for purposes of collective bargaining.

Beachhead demands: Demands that the union does not expect management to meet when they are first made.

Behavior modeling: A training method that utilizes videotapes prepared specifically to illustrate how managers function in various situations for the purpose of developing interpersonal skills.

Behaviorally Anchored Rating Scale (BARS) method: A performance appraisal method that combines elements of the traditional rating scale and critical incidents methods.

Benefits: All financial rewards that generally are not paid directly to the employee.

Biofeedback: A method of learning to control involuntary bodily processes, such as blood pressure or heart rate.

Board interview: A meeting in which one candidate is interviewed by several interviewers.

Bottom-up approach: A forecasting method beginning with the lower organizational units and progressing upward through the organization to ultimately provide an aggregate forecast of employment needs.

Boycott: Refusal by union members to use or buy their firm's products.

Burnout: A state of fatigue or frustration stemming from devotion to a cause, way of life, or relationship that did not provide the expected reward.

Business games: Simulations that represent actual business situations.

Career: A general course of action a person chooses to pursue throughout his or her working life.

Career anchors: Research conducted by Edgar Schein that identified five different motives to account for the way people select and prepare for a career.

Career development: A formal approach taken by the organization to ensure that people with the proper qualifications and experience are available when needed.

Career paths: Flexible lines of progression through which employees typically move during their employment with a company.

Career planning: A process whereby an individual sets career goals and identifies the means to achieve them.

Case study: A training method that utilizes simulated business problems for trainees to solve; a research method that attempts to uncover the underlying reasons for occurrence of a problem in a specific area such as a plant, a department, or a section.

Central tendency: A common error that occurs when employees are incorrectly rated near the average or middle of the scale.

Checkoff of dues: An agreement in which the company agrees to withhold union dues from members' checks and forward the money directly to the union.

Classification method: A job evaluation method by which classes or grades are defined to describe a group of jobs.

Closed shop: An arrangement whereby union membership is a prerequisite to employment.

Coaching: An on-the-job approach to management development in which the manager is given an opportunity to teach on a one-to-one basis.

Cognitive aptitude tests: Tests to measure an individual's ability to learn, as well as to perform a job.

Collective bargaining: The performance of the mutual obligation of the employer and the representative of the employees to meet at reasonable times and confer in good faith with respect to wages, hours, and other terms and conditions of employment, or the negotiation of an agreement, or any question arising thereunder, and the execution of a written contract incorporating any agreement reached if requested by either party, but such obligation does not compel either party to agree to a proposal or require the making of a concession.

Committee on Political Education (COPE): The political arm of the AFL-CIO.

Communication: The transfer of information, ideas, understanding, or feelings between people.

Comparable worth (CW): Determination of the values of dissimilar jobs (such as company nurse and welder), by comparison, under some form of job evaluation and assignment of pay rates according to the jobs' evaluated worth.

Compensation: Every type of reward that individuals receive in return for their labor.

Compressed workweek: Any arrangement of work hours that permits an employee to fulfill a work obligation in fewer days than the typical five-day workweek.

Computer-based training: A teaching method that takes advantage of the speed, memory, and data manipulation capabilities of the computer for greater flexibility.

Concurrent validity: A validation method in which test scores and criterion data are obtained at essentially the same time.

Conference method: A widely used instructional approach that brings together individuals with common interests to discuss and attempt to solve problems (also known as the discussion method).

Conspiracy: The combination of two or more persons who band together to prejudice the rights of others or of society (such as by refusing to work or demanding higher wages).

Construct validity: A test validation method to determine whether a test measures certain traits or qualities that have been identified as important in performing the job.

Content validity: A test validation method whereby a person performs certain tasks that are actual samples of the kind of work the job requires or completes a paper-and-pencil test that measures relevant job knowledge.

Corporate culture: The system of shared values, beliefs, and habits within an organization that interacts with the formal structure to produce behavioral norms.

Correlation analysis: A method of measuring the degree of association between two or more variables.

Cost-of-living allowance (COLA): An escalator clause in a labor agreement that automatically increases wages as the U.S. Bureau of Labor Statistics cost of living index rises.

Craft unions: Bargaining units, such as the Carpenters and Joiners, that are typically composed of members of a particular trade or skill in a locality.

Criterion-related validity: A test validation method that compares the scores on selection tests to some aspect of job performance as determined, for example, by performance appraisal.

Critical incident method: A performance appraisal technique that requires a written record of highly favorable and highly unfavorable employee work behavior.

Cutoff score: The score below which an applicant will not be considered further for employment.

Cyclical variations: Reasonably predictable movements about a trend line that occur over a period of more than a year.

Data communication: Sending computer data over some form of communication medium, such as telephone lines.

Database management: Integration of information subsystems in order to reduce duplication of information, effort, and cost.

Decertification: Election by a group of employees to withdraw a union's right to act as their exclusive bargaining representative.

Decision support system: An information system that allows users to interact directly with a mainframe computer to quickly process and retrieve information.

Deferred compensation: Pay that is held in trust for a manager until retirement.

Demotion: The process of moving a worker to a lower level of duties and responsibilities, which typically involves a pay cut.

Development: Individual growth not related to a specific present or future job.

Direct financial compensation: Pay that a person receives in the form of wages, salary, bonuses, and commissions.

Disciplinary action: Invoking a penalty against an employee who fails to meet organizational standards or comply with organizational rules.

Disciplinary action without punishment: A process whereby a worker is given time off with pay to think about whether he or she really wants to follow the rules and continue working for the company.

Discipline: The state of employee self-control and orderly conduct.

Dual career path: A method of rewarding technical specialists and professionals who can, and should be allowed to, continue to contribute significantly to a company without having to become managers.

Education: Activities conducted to improve the overall competence of an individual in a specific direction and beyond the current job.

Employee assistance program (EAP): One comprehensive approach that many organizations have taken to deal with burnout, alcohol and drug abuse, and other emotional disturbances.

Employee-centered work redesign: An innovative concept designed to link the mission of the company with the job satisfaction needs of employees.

Employee equity: Payment of individuals performing similar jobs for the same firm commensurate with factors unique to each employee.

Employee requisition: A document that specifies job title, department, and the date by which an open job should be filled.

Employee stock ownership plan (ESOP): A companywide incentive plan whereby the company provides its employees with common stock.

Employment agency: An organization that assists firms in recruiting employees and also aids individuals in their attempts to locate jobs.

Employment at will: An unwritten contract that is created when an employee agrees to work for an employer with no agreement as to how long the parties expect the employment to last.

Employment interview: A goal-oriented conversation in which the interviewer and applicant exchange information.

Equity: The perception by workers that they are being treated fairly.

Equivalent forms method: Verification of selection test reliability by correlating the results of tests that are similar but not identical.

Ergonomics: The study of equipment design that reduces operator fatigue and discomfort.

Essay method: A performance appraisal method whereby the rater simply writes a brief narrative describing the employee's performance.

Ethics: The discipline dealing with what is good and bad, or right and wrong, or with moral duty and obligation.

Executive orders: Directives issued by the president, which have the force and effect of laws enacted by the Congress.

Executive search firms: Organizations that are retained by a company to search for the most qualified executive available for a specific position.

Executives: Top-level managers, who report directly to the corporation's chief executive officer or the head of a major division.

Exempt employees: Employees who are categorized as executive, administrative, or professional employees and outside salespersons.

Experiment: A method of inquiry that involves the manipulation of certain variables while others are held constant.

Expert system: A system that uses knowledge about a narrowly-defined, complex area to act as a consultant to a human.

External environment: The factors that affect a firm's human resources from outside the organization's boundaries.

External equity: Payment of employees at rates comparable to those paid for similar jobs elsewhere.

Factor comparison method: A job evaluation method in which (1) raters need not keep the entire job in mind as they evaluate and (2) raters make decisions on separate aspects, or factors, of the job; the method is based on the assumption that there are five universal job factors.

Finger dexterity: The ability to make precise, coordinated finger movements, such as those performed by an electronics assembler or a watchmaker.

Flexible compensation plans: A method that permits employees to choose from among many alternatives the way in which their financial compensation will be allocated.

Flextime: The practice of permitting employees to choose, with certain limitations, their own working hours.

Forced-choice performance report: A performance appraisal technique in which the rater is given a series of statements about an individual and indicates which items are most or least descriptive of the employee.

Forced distribution method: An appraisal approach in which the rater is required to assign individuals in the work group to a limited number of categories similar to a normal frequency distribution.

Frequency rate: A formula used to calculate the number of lost-time accidents per million person-hours worked.

Functional job analysis (FJA): A comprehensive approach to formulating job descriptions that concentrates on the interactions among the work, the worker, and the work organization.

Generalists: Persons who perform tasks in a wide variety of human resource-related areas.

Glass ceiling: The invisible barrier in organizations that prevents many women from achieving top-level management positions.

Going rate: The average pay that most employers provide for the same job in a particular area or industry.

"Golden parachute" contract: An executive perquisite provided for the purpose of protecting executives in the event their firm is acquired by another.

Graphical user interface (GUI): An interface in which graphic figures (or icons) or framed written commands are touched or aimed at to communicate with the computer program.

Grievance: An employee's dissatisfaction or feeling of personal injustice relating to his or her employment.

Grievance procedure: A formal, systematic process that permits employees to complain about matters affecting them and their work.

Group appraisal: The use of a team of two or more managers who are familiar with an employee's performance to appraise it.

Group interview: A meeting in which several job applicants interact in the presence of one or more company representatives.

Guidelines oriented job analysis (GOJA): A method that responds to the growing amount of legislation affecting employment decisions by utilizing a step-by-step procedure to describe the work of a particular job classification.

Halo error: The perception by an evaluator—that one factor is of paramount importance—who gives a good or bad overall rating to an employee based on that one factor.

Hay guide chart-profile method: A highly refined version of the point method of job evaluation that uses the factors of know-how, problem solving, accountability, and where appropriate, working conditions.

Hazard pay: Additional pay provided to employees who work under extremely dangerous conditions.

Health: An employee's freedom from physical or emotional illness.

Human resource development (HRD): A planned, continuous effort by management to improve employee competency levels and organizational performance through training, education, and development programs.

Human resource information system (HRIS): Any organized approach to obtaining relevant and timely information on which to base human resource decisions.

Human resource management (HRM): Utilization of the firm's human resources to achieve organizational objectives.

Human resource managers: Individuals who normally act in an advisory (staff) capacity when working with other (line) managers regarding human resource matters.

Human resource planning: The process of systematically reviewing human resource requirements to ensure that the required number of employees, with the required skills, are available when they are needed.

Human resource research: The systematic study of a firm's human resources for the purpose of maximizing personal and organizational goal achievement.

Hypnosis: An altered state of consciousness that is artificially induced and characterized by increased receptiveness to suggestions.

In-basket training: A simulation in which the participant is asked to establish priorities for handling a number of business papers, such as memoranda, reports, and telephone messages, that would typically cross a manager's desk.

Incentive compensation: Directly relating pay to productivity.

Indirect financial compensation: All financial rewards that are not included in direct compensation.

Industrial unions: Bargaining units that generally consist of all the workers in a particular plant or group of plants.

Informal organization: The set of evolving relationships and patterns of human interaction within an organization that are not officially prescribed.

Injunction: A prohibiting legal procedure used by employers to prevent certain union activities, such as strikes and unionization attempts.

Internal employee relations: Those human resource management activities associated with promotion, transfer, demotion, resignation, discharge, layoffs, and retirement.

Internal environment: The factors that affect a firm's human resources from inside the organization's boundaries.

Internal equity: Payment of employees according to the relative values of their jobs within an organization.

Internship: A special form of recruitment that involves placing students in temporary jobs with no obligation either by the company to permanently hire the student or by the student to accept a permanent position with the firm.

Job: A group of tasks that must be performed if an organization is to achieve its goals.

Job analysis: The systematic process of determining the skills and knowledge required for performing specific jobs in the organization.

Job analysis schedule (JAS): A systematic method of studying jobs and occupations developed by the U.S. Department of Labor.

Job bidding: A technique that permits individuals in the organization who believe that they possess the required qualifications to apply for a posted job.

Job description: A document that provides information regarding the tasks, duties, and responsibilities of the job.

Job design: The process of determining the specific tasks to be performed, the methods used in performing these tasks, and how the job relates to other work in the organization.

Job enlargement: A change in the scope of a job so as to provide greater variety to the worker.

Job enrichment: Restructuring the content and level of responsibility of a job to make it more challenging, meaningful, and interesting to the worker.

Job evaluation: That part of a compensation system in which management determines the relative values of various jobs.

Job knowledge questions: Questions that assess the knowledge required for performing a job, which a person must possess prior to filling the job.

Job knowledge tests: Tests designed to measure a candidate's knowledge of the duties of the position for which he or she is applying.

Job overload: A condition that exists when employees are given more work than they can reasonably handle.

Job posting: A procedure for communicating to company employees the fact that job openings exist.

Job pricing: Placing a dollar value on the worth of a job.

Job rotation: A training method that involves moving employees from one job to another for the purpose of giving them broader experience.

Job-sample simulation questions: Situations in which an applicant may be required to actually perform a sample task from the job.

Job sharing: The filling of a job by two part-time people who split the duties of one full-time job in some agreed-on manner and are paid according to their contributions.

Job specification: The minimum acceptable qualifications that a person should possess in order to perform a particular job.

Job Training Partnership Act (JTPA): A federal law that provides job training and employment services for economically disadvantaged adults and youth, dislocated workers, and other persons who face exceptional employment hurdles.

Key job: A job that is well known in the company and industry and can be easily defined.

Know-how: The total of all knowledge and skills needed for satisfactory job performance.

Labor market: The geographical area from which employees are recruited for a particular job.

Leadership: Influencing others to do what the leader wants them to do.

Leased employees: Individuals provided by an outside firm at a fixed hourly rate, similar to a rental fee, often for extended periods.

Leniency: Giving undeserved high performance appraisal ratings.

Likes and dislikes survey: A procedure that helps individuals recognize restrictions they place on themselves.

Local union: The basic element in the structure of the U.S. labor movement.

Lockout: A management decision to keep employees out of the workplace and to operate with management personnel and/or temporary replacements.

Long-term trend: A projection of demand for a firm's products, typically five years or more into the future.

Management by objectives (MBO): A philosophy of management that emphasizes the setting of agreed-on objectives by superior and subordinate managers and the use of these objectives as the primary basis of motivation, evaluation, and control efforts.

Management development: learning experiences provided by an organization for the purpose of upgrading skills and knowledge required in current and future managerial positions.

Management inventory: Detailed data regarding each manager to be used in identifying individuals possessing the potential to move into higher level positions.

Management position description questionnaire (MPDQ): A form of job analysis designed for management positions that uses a checklist method to analyze jobs.

Managing diversity: Having an acute awareness of characteristics common to a culture, race, gender, age, or sexual preference, while at the same time managing employees with these characteristics as individuals.

Mandatory bargaining issues: Those issues that fall within the definition of wages, hours, and other terms and conditions of employment.

Manual dexterity: The coordinated movements of both hands and arms, such as those required by large assembly jobs.

Media: Special methods of communicating ideas and concepts in training and development.

Mediation: A process whereby a neutral third party enters and attempts to resolve a labor dispute when a bargaining impasse has occurred.

Mentoring: An on-the-job approach to management development in which the trainee is given the opportunity to learn on a one-to-one basis from more experienced organizational members.

Mission: The organization's continuing purpose or reason for being.

Motivation: The willingness to put forth effort in the pursuit of organizational goals.

Multimedia: A computer application that produces presentations combining automation, stereo sound, full-motion video, and graphics.

Multinational corporation (MNC): An organization that conducts a large part of its business outside the country in which it is headquartered and has a significant percentage of its physical facilities and employees in other countries.

National union: An organization composed of local unions, which it charters.

Network career path: A method of job progression that contains both vertical and horizontal opportunities.

Nonfinancial compensation: The satisfaction that a person receives by performing meaningful job tasks or from the psychological and/or physical environment in which the job is performed.

Norm: The distribution of many scores obtained by people similar to the applicants being tested.

Objectivity: The condition that is achieved when all individuals scoring a given test obtain the same results.

Occupational Measurement System (OMS): A method of job analysis that enables organizations to collect, store, and analyze information pertinent to human resources by means of an electronic database.

Ombudsperson: A complaint officer with access to top management who hears employees' complaints, investigates them, and sometimes recommends appropriate action.

On-the-job training (OJT): An informal approach to training in which the person learns job tasks by actually performing them.

Open-door policy: A company policy whereby employees have the right to take any grievance to the person next in the chain of command if a satisfactory solution cannot be obtained from their immediate supervisor.

Open shop: Employment that is open on equal terms to union members and nonmembers alike.

Operative employees: All workers in a firm except managers and professionals such as engineers or accountants.

Organization development (OD): An organization-wide application of behavioral science knowledge to the planned development and reinforcement of a firm's strategies, structures, and processes for improving its effectiveness.

Organizational career planning: The process of establishing career paths within a firm.

Organizational structure: The purposeful way in which the human resources of the firm are related or arranged.

Orientation: The guided adjustment of new employees to the company, the job, and the work group.

Outplacement: A process whereby a terminated employee is given assistance in finding employment elsewhere.

Paired comparison: A variation of the ranking method of performance appraisal that involves comparing the performance of each employee with that of every other employee in the group.

Pay compression: A situation which occurs when workers perceive that the pay differential between their pay and that of employees in jobs above or below them is too small.

Pay followers: Companies that choose to pay below the going rate because of a poor financial condition or a belief that they simply do not require highly capable employees.

Pay grade: The grouping of similar jobs to simplify the job-pricing process.

Pay leaders: Those organizations that pay higher wages and salaries than competing firms.

Pay range: A minimum and maximum pay rate for a job, with enough variance between the two to allow some significant pay difference.

Performance appraisal: A formal system of periodic review and evaluation of an individual's job performance.

Permissive bargaining issues: Issues that may be raised, but neither side may insist that they be bargained over.

Perquisites (perks): Special benefits provided by a firm to key executives to give them something extra.

Plateauing: A career condition that occurs when job functions and work content remain the same because of a lack of promotional opportunities within the firm.

Point method: An approach to job evaluation in which numerical values are assigned to specific job components and the sum of these values provides a quantitative assessment of a job's relative worth.

Policy: A predetermined guide established to provide direction in decision making.

Position: The tasks and responsibilities performed by one person; there is a position for every individual in an organization.

Position analysis questionnaire (PAQ): A structured job analysis questionnaire that uses a checklist approach to identify job elements.

Predictive validity: A validation method that involves administering a test and later obtaining the criterion information.

Predictor variables: Factors known to have had an impact on employment levels.

Premium pay: Compensation paid to employees for working long periods of time or working under dangerous or undesirable conditions.

Proactive response: Taking action in anticipation of environmental changes.

Problem-solving: The degree of original thinking required by the job for analyzing, evaluating, creating, reasoning, and arriving at and making conclusions.

Productivity: A measure of the relationship between inputs (labor, capital, natural resources, and energy) and the quality and quantity of outputs (goods and services).

Profession: A vocation characterized by the existence of a common body of knowledge and a procedure for certifying its practitioners.

Profit sharing: A compensation plan that distributes a predetermined percentage of the firm's profits to employees.

Programmed instruction: A teaching method that requires no intervention by an instructor.

Progressive disciplinary action: An approach to disciplinary action designed to ensure that the minimum penalty appropriate to the offense is imposed, which involves answering a series of questions about the severity of the offense.

Prohibited bargaining issues: Those issues that are statutorily outlawed from collective bargaining.

Promotion: The movement of a person to a higher level position in the company.

Promotion from within: The policy of filling vacancies above entry-level positions with present employees.

Psychomotor abilities tests: Aptitude tests that measure strength, coordination, and dexterity.

Quality circles: Groups of employees who meet regularly with their supervisors to identify production problems and recommend actions for solutions.

Quality of work life (QWL): The extent to which employees satisfy signficant personal needs through their organizational experiences.

Random variations: Changes for which there are no patterns.

Ranking method: A job evaluation method in which the raters examine the description of each job being evaluated and arrange the jobs in order according to their value to the company; a performance appraisal method in which the rater places all employees in a given group in rank order on the basis of their overall performance.

Rating scales method: A widely used performance appraisal method that rates employees according to defined factors.

Reactive response: Simply reacting to environmental changes after they occur.

Realistic job preview (RJP): A method of conveying job information to an applicant in an unbiased manner, including both positive and negative factors.

Recruitment: The process of attracting individuals on a timely basis, in sufficient numbers and with appropriate qualifications, and encouraging them to apply for jobs with an organization.

Recruitment methods: The specific means by which potential employees are attracted to an organization.

Recruitment sources: Where qualified individuals are located.

Reference checks: A means of providing additional insight into the information provided by an applicant and a way to verify the accuracy of the information provided.

Regression analysis: A quantitative technique used to predict one item (known as the dependent variable) through knowledge of other items (known as the independent variables).

Reliability: The extent to which a selection test provides consistent results.

Requirements forecast: An estimate of the numbers and kinds of employees the organization will need at future dates in order for it to realize its stated objectives.

Right-to-work laws: Laws that prohibit management and unions from agreements requiring union membership as a condition of employment.

Role ambiguity: A condition that exists when employees lack clear information about the content of their jobs.

Role conflict: A condition that occurs when an individual is expected to achieve opposing goals.

Role playing: A training method in which training participants "act out" job techniques needed in specific situations without the benefit of either a script or rehearsal.

Safety: Protecting employees from injuries caused by work-related accidents.

Sampling: The process by which only a portion of the total number of individuals are studied, from which conclusions are drawn for the entire group.

Scanlon Plan: A gain-sharing plan designed to bind employees to the firm's performance.

Seasonal variations: Reasonably predictable changes that occur over a period of a year.

Secondary boycott: The practice of a union attempting to encourage third parties (such as suppliers and customers) to stop doing business with a firm.

Selection: The process of choosing from a group of applicants those individuals best suited for a particular position.

Selection ratio: The number of people hired for a particular job compared to the total number of individuals in the applicant pool.

Self-assessment: The process of learning about oneself.

Sensitivity training: An organizational development technique that is designed to make people aware of themselves and their impact on others.

Severity rate: A formula that is used to calculate the number of days lost because of accidents per million person-hours worked.

Shareholders: The owners of a corporation.

Shift differentials: Additional money paid to reward employees for the inconvenience of working undesirable hours.

Simulation: A technique for experimenting with a real-world situation by means of a mathematical model that represents the actual situation.

Simulators: Training devices of varying degrees of complexity that duplicate the real world.

Situational questions: Questions that pose a hypothetical job situation to determine what the applicant would do in such a situation.

Skill-based pay: A system that compensates employees on the basis of job-related skills and the knowledge they possess.

Skills inventory: Information maintained on nonmanagerial employees as to their availability and preparedness to move into higher level positions or laterally.

Social responsibility: The implied, enforced, or felt obligation of managers, acting in their official capacities, to serve or protect the interests of groups other than themselves.

Special events: A recruitment method that involves an effort on the part of a single employer, or group of employers, to attract a larger number of applicants for interviews.

Specialist: An individual who may be a human resource executive, a human resource manager, or a nonmanager, who is typically concerned with only one of the six functional areas of human resource management.

Split-halves method: A method of determining the reliability of a test by dividing the results into two parts and then correlating the results of the two parts.

Standard hour plan: An individual incentive plan under which time allowances are calculated for each unit of output.

Standardization: The degree of uniformity of the procedures and conditions related to administering tests.

Stock option plan: The opportunity for a manager to buy a specified amount of stock in the company in the future at or below the current market price.

Straight piecework plan: A predetermined amount of money is paid for each unit produced.

Strategic planning: The determination of overall organizational purposes and goals and how they are to be achieved.

Strength/weakness balance sheet: A self-evaluation procedure developed originally by Ben Franklin that helps people to become aware of their strengths and weaknesses.

Stress: The body's reaction to any demand made on it.

Stress interview: A form of interview that intentionally creates anxiety to determine how an applicant will react in certain types of situations.

Strictness: Being unduly critical of an employee's work performance.

Strike: An action by union members who refuse to work in order to exert pressure on management in negotiations.

Structured interview: Consistently asking each applicant for a particular job the same series of job-related questions.

Survey feedback: A survey method and research technique that systematically collects information about organizations and employee attitudes and makes the data available in aggregate form to employees and management so that problems can be diagnosed and plans developed to solve them.

Team building: A conscious effort to develop effective work groups throughout the organization.

Telecommuting: A procedure whereby workers are able to remain at home or otherwise away from the office and perform their work (as if they were at the office) over telephone lines tied to a computer.

Teleconferencing: A method of conducting or participating in multiparty discussions by telephone or videophone.

Teletraining: A method of training people efficiently and effectively, utilizing teleconferencing.

Test-retest method: Determining selection test reliability by giving the test twice to the same group of individuals and correlating the two sets of scores.

Total quality management (TQM): A top management philosophy which emphasizes the continuous improvement of the processes that result in goods or services.

Traditional career path: A vertical line of career progression from one specific job to the next.

Training: Those activities that serve to improve an individual's performance on a currently held job or one related to it.

Transactional analysis (TA): An organizational development method that considers the three ego states of the Parent, the Adult, and the Child in helping people understand interpersonal relations and thus assists in improving an organization's effectiveness.

Transcendental meditation: A stress-reduction technique whereby an individual mentally repeats a secret word or phrase (mantra), provided by a trained instructor, while comfortably seated.

Transfer: The lateral movement of a worker within an organization.

Two-tier wage system: A wage structure that pays newly hired employees less than established employees for performing the same or similar jobs.

Union: A group of employees who have joined together for the purpose of dealing collectively with their employer.

Union shop: A requirement that all employees become members of the union after a specified period of employment (the legal minimum is thirty days) or after a union shop provision has been negotiated.

Unstructured interview: A meeting with a job applicant during which the interviewer asks probing, open-ended questions.

Utility analysis: Determination of the ratio of benefits to costs for any selection technique.

Utilization review: A process that scrutinizes medical diagnoses, hospitalization, surgery, and other medical treatment and care prescribed by doctors.

Validity: The extent to which a test measures what it purports to measure.

Vestibule training: Training that takes place away from the production area on equipment that closely resembles the actual equipment used on the job.

Vocational interest tests: A method of determining the occupation in which a person has the greatest interest and from which the person is most likely to receive satisfaction.

Voice mail: Spoken messages transmitted electronically and stored for delivery to the recipient at a later time.

Wage curve (or pay curve): The fitting of a curve to plotted points in order to create a smooth progression between pay grades.

Weighted application blank (WAB): One technique for identifying factors that differentiate successful and less successful employees.

Weighted checklist performance report: A performance appraisal technique whereby the rater completes a form similar to the forced-choice performance report but in which the various responses have been assigned different weights.

Wellness: A concept that focuses on the prevention of illness and disease.

Word processing: A computer application that permits an operator to create and edit written material.

Work-sample tests: Identification of a task or set of tasks that are representative of the job and use of these tasks for selection testing.

Work standards method: A performance appraisal method that compares each employee's performance to a predetermined standard or an expected level of output.

Worker requirements questions: Questions that seek to determine the applicant's willingness to conform to the requirements of the job.

Wrist-finger speed: The ability to make rapid wrist and finger movements, such as those required in inspector-packers and assembly operations jobs.

Yellow-dog contract: A written agreement between the employee and the company made at the time of employment, prohibiting a worker from joining a union or engaging in union activities.

Zero-base forecasting: A method for estimating future employment needs using the organization's current level of employment as the starting point.

Index